JOURNEY INTO
NORTHERN PENNSYLVANIA AND
THE STATE OF NEW YORK

JOURNEY INTO
NORTHERN PENNSYLVANIA AND
THE STATE OF NEW YORK

by MICHEL-GUILLAUME ST. JEAN DE CRÈVECOEUR

Translated by CLARISSA SPENCER BOSTELMANN

THE UNIVERSITY OF MICHIGAN PRESS · ANN ARBOR

Published in the United States of America by
The University of Michigan Press and simultaneously
in Toronto, Canada, by Ambassador Books Limited

Manufactured in the United States of America
by Vail-Ballou Press, Inc., Binghamton, N.Y.

For my daughter, Pamela

BIOGRAPHICAL SKETCH AND
TRANSLATOR'S FOREWORD

MICHEL-GUILLAUME ST. JEAN DE CRÈVECOEUR was born of a well-to-do family in Caen, in 1735. As a lad he loved antiquarian subjects and the solitude of cemeteries and old churches. His literary flair was early evident, for often he recorded his thoughts and impressions to read them aloud to his mother.

During his years at the Jesuit College in Caen where his instruction included religion, Latin literature and composition, dialectics and geometry, his favorite author was the Abbé Reynal, whose *Memoirs* kindled in the youth a fire of enthusiasm for the New World.

When he was nineteen, Crèvecoeur went to Salisbury, England, where he studied a wide assortment of subjects including English and economics. Before the year was out, and shortly after the death of his English fiancée, Crèvecoeur sailed for Canada as a soldier of fortune, not as a man of letters seeking inspiration in greener pastures or collecting copy, but as an adventurous young man with his eyes agleam for a glimpse of the New World. The writings which subsequently poured forth from his prolific pen are thus a result of, not a pretext for, his journey westward across the sea to the American colonies.

The years 1755–59 found Crèvecoeur with Montcalm's army in Canada, occupied chiefly as scout and cartographer, an assignment which involved extensive travel south and westward into the Ohio River country.

Embarking from Canada for New York at the war's end, Crèvecoeur, now twenty-five, engaged in professional surveying. This naturally piqued his curiosity and pushed his peregrinations far and wide: to Vermont in 1764; to New York (where he became a naturalized citizen and also met his future wife) in 1765; from New Hampshire, southward to Virginia in 1766 and finally, in 1767 (a trek westward again), to the Ohio River and Great Lakes country.

This journey he described in "Mémoire pour le Maréchal de Castries (Ministre de Marine) sur la Région située à l'ouest des montagnes d'Alleghany, arosées par les Rivières Ohyo, Mississippi, Illinois et Cherokee." The account was based on observations made by travelers and colonists "les plus instruits qui habitent ces contrées avec ce que je (Crèvecoeur) fis sur les lieux en 1767.'' This trip totaled one hundred sixty-one days and covered three thousand one hundred ninety miles.

In 1769 Crèvecoeur married Mehitabel Tippett, daughter of a wealthy Yonkers merchant. They settled on a three hundred fifty acre farm, Pine-Hill, in Orange County, twenty-five miles from the Hudson, near the present site of Bloomingburg. Three children, America-Frances, Guillaume-Alexandre, and Philippe-Louis, were born in the happy years of gentleman farming, occasional travel, and indefatigable correspondence which followed. During these years *Letters from an American Farmer and Sketches of Eighteenth Century America* were flowing from his pen.

Although a small farmer, his aristocratic sympathies led him, unlike most of his compatriots of French blood, to join the Loyalist cause. He sought protection of the British army in New York, only to be imprisoned as suspect. It was at this time that he was summoned to France on estate matters. Finally, after much anxiety and many mishaps, Crèvecoeur and his son landed in England, where he sold the manuscript of the *Letters*.

Back in France after many years absence, the author was literally lionized by the Countess d'Houdetôt and her coterie of friends. Indeed, he took up his abode in her town house to embark on his ''éducation mondaine'' for, according to Brissot de Warville, a contemporary, ''fière de posséder un sauvage américain, la comtesse voulut le former et le jeter dans le monde.'' There was no element of reflected glory in this liaison, for Crèvecoeur's colorful life and writings afforded him a perfect entrée to the brilliant society of scientists like Buffon, American and French diplomatic dignitaries, and French men of letters. That Crèvecoeur was the victim of a sort of schizophrenic style was due in large measure to the counsels of the fascinating Countess d'Houdetôt and her friends, all of whom assumed extended editorial guidance over him as he wove his notes into the *Voyage*. These had been compiled over a period of about twenty-seven years spent in America.

Having curried favor years earlier with his ''Mémoire'' to the Maréchal de Castries, Crèvecoeur received an appointment as French consul in New York in 1783. The same year he was elected to the Académie des Sciences.

His consulship continued with occasional leaves of absence until 1790, when the Revolutionary government of France recalled him. As consul, Crèvecoeur's activities were boundless. He implemented the founding of a Botanical Garden, the first in America, in New Haven; published and lectured widely under the name 'Agricola'; stirred up an *esprit paquebotique* which culminated in the first transatlantic shipping line between Lorient and New York, backed by Lecoulteux Bankers; and encouraged domestic inventions in an organizaton known as Le Bureau des Lumières, whose aim was the political, industrial, and moral welfare of the United States and France. His efforts in encouraging Franco-American trade were indefatigable.

Recalled, as we have noted, by the Revolutionary government, Crèvecoeur left America to spend his latter years in travel on the continent, then retirement. He died in 1813 at the age of seventy-eight.

At the beginning of the nineteenth century there appeared in France a book whose title page read *"Voyage dans la Haute Pensylvanie et dans l'Etat de New-York* par un Membre adoptif de la Nation Onéida." Traduit et publié par l'auteur des *Lettres d'Un Cultivateur Américain.* De l'imprimerie de Crapelet, à Paris, Chez Maradan, Libraire. ... An IX (1801) 3 volumes en 8, sept gravures et trois cartes avec un épître dédicatoire à Washington, signé "S.J.D.C."

This work Crèvecoeur—St. Jean de Crèvecoeur—had written in his declining years. It had been translated only into German, except for an English translation of Chapter II, Volume 1, in *Duyckinck: History of American Literature* and a translation of 15 (of the total 45) chapters, many chapters only partly translated, by Percy G. Adams, *Crèvecoeur's Eighteenth-Century Travels in Pennsylvania & New York.*

In a biography of his great-grandfather, Robert de Crèvecoeur says: "Crèvecoeur alleges in his Introduction that the *Voyage* is a manuscript found in a shipwreck, as indicated in the author's preface, pages —and even whole chapters of which are either lost or water-soaked beyond legibility, and that he is the translator of this work, NOT its author. It seems reasonable to assume that in re-working notes he took while in America, there were certain *non sequitur* passages, and certainly many lapses of memory ... yet this ancient literary device is not overworked and the *Voyage* is comparatively smooth. ... Written with greater care than were the *Letters,* the work, except for several fanciful chapters, offers very real interest and authenticity. The numerous notes (of the total 1,272 pages in the 3 volumes, there are well over two hundred pages of notes) have appreciable interest."

During many years prior to 1801, the year Crèvecoeur's *Voyage* was published in Paris, a host of Europeans had visited the New World and reported with varying accuracy what they saw. Such men were Charlevoix, La Hontan, Josselyn, Carver, Bartram, Imlay, Chastellux, Brissot de Warville, and numerous others. Crèvecoeur was well acquainted with the eastern United States. In fact, he believed himself an authority on this section. He wished to substantiate his position and also to rekindle in the public mind a waning flame of enthusiasm for his writings. The *Voyage* was the result. In justification of a sometimes apparent "magic-carpet" travel treatment, it should be made clear that in the *Voyage* Crèvecoeur and his imaginary traveling companion, Mr. Herman, an eighteenth-century "Harvey," remain in the East, but are made to encounter persons who have journeyed through the South and West. For material on these places, Crèvecoeur often politely "lifted" from whatever travel and descriptive literature that struck his fancy: Jefferson, Bartram, Chastellux, Imlay, *et al.*, to cite a few; but plagiarism, it should be remembered, was common in Crèvecoeur's day. His *Voyage* attempts to recapture—nay, to capitalize on—his earlier *succès fou* with the *Letters*, their several editions and translations.

In the *Voyage* he is still writing of an agrarian Utopia, but nevertheless a cultured Utopia. Pastoral descriptions abound—farmlands, irrigation projects, cattle, salt-feeding, etc., are all part and parcel of the subject-matter (as they were in the famous *Letters*)—but in Crèvecoeur's last work one reads of a landed gentry who have impressive libraries and private chamber music ensembles—a far cry from the humble man of homespun tastes characteristic of the *Letters*.

"Oddly enough, the element of travel in the *Voyage* is secondary; visiting and conversation are primary. For the unsympathetic reader, this makes for monotonous disorganization, a discursive style with a prose that is perforated with errors, indifferent to spelling, rambling in redundant eighteenth-century rhetoric, dangling participles with abandon, strutting superlatives, and sentences saturated with sentiment. Despite this, the man of letters, if not repelled by the occasional repetition in parts of the *Voyage*, will discover many literary gems; Indian lore, magnificent pastoral descriptions, adventure sagas, fanciful and romantic legends withal, a vivid account of life and thought in eighteenth-century America." (Bourdin-Williams, ed. "Sketches.")

The translator's mission is one of pouring prose or poetry from one language into another without losing the flavor, without letting the result smack of translation. He must scrupulously communicate content. The shackles of blind servitude to the literal meaning must not clank.

In the translation of this work, the aim, of course, has been to achieve the kind of English Crèvecoeur might have written had he been bilingual, which he almost was. Accurate rendition is the translator's absolute and inviolable responsibility. Yet there are times when some freedom with the precise text is necessary in order to preserve some other quality which might escape in merely mechanical translation: rhythm of the phrase, melifluent, albeit sometimes mixed metaphors, etc.—not to mention the single word, which often gets a very whimsical treatment from Crèvecoeur! A kind of temperamental compatibility is what I have aimed at, for violation of the author's stylistic intent would be as great an injustice as distortion of content.

In this connection, deliberate concessions have been made to occasional archaisms, quaint turns of phrase, expletives, and other "period" devices. Also, Crèvecoeur's spelling, abuse of capitals, and other slips of the quill have been retained intact (and have not been signaled by the use of *sic*). Otherwise, eighteenth-century idiom would have been violated and the flavor lost. Since English is more elliptical than French, this concession, it is hoped, will not jolt the reader.

Only textual liberties consistent with achieving clarity have been taken, for occasional obscurity in the *Voyage* borders on the absurd. Modern vocabulary and word order will seem inconsistent, incongruous even with the incredible length of the typical Crèvecoeur sentence, which has not been shortened. The sonority of these sentences would have been sacrificed had I submitted them to the mercy of the modern sentence, short and staccato. Even though many, many sentences are sheer declamation, the result, it is hoped, will thus be harmonious with eighteenth-century style, which was rhetoric, pure and often complex! Crèvecoeur's prose flights of fancy, his overemphasis, his redundancy, his tirades of sentimental and passionate bombast will stand out in wild crescendoes. But there are legato passages, too.

Names and places referred to in the *Voyage* are readily identifiable, despite spelling vagaries. Thanks to the numerous pages of notes by Crèvecoeur at the end, one is not compelled to plow through indigestible footnotes which would prevent him from getting along with the book. The Crèvecoeur convert whose curiosity is further aroused by the *Voyage* will find a very informative and scholarly discussion by Dr. Percy G. Adams in his doctoral dissertation, "Crèvecoeur's *Voyage*" (University of Texas, 1946).

The reader should be reminded that all footnotes and insertions anywhere and everywhere in the *Voyage* are Crèvecoeur's. These footnotes are frequently followed by "Note du Traducteur" ("Translator's Note"), i.e., Crèvecoeur in disguise. For Crèvecoeur purports to be merely *translating* a "ship-wrecked manuscript" and does not admit authorship anywhere in this except by his initials, "S.J.D.C." (St. Jean de Crèvecoeur) at the end of the dedicatory letter to Washington.

In a *Voyage* as long as this, I can scarcely hope to have escaped all the reefs, or buffeted successfully all the waves. The seas have been sometimes rough, never disheartening, always exciting. The translator confesses to an incurable enthusiasm for Crèvecoeur.

I should like to express my deep appreciation to Dr. Albert J. George, Dr. Winthrop H. Rice, and Dr. Harry Elmer Barnes for their counsel and encouragement, and to Professor Morris G. Bishop, who launched me on the *Voyage*. . . .

To Dr. Jay W. Gossner and Mr. Richard Berchan: sincere gratitude for patient, scholarly, and sensitive reading of much of the manuscript.

To my mother and father, a very special and boundless gratitude: their countless queries and comments have helped to make the *Voyage* smoother.

CLARISSA SPENCER BOSTELMANN

Glen Acres
Skaneateles Lake
Homer, New York

To His Excellency GEORGE WASHINGTON

The one who saw you come as deputy from Virginia to the First Continental Congress which came to be known as the "Venerable," and which guided the revolution with such wisdom and steadfastness; [1]

The one who in 1775 heard the voice of this same Congress, and that of your country, summoning you to the command of her armies, to assure her liberty and independence; [2]

The one who, like so many others, judged your conduct to be as sublime as it was unselfish, at the critical time of the disbanding of the Continental army; [3]

The one who read with unmixed admiration the letter that you addressed at that time to the Governors of the Thirteen States, a letter so worthy of being handed down to posterity; [4]

The one who shared the emotion of the citizens of New York when, after having taken possession of that city and re-establishing the Government, you took leave of it to go to Annapolis; [5]

The one in whose ears sounded the blessings which the inhabitants of town and country alike showered on you during that journey of eighty leagues; [6]

The one who witnessed that memorable day when, having raised your country to the rank of nations, you laid your military obligations in the hands of the Chief of State, to become once more a private citizen; [7]

The one who during your four years of repose found you to be as great, as exemplary, while you were perfecting the navigation of the Potomac and Shenandoah rivers and overseeing your vast farm lands, as when you were at the head of armies; [8]

The one who was present in Philadelphia at the time when you were elected President of the Constitutional Convention, to whose sagacity and inspiration the United States owe the wise government which directs them; [9]

The one who, in 1789, saw you, like another Cincinnatus, regretfully abandon your pastoral pursuits to become Supreme Chief of the Union, in accordance with the unanimous vote of your fellow-citizens; a post which you resigned after eight years of wise and worthy administration; [10]

To His Excellency George Washington

The one who, in 1797, saw you, for the second time a private citizen, dedicating anew your leisure to the duties of husbandry; [11]

Finally, the one whom you have long honored with your kindly good will and who now, conscious of the lofty virtues of which your life has been a constant exemplar, begs you to accept the dedication of this humble work as the only public token he can offer you of his esteem.

S. J. D. C.

Among the vessels that were shipwrecked a few months ago at the mouth of the Elbe River was the ''Morning Star,'' coming from Philadelphia and bound for Copenhagen. Within sight of Heligoland its longboat went down with the crew who, unfortunately, perished.

One of the items washed ashore on this little island was a chest containing some newspapers, a few pamphlets, and some manuscripts. Inasmuch as the chest was claimed by none of the persons who survived the shipwreck, it was put aside with the other damaged goods and sent, according to regulations, to the Copenhagen customs house, where it was put up for sale.

I happened to be in this capital on business at the time and was referred quite by chance to the merchant who had just bought most of the goods. He told me about the chest that fortune had thrown his way, of the deplorable condition in which he had found the manuscripts and the extreme care he had taken to save them from total loss.

''In spite of the interest I took in these manuscripts, I do not yet know their titles: they are written in English and I am not familiar with that language,'' he told me. ''You should be able to tell me their value: whether I was justified in saving the manuscripts, virtually snatching them from annihilation. There they are: I entrust them to you. Read them and give me your opinion of the matter.''

Piqued as much by curiosity as by desire to accommodate Mr. ———, I accepted them with great enthusiasm.

''Well now,'' he asked me several days later, ''what do you think of the work?''

''It is a journey through the United States,'' I replied, ''a country that has become very interesting since attaining its freedom. The transition it has made from colonial status to independence is one of the most memorable events of this century.

''Although many chapters of this work have been lost or have become illegible and although the sea water has defaced most of the dates, I think that with the aid of the notes it would still be possible to reconstruct what remains into approximately its original sequence. Furthermore, despite the missing parts, the imperfections of style, and considerable repetition, the account of the journey would be read with interest. But let me assure you, I am far from considering myself a good judge.''

Convinced that the author was one of the hapless group who had perished within sight of Heligoland, the merchant readily granted me permission to make a copy of the manuscript.

I had just completed a translation of it, in fact, I had already decided to have it published, when it occurred to me that I should first consult some friends whose knowledge and judgment I had valued for a long time. Here is what I was told:

''Freed from the chaos and horror of one of the most appalling revolutions that has ever drenched our land in blood, in fear and trembling even now at the memory of those laws of exile, expropriation, servitude, and disgrace, from which by a miracle the vision and courage of a young man (Napoleon Bonaparte) of thirty-one has just delivered us, we are now like the sailor who watches with mingled feelings of fright and gratitude from the harbor he has safely entered the reefs he has had the good fortune to avoid. What interest, pray tell, can we possibly take in the progress of a land so far away? In the growth of a nation which, more fortunate than we, has made the transition from a state of subservience to independence without experiencing the bloody fury of anarchy? What significance to us: the immensity of their lakes the height of their cataracts, the adventures of some backwoods colonists, or the metaphorical harangues of their natives?''

''To read with pleasure,'' another said, ''one must enjoy comfort, tranquillity, and especially that feeling of security which only the blessings of peace and a good government can procure. Wait until the new sun, which already brightens our horizon, has reached its zenith; until the Washington of France has had time to extend to the administration of our country the talents he exhibited as head of the armies. Who can predict what fate will direct him to do some day in repairing so many disasters and healing so many wounds?

''In the meantime, why do you not busy yourself correcting the mistakes that abound in your translation: put the final touches on the several chapters that seem to have been left unfinished by the author; make the notes what they should be: simple, short explanations, not narratives and lengthy recitals. You know, of course, that readers are usually severe judges, more inclined to criticize the defects of a work than to praise its fine qualities. Like the ripple of a soft breeze, the voice of approval will scarcely be heard, while that of censure, like the rumble of thunder, will sound and resound afar. Moreover, it would be extremely indiscreet to publish the translation of an unedited work whose original is neither your property nor that of the person who permitted you to make a copy. Wait until some reliable information concerning the fate of the author turns up. Until that time, correct and edit.''

''On the contrary,'' said some of my other friends, ''we think that despite the numerous imperfections of the work (whose translation, one must admit, should have been undertaken by a pen more skillful than yours), and despite the loss and illegibility of many chapters, what remains will be favorably received by the public because it contains a great number of details that are bound to stir curiosity and interest. And at what more fitting time could this work appear than during the return to peace, justice, and true liberty, after so many years spent amid the violent upheavals, convulsive storms, and volcanic eruptions of the revolution?

''To erase from their minds the gloomy, ghoulish impression made by this long and bloody tragedy, men need to turn their attention to scenes that are instructive, pleasing, and consoling. Are there any more appropriate to our present state of mind than the descriptions of the civil peace and prosperity of a young nation which, like us, has won its liberty and, since that memorable event has made such good use of that liberty? Can there be any reading more inspiring than that of the early efforts of those families who scatter every year over the new and rich soil of the United States? Or any pages more stimulating than those dealing with the structure and character of a paternal government to which, do you realize, the colonists of certain states pay no tribute other than affection and gratitude?

''And those crude orations, prompted by the uncultivated eloquence of the Indians! And the description of Niagara Falls seen during the rigors of winter! And the majestic passage of the Hudson River through the mountains! We believe that these accounts and many others will be read with decided interest.

''As for the indiscretion of publishing the translation of a work whose unedited manuscript may be claimed some day by its author, we are satisfied that the warm reception shown by the public to this translation will not be at all harmful to the original when the author, if he is still alive, decides to publish it in his own country. You need have no hesitation in giving it to the printer. The laws under which we live today are the results of experience and reason; one is permitted to express oneself frankly, and one need not fear that the blind caprice of tyrants will condemn us to exile and death.''

This last opinion seemed to be that of the majority of my critics, and I resolved to act in accordance with it. May my readers share their enthusiasm!

The dedicatory letter, of which I found only an outline, was not signed, and in no part of the book did I discover the name of the author, who in some chapters designated himself only as an adopted member of the Oneida tribe, and in others only by four initials which I have indicated at the close of the dedication letter. Although the newspapers have just informed us of the death of the founder of the independence of the United States, it is to commemorate a man so justly famous, as well as to conform with the intentions of the unknown author, that I believed I should include the dedication in this translation.

The Translator

Paris, 17 April 1800

VOLUME ONE

CHAPTER SUMMARIES

VOLUME ONE

from the north of Europe.—Improbability that the others came from Tartarie.
—Reasons for these opinions.—The warm climates must have been the cradle
of mankind.—Details on the origin of the tribes which inhabit the Australian
lands.—This planet is older than one thinks.—Indications of this high antiquity.—Details on the entrenched Camp at Muskinghum.—Other fortifications
discovered in the region of the Ohio River.—Obvious traces of an ancient
population.—Human bones.—Tombs discovered in Kentukey, Tenessee, and
the two Floridas.—Conjectures on the degree of civilization which these ancient nations had reached.

CHAPTER III   24

Two great councils are to be held; one at Onondaga, the other at Fort Stanwick.—Desire to be present.—Inconveniences of the journey.—Uncertainty
of the author.—The arrival of Mr. Herman from Europe is the deciding
factor.—Departure from Shippenbourg.—Arrival at Carlisle.—College at
Dikenson.—Thoughts of Mr. Herman.—Story of Mr. B.—Departure.—Arrival on the banks of the Juniata.—Observations on the course of this river
and its picturesque banks.—Mahatango-Creek.—Penn's-Creek.—Passage of
the Susquehannah.—Arrival at Northumberland.—Interesting conversation of
the Surveyor-General.—Reflections on the population and culture of this
continent.—Cause of the state of infancy of this town.—Destroyed in 1780.—
Rebuilt five years later.—Difference between Pensylvanie and Connecticut.—
Navigation of the upper Susquéhannah.—Obstacles that hinder its lower
navigation.—Departure for the Mashoping ferry.—Difficulties of the journey.
—Discouragement of Mr. Herman.—Reflections on the wild appearance of the
soil and the forests.—Observations of the first traveler.—Arrival on the banks
of the Chiquisquaqué.—Encounter with a colonist.—His hospitality.—Details
about his industriousness, his happiness, and his hopes.—Discouragement of
the early colonists.—Paths recently made.—Happy effects of a flourishing
trade for farming.—Religious tendencies of this colonist.—Reflections of
Mr. Herman.—Departure.

CHAPTER IV   31

The travelers swim across the two branches of Fishing-Creek.—Observations
of Mr. Herman on the present state of things.—Monotony of the journey.
—What a Swedish settler tells them.—A Westphalian and a Savoyard.—Passage of the Susquéhannah to the ferry at Mashoping.—Entrance into Luzerne
county.—Reflections of Mr. Herman on the origin of societies.—Contrast between the early clearings of this land and those of Europe.—North America's
advantages.—Observations on the small number of colonists who succeed.—
Causes of this lack of success.—Entrance into the district of Philippopolis.—
The travelers hear the sound of a town clock.—They come upon a dwelling.—
The owner invites them to spend the night.—His story.—From the town of
Orsa on the Dnieper River, he finds himself in New-York.—He sets himself
up as a surgeon on the Mohawk River.—He marries the daughter of the
minister in this region.—Instructive conversation with this minister who has
been pastor, farmer, and doctor for forty years.—Qualities which a settler
must have.—Notion of his duties, if he is called to Congress.—What he owes

to his new country.—Happy results of irrigation.—Disappearance of many streams.—Luxury of the guests.—The wife of this settler explains.—Curious tableau.—What Mr. Herman says in taking leave of this family.—Departure.

CHAPTER V   42

Arrival at Seely ferry on the Susquéhannah.—Harmony and Stockport, recently founded marketplaces.—The great line of demarkation between the States of New-York and Pensylvanie.—Salt springs.—Passage of the Susquéhannah.—Entrance into the state of New-York.—Great number of streams and of maple sugar trees.—Raft on the Ononquagé.—Reflections of Mr. Herman.—Natural meadow.—Approach of a storm.—Discovery of a dwelling.—Kind reception by the owner.—His education.—He orders his dogs to fetch the cows.—The cows return.—Thoughts on the perfectibility of instinct.—Wisdom of two Floridan dogs.—Autumn fevers.—Reclamation of many natural prairies.—This colonist is a member of the legislature.—Details.—Hope of making a fortune, founded on the presence of falls of seventeen feet.—Wise law, promulgated by the two States of New-York and Pensylvanie, declaring rivers free.—Reflections of this colonist on the loneliness of his location.—On the misfortunes of Europe.—Departure.—Passage of the Tiénaderha and Adiga rivers.—Approaches of Lake Otzégé.—Encounter with a great number of persons busy building the framework of a mill.—Reflections of Mr. Herman on the great number of falls one sees in this country.—Hospitality of Mr. J. V.—What this colonist says about the rapidity of the clearings. —Heterogeneous mixture of all the nations of Europe.—Causes of this amalgamation.—This colonist promises to tell his life story when the travelers return.—Departure.—Fertility of the regions through which the travelers pass before arriving in Albany.—Arrival at Skénéctady.—They embark on the Mohawk to go to Fort Stanwick.

The chapter which contained the details of the voyage to this Fort, was so damaged, except for a few lines, that it could not be translated.

CHAPTER VI   50

Arrival at Onondaga.—The travelers seek out two Indians with whom they relax.—Reflections of Mr. Herman on primitive life.—Reply of the first traveler.—Ignorance, brutality, misery necessarily attached to the immaturity of these nations.—Error of the savants who extoll the savage life and scorn the advantages of civilization.—Visit to old Keskétomah.—His hospitality.—Conversation.—Effects of music on the faces of many chiefs.

CHAPTER VII   53

Opening of the Council.—Details relative to this new spectacle.—Silence.—Manner of smoking.—Fine proportions of their bodies.—Next day's council.—The chiefs appear, ornamented with their feathers and paints.—They are to speak of adoption and of farming.—Chédabooktoo rises.—He recounts the woes of Wéquash.—The reproaches he makes him.—Wéquash's reply.—Advice of Chédabooktoo.

Yoyoghény rises and tells what happened between him and Muskanéhong.—

She has lost her husband.—He mitigates her anguish.—What she tells him.— She regrets not having offered a roll of tobacco to the Evil Spirit.—Thoughts of Yoyoghény.—He advises her to adopt a white man.—Reply of Muskanhé- hong.—Yoyoghény justifies the advice he has given and deplores the evil that is experienced on the earth.—Muskanéhong's question.—Yoyoghény's answer.

Siasconset, third speaker, rises and tells of his meeting with Kahawabash. —Ravages of smallpox which killed his wife, destroyed almost all his village. —Woes of Kahawabash.—Unhappy is the lot of men on earth.—Desolation of Siasconset.—He consoles Kahawabash, telling him of the death of his three children, and of his old age.—He recommends to him the remedy of adoption and counsels him not to drop tears when he is before the old men.— Touching reply of Kahawabash.—New question which he asks Siasconset.— Wise answer of the latter.

Aquidnunck rises and tells the Council of the woes of Tienaderha relative to the death of her daughter.—What happened to her near her daughter's tomb.—Her desire to join her.—Aquidnunck consoles her, entreating her to summon courage in order to bear up under her difficulties, to cry in order to assuage her troubles, and to work in order to forget them.

Keskétomah speaks of the necessity of farming the land in order to repair all these losses.—Recounts the prophecy of Koreyhoosta, recalling the plight of the nations that have disappeared.—He would like to have the wings of the eagle in order to be understood better; he predicts the ruin of the nation. —He prescribes what must be done to resist the white men: he stops.

Koohassen answers him.—Farming is unworthy of a warrior.—Laws, pris- ons, judges, and chains are the consequences of farming.—Children will no longer have examples of bravery and intrepidity.—His scorn for the tribes that have become agricultural.—He swears to abandon the Oneidas if they become scrapers of the earth.

Keskétomah rises and refutes what Koohassen has just said.—Invites those people who scorn farming to leave the tribe.—Predicts anew the ruin of the village if they do not adopt his advice.

CHAPTER VIII   66

Third meeting of the Council.—Several adoptions are consummated.—The oldest takes the afflicted by the hand, consoles them.—Touching reflections that he addresses to the womenfolk.

CHAPTER IX   69

Speech of the travelers to the Council.—Recalls the time of his and his chil- dren's adoption.—His attachment for his adoptive tribe.—He addresses him- self to their young people, predicts the breaking up of their nation if they continue to scorn the advice of the old men and of their friend.—

Answer of Kanajohary.—His reflections on what the traveler has just said.—He passes pipe of friendship to him, presents him with a Belt of Wampun.—Adoption of Mr. Herman.—Details relative to the dances and games of the young people.—What Koohassen says.

The translator did not find the next two chapters which probably contained the details of the Congress which the Governor of New-York held at Fort Stanwick.

Here there appears to be a great lapse of time or loss of chapters.

There appears to be a great portion missing here.

CHAPTER I

(Although the first and last pages of this chapter * are damaged beyond legibility, we believe that the remainder is interesting enough to merit translation. According to some of the notes, the year is 1785.)

"What a vast subject for speculation the old and new inhabitants of North America offer!" continued Colonel Crawghan.[1]

"Quite different from the European nations whose complexion and very features vary according to latitude, one can observe an invariable uniformity among the inhabitants whom one meets—from the sunny, scorching banks of the lower Mississippi of 30° latitude to the foggy regions of the Saguenay [2] of 50°. The Mistassing, the Missisagé of the North, resemble the Musk-Kogulgés and the Chectaw of Florida, the Arcansa of the South. They all have coarse black hair; all the same general appearance: their skin the color of copper, the whites of their eyes tinted with yellow. Wouldn't this analogy suggest that these nations are descendants of the same stock, and not of an old race, since the difference in climates has not yet produced any differences in their skin? On the other hand, the differences one notices among the languages of the South, the West, and the North are so great that such an opinion seems out of the question.

"Various confederations existed at the time of the discovery of the Continent. The best known were the Creeks in the two Floridas and Georgia; [3] the Poohatans in Virginia,[4] the Whelenys, or Illinois in upper Louisiana; [5] the Mohawks in New York; and the Lénopys in lower Pennsylvania and Jersey. Only the first tribe has persisted: of the Illinois, there remain only a few families who dwell on the banks of the river which bears their name. Nowadays one would not meet a single Poohatan in all of Virginia, nor a single Lénopy in the region which that tribe once inhabited. Of the Mohawks, now only the Oneidas are left, and some scatterings of the Cayugas and Senecas, for the Mohawks were forced to flee to Canada, where their number has diminished substantially in recent years.

"The nations of the Great Lakes and of Ohio,[6] although more agricultural, living as they are in one of the most fertile regions on this continent, are rapidly heading toward extinction, because they are exposed, like other nations, to the ravages of smallpox, the corruptions

* According to the details in this chapter, it appears evident that it must have been preceded by a great number of others which very likely disappeared when the chest containing the manuscripts was opened. The first five pages of the manuscript were so obliterated that the translation could begin only with Colonel Crawghan's observations.

of liquor. They are our dependents because of their fascination for European foods and it would seem that they are destined to disappear before the ascendency of the white man. In another few years there will be no trace of their existence other than the names given by their ancestors to the rivers, mountains and lakes of their land.''

"What could be," I asked him, "the cause of the inconceivable blindness which today, just as centuries ago, makes them prefer the roaming and precarious life of the woods to the more secure and settled life of farming? How could they close their eyes to the evidence of their gradual disintegration, to the disasters of drunkenness, as well as to the example and advice of people who came to live among them?"

"That does seem inconceivable," he replied. "I was here twenty years ago at the time when the first settlements were made on the fertile banks of this river and in the region occupied by the Mohawk nation. Never in the history of the colonies had there been such peaceful and friendly bonds. This state of affairs promised long continuance. The savages did not violate the agreements made in the sale of these lands; on the other hand, colonial laws protected their own lands from any invasion. In several cantons, Indian and white children playing together learned both languages. Contrary to our expectations, the harvests which they often helped to gather, the hay of the green meadows that they used to turn and dry, all the results of industry and harmony were fruitless. This long-lasting example of prosperity was futile. Although witnesses of the clearing of highlands and the draining of lowlands, although knowing the methods of these two important operations, and despite having lived for several years among colonists who had become rich and happy from farming, not one of them has been tempted to follow such a fine example.[7]

"This constant aversion to work and a sedentary life, the capriciousness of their conduct, the habitual state of thoughtlessness and childishness in which they live, wouldn't all these causes which betoken inferior intelligence be considered an insurmountable obstacle which has stood, and always will stand, in their way to a better life? Indeed, how strange that for centuries they have not participated in the progress of time which in the long run brings about those changes and circumstances to which other countries owed so many useful discoveries and inventions. To think, for example, that they have never tried to domesticate the buffalo which roam their prairies;[8] that they have never known the use of iron whose deposits are found on the surface of many meadows;[9] they have never cultivated rice which grows wild on the banks of Lake Ontario, Lake Michigan, Green Bay, and the Outagamy![10] Yes, I repeat, their peculiar lack of foresight which prevents the immediate future from meaning anything for them, the futility of the education which many of their children received in our colleges, the same futility of our missionaries' zeal in the teaching of the salutary precepts of the gospel have been coupled with the futility of their farming. All this proves that their intelligence is less susceptible to perfectibility than ours and that these races are inferior to those of Europe and of Asia. For the latter two, having lived like the North American Indians, from hunting and fishing for many centuries, succeeded finally in forging iron, and in domesticating wild animals.

"The plight of the great tribes, the Natticks, Pecods, Narragansets, Catawbas,[11] etc., confirms this opinion: for in the very heart of peace and plenty they have disintegrated while making feeble efforts at farming the land which colonial law had declared theirs, inviolable and untransferrable. An inconceivable thing! Their new condition has proven to be more disastrous to them than their former status.

"During the one hundred seventy years that we have known them, has anyone ever seen among them a single individual who has shown any spark of that celestial fire whence spring practical ideas and great concepts? No. Their relationships with us white men putting a stop to their wars, their revenges, and their cannibalism have not given them any new tastes. Even today, they do not feel the pride nor the advantages which result from the exclusive ownership and cultivation of a field. They have no conception of the pleasure of planting a tree, and the even more delightful pleasure of watching it grow and bear flowers and fruit, nor finally, that instinctive attachment that all men have for the place of their birth. Like wild animals, they leave it without regret and pitch their wigwams [12] elsewhere.

"On the other hand, how could one call them savage after having observed the unfailing gentleness of their domestic customs, their peace of mind, their unselfishness, their constant disposition to help one another in need or in distress (for among themselves they are really brothers)? How can one reconcile their barbarism with the tenderness with which they raise their children, the regrets, and the tears they shed when they lose these children, their respect for old age, as well as their reverence for the ashes of their ancestors? And what of the attachment they feel for their tribe and their nation, the heroic courage with which they endure hunger, illnesses, sufferings, and death? I know no friends more dependable, none more faithful. If occasionally one observes among them traits of bad faith, it is from us they have learned lying and cunning. Considered in this respect, who would not regret seeing their number shrink day after day?

"How can one reconcile the mildness of their customs with their ferocity in war, and their maltreatment of prisoners? This amazing contradiction is just as striking among all the nations I know: from the Mississippi to the north of Lake Ontario, they all have the same physiognomy, the same opinions, the same customs. What can have been their prototype? This racial leveling results from similar ways of life and occupations and must have developed in them the same needs and pleasures, producing analogous states of mind among them. Thus, one observes among these nations the same degree of indolence which prevents them from working and inspires in them only the deepest scorn for farming. The same impatience makes them disdain the repose of a quiet and sedentary life and lures them to the more remote and exhausting hunts, as well as to war. All of them reflect the imprint of a vacant mind and an inclination toward sadness. Yet, they do not truly know melancholy. All of them have to the same extent a carefreeness and lack of foresight, and, in spite of the recurring famines for which they are to blame, they become neither wiser nor more foresighted.''

"I was extremely impressed," I told him, "during the session of the last council, when the chiefs and warriors of eleven different nations were gathered, in observing among them not only the resemblance of the facial characteristics you just mentioned, but also the absolute lack of expression on their faces. Although they were curiously attentive to what you were saying to them, I saw on their sphinx-like faces no change, nor any of those subtle shifts of expression which mirror one's thoughts and are character indices."

"Where would any changes of expression come from?" he queried. "They know nothing of the effervescence of desire, the conflicts of passion, nor the anxiety of planning. Not clinging to life as we do, by the hope of fortune or self-betterment, they are rarely occupied with extremes of pleasant or heart-rending thoughts except when they lose their wives or children. Besides, one of the principles most deeply impressed on the young people is to preserve an unfailing impassiveness in all situations of life. Nevertheless, they sometimes lose this stoicism when they speak in public; then their faces light up; sparks sometimes flash from their imaginations, to scintillate for a moment. And lo! these very chiefs, who express themselves with so much vigor and zeal around the fires of their tribal councils, are in fact only capricious, unreflecting beings, to whom years add habits but rarely experience.

" 'Neath their roofs, the passing of time is nothing: they neither measure nor calculate its duration except when they hunt, fish or take to the war path. According to them, only these three occupations are worthy of a Nishynorbay.[13]

"Their womenfolk, less hardy and less cruel than the men, are all subjected to a hard and often painful life: they plant the corn, potatoes, tobacco, smoke the meat, carry all the burdens, and often accompany their husbands to the winter hunts,[14] as well as to war. Nevertheless, they enjoy a great influence in all tribal decisions (although they are not permitted to speak there), as well as in matters of adoption of prisoners.

"This adoption ceremony which, next to marriage, is the most important, endows the adopted individual with all the rights of friendship, kinship, and hospitality. It is a means for replacing losses created by war, by the devastation of nature and of time. Sometimes adoption is the cry of a broken heart which needs love again. I have occasionally seen very touching evidences of this, especially among the Wyandottes.

"Almost all their wars, although less frequent in recent years,[15] have sprung from one cause. They are impelled by revenge, for never has either avarice or desire for conquest caused the Indians to take up their tomahawks. That is why the ferocity of the conqueror and the resistance of the conquered produce scenes of fury and rage, tales of which make one shiver, suggesting as they do, bloodthirsty tigers in combat with angry lions.

" 'We are as destructive as fire,' Pontiac [16] once told me; 'fickle as the wind, inexorable as the tomb.'

"Often it happens that, thanks to the intercession of women, they adopt the prisoners instead of appeasing the memory of their dead ones by their destruction. Then they say:

" 'Don't bear us any malice for you will not be tossed into the cauldron; I will not drink the soup of your flesh. I will even let you share my bearskin.'

"But how can one depict the cruelties which they inflict upon victims who are doomed to die? If they struck them down with a quick blow, such a death would be a boon. But no, they draw life from them only in slow ways, submitting them to all the kinds of torture which their perverse minds can conjure up. Then arises an almost supernatural battle between the most heroic courage conceivable and the most unspeakable ferocity. The victim's resistance equals the torturer's persistance. Life which, in certain circumstances seems to hang by a mere thread, sometimes survives long hours of deep wounds, scalpings, and excoriations. And these, my friend, are human beings who, in order to wreak their relentless revenge upon an unfortunate captive, inflict on him such excruciating tortures. Yet in their villages, these same men are mild and compassionate.

"It is in the midst of these hellish torments which sometimes wring from the wretched victims piercing cries of pain, that the prisoner, tied to the stake, proudly intones the war chant, excites and calls upon the anger of the monstrous captor surrounding him, saying:

" 'If *I* had been the conqueror, I would have had *you* roasted slowly; I would have eaten your flesh and tossed your bones to the dogs.'

"'Here is what they told me when I would reproach them for their excessive barbarism:

" 'If we were to adopt all the prisoners we take, how would we appease the shades of our warriors? How would the village share in our triumph? Isn't it necessary that our young people, in watching these prisoners die, like braves, learn to endure such torture with that same courage?'

"What an education! What a state of things!" [17]

"Whether cannibalism was provoked by the irritation of hunger, or by craze for revenge or victory, it is certain that in their primitive state all nations were cannibalistic like the tribes of this continent. In reading Herodotus, one discovers that the ancient Egyptians worshipped Osiris for having taught them to eat vegetables instead of the flesh of their enemies. At the time of the Europeans' arrival on this continent, carnivorous customs were known from one border to the other. The interior of Brazil is still filled with tribes who, like their ancestors, are cannibalistic. The Ibo Negroes on the Côte des Dents, those of the Arsacides and Andaman Islands are all cannibals.[18] In fact, wherever Cook landed, he saw traces of cannibalism. You have doubtless read, and with shivers, too, the voyages of Captain Viaudi! How many times one has seen the same cause produce the same results among starving crews in mutiny at sea as well as in riots on land?

"Indeed," continued Colonel Crawghan, "a weak, bare being whom chance has thrust in the woods, finding neither fruit nor vegetable, devotes himself to hunting. Necessarily he has formed the habit of killing, of bloodspilling, of slaughtering animals to appease his hunger. Out of necessity he has become bloodthirsty and ferocious. The hunter loves solitude, hating his neighbors with whom he fears having to share his prey. Hunting, you see, has produced rivalries, revenges, and war; hence, no doubt, sprang the first fighting which drenched the land with blood, and likewise the fact that in the extreme irritation of need, or in the frenzy of victory, the victors assumed the right to eat their victims. Tragic and deplorable results of the cruelest of passions or of the starkest necessity.

"Therefore, you see, it is only at the moment when man became graminivorous that he could come to know compassion and pity! Only then did his savage and fierce habits become milder and his neighbors his friends.

"And yet that is the character of man as he emerged from the hand of his Maker, this person whose destinies have only too obviously justified the sinister circumstances under which he appeared on earth! There is that age of innocence and of happiness, that springtime of nature so often celebrated by the poets. This primitive state of degradation and misery probably lasted a number of centuries, until a time when some happy circumstance witnessed the emergence of men who were superior to their contemporaries. Instructed by experience and profiting by favorable conditions, these men united several bands of these fish-and-flesh-eating bipeds and taught them to cultivate the soil. They softened their ferocity by teaching them noble notions of what is just and what is unjust: virtue, remorse, ideas of rewarding and vengeful Gods. If, under these new conditions man came to know times of peace and prosperity, it is to man, himself, that he owes it, and not to nature.*

"Like the wild vine of the forest, whose fruits were bitter until the time when the marvelous invention of the graft, modifying the sap, made trees bear finer fruits, man in his primitive state was but an uncultivated being, unsociable and savage, until the time when civilization, developing his intellect, created in him a feeling of power, together with means for using this power to increase his enjoyment and happiness. What ingenuity had to be used before man was intellectually ready for the sacrifices necessary in civilized society! And to make that wild, thorny plant produce the magnificent fruits which are developed by civilization! If in traveling this new course, man has encountered fresh sources of disappointment and doom, and if he has perhaps regretted the passing of his earlier freedom in the forests, this doom and disappointment are inevitable for their sources are in the passions which he can neither repress nor alter.**

"The Indians' bodies, almost continually exposed to the inclemency of the air, are far less susceptible than are ours to atmospheric changes and change of seasons.

---

* Is this plaintive plea uttered by a sensitive soul, well considered? Above all, is it justified? Rather, isn't it a genuine benefit granted by the Creator to mankind that he has assured the permanence of civilization, by the very comparison that man would have to make some day between the rigors of his primitive state and the advantages of his later social state? An examination of this question would take us far. Weak and limited beings that we are, let us not pass judgment on Providence; especially, let us refrain from inveighing against her. Let us remember, rather, that every doubt raised against her existence by a worthy man, is greedily grabbed by a materialist or an atheist (if there are any who are sincere) and becomes for them a pretext for triumph.

(Note written to the editor by Citizen Bilocq.)

** This last suggestion need not be refuted: the paradox is obvious. Man unquestionably has violent passions, often tyrannical. But, that he is unable to quell those passions by dint of combat or virtue, Colonel Crawghan will never fortunately be able to convince anyone.

" 'Aren't you cold?' I inquired of a nearly naked Powatooatami [19] one freezing day.

" 'Is your face cold?' he countered haughtily.

" 'No.' I told him, 'my face is accustomed to the whip of the wind and ice.'

" 'Well, my body is all face!'

"Healthy and vigorous, although less able than we are to endure the drudgery of farming, those who manage to escape the dangers of smallpox, and the abuse of spirits, live to a ripe old age.

"The education of their children is based simply enough on the example of their parents who seldom discipline or punish them. Nudity, almost constant exercise, especially swimming—in which they excel, fortifies them and gives them an agility and suppleness which has often amazed me. I have never seen any deformed bodies among them. Most of the men are tall and well proportioned; they are proud without being brutal, more serious than gay. This frame of mind often produces on their faces the suggestion of 'inanimation' yet different from a look of sadness.

"Like all primitive tribes, they believe that the world is subject to two principles or spirits: they claim that the good one is too far up to be aware of what is happening on earth—that is Agan-Kitchee-Ockemaw, the organizer and animating spirit of all matter. Never do they appeal to him.... The other, an evil spirit who haunts the shadows of the night, whence he sends baleful dreams, illnesses, misfortunes, tempests, snow, ice, and war. That is Agan-Matchee-Manitoo, whose anger these men believe they are appeasing, when, from their wigwams,[20] they offer up to him a twist of tobacco * and the red pipe of peace.[21] Countless incidents, such as dreams, the behavior of beavers, the appearance of the full moon, the arrival of the bees,[22] burglary in their wigwams, provoke either favorable or ominous presentiments about which they consult their medicine men and witch doctors. Such is the narrow range of their religious ideas, based on a fear of evil, rather than the hope of a future happiness, of which few nations have the remotest notion. The Shawnees,[23] the Ottawas, and the Wyandottes of the Sandusky [24] River valley all believe that after death the souls of good hunters and brave warriors will depart for a western land where there will be abundant hunting and fishing and where war will be unknown; from this, the expression *to go west* has become synony-

---

* On this subject, consult Chapter VII of the *Journey of J. Long Among Various Uncivilized Nations of North America*. Translated and published in the Year II by Citizen Billecocq. This account by an ordinary fur trader is one of the most reliable, accurate and interesting ones I know.

Ed. note.

mous with that of death. Among the tribes I have known, I have observed no evidence of prayers nor of sacrifices. For these ideas, fruits of civilization, are still foreign to them; they all have a sincere respect for the memory of their ancestors as well as for the hallowed places where their ashes lie.

"After many years of effort and perseverance, our missionaries finally christened some tribes. Of all the sects, the Moravians and the Quakers have proven themselves the most zealous in the accomplishment of this great work. On the banks of the Muskingum,[25] the former founded a respectable and fair-sized colony of converts whom unforeseen events have since scattered. In an attempt to compensate for this disaster, the federal government has just granted them a site of ten thousand acres of land where these pious missionaries feel sure they will unite the scattered remainder. May their new efforts be crowned with success!

"Each family is governed, or rather presided over, by the father or grandfather; and in the villages the Sachems rule. The latter are elected to these positions, the former of course inherit their authority, which is more fatherly than forceful: but so great is the young peoples' respect for their elders that the title alone suffices to impress them.

"The peace of these villages is seldom broken by quarrels, unless drunkenness has been rampant. Barring this fatal source of dissension, which often has murderous consequences, there would never be any discord among these dispassionate men who have neither ambitions nor property. Provided they have something to eat, they are satisfied and content."

" 'If you use up all your food today, what will you eat tomorrow?'

" 'Where is tomorrow? Perhaps we will never live to see it,' they retort.

"The quarrels and the fights which often arise among them following drunken orgies are a reflection of the most extreme excess of degradation into which human nature can fall. Armed with knives or their tomahawks, they spring to their feet, strike up their war cry, stamping in rhythm around the fires which always constitute the center of their gatherings, and yell their war whoop.[26] And if one of them should try to vaunt his prowess and tell of his most daring deed, immediately the others, believing themselves insulted, stop and deny his story. Then to anger and indignation; threats follow, then insults and finally blows. In the midst of this tumult, or rather frenzy, brothers and friends cease to recognize one another. Fathers and sons often become enemies of each other. Bonds of brotherhood and association are broken. It becomes now a war of every man against his brother. There is not an old man or a chief who can interpose his authority. These mad men, foaming with rage, their eyes flashing with anger, know no one.

"It is their wives and their daughters who, like angels of peace risking their very lives, dash into the midst of this horrible brawl, disarm, and often succeed in knocking down the most enraged and in restraining them until sleep overtakes them."

" 'I was crazy,' they solemnly say on awakening.

"Unbelievable though it may seem, the disorder occasioned by these frightful scenes, the experience of their fatal results make absolutely no impression on their minds and provoke no regrets whatsoever. Carried away by an unimaginable sense of fatality, they would begin again the next day, if on the next day, they were able to procure a fresh supply of firewater. For that is the scourge that day by day shrinks their numbers. In the light of all this, you can judge what services the missionaries perform for the inhabitants of these villages whence they have forbidden this liquor of madness and death.

"Games of chance are very common among the hunters; the craze for them produces the same results one sees in Europe. Only instead of guineas or dollars, they bet furs, skins or kettles. One of their greatest pleasures is that of listening, while they smoke, to the telling of stories to which their empty, idle minds pay the deepest attention. What an influence one could exert over them if one cared to take the trouble to compose tales to their taste.

"Dreams are always considered as forecasts to which one must pay strict attention. Nothing is more irritating to them than to have had bad dreams. And, to wish someone happy dreams is always considered a compliment: sometimes it is a device for begging."

" 'One day,' Sir William Johnson [27] told me, 'old Nissooassou [28] came to my home and said:

" 'O father, last night I dreamed that you gave me a fine scarlet-coloured suit, trimmed with gold, with a hat to match.'

" 'You don't say!'

" 'Yes, on my word as a Sachem,' he replied.

" 'Well, then, you shall not have dreamed in vain, for I shall present you with them, and gladly.'

" 'The next day,' continued Sir William, 'having invited him to dinner, I saw my chance, saying:

" 'Henrique, I, too, had a dream last night.'

" 'What did you dream, father?' he asked me.

" 'That in the name of your tribe, you gave me a small piece of land on the Tienaderhah, known as Acerouni.'

" 'In terms of acres, how much land does this include?'

" 'Ten thousand,' I replied.

" 'After a few moments of thought, he said to me:

" 'Well, you shall not have dreamed in vain either, for I shall give you this little piece of land: but don't take it into your head to dream any more, good father.'

" 'And why not, Henrique? Dreams are involuntary, aren't they?'

" 'You dream too hard for me and soon you wouldn't leave any more land for our people.'

"The law of retaliation," he continued, "prevents murders: nothing is rarer among these Indians, except for those occasioned by drunkenness, which they excuse, because, they claim, these acts result from madness, not from malice aforethought. Although any manner of checks and restraints is unbearable to them, and provokes them to fury, they know neither the disorder of anarchy nor the hell of license. That fact one can attribute to their respect for old age, as well as to their aversion to ownership. Whether it be in war, sickness, calamity, or wounds, they push courage to the point of heroism, and die without uttering any wails, moans, or regrets. The tribes distant from our frontier, less exposed to the ravages of smallpox and the overindulgence of liquor, are far more respectable and numerous than those near to us. They preserve something of the independence and pride that is their tribal characteristic. One can still see in their warriors an alert and penetrating eye, and when they frown, those hints of primitive savagery. But unfortunately for these nations, they can no longer do without European merchandise. What would they do today without our kettles and blankets, for instance? Without the powder and lead necessary in hunting? They are doomed to disappear somewhat later than the other tribes, for as Korey-Hoosta, chief of the Missisages [29] said some thirty years ago:

" 'The race of sowers of those wonderful little seeds,[30] wheat, and rye, is certainly destined to outlast men who live by what they kill, unless these hunters soon stir themselves to an agrarian way of life.' "

(There appears to be a considerable portion missing here.) *

---

* This remark between parentheses is Crèvecoeur's, NOT Crèvecoeur's translator's. Almost every chapter has some such remark. These remarks were used by Crèvecoeur to explain abrupt transitions, sudden plunges, quick cut-offs. Although they are not always followed by "Translator's (i.e., Crèvecoeur) Note," THEY ARE ALL NOTES BY CRÈVECOEUR.

CHAPTER II

In 1787 I accompanied the venerable Franklin, then governor of Pennsylvania, on a trip to Lancaster where he had been invited to lay the cornerstone of the college [A] he had recently founded for the Pennsylvania Dutch. On the eve of that ceremony, we were discussing the different races that inhabit this continent, their aversion to farming, etc., when one of the leading citizens of the town addressed Mr. Franklin:

"Your Excellency, whence do you think these nations may have come? Do you think they are aborigines? Have you heard about the ancient fortifications and the tombs that have been discovered quite recently in the west?"

He replied: "The nations of the two Floridas and Louisiana allege that they came from the mountains of Mexico. I should be inclined to believe it. If one can judge from the Esquimo [1] tribes (the most savage men known) along the Labrador coast, by the fairness of their skin, the color of their eyes, and their enormous beards, they originated in northern Europe whence they migrated a long time ago. As for the other nations of this continent, it would be difficult to imagine from what stock they are descended. To attribute to them an Asiatic and Tartar origin, to suggest that they must have crossed the Behring Strait [2] and roamed this continent, in my opinion, would shock all probability. Indeed, how can one conceive of a band of almost naked men, armed only with bows and arrows, undertaking a journey of one thousand leagues, through deep forests and impenetrable swamps, accompanied by their wives and children and absolutely dependent on hunting to keep alive? What motives could have prompted their migration? If it was the cruel cold of their native country, why then, would they have penetrated as far north as lower Canada and Hudson Bay? Why, I wonder, would they not have settled along the beautiful plains of the Missouri, Minnesota,[3] Mississippi, or Illinois? But, one might suggest, perhaps they did linger in those places and mayhap the tribes we know today are merely the overflow of the ancient migrations. If this were true, we would discover some similarities in language, and we know beyond a doubt that the Nadouasses' and the Padoukas' [4] languages no more resemble the Chippeway the Mohawk, nor the Abenaky, than they resemble the Kamchatka tongue.

"On the other hand, how can we presume that they originated in a region such as this, which produces almost no fruit or plant on which early man could have lived until he knew how to make a bow and arrow,

spear a fish and light a fire? How could these early families endure
the bad weather, the bite of insects, the attacks of carnivorous animals? Assuredly, the warm climate fostering an abundance of wild
fruit must have been the cradle of settlement of human kind. It is from
the heart of these favored regions that the exuberant members of early
society by slow degrees spread over the rest of the earth. Whence
came these nations inhabiting this land? Whence came those whom
one sees on the beaches of Zealand and New Holland as well as those
dwelling on the Pacific Ocean Islands. Why have the nations of the old
world been civilized for thousands of centuries while those of the
new world are still plunged in ignorance and barbarism? Is it possible that this hemisphere has more recently emerged from the waters?
These questions, and a thousand others one could ask, will for us, mere
transitory beings, be like a vast desert where the wandering eye can
not see the tiniest bush.

"This planet is quite old. Like the works of Homer and Hesiod,
who can say with certainty through how many 'editions' it has passed
since time began? The ragged continents, the straits, gulfs, islands, shal-
lows, and shoals of the ocean are vast fragments of debris on which in
early times men, as on the planks of a wrecked vessel surviving the
chaos, finally succeeded in refashioning new lives for themselves. Time,
so precious to us who are here on earth for so short a time, means nothing to nature. Who can tell in what future epoch there will be a recurrence of these deadly catastrophes to which the earth in its rotations
seems as obviously exposed as ships at sea are to dashing against reefs
and rocks on uncharted seas? What will have to take place to change climates and make the earth habitable for long? The near approach, or
collision with one of these orbs whose elliptical and mysterious courses
are perhaps the agents of our destiny; some variation in its annual
or diurnal rotation, in the inclination of the poles, or the balance of
the seas.

"As to your third question," Governor Franklin continued, "here
are a few ideas provoked by the reading of some papers, recently presented to our Philosophical Society by Generals Varnum and Parsons,
and Captains John Hart and Serjeant, relative to entrenched camps
and other indications of an ancient people whose traditions seem to
mean nothing to our Indians. In traveling through the regions beyond
the Alleghanies in this state, one often finds on elevations near the
rivers evidences of walls and ditches covered with very high trees.
In fact almost the entire Muskinghum peninsula is occupied by a vast
fortified camp, divided into three squared enclosures. The one in the
middle, larger than the others, communicates with the former bed of

the Muskingham whose waters appear to have retreated almost three hundred feet. These enclosures are formed by ditches and parapets of earth, in which no cut stones or brick have been found. In the middle there are cone-shaped elevations of varying diameters and heights. Each of these fortifications appears to have had a cemetery. As proof of the great antiquity we are told that the bones have been converted into calcareous matter and that the vegetable soil with which these fortifications are covered (caused by nothing more than the fall of leaves and debris from trees) was almost as thick as that of the surrounding area. In like manner, two similar settlements have been discovered in the region of Lexington.[5] One covers six acres; the other three. The fragments of earthenware that have been found during cultivation of the land are of a composition unknown to our Indians.

"Along Paint Creek a branch of the Scioto, can be seen a series of fortified enclosures extending as far as the Ohio and even south of that river. Similar structures are located along the two Miami[6] branches at a distance of twenty miles, as well as along Big-Grave Creek.[7] These last however, are only a series of elevated redoubts erected along the banks of these rivers at unequal distances apart. Those which were found on Big Black Creek and at Byo-Pierre, in the Mississippi River region, appear to have been a kind of levee designed to shelter men from the floods.

"Five hundred leagues from the sea, on the eastern shore of Lake Peppin (which is merely an extension of the Mississippi) Carver found substantial evidence of retrenchments, made of earth and covered with full grown trees like those I described. The barrows (burial mounds) recently discovered in Kentucky and elsewhere are cone-shaped structures of varying diameters and heights. They are reinforced with a thick layer of earth, and though smaller, resemble those one can still see in Asia and in some parts of Europe. On the first layer of bodies piled on flat stones which cover the entire floor is piled another layer, which serves, in turn, as a bed for other bodies and so on to the very top. Just as in the fortifications along the Muskinghum River, no evidence of the use of mortar nor of the hammer has been found. The new state of Tennessee is filled with these tombs. Some caverns, containing bones have also been found there.

"In the vicinity of some villages of the Cherokees, at Keowe, Steccoe, Sinica, etc., one can see embankments, very high pyramid-shaped artificial hills: their origin was unknown to the inhabitants whom the Cherokees drove out at the time of their invasion nearly two centuries ago. The same artificial elevations, the same proofs of the presence and power of early tribes, are evident also in the two Floridas, along the banks of the Oakmulgé, at Taensa, on the Alabama,[8] etc.

"When and by what nation were these structures built? What degree of civilization had that nation attained? Were they familiar with the use of iron? What became of them? Can one conceive of nations powerful enough to raise such substantial fortifications, and burying their dead with such reverence, being destroyed and replaced by these ignorant, barbarous hordes we see today? Is it possible that disasters caused by a prolonged state of war have blotted out the last traces of civilization and made them retrogress to the primitive state of the hunter? Could it be that our Indians today are descendants of that ancient people?

"These are some of the doubts and conjectures which are provoked by the evidence of the migrations and existence of tribes which inhabited the regions in the West: traces which are not really clear enough to guide us through the mysterious past. Although neither weapons nor tools of iron have been discovered, how can one visualize their digging such deep ditches and building earthworks of such proportions without the aid of this metal? This ancient people must have had leaders and they must have had laws. For without bonds of subordination, how could they have united and kept in check such a great number of workers? Such a nation must have known how to farm, for game could never have been plentiful enough to suffice them. The extent of these camps serves as evidence of the great number of warriors who must have been assigned to their defense, as well as the number of families who must have sought here a refuge from danger. The existence of cemeteries proves that before these people must have made long sojourns in these areas, it would seem then that this nation was far more advanced in civilization than our Indians today.

"When the population of the United States has spread over all parts of this great, wide, beautiful land, our descendants, aided by new discoveries will be able to make more satisfactory guesses. What a fertile field for conjecture! A new continent which, at some unknown date, appears to have been occupied by agrarian and warlike tribes! Were it not for my advanced years, I myself would cross the mountains to examine these ancient fortification works. Perhaps a close, detailed inspection would give rise to some conjectures, which elude us today."

CHAPTER III

For a long time I had planned to attend the two great councils which the newspapers in New York had announced. The first was to be held at Onondaga [1] in the Mohawk region by the chiefs of the Oneida, Cayuga, Seneca, and Tuscarora tribes. The second at Fort Stanwix [2] where these same tribal chieftains had been invited by the governor of New York. But, apprehensive of the distance as well as of the discomforts of such a long journey through territory which I knew was only recently settled, I was undecided until, inveigled by the enthusiastic entreaties of Mr. Herman, a well-educated young man who had just arrived from Europe, and had been highly recommended to me, I resolved to undertake the journey. Furnished with much information, which unfortunately would be of little use beyond Northumberland, the last outpost of the cultivated region, we left Shippenbourg [3] and arrived that same evening in Carlisle, having crossed seventeen miles of the most fertile land in Pennsylvania.

This little place, county seat of Cumberland county, and located 140 miles from Philadelphia, on the route which leads over the mountains to the western regions, and very near the Susquehanna, gives the impression of youth to the traveler. Some of the most beautiful trees, preserved by the first colonists, still stand, beautifying the surroundings. Almost all built of stone, the houses, instead of adjoining one another, are separated either by an orchard or by a garden or a barn; often by all three. All this, of course, enhances their natural beauty and in summer assures coolness. Although there are only three hundred seventy houses and about eighteen hundred inhabitants in this town, it covers an area that in Europe would suffice for twenty thousand persons.

That region is so fertile and so healthful that it was chosen by Governor Dickinson as the most appropriate place for the establishment of the college which he founded there in 1783. This fine institution, fruit of the patriotic spirit of this famous man,[4] already boasts three professorships, a small library, and the beginnings of a physics laboratory. On seeing all this improvement, Mr. Herman could scarcely bring himself to believe that we were more than three hundred miles from the sea and that this section of Pennsylvania had been under cultivation only forty years.

Mr. B., a wealthy, well-educated man to whom we were commended, entertained us by the hour with episodes from his life. He had come

over from Ireland, a mere lad of eleven, as an indentured servant.*
Mr. P. S., to whose home chance had steered him, was so pleased with
his aptitudes and services that he cut short his time, gave him a fine
education, and set him up in business. At the end of several conscientious years of work, fortune, as though to compensate for its
oversight, overwhelmed him with favor. Now owner of a fine waterfall
near the town, he built on it a large mill according to the principles
of Oliver Evans, the leading engineer of the continent. In this mill he
converted annually forty thousand bushels of wheat into flour and
meal.

Exceedingly pleased with this auspicious beginning, we left Mr. B.
the next day and went to sleep that night on the banks of the Juniata,
three miles above its junction with the Susquehanna, twenty-five miles
from Carlisle. Despite the roughness of the road, we arrived early
enough in the evening to enjoy a few hours of shad fishing. The judge
in that region, Mr. Jenning, imparted some interesting observations
relative to the course of this river from the Alleghany mountains, as
well as to the progress of the farming in the different counties that
it waters.

"I know of no other river," he said, "whose banks offer more magnificent, yet wilder views. Just twenty miles from here one can see
great grottoes filled with concretions and stalactites. But we are still
too young a nation to have among us mineralogists and lovers of
natural history."

The next day we dined at Mahatango Creek, fifteen miles further.
Its turbulent waters turn many mills. The third day we had our evening meal at Penn's Creek. Some time before arriving there from the
mountains to the east of our route, we saw the town of Sunbury, located
on a little plain, on the east bank of the Susquehanna, which we crossed
in the evening in order to reach Northumberland.

Having landed on this beautiful peninsula we hastened to take our
letters of introduction to Mr. Plunkett, the general surveyor of the
county. His father, we knew, had been killed in one of the uprisings
which were caused by the arrival of people from Connecticut on the
east branch of the river. He occupied the only stone house there was
in this town, the rest being log houses.[5]

After supper he said to us, "You came a few years too soon, gentlemen. We are still only in the first stages of land clearing and cultivation. Our creeks have no bridges, the roads in many sections are mere
paths, rarely used. Despite your courage, I fear that crude lodgings,
the sight of such wild and uncultivated land, rough log cabins covered

* A guess, but a likely one.

only with bark, all this melancholy monotony of the woods will arouse your distaste and boredom, rather than inspire you with new and instructive observations. Indeed, what a contrast there is between the countrysides of Europe and these provinces whose surveying is scarcely completed! What a difference between our fields, bristling with stumps, badly worked, enclosed by clumsy-looking fences, and an open land beautified with green hedges, twining vines, and thriving orchards! Many years will elapse before this one will deserve the traveler's attention, before each section shut in by mountain gorges of rivers will give easy access to the neighboring countryside. On the other hand, the clearing, the rapidly increasing population of this continent, presents an exciting new prospect. Little by little we are shaping a new order, perhaps the most interesting one that has been presented to man in many a century.

"Almost all of the families that have settled along the road that leads to the Meshoppen [6] ferry come from Europe. Their methods, as you will see, are still quite imperfect. A few years of the useful apprenticeship that they are serving will make them more hard working and more resourceful. For the first time in their lives these colonists are working for themselves, clearing forests from the land which belongs to them. They are the precursors of the vast throng of people who will follow in their wake and who in four or five years will replace those who succumb to laziness or bad habits. They are quite different from the New England [7] colonists who, wherever they migrate, carry with them the precious qualities of industriousness, religion, refinement.[8] Scarcely have they cleared and planted some of their fields, when they meet to build a church and a school. My dear friends, it is laborers that we lack: he who in the autumn has sown twenty acres of wheat is often very embarrassed when harvest time arrives, for where will he find reapers? Yet, the childhood of this land of ours will not last as long as you may think, especially if by good hap, the new ideas raging in Europe do not come to agitate our wise and young government and prevent its consolidation.

"Founded in 1774, this town was destroyed six years later by the Indians," he continued. "Only since 1785 has it emerged slowly from the ashes. The cause of this slowness stems from the difference which has existed so long between the state of Connecticut and this one, relative to the ownership of lands irrigated by the eastern branch of the Susquehanna River. It has been finally settled as far as jurisdiction goes, but not insofar as ownership is concerned. The government is working on the problem and we hope that, at the next meeting of the legislative branch, everyone will receive the land to which he is entitled. Then the prosperity of this little town will increase rapidly. Then these crude cabins will be replaced by fine homes and we will enjoy all the advantages promised by the junction of these two rivers, navigable to their very source six months a year, for more than two hundred miles—especially after the State has eliminated the obstacles which obstruct inland navigation from the mouth of the Juniata to the Swatara.[9] The fine spirit of our legislative body makes us hope that this great work will be accomplished within a few years. Already the state has appropriated 800,000 piastres (four million two hundred thousand pounds) for a bid on the work.''

Very eager to see the beautiful plains of Wilkesbury, Wyoming, and Mashaney from which the Indians chased the Connecticut settlers during the Revolution, my companion and I tried to rent a boat in order to get upstream to the Meshoppen ferry, one hundred thirty miles from Northumberland. Unable to find any sturdy enough to bear the weight of our horses, we decided to cut across the middle of this county, taking the path indicated by Mr. Plunkett. It was the most direct route we could follow to enter the northern section of the Luzerne region, located east of the river, and bringing us closer to the dividing line separating the state of Pennsylvania from that of New York. From there we could easily reach Lake Otsego, Albany, and Schenectady on the Mohawk River, whose waters would transport us to Fort Stanwick.

After leaving Mr. Plunkett, for some time we followed the banks of the Mahoning which we found rather well cultivated, but from the source of this river on, we encountered only winding trails and from time to time scattered cabins occupied by settlers who had only recently arrived. Occasionally trees, fallen from decay or uprooted by violent storms, obstructed our way and forced us to make a considerable number of detours. We were traveling slowly, and it was only on the third day of our journey, that I observed how impressed Mr. Herman was with the difficulties of traveling, the poor lodgings, and above all, the silence and obscurity of the woods.

''Can this be the usual appearance and primitive state of the forests in the New World?'' he queried. ''I don't know why, but I had an entirely different idea of them! It is the homeland of bears and wolves, not of men.

''How rough and dismal the land seems, how dark and gloomy these solitudes! How can one think that these hills, so heavily wooded, and these swamps, filled with dense undergrowth are destined some day to become smiling slopes and greening meadows!''

''Well,'' I answered, ''the beautiful regions of Shippensbourg,

Carlisle, Reading, and Lancaster and so many others resemble what you see here at the time of the arrival of the first colonists. What would you think if we were to penetrate even thicker forests, and swamps whose surface is but a bed of uprooted trees, one wots not why nor for how long? When you have seen what man's strength and intelligence is capable of in a short span of time, then and only then will you realize that these obstacles are easy to surmount and that it is easier than you would think to destroy these giant trees, to let the sun penetrate the soil and cover their land with fine crops.''

''I find that difficult to understand,'' he replied, ''for after all, no matter how industrious the colonists are, they have not the strength of Hercules, and their powers can hardly match the resistance that nature offers.''

''This long series of work and projects,'' I replied, ''require more skill and perseverance than actual strength; fire does a good half of the task. Would you believe that within one year after their arrival in the autumn [10] ten men can sow twenty acres of wheat? Yet it is very true: after clearing the ground, piling and burning the brush and the shrub, they ring the bark of the trees, causing them to die. Then they merely harrow the ground.[11] Fencing these fields, the most toilsome task, is necessary because of the great number of beasts that roam the woods.''

Meanwhile we were making our way slowly, keeping to the left branch of the Chiquisquaque Creek, that we had already twice crossed, when we sighted a dwelling covered with shingles in the midst of a fairly wide clearing. The owner whom we met very soon afterward offered us shelter for the night with charming alacrity. We followed him across a good-sized field of wheat. After taking care of our horses, this worthy settler showed us with a kind of reverence the stump of the first pine tree that he had cut down a few years before. He pointed out what he had already accomplished, what he still had to do before he could settle down to a life of ease and affluence. He reckoned the time when a certain part of his swamp land would be converted into pasture land, when one hillside would be covered with wheat, another with clover, and another planted with apple and peach [12] trees—all this with an air of joy and satisfaction that we shared spontaneously. It seemed to me I had never seen hope in such a humble and touching light. It was like the plenitude of a happiness not yet realized.

''The desire to contribute to the happiness of my family, to assure their independence after my death, made me decide a few years ago to leave the town of Fairfield [13] where I taught a Greek and Latin School. Content with my lot, I was teaching the young people entrusted to me as best I could, when one day I learned of the death of one of my relatives who had just passed away in Bengal, leaving me nineteen hundred dollars. Fearing to risk such a sum in business, I resolved to invest it in some new land, the only speculation that rarely disappoints us if we join thereto industry and activity. Learning that the government of Pensylvanie had just formed a county of this part of the state, I came here. After an inspection, I bought the four hundred twenty-six acres that I own here for three hundred seventy-five dollars (the price has more than doubled since the uprisings in Europe). I hired a fellow-countryman who is still with me. Together we built this house from the trunks of the first trees that we felled. At Wilkesbury, we bought enough provisions for one year, a team of oxen, two foal-mares, and necessary work tools. Finally after six months of labor, occupied chiefly in draining a few acres of swamp land and in clearing seventeen acres in which we planted wheat, I went to fetch my family. Since their arrival, hope has never abandoned me for a single moment. Between the fertility of the soils and the price of provisions, I see sure reward to him who wants to earn it by virtue of intelligence and work. I sow much less than my neighbors, yet I harvest more because my methods of cultivation are better. Since my arrival here I haven't been the least bit smitten by discouragement, despite countless obstacles to overcome. Quite different from me is my nearest neighbor, five miles from here. He is very dissatisfied with his plight, his location, the condition of his land, which is every bit as fertile as mine; he plans to make some profit from his miserable improvements and move elsewhere. But he will never be happy anywhere and will waste his life away in false starts. Such a character is fairly common among the early colonists. As for me, I have such confidence in my own strength and courage, that I often do much more than I thought myself capable of. This, only because I believe in myself, and that is a powerful lever when one is faced with the business of uprooting a stump or tree.

"I had the foresight to bring with me a great quantity of fruit stones and pits, which I carefully planted. In a few years my nursery will be the source of all the fruit trees and orchards of the region. I am in debt to no one. Already I am beginning to sell the surplus of my little harvests to colonists who settled after me and whose progress is not so far along as mine. The only inconvenience I experience is the distance from a mill, a church, and a smithy. Eight shillings a year to encourage the destruction of wolves and panthers! This is the only tax that the government imposes, or rather the contribution we offer with pleasure and gratitude. The government is engaged in opening extremely useful roads. Tomorrow you will travel on the one known as Bridle Road which starts at the source of the Monsey on the east branch and ends at the head of the Sissheny source which empties into the west branch. There are still some stumps remaining, it is true, but the bridges have just been completed. As we drain our swamps, the insects disappear. Congressional law encourages maritime trade. This flourishing trade encourages farming. Our country is now enjoying peace and harmony. Until now heaven has blessed the works of its children and the seasons have been favorable to us. Morning and night we entreat its instruction and its favor, which we try to deserve not only through prayer but also by hard work and co-operation. I fear only the flight of time, which, like water in a stream, so swiftly flows away.

"That, gentlemen, is how the schoolmaster from Fairfield became a citizen of Pennsylvania and a freeholder of Northumberland County."

Impressed with what he had just heard, Mr. Herman said to me that evening:

"The candid tone in the conversation of this fine settler from Connecticut has made a very deep impression on me. I blush at my own weakness. Think of it! This man, transported from the snugness of a town to the heart of the woods, traversed only by a few trails, subject to hard work and painful toil, compared to his former occupation, and separated from his family and friends and from the succor of society, is gay and content withal. In the evening, happy in the thought that he has accomplished the day's tasks, he thanks heaven for its mercy and the next day begins anew with the same courage and blithe spirit. Hope of ease and independence spurs him on, encouraging him; it takes the place of his present happiness. He is both a good father, a devoted husband and a fine farmer. While I, whom fortune has favored, I, who crossed the ocean to enjoy meditating upon the origin and development of these young societies, I would not have the fortitude to overcome even temporary disgust and to stand even a few temporary inconveniences which habit would soon banish. Suddenly I feel myself a new man. If ever the obstacles and hazards of travel, the inconvenience of lodging cause a recurrence of this shameful pusillanimity, I shall remember what Mr. Doolittle has just told us."

The next day in accordance with our host's intention, we followed a new route just completed and known as the Bridle Road. It led from the Monsey, on the west branch, to the Sissheny, which empties into the eastern branch.

CHAPTER IV

We were journeying on in much gayer spirits through exceedingly dark and dense forests when Mr. Herman's courage was again challenged by the necessity of swimming across two branches of Fishing-Creek, amid the trees and bushes brought down by the spring floods.

"How much time and labor lie ahead before the beds of these rivers are completely cleaned and their banks, so marshy and of such negligible value to the traveler today, will become smiling meadows, like those which border the Elbe from Magdeburg to Cuxhaven!" mused Mr. Herman. "How many hardships and worries face these colonists till, from their thresholds on a fine summer's evening, they can behold their fields covered with a wealth of cultivation and their orchards laden with fruit!"

The monotony of this long and difficult journey of sixty-seven miles to the ferry at Mashoping on the great river was eased for us a little only because we encountered numerous families, mostly all European, but so recently settled that we had difficulty finding shelter and nourishment for ourselves and our horses. Busy as they were, in putting up fences, ringing the bark of the huge trees for felling, piling up and burning the dry brush, they had as yet harvested only vegetables.

"Ah!" said a Swede at whose dwelling we baited our horses, "I can pass on without being uneasy over the future of my children, since I am living in a land of plenty where work is amply rewarded: assuredly they will not be exposed to the shame of begging, of remorse, nor to the dangers of crime."

"Indeed," another told us, "I shall no longer have to harness my poor cows to my old plow as I used to in order to stir in vain the barren soil of my fatherland, for here oxen and horses will work the rich soil which belongs to me."

"As for me, I was born in Savoy, in the region of avalanches and glaciers," said a third. "I worked hard and lacked nothing for my happiness except the protection of the law and that of the earth—which is everything! Here I have found everything I need and more too, since the god of harvest and our government require only our prayers and gratitude."

After crossing the Susquehanna, we were continuing on our way slowly in Lucerne County when my companion said to me:

"Yes, only since my arrival at the Fairfield Plantation I confess, I have begun to fulfill the aim of my journey; for since my visit there,

I find myself more interested not only in these wood or bark cabins, the first shelter of the colonists, and destined some day to be replaced by prosperous homes, but also in the preliminary clearings which, in accordance with the dictates of industry and necessity, will transform all this wild, uncultivated land into fertile fields. I am far less repelled by exploring these woods whose soil, till now rough and unproductive, will soon nourish thousands of families; and by these boggy and impenetrable marshlands on which countless flocks will soon graze. Finally, I have arrived in the midst of what can properly be called the very origin of society! Yes, surely; for in this region where a mere seven months ago one could hear the panther screech and the wolf howl, we see the plow trace the first furrows, fire devour bushes and useless growth; we hear the noise of axes, the songs of gaiety: everywhere, activity and life. Indeed, we are following paths which will one day become great and beautiful roads, and we even talk with high ranking public officers who are busy like the other colonists in clearing their land, planting their corn, or sowing their first crop of wheat in the midst of trees, ringed, but not yet felled, and branches, stumps, and roots that are piled up and still burning.''

"This," I replied, "is how Europe had its beginning. But what a difference between the customs, the laws of those bygone times and what one sees here! Such a difference in centuries and progress! As obscure rivers like these, hidden in the bosom of mountains, whose imperceptible reunion makes rivulets, streams, and rivers, these minute centers of population we have noticed while crossing these ancient forests, will change this land into fertile fields, into meadows pied with flowers. In just a few years, one will see emerge from these beehives of activity countless swarms of people who will bring even more remote regions under cultivation. What resources an industrious, ambitious, and conscientious man can find here! An abundance of food, of low-priced land, of rich, unworked soil, of protective laws, and flourishing commerce. These rare and precious advantages are bound to provide human growth with all the vigor and richness it can assimilate. Who knows how far all this progress can expand in a half-century.

"Here," I continued, "the universal desire is to possess a certain amount of land and to cultivate it. Thus, agriculture, though still quite crude as it has been since the beginning of the colonies, has become the favorite occupation of two-thirds of society and the foundation for the prosperity of the states. However, all the colonists do not succeed: here, as elsewhere, success does not crown all enterprises, for man is exposed to the dangers of accidents, to bad seasons, and to the caprice of fate. Everyone does not bring with him the necessary temperament, customs, nor the intelligence which this new way of life demands. Everyone does not have the same degree of strength, courage, and good sense. And, all people are not equally happy: sickness, insects, neglect, and laziness often destroy their hopes. If one is not in a position to pay the agreed price when due, the law restores his land to the seller after compensating the purchaser for his improvements. But even among those who have no debts, how many become 'do-nothings' as soon as they see that with but two days of work, they can live the rest of the week. Such people are found more frequently among foreign colonists than among those who come from the Northern States, for their habits, customs, ingenuity, and industry are generally very praiseworthy.''

Meanwhile, we were approaching the Salt-Lick Farms, in the district of Philippopolis, to the west of Mount Ararat, when, in the evening of the third day since reaching the great river, while crossing a good-sized swamp from which springs (I have since learned) one of the branches of the Wyotucing, we heard the sound of a town clock. Encouraged by this noise, extraordinary in a region so sparsely settled, we continued our way more gaily and soon we came upon a cornfield, a young orchard, and a dwelling. The latter, though crude, it is true, possessed four casement windows.

"All this," observed Mr. Herman, "suggests a good lodging; let us rejoice and forget the hardships of our long day."

We were still a little distance away when a distinguished looking gentlemen approached us and said:

"Welcome, gentlemen. You must have mighty compelling reasons or else great courage to venture into a land still so sparsely settled. Aren't you perhaps lost?"

"One is never lost," my companion replied, "when one has the good fortune to meet a fine colonist like you, and to be invited to spend the night under such a hospitable roof."

"Ah, gentlemen, don't prize the hospitality of the woods more than it deserves; if only you knew how keen is the pleasure and the need to see and hear educated travelers, you would realize that it is I who should thank you for such a great boon."

"You underestimate the value of the service you would do us, kind sir."

"Very well, consider it mutual and I am satisfied."

"How many years have you been here?" I asked him.

"Seven," he replied. "Tomorrow I shall show you that I have not wasted my time. For when one wishes to enjoy soon the fruits of his labors, the cost is heavy. But money shrewdly spent in the clearing of lands and reclaiming of swamps pays back more than one hundred per cent. My ambition is to have some day many meadows and fields so that I can raise and maintain a great number of cattle and horses. I have a high respect for the plow but I value even more the scythe, because this technique in farming requires fewer hands. Only ten years ago this land was scarcely known and frequented only by hunters. The land was worth a scant six pounds sterling an acre. What a difference today! All over it is the same. Lots of one hundred ten acres which the Penns have sold beyond the Alleghenies for twenty-five dollars are worth right now more than ninety. Yet, we have been enjoying the benefit of municipal law only three years!''

"Is this countryside healthful?" Mr. Herman asked.

"Here so far we have experienced only fever and that only in certain seasons of the year," he replied. "But it comes because of the colonists' ignorance, rather than because of the climate. After getting thoroughly overheated from work, they lie down under the shade of a tree; perspiring ceases and they catch cold. I have brought with me a simple, sure remedy which many of the colonists have tried with success."

"You talk like a man who knows medicine," I observed.

"I practiced for a short time in Europe," he answered.

"Oh, you are a European, then?"

"Alas, indeed, I was Polish and Poland no longer exists. You must have heard talk about our confederation—about the first partition of our provinces which took five million people from the king of that unhappy country, when you heard of the general dismemberment of the Northern Powers. Since that time, the complaints of my unfortunate compatriots have echoed through the world in vain. What an event, forever deplorable! After Russia seized the province where I was born, I was obliged to serve as a surgeon in their hospitals and to dress the wounds of those who had ravaged and enslaved my country. Incensed over this shameful servitude, I decided to break my chains or die in the attempt. Everything in this world, as you well know, depends on a mere nothing: I owed to a mere nothing my flight, my lucky arrival in Copenhagen, and the good fortune of making myself useful to a captain of a ship that was about to leave for Lisbon. There he had scarcely discharged his cargo, when he took on another, bound for New York, where we arrived in forty-seven days; and in less than four months—from the town of Orsa on the Dneiper, I found myself on these shores. On what does the fate and fortune of men depend? Several days after my arrival, thanks to my knowledge of German, I became the friend of Doctor Ebeling, the Lutheran minister of that city; he recommended me to his colleague, Mr. Mulhausen, the pastor of German-Flats on the Mohawk River. This worthy and respectable ecclesiastic received me as though I might have been one of his compatriots and when I had told him my misfortune, he showed me even more affection and interest. After making me known to the countryside as a surgeon, he was kind enough to direct my first enterprises and help me to become oriented.

"Ah!" he continued, "how refreshing and welcome this independence and consideration which I soon enjoyed, compared to the servile state whence I had come! It was like a rebirth for me. The moment of awakening was the most charming for me: after dwelling in Poland in my dreams, to find myself a citizen of this state was a novel and exquisite joy.

"Finally, enjoying for the first time a real zest for life, I resolved to forget the past and to turn my attention only to the hopes of the future. If my imagination was keenly struck by the sight of beautiful rivers, great lakes, and the magnificent cataracts of this country, so were my heart and mind too, as I carefully studied the bases on which this new society is founded! The mildness and justice of the laws; the ease with which one can acquire land; the weight accorded to individual ownership; the bountiful reward assured to work and industry; the harmony and the great number of children that one sees in most families; in a word, the general air of well-being! Seeing this wonderful state of affairs, I began to have a better opinion of human nature and love for my fellow men. After I had practiced medicine several years in the Mohawk country, Mr. Mulhausen accepted me as his son-in-law and presented me with seven hundred and fifty acres of land which I own here. And thus it is from him that I hold the greatest, the most precious of all benefits: the best of all womanhood. There she is yonder, this angel of goodness and sweetness, to whom I owe everything: the children she bore me, the land which I cleared, the happiness of my life, as well as the order, peace, and cleanliness of my little home.

"I owe to the long and interesting conversations with her esteemed father," he continued, "the advantage of knowing the history of these States: during their colonial infancy, the details relative to the new social pact which has united them since their separation from the mother country; the limits of the three powers of which that pact is composed; the code of civil laws on which rest an individual's personal and religious rights. What a contrast between the absurd and barbaric feudal customs extant in Poland for centuries, and the protective system of life and liberty adopted by these states! What a contrast between the religious oppression, source of almost all the evils that have flooded my fatherland, and the constant equal protection that this government accords: a protection which is not one of tolerance, but of justice, since it is founded not on opinion, but on natural right!

"One day my esteemed father-in-law told me: 'I have been minister of the gospel, doctor and farmer by turns. I dare to appeal to the divine Scrutinizer of hearts, as well as my neighbors: they will judge if I have not done what was in my power to fulfill the duties of these three callings. I have directed the clearing of four hundred acres of land which the government gave to the church of this district, granting it a charter for corporation[1] in which it has since authorized me to allot two-thirds to the maintenance of a free school. I have grown old while pursuing the noble and interesting career that you are embarking on. But the fruits of this old age are neither sad nor bitter, such as are experienced by those who pursue a career in enterprises less honorable. The experience I have acquired is a little treasure which I wish to impart to you before that day when I must bequeath it to you as my daughter's protector. In this way I shall enjoy a share in your success. This desire is but a token of my friendship and affection for the man whom I have esteemed enough to have made my son-in-law.

" 'Those people who believe they'll become rich by farming deceive themselves. There is no money in farming in these Northern States. The seasons move too swiftly; winters are too long and labor still too dear. There is a fair yield—for those who are industrious—of ease and abundance. To succeed in the backwoods, one must have capital, so that he will not be wiped out by the annual interest on borrowed sums. He must also have knowledge of this new way of life. Farm work being composed of several branches, everything pertaining to work, supervision, and precaution must be concomitantly the objects of your daily care. Knowledge of the nature and quality of soils is indispensable for proper planting technique; one should have some works on veterinary medicine, although beasts that roam freely and eat salt are rarely sick.[2]

" 'The first among the valuable qualities a colonist should possess, after love of work, is a mild and conciliatory spirit, indispensable to happy living with one's neighbors. For one is not isolated long. The peace of a region is a never-ending source of prosperity. You will see what wonderful fraternal harmony can exist among men who help one another in the great and difficult tasks of settling. I know of no obstacles that the blend of communal will and effort won't surmount. Everything improves and brightens; in just a few years, the most somber forests, the most uncultivated land will burst forth with flowers, fruits, and harvests.

" 'After uprooting the first trees from your plantation,' added my venerable father, 'pray to God that He grant you good health, which is really the mother of strength and a very real aid to perseverance and courage. Yes, health is more necessary than you realize: to endure the solitude of forests, to clear the land's surface of these giant trees at the foot of which man feels so insignificant, to clean and burn everything that encumbers growth, to drain the swamps, to plant and to fence in the orchards and to keep the roads open, and to build homes and barns. And if ever you experience any disgust, the forerunner of discouragement, think, my son, of the woman I entrusted to you, and of the children she will bear you: if this powerful incentive summons neither activity nor devotion, you are not destined to be a good and true colonist.

" 'Beware of the illusions of your imagination which all too often paint a rosy future; for nothing is so tempting as planning a new home. And don't make the mistake of many farmers I have known: chop down only those trees which will be injurious to your land, for the cold of these long winters, the construction, the repair of barns and sheds, the upkeep of fences will require constant replenishment of wood. The second generation will regret bitterly that their fathers destroyed so much. This has already been proven in various regions of New Jersey and Connecticut, where for lack of wood, the value of land has diminished considerably.

" 'Even considering the forests as an adornment, a magnificent cloak with which nature in her indulgence has covered the continent: are they not beautiful and majestic beyond words? How can one help but revere these gigantic pines, which neither art nor artifice will ever be able to replace? These oaks, whose origin is much older than the capitals of Europe! This respect for forests and their beautiful trees is so natural that in spite of the work and expense necessary to break up the ground, fence and cultivate the land, in spite of the distressing habit of sometimes treating trees as enemies, as intruders using up sorely needed land, a prosperous proprietor, after several years, is more deeply affected, more flattered when walking through his woods than through his fields. True, once cleared and plowed, the latter seem like his very own creation: nothing lives there that he hasn't sown or planted. Yet in his forests, everything bears the compelling imprint of magnificence and enduring time, a feeling which impresses men, even the most ignorant.[3]

" 'The colonist who has overcome the first obstacles of his settling and who owes nothing is happier and richer than he realizes; likewise, as free as he wishes socially. His fortune is more assured than in any other occupation. He has only a few relations with the world outside.

The source of his independence and of his happiness is at his hearth and on his land: if he learns peace and moderation of desires, his enjoyments, long earned through work and industry, are keen and sincere. Finally, the laws which in other countries favor some and oppress others are equal for everyone on these shores.

" 'Do you wish to increase your happiness? Well, then, contribute to that of your neighbors: help them when they are sick and give them preventive advice about their health. That is what I have done for many years. Do you wish to become a distinguished and respectable colonist? Instill in your neighbors by precedent and by your conversation a love of work, of order, of justice as well as the worship of a God who rewards virtue and punishes crime. If ever your talents and the esteem of the public open to you the doors of representation in the government, never forget that union makes for strength in united States; that the grandeur and the prosperity of this new empire are founded only on this unity. All the laws destined to cement it will obtain your vote and your support, as well as the ones whose aim will be the encouragement of clearing land and the perfection of farming methods. That is the national character, the guarantee of religion and virtue which has brought us so rapidly from the weakness of infancy to the vigor of adolescence. And it is that which in less than a half-century will give us manly strength.

" 'As a son loves and cherishes his parents, love and cherish your country. Exert all your efforts to establish a system of public instruction which, as long practiced in the Northern States, is perhaps the most effective that has appeared in these modern times. The enlightenment of a good education reaching all classes of society, both establishes the good fortune of families and assures the peace and glory of a nation. Respect a government which reason has founded on the eternal bases of justice and liberty. During peace time, devote to it your talent and set an example; for your fellow-men during war, give your courage and your blood, if necessary. For only at this price can a good citizen do his duty for his country. Beware of those so-called orators who, in order to curry public favor, unceasingly undermine the government: its form, its acts, everything. As though what is man-made can be perfect! To strain beyond the limitations of the human mind must be considered folly and these frenzied fanatics, as enemies of public peace.

" 'As you have, I first saw the light of day in a country where for centuries men have been slaves to the soil. I arrived, as you did, despite innumerable difficulties, on the shores of this new world, to which want, despair, intolerance, and misfortune have guided the shattered remnants of the old world, just as the surf of the sea washes ashore ship-wrecked victims. And just as a plant, withered by the shadow of trees, revives and bursts forth as soon as it has been transplanted to a place where it has enjoyed the dew and sunshine, so the good qualities with which nature has endowed me, long stifled by misery and ignorance, developed soon after my arrival, and have borne fruit. I still recall the day after my naturalization when, full of joy and hope in a town where work and talent were so amply rewarded and where there was so much space, I quite forgot my allegiance to Salzburg to become a member of the new family of the United States.'

"That, gentlemen, is what this worthy minister of the Gospel told me."

The next day, impressed by the size and beauty of his barn, I asked him how it happened that it was a fine frame construction, while his house was only of hewn logs.

"My father-in-law," he said, "insisted that I postpone building a proper dwelling until after the ninth harvest. If the new colonists followed this practice, misfortunes would be less frequent among them, for most of them build before they are ready. I myself hauled across the snow the pines and oaks of which my barn is constructed and took them to the sawmill of one of my neighbors. Although the barn is very large, it cost me much less than you think, perhaps: I spent, gentle-men, only three hundred dollars.

"There is an orchard whose trees come from Schoharie. I planted it on the southern slope of this knoll so that it would be more easily irrigated by the waters of the stream that you have just crossed. That is why it gives the air of freshness which has impressed you. But I shall not enjoy this advantage very long, for the creek is drying up gradually as the land clearing increases.[4] I know some people, who, not realizing that their stream sources were from swamps, constructed mills which today are of course, useless. If ever this creek dries up, it will be an irreparable loss for me, for it is difficult to understand, if one has not actually seen it, the effect of irrigation on the growth of vegetation and trees, particularly in the month of August, when this orchard will be covered with flowers and fruits long before those of my neighbors."

"But why," Mr. Herman queried, "are your roads still so bad?"

"That comes from the great territorial dispute which took place between this state and Connecticut: fortunately for us, it is over now. Since then everything has changed: the Governor has subdivided our land into counties and subdivided those into districts, according to custom. In order that all parts of our land may come under the jurisdiction of the laws, he has just opened a road from the Susquehanna to the dividing line. They say that the government of New York is going to extend the road through Tiogo, Otsego, and Albany counties. Already we have almost three hundred families, all freeholders in this part of the state, as well as various saw and wheat mills, two churches, and some schools. Next year they are going to build bridges over the main creeks. And, gentlemen, to think I was virtually alone only a few years ago!

"Several causes have contributed to this progress; the navigation of the Susquehanna as far as Northumberland, the great number of lowlands, the encouragement which Congress gives to the cultivation of hemp,[5] and the introduction of two branches of industry, until recently unknown in these cantons. The first is potassium,[6] the second, the extraction of maple sugar.[7] It is to the philanthropic efforts of the Quakers that we owe the latter. What would you say if I assured you that five thousand quintals have been sold on the Philadelphia Exchange in the space of two years? What a benefactor is nature! One finds this precious resource from the plains of Kentucky in latitude 35° and as far north as Canada in 47°."

On our return from the fields, his wife led us into what she smilingly called her parlor; on the table was laid one of the most delightful dinners I had had since our departure from Carlisle.

"What luxury for new colonists!" my friend observed.

"Why do you speak of it thus?" she asked. "It is but the fruits of our labor. The tea comes from China, yes, but we pay for it with the ginseng from our woods.[8] The shad, the ham, the beef, the cakes, the jam, and the sugar, everything is the product of our land. My husband has the eighteenth part of a seine [9] from the great river which brings him nearly two hundred fish a year and we know how to preserve them with smoke, just as we do beef and ham."

During this conversation, Mr. Nadowisky, noticing that we frequently turned our eyes toward a little oil painting, on which one could see only the following three words, "Property, Protection, Justice," in great Saxon letters, explained to us:

"Gentlemen, the names that you see are the names of three beneficent spirits, whose help I sought vainly in my old country. Here, being placed by the laws under their tutelary aegis, I have worshipped them with gratitude."

On leaving this fine family, Mr. Herman took Mr. Nadowisky's hand, saying:

"Having lived a long time 'mid old social institutions, and having experienced their degradation and misfortunes, how happy one should consider oneself in having escaped it all, in having become a member of a group founded on such different principles! How much this striking contrast should contribute toward making life in a forest less lonely and gloomy and in easing the task that you have imposed upon yourselves. I shall never forget what I have seen and heard under this blessed roof of happiness and well-being.''

CHAPTER V

In accordance with Mr. Nadowiski's counsels, we steered our course in the direction of the 24th milestone of the great boundary line crossing the Susquehanna a little north of the Seely salt works and ferry. This place, important because of its meeting with several other routes, is only ten miles from Harmony, a town recently founded at the bend of the Susquehanna nearest the Delaware. From there a portage of nineteen miles takes one to Stockport, another small town built two years ago on the west shore of the Delaware. It is at a little distance above at 42° latitude that this boundary stretches right to Lake Erie where the line runs north at 88° 10″ west.* Mr. Seely, who furnished us with this information, showed us the spring with the waters from which he had already begun to make salt.[1] He was awaiting, from the Sterling foundry,[2] boilers of a new shape that would be more suitable for the evaporation process.

After crossing the river for the third time, we left Pennsylvania and Lucerne county to enter New York State and the Tiogo region. What rich pasture land the colonists of this region will enjoy when the river banks, the brooklets' beds, the swamps, and the bottom lands are drained, converted into pasture land and plied with the scythe! From Shippensbourg on we had not seen as great a number of hard maples: in certain sections the forests contained only these valuable trees that are found in abundance (we were told by a well-informed settler with whom we lodged one night), as far as the eastern branch of the Delaware, known as Popackton. The part of Tiogo county that we crossed was as well watered as Lucerne County. Its streams flowed into the Chenango, or the Susquehanna, and none had bridges. Fortunately on reaching the banks of the Ouaquaga, a sizeable creek, we found a white cedar raft, which travelers were earnestly adjured to treat with care by means of a warning posted on nearby trees.

"Nothing is more just," said my companion. "I would banish to the infernal furies any individuals who would be ungrateful and careless enough not to follow the thoughtful example of those who preceded them."

"In another few years," I told him, "we will find bridges or ferries on all the rivers and even direction signs, as these have been common in this state for more than thirty years."

Scarcely had we gone more than a few miles north of the Ononquage when the sun disappeared and the rumbling noise of thunder sounded.

* In fact, at 79° 46″.

We were journeying, absorbed in that melancholy mood that twilight inspires, especially in the woods, when the eye becomes more alert to distinguish objects as darkness closes in. Making our way slowly, following the edge of a Bog meadow whose area seemed quite considerable to us, we suddenly spied a good-looking frame house.

"Even though this is not the house they told us about this morning," said Mr. Herman, "let's go in, for I am afraid of thunder and more so of lightning."

"Dismount and come in, gentlemen," the owner greeted us cordially, for his dogs had warned of our approach. "My man here will take care of your horses."

His wife, whose features, manner, and speech all betokened a fine background, received us with great courtesy. We were talking with her about the remoteness of her home, and the fine brood of youngsters who were clinging to her skirts, when her husband reappeared. Without asking us the customary questions, he plunged right into a discussion of the soil in that district, of the marl that had already been discovered, of his speculations relative to the nature of the soil in that section, of the increase of population—all of this with such logical reasoning and in such elegant language that we readily surmised that he had not been born to swing an axe. He was telling us of the expected arrival from Scotland and Ireland, of a great number of colonists when his wife said:

"A storm is coming; it's time to bring the cows in."

Immediately her husband rose, called the two dogs, transmitting the errand to them as though he were speaking to men. Shortly afterward, we could see the cows coming through the gate.

"You certainly have two very useful servants," I remarked.

"Without their help and that of the soil," he replied, "what would we have done in these woods, especially during the first years? At night these dogs chase from my fields wolves, as well as bears, foxes, and weasels, who do not willingly give up their ancient rights. During the day, they watch over my cattle. The older taught the younger one. As for the first born, all his knowledge is the product of his own experience. One couldn't ask for more faithful and unselfish friends. You must have noticed that island yonder in the middle of the river. Well, morning and night the dogs swim across to lead forth and bring back my herd."

"That reminds me," I said, "of something I saw in Florida in 1783. Oweecomewée, chief of the fifth Seminole tribe (Creek), owned a good-sized savannah several miles from his village. There he raised a great number of horses. His dogs, after keeping watch over them during the day and taking them to a wooded island nearby to spend the night, would return home to their master to seek their meal, and at the break of dawn, back they went to their post. And mark you, they were obliged to cross the great Saint Joan River twice.''

''That does not surprise me,'' replied Mr. J. M. ''The instinct of these humble friends that man doesn't respect as much as they deserve is sensitive to a point that arouses both astonishment and admiration. How many examples I could cite you in support of that statement! It is the same with horses and cattle: the more primitive their life, that is to say, the more they are left to themselves, the more experience and wisdom they acquire. Especially in the woods does this faculty become the rival of reason: more fortunate than are we, creatures who possess this instinct know neither vices nor unbridled passions. Such creatures enjoy the only perfect happiness that exists on earth.''

''Isn't the region of the great swamp that we skirted for almost three miles often dangerous?'' asked Mr. Herman.

''Some people living to the leeward, that is, northeast, often experience autumnal fevers; others never do. This drawback, inevitable in the early years of clearing land, will soon disappear altogether. We plan to follow the example that was given us three years ago by the inhabitants of the region of Cornwall, Florida, and Walkill, in Orange County. They secured from the legislature a law which forced landowners to drain their swamplands (Bog Meadows), opening the streams formerly choked by beaver dams, and also to surround their grants with deep ditches. This law, which the government passed with an appropriation of twelve thousand dollars, has produced very healthful results: not only has the land been improved, but also, the wild meadows submerged for so many centuries are today either covered with hemp or corn, or else they have become rich grazing land. I hope we can get such a law passed in our legislature. My colleagues regard it as their duty to agree, without argument, to the passing of laws pertaining to the local advantage of the counties which they represent. How desirable it would be if these drainage laws should become universal! At the moment I am engaged in making a list of such lands, which I shall present to the legislative body at its next session. The number of swamps is prodigious. But I am well acquainted with the fine motives that stimulate the legislative group and I haven't a doubt in the world that it will vote a sizeable appropriation to encourage the colonists in the regions most settled. One of these bog meadows has seventy thousand acres and this state may well have more than one million, eight hundred thousand acres! What riches, what treasures for farming these lowlands, formed from the silt of waters through the centuries, will provide some day! This conquest will be more useful, and more important than that of a sugar island or a new business enterprise. Only labor is lacking. But, every day new hands are born and every day new sources of labor arrive.''

''You don't mean to tell me that as assemblyman from this county, you also work!'' my companion queried.

''Why not?'' replied Mr. J. M. ''Necessity demands it. And necessity knows no exception. I was elected immediately after the Government had set up this region into counties. At that time there was only the number of inhabitants required by law for representation. Satisfied with my services, they have re-elected me. But I confess, if it weren't for the fact that I am stimulated by the desire to obtain local legislation needed so urgently in this young region, I would have asked them to elect another. The annual three months of the sessions represent a substantial loss of time for me.''

''Don't you receive any pay for your service?'' asked Mr. Herman.

''Oh, they pay us three dollars a day, but this sum doesn't compensate for the inconvenience occasioned by such a long absence: a good farmer should never leave his fields.''

''What coincidence brought such an educated man as you to be one of the first founders of this country? For I know how toilsome and dull the wearisome work of clearing and planting is.''

''After losing an enormous fortune in business, I counted myself lucky beyond words to be able to turn to these five hundred acres belonging to my wife. I confess, it was not without regret or conflict that we left our town and our friends to embark on such a rude adventure, subjecting ourselves to a way of life so different from the one we were brought up in. Fortunately, we were young, and that is the time of greatest mental vigor and courage. And well did we need it, especially in the early years when we were twenty-five miles from our nearest neighbor and we trod the solitary trails of these unknown woods. But if, following the example of all new colonists, we had to begin by clearing out the thorns, today we are gathering flowers and fruits!

''We are comfortable and snug in our little home and live in comparative ease. The high price of wheat has rapidly added to our little fortune: I sell annually five hundred bushels. With the assistance of four faithful servants, I put my strength to the test. The god of harvest has seen fit to reward our care and efforts. However, my fondest hopes are founded on a seventeen-foot waterfall (the only one within a ten-mile radius) and on a law which the two adjacent states have just passed to encourage inland navigation. This law declares all

rivers open to anyone; in addition, it forestalls the innumerable inconveniences resulting from the building of dams which would flood
the lowlands and create infected air. The mill that I plan to build
according to Oliver Evans' [3] principles will yield great returns. After
it is finished, we will be able to relax, busying ourselves with the
breeding of cattle and the cultivation of hemp.

"Since the advent of easier times, I regret even more keenly the
separation from our old friends, that out-pouring of hearts, those conversations which, like steel in contact with flint, ignite ideas. Almost
all my neighbors are Swiss, Irish, or German. They can scarcely
understand our language. I compensate for my loss of outside contacts by reading good books. They are my friends, consoling, amusing,
or instructing me, according to my mood. Thanks to the paternal
vigilance of the Government, we are beginning to receive newspapers
regularly. What wonderful grazing they offer one's interest as well as
one's curiosity. How many ideas are bursting to come to light in the
Old World! Could the strength of these new ideas be sufficient to overthrow such ancient, massive structures? Will the distance fortunately
separating us from it save us from its havoc? Would Peace, without
which life is but a gift of evil, and so vital to us in these woods, give
place to civil strife? Would the demon of human nature again exert on
the land its redoubtable prowess? It is possible that we have men in
this land who might wish to overthrow the government, to which we
owe the astonishing prosperity of this republic, the peace, the inviolable
security of life, and of property, as well as the very laws for the encouragement of farming, trade, and the arts? Can there be men who,
to introduce among us new opinions from Europe, have resolved to
plunge us into the horrors of chaos and the bloody furies of anarchy?"

The next day we left this interesting farmer-legislator, promising to
see him again in New York the following winter. This meeting subsequently took place and we also had the opportunity of meeting several
of his colleagues.

After four days' journey, we easily reached the Tionaderha, the
Adiga, and the Unadilla, branches of the east Susquehanna over which
we found convenient ferries. In the distance of fifty-four miles, we
were obliged to sleep only one night in the woods, and even that was
an inconvenience that we might have avoided, had we not strayed in
our search for Harper's mill, located on the main river. After crossing
the Adiga, we entered Otsego county, which had been settled nine or
ten years. Here we found passable roads, abundance of provisions for
ourselves and our horses, comfortable enough lodgings and, to our
great satisfaction: some well-educated settlers.

We were still three miles from Otsego Lake when we heard the noise of a waterfall and soon afterward we came upon a great number of persons busy erecting the framework of a mill by its side. The owner, we learned, had settled there six years before.

"Although the son of an English lord," one of them said, "and formerly a lieutenant in the royal navy, he is as intelligent, as active, and as hardworking as though he were born in the woods."

"How fortunate you are to possess such a beautiful falls," said my companion to him after entering his home. "Never do I encounter cascades without becoming involuntarily dreamy and pensive. The motion, the mass of these waters are a source of power applicable to so many uses, the mill-ponds are almost always so beautiful and so varied, the forms you see so bizarre and picturesque, that it seems impossible that the combination of beauty and utility could fail to impress the mind and the eyes of a traveler. One must admit that nature has been wonderfully bountiful here. Located in the midst of these vast forests, I can readily see how your sawmill is so useful to you. But what about the flour-mill that you are building: where will the wheat come from that you plan to convert into flour? This region, although more populated than those through which we traveled, appears to have only a very few inhabitants."

"This continent," replied Mr. J. U., "has for a long time become a haven, not only for victims of want, oppression, and unhappiness in the Old World, but also for a great number of restless persons, disgusted with the government of their country. It is difficult to imagine, without having witnessed, how rapidly the farming of this county is daily increasing. I estimate at seventy-four thousand acres the quantity of land which has been cleared in the last seven years and of which more than one-sixth is today scythed or converted to pasture land. The fertility of the soil and the location of this region at the source of such a beautiful river as the Susquehanna, the great number of the sugar maple trees, the roads that the Government is opening at various points, all these advantages attract not only the industrious colonist, but families well off, commendable for their zealous industry as well as by the refinement of their habits. Wealthy Dutch and Flemish companies have purchased whole townships. Six years ago I was the nineteenth colonist; today you can count more than eighteen hundred freeholders. Far from fearing that this mill will lie idle, I plan to add to it a third factory to spin woolen stuffs and a fourth to extract oil from the flax seed which is already under abundant cultivation.

"Among the people who have come to help men build this structure, there are some from the four Northern states of the Union, as well as

men from Scotland, Saxony, Brandenburg, Sweden, and even from
the Morea. What an interesting sight it is to watch daily the arrival in
their adoptive land of these victims of tyranny, need, or civil strife!
And these men, although speaking different languages, raised in different religions, are forming a new nation whose posterity is destined to
play an important role in the world!

"This happy blend is the result of the temperate influence of laws,
founded on liberty, on tolerance, on justice, and on pride of ownership
whence emanate the finest rights of a citizen: further, it is the effect of
work and industry on the customs of these colonists. These, no doubt,
are the causes which identify them in such a short time with the new
society, rooting them to the soil as well as to the government which
protects and encourages them."

"You are Scottish," Mr. Herman observed, "and you have served
for a long time on warships?"

"True," replied Mr. J. U., "for several years I saw nothing but
clouds and the sea and now here I am in the heart of the woods. What
about you, Gentlemen? Where did you come from? And where are you
going? I hope you will pardon the questions. Your replies are a debt
that it would be cruel not to acquit toward a person who, like myself,
rarely sees educated travelers."

After we had satisfied his curiosity, Mr. J. U. exclaimed:

"You don't say! From the middle of Pennsylvania you are going
all the way to Fort Stanwick to Onondaga, to attend the two councils
that are soon to be held there! If I were not tied down by my obligations here, I would accompany you with pleasure. But I hope that on
your return you will be kind enough to tell me what you have seen
and heard."

"Very gladly," said Mr. Herman, "on condition that you will tell
us the adventures, doubtless extraordinary, which induced you to quit
your military career and your country to come here and toil so long
and arduously for a home."

"Agreed," he replied. "But rest assured that I have the better part
of this bargain. What can there possibly be of interest in the career
of a man of thirty-two who is not an adventurer and who has served
almost ten years of his life on the high seas?"

The following day, having learned that several boats were to leave
from Schenectady to go up the Mohawk, we took leave of Mr. J. U.,
promising to see him again on our return from Fort Stanwick. The
regions of Harper's Field, Cherry Valley, and Schoharie, through
which we traveled, seemed to Mr. Herman to be the richest in wheat
that we had seen in a long time. We were informed that the soil of the

Schoharie region especially was of an extraordinary fertility; that wheat grown there sold as high as in Europe; that the majority of the inhabitants were descended from the first colonists who founded New York in 1626. Indeed, the beauty, the symmetry of the fences, some of quickset hedges, the elegance of the houses, the fine, sleek horse teams, all betokened the wealth and prosperity of the colonists.

We reached Albany and finally Schenectady the evening of the fourth day after our departure from Otsego Lake. The very next day we had embarked on the waters of the Mohawk which would take us to Fort Stanwick, one hundred ten miles away.

(The chapter containing the details of the journey to the fort was so damaged —except for a few lines—that it could not be translated.)

CHAPTER VI

The first two people we met on our arrival at Onondaga were Siategan, former chief of the Chippaways,[1] and Yoyowassy, sachem of the Outaways,[2] whom I had met once in Montreal. They invited us to smoke the pipe of friendship, telling us how their numbers had diminished to such an extent in recent years because of smallpox [3] that they had resolved to unite the remainder of their tribe with the old Oneidas.[4]

Fortunately the lighting of the ceremonial council fire was a few days off and thus we had time to see to the care and feeding of our horses, a rather complicated detail in an Indian village. My companion had the opportunity to accustom himself gradually to the appearance of the Indians, their customs and their way of life.

How different mankind must have appeared to this man who only four months previous had lived in one of the capitals of Europe!

"Is this all that nature and time have done for them?" he asked me.

"Yes," I replied, "how truly insignificant man is before time and nature! When you consider the brutishness, the baseness of his delayed, wretched childhood, you cannot conceive how such a weak creature has been able to survive the reverses and disasters that he has experienced for so many centuries of ignorance and misery; nor by what happy chance he has finally learned: how to light a fire, how to forge iron, domesticate animals, till the soil, instruct himself by his own mental faculties in the understanding of the arts and sciences.

"What was mankind like before these memorable times? The land at that time was inhabited only by nomadic bands divided into tribes similar to those one sees today on the beaches of New Holland, New Zealand, the Straits of Magellan, etc. This primitive organization, while destroying the idea of a common interest, was for all time a never ending source of quarrels, hatreds, revenges, and wars more implacable than those of tigers, since the conqueror devoured the conquered, as they still do today; while the tiger, however hungry, never eats his own kind. What a span between savage and civilized man! Between the primitive ages of the world, so often celebrated by the poets, and the present state of Europe!

"The Indians such as you see today, except for trifling differences, were like their ancestors at the time of the discovery of the Continent. Stubbornly they cling to the same customs, the same beliefs, and still prefer a nomadic to a sedentary kind of life: the blind ignorance that goes with a carefree existence to one of safe foresight. Nothing has ever succeeded in opening their eyes: neither the example of the whites, nor the rapid decrease of their number; not even the annihilation of so many nations some of which have disappeared completely in recent years.''

"What can be the cause of this inconceivably blind ignorance?" Mr. Herman asked me. "Could their intelligence be inferior to that of the Europeans who themselves were once hunters and nomads? Why hasn't the energy of nature, that gouged out the great lakes and rivers of this continent, that covered it with magnificent forests and peopled it with animals and birds of such amazing instincts, done nothing for these wretched Indians? Why do all the creatures that she endowed with this sublime gift of instinct attain the highest peak of perfection of which they are capable in the short time of their education? Why, on the contrary, does man, to whom she gave the pre-eminence of reason, leave in her hands a ferocious, cannibalistic and unsocial creature? Can it be that this state is the one for which we were destined?"

"Very possible," I replied. "This continent, that of the Papoos, of New Holland, New Zealand, and so many other lands discovered by our modern navigators—aren't these all inhabited by the hordes which for thousands of centuries have been wallowing in the mire of their primitive state? Of what importance is it to the great Creator whether we are living under a birch bark shelter or in marble halls? In occupying the place for which she destined us in her scheme, her designs are realized whether we be hunters, nomads, or farmers.

"In examining closely this long chain of disasters which early generations must have experienced before they succeeded in spearing the fish, lighting the fire, and slaying the bear, the wolf, and the deer, one is astonished that such tribes have been able to survive the dangers and misfortunes of this long and delayed childhood. What superiority of intelligence, of ingenuity, and of strength these animals had, compared to man, helpless, stupid, and unclad! Well protected, well armed, clever and cunning, the animals ruled the wild; they must have been deadly to the first groups of men whom providence put in these forests. How could man pull himself out of these sorry and dismal beginnings and attain the degree of power and pre-eminence which the nations of Europe and Asia possess today? That seems difficult to understand.''

"Yet there have been great writers," replied Mr. Herman, "who have written wondrous dissertations to prove that civilization is scarcely an advantage at all: merely evil retrogression from the primitive, sublime character stamp which we received from the Great Creator. I, myself, had long ago almost been convinced of it.''

"What those writers have said," I answered, "was inspired only by a spirit of censure and eccentricity. They assumed a type of primitive man, whom they didn't know at all—in order to satirize their contemporaries. If, like me, they had accompanied these Indians in their devastating wars, if their eyes had witnessed, as mine have, the torments which they inflict on their prisoners, as well as these cruel periods of famine, result of the lack of foresight! If, finally, they had been present during these cannibalistic, these drunken orgies, whose very memory causes a shudder, very certainly they would not have looked to the natural men for the originals of their illusory descriptions."

After finishing our discussion of these matters, together with some questions to our hosts, Siategan and Yoyawassy, we left them to go to the wigwam of old Keskétomah, my old guide and companion, whom I knew to be one of the best lodged in the village.

"I have come," I told him, "from the land of the Onas [5] to be present at the council fire. I am tired from this long journey and should like to rest in your wigwam. Do you have bearskins to lend me? For, as you see, I have brought with me a friend who hails from the land of the rising sun."

"Plenty bearskin. Grateful for your confidence. My fire is lit, my kettle full; smoke my pipe, and you too, Cherryhum-Sagat [6] since you are the friend of my brother, rest your tired body here."

We spent part of the day in discussing general news of the tribe, the beginnings of farming which several of the chiefs had undertaken, the ever present aversion of the young people to a farming life, the folly of the Cayugas, the ways and means to open their eyes, the danger of selling their hunting grounds to the Government of New York. Keskétomah also gave me news of my adoptive family of whom I was rather amazed to see no member. That evening we witnessed a dance of young people. The next day after dining in the wigwam of Tocksikanehiow-Anier [7] on the salmon which he had caught the day before, we were invited to sup in the wigwam of the venerable and esteemed sachem Chedaboocktoo, from the Ossewingo [8] village. He had learned, I know not how, that we had brought our flutes, and wanted us to give a little concert. Even now I recall the rapt attention with which he and the numerous gathering he had invited listened; and the effect which the eerie passages, especially the chords in thirds and fifths,[9] produced on their faces, until then, immobile. The council fire having been lit, we accompanied our aged host, and as, of all sachems of the tribes I knew, he spoke English best, we seated ourselves beside him that he might interpret what we could not understand.

CHAPTER VII

Seventy-eight persons, chiefs, old men, sachems, and warriors were squatted according to custom around a fire lit in the middle of a great shelter whose walls were made of beams, neatly squared and dovetailed at the corners. Their heads bowed, their eyes fixed on the ground, they inhaled the smoke of their peace pipes, pausing deliberately, then exhaling two long columns through their nostrils. This was an indication of their deep meditation on important issues. None among them was painted, nor were their heads and ears bedecked with feathers. Their blankets of beaverskin fell off their shoulders, revealing their mighty chests and muscular arms on which in their youth various animal and insect figures had been tattooed. At such a scene a painter could have drawn bodies that were perfect in proportion, limbs controlled by muscles lightly covered with a kind of swelling that was unknown to the whites, and which among the Indians attests to their vigor, strength, and health: heads and faces of a special type, the like of which one sees only in the depths of the New World's forests. This meeting of almost naked men, so ferocious in war, so implacable in sating their vengeance, so mild, so quiet in their villages, presented to the eye an impressive spectacle and to the mind, a fruitful subject for reflection.

The speeches of this first meeting were devoted exclusively to the demarkation of their land, the Cayuga's plans to dispose of theirs, and the encroachments made by some white families. It held interest for none save those who were familiar with the local geography, as well as the facts relating to agreements with the neighboring Governments, and therefore I shall refrain from describing it, instead, confining myself to the next day's meeting where it was a question of adoption and of farming.

It was the first time there had ever been public discussion of farming and the need they felt for its use. Their appeal was directed to the young warriors. To my great surprise, our host, the worthy Keskétomah, offered to be the spokesman.

On the second day the assemblage was more numerous and more brilliant; this time the chiefs and warriors wore their paint, their arms were decorated with silver bracelets, their heads with warhead dresses, and from each of their noses hung a pearl. After the period of ceremonial silence, or rather of deepest self-communion and meditation, after we had slowly smoked our peace pipes, Chedaboocktoo, from the Ossewingo village of the Sturgeon tribe, rose and said:

"As I was smoking my pipe by the light of the moon the other night a voice caught my ears. I advanced and listened. It was Wequash, one of our tribe.

" 'What! you! A man—moaning! To whom are you addressing your woe and your wail? Don't you know that the Good Spirit is too far up to see what takes place here on earth? And that the bad spirit who dwells in the shadows of the night only mocks our misery? I have watched you, suffering from hunger, thirst, fatigue, exposure, and wounds. Why did you not then complain?'

" 'I do not complain, Chedaboocktoo,' he answered. 'I am thinking neither of the Evil nor of the Good Spirit, for I don't know where they are nor even whether they exist. Some say yes; others say no. When you throw green wood on the fire, haven't you ever watched how the air and the sap exude noisily? As the sap of a tree whose bark you have wounded flows, as the spring streams and rivers swell in the autumn after the rain, so is my heart smitten. It is that which laments, not my spirit whose fiber is as sturdy as yours. Temiskaming has left me, Chedaboocktoo. I am alone. My bearskin is cold. My fire is out. The ashes of my hearth have scattered and my kettle is empty. I no longer have the will to fill it. When one hunts or fishes only for oneself, can one be as patient or skillful as when one hunts or fishes for his wife? If I were to continue hunting, who would encourage me and clasp my hand?'

" 'Ah, Chedaboocktoo, evil befalls us like the autumn rains; good comes drop by drop like the dew of spring.'

" 'Everything that has come, Wequash,' I said to him, 'must pass away. We, too, must pass away, since we have come: like the dugout canoe of a traveler, dragged along by the weight of the current, like the waters of rivers which hurry toward great cataracts. I have heard said by the white medicine men that the child who is born is arriving just as the man who dies goes away. Where does the infant come from? Where is man going? This I asked them and they told me such extraordinary things that I did not try even to remember them. Everything which is on earth comes from it. I said to them: all that has come from it will return to it again. They made fun of me. I turned my back on them and left them there.

" 'I haven't grown old, Wequash, without having often been struck by the great arrow of Agan-Kitchee Manitou.[1] Each time I snatched it out and put it under the ground. In my whole life I have spilled more blood than tears—tears that should never fall except from the eyes of a woman, and never from yours, which have seen more than once with dry lids the sting of death and tragedy. Live if you are a man! Tomorrow you will deplore your plight less and after tomorrow less yet and so on until oblivion, the son of time, heals the scars of your heart. Do as Keskétomah, your ancestor, whom I knew in my younger days did: avenge the Evil Spirit. Seek another Temiskaming. You know the cure that adoption offers. Who can tell: maybe your new spouse will cultivate your corn and cook better than the one who has just passed on!'

" 'You speak, Chedaboocktoo,' he replied, 'like the old man that you are. You have forgotten the time of your youth when your heart was overflowing and your breath hot. Everything comes, everything goes, just as you say. But I who am arriving, I am not yet gone. I haven't heard yet the noise of my cataract. And you speak to me of another Temiskaming! How can I ever forget the one I loved and whose love I had. It isn't the task of a day. When ice has crushed my canoe, or fire has destroyed my wigwam, I can easily rebuild another; but a companion of so many moons, whom one has lost—don't you realize that a fine woman, like an ermine, is difficult to find? And if, among the daughters of our tribe, I can find none who wishes to blow upon my brand [2] nor listen to my war songs, will I, then, remain like an old man—alone on my bearskin? What shall I do? Where will I go?'

" 'Well,' I replied, 'go and seek one among the other tribes, as Ockwacock and Matamusket did. They had good fortune finding someone. They live in perfect harmony with their wives. Their families grow. They are as united as the branches of the same tree, like the shells of the oyster. Is their kettle empty? Straightway it is filled. Do ashes begin to choke their fire? Immediately they put on wood. They live under a happy sun. On the morrow of the next full moon go, by the Onondaga fire, and seek for yourself. You will hear what the sachems have to say to you.' That is what I told him. I have spoken."

After quite a long silence, Yoyogaheny from the Lackawack village of the eagle tribe, rose and said:

"As I was returning from fishing, I saw Muskanehong at the opening of her wigwam. She was sobbing, weeping, and beating her breast.

" 'Who caused you such grief?' I asked her. 'Has the Evil Spirit during the night broken your doorstep? [3] Has your memory recalled some bad dream? Could you have seen some falling stars when you were honoring the full moon? ... You don't answer me. Why, then, do you interrupt the peace of the night which is the time of sleep? Is not the sun's day long enough for your lamentations?'

" 'You speak of rest! There is no more rest for me on earth,' she replied. 'My spirit is in the shadows; the clouds obscure the sun of my life. The wind of the night has chased away my sleep. I have lost

Mondajewot, the companion of my days, the friend of my youth. When I followed him into the woods, I feared neither ravenous wolves nor catamounts [4] nor the ferocious panthers. As I paddled in the bow of his canoe across the lakes, I felt proud and free. Like my man, without complaint, I kept my face to the wind. I did his bidding: moving whenever he wished, for his wish was always mine, and mine, when I had one, was always his. He who swam like the tewtag and the muskallunge has disappeared under the waters while crossing the Nepinah rapids. His body has become the food of fish. Who will console me? Who will take me by the hand when I am old? No one, since I am now alone in the land. Ah, why didn't I offer a twist of tobacco to the Evil Spirit! He might have prevented the canoe from capsizing, then I would not have had to interrupt the night's rest, nor would I have aroused your anger.'

" 'In vain you would have offered all the tobacco of your crop to the Evil Spirit,' I said. 'The canoe of Mondajewot would none the less have capsized. Don't you know that he is impassive and deaf? That it is he who sends the hailstorms and the hurricanes; that it is he who swells the river and unleashes the storms; that the thunder is the noise of his voice, and lightning the sparkle of his eyes; that he is no more interested in the success of our hunts, of our wars, nor of our fate here on earth than in that of the migrant birds nor of the fish which the current drags over the waterfalls among the rocks? Your loss is great, Muskanehong.' You are a woman, therefore cry: tears and time will heal your wound. For time either kills or cures us. With time, storms blow over and the sun shines again. Time is like a long path: he who follows it soon finds oblivion crouching on the ground or huddled at the foot of a tree. Muskanehong, isn't there in the village or elsewhere some white man whom you could adopt?'

" 'Yes,' she replied, 'but can wolves and foxes [5] hunt together? What is a white man worth in the woods? As soon as the clouds conceal the sun, he is lost, knowing neither whither he goes nor whence he came. When snow falls he is at a standstill; if he comes upon a river, he needs a raft in order to get across; if hunger seizes him, he knows neither how to combat it nor how to satisfy it.'

" 'Muskanehong,' I said to her, 'there are good and bad among us, just as there are among them. Examine the trees in the forest: are they of equal height? No. Are the corn stalks equally tender and grainy? No. The same is true among men. I know some white men who, like us, are brave warriors, good hunters, and who in the woods are as skilled as we are. How many there are among our people who will sell everything they own to get their hands on firewater! Wouldn't you rather light your own fire than to have one of these fools as a husband? For such a one would keep neither your wigwam nor your canoe in repair. Whatever we do, Muskanehong: we meet everywhere more evil than good, more thorns and brambles than blooming bushes.'

" 'Why is that?' she queried.

" 'When you poke your head outside on a very dark night, what do you see?'

" 'Nothing,' she replied.

" 'Well, you see, your question and my answer are like that black night. Perhaps, though, if men were less wretched, they would multiply too much in the land and for lack of fish or game the strong would devour the weak, as sometimes happens. Go to Onondaga the morrow of the full moon: your heart and your mind will hear what the wise men say.' That is what I told her. I have spoken.''

Siasconet, from the village of the Pentagoet of the Outagamy (fox) tribe rose and said:

"As I was leaving Naponset's wigwam, I met Kahawabash, of my blood, although born among the Outawa. Instead of carrying his head high, according to the habit of warriors, he had it covered with his blanket and was making his way slowly.

" 'What are you doing in this village?' I asked him. 'You look like an old man or one who is sick, or perhaps you have just returned from far off hunting?'

" 'I hunt no more,' he replied. 'I fish when I am hungry. I left the flap of my wigwam open to the birds of the night and abandoned the village of Togarahanock.'

" 'But why?' I inquired.

" 'My heart bleeds like the stag struck by the hunter's arrow. My eyes burn; sleep abides just beyond my reach, perches on the roof of my lodge and will not descend. I am tired; yet I do nothing. I no longer feel cold nor warmth. Matchee-Manitoo sent down into the village a great black snake which bit my wife, Nezalanga, and nearly all my family and almost all our people. I have come to warm myself by your fire and consult your wisdom.'

" 'Wisdom is struck dumb,' I replied, 'when misfortune speaks. I knew your wife well. Wasn't she of the Pakatakan family?'

" 'Yes,' he answered me.

" 'Well, why did you not go by their fire to warm yourself? The mother, father, the sisters, and brothers of Nezalanga would have received you warmly, for the bond of blood is closer than that of a stranger, or even of a friend.'

" 'Not a single drop of Pakatakan blood flows anymore. The mergum-mergat (scourge) [6] of the white man, like the fire from the clouds consuming the forests, has destroyed almost the entire village, while I was beaver hunting in the highlands. On my return, I found only the skeletons of our people; their bodies had been feasted on by wolves and flies. Not one fire was lighted, not one wigwam was closed: nothing except their dogs were alive,[7] for beasts are less unfortunate than we are, Siasconset. If, as someone has said, the Good Spirit is the father of man, why doesn't he come among us, and rid us of the Evil Spirit? Why doesn't he hurl the war tomahawk to the bottom of the lake? With his hot breath, why doesn't he melt the snows of winter? He has given us the power to speak, they say, to raise us above the level of wolves, bears, and beavers; yet, we are more wretched than these wild beasts. Is there nothing on earth, nor above the clouds, which can protect our weakness?'

" 'You make me shudder,' I replied. 'Your wife, your kin, your friends—almost your entire village destroyed by the greatest of scourges! Kahawabash, when we learn some bad news, when great misfortunes befall us, then, our minds are struck with dismay, our hearts are chilled, like the canoes crushed by the winter ice, like the roots of a cedar tree, caught in the crevice of a rock. At such a time one cannot speak, one is absorbed only in his misfortune. The next day while hunting or fishing, he thinks a little less of it. Little by little first impressions shrink and fade, as do the tracings that our children make on the river's sand banks only to have the waves come and wash them away. Thus will it be with your loss, Kahawabash. It is great and very difficult to forget, I know, and as for me whom you have come to consult because you believed me less unfortunate, did you know that I had three fine sons, Tienaderhah, Tiogo, and Nobscusset? Well, the Evil Spirit struck them down. They are no longer here to fill my kettle and to carry Siasconset's tomahawk to war! You are young and I have seen many moons. Stay with me in my wigwam until the fire of the Great Council is lighted. There you will see old men and sachems who, like you, have suffered great losses and have compensated for them by adoption. But avoid shedding tears before them. They would scorn you and refuse to speak to you.'

"And this is what he answered:

" 'Siasconset! Have you not often heard the plaintive cry of the bear whose mate has been killed?[8] Have you not often seen the beaver's eyes filled with tears after he has lost his mate or little ones?[9] Well, am I inferior to the bear or beaver? No. I am a man, as good a hunter, as brave a warrior as your sachems. How can you prevent the bow from straightening when the bowstring breaks, or the oak tree or the stalk of the sweet rush from bending when a storm bursts? When the body is wounded, Siasconset, blood flows forth; when the heart is grieved, tears flow: that is what I shall tell your old men. I shall see how they will answer me.'

" 'Well, Kahawabash,' I told him, 'weep underneath my wigwam, since your guardian spirit wills it. To appease the Evil One, may your eyes be dry when you go to the Onondaga council fire.'

" 'Here on earth, what can one do: one spirit wishes what the other disdains—repudiates?

"What should one do? Consider life as a crossing from Toronto [10] to Niagara.[11] How many difficulties we endure in rounding a cape to find our way out of bays which the winds force us to enter! What odds against canoes as frail as ours.

" 'Nevertheless, we must take things as they come; since we have no choice. We must feed and love our wives and children; respect our tribe and nation; rejoice in good when it falls our way; bear up under evil with courage and patience; hunt and fish when we are hungry; sleep and smoke when we are tired; expect to meet misfortune, since we are born men to rejoice when it does not befall us; consider ourselves as birds of passage who, perched for the night on the branch of a tree, fly away and disappear forever at daybreak.'

"That is what I told him. I have spoken."

Aquidnunck, from the village of Acquakanunck, of the Skenonton stag tribe, rose and said:

"As I was smoking around my fire, Tienaderhah, from the Marneck (esturgeon) tribe, opened my door and entered, seating herself beside me.

" 'What do you want of me at this late hour?' I asked her.

" 'I have come to tell you my troubles and to consult you.'

" 'What has befallen you?'

" 'The wind of misfortune, like the burning breath of midsummer has dried up the tree of my life and has carried away its shade and its leaves. My little Tigheny has gone to the great west. I want to go there, too, before her father, Venango, returns from the hunts. Why should I remain on this earth, since joy and happiness no longer exist here for me? During the nights of full moons when I visit her resting place, shedding tears from my eyes and drops of milk from my breast, I think I hear her voice calling to me. I want to join her. All I ask of you, Aquidnunck, is to put my body in shelter from the wolves' teeth.'

" 'Has the evil spirit carried off your very threshold?' I asked her.

" 'No, he has snatched something far more cherished.'

" 'Well, then, why would you want to extinguish your fire and leave your wigwam? Can one reach the bank from the middle of rapids? No! One must have the courage to steer safely to a portage: you have borne a child; and this happiness will be yours again. Why do you wish to die before your sun has set?'

" 'What will Venango say when he discovers that his first life-blood is no longer on earth?'

" 'He will pity you; to calm and ease your sorrow, he will conceal his own, as the brave hides the arrow which has just struck him. He will dry your tears and light your fire again; it is a wicked thought, Tienaderhah, wishing to shorten your life: is it not true that old time is ever at his task, abridging it day by day. You have lost your daughter, but Venango still lives: would you kill him, too? Summon courage! Make it your daily companion. Soon he will bring his sister, Patience; you will understand what they will tell you. Weep, my child, weep!

" 'Your tears will soften the anguish in your heart as the rain calms the violence of storms. Busy yourself and you will think less. It is thinking which detains and increases evil. Go to the Onondaga council fire on the morrow of the full moon. There your ears will hear and be consoled by the wisdom of the sachems.'

"Those are the words that were spoken between Tienaderhah and Aquidnunck. I have spoken."

After a long silence, devoted to gravely smoking the peace pipes, Keskétomah, from the village of the Onondaga, of the Maskinonge tribe, rose and said:

"Brothers and friends, the greatest of all our tragedies is the decrease of our race and the increase of that of the white man. And yet today, we smoke, we sleep, weakened as we are, as though we were as numerous and formidable as of yore! Where did these white men come from? Who brought them across the great salt lake? Why didn't our forefathers who lived at that time along the coast close their ears to the fine words of these foxes—all false and deceiving like the shadow of the setting sun? Since that time they have multiplied like ants at the return of spring and like these tiny insects, they need only a small space to live in. Why is that? Because they know how to cultivate the soil. Brothers and friends, that is the remedy that can cure our evils yet. But—so that it can be efficacious, let us be joined, like the fingers of the same hand, like the paddles of the same canoe. Otherwise our hopes, our very plans will flutter away with the breath of the wind.

"Let us hunt in order to preserve these precious habits of patience, perseverance, and skill which make us so formidable in war and let us at last begin farming the soil on which we were born. Let us procure oxen, cows, pigs, and horses. Let us learn to forge this iron which makes the white men so powerful. Then we will know how to keep them in check; when hunger and want come knocking at our doors, as they have in the past, we will have something with which to combat them. I remember that Koreyhoosta, former chief of the Mississagee tribe, used to shed tears every time he returned from Hotchelaga [12] (Montreal). When anyone asked him why he wept he would reply:

" 'Don't you see, the white men live on grain while we live on flesh? That this flesh takes more than thirty moons to mature, and it is often difficult to find? That each of the wonderful seeds the white men plant in the earth yields them more than one hundred? That the animals on which we live have four legs to flee with, and we, but two to pursue them? That where the white men plant these seeds, they stay, and grow? That the winter, the time of our arduous hunts, is for them a time of repose? That is why they have so many children and why they live so much longer than we do. I say this for the benefit of any who may care to listen: before the cedar trees of our village die from old age, and before the maple trees of our valley cease to yield sugar, the race of sowers of little seeds will have extinguished that of the game hunters, unless these hunters take it upon themselves to start planting seeds, too.'

"The words of Koreyhoosta have been borne out among the tribes of the Pecod, Nattick, Narraganset, and so many others. Go and see the places where they used to live. You will find not a single member of their stock, nor any trace whatsoever of their villages, where once Indian life and liberty reigned. White men's dwellings replace them now: today their plows work the land 'neath which lie the remains of the redskins' ancestors.[13] And if you continue to refuse to farm the land, you may anticipate the same destiny.

"Ah, if only I had the wings of an eagle, I would soar as high as our mountains, then my words, windborne, would resound among all the nations which live in our land. If only the evidence of truth would penetrate your hearts, like the blade of the tomahawk in the body of my enemy! Then you would never forget what I have yet to say to you: you are lost, brave Oneidas, if you continue wishing to be merely hunters. Today's sun is different from that of yesterday. You are lost, if you do not stifle the voice of old custom and open your ears to that of imperious necessity. Brothers and friends, why wouldn't you harken to this necessity, for its voice is as loud as thunder? I shall tell you what it says to you, through my lips:

"A musket is good, a plow is better; a tomahawk [14] is good, an axe well helved is better; a wigwam is good, a house and barn better still.

"The white men approach our borders and are threatening us like the distant waves of the lake, which pound incessantly against the shores. Already the bees, their precursors, have arrived among us. Are you going to resist them? To the products of hunting, add those of the land; to your wives' milk, add that of the cows. Is their soil more fertile than ours? No, and the white man knows it well. Have we not red and white cedars, marshy ash trees, and black birches in abundance for the construction of our canoes? Do not the salmon of Katarakouy penetrate inland to our very lakes? With our furs let us buy hatchets and iron, or better, let us learn to forge this iron. Ah, if only we had been aware of these iron deposits over which we have long walked, we would not be reduced to speak in this manner. We would have forced the white men to return to their land whose sun sets, they say, as ours rises. Let us make laws governing our trade; let us forbid the introduction of the liquor of fire and death into our villages, for that is the fatal source whence all our misfortunes sprang. With this poison, they have rendered us mad and wicked and have bought so much of our land; with this same trap which we should now well recognize, these foxes of the dawn-land have tricked the wolves of this great continent; succeeding finally in destroying so many of the Nishynorbay nations. Let us define the limits of our lands, live in peace with the white men, yes, but uphold our rights at the risk of our lives. Of what value is the life of a warrior, if in losing it, he assures that of his wife and his children, the independence of his village, his tribe and his nation, which is for him like the sun is to trees and plants?

"But I make an end: perhaps among our young warriors there are some who, in disapproval of my words, would like to shut my mouth."

Scarcely had he uttered these last words, when Koohassen, from the Wawassing village, of the Mawhingon (wolf) tribe, throwing aside his blanket, pride virtually painted on his face, tomahawk in hand, rose and said:

"Yes, there are many who would wish just that! I have not spoken sooner because I respect old age, not because I lack thoughts that are strong and good."

Flashing his eyes around the group, chest bare, his head and ears bedecked in his feather headdress, his arms adorned with shining knuckle-bones, he continued thus:

"Before the white man's arrival, the powerful Mohawk league, of which our nation was a part, conquered several coastal tribes and ever since, this league has caused quaking among the tribes of Hotchelaga and of Corlear.[15] Yet, these warriors lived well without stirring the earth like women; why don't we follow their example today? Game is scarce only to the fainthearted and lazy. Can one be brave, unyielding, and indifferent in the face of danger when one possesses land which produces corn, when one keeps cows and horses? No, I say. We regret life too much to risk losing it. And when war breaks out, how can one split oneself in two? Can one be in the woods, wielding his tomahawk at the same time he is guiding a plow? No. Those who farm the soil spend too much time on the bearskins of their wives: he who would strike his enemy down must long since have renounced the wigwam's ease. In living like the white man, we will cease to be what we are: children of our God, who made us hunters and warriors. We shall think, we shall act like them; and like them, we shall become liars, cheats, parasites, slaves to the soil which we cultivate, enchained by laws governed by papers and by the writings of lies. Tell me, with their fields, their cows, and their horses, are the palefaces happier, and do they live any longer than we do? Can they sleep in the snow or at the foot of a tree as we do? No. They have so many things to love that their minds are wakeful with worry. Can they scorn life, suffer or die as we do without means or regrets? No. They are shackled to it by too many fetters. Of what use to them is the silver for which they labor so hard. Only to make rich and poor, only to breed among them crime, ill-will, and jealousy. If we became farmers, we would have to call into our villages judges who would torment us, build prisons with high walls to shut us in, and forge chains to restrain us! Then would we be fearless, proud, and brave like our ancestors, forgetting the past, content with the present and unconcerned over the future? No. Hospitality would disappear I know not whither, never to return among us, for each, desirous of hoarding at the expense of others, would have nothing to give his neighbor who would cease to be his friend. Like the white men, we would obey any behest for money. Our very will would vanish. Of what good is a man who could no longer wander at will, smoke, sleep, rest? The rich would want to rule the poor! And what would become of these poor? Would they be doomed to slavery, toiling for masters greasy with their fat? Then would strength, courage, skill, and patience any longer be the measure of manliness? No: these measures would be money and an overflowing kettle. Could, aye, would, a brave in whose veins throbbed the blood of a true Oneida ever stoop to serve a rich poltroon, should misfortune befall his wigwam? No, no more than the mountain eagle would enslave himself to the faint-hearted and miserable osprey; no more than the proud vulture would serve the shy wood pigeon. Instead of bending down like the riverside reed, he would resist like the mountain oak, or—like the bees, he would hie to the forest to seek his freedom. If ever I lose my will and am obliged to take orders from another, simply because he is richer than I, at that moment I will tomahawk him.[16] I will scalp him after setting fire to his wigwam. For he who scorns me is my enemy. I will then go up the rivers of the west and seek out the chiefs of the tribes in the Mississippi region, telling them that the Oneidas have become like the bearded palefaces, scratchers of the soil and lowly day laborers. Aye, rather than submit to the orders of a master and become a wretched hireling, I will join my worthy ancestors. For what is this death, so feared by cowards? For the hunter, it is his hour of rest, the end of his need, for the warrior, everlasting peace, for the unhappy, the term of their misery: it is confidence and consolation for all those who suffer and starve, and the haven whence one can defy oppression and tyranny.

"And what of our womenfolk and children? What would become of them with their fields of corn and wheat? What models of courage and patience would they find to follow in this new state? Busy with domestic labors from infancy to ripe old age, would they ever learn how to endure hunger, thirst and misfortune, and death? Who would teach them not to fear the devouring man or the kettle of their enemies,[17] but to die instead like braves, proudly chanting their war song? Observe the nations that have ceased to hunt, only to bend their backs over the land! What is their plight now that they have cows and horses and turn to the white man's God? I will tell you! The palefaces and their God scorn such men and do not extend to them the hand of fellowship. Their numbers diminish daily. If ever such men dared to offer me their peace pipes, I would say to them proudly: Cawen! Cawen! (No! No!) [18]

"Let us continue being what we have always been: good hunters, fearless fighters. I hope my opinion is shared by most of you who are listening. For your blood has not yet been blanched by the snows of winter, nor has it been chilled in your veins by the ice of old age. I have spoken." *

This speech, delivered with much vigor, was followed by a very long pause. Finally Keskétomah, after calmly exhaling the smoke of his pipe through his nostrils, rose for the second time and spoke:

"Brave, but unthinking rash youth, for whom today is like yesterday, tomorrow like today, for whom moons and events leave no trace as

---

* This speech, whose wild virile eloquence is truly admirable, recalls the fine orations of the Scythian ambassadors sent to Alexander, recorded by Quintus Curtius in the seventh book of his history. The same simplicity, the same loftiness of thought, the same accumulation of metaphors, the same feeling of ardor. There is one language of men of nature and another language for men of civilization. But what a difference between the two!

(Note communicated to the editor by Citizen Billecocq.)

they pass, like the arrow which whirs through the air, or the hawk which pursues its prey; whose thoughts resemble sterile flowers; who close the door to experience, instead of inviting it to the Council: do you not realize that circumstances have changed markedly since the old days of which Koohassen has just spoken, and that we, too must change—or perish! What would you do if the waters of the lake overflowed? Instead of moving our wigwams elsewhere as your young people would choose to do, I—old as I am—would advise building a dike to keep them off and thus defend our village. Hear me, all you young people who are listening: such is the case today. The pale-faces are threatening us, encroaching beyond the limits set for them by our ancestors. Let us, therefore, build this dike here, not elsewhere, before this flood engulfs us, with our wives and children.

"By virtue of their numbers and their cultivation of corn and wheat, they have become proud and strong. By these same means, we, too, must become proud and strong. Let us hold in respect our forests, our native haunt and ancient heritage; let us cultivate the soil which will swell our numbers and our power, for since each man is welcome to as much land as he wishes, he will never know the shameful inequality of which Koohassen has spoken. As for judges, chains, prisons—they are all for the wicked and we have no such people here.

"May those among us who might be so blinded in their opinion as to prefer that the Oneidas disappear from the face of the earth than to see them prosper and multiply by the adoption of farming: I say, let such people seek the company of Cayugas, Tuskaroras, and Senecas,[19] and pitch their wigwams on land that is foreign and will not be theirs for long. On the other hand, let those who are frightened by the fate of so many tribes once as powerful as ours and today reduced to nothing, unite in heart and spirit with the opinion of the old men, which is that of a great number of our braves, and, tomorrow, let them do everything in their power to effect this great change on which hang our safety and our very life. I hope truth has illuminated my words as the sun shines on the surface of the lake. I have answered what the Great Spirit has inspired in Koohassen; he inspires me to say nothing against that which anger has placed on his tongue. I have spoken."

Here ended the second day of the Council.

CHAPTER VIII

The third meeting was devoted to the business of several adoptions, delayed over a long period of time, and to the discussion of ways of encouraging white families to settle among the Indians. Many of the chiefs disapproved of this latter idea, reminding the Council that almost all the families to whom land had been given had become do-nothings and drunkards; that, in a word, they were far from setting the good example that had been expected of them. As soon as these matters were settled, the blind Kanajoharry, a venerable sachem from the Skenonton (roebuck) tribe, rose and said:

"Where are the bereaved? Have them come forth. Even if I cannot see them, at least I can touch them. They will be able to hear me better, for my feeble voice is no more than that of a dying echo. Where are their hands? Ah, here are two that I don't know. Yet, these I recall having shaken for the first time many moons ago!

"Ah, it is your hands I am clasping, Wequash! Tragedy has tracked you down and the Good Spirit has turned his back on you. Your wife, Temiskaming, has fallen from the height of the great cataract into the abyss. I mourn her passing almost as much as you do. Was she not of the Arianchée family? And now she has departed before increasing your blood, which for so long has produced brave warriors. We arrive, Wequash, like trees uprooted by torrents which our rivers drag along: in the morning we see them; in the evening they are gone; thus does time and its moons drag us along, too. We are born only to die; we arrive only to leave. Today or yesterday; it would be the same thing unless we were needed in our village. You, whom I have observed so patient in the face of misfortune, so little concerned over a future which you may never come to know, continue to be thus, until the Great Spirit helps you to forget your first love, Temiskaming, and gives you another! I know where to find such a one; old and blind as I am: the day when you take her for your own, I shall come to light your fire and fill your kettle.

"And you, Muskanehong, give me your hand! So young! And to have lost the father of your children, the guardian of your nights, the hearthstone of your fire, the prop of your wigwam when the wind of woe was blowing. I grieve for you as though you were of my blood, and I mourn Mondajewot's passing as though he had been my friend. Do you not know that life is like those rivers on which one meets more falls and rapids than quiet and navigable waters? How many accidents and shipwrecks one experiences before arriving at safe portage! How small the number often is of those who, after greeting their sun in the morning, still see its last rays that evening! And I who speak to you, Mondajewot, no longer do I have anyone of my blood to keep my fire going. The clouds of life were just beginning to weigh heavily over my head. I was drying up of old age, when Matchee-Manitou struck my children with his great arrow. With their passing, went the hope, the joy, and repose of my declining years. Eleven times have the winter snows whitened the earth since they guided me through the darkness which surrounds me. Since that time the birds of the night, aware of my weakness, abide aloft my roof; yet I am still alive, though bowed like an old oak tree that is but a reed broken by the wind from the northwest. And Mondajewot, that tireless hunter, protector of the weak in a moment of danger, that mighty warrior said to us:

"'To the brave, death is nothing; it hides behind him, barely noticed.'

"And what became of the mighty Mondajewot? In his prime, in the full strength and vigor of manhood, he left us to go to the Happy Hunting Ground of our ancestors. Why does Matchee-Manitou snatch from us so soon the life-giving spirit that the Great One gave us? Why is it that the full term of our earthly existence is never reached? Why are our lives almost never fulfilled? What shall we do, Musk-anehong? Bow our heads, as when it snows or hails? Lean against a tree until the storm has passed? Supposing, though, the Evil Spirit should uproot this haven! Should we then close our eyes and abandon ourselves to blind destiny? May the Great Spirit keep clear the paths of the rest of your life, give you days without clouds and nights without disturbing dreams.

"And you, Mahawabash, come closer! Smoke my pipe! It is the pipe of an old man who has become blind because he lived too long, and who a thousand times more than you has frowned upon the violence of tempests and the blows of fate. You have lost your wife Nezalanga! The story of that catastrophe has chilled my blood, like the northwest wind of woe when it blows against my chest. You did well to abandon a place on which Agan-Matchee Manitou unleashed such a wicked wind. Summon courage! If it does not come today, summon it again tomorrow. Soon it will come to you; for it loves youth: moreover, our sachems are concerned over you and would console you.

"And you, Tienaderah of my blood who has lost the first fruit of your womb: your head hangs heavy with sadness. Your face is covered with clouds of melancholy; silent tears of sadness fall from your eyes. Weep, Tienaderah, weep! Though my blinded eyes can no longer watch the tears fall, my ears can still hear your sobs, and my heart can share your bitter sorrow. Often, you say, deluded in your dreams at night, you believe that you see once again, and that you hold once again, the child of your youth. Even in the days during the full moon when you go forth to her resting place, from your breast pour forth some drops of milk, mingled with fright and hope, as you think you recognize the plaintive tone of her cries. Unhappy Tienaderah! These utterances are but the voice of the wind whistling through the nearby branches. That is what life really is: the illusion of a dream, that phantom of happiness which the dawn of a new day dispels, a ray of light never-endingly obscured by clouds, a fire which lights, one wots not how, sparkles, and becomes covered with ashes or is extinguished at the whim of the breeze that fans it, the winds that blow it, or the tempest which scatters it. Remember that you are the wife of an Oneida, who was a mighty brave hunter and warrior. What would Verango say if he were to see you so saddened? Your sun is still high, the season of your youth is not yet passed: the old days meandering aimlessly will take you by the hand, consoling you, until, becoming a mother once again, you forget the one who has left you, absorbed completely in the little one who will become the light and joy of your life, just as your first-born was.

"I have spoken."

CHAPTER IX

We were informed that the Council was to be adjourned until more definite pledges were received relative to the secret negotiations of the Cayugas with the agents of the Government of New York. Presuming that I would never again see the Oneida chiefs united, and being, moreover, an adopted member of the Maskinonge tribe, I thought I ought to speak. But, not possessing adequate command of their language for public purposes, I addressed them through a native interpreter:

"Brothers and friends, ockemaws, sachems, old men, and warriors: this fire recalls to my mind the time when I was adopted into the Osséwingo village, to replace the chief of the Kayo family. Even if I have not since that time helped to bring warmth to his wigwam during the winter snows, I have provided, as much as I have been able, for his other needs. I renewed the bonds of my affection when the Osséwingos dispatched one of their members to bring me three belts of wampaum,[1] which confirmed the adoption of my children, Mataxen, Téwénissa, and Winésimet. As to my attachment for this nation, I have manifested that as often as I could. Every time that our revered Aliab-Hoking, recently departed for the Happy Hunting Ground of your ancestors, and Tocksikanehyou, whom I see around this fire, were sent to Corlear, to speak there concerning your affairs with the great white chief, they found under my roof the fire and hospitality of a brother, as well as friendly zeal and co-operation. Your memory, Tocksikanehyou, fresh as the footsteps of a traveler on new-fallen snow, still recalls all that, as well as the message I delivered at the village of Tanganock, on the occasion of old Mashapongo's death.

"When will these old eyes of mine see shine the light of day, prayed for by the ancients, when young people like you listening now will cease forever scorning work done by hands, and will cultivate the soil? Like a good mother, she calls you today, young people, and perhaps for the last time, saying:

" 'If you probe and plow beneath my surface as your neighbors do, I will clothe you, feed you, and increase your power manifold just as I do for them. Then you will see that men can plow, sow, reap without losing their bravery, and they can yet defend themselves when their land is invaded, with the same courage that they would have were they still hunters and warriors. If, on the other hand, you scorn much longer the nourishment of my fertile bosom, you will vanish like the cranes of the Savannah at the approach of winter, and like the emptiness of the past, the remembrance of your existence will be erased from the memory of man. The race of whites will replace that of the Nishynorbays. Brother and friends, may you never forget these words':

"I wish you happy hunting and fishing, anticipating the time when you will put the sickle to your first harvest. I have spoken."

Canajoharie, being the eldest, rose and said:

"Kayo, your arrival in this village has gladdened us all; the young folks have said:

" 'This is one of our friends!'

"Our old men very quickly recalled your words in the village at Taughannock, but alas, those words and those of so many others haven't yet persuaded our youth, who listen only to the Evil Spirit.

" 'Do you wish to rejoice,' says the Evil Spirit to them, 'and forget the fatigue of your great chase? Drink white man's fire-water. Do you wish to intone proudly your war chant? Drink white man's fire-water.'

"In their obstinacy, they cast aside the advice of experienced ones, who implore:

" 'Don't you realize that this liquor creates folly, will burn you, destroy you as it has destroyed so many nations? You fear an encounter with a wild cat, or the bite of a snake? But, blind as you are, you have no fear of this poison, a thousand times more dangerous, for it kills men by the hundreds.'

"What are we to do, Kayo, after so many futile efforts? Lament and wail? But the old days haunt us; the introduction of liquor to our village will soon be forbidden just as one shuts one's door on a wicked wind. Ah! If only we had shut it sooner!

"Smoke, Kayo, the great pipe of peace and friendship that I offer you in the name of my tribe, who present you also with this wampaum belt of blue and white, so that you will never forget your friends the Onondagas, nor your family of Osséwingo.

"May you find, every night in your journeyings, a shelter for your canoe, wood to light your fire and if game is scarce, fish to nourish you. On your return to your hearth, may health, your kin and your friends take you as warmly by the hand, as we do today. I have spoken."

The speaker, remembering that shortly after our arrival Mr. Herman had expressed a desire to be taken in to the family of the Kesketomah by bonds of adoption, received him under the name of Towaneganda, and as a final token of his friendship for me, he also wished that his daughter, Bennsivassika, should adopt under this same name the daughter of my family. Finally, having exchanged the customary presents, we took leave of the Council.

The following day, we were congratulating our host on his speech, and discoursing on the effect that it must have produced, when he stopped us, saying:

"May it last, for you don't know, as I do, my compatriots' minds, nor the heads in which their spirit is lodged: they are capricious as the breeze and as fickle as the wind on the lake."

In the evening we were invited to dance with the young people; we found it only moderately amusing. Their heavy, labored breathing, the rhythmic stamping of their feet, the hideous shrieking warhoop accompanying their steps, all this appeared odd and irritating to Mr. Herman. Nevertheless, he was obliged to admit that the dances of discovery, victory, and retreat were well performed. They also invited us to join in the tomahawk ceremony, but we preferred to watch. One of the most accomplished performers was Koohassen, who, only a little while ago, with so much nerve and vehemence, wanted to shut Kesketomah up. The finely chiseled features of his face, his tall figure, the fire in his eyes, the puckering of his brow all betokened an indomitable personality and an untamable soul. He seemed to us so deeply stirred by what he had said at the Council when he swore by the bones of his ancestors that if the Oneidas ever became scrapers of the earth, he would desert them and go to the Shawnees of the Scioto. Finally, after smoking the pipe of happy memory with our friends, and expressing our gratitude, we left the Onondagas to proceed to Fort Stanwick.

(The translator did not find the next two chapters which probably contained the details of the Congress which the Government of New York held.)

CHAPTER X

Several days before the close of Congress, my companion and I, wishing to return to Shippensbourg as promptly as possible, consulted Governor Clinton about the possibility of reaching Otsego Lake through the forests, instead of returning via the Mohawk and resuming our former route.

"Simple enough," he answered, "especially at this season of the year when the woods are filled with wild pea-vine, excellent provender for the horses. But this district, although already granted to a great number of families, is not inhabited yet. Therefore it is necessary for you to get yourselves two Indians who will serve you as both guides and purveyors. Tomorrow I shall speak to old Nabahojé whose sons are excellent hunters and gentle in character. I do not doubt that he will permit them to go with you as far as the nearest dwellings, which, if I am not mistaken, are forty miles distant. Everything will be quite changed next year: one hundred thirty families, coming from Long Island, Orange, Fishkill, and Richmond Counties are expected there in the spring.

"But I warn you," he continued, "from here to the nearest dwellings, you can count on your food only by virtue of the good fortune and skill of your guides. At night you will have for shelter only a light roof of bark which you can set up while they are off hunting or fishing, according to their instructions; leaves will be your bed.

"Do you think," he said, addressing my companion, whom he knew had only recently arrived from Europe, "that you have enough courage to withstand the fatigue and privations of this three or four day journey, so different from those you have made before?"

"I have already served quite an apprenticeship," Mr. Herman replied, "in going from Shippensburg to Onondaga, through land so recently settled. I know what it is to sleep on straw—if the new colonists are rich enough to have any—and what it is like to spend the night on leaves under a tree when one finds no dwellings. Among so many new things that this continent offers one's curiosity, even at the risk of some inconveniences, I have the greatest desire to see by what means your Indians find their way through strange forests, with the aid of neither compass nor sun; and how these Indians live by whatever skill and chance bring them. As long as our horses easily find food, I am relatively unconcerned for myself; a few pounds of chocolate—as well as the ham that Your Excellency has been kind enough to give us—will more than stay us until we reach the first dwellings. I hope that the two guides of whom you spoke will be from the Oneida tribe. Since we spent nearly two weeks in their village, they will be far more interested in us than in strangers of whom they might never have heard.''

''Rest assured,'' Mr. Clinton replied, ''I have known their family several years. It is not the first time I have hired them; never does my brother, a surveyor by profession, venture into the woods without them. Moreover, this is the most favorable season of the year for fish and game. The soil of the land you are going to cross is one of the richest I know, as you will discover, from the beauty and majesty of the trees, the height of the grass, and the luxuriant growth in the lowlands. It is also one of the best watered. As soon as you have crossed the streams and creeks whose meeting forms the Oriskany, you will come upon numerous branches of the Chenango, which empties into the Susquehannah. The location of this region, crossed by so many little navigable waterways near the Mohawk, adds to the tremendous advantages which assure its prosperity. The one hundred thirty families that I mentioned, according to an estimate given me, form a total of nearly eight hundred individuals who are to bring with them one hundred thirty teams of oxen, as many cows, and two hundred sixty horses. In addition, there are several carpenters, weavers and smiths, two ministers of the Gospel, and five schoolmasters to each of whom one hundred acres of land are given. The oldest of these family heads is not yet twenty-seven. It makes one of the finest swarms I have ever seen leave our old beehives. If anyone other than myself told you that, for thirty years now, Long Island alone has furnished more than twenty-seven thousand colonists who have settled in the heart of New York state, you would hardly believe it; not to mention the great number of other young people who have been employed in coastal traffic, in the fisheries of New Foundland and in the whaling industry, and in European trade. Of all parts of this continent, I know of none where the human race multiplies with as great rapidity: as soon as the leaves begin to fall, I am going to have the main routes opened and have some bridges built which they will need in order to settle in their own regions.''

The first day of our departure, our young guides, Ock-Negah and Cohgna-Wassy, had the good fortune to come upon a hunting path which they followed with skill. Although these faint clues were merely bushes broken long ago, they led us to the banks of the west branch of the Oriskany, where we found the remains of an old bark roof that Mr. Herman and I raised as best we could while our guides were busy fishing. Soon they brought us eleven fine salmon trout from which we made an excellent supper. Despite the inconveniencies of the shelter, the smoke, and mosquitoes, we slept soundly.

Early in the afternoon of the second day we stopped beside another branch of the same creek, in order to have time to raise our night shelter, to cut wood, light the fire, and gather leaves, while our hunters pursued some partridge whose drummings we heard.[1] Fearing lest we lose our way, they had not wanted to hunt on the journey.

"One can easily see," said my companion, "that the forests are the real home of these Indians and their favorite retreat. In the village, these young warriors were lazy and sullen; here you see how gay they are, how active and even how accommodating!"

"They are flattered by our confidence," I told him. "Moreover, they are fulfilling the intentions of their father and of the governor: each creek they come upon toward twilight is for them a haven where they almost always find game, fish, and undisturbed sleep. Such is the way of life preferred by them far above any having to do with farming and labor, and the one for which they appear to have been created; how many Europeans, captured by the charm of this life, have adopted it forever? The number is greater than one thinks; especially in the warm climes of Georgia and the two Floridas, where the examples of this regression toward primitive life are much more frequent."

"That doesn't astonish me in the slightest, for this taste seems to be innate," he observed.

It was late on the morning of the third day when we left our camp on one of the branches of the Chenango, because our guides had had difficulty in rounding up our horses. Scarcely had we gone three miles when we met a band of Senecas and Tuscaroras who were on their way to the great Buffalo Plains in northern Pennsylvania. The fourth day we camped on a swollen creek which, we were told, emptied into Unadilla creek. The next day we were making our way slowly through a heavily wooded swamp, when one of our guides who was walking ahead stopped suddenly and called our attention to the faint light of a clearing, and soon after we discovered a dwelling of tree trunks known as a log cabin toward which we made our way with haste. It belonged to a Dane who had two cows and some chickens; he offered us corn cakes, butter, and even peach brandy with which, in addition to maple syrup in which the entire country abounds, we made milk punch, which our young guides found delicious. Although my companion had borne gaily and courageously the inconveniencies and fatigues of this journey, he was so fortunate to have emerged safe and sound from the depths of these somber forests, and so grateful for the little attentions our two hunters had given us, that, not knowing how to reward them, he offered to one his pistols and to the other his watch. They refused these presents with a smile of astonishment and would accept only a few dollars with which they would buy powder and shot.

The next day, after taking leave of these worthy Oneidas, we continued our journey on a path that was fairly well trodden. Rarely did we go a mile without encountering a clearing and a new little dwelling. Most of the settlers were young people recently arrived from Connecticut and New Hampshire. They seemed to us full of hope and happy over settling in one of the most fertile and most ideally situated districts of the state of New York.

"What we see here," said my companion, "is a reflection of what we saw in the counties of Northumberland, Luzerne, Tioga, Montgomery, Otsego, etc. During this long journey we have not traveled ten miles without finding families recently arrived: surveyors busy subdividing land, men busy opening roads, or building bridges. What vast new fields man's industry can prepare by the plow!"

"That is certainly true," I replied. "Everything here grows and flourishes with a rapidity that one cannot conceive in the land whence you have come. That is why, at the end of only a few years, what was true last year is today no longer true. You can no longer recognize the scenes they have described from their tales."

Instead of sleeping in the woods as we had done since leaving Fort Stanwix, in accordance with the information given us, we realized with delight that if we regulated our itinerary it would be easy for us each evening to come upon a shelter with provisions for us and our animals. Toward the end of the third day since leaving the Danish plantation, we arrived at the home of a prosperous farmer, located on one of the branches of the Butternut, which empties into the Tienaderhah. His settlement, we were told, was already five years old. Scarcely had his dogs announced our approach, when the farmer was out of the house and begging us politely to dismount.

"I never permit travelers to proceed without insisting that they refresh themselves if it be morning, or persuading them to sleep, if it be night. My home, although far from perfect, is large and roomy. The sight of people such as you, gentlemen, is a pleasure for people like us who are so weary of the silence and solitude of these forests."

We followed Mr. Wilson. When we entered his home, in accordance with the custom of the land, he introduced us to his wife, his children, his brother, and his sister.

"What is the purpose of that great framework not far from here at the junction of the two paths?" my companion asked him.

"It is the framework of a church," he replied.

"What! A church!" exclaimed Mr. Herman. "The country we have just explored seems rather young to be able to stand that expense; no doubt the Government advances funds for it."

"No: it protects and incorporates by legislative act all those churches which the inhabitants choose to erect. But it makes available only two hundred acres of land to serve as endowment. The building is the work of fifty-seven families, scattered over an area of more than thirty miles; because land and the wood cost nothing; since we already have several sawmills, and since each subscriber gives one week of his labor and his equipment and, besides is a carpenter, this construction will be much less costly than you might think. We will be obliged to buy only the nails, the window panes, and the paint. Here we need three things, without which we cannot prosper, not to mention health, the mother of strength. We need a smith to repair our tools (for, as you know, iron is the sceptre of our power); a schoolmaster who will go from family to family instructing the young; finally, a minister of the Gospel and a church where through prayers every Sunday we can seek and obtain the protection of the Lord over our new and difficult tasks. All men need this divine protection; but especially those who, having left a cultured land where they enjoyed all the advantages of society, had the courage to go afar. Without religious principles, what would we be on earth? The most wretched of human beings! For religion is one of the bases of our social structure, one of the props of our political system. Without the influence of religious opinions, who would guarantee the faith of vows, the morality of individuals and even that of our Government? I have observed that in regions whose inhabitants are indifferent to worship, lawsuits and quarrels, drunkenness and idleness were very common. The education of children, the union of families, the peace and prosperity of a land depend in great measure on this religious disposition which impresses on all minds respect for laws, gratitude toward the most paternal Government in the world, and that subordination of desires that fosters order, peace, and industry. Besides, remote from one another, how would we know what is going on in the world of which we have not forgotten for a moment we are a part? How would we learn the conditions of trade, the price of commodites, the news of Europe? Without these Sunday meetings, we would soon lose the refined and social ideas in which we have been raised. To see one another too frequently would be detrimental to men whose time must be devoted to work; to see another occasionally is a useful and even indispensable practice."

"Where did you imbibe these ideas which are so just?" asked Mr. Herman.

"From the experience and observations that I had in traveling through the states of the union."

"You have certainly not traveled in vain. May I be so bold as to inquire where you came from?" he asked.

"From the state of Connecticut," Mr. Wilson answered. "I spent my youth at sea and my mature years at New Haven,[2] where I had a store. I have tasted good and bad luck; been shipwrecked on the coast of Cuba and at the mouth of the Mississippi. I have repaired my misfortunes by new efforts and I have always mingled a little reading with my daily work; for good books, like the good earth, are the source of useful and satisfying fruits. Yet I do not wish to imply that I am a savant."

"And why did you abandon a business career and your native town to make a laborious settlement here where progress must seem so slow and painful to you?"

"This project springs from reading the work of a Doctor Styles who for thirty years was president of our college.[3] This work contains a series of judicious and profound observations on the progress of enlightenment and what is called philosophy, from the discovery of printing to the end of our revolution, the time of the author's death. This progress, at first imperceptible, like the first rays of the sun obscured by the mists of a long night, nevertheless prepared men, according to Doctor Styles, for the understanding of new ideas. In tracing with admirable sagacity the development of these germinating ideas, the effects of this cause, so feeble in appearance, Doctor Styles thought he discovered that from the beginning of the century, the momentum had become so rapid that before the century ends, the bases on which societies are founded will undergo perhaps a great change, or at least will be very much shaken.

"On the other hand, knowing through the study of history that good never comes to men except in the wake of great abuses, just as light emanates from combustion, he foresaw also that should this paroxysm take place, it would precipitate a long series of misfortunes and disasters.

"Impressed by this peculiar foreboding, and fearing that these germs crossing the ocean might prevent our Government, still so young, from becoming strong, I put in safekeeping part of my capital, and came here, far from the sea and the cities, to found a useful settlement. It is founded on the clearing and cultivation of 4,800 acres situated on the banks of a navigable river. My brother and sister have a third interest. This happy future can elude us only through the overthrow of our Government; but this Government is founded on reason, the work of deep thought and collective wisdom of the Constitutional Convention, and it seems impossible that those who planned it and those who daily derive benefits from it would consent and contribute to its overthrow, replacing it with new systems. Like a shining beacon mounted on the peak of a promontory, is not the experience of the past supposed to illuminate the present and the future?

"Yet the solitary life of the woods, the separation from my former associates, would have been too bitter a sacrifice and one to which perhaps I would never have been able to subject myself, had my brother and sister not consented to share and lighten my work. We relieve the tedious tasks and inevitable privations of this new way of life through helping each other as well as through gaiety and serenity of mind. Satisfied with our lot, we lead an active life, hardworking, it is true, but one that is peaceful and moderate, which the agitations of business and trade can no longer envenom. In a few years this clumsy-looking shelter will become a snug and charming dwelling, and this region a rich and cultivated land.

"I raise my children to know farming, the source of health, independence, and happiness, if any is to be had on earth. Each of them has a colt, a heifer, and some garden space. The oldest takes care of my nursery, which already boasts pear, apple, and other fruit-bearing trees. And that is an unusual thing for early colonists who rarely bother to replace trees which they uproot and destroy. My brother hopes (soon) for a wife, and my sister for a husband. One day, and it is not too distant, our three families, closely united by bonds of blood and affection, as well as by similarity of taste, will become neighbors and friends.

"The Government has honored me with a commission of Justice of the Peace, for everything in these woods is organized just as though we were already numerous; this is one of the best methods of increasing the population of new areas. This region, incidentally, already enjoys great advantages."

Scarcely had Mr. Wilson finished speaking, when we heard in the adjacent room, a concert of various instruments.

"What!" I exclaimed. "Music under a roof still so rustic! and in a land which has been under cultivation so few years! Whence comes all this talent?"

"We brought our talents from New Haven," he replied, "they cheer us and divert us from our hard tasks. We devote a part of our evenings to this charming activity. You would not believe how much it brightens our hearts, sustaining friendship and affection. It is one of the bases of the bond that exists among us. A few years ago, one of our vessels returning from Bremen brought over a number of Germans, among whom was a Saxon, a fine musician who even composes! It is he who taught us. We colonists do not appreciate enough the need, the utility, and the charm of music.

"But let us go outside. I am very eager to show you what I call my conquests. You know there enters always a little vanity in what we do."

We followed him.

"Everything you see," he resumed, "is the work of courage, toil, and the most stubborn perseverance. Before bringing in the harvest from this soil, fertile though it is, how many obstacles we must surmount! how many difficulties we have to overcome! how much loathing we must swallow! Yes, I am sure of it: from the first day of his arrival, if the colonist could see a true picture of it, he would wish he had never left his homeland hearth. But the hope that guided him smilingly to this foreign land hides from him carefully any harshness, permitting him to see in the distance only fertile fields, lush meadows and blooming orchards, ease, and independence.

"Do you see over there on the right, that great pasture through which this fine little stream meanders and flows? Well, five years ago, it was an impenetrable, miry swamp. The dams which the beavers so artfully built there and which cost us so much effort to demolish, caused these waters to overflow to the level of the highlands. Today, as you see, my herd grazes on clover in the same area where the first of my stock found only birch, willow, and alder trees. Here on the left are sixty-five acres of cultivated land which tool and fire have finally subdued for plowing. One part is wheat, the other clover. Only the swamps remain and their destruction is but the work of time."

"Why," I asked him, "did you allow several of these trees to grow in the midst of your fields? Isn't their shade unfavorable to the wheat that you have sown?"

"That is true; but I must confess that the charm of their majesty, their beauty paralyzed our hands just as we were about to fell them. I admire them too much to dare to uproot them."

"I must agree," I told him, "these superb and gigantic trunks do have an imposing majesty which instinctively inspires respect. In time, they will contribute immeasurably to the beautification of the land."

Further on was a tulip tree of prodigious height. Its pyramid shape seemed to have been formed by a special will, and it is that same will which has preserved it. In laying out the first path destined to become some day the main road of the district, at about one hundred paces from the house, all nature's great and beautiful structures untouched, made an avenue.

After exploring almost the entire plantation, our host took us to a valley that he had just fenced in. It was covered with maple trees.

"Every year," he told us, "I extract four hundred seventy pounds of maple sugar without sapping the tree's strength. What a splendid gift nature has bestowed on this continent! Why is this tree not known and cultivated in the four corners of the world! On the neighboring slope, I planted a triple orchard: the first, apple trees; the second, cherry trees; and the third, peach trees. One will give us cider, the other wine [4] which my wife knows how to make to perfection; the third brandy." [5]

From there he led us to the falls of one of his rivers.

"Here is another of nature's boons," he told us, "and never, in this connection as well as in various others, has she been more bountiful in any other land. This great source of water has fallen futilely for centuries. Before eighteen months I hope to put into motion wheels of mills that I plan to build. Here we have everything that is needed: industry, knowledge, iron, wood, stone, and limestone. From the state of Pennsylvania come the most skillful artisans of the continent; they know how to bring to these superb machines a degree of perfection that no one had ever attained prior to the discoveries of the famous mechanic, Evans. Grain, being one of the most important items among our exports, the price of labor very dear, it is not astonishing that man has sought to perfect and simplify the art of milling."

The next day, with the information we needed, we bade farewell to this fine, upstanding family. The memory of them will never leave me.

CHAPTER XI

Although we had but fourteen or fifteen miles farther to travel before we would reach the settlement mentioned by Mr. Wilson, we did not arrive there before four o'clock in the afternoon. Since our departure from Onondaga, we had not yet come upon a land so thickly wooded nor one with swamps whose crossings were so difficult.[1] Our horses were tired and Mr. Herman was almost discouraged when we finally sighted a house of very elegant appearance. The entire front was adorned with a piazza[2] supported, according to custom, by columns of white cedar. The windows, equipped with shutters, were handsomely painted. Since leaving Pennsylvania, our eyes had become unaccustomed to the fastidious taste suggested by all this.

"Here at last," said my companion, "is a haven which promises us good beds and a fine stable for our horses. To whom does this fine house belong?" he asked of a man who happened by.

"To a Jamaican. And no one knows why he labors, for he has neither wife nor child."

"What!" Mr. Herman said to me. "To come here from the rich and magnificent land of Jamaica to settle in the depths of somber, lonely forests of New York! To prefer the cultivation of grain and forage in a climate which for three months yearly knows only snows and frosts, to raising sugar and cotton in a climate of eternal spring! This seems strange indeed!"

Both of us, stirred by the desire to learn of the motives behind all this, as well as by the need to rest, stopped at the door to ask for a night's hospitality.

"Need you *ask* shelter?" said the householder to our request. "How else could one travel in these forests if peoples' homes were not open to travelers? In bidding you welcome, I return a favor I have often received."

His house was spacious, clean, and conveniently arranged. I noticed even some beautiful mahogany furniture but I saw neither wife nor children. Immediately he ordered our horses baited and had refreshments served to us, of which we were indeed in great need. When this was done, in accordance with the custom of the land, he asked us who we were, whence we came, and whither we were bound. We answered his questions in a manner that seemed to satisfy him so well that we thought we were justified in asking him his reasons for leaving Jamaica.

"Slavery and the climate," he answered. "My father was unhappily carried away in the prime of life by one of those epidemic diseases to which our island is so often exposed. He had Negro servants and, while he was more their friend than master, he always regretted being obliged to command their wills and profit by their services. He often talked to me about it. These sparks ignited me during my youth and were not without benefit. But, since the government of the island permitted emancipation only with great complications, I was not able to follow the inclinations of my heart in the matter.

"A hundred times I asked whence came this impious and sacrilegious trade?"

" 'From power and from need,' they told me.

" 'But why should a man, born 'neath the equator, be condemned to work his whole life for another who happened to see the light of day under the fiftieth degree of latitude? Could it be from this latitude that strength and preëminence spring?'

" 'That is likely; but the Europeans are not the first who sought slaves in Africa; for centuries the Moors, as well as other nations, have carried on this trade. Negro slavery dates from earliest antiquity.'

" 'What a state of things,' I said. 'Is it not possible that some day the greater number may subject the smaller number? Then the avengers of so many years of oppression will soil the land with new crimes and their vengeance will erase neither the horror nor the memory of those crimes that their oppressors have committed.'

"If the colonists of these islands had thought as I do, sugar would soon have risen in price in Europe—or rather it would have become more common, because, instead of stirring up wars in Africa, instead of corrupting the unhappy and guilty chieftains, the colonists, acting in concert with the sensible Europeans, would have joined their efforts to those of that worthy and famous company which has conceived the magnificent scheme of liberation, has obtained sufficient funds, and has acquired land on the coast of Africa in order to establish there colonies of free Negroes whose industry and example would have encouraged the black princes to have the sugar cane cultivated by their subjects.

"Humanity will not cease to regret that so holy and laudable a motive has not sheltered from the violences of war the colonies it made on the island of Bulama and at Sierra-Leone.[3] Men, armed supposedly in the name of liberty, have destroyed, annihilated everything that the most ardent desire, the purest zeal for that same liberty had conceived and realized. When man wishes to do evil, every means of accomplishing it presents itself; often he is embarrassed only by the choice of evils. Does he want to do good? Everything, even unto Nature, opposes itself to his plans. Need one be astonished that food is so rare on the earth whose surface appears sometimes to have been poisoned by his presence? *

"The wasting climate of this little island was the second reason for my leaving it. What is life without health? A burden, a continual source of regret—especially for a man of my age—for I am only thirty-five. Well, I spent twelve of them suffering, languishing, wishing the end to a life so painful. I had to battle against the rays of a sun that was well nigh vertical, of which anyone in this climate can conceive only a very imperfect idea. If, on one hand, its extreme heat produces a nature that is smiling, vigorous, and fertile to excess, on the other hand, this heat leaves only the slightest interval between the domain of life and that of its destruction, the debris of which often arrests and stifles its productive power. Danger goes hand in hand with work. Rest and inactivity are equally harmful. Sobriety and temperance are not, as they are here, the guarantees of health. In certain seasons deadly vapors rise from our swamps, polluting the very air we breathe. Life is but the flower of one day, a fugitive dream, and as if the intemperance of climate were not sufficient to shorten it, the violence of passions accelerates even more swiftly its ruin and destruction.

"I came to New York seeking health. I have found it but from fear of losing this inestimable gift a second time, I obtained naturalization papers, and after exploring various regions, I purchased the six hundred fifty acres which I own here, and I found what I was seeking: a little lake about one hundred fifty acres in area whose waters flow into the Charlotte River (for I am passionately fond of fishing), and a knoll whence some day my view will reach far. Here I breathe fresh and pure air. Here I enjoy every moment of my life, far from the tumult and squalor of the towns, sheltered from the threat of bankruptcies and fires, and far from those destructive storms which cover the land with ruin and fill hearts with terror and tragedy. Elsewhere people would like to rid themselves of the pressure of time; here I would like to prolong its duration.

"To make over a new land that becomes dearer through the work it exacts, to fell from it the useless trees that encumber it, to plant on it fine, useful ones, to dam up and guide waters wherever necessary, to cultivate and plant the new and rich soil—these activities, so new

---

* This is an assertion that is probably too absolute. Evil here on earth is more common than good—agreed. But to allege that nature (and to what blasphemous notions would such a proposition lead us!) opposes and resists the good that men sometimes wish to do, is to exaggerate, is to transcend the bounds of indignation that are permissible and natural to virtue.
(Note communicated to the editor by Citizen Billecocq.)

to me, bring me enjoyment of which I had never before even the remotest notion. Healthy, vigorous, active, I am busy from dawn till
dusk; I have a fine collection of choice books, the reading of which
both entertains and instructs me in my moments of leisure. Six months
ago, the Director-General of the Post Office set up a mail route which
comes through this region on its way to the Ontario country. In order
to express my gratitude for such a benefit premature in view of the
size of our population, I offered him my house and my services. The
more I read newspapers and details of everything transpiring in the
Old World, the more I congratulate myself on the decision I made to
settle in this world.

"I have neither wife nor child. Sometimes indeed I regret that I am
alone and working only for myself. But to give life to beings condemned to experience all the evils that once escaped Pandora's box,
who would be necessarily exposed to the scourges that ceaselessly afflict
the inhabitants of the earth, that vast arena of plunder, murder, and
misfortune would be like sending out to sea one's dearest friends in
a frail skiff 'mid storm and tempest. The reflective reading of history
whose pages are stained with blood or soiled with crime and trans-
gression has long made a deep impression on my mind. No, it is not
the impression of man as I had pictured him in my youth, but that of
a tiger. One cannot comprehend the intentions of creative power
when, having called us from nothingness, she put in our hearts the
source of passions which were necessarily fatal to us, and condemned
us to suffer during the short span of our lifetime, all kinds of misery,
pain, and anguish to which we might be susceptible. No, never will
I have to reproach myself for having introduced new victims to this
theatre of tears and misery, where crime and dishonesty triumph.
No, never will I expose myself to the severe and heartrending pains
that a father must feel in watching languish and die in his arms the
child of his tenderness, without being able to relieve his suffering. The
enjoyments of this exquisite and sublime feeling are bought with too
many risks and dangers. I prefer to make the journey alone, rather
than accompanied by cherished beings whom I might perhaps have the
misfortune to survive.

"To console me in these sad reflections, I study Buffon, the outstanding painter of nature. I have made some interesting experiments
on the transpiration of leaves and the grafting of trees.

"I have one friend—for one must love, if not life, at least those
who among men are kind and loving. By preference this friend is a
turner and cabinet-maker. He made the beautiful furniture you see
with wood sent to me from Jamaica. I am not alone any more than is

good for me. I deplore only the too rapid passing of time. The acquaintance I made with the Wilson family fills and enriches my leisure time —I refer to Sundays and holidays.''

The next day we took leave of this young misanthrope who, although appearing to enjoy all the attractions of life, health, activity, and ease, had nevertheless certainly conceived gloomy and disheartening notions of human nature. Perhaps he had looked only on the dark side of life.

CHAPTER XII

Despite the most scrupulous attention in following the directions that Mr. Seagrove had given us, such was the condition and multiplicity of the paths, that we strayed over twenty-eight miles before arriving at Mr. J. U.'s dwelling. His hospitality soon made us forget our fatigue and privations. Recalling to us on the very next day our old promise to tell him what we had seen at Onondaga and at Fort Stanwix, I, as the older, was seeking to put a little order to my recital, when Mr. Herman offered to read to him the journal of our trip.

"Ah," said Mr. J. U., whom the prospect of this reading seemed to interest, "if the Europeans who travel here took the trouble to see things as carefully as you, Gentlemen, they would render more justice to our efforts and to our industry, as imperfect as it still is. They consider neither the paucity of men, nor the high cost of man power, nor the time involved in building, nor the multitude of obstacles which untamed nature presents, nor the difficulties of communication for several years, nor finally the special disposition of the early colonists. How much time must necessarily elapse before the houses, barns, fields, and prairies can acquire that degree of perfection, and our countryside that elegance and pleasing appearance to which the eyes of Europeans are accustomed! Yet, if you were to travel through the great sections of Connecticut and Massachusetts, in the land of the Mohawks, and the regions about Reading, Lancaster, Ulster, Fishkill, Duchess, Columbia, and so many other counties, you would notice that already luxury in homes is known: the art of irrigation, the planting of useful, fine-looking trees. And furthermore, already there are indications of clay and rich pasture land.

"Whatever superficial travelers say," he continued, "I am convinced of this: never have there been colonies in modern times situated in the same climate where mechanization and useful arts have contributed so much to lightening and accelerating the work of man, and where growth and population increase have been so rapid. In vain could we attempt to measure this progress. What was true only a year ago is no longer true; on the one hand, never has the Government been so favorable to the development of active enterprises and in creating and stimulating this energy which leads both to speculation in trade and manufacture and land development. The example of the United States offers a vast proof of this activity and enterprise.

"More than one hundred twenty thousand colonists live today in the land known as Vermont.[1] And what was this land twenty years ago? Nothing more than ten or twelve small, straggling villages, scattered as if by chance over a vast territory, part of which was claimed at the time by the state of New Hampshire, and the other part by New York. One never spoke of those young colonists save under the derisive name of Green Mountain Boys. Suddenly, irritated by the injustice of colonial government, and threatened by a kind of tyranny unknown in this region,[2] as soon as Congress had proclaimed its independence, they had the spirit and the courage to unite, the wisdom to establish a democratic, but wise constitution, and the good fortune to enter the confederacy of states. As a result, today Vermont has numerous flourishing settlements linked by good roads, each with its church and school. A University endowed wth ten thousand acres of land has just been founded at Burlington. The militia is composed of twenty-two regiments whose martial spirit is well known. All that was the work of only twenty-four years!

"If ever you go to Canada by way of Lake Champlain [3] you will admire, as I have, its picturesque banks alternately wild, cultivated, or wooded. This mixture of slopes is more or less mountainous, covered with moss, meadows, orchards, and pasture land, scattered with farm houses—some of which are elegant and well painted. If the wind is favorable, stop at Plattsburgh. This town, which has become the county seat of Clinton County, the countryside which surrounds it, and the meadows which the Saranac River waters, present paragons of improved cultivation. And think! Colonel Platt, founder of this settlement arrived there only in May of 1782. The year previous deer and beaver were still being hunted there. Salmon fishing has already become a very lucrative industry for the inhabitants of the fertile islands of this beautiful lake.

"And the town of Hudson, whose very birth I witnessed in 1783 on the banks of that very river, today boasts five thousand inhabitants, many fair-sized factories of sail cloth and rope, and thirty-four ships, whaling vessels, coasters, and trading ships!

"What was being grown there before the Revolution and what was the population of the state? Hardly did one know the extent and limits. There were scarcely two hundred-forty thousand inhabitants: today there are more than four hundred thousand. The population of the capital city has increased ten thousand in a period of four years. Everything is bustling in the new sections of Tioga, Bath, Ontario, Montgomery, Otsego, Onondaga, etc. The colonists have come there from northern countries as well as from Europe. To encourage them, the Government at great expense has opened roads at various junctures, and through gifts and loans has encouraged companies to undertake the building of canals and useful bridges. It gave seven thousand five hundred piastros to the company that contracted to build the bridge at Cohoes [4] on the Mohawk River and perhaps as much for the completion of the canal at Little Falls. It has been no less generous toward those who built the ones at Wood Creek and Onondaga.

"Look at Pennsylvania, whose population has already reached the southern banks of the Erie, where a port has just been developed.[5] See with what wisdom and perseverance this government directs the making of roads and canals destined to link the different parts of this great Republic—all this in order to encourage agriculture!

"The same spirit has been evident for a long time in Virginia. Before four years the Potomac [6] will be navigable to the remotest wrinkle of the Alleghanies. The Shenandoah will perhaps become navigable inland as far as to the foot of the Blue Ridge Mountains. Soon the waters of the North Carolina River will meet with the Chesapeake.[7] The canal at Richmond is already finished.[8] The desert that separates this state from Kentucky is shrinking daily because of the new settlements.

"And this new state in a land so attractive by virtue of its climate, the fertility of its soil, and the cosmopolitanism of its inhabitants! There are already one hundred fifty thousand persons there. Already one can see well-built towns, a university richly endowed (Salem), machines for carding and spinning cotton, many educated persons, several printeries. Well! all that is the work of only a few years; for the first furrow was not plowed until 1774 by Colonel Boon.

"And Judge Symmes' colony on the banks of the great Miami, known as Columbia! The colonies of the Wabash and the Illinois; and the various military concessions, granted by Congress and the states to the different divisions of the continental army! How these seeds sprout!

"Let us not forget Tennessee, a land whose geographical location is still so little known. A land which, from the mountains of North Carolina (the Ironhills), stretching to the Mississippi over a space of four hundred miles, irrigated its entire length by the beautiful river whose name it borrowed, as well as by various other rivers. This region is destined to become one day the Quito of our hemisphere because of its beauty and the mild temperature of its climate. And finally the new state of Washington, on the Muskinghum, founded in 1788 by three generals of the Massachusetts Company.[9] Despite war with the Indians lasting three years, there are more than eighteen thousand inhabitants and several very interesting factories. You must pardon, gentlemen, the length of these reflexions which the reading of your

journal stirred. I wanted to confirm some of your conjectures by telling you facts of public information, which, as foreigners in this land,
perhaps you might not know.

"Eager to do something that might be pleasant for you, I entertained myself during your absence by sketching what you might wish
to call the story of my emigration. I was going to read it to you; but
I note that it is late, so if you will permit me, I shall postpone reading it until tomorrow."

CHAPTER XIII

"I was first lieutenant aboard 'The Galathea' in 1783 when the admiralty sent that frigate to New York where it was not long before I experienced the hospitality for which the inhabitants of that town were so renowned in colonial times. I was all the more moved by it because the impressions occasioned by the misfortunes of war could not yet be erased. Soon I was to observe that the principal topics of conversation were relative to the purchase and sale of land, the amount of which seemed exaggerated to me. It was still a question of concessions of ten, twenty, or often even fifty thousand acres, as well as the settlements, the clearing of sites, talk of bridges, mills, and new communications. Imagine how much these topics, so new to a European, must have aroused my imagination and stirred my curiosity! On my return, meditating over what I had heard, I often spoke of it to the captain who said to me one day:

" 'Here we are in a world newly discovered: not even one hundred sixty-five years have elapsed since the Dutch disembarked on this island, founded this town, and made settlements in the neighboring countrysides. The greatest portion of the soil in this hemisphere is still covered by forests and awaits only the progress of population, industry, and time before gathering the harvests and producing all the riches of abundance; the purchase, sale, and clearing of lands must then be the chief object of speculation and the topic of daily conversations. It is not astonishing that the colonists are busy in these new ventures; but the value of land being proportionate to the population and the population of this land being still quite undetermined, even twenty thousand acres are perhaps not worth those that are located in the neighborhood of London or of Edinborough.'

"That is quite true," I replied. "But since this value increases every year with the number of colonists, would it not be very advantageous to acquire a certain amount of land? It would seem to me that this would be investing one's money at a high interest.

" 'Quite true; then one would have to cease being European, obtain naturalization papers, and renounce his country.

" 'In some of the states of the Union, it is necessary to be naturalized, I admit, but here in Pennsylvania and Virginia, a Russian, a Neapolitan, or a Turk may become a landowner provided that at the end of three years he has a house built, a garden planted, and a ditch dug around each thousand acres.'

"The next day on my way to see a friend who would inform me of the price of land, of its revenue, of the necessary forms to obtain, of the expenses of clearing, and of those expenses involved in the construction of houses and barns, I met several former officers of the forty-second regiment who, at the time of the peace of 1763, had come to settle here. What they told me was like a ray of light that suddenly gave me an idea. I bought some maps and as soon as the geography of the continent and that of this state became familiar to me, I decided to follow their example and become a landowner. This plan was becoming firmer day by day in my mind, when comparing our barren mountains, our rude climate, our meagre and worn out soil with the freshness, the fertility, the expanse, the majestic rivers, and the immense lakes of this continent. My father, I told myself, can leave me only a small fortune; without some other income, I shall never be more than a lieutenant and soon I shall have only half pay; young, healthy as I am, why should I not devote my strength and vitality to the undertaking of so useful an enterprise? Is there any channel more worthwhile for a man's energy?

"One day, filled with these ideas, I talked with Mr. William Seton, a man of great experience with whom I formed a steadfast friendship.

" 'Could you not obtain a six weeks' leave from your captain? Then you would be able to explore the region I pointed out to you; you could judge the condition of the soil, its quality, that of the trees, and according to what the colonists with whom you would lodge have done, you would discover whether you are capable of the same; in any case, this excursion into the great forests, and the sight of so many new things, is bound to be very interesting.'

"I had no trouble in obtaining this leave and a few days later I set sail for Albany, arriving in fifty-four hours.[1] How peaceful and comfortable this trip of two hundred seventy-five miles seemed! What a majestic river! Above all, how much I admired its passage through the chain of highlands. The freshness and the greenness of these mountains aroused my curiosity especially when I recalled the sterility and nudity of those mountains in Northern Scotland. What a contrast indeed! Here these mountains give the impressions of youth—while those of my native land are the shadow of old age.

"From Albany I easily reached Cherry Valley, through well-cultivated countryside, though part had been devastated during the war. There I took a guide, a good hunter, and after four days of travel through very recent settlements, we finally entered a great forest where we made our way by means of a compass. At first we explored the banks of Caniaderague Lake, but having learned that the best lands had been granted two years ago, we crossed the six mile peninsula that separates it from Otzegue Lake and easily reached the latter whose banks appeared to be of a gentle and pleasant slope: with the aid of a borrowed canoe, we paddled up several of the small rivers which empty into Otsego, while I examined their banks carefully. At a point five miles from the mouth of the Seneca, a creek coming from the west, I discovered a spot that pleased me immensely, and at a little distance farther on in the woods was a great and magnificent waterfall fourteen feet high, formed by the union of two swollen streams whose waters, after falling, formed a canal that was navigable as far as the lake. This site was what gave me the idea of a sawmill, whose advantages I already knew quite well. The trees of the forest were a mixture of oaks, pines, hickories, and very high chestnuts, evidence of a fine soil. Finally, after spending seven days in the woods for the first time in my life, with the record of my notes that I took care to write out every evening, I returned to New York. There with the help of the same friend, I bought one thousand eight hundred fifty acres at the rate of four shillings sterling an acre, half of which was payable yearly and the other half at the end of the third year.

"From the moment this important and interesting transaction was completed, I began to think of myself as a member of a new society. My name had just been added to those of the citizens of this state and here I was, a man who had possessed nothing in the Old World, belonging by the mere acquisition of this land to the New World. I no longer felt like a European. What a curious and powerful effect ownership of land exerts on the mind and heart of man! This feeling, so heart-warming and so flattering, gives new aim to his character and conduct: that is what convinced me, not only by my own thoughts and sensations, but also by the observations of my comrades during our return voyage to England. The prospect of resigning my commission, renouncing my old habits, and above all that of some day having well-cultivated fields, pasture lands covered with cattle, the hope of creating during my youth a farm that would enrich me at no one else's expense, a place where I could lead a quiet, peaceful life and spend my old age in independence and repose—all of these ideas occupied my mind so intensely that my comrades, to whom I had said nothing of my plans, were struck at the change they observed in my attitude and conversation.

"On returning to Scotland, I obtained some help from my father and from an uncle who had become wealthy in Bengal: the former even had the generosity to add a considerable legacy which he might have enjoyed until death, according to the laws of the realm. I hired for a period of four years three Erse families,[2] strong, rugged people to each of whom I promised two hundred acres of land at the expiration of the four years. Finally, with all my affairs in order, I arrived without incident in New York seven months after leaving it.

"To be sure, the first two years were costly and difficult. Yet, never did I chance to regret the decision I made, even when surrounded by uprooted trees, thin branches, heaped up bushes burning; in the midst of smoke and fire, I compared this work, so new to me, to my military functions, and to my former pursuits.

"Like the signal light of a flagship on a black night, hope guided me, consoled me, and surrounded me with its beneficent illusions, for it is at such a time that one has a constant need of this hope. The more obstacles I met, the more Spartan I became, the more I summoned to my side courage and perseverance, those guardian divinities on whom one must frequently call, but who, in place of lofty altars of fragrant incense from Arabia, demand from the colonists only that of trees and destructive objects which clutter the land. I confess with gratitude the example, the advice, and often the fraternal help of some neighbors (if one can call by this name persons who live ten or twenty miles distant) have been of the greatest help to me. They encouraged me in my difficult undertakings, showing me what they themselves had done. Without this camaraderie and this happy disposition to helping one another, what would the early colonists do? How the obstacles disappear before them when, impressed by their own weakness, they call forth union and harmony among themselves. Always favorable to those who implore them, these daughters of heaven never miss heaping all the blessing needed by these colonists to bear up under the disgusts and fatigues of this state.

"I dare boast of having the most powerful mill in these regions, because I can control enough water to turn seven or eight saws simultaneously, and bring down, with one fell swoop, a tree of the greatest diameter. In building this mill, I did not forget to set up a weir; it nets me annually a great quantity of eels of a species very special in this region. At the beginning of autumn they leave the mud of our swamps and make their way seaward.[3] They are a manna-like occurrence coming twice yearly like that of the flight of pigeons we see covering our countryside in their passage into the interior twice yearly on their way to the seacoast where they replenish their supply of salt. This is not the only gift nature offers us. She permits us to share with inhabitants of the coast several kinds of fish that enter our rivers from the ocean every spring. Would you believe that the shad, the salmon, the herring, the sturgeon, and the bass come regularly to our lakes to deposit their spawn? Our creeks and our streams are filled with salmon trout that are from ten to eighteen inches long. The pleasure of catching them with the aid of artificial flies that I now know how to make is a relaxation and recreation that I frequently need.

"Already I have one hundred acres of land plowed and fenced. One part is covered with wheat and the other with clover; they are the admiration of the countryside. Seventy-two acres of swampland are drained and cleared and part is being cut down with the scythe, while the other part serves as pasture land. I have as many cattle, sheep, and horses as I can take care of in the winter.

"The lowlands that border on my little river are of a remarkable richness. I have devoted one part to the raising of corn and the other to hemp, for each quintal of which the Government pays us a dollar in gratitude. No where else other than on these irrigated lands, does one see such luxuriant vegetation; thus these banks have become my delight. Their soil is so light and rich that cultivation of it involves little expense. We have to battle only against the quantity and vegetative strength of weeds whose growth in the spring brings new seeds. If it were not for the fact that I plant my corn five or six feet apart, the stalks would bear nothing, so much space do the branches and leaves occupy. Imagine a forest of young palm trees, or a sugar plantation whose cane is ten feet high: one can scarcely walk through at the time of its full growth.

"Thanks to my fine oaks, my superb pines, and my mill, my house is spacious and comfortable. My young orchard is beginning to yield. Ah, how eager I am to see it laden with apples! As to the peach orchard, it provides me with an abundance of its fruit, for nothing grows more rapidly than these trees.[4] One part provides me with a necessary supply of brandy; the other serves to fatten my pigs.

"I devised a little system that I have been long in perfecting in order to regulate my life. From it, I have summed up and written down the essential principles, hanging the list over my bed, so that I would have them constantly in view, for it is wise to distrust oneself somewhat. My three Erse families settled in my neighborhood, work for me whenever I need them. I am happy in the thought that they owe to my efforts the happiness they enjoy. These worthy people, raised in the mountains, having known nothing but oats, were not, as I was, spoiled by idleness and luxury; they feel more keenly the advantages of their emigration.

"Instead of sending my products to Philadelphia by way of the Susquehanna, I sell them to the colonists who are already beginning to settle in the districts of Tiogo, Bath, and Ontario. This advantage is reciprocal: without the convenience of buying here the provisions they need, how would they have them brought from Scoharie, from Albany, or German Flats? That is how a region inhabited for six years contributed to the progress of clearing and populating distant regions; that is how, step by step, we arrived from the seacoast to the shores of the Ontario; such has been and will be the march of our colonization, until we have reached the remotest cultivatable limits of the territory of the United States.[5]

"In 1783 there were only seven families in what is today known as Otsego County. Chance had placed them so far from one another that they believed themselves alone, isolated in the heart of these forests. At Cherry Valley, Albany, or Lunenbourg, one would not suspect that men who were not hunters could settle at so great a distance from inhabited frontiers. The head of one of these families was an Englishman, formerly a captain in the regiment, who, they say, wanted to kill himself when he knew that he had to be reclassified as unfit for duty. His wife, endowed with great strength of character, recalling that in her youth she had watched the making of cheese, conceived the notion of coming to this country, long a haven for unhappy folk. After persuading her husband to waive his rights to half pay, his pitiful patrimony, and what she possessed, they crossed the ocean and disembarked in New York. Guided by good advice, they bought five hundred acres of land at the rate of two shillings sterling an acre (this was before the independence of the states) and came to bury themselves in this deep loneliness. They were completely forgotten until some years later there appeared in the market places of Albany cheeses of attractive shape and quality superior to any that had been seen before. Everyone wanted Turnicleaf cheese. Imagine what must have been the happiness of this family on seeing, after so many years of loneliness, the arrival in their neighborhood of men, new roads opening by Government order, mills built, artisans following farmers; to find oneself finally surrounded by the help of civilized society of whom they had been deprived so many years. This worthy captain is a colonel in the militia, and one of the judges of the lower court. Think of the progress of people and their industry! What a difference between the day when, despairing, this officer wanted to put a bullet through his head and the day when, as a colonel in America, he could count through his own enterprise eighteen hundred twenty free tenant families, all prospering in a territory where in 1778 there had been no one save himself and family!

"Already we have several churches, a great number of schools, some fairly decent inns and bridges over the principal rivers. As for the roads, they will soon feel the effects of the young vigor of our region, for everything is progressing. Ten or twelve well-to-do families from New York have come here to settle; their enlightened ideas, their wealth have already paid great dividends. The charm of society has already begun to lessen our loneliness and lighten our tasks. Distance, however great, cannot prevent our meeting on certain days—even in the wintertime. Together we are sure of finding happiness, not to mention a little amusement.

"Once a week a branch of the postal system brings us our mail and newspapers. How wonderful and useful these social institutions are! How they link and unite men! How effectively they serve to sustain friendship, encourage business, and promote knowledge! Never do I watch the arrival of the mail without feeling a deep gratitude toward the Government that made possible this advantage before we have grown old, and long before we hoped for it. Ah, if, like me, you had spent six years of your life without hearing the voices of your relatives and your friends, or news of what was going on in the world outside, you would be even more grateful to Congress, just as I am for this mail, than for the fine laws that it made.

"I have a plentiful supply of everything of essential need: woolens, linens, seeds, cattle, butter, cheese, lard, etc. Annually I market three hundred fifty bushels of wheat; a proportionate amount of oats, peas, and corn. Thus you see that with good land, one can become well-off, even opulent, without having much money and above all happy in pleasant comfort through the fortuitous necessity of work and activity.

"My neighbor is a former shipmate, with whom I served for a long time on the same vessel. He came here three years ago chiefly out of curiosity to find out whether I regretted having resigned from the service, and to see what my home was like; it is very difficult for a European to get a clear picture of all this. He was horrified by the woods; instead of stirring his admiration the height and the somber majesty of the trees of our forests aroused only disgust and aversion. Never did we go for a walk without his imagining that he saw behind each great oak or pine an Indian armed with a tomahawk. He would scarcely venture to take a step for fear of walking on a rattlesnake.

"In observing what it costs in work and care to clear the land and reap harvests, he could not possibly realize how I could have given up the certainty of a career in the navy (where, as the son of a lord, as he candidly pointed out to me, I had excellent chances for promotion) to become a hardworking colonist and bury myself in this solitude. However, he gave me credit for the courage and perseverance with which I had surmounted so many obstacles and dissatisfactions. For a long time he tried to persuade me to sell my lands and return with him to Europe. But I needed neither deliberated eloquence nor subtle reasoning to make him feel the nature and impact of the motives which had determined my course. I pointed out to him the probable chance of fulfillment for my hopes; the stability of my little fortune in the shadow of reverses, wars, revolutions, as well as those unforeseen events which happen so often in societies established long ago. In the course of my talk with him I compared the wonderfully pleasant ease that my labors had already made possible, with the mediocrity of my former lot; the liberty and independence in which I lived now with the constraint of my former state; the civil importance, the prestige that I enjoyed now with the anonymity of a man lost amid crowded society in Europe.

" 'What was I in Scotland,' I said to him, 'where I occupied a place so easily filled by another? What good could I do there? What could my hopes be? I was useless there, since I lived only to consume. Here, now as a member of a growing society, property, laws, local circumstances have invested me with a certain weight in the social scale. As for the state, I am a citizen (a condition I did not enjoy when I first settled). As for Otsego County, I am one of its useful citizens who clears, works, labors, and covers with seed a land formerly unproductive. As for business, I am a consumer and producer of considerable measure, since I add annually to the export of this state more than five hundred bushels of grain; I have the right to vote and to be elected deputy to the legislative body or to the Federal Congress. I do not refer to the municipal positions of the district which can be filled only by free landowners. All this is not the expression of childish vanity but rather that of reason. Show me a country where for twelve thousand piastres I might possess twelve hundred fifty acres of land (for you realize that I gave six hundred of them to my three Erse families in return for four years of work), free and clear of all taxes, in the same state of improvement as are mine; all this under the influence of fair and just laws whose protection would cost me only six piastres a year for municipal expense. Assuming that I sell this farm for twenty thousand piastres, and that I invest this sum in Europe, would the interest, I ask you, that I would draw from it enable me to live as I do here—in the lap of plenty, surrounded by people who are devoted to me, with cattle and horses and barns well stocked? Assuredly not; and furthermore, who would guarantee to me that fire, bankruptcy, or war would not wrest from me my capital?'

" 'As to the inconveniencies you mention, such as our long winters, during which we are obliged to consume part of the profits from summer, the necessity of fencing our fields, the high price of labor, the insects that sometimes harm our harvests and inconvenience us, the lack of good roads, the remoteness of waterways and the towns, the distances one must travel to see his friends and neighbors, all these inconveniencies are balanced by so many advantages, I daresay by so many essential enjoyments, that after the experience of six years I am convinced that for a man who has nothing, or very little of anything, it is infinitely more advantageous to be here than in Scotland. Everything around me moves at so swift a pace, that before ten years are spent, two-thirds of the inconveniencies will no longer exist. Our lands will be cleared, most of the stumps rotted or removed, roads and bridges will be finished, and the insects will have disappeared as soon as our swamps are drained.'

" 'These are the thoughts that experience has provoked since I have come here. I could add many others that a sensible man should not forget. I refer to the moral enjoyments which have so great an influence on the mind. For myself, I benefit enormously from the mere fact of finding myself in a new society that is in the making one thousand leagues from Europe, in virtually the same uniform climate and on fertile soil. From a society founded on the principles of most favorable legislation for the stimulation of industry and the assurance of civil and religious liberty: I hold as very important the happiness derived from becoming one of the first sprouts of this society, of seeing fields and orchards replace useless forests; muddy swamps converted to pasture land; the upstanding immigrant considered in Europe the riff-raff, becoming a substantial colonist and respectable citizen. Finally, the good fortune of watching the growth of this vast land under the guidance of a Government which is preserver of order and peace. Ah, my friend, with how many other distinctions I could color richly this feebly drawn picture, were I not fearful of tiring your European ears! You are wealthier than I. Invest part of the funds you have in the buying of a parcel of land. I know of one right in this vicinity on which a drunken, lazy colonist has been vegetating for three years. I will help you with my advice, teaching you everything that experience has taught me. My sawmill, that faithful, obedient servant, will do for you whatever you command. If ever it should happen that you were to regret this purchase, tell me, and I will return your investment, I will pay you for your improvements and take back your land.'

" 'Bide your time; it will not be long before you feel the self-respect and pride which ownership and cultivation of your own land inspires in us—above all in a land such as this, where three-fourths of the men are farmers and where neither a privileged clergy nor favored classes exist. Soldier though you are, work, and the improvements you will make will be a delightful and novel enjoyment. The honest, sensitive man, when he can, loves to create and give life, and he gets great pleasure out of watching the result of his labors.'

" 'Base your hopes of future retirement and of freedom as I have, on the property I suggest to you; one which in time, believe me, will become in all likelihood as pleasant as it will be useful. The island near it alone would suffice to make you rich through the cultivation of oats. Your place on board ship will soon be taken, as has mine. As soon as the neighboring forests are yours, you will see that their gloom will repel you less, and soon you will come, as I do, to respect a gigantic pine, a majestic oak; before long you will consider them one of the most beautiful presents nature has bestowed on us.'

"Imagine the astonishment and pleasure I felt when several days after this conversation he expressed the desire to see this land I had mentioned to him. He was enchanted by its location on the banks of our lovely river and above all by the island which alone is a treasure because of the richness of its soil. He bought the property. Since that time my friend has become as active and as enterprising as I. Everything I foresaw happened: he built an elegant and attractively painted house. He has a small library. Hunting and fishing amuse and busy him. In his schooner of cedar, he has become the commodore of the lake and never was a vessel of 118 cannon admired more. One cannot please him more than by asking him to navigate it. He has brought several industrious and honest Erse families from the part of Scotland where he used to live. He is no longer the same man: you will see him this evening and you will never believe that he was one of those fanatic Scotsmen who do not imagine that there is anything beautiful or good beyond the limits of Great Britain.

"So you see, I have now the good fortune to have as neighbor, my former shipmate, now my intimate friend, a precious possession any place, but above all in the woods.

"We will grow old together, we often tell ourselves, we will help each other constantly at harvest and hay making time. May Nature give us health and favorable seasons; that is all we ask.

"Yet, something is lacking in my happiness. I feel it more and more. I am tired and almost ashamed of working only for myself. I feel a need to divide the fruits of my labors with a good and sensitive person who by her presence would make these labors seem less harsh; someone who would make my home beautiful, who would fill the void, as well as someone whom my heart would love. After the harvest, when I think my hay is well stacked in the fields, my barn full of grain; when I watch my cattle and sheep return to their sheds; it is then when I want to be united with a person who would praise my industry and approve my activity. You see that it is of a wife whom I speak: but I should like her to be such a one as my imagination presents to me: hard-working, gentle, sensitive, and fertile as much as is necessary to assure the prosperity of a family of farmers. I would want her to unite gentleness with reason, cleanliness to a great knowledge of house-keeping; she should know how to direct and oversee the spinning of linen, woolen, and cotton, sufficient to procure clothing necessary to a family; for, woe to the man who depends more on the yardstuff from Europe than on the wool from his sheep. This woman must inspect the dyes, she must know everything concerning the making of cheeses, needlework, and repairs necessary to the upkeep of a house, all this makes for a very extensive schedule indeed in a land like this, where a colonist must do everything for himself. I should like her mind to be somewhat cultivated so that she can enjoy with me the fruits from the reading of good books, of which, as you see, I have made a con-siderable collection.

"I am hard to please and that is why I do not hurry in this decision. I seek such a one for my neighbor and former shipmate. If heaven is favorable to us, then we will leave our homes less, since we will have brought to them their happiness. We will find in the reunion of our families everything necessary for us to relax from our work, inspire our activity, thrill our hearts, especially when we have become fathers."

(Here there appears to be a great lapse of time or loss of several chapters.)

CHAPTER XIV

New York, June 25, 1791

It appeared that Fort George, built in 1670 at the western end of the island on which the city of New York stands, would now become useless because of the crossed guns that were being set up on Governor's Island and on the banks of the Narrows.[1] These would be sufficient to protect the town along the sea coast. Consequently it was decided to build on this fine site a mansion to house the Governor: in searching through the casemates of this fort, the workmen discovered several kinds of money, and some epitaphs, elegantly engraved. These were taken to the mayor of the town: but instead of ordering that they be placed in the public library, he permitted those who found them to do as they wished with them.

Mr. Herman, who found this thoughtlessness unforgivable, bought them for a price beyond their value and presented them to the Directors of the library.

"What motives prompted you to decide to pay so high a price for items which I found quite uninteresting?" I asked.

"Their antiquity," he replied.

"If they were Greek, or Roman medals, your enthusiasm would have some foundation, but a few crowns of the two Charles, some Batavian money, some from Russia, Norway, or Courland and two or three epitaphs of former governors of the Colonies—I see nothing in all that which could justify what you have just done nor even anything that would arouse your curiosity. These pieces are not yet interesting enough to be imbued with that prestige that would capture your fancy. These have not yet been vested from the passing of centuries with that sanction which inspires involuntary respect."

"Nevertheless," he replied, "they represent the most ancient things one can find in a country so new."

"If ever you pass through the Alleghenies, you will see fortifications that are made of earth, but otherwise quite respectable, for they have survived the very nations that erected them, and tradition is dumbfounded in contemplation of them, even among the Indians."

"This taste," I queried, "is it instinctive, do you suppose or is it the fruit of your education?"

"I grew up," he replied, "not far from a château whose origin may well date back to the Crusades, and which has seized hold of me from the moment it ceased to be inhabited; from that I absorbed the fabulous tales, legends, and ghost stories whose telling fired my curiosity and stimulated early stirrings of my adolescent imagination and even the first spurts of my pen, if I may make so bold.

"Everything that has survived the destructive power of time and men captures my imagination, I know not why. The more remote and uncertain I think its origin, the more interesting it appears to me. I enjoy delving into the past, that sea of historic memories, just as one likes to contemplate a vast horizon after reaching the summit of a mountain; just as one likes to hear the tales of travelers home from distant lands. The idea of great distance, of remoteness, of immensity, exalts my feeble faculties and gives wings to my thoughts. That is why, of all the planets, it is Herschell's, accompanied by his numerous cohorts of satellites [2] toward which I have most often turned my telescope. Who would have predicted, several centuries ago, that with the aid of this marvelous instrument, human intelligence could carry its eye to the remotest limits of our universe?

"In considering what is still left of the old buildings that escaped the ravages of destruction, I seem to see the men whose contemporaries they have been, as they were when surrounded by prejudices, driven by opinions so different from ours; and then I am back in my den again, as though home from very distant lands. How can anyone be insensible to the sight of these respectable ruins, covered with brambles and dead weeds, remains of monuments that required so much work before becoming a great and majestic unity? In exploring these places, today solitary and abandoned, one is, in spite of himself, assailed by a myriad of memories, as well as by the need to satisfy one's curiosity.

"But perhaps you consider all this the effect of wildness, or illusions belonging to a head still very young."

"You are not the first person," I said, "in whom I have observed this respect for ancient monuments, ruins, and tombs. Without being an amateur, I can imagine how much the obscurity of several intermediary centuries must contribute toward stimulating interest and discussion. Like these countrysides that offer to the eyes of the imagination mountains seen through mist which one cannot approach, the contemplation of this debris must inspire melancholic and touching ideas, bringing the mind back to times of disaster, wars, and revolutions: they are traces of the passing of generations that preceded us; the chain linking the nebulous past with the fugitive present and one which will link the present to the future. Therefore, instead of hastening the ruin of this debris, one should consider its destruction a sacrilege; its conservation a religious act.

"Amateurs of dubious antiquity," I continued, "will not find in the research that they will some day make here the same causes for discussion, interest, or instruction that the old monuments of Europe and Asia offer. The foundation of these colonies, that of towns, the progress of this new nation, the events that will fill the pages of its history, illuminated by the flame of knowledge and printing, will never be extinguished by clouds of ignorance nor falsified by errors of tradition. This land will never become one of shadows or fables.

"Well, since you love antiquity so much, why did you not wend your way toward Asia Minor, Greece, or Italy, instead of coming to see a land which is not yet two centuries old?" I asked.

"I am young," he replied, "I wanted first to explore a continent whose emancipation interested me so keenly. I wanted to see what comprised the progress, the early beginnings of these little tribes that annually go to found new societies in the depth of the forests; I wanted to watch their progress and their industry; discover by what means trust and confidence extend their salutary influence from coastal cities to the most inland regions, and encourage their clearings and enterprises; I wanted to study the principles of their civil economy, their code of laws, the forms of administration that unite the parts that are so divided of this great country, encouraging and protecting so much work and activity. The result of all these observations will form the prologue to my adventure; I reserve the main drama for ancient Egypt, the aqueducts of old Mesopotamia, the ruins of Balbec and Palmyra, and lastly, for the classical land of the beautiful and fertile Ausonia."

"Your undertaking is vast," I replied, "and quite worthy of a head as young and ambitious as yours. But I fear that the storms menacing Europe may not permit you to carry it through."

"Well," he said, "I shall console myself by staying several years longer on this Continent. After visiting the coastal states, I shall go to the Alleghanies and leisurely explore this new area [3] in which industry and courage have already accomplished so many astonishing things. The settling, the rapid progress of these young colonies situated on a soil so fertile, and in a climate so mild and temperate, is one of my most tempting objectives. I am charmed by the prospect of going down the Ohio, so justly called the beautiful, for three hundred ninety-six leagues, that of seeing what the new colonists on the river banks do— those along the Muskinghum, the Indiana,[4] the Limestone,[5] the great Kanhawa,[6] the Gallipolis,[7] the Scioto,[8] the Ménóamy, the Kentucky,[9] and various other settlements recently formed on the southwest and northwest banks of the Ohio. From the mouth of this fine river I shall proceed down the majestic Mississippi to New Orleans, the distance of two hundred seventy-seven leagues and even as far as the remotest bayous of its great delta, seventy leagues beyond. After admiring the rich and superb forests of magnolias, cypress, and sycamores that enhance the beauty of its shore, and after observing the agriculture and commerce of lower Louisiana from there I shall embark on one of the great boats that leave every year for the land of Illinois, situated four hundred leagues from the sea and even if I find the opportunity, I shall go as far as Lake Peppin [10] and St. Anthony's Falls, located five hundred sixty-six leagues from the sea.

"I shall spend some time among the Nadooasses and the Padookas [11] who hunt mounted on horseback on the vast prairies that are watered by the Wadappa-Ménésotr and the different branches of the Missouri; [12] they are tribes renowned for their hospitality and for the refinement of their customs. Returning from the Illinois, going up the river of that same name for about 100 leagues, I shall arrive at Chicago on Lake Michigan [13] whence trading vessels will take me to Michillimakinac [14] situated near this vast 'Mediterranean' sea, greater than the Euxin.[15] From there, I shall easily be able to visit the different Ottawa villages on the banks of Lake Huron. There the chiefs will conduct me in their canoes as far as the strait.[16] I shall embark there on one of the local vessels that are laden with furs going to Ft. Erie near the great falls of Niagara, crossing Lake St. Clair (Otsiketa) and Erie. That journey is certainly enough to occupy several years."

"Such a plan," I told him, "suggests a hope of longevity which characterizes youth: distances do not frighten you.

"I know two persons who accomplished it in less than three years, including their long visits and two winters, encountering not one enemy and only one obstacle, the short portage from Chicago. According to their diaries, they covered two thousand five hundred seventy-four leagues in the interior of the continent. What other part of the globe offers human curiosity and industry lovelier rivers, easier communications, a more fertile soil, in climates more temperate? This immense region, of which one part consists of natural prairies or swamplands, will some day become the glory of this hemisphere.

"According to what you have told me," I continued, "it would seem that your imagination, inflamed by the recital of romantic adventures, fabulous tales, as well as by the sight of imposing ruins of the château of ———, has felt very early in your life the need to describe and paint. Aware that in the first essays of a natural talent, one often perceives the characteristics which equal perfection in art, tell me if there would be any indiscretion in requesting that you read us some of these pages?"

"Gladly will I read to you the sketch that I wrote on the very scene four years ago, during my last stay in that country; for since that time my family has been living in the north of Germany; but as you will see, it is a plant that has sprung from itself, without the aid of art or cultivation.''

He read me what follows:

''I like to gaze on these ancient temples devoted to religion; the towering slenderness of their architecture is beautiful and imposing. Impressed by the mysterious obscurity and solemn silence that reign there, I lift my thoughts toward that incomprehensible Being, Author of nature and life, and wander in meditation among these tombs placed under their somber vaults whose epitaphs, those enfeebled voices of centuries past, still speak so eloquently. What faded glory! What forgotten names and honors! I like to examine what still remains of these towers from whose heights one could once sight the progress and approach of the enemy; the ruins of these bridges once so useful that war and time have now destroyed; the ruins of these old donjons, of these huge châteaux which feudal power raised on the banks of precipices or rivers. I like to examine this unexceptionable evidence, witnesses of the fragility and instability of human things. My mind, unable (as it is) to pierce through the impenetrable obscurity of the future, plunges backward into those interesting infinities that our ancestors explored, and suddenly, as though transported to the summit of a promontory, I seem to discover a new horizon, new objects, long hidden, obscured by the clouds of oblivion and remoteness. Like the waves of a swift river, ceaselessly flowing and following each other, I see in these backward excursions, the generations, laws, and opinions renewing themselves unceasingly, each century bearing a different stamp. Among so many epochs, more or less interesting or famous, I distinguish with the keenest gratitude the one in which my compatriots found the secret of casting the movable printing blocks, a sublime invention, a marvelous art, unknown to the most enlightened nations of antiquity; truly an art to which man owes more than he realizes and one to which it is inconceivable that the remarkable art of writing did not sooner give birth. Thousands of centuries elapsed between these two epochs, ever memorable.

''In the shadow of one of the greatest oak trees in the land, formerly growing in the middle of an old cemetery, surrounded by the ruins of a chapel that piety had built on the smooth ground of a mound, I admire the vast and venerable ruins of the château of ———. Contemplating so many efforts and so much work, I wonder about the motives that prompted strong men of these bygone times to raise such enormous and fabulous masses, making of them arsenals and ramparts of war. What could have been the state of society, the plight of men at that time, when the yoke of servitude weighed heavily on their heads? What was that of agriculture, industry, commerce, and the arts when everything submitted to the sway of violence and clouds of ignorance covered the surface of the earth? When protective laws were unknown and governments weak, men were but a lowly herd whose blood was prostituted by the chiefs in the unceasing quarrels of their ambition and jealousies?

"But soon, tired of this gloomy review of the past, with a single glance, I embrace this vast assemblage of Gothic grandeur, only a short distance from me, and I study its different parts. How to represent in the same grouping these points of view so different, these buildings detached, yet united by the same perspective, these masses still rich and mighty by their elevation and the sturdiness of their structure as well as by their immutable firmness? Where to put these ancient walls, these thick and heavy donjons, these embattled ramparts, which in their state of decadence still seem to weigh upon the land? How to describe, unaided by any design, these remarkable towers built at intervals and part of whose crowns have given in to the pressure of time; these flying buttresses, which for centuries have resisted the violence of tempests and have dared so many storms, and those frowning bulwarks which from the ridge of rocks slope downward and, faithful to the vagaries of the terrain, reappear again beyond nearby heights? How to indicate what remains of so many other structures, of those subtle accessories which attest to the genius and skill of ancient architects, those angular piles, each atop an enormous block, those flying buttresses whose resistance and strength, seemingly eternal, have in part succumbed to the irresistible weight of centuries?

"The colors of the most skillful painter would scarcely be able to capture from this great collection of objects the lighting and shading they demand; nor could he catch the reflections that are so varied, nor those contrasting shadows produced by strokes more or less great, yet guided, and which from the bottom rise to the top of the painting? How without this help, can we paint the magic effect produced by the light of a beautiful day, when the rays of the sun bathe with their splendor so much surface, rounded, square, or plain, placed at distances that appear so different to each observer? How to describe the effect produced on the mind by these images, of a grandeur now passed, traces of degradation and ruin so different?

"Tired from this long scrutiny, my eyes sometimes rest with delight on these bushes, children of chance and nature growing 'mid crevices and on these trees whose roots seized the life-giving substance of foundation that has become tillable soil, and whose greenish heads shade the ledges and decorate the most elevated parts as well as the eternal ivy whose luxuriant growth and nervous twinage veil the sun-bathed surfaces and sustain the decadence of these ancient structures.

"But for lack of dates engraved on the key to the vaults or on the architrave of the façade, the period of the building is unknown. One is astonished that the desire—so natural—of transmitting knowledge to posterity, that vanity, that undying sentiment, have not inspired in these barons the urge to consecrate, by some inscription, the erection of buildings, to which they wanted to give the same firmness of the rocks on which they had been built: but in the centuries of barbarism and shadows preceding and following the Crusades, one knew the art of military fortifications, and that of writing was unknown.

"Scarcely had I entered the outside court when I was struck with astonishment and shaken by a shiver of fright in contemplating this vast domain of desolation and death, this debris scattered over nearly the entire stronghold, as I walked over the grass, the slopes, and the ridges that cross 'mid these ruins. Some of these buildings, entirely thrown down, have piled their debris over the entire space that they used to occupy; it is impossible to get near them. Others appear to have resisted the impact of time, the pressure of winds, only because of their weight and uprightness. Here one sees collapsed roofs whose worm-eaten and rusty rafters betoken antiquity and decadence; there, isolated masses, immovable on their bases, which, like pyramids, must be eternal; farther on, bare pieces of wall in which one can still distinguish the flattened plinth course, and the unsteady jambposts. Wherever one walks, there is debris of a thousand different forms making a work whose every page attests to the ravages of men and time.

"I called forth the shadow of the old masters of these haunts, and I dared ask them what means they used to transport such great masses and how, in a climate as quixotic as that one, they could imprint on these structures such everlastingness: why, in erecting their dwellings in the midst of these lofty ramparts, had they shut out from them the light of the sun? Why hadn't they known and felt the pleasure of planting and watching the growth of trees, and that of cultivating gardens? Why had their power become the curse of peaceful farmers, those humble artisans of plenty and of real riches?

"But the abrupt arrival of the keeper interrupted these thoughts and I went with him. He was eighty-seven years old, and the only person in this gloomy place: his advanced years, white hair, ancient and venerable face and demeanor, all seemed to blend with the sad and solitary functions which were his.

" 'Once upon a time,' he told me, 'these places were bustling with the noise and movement of life and the confusion of a full garrison, as well as with the presence of our old masters. What a difference today! This great stronghold is nothing but a lonely spot in the midst of which I often wander when I leave my ordinary paths. The silence of nothingness, the sterile nothingness of the desert, the inactivity and shadows of death have replaced the reverberation of firearms, the voices of the men in command, the songs of gaiety and those of religion. Nothing of olden times is alive; only echoes which have fled to the height of towers and ramparts are left and they rarely speak anymore.'

" 'This site on the right,' I asked him, 'whose interior is covered with arched fragments, chiseled stone, Gothic moldings, of what use was it?'

" 'I do not know,' he replied.

" 'And that formless chunk of masonry, so wide and so high, from which spring three fine and light archings, what has become of its corresponding part?'

" 'Even my grandfather who lived here one hundred fifty-six years ago did not know.'

" 'And this circular platform built on that rock?'

" 'That was the signal tower.'

" 'And that building of which there remain only fluted pillars painted cinnamon-color?'

" 'That was the chapel of the château and under its vaults before the invasion of the fanatics of Munster, lay the ashes of nine generations of ———, our former masters. For several centuries prayers were recited there; incense was burned and mystery plays were given. Today, as you see, the altar, the priests, and their religion have disappeared; it is the haunt of all the screech owls of the land.'

"A wide ditch separated the outside court from the inside; its entrance was guarded by a draw-bridge placed against an enormous belfry: but the bridges have disappeared centuries ago; the ditches are partially filled by the fall of nearby ramparts, as well as by the heavy growth of willows that spread over the entire area. The surfaces are bristling with saxifrages whose seeds, windborne, drop into the merest spot, for nothing escapes nature's fertility. Their vagabonding stems even penetrate to the bas-relief, to the arms and trophies that form the great crown of which there still remain some vestiges. Just as in the outer court, I saw around me only accumulated debris or unsteady ruins in the midst of which one was forbidden to speak, just as in crossing through the Alps during the season of snows: the breath of a breeze could bring down stones once firmly imbedded and which for years had resisted the wickedness of winds. On all sides, I was surrounded by rubbish and sinister-looking objects: on the right, I saw shaky-looking stones jutting out, having lost their sub-foundations; on the left, consoles, entablatures that seemed to await only the passing of several winters, or a few days perhaps, before detaching themselves from their foundations; farther on were look-out slits that owed their precarious existence to the spritely and wiry growth of branches at their ledge.

"From the midst of the ruins of this second surrounding wall, I saw several of those turrets that people dared erect on three stones of an enormous projection: such is the height of the towers whose supports they are, that one would believe them suspended in midair. Despite the effects of winds, rains, sleet and the devastating power of time, they are still intact, but since the destruction of the staircase leading to them has made them inaccessible to men, they serve as retreats for birds of the night. Flocks of crows roost on the highest perches, as well as in the holes and hollows made by the wind and the rain; scarcely is a new gap made when a new family takes possession; unceasing they fly, bestir themselves, soaring gracefully over the area enjoying happiness and freedom far from the deadly lead of men.

"It is here that the ivy, both protector and tyrant of old structures, reigns supreme: clandestine crony of shadowy and solitary haunts, it flourishes far from the rays of the sun, in the bosom of the darkest woods, under the thickets, as well as the dryest debris; just as the gloomy cypress and yew-tree, companions of death, one can see ivy in cemeteries on whose ancient and venerable fences it hangs; now its bendable and twining twigs hide forgotten epitaphs, now they surround from the base to the summit those antique crosses of ancient, uncut stone that the hand of poverty consecrated to the memory of relative or friend. Everything begins to lose itself in the remoteness of oblivion, everything which chance or intention has pushed from sight or from the destructive hands of man: the mutilated door, the various legends of which still attest to some Gothic origin; those elliptical roses, masterpieces of the Twelfth Century; tottering columns of which still abound in broken fragments—these, as well as the hovels of the poor, all become the exclusive domain of the ivy.

"No sooner has the weight of years destroyed the roof of a structure, shaken the supports of the rafter, crushed the spring of an arch than the ivy appears in the midst of ruins, overrunning everywhere, pressing with all its might. Soon its branches, reaching the foot of the walls, rise, attach themselves to crevices or the emptiness of a casement that might be in their way. They seize upon them rapidly until their flexible extremities, driven by wind or chance, cling to the exterior walls, then borne by the support of these new holds, they resume a vertical direction and gradually reach the cornices and superelevations which they cover with their gloomy green growth.

"When exploring the depths of the old buildings, one observes what degree of thickness the hard, tortuous roots of the ivy has reached, and it is impossible not to be amazed at the great number of years which must have elapsed for such slow growth; and impossible, too, not to be persuaded that the longevity of this plant is perhaps equal to that of the oak; and as though the enormous diameter of its rootstock did not attest to its age, nature has seen fit to cover them with hair of old age and special moss, for in her inexhaustible laboratory she has manufactured something for everything exposed to the air.

"In addition to the juice which the great roots draw from the earth to furnish their most remote branches, these roots, by means of tendrils with which they are supplied, also pump minerals from the earth. These tendrils are admirable tools, seizing on everything they touch, becoming thus either ingenious hands or spirally coiling fibers that penetrate the merest openings. That is why with this great array of resources and supports the ivy I observed while exploring the interior of this château has, in the course of centuries, risen from the base of ramparts to their uppermost parapets, from the foot of towers to their highest embrasures.

"Emblem of perseverance, friend of solitude and silence, companion of oblivion, faithful unto death, it perishes only with the trees, the buildings, and the ruins to which it is attached, after having long protected their old age and prolonged their decrepitude.

"From this second enclosure, one enters a third, crossing under two enormous arches fairly well preserved, where there had formerly been great cross-beams and iron grill work. It was far less cluttered by ruin than the others. A walnut tree, bereft of all but two lower branches, a wild vine whose barren boughs entwined the sides, the far-off cooing of pigeons, some windows, two or three closed doors, such were the objects whose unexpected appearance gladdened the eyes of the traveler, tired from this sojourn in desolation. It seemed to recall him to life.

" 'Of all the wings in this château,' the keeper told me, 'the only habitable one is this sad and gloomy one in which alone and isolated I vegetate like the thorn-bush in the middle of the desert.'

" 'Why is that so?' I asked him.

" 'I am unfortunate in having survived what was dearest on earth to me; the outrages of time and nature have broken the bonds that attached me to it! I am still here. If I could only forget myself during the peace and quiet of the nights, the hours of my existence would not seem so long. But no, in the midst of these ruins, just as in cemeteries, the night, I know not why, knows neither peace nor sleep. The cracking of these old walls, the muffled sounds, the ominous cries of the osprey and screech owl repeated and amplified by echoes, the whir of wind through the huge hollows, the cracked walls and withered thickets murmuring what seems to me a cacaphonous mixture of sounds, sighs, and swishing of varying sharpness, all that freezes me into fright, chasing sleep from my old eyelids. It is toward midnight when I sometimes seem to hear far off the voices of my dear ones, those of my ancestors, who, from the depths of their tombs, call to me to share the repose which they are enjoying. At other times the plaintive sounds of ghosts of our former masters, wailing from the height of the towers and ramparts over the savagery of men who have scattered their long-forgotten ashes, moaning over the instability of glory and grandeur, over the destruction of their family, their name, their former power; groaning over the ruin and degradation of this château which they believed to be indestructible. How can anyone enjoy sleep in the midst of this visit of spirits? I call on heaven and I grow calmer, until finally the delayed dawn of day dispels these baleful impressions.'

"The righteous and respectable tears of old age and unhappiness escaped from the eyes of this venerable gentleman, he would sigh out. I wanted to console him; I even ventured to offer him money.

" 'No, no; that is not what I need.'

" 'Well, what then?'

" 'My journey began long ago. I have been traveling eighty-seven years; I am anxious to reach the end.'

"At the other end of this stronghold one could see a very high tower whose center was occupied by a great winding staircase. This fine bit of ancient architecture was very well preserved for with the exception of its steps, part of which though were worn by the traffic of so many generations, it was perfectly solid. A dome made of nine cut stones and placed with amazing artistry crowned it.

"This stairway led to the different balconies cut into the thickness of the walls, leading out to the platforms, ramparts and apartments; one could still see there some vestige of former magnificence: some traces of the rude luxury of bygone days; no sooner had the keeper taken me into these parts, when the birds of the night, frightened by the sight of men and daylight, took flight clumsily and silently.

"How gloomy and dismal these abodes must now be, scenes for centuries of power and wealth! How incommodious, cold, and damp must have been those donjons, situated in such inaccessible and savage places, admitting neither the enjoyments of agriculture, nay, scarcely the enlivening strength from the sun! What was the source of happiness and pleasure then? Before the invention of printing, before the rebirth of knowledge, the arts and music, before glasses were invented, what education could the children receive? How could old men avoid the languor of boredom in the twilight of life?

"Yet, here at one time lived youth, beauty, opulence; here Silvia ———— had lived; tradition has kept alive her memory as being one of the most beautiful women of her time and the heroine of her century: her courage and her beauty made her justly famous. There several generations of ———— were born, redoubtable for so long a period: their name exists no longer, save in popular sayings. These sayings expressed opinions about feudal tyranny. That ancient system of tyranny has been replaced by new forms of pressure and evil known under other names. This rendezvous of warriors, this abode of men whose power and influence often matched that of emperors, is today nothing more than a vast scene of ruin and decay. Such is the emptiness of human greatness, riches, and fame!

"From these apartments, I walked down to the subterranean passageways, the best preserved parts of this old château. It seems that time can destroy only works built above the ground. How vast, great, beautiful, and resounding our steps through these majestic arches! How sturdy yet, their groins and bends! Nowhere did I see the file of time; their firmness matches that of the rocks on which they were built; yet they date back to the time of the Crusades. Of all man's works, arches are the only ones to which have been given a lasting quality equal to that of the earth. Of such a quality were the reservoirs of the Carthaginians (a work far more ancient), above which the Tunisians work and plant today, without even suspecting their existence; such were the reservoirs of Alexandria, and the great sewers of Rome, whose origins were unknown at the time of its founding.

"Not far from the immense cone that once served as a kitchen, one can see a deep, wide well; whether one lets fall a stone or raises his voice, the echoes from this great subterranean depth, so long solitary and soundless, hasten to repeat these sounds and to exaggerate them in a strange and striking manner. It seems as though one might have descended into an unknown world.

"Until the time of the war of the Anabaptists in 1503, this château had resisted the abuses of time. But then these fanatics spread themselves throughout the land, and wrought more havoc in the space of a few days than six or seven centuries had. And as though the surface of the earth had not been surfeit with the spread of crime, these monsters searched its very bowels, where with insatiable greed they seized the lead of coffins, committed sacrilegious impiety, and despoiled ruthlessly the remains of humanity. This redoubtable sanctuary was invaded, and the rest of the dead violated. Daylight penetrated these places consecrated to eternal oblivion; the ashes they contained were scattered and these sepulchral shadows forever obliterated.

"Plaintive, roving shadows, why were you not born in Athens or in Rome, under the influence of laws and religious dicta, that brought execration to those who dared invade and dishonor this sacred haven!"

"My sincere gratitude," I told Mr. Herman, "for the pleasure that you have just given me. If, as you said a moment ago, this is merely a plant, spontaneously sprouted, what will be the nature of those you cultivate some day when you have summoned your muse? What finer gift is there than that of an imagination that can make an interesting story of crumbled walls, old donjons, things which most men view only with indifference! Lose no time in going to Greece and Syria, to see the precious remains of exquisite antiquity, a thousand times worthier of your pen than the gloomy abodes of these ancient barons." *

* Could one define effectively this melancholy affection, shared by sensitive souls, that inspired in them the enthusiasm of rambling around in ruins, that sad wreckage of the magnificence and industry of mankind? What, then, is the secret of this pleasure, real though it is, that we find in the contemplation of old monuments stamped by the rust of centuries? Why do ancient buildings, tombs on which time in its flight seems to have sharpened its murderous scythe,—and epitaphs, half defaced—why do they offer enjoyment to our imagination? Would it be because man, unhappy with the present, prefers to concern himself with thoughts of the past rather than think of the future—preferring to live on memories rather than on hopes?

(Note communicated to the editor by Citizen B.)

CHAPTER XV

New York, 1790

"How rapidly time passes when it is usefully filled!"

These were the words of Mr. Herman, whom I had the good fortune to meet here on my return from Virginia. "Since I have been on this continent," he continued, "I have not yet had the opportunity to see Natural Bridge nor the passage of the Potomac [1] through the Chain of Laurier, nor the descent of the Ouasioto,[2] nor the falls at Niagara, the most astonishing phenomenon on earth. It is rather the great distance than the multiplicity of objects that consumes a considerable part of the traveler's time. This, as well as communication difficulties. Everything will be quite changed in twenty years; then one will be able to travel here as easily as he does in Europe; then one will be able to see in a year, what today takes two years to see.

"Yet, I must not complain, for on my last journey lasting only six months, I observed closely what was most interesting in the states of Connecticut, Massachusetts, and New Hampshire. What movement! What activity! In the countryside as well as the towns! Everywhere one sees the vigor of youth. Twenty or thirty miles from most of the towns, I found a perfection of farming that seemed only slightly inferior to that of Europe, especially along the great highway from Worcester to Cambridge and Boston. The beauty of the fields, the freshness of the pasture lands, nearly all dotted with clumps of trees: and the cleanliness! What shall I say? Everything—the elegance of the homes, the size of the cattle, the fine quality of the roads—everything betokened taste, intelligence, happiness, and the prosperity of the colonists: the same is true in the regions around Salem, Marblehead, Beverly, Newburyport, etc.

"In almost all the small towns along the Connecticut River," Mr. Herman observed, "factories have been set up for the manufacture of cloth, linen, cotton fabrics, and hats whose use has become quite common. What a pity that the exorbitant price of labor and emigration prevents a higher degree of prosperity. The mills for the manufacture of sail cloth, already numerous, appear to persist and increase every day. The threads are made, it is said, with a fishglue that makes the cloth less subject to moisture than the cloth imported from Russia. I spent several days at Norwick, on the New Tamise; it is the Birmingham of Connecticut. I believe that there doesn't exist in this town of 3,000 inhabitants a single idle man or woman. There steel and iron are manufactured to great perfection. From the workshops of this town emerge the machines for the manufacture of stockings, fulling shears, scythes, and the sickles, used in this part of the continent; here are made all the seabiscuits necessary for supplying numerous vessels of New London; here, too, watches, clocks, buttons, paper, iron wire, oils, chocolate, chimes, etc., are made. The waters of a falls 60 feet high, formed by the union of the Quinibaw and the Shetuket, put into motion a great number of machines and factories. Moreover the area abounds in streams on which have been built many mills, tanneries, forges, etc.

"Mighty rapids obstructed navigation on the Connecticut River.[3] By means of canals which a company incorporated by the Government has just finished, boats come and go, as far north as Dartmouth and even into the Coohaw country, very near the frontiers of Canada under the 45th parallel and 380 miles from the sea. The abundance of wood and that of sandlike matter have given rise to the formation of several good-sized glassworks: the one at Albany has already become famous.

"The great fisheries have been an inexhaustible source of riches. Near the sandbanks of St. George, New Foundland, is a large school for boys of these sea-minded states who wish to become sailors. The number of schooners used is prodigious; those used by fishermen, they say, has reached 15,000. What a fleet! The day when I arrived in Marblehead, the weather being extremely stormy, the port impressed me as one of the most amazing sights I had ever seen. As far off as my eyes could discern, the area seemed to me to be covered with isolated rocks, similar to cones, against which waves broke, roaring and rising to a great height. I was seized simultaneously with a feeling of fright and admiration on seeing these hardy sailors sail, tacking their schooners around the numerous reefs with an audacity, a presence and a precision that I cannot describe exactly, not being a sea-faring man. They say that some of these cod fishermen, converted from piracy during the revolution, captured eleven hundred eight English merchant vessels. That made one-seventh of the entire English navy; and from another were formed two regiments whose courage and fearlessness history has not forgotten.

"The only things I have not seen in this part of the continent," he continued, "are the huge forges, foundries, and refineries which, they tell me, are situated in the mountains."

"The desire to see these," I replied, "is very praiseworthy and a visit to them would be easy to accomplish. The regions of New Jersey and those in the part of this state have been cultivated for nearly a century. Instead of those temporary and inconvenient shelters which we meet so often in the newer settlements, we shall lodge in good homes, inhabited by people whose hospitality will leave us nothing to be desired. But to make the journey doubly interesting, let us not travel by land. Let us go up the great river for 75 miles, as far as the wharf at New Windsor; from there we will easily reach the home of Mr. Jesse Woodhull, one of my old friends, an educated man, and one of the most respected in this region. You will admire, as I have, his ingenious industry, his activity, and his large family. You will be astonished, as I was, at the great work he has had done over a period of thirty years, as well as the tremendous farming project that he has supervised. You will scarcely believe that a single man has dared undertake, and has had enough courage and perseverance to carry out, the clearing of a valley that contains almost 1,500 acres of land: in addition, he is one of the first farmers of this state, colonel of the militia and sheriff of Orange county. From his home to the great foundries at Sterling and Ringwood is a distance of only ten or twelve miles. He will gladly accompany us and furnish us with horses, for he raises a great number of them and no one has a finer breed.

"I wish circumstances might have made it possible for both of us to go back together up the river, as far as Albany, because I am convinced that you have seen nothing in Europe as imposing as the navigation of this beautiful river. Do you recall what M. J. U. told us two years ago? Yet I do not propose to compare it with the St. Lawrence in width, for one does not experience storms such as those on the St. Lawrence; nor does the Hudson present the perpetual difficulty of a current against which one must ceaselessly battle. When the wind is favorable, the same tide often brings a vessel from here to Albany, the last navigable point, although it is 275 miles from here.

"In order to appreciate the numerous advantages that this inland navigation and that of its different branches bring to the capital (Albany), one would have to be well acquainted with the geography of this part of the United States, the elevation of the land in relation to the Ocean and to Lakes Ontario, Erie, and Champlain which are virtually Mediterranean Seas—as well as to the Genesee, Alleghany, and Susquehanna rivers. The day is not far off when the produce of all the western and northwestern regions in this state will go down to Albany via the Mohawk; that of the eastern, by the different branches of the Hudson and the canal of the South Bay.[4] From the other side, the inhabitants of Vermont, Massachusetts, and Connecticut, nearer the waters of these rivers, than that of their own rivers, have been transporting the products of their agriculture and industry for a long time.

"As to the facility of landing places, the navigation of the Sound, the relative position of the neighboring states, the beauty and safety of the port, this town enjoys incredible advantages which some day are bound to raise it to a high degree of prosperity. All foods come there by water, and that is why everything runs quietly. I have been told with assurance that the exports of the last year amounted to more than twelve million piastres; in 1791 they were no more than two and one half million."

Everything in readiness, we took passage aboard a fine sloop of 90 tonnage bound for the town of Poughkeepsie.[5] The captain agreed to put us ashore at New Windsor, a little town situated on the west bank of the Hudson River. Several reasons made us prefer this sloop to those that customarily plied the river: the fineness of its construction, the unusual comfort of its staterooms, and especially the hope that the conversation of Captain Dean, who had just returned from a voyage to China in that same sloop, would be interesting. We were not mistaken; he told us that if the Chinese customs at Canton had demanded a sum proportionate to the size of his ship, he would have had a profitable trip.

"I think," I told him, "that you are the first navigator who has dared to cross as great an expanse of seas in so small a vessel."

"And do you know," he replied, "I had no mishap."

The day was a beautiful one, the wind and the tide favorable when we left the wharf to skirt around the battery, located on the western extremity of the town, to enter the river which is more than two miles wide. On the right, its waters bathe the banks of the island [6] on which New York is built; on the left, those of New Jersey; but so great was the speed of our vessel, that in less than forty minutes, we lost sight of the Narrows, Staten Island, and the islands of the Great Bay. Soon after, the shops, the churches and their steeples, imperceptibly obscured by the mists of the horizon, disappeared from our sight.

What a contrast between the appearances of the two banks of this beautiful river. Off starboard, were wooded, lush, fertile lands, covered with well-cultivated fields, orchards evenly planted, dotted with homes belonging to the merchants of the town, almost all handsome and painted white; some appeared hidden in the thickness of the trees; others, situated in the midst of gardens surrounded by acacias, plane trees, or tulip trees.

Those on the left, or strictly speaking, New Jersey, although withered, dry, and deserted, merited attention no less, above all by lovers of botany. For the distance of 25 miles or more, the river is held back by a perpendicular wall of rock formation more than fifty feet high, whose summit is crowned by great trees; enormous heaps of rock that one would believe to have been quarried, very much like the rubble of some building, make up the base that leans slightly over the bank of the river and is partly covered with trees and thick bushes as well as interesting plants. At intervals less rocky and more fertile, man's industry has already erected houses, surrounded by peach and cherry trees. We passed not far from these houses.

Mr. Herman and I were exchanging the impressions that so many new and striking objects were awakening, when the captain said to us:

"You are now in a region known as Tappan Sea; but that is merely an extension of the river; almost five miles wide."

"What!" said my companion. "We are sailing, full rigged on a salt lake, though far from the ocean, and yet we feel no greater movement than were we sailing on a pond in a park!"

"It is not like this during the autumn season," replied the captain, "the winds demand more prudence in sail rigging, and some knowledge of the channel too."

"What is the use for those cranes and long piers and warehouses that I see on the east and west banks of the river?"

"They are landings where the great highways of the interior end. The various items of produce are speeded from here to New York. From New York merchandise is shipped to Europe, the Indies, and the islands; these are mainly necessities for the inhabitants.

"Each landing has a certain number of sloops regularly serving it; they are the channels of trade, whose progress follows the progress of population: but often it happens that part of the profits of farmers is used to pay for this foreign merchandise. That is why public sentiment is so strongly in favor of domestic-made goods; that is why the Government protects and encourages them by the wisest laws possible. But I fear the time has not yet come for the exclusion of foreign goods."

The captain was entertaining us with all these interesting details, when while rounding Cape Vrederickhook, we suddenly came in sight of a magnificent chain of mountains that seemed to shut in the river.

"Is it here where the river ends?" Mr. Herman asked. "I see neither opening nor passageway."

"Nevertheless it crosses them for a distance of 21 miles," the captain replied, "and separates them by a deep and wide winding canal. This passage is one of the most interesting phenomena that one can see on this continent; and something that will astonish you even more: the tide rises more than 135 miles beyond in these mountains. This opening must have existed from the very beginning, and preceded even the beginning of this river: for if, like the Shenandoah, the Potomac, the Great Kanahawa, the Tennessee, etc., these waters had worn a passage through these High Lands, we would have come upon reefs, islands, debris—some evidence of this great upheaval; yet we have seen none. From here to the town, the river is quite smooth. We are approaching the truly magic spots: you will see.''

''What a superb curtain!'' said Mr. Herman. ''How fresh and green, from the river level, to the highest summit! I do not see the bare top of a single rock; everything is covered with beautiful trees: would this not confirm the opinion of those who claim that it sprang more recently from the depths of the sea than Europe and Asia?''

After crossing the bay at Haverstraw, while my companion and I were discussing the captain's various ideas, we rounded without our noticing, a long peninsula, Verplanck's Point, that formed the foreground of this great and magnificent scene. Suddenly we found ourselves in the midst of a superb canal of more than 600 fathoms, formed by the almost perpendicular walls of very high mountains (Tonder-Berg and Anthony's Nose), whose bases, the captain informed us, were more than 100 feet deep underwater. Their crests were crowned with cedars that appeared to us like dwarfed trees. Glancing back off the stern of the vessel, everything was shut off, out of sight; one could no longer see Haverstraw Bay that we had just sailed from. Watching off the bow, we saw what appeared to be one long series of more or less jutting summits, promontories of varying heights, covered with pines, hemlocks, cedars, whose shape all appeared more or less lengthened and blurred by the various shadings due to remoteness and optical illusion. The extremity of this channel toward which we were making our way appeared to be closed.

We were sailing full rigged, when Mr. Herman, after a few moments of silence, exclaimed:

''How beautiful and impressive all this is! What grandeur! What majesty nature imprints on her works! For even the coldest or deafest imagination, it would be difficult to be unmoved or inarticulate! The fantastic shape of the rocks scattered along these banks, their curious primitiveness, the height of the trees, the tremendous elevation of these mountains in the midst of which this vessel seems like a mere speck, the refreshing coolness of the air we breathe, the murmur of the gentle waves that break on the river bank, the multitude of birds that stir and furrow the water surface—all this arouses great pleasure, astonishment, and admiration. It is but the illusion of a beautiful dream. It is indeed merely a dream for the speed of the vessel is so rapid that it is impossible to enjoy fully the ensemble of these great views. Scarcely have the eyes rested on some arresting sight when soon the change of location presents new views; the succession is so rapid and so fleeting that one scarcely has time enough in which to grasp the ideas that they awaken. In order to enjoy this spectacle, which alone merits crossing the Ocean, one would have to stop at each place, to review what should be most attentively considered, taking several days in coming down this beautiful strait.''

We had no sooner passed the second peninsula when the river, winding westward, offered us a new vista whose details were less imposing, but more pleasant, more picturesque, and more varied. Less rough mountains appeared to be on accessible bases, where one would have breathed with delight the coolness of the trees covering them.

When the wind and the wash of the ship permitted, we heard from every direction the reverberation of falls and cascades whose echoes increased or softened at the whim of the breeze, without our being able to distinguish the course of these waters because of the denseness of the woods.

''They are great streams coming from the slopes of far-off hills,'' the captain told us; ''they reach the river only after falling from the height of rocks and after crossing many obstacles some of which, extremely picturesque, would be worthy of the paintbrush of an artist. Modest as a young virgin who carefully hides her beauty behind her veil, it is only in the mysterious obscurity of the woods, and especially the mountains, that nature unfolds her beauties and her treasures, and only then that she is lavish with them. Indeed, when I go on journeys, it is almost always in the mountains that I prefer to wander.

''In the course of time, when farming, trade, and industry have accumulated riches in our coastal cities, and our population is increased, it is here where luxury and the arts will build homes of elegance, direct and harness these fine waters, seize the most advantageous sites, convert these deserts, today so arid, into healthful, happy and delightful homes; it is here where the rich, the unemployed, and the wretched will come to seek repose, new outlooks, and good health. Nature has done everything to make these retreats charming during the hot days of August: she has favored them with proximity to a river as abundant in fish as the sea; fertile valleys, cool and shaded shores, steady breezes borne by the ebb and flow of tides, abundant, clear waters; finally, the enjoyment of all these advantages is furthered by proximity to the town.

''Never do I go upstream or downstream without my imagination involuntarily entertaining itself in exploring these delightful sites, so numerous and so varied. Here in the shadow of fine oaks planted by nature on the banks of this roaring river, my imagination can already see a spacious and attractive home. There on the western slope cut off from the north wind by neighboring heights, it can already see a little farm in which ingenuity has united the useful with the pleasant. On the edges of a steep cliff whose foundation is bathed by the riverwaters, she places a pavillion whence lovers of fishing can throw bait and amuse themselves fishing. On the flattened crest of a promontory, nature imagines a fine summerhouse whence one can admire some day the magnificence of the sunrise and sunset during the beautiful summer days, the breaking up of the ice at the return of spring, the maneuvering of vessels, that ply up and down this beautiful river. My imagination penetrates even to the most magnificent yet least accessible places in these mountains on which nature has planted cedars: there for a moment it forgets the storms, the misfortunes, and the annoying things of life, for this is the tree of meditation. The aeolian sounds produced by the wind whistling through its pointed leaves in which the soul perhaps more than the ear seems to hear harmonies; the amazing span of life, especially of the cedar and of the stone in whose crevices it grows, its elevation, the pure air one breathes there—everything excites and gives birth to thoughts. Only with a kind of instinctive respect does one walk over these indestructible witnesses of the upheavals and changes which the earth has undergone and will continue to undergo in the course of centuries. Such are the ideas that my imagination often plays with while we tack about exploring in their great length the divers meanderings of this magnificent and winding channel. May future generations carefully preserve these beautiful cedars, these gigantic pines, these venerable hemlocks, these God-like oaks, which human industry could never replace, and whose peaks stirred by the wind sway over every height, as well as over the crest of these riverbanks!

"This is the land of echoes, their favorite haunt; elsewhere they mumble out; here they express themselves distinctly; nowhere are they so numerous nor as attentive in replying. The different intonations of their voices resemble the conversations of people at different heights and distances; some whisper right into your ear; the voices of others are stronger; their sounds more clearly articulated; some reply immediately, others after an interval, as though they were thinking, before speaking; some answer in unison. It is especially when one laughs that the mixture of their outbursts makes the illusion complete. When vessels approach, tacking about, from the river bank, it is impossible not to believe that people are seated behind the rocks; those who reply from the mountains always do so distinctly that the eye, guided by the ear, thinks it perceives the tree behind which they are hiding. Of all illusions, the latter has always impressed me most. One of my passengers was very astonished sometime ago. While we were skirting the west bank, he heard the echo coming from the nearest cliff whisper to him. So astonished was he that for a moment he could not decide whether this whispering came from the person nearest him.

"These hamadriads understand all languages, and repeat with delight the songs of travelers. Does one play the flute or clarinet? In a moment they seize these very instruments; then it is a veritable concert played with precision and rhythm; above all, it is their simple harmonies whose repetition, softened by the ripples of the breeze and the uncertain vagueness of something remote, that is delightful to hear. Animated by pleasure, they seem to add to their performance grace and taste; but in order that this enjoyment of such a novel musical entertainment be more lasting, the vessel should be at anchor in a favorable spot. I know two or three such places situated on the west bank from which one can enjoy these aerial and invisible concerts, without being able to distinguish whence came the sounds that produce them—and often the distance is one mile away![7]

"Every time I wanted to count the number of echoes, I was unable to count more than eight, not that I could not hear more, but because my perception was not quick enough, and they repeated themselves too rapidly. This task became even more difficult on being able to count 17, when I tried to use my megaphone. Then a great drove of dryads who had not yet opened their mouths burst forth and their sounds escaped my ear. Imagine my astonishment when in the midst of these attempts, I observed that the ones that were too far off for me to hear, repeated what the nearest ones said, and this was repeated in turn by those farther away. In such a manner did all this happen that in the progression of remoteness, each echo became another *me* to whom his neighbors replied. I still recall the phrase, divided into four syllables, that I distinctly heard repeated 17 times: 'Hail! fair hamadriads!' Would it not be possible during the calm of a beautiful day to determine at what distance a sentence, shouted through the megaphone, can be repeated from echo to echo, in a manner so distinct as to strike the ear?"

In uttering these last words, the captain bellowed, "hail passengers!" but the wind and the noise of the wash permitted us to hear only our near neighbors.

It was then that the mountain tops, the slopes, the hollows of the valleys, the peaks and surfaces of the rocks, the tops of the trees and bushes seemed inhabited, filled with invisible or hidden beings who greeted us, repeating, "hail passengers!" Their voices were so distinct, the place we supposed they were inhabiting so well located, that none of us was able to conceive how it could happen that our eyes could not see them, and our ears could be contradicted.

"The time and height of the tides," said the captain, "the strength and direction of the wind, the stratum of the mountains, the position of the promontories, the soundings of the bays and inlets, the season of the year, the hour of the day; such are the causes that modify infinitely the number, the effect, and the mixture of these echoes. Like the birds, they are gayer and more numerous when the bushes and trees are covered with leaves, than during the nudity of autumn and winter.[8]

"What would a man think, a Dutchman for example, born in a flat country where this phenomenon is unknown, if he found himself in the midst of this great solitude, hearing for the first time these hamadriads repeat clearly everything he said. And as if there were still some nuance lacking to the variety and the magnificence of this superb drama, as soon as the bass leaves the Ocean to enter this great river, the fishing hawk comes to live in these mountains. After soaring into the air at a great height, in order to identify his prey more effectively under water, he rushes with the speed of lightning, dives, and soon reappears holding in his talons this enormous fish whose weight and convulsive movements make his flight slower and more difficult. But in his neighborhood there also lives a formidable enemy, the bald eagle, that loves fish but is unable to catch any: and because of the rarity of game in this season, he is obliged to leave the mountains: no sooner does he see the fishing hawk arrive at the height of his eyrie, when the bald eagle, that monarch of all birds, leaves his own eyrie, follows him swiftly until the fishing-hawk, convinced of his inferiority, abandons his prey. Then this proud antagonist, wings folded under, flies like an arrow, and with inconceivable skill recovers possession of his prey before it reaches the river. Sovereign arbiter of great as well as petty disputes, the so-called right of might wields supreme throughout the universe, in the stratosphere as well as on land and under water.[9]

"It is in these mountains that the wind from the sea meets and battles with the wind from the interior. It happens that often (especially in the summertime), their strength being equal, each of them dominates in his region. Then the vessels, returning from New York or Albany, are obliged, if the wind is against them, to drop anchor when they approach these mountains. Consequently, the interval is a variable zone. As a result, in this area the cool breezes rise in the summer; and the mighty blasts of wind coming from the valleys beyond reach the river in the autumn, causing disasters if skill and experience have not taught sailors to anticipate them. Besides, sure of a great depth of water, they can move along, tack, obey the currents and the eddies, until the bowsprit of their vessel touches the branches of the shrubby trees along the river bank.''

We were steering our course through the middle of the fourth channel, extremely imposing by virtue of its length and the awe-inspiring majesty of the mountains that border it, when we noticed on the west bank some very high falls (Butter-milk Falls), whose water seemed to us to be as white as milk; at the foot of these falls a good-sized building had been erected.

''If that is not one of the most beautiful wheat mills in this state,'' the captain told us, ''certainly it is one of the most advantageously situated and one of the most active and prosperous. The base of the granite rock on which it is built is three hundred feet long by forty to sixty feet wide; that is the only land which the owner could buy; but the advantage of a falls forty-five feet high is incredible for this establishment, as well as its location on the banks of a great river, whose waters bring it seeds and take back flour to the capital. You would be amazed at how little water these windmills require, because their weight and speed compensate for the small amount they grind at a time. The fine construction of the building, the number of wheels, the ingenious use made of the cylinders, simplifying the motion and thereby diminishing the friction, as well as the fine wheat products that leave this mill, have justifiably provoked the praise of experts. The vessels coming from the interior laden with wheat, and those from New York which load on cereal products, tie up at the very door of the mill, at whose foot there is always forty feet of water. What a pity that the elevation of the mountains deprives the mill of the sun during part of the day. They say that this beautiful construction cost 18,500 piastres (97,125 pounds).''

The wind and the tide failing us, we had strayed several miles from this mill, when we dropped anchor at a few fathoms in a lovely inlet surrounded by white poplars with silverish leaves and hemlocks that were very impressive because of their moss. At the other end of the inlet we heard the noise of falls; this, we were told, was Pooplos-Kill.[10] It was six o'clock and the sun had long since disappeared behind the mountains of the west bank. We were busy watching this beautiful and bounteous cascade which ingenuity will some day harness, when suddenly we were startled by a violent explosion.

The echoes which had diverted us a short while ago were only feeble sounds, compared with those which repeated the rumblings and burstings, whose strength and violence it is impossible for me to describe. They surrounded us on all sides, and we entertained ourselves by listening to them with an attentive ear, until gradually they were swallowed up in silence and distance.

"It is the cannon-volley announcing retreat," the captain told us.[11]

"I thought I was 1,500 leagues from Europe, in a country of peace and calm and yet there is a cannon!" said Mr. Herman.

"We are only three miles from West Point," the captain answered. "Haven't you ever heard about the fortifications that our first Congress built there during the war for independence? Indeed, never has a fortified site been more strategically located. The river forms a considerable elbow, and the very long peninsula formed obliges vessels to make a great detour as they approach; the steepness of the river banks, the relative position of the neighboring heights—all of these factors made Congress decide to close this passage; peaks were converted into sites for cross-fire guns, formidable redoubts whose gunfire intersected at several points along the river. Tomorrow, as we sail by, you will see what remains of these great works; we will touch the rock to which was attached the east end of the cable chain that closed it in; each link in this chain weighed more than 400 pounds. Among the causes that have assured the liberty and independence of these states, unquestionably these impregnable fortifications can count for much."

The darkness of the night having little by little obscured the objects that surrounded us, the captain invited us to go below in the stateroom of the vessel. It was furnished in Chinese fashion, lighted by candles from that same land, each in its wide-mouthed, short-necked bottle; he showed us the map made during the war under the supervision and by order of General Washington: it showed the peninsulas, and the promontories, the capes, the contours, and the most defendable parts of this celebrated strait which the great man regarded as the key to this part of the continent. He entertained us then with an account of the interior of these mountains which he had explored on one side as far as the boundaries of Connecticut, and on the other, as far as New Jersey.

"If I were a farmer," he told us, " (and I sail only because I want to realize that ambition some day), I would prefer living here to living in the areas of Fish-Kill, Duchess, and Columbia.[12] Everything here is favorable to farming: fertility of the valleys, the clearness of the streams, the utility of irrigation facilities, abundance of these beautiful woods, and proximity to several great forges. Some foreign officers, discharged after the peace of 1763, came here to found settlements which have long since evoked great praise from connoisseurs and admiration from the public. To love of work and knowledge of farming, they united urban ways, the refinement of customs as well as the advantages of their divers talents. Often respectable friends left the town to spend time with these families for a while. Such a reunion has long offered the most appealing picture of enlightened industry, comfortable ease, and happiness. Unfortunately the war for independence ruined many of these families."

The moon that we awaited impatiently finally appeared over the mountains; up on deck once again, it was then that we saw a thousand strange and new forms. They were no longer optical illusions, gradations of perspective, nor that variety of well-known objects that during daylight are illuminated by the sun, but more curious and more bizarre illusions to which one could give no name. What seemed more amusing to me was that each of us, impressed by the beauty of the objects which his imagination painted, accused his neighbor of "seeing things" if different from what he saw! Indeed, what a spectacle was this deep darkness, this mixture of rather brilliant light, changing to feeble rays, surrounded as we were by forests, those veritable mountains which the mists of the night appear to have folded over us! It was scarcely astonishing, therefore, that in the midst of this novel, imposing scene, our imagination might borrow the peculiarity and majesty of so many objects, some of the characteristics and even the charms of oddity!

It was midnight and we were still on deck absorbed in contemplating the majesty of nature, those efforts of a power that we will never understand, displayed in the heavens, on earth, and under water. The great calm, the solemn silence of this Chaldean night were only rarely and feebly interrupted by the long and slow rippling of waves that one could scarcely hear breaking on remote river banks, or washing against our ship as they made the anchor of our ship shake, or finally, by the far-off stir of leaves, or by the distant sound of the flow of this immense body of water as it passed through this long and twisting channel. We were still entertaining ourselves with the echoes of the neighborhood, making them repeat our poetry and song, when suddenly our ears were caught by a most extraordinary noise, as though some giant atop a mountain might have heaved boulders into the river.

"Those are sturgeons," the captain told us, "falling back into the water, after jumping to a great height. I don't really know the reason for such curious exercise."

The next day we raised anchor as soon as the tide permitted, and the captain having trimmed his sails, we had time to watch closely what still remains of the great works at West-Point, or rather what can be seen of it from mid-river. Most of the stone-built redoubts and the batteries erected on the top of boulders as well as at water level seemed to us to be well preserved, although in part hidden under the thick foliage of bushes and shrubby growth; for everything that the foot of man rarely tramples on is soon covered with growth in this region.

"This vast amphitheatre of defenses," the captain told us, "took the hard work of several men for two long years; the warehouse has been converted into an arsenal and in it they have put the big guns of defense (heavy artillery) and the artillery taken at the surrender of Saratoga. The two extremities of the cable marking the defense point of the river were defended by those two impregnable redoubts perfectly conserved, as you can see. It is easy to see that vessels could never have arrived near them, without exposing themselves, for two or more miles, to the crossfire from the banks and neighboring heights."

Finally, after slowly bypassing these buildings representing so much effort and perseverance, we entered the last and most spacious channel, the most imposing in the strait, whose extremity is cut by two mountains which, although almost perpendicular, are partly wooded. It was here where we began to discover the countryside and habitations of the west bank of the river. This river, as it emerges from the strait, is three miles wide between New Windsor and Fish-Kill.

CHAPTER XVI

In accordance with his promise, the captain permitted us to disembark at the first little straggling village soon after leaving the strait; but since it was merely a little landing-stage where several inland roads intersected, and offered virtually nothing of interest to us, we struck out cross country. Scarcely had we covered a few miles in the direction of Bethlehem, when we met Mr. John Allisson, a wealthy landowner of this canton, with whom I had crossed the ocean a few years before, and who, after showing us his fine mill, in which he converted annually 25 to 30,000 bushels of wheat into flour, wanted us to dine with him. He told us that his enterprises would have been much more extensive, if he had not been subjected to low water supply during the heat of the summer, and if he could find means to rid himself of the Hessian Fly,[1] an insect which for many years had wrought considerable damage in all the neighboring regions, and of which no one had ever heard before the arrival of the German troops in New York.

Guided by military marker stones, we continued our journey as far as Blooming-Green, where we had to leave our route to strike off through the mountains; but scarcely had we crossed the bridge built over Murderer's-Creek, when we discovered another mill which excited the insatiable curiosity of Mr. Herman. We had the good fortune to meet the owner, Mr. Thorn, who invited us very politely to come in, and offered to show us around. He began with the ground floor, occupied by four pair of millstones; from there we climbed several stories that were filled with tremendous fans, boilers, and brushes of a new type, and he took us up to the fourth story where the meal was processed for two weeks before being sifted into large barrels. This top story was as big as the entire building, that is, 94 by 40 feet. Finally he took us to his dam.

"Ingenuity and nature have given me a falls 18 feet high; in this way my wheels are propelled and the amount of water I would otherwise need is considerably reduced. Here is my cooperage where I make three to four thousand barrels every year."

"How much wheat do you grind into flour?" my companion asked.

"Forty to fifty bushels."

"Where do you get the wheat?"

"From Sussex, Orange, and Ulster counties, as well as Northern Pennsylvania."

"How much does it cost you a bushel?"

"The prices in the European markets are our gauges; in general, eight or ten shillings."[2]

"What is the purpose of this great wall beyond your mills? It seems to support part of the masonry of your fine mill."

"It is to shelter them from the ice."

"How much does all this cost you?"

"Fourteen thousand piastres including the dam and the piece of ground (73,500 pounds)."

Finally we entered the mountains, almost all well cultivated for many years, and after walking three hours, we came upon the valley of the Skonomonk.

"Everything you see," I told Mr. Herman, "belongs to my friend, Jesse Woodhull; those pastures, that great orchard, those fields beyond view. Would you believe it? He was the first to uproot a tree in this great settlement and this worthy man is not yet fifty. I think I recognize him by his height over on that hillside where three plows are turning up the earth; let's go over."

After we had been received as though hospitality itself had taken us by the hand, my companion, astonished to see that each team had two oxen and two horses harnessed, asked him the reason.

"The soil is of such a type in this valley," he replied, "that our labors require great strength; often even the first break-through is made with four teams. Quite different is the soil in neighboring regions, plowed with only three horses."

"Why do these oxen walk so briskly while those I saw in Connecticut walk so heavily?"

"Those you see here are really not oxen."

Astonishing by this reply Mr. Herman, who did not seem to understand, the Colonel added:

"No, sir, they are not oxen, but a new kind of animal for whom our language, rich as it is, has not found a name.

"They are heifers on whom I operated when they were very young; very simple and not the slightest bit injurious: removing their sex organs. This operation has made them much more agile, although as suited for work and hard toil as males, they are less docile. Every year I perform the same operation on a certain number of mares, making them far superior to my other horses insofar as strength and health and especially surefootedness go."

"Where did you get this new and curious notion? And what surgeon performs this operation?"

"I got the notion out of my own head. I tried it fifteen years ago; the results were favorable and they have continued to be ever since."

"Are you not afraid that you might do harm to the reproduction of the species?"

"No, because around here we never kill calves and we have a great number of horses."

"We have come to spend a few days with you," I told him. "Then when you give us instructions, we are going to see the great foundries of Sterling, Ringwood, Charlottesburg, etc. Will you lend us some horses?"

"Gladly, but I insist that you spend a week with me, then I shall accompany you wherever you wish to go."

"If you enjoy hunting and fishing, you will certainly find a source of amusement."

On returning from looking over his fields and meadows the next day, he brought from his stables two of his geldings.

"I hunt deer only on horseback," he told us, "and there are my mounts; they are tireless and they never stumble; they have another fine quality: that of a fast trot without ever tripping."

"What accounts for these fine qualities?"

"During the summer three times a week I shoe their forefeet; they are taught to walk with this weight—finally to trot. After six months of this exercise they reach a point of adjustment where their hindfeet and forefeet coördinate in perfect cadence, whatever their gait."

"How much land do you have under cultivation?"

"748 acres. That is too much, I know, for a single man can hardly look after such a great enterprise. But the deed is done; I have no alternative; besides, I have nine youngsters, and if all wanted to be farmers like their father, you know that my 1,500 acres would not be enough for each of them to have a good farm. I have provided for all this through a good-sized purchase of land which I have just made in the new county of Otsego." [3]

"I notice scarcely any stumps in your fields," Mr. Herman told him, "I imagine that this great clearing began before your arrival."

"No, I myself uprooted the first tree thirty-one years ago; I was then eighteen. I was not alone, as you can well imagine. What a hideous sight the bed of this valley presented at that time! The beneficent riches of nature were buried under the most forbidding debris, and in part covered with earth; these fine pastures, these meadows, today so uniform and so green, were once swamplands filled with willows, whose branch-ends took new roots that produced new stalks; black briars and thorny vines whose innumerable sprouts intertwined with the bushes and made them impenetrable; finally ash-trees and red maples of great height. Most assuredly, future generations will owe us some gratitude; but will they ever realize what have been the discouragements and the difficulties, the disgusts and the boredom that accompanied these painful beginnings?''

"One day," said Mr. Woodhull, "after seventeen months of the most assiduous work, realizing the little progress we had made, I thought I would never reach the end of the great interval that lay ahead before I could have the enjoyment of some fenced fields, some acres of grazing land, a house, and a barn; this thought depressed me. Suddenly I was seized with a despondency such as I had never known; my courage and strength left me; hope, which, every morning preceded my steps when I went into the woods, and followed me every evening when I returned, abandoned me altogether. I ceased looking on this fine property given me by my father as the way that would lead me some day to ease and independence. I deplored my plight and lamented over seeing myself condemned to spend the best days of my youth far from the pleasures of society, in the midst of these somber forests, these impenetrable swamps, which even perseverance and courage, iron and fire could not destroy. So many obstacles to overcome, I told myself, so many difficulties to surmount, would require the strength of Hercules or of Milo and the longevity of a patriarch. In vain did one of my uncles, settled in Blooming-Grove in the vicinity, come often to see me and encourage me; in vain did my father write me many letters, most conducive to reviving my enthusiasm; for many months I fought with myself; then I learned of the imminent departure of one of my uncles for Dutch Guiana, with a cargo of horses.[4] Seized by some sort of fascination, I went to him in New York and did not inform my father of my flight until the very day of our departure.

"We were no sooner on the high seas than I felt as though I had been relieved of a great burden; I felt like a man brought back to good health after a long sickness; I congratulated myself on having left a way of life so difficult and so monotonous; all my ideas and my thoughts were directed toward another goal. Never was a turn of mind so complete. If ever I thought of this valley, I congratulated myself again on having abandoned it, as well as that long series of chores that appeared to me now anything but lowly work, a vile kind of slavery. I figured out what would be the length of my apprenticeship and how many years must elapse before I might obtain the command of a ship. The only thought that sometimes saddened me was that of having displeased my good parents in leaving Skenomonk.

"Until this time the wind had been favorable and the sea calm; but in making the crossing between Cape Hatteras and the Bermudas,[5] we were assailed by a very violent wind that obliged the captain to get rid of the horses, by pushing them overboard. This storm, the first I had seen, filled my heart with fear and terror and in a moment shattered my new plans. I was seized with seasickness: during my sorrowful anguish, my mind returned involuntarily to this valley which I began to look upon under less somber colors. Sometimes in my dreams I seemed to see the swamplands converted into green pastures and covered with cattle; the wooded lands into fields of corn and wheat.

" 'Ah!' I often said to myself on awakening, 'if only a part of what my imagination has just seen might have existed, I would not have left this fine heritage and today I would not be exposed to the fury of winds and waves!'

"Finally after a long and difficult crossing, we arrived in Dutch Guiana.[6] The excessive heat of this oppressive climate; the disgusting insects that ceaselessly surrounded us; those thunder storms, those frightful lightning storms that appeared to me to be the precursors of the destruction of the world; the extreme subservience that my uncle demanded; that whirlpool in the hold of the ship where I was daily obliged to go below for the loading and unloading of the ship; all these unforeseen sufferings awakened regrets in my heart and brought repentance to my heart. In comparing the disadvantages of these two ways of life, it was not long before I realized that there are disadvantages in everything; that everywhere nature eludes us or arms herself against us; that it was a thousand times better, whatever it cost, to uproot trees, burn them, and little by little destroy the surface of a fertile soil which would some day reward me hundredfold, than to sail over the tempestuous ocean, than to cross through these burning climates and brave the storms of the torrid zone. If in the woods one experiences disgust, boredom, fatigue, I told myself, at least all this activity does not permit hope to disappear, as it does in the dangers of this climate where one spends half his days in trembling under upright thunderbolts that shake the atmosphere and the earth.

"Returning to New York after five months absence (for we had been obliged to go to Essequibo [7] to complete our loading operations) I resigned my commission the day after my arrival to go to Long Island, to throw myself at the mercy of my parents, whose wrath I feared. Imagine my surprise and joy when I learned that my father was here, in this country, and when my mother told me what he had said after receiving my letter!

" 'The discouragement that seized this young man does not surprise me in the least; he is not the first who, in similar circumstances, has reached such a point; but instead of sailing away, fleeing his native land, why did he not seek me out? Didn't he realize that as his father I was also his friend, and you his mother, his devoted mother? To discourage him from his plans for going to sea and settle him here once and for all, I know only two ways: I am going to hire six good workers who, with the four left in Skonomonk, will do a great deal of work during his absence. On his return, astonished and flattered at our progress, he will blush at this outburst and will feel the price of the lesson I wanted to teach him. Will that not be worth more than any other kind of reprimand? Soon he will forget the past; and so will I. As to the second way, I shall tell you of that only when he returns.'

"This was one of the greatest moments of my life. Some days later, I came here to find this good father of mine who told me while embracing me tenderly, his eyes dim with tears:

" 'Come now, Jesse! Isn't this land worth more than Surinam? To tell the truth, one does not become a rich and luxury-loving colonist, or a millionaire, but a farmer, a laborer, healthy and well-off who does not blush over wielding the axe or laying hold of the plow.'

" 'Ah, father!' I replied, 'today this climate, this land appears to me like an earthly paradise compared with the one whence I came; if you will forgive me, I shall never cease devoting myself to the most steady work until I have accomplished the plans that were yours and have now become mine!'

" 'Since your departure,' he replied, 'I have cleared, fenced, and planted a wheat field of 27 acres, removed and burned a great number of stumps, destroyed two beaver dams, built a sawmill in order that you will be able some day to build a fine, attractive home as well as a barn suitable for the good-sized crops that you will have. Have I not used these five months of your absence to good advantage?'

" 'I have another present for you, Jesse: a wife, such as you deserve; one who is wise, healthy, hard-working, and sensible. You know S. B. from the region around Cornwall. Here, let me take your hand. If you have fetched from Surinam neither sugar, nor indigo, during your voyage, you have acquired something far better, a thousand times better for a young man like you: that is experience. Life is like the ice of winter, on which one learns to walk, to balance, only after picking himself up from his first falls: and after all, you can trust your father's good judgment.'

" 'What a mistake I made,' I replied. 'And if you will forgive me, it will be my last.'

" 'Yes, I am sure of it,' he told me. 'Embrace me; let's forget all this!'

"Fortunate are the children to whom nature has given fathers, or rather friends such as mine. They owe them more than life. He is dead now unfortunately; but his memory, which I bless every day after offering my prayers to the Supreme Being, will linger with me until I die. My good mother is still living at St. George, on Long Island in the region known as Nassau.[8]

"The next day, hatchet in hand, I was about to leave for the woods, when he stopped me and said:

" 'Jesse, why don't you rest from your labors; go see the lady whom I have chosen for you; be worthy of her affection; I shall stay on here until winter begins.'

"I married her six months later, that dear and priceless woman; ever since she has been my happiness. She has borne me nine children and is justly acclaimed for her intelligence in the management of a household, a very important department in this part of the country.

"As though to crown all my happiness, a dear brother, professor at the college in New Haven, spent his vacation that very year with me and it is to him whom I owe various important agricultural improvements. In the outskirts of this town he owns a small farm on which by virtue of great care, perseverance, and knowledge, he has brought together in one area everything useful and beautiful that is cultivated in these states. His garden and land are a model for the countryside. Once a year he gives a great dinner for the president of the college and his colleagues; the group has a Greek name which I have forgotten. The linen for his table comes from flax trees which he grows; his napkins have blue borders dyed with indigo, a two or three ounce supply of which he makes annually. I haven't even mentioned the meat, vegetables, and fruit coming from his farm yard and his kitchen garden, oil from sesamen, brandy from peaches, maple syrup and vinegar,[9] cider, hydromel, wine from cherries, jams, a kind of tea peculiar to that country (Labrador), even coffee, everything comes from his fields, his garden, or green-house; yes, everything, even to his candles.[10] But what will astonish you even more is the punch which they will treat you to: the fruit of this liquor also comes from his garden. I was the one who discovered this charming little shrub while wandering through the woods one day; it bears reddish berries that are as large as pigeon's eggs, filled with a transparent juice of the same color; this juice our doctors have found to be as good as that of lemons from Jamaica or Bahama; it is precisely the same as the juice of the cranberry [11] in the bogs. It is quite curious that a tree and a plant bear the same fruit, with no difference other than size."

The next day, failing to find the Colonel in his living room, we discovered him repairing the plowshare of his plows.

"It is not for reasons of economy that I sometimes strike my own anvil, but to save time, the greatest factor in promoting our prosperity. Time moves more swiftly than the water in my river. How many days have I not frequently lost for the work of a half-hour when I used a neighbor's smithy."

"Why should time move more swiftly here than any other place?" asked Mr. Herman.

"Because we have virtually no spring, and summer succeeds winter so quickly that often it is difficult to plant all the season's crops before harvest comes. On the other hand, the length of our winters obliges us to lay up a great quantity of provender; the work necessary to accomplish this sometimes takes six weeks; annually I reap nearly one hundred acres and during that time our plows are idle. You can see then that we have no time to lose and that if our winters were shorter, our harvests would be far more abundant."

"Furthermore," continued Mr. Woodhull, "as sheriff of the county, I am obliged to spend several days in Goshen [12] everytime the lower and higher courts hold their sessions. As Colonel in the militia of the same county, four long training periods and frequent inspections oblige me to leave my fields often. All these outside duties, together with the indispensable details that such a great undertaking exacts, together with a family of thirty-five individuals, who must be fed and clad, contribute toward making time more precious and more rapid for me than for others."

"But why," Mr. Herman asked him again, "the necessity for militia in a country that enjoys great peace? Do you have no regular troops?"

"We have only what we absolutely need to guard our frontiers and protect the new colonies that have settled beyond the Ohio. There is not a single soldier in our towns; besides the Constitution requires that every citizen between the ages of 18 and 50 be registered, armed, and ready to serve. Since the peace and tranquility of the towns and countrysides are confined only to the safeguarding of laws, it is necessary that in case of emergency, the magistrates can call upon the detachments of militia. By whom can these laws be more effectively guarded and preserved from any evil than by the citizens?"

In the evening, my companion, noticing that the candles which lighted the living room were green, asked the colonel the reason for it.

"It is because they are not made with tallow," he replied, "but with bayberry whose bushes are very common in this region: the plateau of the mountain at Skonomonk is entirely covered with it. Very simple and easy to get as much as one wants of it. Have you noticed how subtle and fragrant the smoke is? People have tried with some success to bleach it. In a few years more we will have reached a stage of perfecting several new branches of industry and commerce. Already they are exporting some of this bayberry, together with beeswax, to the Spanish Islands and the Portuguese Islands, whose religion requires candlelight even though there is abundant sunlight.

"The same activity, the same degree of care and foresight that pervades our work in the field, is also present in the management of our households. Here every year enough cotton, linen, and wool is spun to maintain the household and clothe the entire family. The different stuffs that are made from it are woven 'neath my roof, those that must be dyed undergo this process here too. My wife is our great dyer; ordinarily we dye from 800 to 1,200 ells yearly. The same is true of the soap; every year each family makes as much as it needs with fat and vegetable juices. This process is easier and quicker than the maple sugar processing.

"I owe to nature three or four hundred of these very useful trees that I have carefully fenced in and from which I have pruned all excess growth to increase the vigor as well as the quantity of their sap. This beautiful orchard, now become our little Jamaica, supplies me every year in the month of April with all the sugar, the syrup, and the vinegar we need. Each tree yields three to four pounds; but lest we overdraw them, I have divided them into three classes, and we tap only one group a year. Since I disencumbered them of everything in their way, everything choking their growth, the sun now floods them with its beneficent rays. I notice that their sap annually becomes richer and more abundant. In a few years I hope that each will yield me 5 pounds of sugar. Already they are beginning to refine the sugar. The lot I have just received from New York seemed as white, bright, and beautiful as any I had seen in Jamaica or Antigua. As far as the vinegar, I know of none better, nor stronger."

Finally preceded by the head of this little family, we left Skonomonk for the foundry at Sterling.

The interesting details which conclude this chapter would suffice to prove, if it had not already long since become trivial by dint of being obvious, of knowing that necessity is the mother of invention. I might add that success in industry, always dearly bought, procures happiness for man which he finds neither in the favors of fortune nor in the easy enjoyment of luxury. Of this the active and hardworking colonist must be convinced and through his own experience: that is not even suspected, and far from being understood, by the idle and frivolous inhabitant of the towns in Europe. (Note communicated to the editor by Citizen B.)

CHAPTER XVII

No sooner had we stabled our horses when the owner, Mr. Townsend, came to meet us and received us with that politeness of a man accustomed to seeing strangers and travelers often. Indeed his hospitality has been famous for so long a time that whether one comes from the interior or from New York, one always plans to stay with him when crossing the mountains. Learning that we had come here to inspect his various works, he offered to give us a detailed tour.

First he led us to his great furnace where the raw iron ore was smelted and then converted into "pigs" weighing from 60 to 100 pounds. It was situated at a little distance from the dam, which from its favorable position near the rocks had procured for it a considerable supply of water at very little cost. From a simple stream, he had made a small lake of fifteen thousand square acres. It was filled with fish and had a nice little boat. This furnace was powered by two huge bellows 48 by 7 feet that were made only with wood, with neither iron nor leather. The violence, the noise of the wind they produced, resembled that of a tempest.

"Unless some accident befalls us, this furnace," he told us, "produces every year, from 2,000 to 2,400 tons of iron, three-fourths of which is converted into bars, and the rest into cannon balls, etc. These mountains whose depths bring me coal also furnish various kinds of mineral of an excellent quality known by different names."

From there we went to see the refinery: six great hammers were busy forging bars of iron and anchors, as well as various parts for the use of ships. Further on, on the same stream was the foundry with its reverbatory furnace. He showed us some ingenious furnaces designed for different uses that he had set up with a pinchbeck newly discovered in these mountains, whose grain, after two meltings, acquires the fineness and almost the color of tin.

"I can make from it the lightest and most delicate things," he said. "What a pity you didn't come here eight or ten days sooner! I would have shown you first three new types of plows, most of the main parts of which I cast and which nevertheless are no heavier than the old ones. Each one of them is provided with a kind of graded steelyard, by means of which one can see with the greatest precision the degree of the team's pulling power and consequently the resistance, that is to say, the firmness of the soil; second, a portable mill designed to thresh wheat out of the shavings. This invention is merely the result of another, by means of which all the ears of corn in a field will be easily removed, without being obliged to cut at the base to make sheafs according to the ancient custom. An account of all that has been sent to Mount Vernon [1] for although General Washington fills with distinguished talents the presidency of the Union to which he has been called by unanimous vote, affection and gratitude, and though the seat of Government is 100 miles from his property, he supervises an immense agricultural area and directs its operations with a judgment and attention worthy of praise. Every week like a merchant he receives details about it, the latest status of his business. With the aid of a great map which he showed me, he knows all his fields, knows what their yield is, and advises what should be planted there. Never has anyone pushed order, method, nor economy of time further. The same was true during the war. Congress and the public were not a little astonished when, after resuming citizen status, he gave, at the very beginning, an account of his command, in which were listed the items pertaining to the private expense of secret service for seven years, written entirely in his hand, these expenses amounting to no more than twelve or fourteen thousand guineas. During this long interval, as well as since the time when he became head of the general government, this illustrious Agricola never ceased being one of the most enlightened farmers in the United States. Before the Revolution, he had forty plows and in 1772 he harvested nearly 10,000 bushels of wheat.''

From the furnace we went to see the ovens in which the iron was converted into steel.

''It has not yet reached the degree of perfection that Sweden has,'' Mr. Townsend told us; ''but we are approaching it. A few more years of experience and we will arrive at perfection. The iron that emerges from my hammers enjoys a longer lasting reputation and sells at 28 to 30 pounds sterling the ton weighing in at 367 to 390 pounds (the ton weighs 2,200 pounds).

''Do you see this beautiful and vast pasture land bordered by the two branches of the river? That is what I call the masterpiece of my industry; scarcely ten years ago this swamp was the cesspool of these mountains. I tried to clear it with my hatchet; but the thickets and copses with which they were covered offered such resistance, that this instrument became virtually useless. I did not know what to do about the overgrowth when the idea came to me to turn loose 300 goats and to leave them there until winter fell. Pressed by need, they killed the most spritely bushes, eating their very bark. The following summer a general conflagration destroyed everything. I planted my ground in clover and timothy, and the following year to my great joy this impenetrable mass of bramble bushes and thorn trees was replaced by an abundant harvest of hay. Since that time this island has become one of the best prairies of the region. Several farmers have followed my example.''

We spent two days looking over the results of his labors, admiring the ingenuity with which he had combined the movement of the waters as well as the order and arrangement of cutting of the trees, necessary to furnish the charcoal that such an enterprise requires. We left Mr. Townsend and that very day we arrived in Ringwood whose owner, Mr. Erskine, we knew had spent three years in Europe visiting the principal foundries of Scotland, Sweden, and Germany. Although not quite as extensive, the buildings appeared to us none the less interesting. The combination, the mechanisms of different machines designed to simplify the work of man, were even more perfect than those we had seen at Sterling. A great process designed to flatten and cleave the metal into rod shapes appeared to Mr. Herman to be a masterpiece of simplicity; but what made it even more remarkable was the mill which surmounted it and which one could lower or raise at will. All the parts were made of metal. Not far from there was another machine designed to bore the holes through cannon. Mr. Erskine told us that in a normal year he sold 5,000 tons of iron in bar shapes, 200 tons of steel, not to mention the scrap; but Ringwood, besides the abundance of water and wood, enjoys an appreciable advantage, that of being only a slight distance from the Hackensack River which empties into the great bay of New York.

''What resources these mountains offer to the inhabitants of the two states of New Jersey and New York! The immensity of the forests with which they are covered to their very peaks; the different kinds of minerals which one finds in their bosom with as much ease as abundance; the rich and fertile valleys, the numerous streams irrigated by them—what possibilities for riches and prosperity! If posterity conserves these beautiful woods, it will enjoy centuries of precious advantages of having the coal necessary for the manufacture of iron, the ease of repairing buildings and dams, as well as the means of power that it will need.''

''You are right,'' said Mr. Erskine; ''this may well happen, since for a long time the whole chain has been the property of several individuals extremely interested in the conservation of these forests. From the border of Connecticut to that of Jersey, there are in these mountains seven furnaces and six great forges, not to mention foundries and refineries that produce perhaps annually 140,000 quintals of cast iron, much steel, anchors, cannon, etc. If, on the other hand,

I could know what the sale of these harvests amounts to and the number of cattle raised in the valleys, I am convinced that a rich and fertile plain of 882 square miles (that is what I estimate the space occupied by these mountains) would not be as productive.''

The next day we were in Charlottenbourg going through a very mountainous district. Constructions around there had been erected before the Revolution by an English company which the war had ruined. The furnace had just burst and the proprietor was absent. We saw a great nail-making machine extremely simplified by means of a great number of little hammers that were put into motion by a slewing crane. Here they made bolts as well as various iron fittings for the use of vessels. We saw a sheet metal works necessary for the manufacture of spades and shovels. There as at Sterling and Ringwood, the supply of water is tremendous. We were told that the preceding year 46,000 quintals of ''pigs'' had been smelted.

From Charlottenbourg we were to visit in Bellevale, but after learning that all we could see there were huge hammers, we resolved to abandon this project in favor of seeing a natural prairie containing nearly 70,000 acres [2] located in the middle of a region that was beginning to be cultivated.

As though to dress up, nature embellished these immense prairie lands with several islands of varying size, whose soil is extraordinarily fertile. Some are covered with very high red cedars. It is with the wood of these that the houses and barns are made. A fine cooperage, whose use is so widespread and so varied, is also built from cedars. This expanse of grassland is crossed in its 48 miles' length by a deep, wide river (the Walkill), but from the bridge built at its eastern shore to the Hudson River, its noisy waters serve only as water power for a great number of mills of various purposes.

Accompanied by Mr. John Allison, one of the wealthiest landowners in this region, we went to see an island belonging to him, about a half mile from the riverbank; there we saw 52 cows. The sight of this superb herd, as well as that of his immense creamery and the device used to stir the milk, surprised Mr. Herman.

''What!'' he said, ''you were telling me just a little while go that the hundredth part of the surface of these islands was scarcely under cultivation, subdued by the scythe or converted into pasture land; and already there is such a numerous flock! What will it be like in a matter of a few years?''

''The time when everything you see becomes transformed into grain and useful grass is still far off. The cultivation of this vast plain is a conquest reserved for our posterity; here as in Egypt, we will be obliged to cut draining canals, although this prairie land is not very apt to be flooded over; we will have to build dikes and cause-ways, to divide the properties by a great number of ditches, put lasting boundaries to determine the limits and subdivisions, and to establish the line of demarkation across New Jersey. The boundaries will be trees; then on all sides one will see willows, cypress, poplars, sycamores. What embellishment! What richness! What great utility the coolness of their shade will be during the summer heat! The monotony you see today will be replaced by variety; the green sombreness of this bleak horizon will no longer blend with the brilliant blue of a beautiful day; our population will be increased.

"But how far the increase of men is from contributing to their happiness! In primitive societies enjoying more space and less exposed to the stimulus of needs, men are happier; hence, less perverse. Perhaps our posterity will consider as the golden age the one in which we now live. Labor will be cheaper, it is true; the enjoyments of life will be more keenly felt; the houses more spacious and better arranged; but there will be rich and poor; crimes will become more common and laws more severe; perhaps the very form of our happy government will have changed with circumstances.

"Nevertheless it would be an interesting spectacle for a man born, as I was, in this country during its early infancy, to see it again when these great spaces, today useless and uncultivated, will be covered with fine crops; when these islands and shores are covered with fine dwellings and surrounded by magnificent orchards; when the gentle slopes of the riverbanks of this vast prairie are cultivated to the point where scythe meets plow! What a luxury of vegetation this fat and fertile land will exploit! Especially when spurred on by the perpetual supply of waters! What a great number of horses and cattle will be bred to fatten off this land, today so abundant in useless weeds and wild growth! What a quantity of butter, cheese, hemp, and linen will come out of this region! Yet the seeds of this great productivity exist and await only development by the progress of time and industry; both are advancing with great rapidity."

This educated colonist, magistrate of the region, had just finished an elegant and commodious brick house. We experienced fine hospitality for two days and enjoyed the pleasure of his conversation. He gave us some of his red currant wine, so good and so mellowed by age that Mr. Herman thought it came from Europe. He told us that every year he sent to New York 4,000 pounds of butter, 200 pounds of cheese, 40 barrels of lard, and several casks (tuns) of hemp; [3] all this nets him between twelve and thirteen hundred piastres; and the result of his harvests, his breeding, and his forest of white cedars yielded him nearly as much; his taxes did not exceed four piastres; and his father had begun this settlement only 22 years previous. He also talked to us about a law that the states of Jersey and New York had passed to encourage the reclamation of land; he added that already work had begun with great effect.

"What a conquest," he told us, "when one thinks that for three thousand guineas, a surface of 70,000 acres can be cleared!"

Colonel Woodhull's affairs having obliged us to leave sooner than he had anticipated, we separated at Wawayanda in Northern Jersey, whence we crossed by the Highlands; [4] they appeared even higher than those that border the river. The next day we put up at Basking-Ridge in order to admire the ingenious mechanism of a mill designed to break up and chop hemp and linen. The following day we were at Princeton, where we planned to see the Rittenhouse masterpiece. It is a machine that reproduces with great exactitude the movements of the heavenly bodies, their eclipses, their oppositions, as well as all the astronomical phenomena that modern scientists have discovered.

"This machine," said Mr. Jefferson, "which for lack of a better name we call the Orrery is perhaps the finest piece of apparatus that was ever made by man. Rittenhouse did not create the world, but through powers of imitation, he has approached nearer the great Creator than any man who ever existed."

We had decided to see the copper mines at Rock Hill and Sckyler, but after learning that the damages that they suffered during the war had not yet been repaired, we returned to Newark, the most elegant and rustic village in the United States. From here, after crossing the Passaic and Hackensack Rivers over two bridges that had just been completed, we arrived in New York.

(There appears to be a great portion missing here.)

NOTES

NOTES ON THE DEDICATORY LETTER TO GEORGE WASHINGTON

1 George Washington, born in Virginia on February 11, 1732, in the parish of Washington, country of Westmoreland, was sent by that State, as deputy to the first Congress which met in Philadelphia September 5, 1774.

2 The following year, he was named commander-in-chief of the Continental Army, a commission that he accepted only with distrust, and not without much difficulty. This choice, sanctioned by the voice, or rather the acclamation of the people, produced such a great effect, that a goodly number of young people hastened to join up under his command at Roxbury, near Boston, where he soon found himself at the head of 30,000 volunteers.

3 A general discontent had reigned for several months in the Continental Army, encamped at the time at New-Bourg on the west bank of the Hudson River. It was based on the inadequacy of the measures Congress had taken to pay the soldiers what it owed them and also on the amount of the promised bonuses, the only ones, moreover, that in its extreme destitution of funds it could manage. This discontent was not long in producing a ferment all the more alarming since there was neither licentiousness nor tumult. The soldiers sent several representatives to the General and although I have never known what they were supposed to say to him, it is easy to guess that armed men, irritated, needed only a chief to right the situation; he had the good fortune, not without meeting obstacles, to appease these angry overtures, to mitigate the harshness of their thinking, to dissolve plans that might have had fatal consequences and, finally, to discipline that army. It would be difficult to find oneself in more delicate circumstances and emerge with more honor.

Who is the citizen in the United States today who could remember this period in the life of General Washington without feeling filled with a mixture of admiration and gratitude? What change in the destinies of the continent a single monosyllable might have been able to produce!

4 The letter addressed by the General from that same camp (New-Bourg) June 11, 1783, to the Governors of the thirteen States is a masterpiece of wisdom. Foreseeing from that very time the misfortunes, the heartbreaks which must necessarily result in achieving peace, the inadequacy of the confederation, and the weakness of the Congress, he places the energetic plan under the very eyes of his fellow citizens, together with the one concerning the measures they must adopt in order to guarantee their liberty. He tells them that the dangers of the war from which they have just emerged with so much glory are nothing compared with those dangers that

await them, if the States do not consent to grant to Congress a part of their sovereignty, in order to assure domestic tranquility and to establish justice on a firm basis.

But four long years had to pass before the forewarnings of this man were acted on; the inhabitants of these States had to be dragged to the brink of the precipice before his profound wisdom was pointed out. When one projects his imagination to this critical time, let him recall the circumstances in which these States found themselves at the time of peace, when the feeble bonds that linked them were near the breaking point; it is difficult not to notice something truly extraordinary in that letter, dictated as much by wisdom as by foresight and by the most enlightened patriotism; that, at least, is the effect it produced on my mind.

5 I was witness to the general joy and the outbursts of ecstasy, that his modest but triumphal entrance occasioned in the city of New-York (November 25, 1783), to say nothing of his benevolence toward the royalists whose affairs were not yet in order; I admired, as did so many others, his modesty, his affability; the wisdom of the means he used to mitigate the harshness of the two parties, which, after 7 years of separation, were reunited. I shared with these inhabitants the sadness, the regrets, the consternation that the announcement of his departure, set for December 4, aroused. I was with the troops and the officers of the army who met to receive his farewell. Rarely have human feelings been more moved than they were during this sad scene. What a spectacle! All hearts were stirred, all eyes dimmed with unshed tears betokening respect and tender affection. Never will I forget the last words he addressed to the companions in arms from whom he was going to part forever; * never from my memory will be erased the profound impression made by the imposing dignity of his countenance, the sound of his voice, altered by inner emotions which he endeavored to repress—and many other indescribable nuances.

6 Despite the rigors of winter, the inhabitants of the places through which he passed hastened to come to hail him and offer evidence of their esteem and gratitude; women, even children—everyone wanted to enjoy the pleasure of seeing the man whom they called the father of his country, on whom they heaped heavenly benedictions. It was a whole movement, or rather a widespread impulse throughout New Jersey. Surrounded by some of the inhabitants of Philadelphia who had come forth to greet him, he entered that town 'mid rejoicing, the clang of bells, and the boom of cannon.

Among the numerous eulogies he received during his public life, the ones addressed to him at this time by the groups and societies of this town are truly remarkable, not only for eloquence of style, but also for the

---

* Dear, esteemed comrades: I take leave of you with a heartfull of affection and gratitude. I depart, wishing sincerely that the rest of your lives may be as tranquil and as happy as have been glorious and honorable the days we have spent together. 27 November 1783.

great and interesting ideas they contain. It is difficult to imagine how he could put so much elegance and variety into his acknowledgments. Here are some extracts:

* "The American Philosophical Society, which for so long a time has been proud to count you among its disciples, is happy to have the opportunity of congratulating you on the return of peace, as well as on the occasion of your visit in this town. Foreseeing as we do, the happy influence of this great event on the aim of our institution, we hope that the arts and sciences, companions of liberty and virtue, in offering you just tribute of their praise and acclaim, will contribute toward handing down your name to remote posterity; may you enjoy unalterable happiness in the private life that you are going to lead, and may you add fresh lustre to the fame of your name. In this, you are certain to be accompanied by the love, affection, and gratitude of your country."

7 EXTRACT FROM WASHINGTON'S REPLY.

". . . . . If my heart makes an ardent and sincere wish, it is that of being the associate of virtuous and learned men; its wish is to see the sciences and arts continue to be prized, patronized among us; it is the wish of seeing them lighted with their salutary and beneficent lights, the entire stretch of this continent. I shall think often, be well assured, of the usefulness of your institution in the leisure of my retirement."

"This struggle, uncertain for so long, is finally over, thanks to your wisdom and to your courage. We are hence finally enjoying the blessings of peace and independence.**

"In the name of the various groups whom we represent today, we hail you with emotions of joy, affection, and the sincerest gratitude. Let others speak of your military exploits and compare them with those of ancient heroes of history. We regard you surrounded by a splendor and glory truly superior to that of Alexander and of Caesar. Neither ambition nor criminal folly of conquest led you into battle. You have never sought to advance your own interest on the ruins of your fellow-citizens; it is the voice of your country that has summoned you to its side. It is the love of liberty which has made you take up arms and those arms have been consecrated by religion, law, and humanity. The purest principles have guided your conduct and true piety has evoked heavenly protection over your endeavors.

"The causes of truth and knowledge were keenly interested in the cause you have defended with so much prudence and glory; our liberty is established and confirmed; the sciences will flourish, true philosophy will enlighten us—a new happiness appears for mankind.

"You leave your military career 'mid the acclamations of a grateful people. What finer triumph have moderation and victory merited! May your example, as well as the lessons you have taught us,*** never be for-

* Address of the American Philosophical Society in Philadelphia December 9, 1783.
** Extract from the address of the clergy, lawyers, and doctors of Philadelphia, December 13, 1783.
*** The letter which he made public at New-Bourg June 11, 1783.

gotten. Your country will never lose sight of you and never cease being interested in your happiness. It asks that in your retirement you continue to love and enlighten us.

"The learned professions in particular will always consider you as their protector and friend, and will always remember with the tenderest gratitude the man who, protected by heaven, has just opened a new career of happiness and peace and founded a new era whence date the progress of the sciences and arts."

EXTRACT FROM HIS REPLY

".... Wishing to deserve the esteem of my fellow citizens, that gentle reward of so many solicitudes and services, I confess that the good opinion of virtuous, enlightened men flatters and touches me infinitely. If I have detested the craze of ambition and conquest, if the purest principles have guided my actions, if the object of war and the manner in which it is conducted have been just and in conformance with humanitarian laws, may mankind claim no merit for it! Let us, instead, attribute the glory and success of this happy event to a much higher source. To this, before all else: the principle of all things that we owe the re-establishment of our invaded rights, the confirmation of our independence, the protection of virtue, of philosophy, and of literature, the flourishing state of arts and sciences; and finally the new arena of prosperity and peace which presents itself to mankind.

"Yes! My public and military life is over. Yes, I confess, it is with inexpressible pleasure that I retire to the peaceful paths of the life of a simple citizen. But the happiness of my country will always be the dearest object of my desires. Never will I forget how useful learned societies and learned men are to mankind; how much knowledge and enlightenment and the sciences teach us to enjoy the preservation of liberty; and finally, how much they will contribute some day to the tranquility and glory of this new Union."

8　Of all the periods in the life of General Washington, the one when he resigned his commission as Chief of the Union * is one of the most glorious and most widely known. The keen interest aroused by that scene, vivid even in later times, the idea that this act constituted the closing of the bloody battle, for the price of which these colonies had become independent States; the scene when the man who, 8 years before, had received from the same Congress absolute military authority which he had never abused, was soon to appear before Congress to return to it this authority and to retire to private life, for whose pleasures we know he had long been yearning; the great number of spectators with whom the meeting room was filled; the profound silence that reigned there; the many manifestations of sadness and admiration which suddenly appeared as he entered; the calm and dignity of his countenance, his great stature; the bearing of the aides-de-camp by whom he was surrounded;

---

* At Annapolis, December 23, 1783.

the noble simplicity of his speech, worthy of antiquity * the eloquent and always touching speech of the president—** such were the chief circumstances that impressed the minds of spectators and left them with lasting impressions.

A short time following his return to his plantation, General Washington devoted his time to projects that were extremely useful to his country; among others, that of improving navigation on the Potowmack, obstructed by considerable falls, located at some distance from Alexandria. After carefully studying these major obstacles and being convinced of the possibility of overcoming them, he proposed to his fellow-citizens the plan of contributing 1,500,000 Fr, to be divided into 500 shares. As soon as subscriptions were made, the two bordering States of Virginia and Maryland gave the subscribers a charter of corporation and privilege

* "Mr. President, the great events with which I was charged through my commission, having been accomplished, I have the honor of offering Congress my sincerest congratulations and of presenting myself before it in order to return to it the command with which it charged me, and to seek at the same time permission to retire from the service of my country.

"Happy to witness our independence, confirmed, and the inhabitants of these States become a respected nation, I resign with joy a commission which was accepted only with misgivings and mistrust. This mistrust in my talents has fortunately been encouraged by the righteousness of the cause, by the cooperation of the supreme power of the Union, as well as by Heavenly protection.

"The successes of the war have justified our highest hopes, and my deep gratitude to Providence from whom I have received so many favors, and toward my compatriots who have seconded me so powerfully, increases as I weigh the importance of the great dispute which has just been terminated.

"In setting before you the infinite obligations that I owe to the bravery and to the leadership of the army, I would betray my dearest sentiments, if I were to forget to speak to you of essential services and of the rare merit of the officers who were assigned to me in the course of the war. The choice I made of them could not have been happier. Permit me, too, Mr. President, to commend to you all those who have continued their service to this day; they are worthy of all the attention and all the protection of Congress.

"I regard as an indispensable duty the termination of the last chapter of my public life, in commending the interests of our beloved country to the protection of the Almighty, and also those who are the leaders of the country, to His holy vigil.

"Having accomplished the task imposed on me, I depart from this great hall, taking leave of this august body, under whose orders I have so long acted. Receive herewith my commission. I resign my service to public life."

** "Sir, the United States receives with the keenest emotions, the solemn resignation from the authority under which you have led its troops with so much wisdom and success, in the course of this long and perilous war. Summoned by your country to the defense of its invaded rights, you assumed this sacred duty before your country had formed any alliances, before it had established a treasury and a government. You led this great struggle with wisdom and courage, without ever having invaded the rights of civil authority, and in the very midst of tragedies and disasters.

"Your fellow-citizens, stimulated by the love and confidence you had inspired in them, put forth under your orders, their talents, their military genius, and have assigned their reputation to posterity. You have persevered, without ever dispairing of the public cause, until the time when the United States, having become the ally of a king and of a generous nation, had the good fortune, under providence's auspices, to end the war with honor and to obtain security and independence. We accept your congratulations over this happy event with joy and sincerity. After defending the standard of liberty on this new hemisphere, after teaching a memorable lesson to the oppressed and oppressor, you are retiring from the great theatre of public affairs with the blessings of your fellow-citizens. But the glory of your virtues will not end with your military command; it will extend to the most remote places.

"Like you, we commend the interests of our beloved country to the protection of the Almighty, we beg Him to inspire the hearts and the minds of the inhabitants of these States to profit by the favorable opportunity that divine providence offers them, to become a happy and respectable nation.

"And as for you, we address our most fervent prayers to Providence that the days of our lives, that are also dear to us, may become the object of its special vigil and that these same days will be as happy as they have been until now filled with glory and that He deign to grant you His eternal reward."

of perpetual toll; from their meeting the General was elected president of this great and useful association.

These two canals are finished. The first is 1,320 toises long and has 4 canal locks from 10 to 11 feet, at a pitch of 75. The second, 2,200 toises, with 10 locks, has a pitch of 28 toises, including the height of the cataract, which is 13 toises. Above the first they have erected a wooden bridge, whose span is 120 feet. It was constructed by the same man (John Coxe) to whose genius—without the aid of education—Ireland and some of these States owe the execution of a number of bridges which have earned public acclaim. What would this man have accomplished if, from his early years, he could have been instructed in the great schools of Europe!

The same association is planning to undertake removal of obstacles at the mouth of the Cumberland, as well as in the neighborhood of the Shawanèse-Fields, 200 miles from Alexandria: then from this coastal town, although it is located 400 miles from the Chesapeake capes, one will easily be able to transport merchandise during four months of the year, as far as 35 or 40 miles from one of the branches of the Monongahéla (the Cheat) which empties into the Ohio or Beautiful river; an advantage of greatest importance, since with the exception of this portage, the Potowmack will open communication with the trans-Alléghény country; and since everything is relative, this obstacle is nothing, compared with the immense extent of interior navigation in this vast region.

The perfection of navigation on the Skénando is also one of the objectives indicated in the charter of incorporation with which this same association is to devote itself.

9　After experiencing for 4 years the inconveniences that resulted from the weakness of the confederation, and after seeing Congress make futile efforts to bring some remedies to it, the States, frightened at the progress of anarchy which began to devour this country, determined, in 1786, to send deputies to Annapolis; the following year they met in Annapolis, charged with proposing a new system of Union; a new form of government that might maintain domestic tranquility, establish justice, and promote the general welfare. General Washington was elected one of the three deputies from Virginia. The first time the members of this convention met in Philadelphia * they were going to choose as President the venerable Franklin, then Governor of Pensylvania and member of this same convention; the latter, after reminding them of his long service and his great age (he was then 82), turned his eyes toward the General, saying to the members:

"There is the one who is to fill the duties of the presidency." At the unanimous voice of consent, this worthy old gentleman took him by the hand and settled him in the armchair.

Washington, foreseeing the danger of permitting publicity of their proceedings, proposed and obtained promise of inviolable secrecy until their task was accomplished. Happy thought! thousand upon thousand

* May 12, 1787.

times happy thought, to which united America perhaps owes the wise Government that regulates it today.

When one considers the effervescence of peoples' minds of that time, the diversity of interests of these colonies, suddenly become sovereign, independent States, the new Federal Government, despite its imperfections (why wouldn't it have some, since it is the work of men?) must appear a masterpiece of reason and its acceptance a miraculous, unexpected event. Most assuredly, if the proceedings of the Convention had been made public, the agents of European powers, the men among Americans who dreamed only of Athenian democracy, those whose personal passions and interests made the return of justice and order reprehensible, the Convention would never have completed its important task and the union of these States would never have taken place. On what, then, do the destinies of individuals, nations, and empires hang? In reading the letter which the General wrote from his camp at New-Bourg to the 13 States, one recalls all these circumstances and it is difficult not to admire once more the prophetic sagacity, the profound wisdom of this great man.

10 For 4 years he had been busy with the cares of agriculture; often visited by Europeans, as well as by the most distinguished persons on the continent, he had been enjoying on his beautiful estate at Mount Vernon the pleasures of retirement and repose, when he received the official news of his election to the presidency of the new Government (April 3, 1789). Although extremely flattered by such splendid evidence of esteem and confidence on the part of the electors of the continent, he left his home only with keen regret. His replies to the addresses made in his honor on this occasion by all the public organizations, by the private and religious societies; those he made to his friends * bear witness to the fact that he embarked anew on the stormy sea of public life only with fear and doubt; and indeed, was there anything fine and pure that his glory and reputation lacked? He was well removed from foreseeing the hardships and worries that the new Government would bring him—that new Government of a nation to the generous aid of which America owed in part her very emancipation. Among the great number of addresses that were made in his honor, posterity will not read without sadness the one to his

---

* Here is what he wrote me in response to my letter of congratulations.

Mt. Vernon........April 10, 1789.

....

A combination of circumstances, a series of events that I was quite far from predicting, have rendered indispensable the necessity in which I find myself embarking a second time on the stormy sea of public affairs. I do not need to tell you how contrary this resolution is to my dearest desires and inclinations; my friends, all those who know me, are, I hope, intimately convinced of this. If I accept the presidency of the United States, it is with the purest intentions. I call on the Great Scrutinizer who alone knows what is in our hearts; He knows whether any object, however flattering one might imagine, whether the lure of any advantage, however tempting it might be, finally the fever for fame, however easily it might be gained, would ever have made me decide at my age and in my station to abandon the peaceful paths of private life. Most assuredly not: I know happiness' worth too well. But if the inhabitants of these States believe that my services can still be useful to public welfare, I offer these services to them, since they seek them. This thought alone can compensate for the many sacrifices that I shall make in putting behind me my home and abandoning my retirement..............etc., etc...."

good neighbors, in the town of Alexandria, as well as the fine and touching response they made to him. As to the details of the receptions given to him, in so many of the towns he passed through en route to New York, where the new Congress was then sitting, those receptions of his inauguration of which I was witness, are a matter of historical record. Arriving the 22nd day of April 1789, he was inaugurated the 30th of the same month.

11 Yearning a long time for the peace and tranquility of which his health was in the greatest need, he informed the public as early as the month of October 1796 of the resolution he had taken to return to private life, as soon as his term of office expired. The day after this, March 4, 1797, saw the illustrious Washington become for the second time a simple, private citizen, and John Adams, one of the most learned men on the continent, and for 8 years Vice-President of the United States, elected to the supreme office of the Union. The presence of the General, mingling in the crowd of spectators, added a great deal of interest to the ceremony of that installation which, nevertheless, was as free from pomp and circumstance as was that of the archontes of Athens of yore.

Some time later, after he had retired to his home, a chain of circumstances having arisen, requiring the United States to prepare for war, he was named Lieutenant-General of the troops and militias which were to be activated; but these war clouds, having happily dispersed, his retirement was scarcely disturbed at all. Although considerably aged by the anxieties and fatigues of the war that had lasted 8 years and that had not always gone well, in addition to the labors of administration, and the great changes that had taken place in Europe, making his last years thorny and difficult, he is still riding his horse, tending his fields, and surveying his great plantation.

In the shadow of the glory that he so justly deserves, may the sunset years of a life, illustrious through so many useful deeds, be as happy as have been glorious the years he dedicated to establishing and affirming the liberty and independence of his country.

In order to prove that this praise and these details are but a feeble echo of public opinion, I thought I should include here the inscription which the Legislative body of Virginia ordered engraved on the pedestal of the statue it commissioned December 17, 1781, and which, since that time, has been executed by the famous French sculptor, Houdon; this, in addition to the address by a representative of the town of Alexandria and the response he made to the speech.

The general Assembly of the republic of Virginia had this statue erected "as a monument of affection and gratitude to George Washington who, uniting to the qualities and talents of heroes, the virtues of a citizen, devoting himself to establishing the liberty of his country, rendered his name dear to his fellow-citizens and gave to the world an immortal example of true glory."

Address of the Mayor and municipal magistrates of the town of Alexandria, presented to George Washington the day before his departure for New-York, then the seat of Government where he was to be inaugurated President of the United States.

"The voice of your country calls you again! In order to achieve its aims and fulfill its hopes, it needs once more the employ of your talents and your virtues. No, it is not without a mixture of regret and admiration that we see you on the eve of abandoning the cares of an enlightened farming, as well as the peace of domestic life, to the detriment of your personal happiness, and this, at a time of life when nature prescribes and justifies the choice of calm and peace.

"We shall not speak to you today of the glory you have so justly acquired, nor of the profound recognition earned by the long and arduous services you have rendered to these States which have become, through your valor and wisdom, free and independent. We shall not speak to you of the honor, until now unsurpassed, of the unanimous vote of 3,000,000 men who elect you to the supreme office; nor, finally, of that unselfish devotion, that enlightened patriotism which, for so many years, has directed your leadership. Your neighbors and friends, filled at this time with endeavors less brilliant, it is true, but no less dear to their hearts, offer you their respectful homage and their tender farewells.

"Must you, the first and foremost of our citizens be so far from us? Must our old people lose the leading light of their societies; our youth, its model; our farming the most useful and enlightened improver; our trade, its protector; our college, its founder; our Indians their benefactor and their father? Finally, must the inland navigation on the Potowmack proven possible by your enlightenment, and already begun through your efforts—must it, too, watch you from afar, you, its promotor, its support? Take leave of us, dear and great man; take leave, since you are summoned to contribute to the happiness of a grateful people: it will be doubly grateful, we are certain, on reflecting over the new sacrifice that you are about to make for it. From the deepest part of our hearts, we commend you to the protection of the great Being from whom all human events emanate.

"After finishing the memorable work for which you are destined by universal providence, may it bring back to us the best among men and the most cherished of our citizens."

In public meeting in the name of the corporation and inhabitants of the town of Alexandria,   David Ramsay, Mayor
April 16, 1789

Response:

"Gentlemen, although I cannot hide them, I do not know how to express the heart-rending and sad feelings and disturbances that have assailed me at the time when I had to decide whether I would accept or reject the supreme presidency of the United States. The unanimity of vote, the desire of my friends, the wish, even, of those who do not entirely approve of the new constitution—finally the hope of becoming the feeble spokesman to conciliate, to unite the opinions of my fellow-citizens; such are the great and powerful reasons that made me decide to accept the presidency.

"Those who know me—and you, my good neighbors, more even than the other inhabitants of Virginia—you must know how devoted am I to farming, how much do I love the sweet, peaceful life of the country. Be assured of it: the intimate conviction of a sacred duty, to which it seems

I am summoned, is the only human consideration which could have revoked the decision I made a long time ago not to mingle in public affairs. Indeed, at my age and station, what advantages can I hope for in setting out again on this uncertain and so often surging ocean?

"I do not need recourse to any public declarations to convince you of the sincerity of my attachment, and the keen interest that I take in the prosperity of your young town, as well as everything touching you. Born in this region, my entire life is known to you; the deeds with which my life has been filled will become, I hope, pledges, guarantees of my future conduct—more satisfactory and more secure than anything I could say.

"I thank you for the feelings of affection expressed in your moving tribute to me: I confess, however, that this last proof of interest and friendship renews the deep regrets I feel at this time, when I am obliged to take leave of you, of my family and to abandon all the charms of private life.

"I finish by entrusting myself, as well as you, worthy magistrates, and you, inhabitants of Alexandria, to the protection of the Almighty Being; after an absence of seven years spent in the midst of dangers, difficulties, and worries of war, He brought me back to my home at the end of 1783.

"Now, forced by the inadequacy of my words, I abandon to the eloquence of silence, that of the many emotions stirring within me.

"Dear and good neighbors, receive my tender farewells."
Mt. Vernon, April 17, 1789.

George Washington

NOTES TO VOLUME ONE

CHAPTER I

1   COLONEL CRAWGAN. Employed for a long time by the English Government in what was then called the Department of Indian Affairs: few Europeans knew the Indians better, nor were more highly thought of by them; few people made more efforts to encourage them to cultivate the land and to open their eyes to the dangers of drunkenness. What a pity he did not record the countless observations that his long journeys had permitted him to make on botany, natural history and geography! They would have been, and would now be, tremendously interesting, although the interior of the continent is better known today than it was then.

2   SAGUENAY. A good-sized river in lower Canada, whose junction with the St. Lawrence, 150 miles below Quebec, is known as Tadoussac: it is here where the great fishing in the river begins. The source of this river is lake Mistassing, formed by the union of the waters which water this dismal region, once the favorite haunt of beavers. In going up the Saguenay, one is astonished that under a latitude of 48 degrees 30 seconds, the soil is as fruitless and sterile, the climate as humid and cold, and the forests composed only of spruce, birch, and hemlock. On the bleak banks of this river, and on the shores of the lake from which it comes, once lived the Mistassing nation, now extinct, having left only its name to this lake, as well as another which is much larger, whose waters empty into the southern part of Hudson Bay, not far from Fort Rupert.

3 CREEK OR MUSCOGULGÉ CONFEDERATION. The largest known to this continent. After the annihilation of the Natchée nation, whose allies the Creeks were, they made war on the Florida tribes, and, like the Romans, they had the wisdom to incorporate the vanquished among them. After subjugating their neighbors, they founded what one might call a Power. It has become much more formidable, since the time when they learned the value of land and farming, established a council, and chose chiefs who know how to maintain peace and good order, and how to prevent, as much as possible, the introduction of intoxicating liquors. Of all the nations of this hemisphere, the Muscogulgé is incontestably the most civilized and the most interesting to know. Their towns, such as Uche, Apalachicola (capital), Talasse, Coolome, etc., are laid out with a fair degree of regularity: Uché has more than fifteen hundred inhabitants: the houses are fine frame structures, covered with shingles. Everything about them suggests comfort, cleanliness, and happiness. They have a national religion which appears to spring from the ancient Natchées, just as their dances, games, and regular meetings have. Their womenfolk enjoy much greater consideration than among the Indians of the north; in general, they are clean, skillful, economical: they have fine features and sparkling eyes.

In this land three absolutely distinct languages are spoken, and each person is invincibly attached to his own. The first, I am told, is the Natchées; the second, the Floridas, and the third, the Creek or Seminole language.

It is by this name that the tribes inhabiting the coastal section of the two Floridas are known; as they are less advanced in culture and civilization than their elders, people cross their land only with precaution. Among the superior Creeks, however, travelers are always certain of being received and treated like friends, not for a few days, but for as much time as they wish to stay with them. Nothing is more interesting to see than the peace, plenty, and gaiety that reign there. A young man having neither family, friends, nor fortune and whom chance might lead to them, if he were skilled in hunting, fishing, and the cultivation of corn, would soon be tempted to take a wife and settle down. Surrounded by vast forests, filled with bears, roe, geese, etc., and lakes filled with fish, or savannahs on which they raise as many horses and cattle as they wish, fertile fields, planted with orange trees, fig trees, and other fruit trees, 'neath a mild and temperate climate, they lead a much happier and more independent life than if they were more advanced in civilization.

On the other hand, they have reason to fear the danger of proximity to the whites, the negative influence of their depraved customs, the often immoral and shameful conduct of the traders living among them; and in a word, the bad effect that their craving for European merchandise will eventually have on them. Their confederation is composed of more than sixty towns, villages or tribes, whose population, they say, is nearly twenty thousand.

4 POOHATANS. This confederation, once composed of thirty tribes, occupied all of southern Virginia, that is to say, the region included between the shores of the sea and the first falls. The small nations who inhabited the region between these first heights as far as the great mountains, implacable enemies of coastal tribes, were obliged to unite their forces to resist, not only the Poohatans, but another band, no less formidable, which occupied the entire chain of the Alléghénies, which had for enemies the most remote nations. These hordes were in a continual state of tension or resistance, a state which in Europe as well as here seems to be natural to man. If these tribes had had historiographers, the pages of their history would have presented in miniature the same scenes as those of the great Asiatic and European nations.

The tongues of these various confederated nations were so different that they needed interpreters every time they had any negotiations with one another. What a pity that neither the colonial Government, nor any individual ever thought to make a study of them! Perhaps such a study and comparison of them would have helped us understand whether the difference in their tongues stemmed from their early antiquity, or whether, on the contrary, it indicated the recent arrival of these nations in this part of the continent.

Sixty years after the white man's arrival in Virginia, half of these tribes, having become victims of the new scourges which the white men introduced among them (scarlet fever and intoxicating liquors), no longer existed. What was left of the second and third confederation, known as the Tuscaroras, united in 1712 with the Mohawk league, their former enemy, and this last group association concluded their history. The Indians who inhabited the counties today known as lower Pennsylvania were in the same state of warfare against their neighbors of the Susquehannah, at the time of William Penn's arrival. What still remained of the Lénopys and their confederates, former owners of the lands included between the mountains of Kittatiny and the sea, was to be exterminated, when this famous founder and his peace-loving companions disembarked at the very place where Philadelphia today stands. The curiosity excited by such an extraordinary event mitigated the fury of these tigers: in making presents to the oppressors and the oppressed, in giving them clothes and provisions, it was not long before he made himself loved and respected by them. These Indians did not know what to think of the sudden arrival among them of these white and bearded men, nor of the great vessels that had brought them, nor even what name to give them: without the aid of arms, without violence, by the sole exercise of gentleness, justice, and steadfastness, this man succeeded in disarming them, and in making them know the fine qualities of peace; and beginning with the very following summer, the two nations cultivated potato and corn together. After buying from them the land he needed for his colony, William Penn set forth the laws, established the Government to whose wisdom Pennsylvania owed its astonishing prosperity.

Such were the happy auspices under whose influence he founded this province in the month of October 1682.

The justice and peace of his administration, as well as the exemplary conduct of his colonists with the Indians for a great number of years, inspired in them such a degree of esteem and confidence, that in one of their invasions on the frontiers of Virginia, scarcely knowing the boundaries of these two colonies, they were about to burn the houses and massacre the inhabitants of northern Pennsylvania, when an officer of the militia, having had the presence of mind to represent to them that they were the sons of Onas,* to whom these lands had been sold by their ancestors, suddenly recalling the significance of these words, as well as their ancient respect for the memory of this founder, and for the name they had given him forty years before, they extinguished their torches, and renounced their cruel enterprise.

Today in Virginia only feeble traces of these ancient Poohatan tribes remain: the peace, quiet, cultivation of fertile fields has not been able to delay their annihilation. That is what is impossible to understand, unless one assumes that these races are different from the Old World's, and that, like wolves, they were created only to inhabit the forests. Everywhere the same secret and powerful causes have produced the same effects, except among the Muscogulgés. Not a Poohatan, Pamonky, or Nottoway family has resisted the force of this amazing destiny; not one family did increase by cultivating its own fields, for whose protection the Government had passed laws, naming men whose responsibility it was to listen to and adjust their complaints. The last individual who spoke pure Poohatan died twenty years ago on the banks of the Pamonky.

5   ILLINOIS COUNTRY. This land, located on both banks of the Mississippi 400 leagues from the sea, was a Canadian colony, although seven hundred leagues from Quebec. It extends from the junction of the Ohio, to that of the Missouri, over a space of seventy-five to eighty leagues. There are few regions in the land that have been more favored by nature. Its imposing location in the middle of the continent, its communications with the Gulf of Mexico, the great lakes, the Missouri and northern Louisiana, the fertility of the soil, the natural prairies with which it is intersected, the beauty of the forests, the high banks of the river, a mild and healthful climate protected from the rigors of winter; such are the principal advantages enjoyed by this beautiful land. What activity, what movement one will see there some day when from far off regions, the products of culture and industry will be brought there by inland navigation, to be transported to New Orleans in vessels that will draw more water.

Considering that this colony was founded in the last century, one is astonished at the little progress it has made. At the time of the conquest of this region by the American, General Clark, there were scarcely three thousand white men on the two banks of the Mississippi, and something

---

* Name which they gave to William Penn shortly after his arrival.

no less extraordinary! these colonists had never received titles from the seminary of Saint Sulpice, to whom this land had been granted by Louis XIV. Located in the middle of the continent, living in peace and abundance, having no neighbors other than a few scattered traces of Indian tribes, having sunk to the lowest point of degradation, they never suspected that in order to own lands and pass them on to their children, they would need a survey, contracts, registration, etc. The boundaries of their land increased or decreased at the dictates of their fancy, or rather, according to their industry and their needs. This curious oblivion, stemming no doubt from the ignorance of their ancestors, or their remoteness from the mother country, might have succeeded in exposing them to the bickerings and quarrels with the new nation that had just seized their land, if the justice of Congress had not come to their rescue. As soon as it was informed of this strange circumstance, not only did Congress confirm everything that each person wished to call his possession, but added to it a gift of land whose amount was proportionate to the number of members in each family. Despite the generosity of this procedure, which must have given them a high idea of the justice of the Government of the United States, almost all these Canadian families were settled in Missire, Sainte-Geneviève, Pancore (Saint-Louis) on the west branch of the Mississippi. They say that this procedure was caused by the fear of losing their Negroes, as well as by the great remoteness they felt toward the laws, customs, and above all the religion of the Americans; they preferred the Spanish religion and rule.

The land of the Illinois has long furnished flour, bacon, hams, etc., and even wine to the inhabitants of New Orleans. They say that, in 1745, 400 casks of wines were sent off. Impressed by the great quantity of grapes produced every year from the vines which everywhere grow spontaneously, some of the colonists tried to make wine from them and succeeded: no doubt they would have succeeded in making an even better quality wine had they thought of making regular vineyards from this fine wildstock or if they had grafted them with the young Madeira or European plant. On almost all the banks and islands of the Mississippi and the Ohio, one notices some vines whose vegetative growth seems quite extraordinary; some envelop with their boughs the bushes and shrubs in their way; others, with the aid of branches, rise above the summit of the highest trees. I have seen some near Louisville whose height is estimated at 80 feet, and whose grapes could have made a whole cask of wine. Three species of these grapes are known: the first grows on wet ground; the second on high land; and the third, on the southern slope of mountains. Perhaps in the course of time, people will speak of wines from Missire, Pancore, Illinois, Kentukey, etc., as people speak today of wines from Bordeaux, Burgundy, or Champagne.

Two companies have obtained from the federal Government concession of a great quantity of land in this beautiful country which in a few years will be filled with activity and inhabitants. To judge by the eagerness with which the small landowners of coastal states sell their property, in order to venture forth to found new settlements five hundred leagues from their country, one would think that the population of these states has reached its limit; that is very far from the case. It is to that desire to be even better, when one is passably good (a ceaselessly agitating illusion, and so often deceiving), that is due the great number of these little colonies, scattered like dots over the vast surface of the United States; in a short span of time, these will become flourishing regions. After having lost them from sight for a few years, suddenly one hears talk of their number and of the extent of their clearings.

Today no one knows the names of the different tribes of which the confederation of Wheylenis was composed: on the edge of the Kaskaskia, Kahokia, and Illinois rivers only a few families remain: they have fallen into the lowest abyss of brutality: they can scarcely summon themselves to hunt enough to procure provisions and brandy. In living among the white men, these Indians have become liars, cheats, thieves, and most assuredly the most lowly of any men I have ever known.

6 NATIONS OF THE GREAT LAKES AND THE OHIO. The largest are the Chippaway, Winébago, Outagamy, who have settled on the banks and rivers around Green Bay; the Kikapoos, Menomonies, Pootooatamys on Lake Michigan; the Outawas, Missisagés on the Huron; the Delawares, Wyandots, Cagnawagas, Shawaneses, Mingots, Oyatanons on Lake Erie, the Ohio, and the Wabash River. These nations, once mighty and powerful, vanquished by the dual poison of scarlet fever and intoxicating liquors, are rapidly heading toward annihilation. The last war (in 1791), in which the English involved them under pretext of preventing the establishment of American colonies in northwest Ohio, was disastrous for them by virtue of the fact that it cost them the lives of their bravest warriors, and the destruction of their principal villages. And now at long last they are enjoying the sweet benefits of peace; the limits of their lands are fixed; the Government has built forts, passed laws to prevent invasions, injustices, and quarrels. But a new danger is menacing them; it is the proximity of some colonists who are soon to settle on lands granted them by the treaty made with them. Closer to the Europeans than they have ever been before, they will easily obtain from them intoxicating liquors, and will be more exposed to smallpox, a disease which would be as disastrous for them as the plague is for us. Had they forgotten their rivalries and their national hatreds thirty years ago, they might have united their forces, with the Cherokées and the Creeks, and it is probable that the progress of the European colonies would have been considerably retarded.

The decadence of these nations has been much more rapid since the conquest of Canada. Masters of the entire northern part of the continent, the English have brought their trade to great distances, and are making known to all these nations the attraction of European merchandise and the even more pernicious one of intoxicating liquors. In order to get a

good idea of the extent of these important discoveries, one must see the
fine maps of Arrow-Smith, published in London in 1796. On them are
traced the voyages of Hearne, who, having left from Hudson Bay for a
northwesterly destination, arrived at the sea by following the course of
a river called the Copper River; even more important are those of
Mackenzie, who, from Lake Superior went to Cook River, or rather Cook
Gulf, under the 60th parallel of latitude, whence an English vessel, loaded
with furs, had just set sail for Canton. This journey of from 800 to 900
leagues, across vast and inhospitable regions, is perhaps one of the boldest
and most extraordinary that has ever been made on earth.

7 MOHAWK NATION. Once considered the most powerful of the middle
states, and chief of a confederation long known under this name, composed of tribes or nations such as the Onondagas, Oneidas, Cayugas, and
Seneccas. At the time of the arrival in 1614 of the first Dutch, at what is
today called New York, this confederation had just subjugated the
Wabingas, Mohégans, Manhattans, Méhicanders, etc., coastal and fish-
eating tribes. It had already reached its zenith of power, for it numbered
10,000 warriors. These confederated nations were living on the banks
of the Mohawk river, the upper Susquehannah, as well as the banks of
rivers and little lakes emptying into Lake Ontario.

The alliance which the Dutch made with them, and which their successors, the English, carefully maintained until the eve of the Revolution,
contributed a great deal toward facilitating the beginnings of this fine
Colony and was one of the principal causes to retard for a long time
the progress of the Colony which the French founded at the same time in
Canada. This national jealousy, which in Europe has occasioned such
long and frequent wars, was the cause of all the tragedies which this
little colony experienced during its infancy. Less numerous, more remote
from the sea, from which it was separated by ice for six months of the
year, one cannot conceive *how* it could have resisted the invasions and
attacks of this powerful league. In the pages of history, one must see
the frequent attacks which these brave colonists had to weather, their
indefatigable perseverance and their resources. Men much less patient
and less disciplined would have succumbed and Canada would then have
become an English colony.

Ah! if from the very beginning, a less exclusive religion, a government like that of Massachussetts or Pensylvanie, for example, might
have been given to this land, never would the English fleet have gone up
the Saint-Lawrence River, never would General Amherst have come down
it from Katarakouy to Montreal, because, instead of 90,000 inhabitants
which it boasted at the time of the conquest, there would have been
400,000. But unfortunately from the origin of this colony, they wished,
just as the people of Arcadia,* that no tree be uprooted, no child be
procreated except by Roman Catholics; just as if the sun and the dews
might not fertilize cleared fields, planted by Lutheran or Calvinistic
hands!

* Today New Scotland (Nova Scotia).

The Mohawks, influenced by their former attachment for the English, followed them to Canada, where they say their number has considerably diminished; and their land is covered with dwellings and cultivated fields. Of their confederates, only Oneida, Cayuga, Onondaga, Tuscarora, and Sennecca families remain; they have recently sold their lands, with the exception of some reserves, to the Government of New-York. Thanks to the zeal of missionaries, books in their tongues and in the Nattick tongue have been printed, also several books on religion and prayer: I have even seen some grammar books.

8 BUFFALOES OF THE PLAINS (SAVANNAHS). Before the white men had crossed the Alléghénys, and founded the beautiful colonies of Ténézée, Kentukey, Cumberland, Washington, etc., large herds of buffaloes or bison grazed on the natural prairies of these vast regions, and had increased prodigiously; but for several years now, none have been seen: a great number have been destroyed, and the others, fleeing such a redoubtable enemy, have crossed the Mississippi, and are rejoining their buffalo brethren in the vast grassy plains which stretch from the west bank of this river to unknown distances. Considering the number of these bisons, the ease of coming upon them and slaying them, one can scarcely imagine how in the course of centuries it never occurred to the Indians to domesticate the young animals, fence in some acres of these natural prairies to raise them, and, little by little, tame them. It is probable that the stock of European cattle originally came from bison like these, which the early societies tamed. What inappreciable advantages these American Indian nations would have derived from these attempts which would have gradually brought them to farming! From the fact that such a simple idea, a project so easy to execute never occurred to them, is one not to conclude that their intellectual potential is inferior to that of the European and Asiatic nations?

9 IRON ORE. At a little distance underground and often even at the surface of the natural prairies of New-Jersey and Pensylvanie, one finds this ore (known as bog ore), weighing from 25 to 100 pounds. In examining it carefully, one would think it had been exposed to fire. I know some bloomeries, or small forges in which only this ore is found. They say it is harder than that kind which is found in probing the mountains.

10 WILD RICE. It grows on the shores of Lakes Ontario and Michigan, on the little lake of the Winebagos, as well as on the banks of the rivers that empty their waters there; the Canadians know it as wild oats, the Americans know it as wild rice. It is extremely nourishing, and grows in certain regions in such abundance that the Indians gather good-sized harvests of it; they bundle handfuls of the stalks; each family makes its mark, cutting them at water level when their maturity is reached, and carrying them off in its canoe.

This grain has become the principal nourishment of the Outagamis, Menomonis, and Winébago who inhabit the region included between the west shore of Lake Michigan and the Mississippi River. After experiencing advantages and harvests for so many years, it is inconceivable that

the desire to augment them and that of obtaining a more assured livelihood has not made them decide to plant them in more convenient places,
and, imitating nature, make them grow in water. The indifference, or
rather blindness of the other nations, who, for centuries have heard
this grain discussed, without seeking any means of "domesticating" it,
seems even more inconceivable to me, and proves what I have already suggested: the inferiority of their intelligence.

11   THE DECAY OF THE NATTICK AND PECOD NATIONS. When
one thinks of the obstacles of all kinds which the colonists of the four
northern States (once known as New England) had in vanquishing during the infancy of their early settlements, one is astonished that they
were able to overcome them; one is no less astonished when considering
that their perseverance and their industry have since become the model
for the continent. For how many years did they have to struggle against
the stubborn resistance of the Indians who never ceased harassing them.
Like the inhabitants of Canada, never did they venture into the fields
without attaching their guns to their plows; law commanded them to fetch
them to church, where, seizing the moment of their prayers, the Indians
would come to attack them.

From this long state of warfare came this great number of sites,
known on the map as towns, which were once merely palisaded enclosures,
scattered over the farms in the vicinity, where the colonists would take
refuge at the first alarm signal. Perhaps, even, these four colonies might
have succumbed, in 1668, to the efforts of the coalition of all the neighboring nations, if they had not united and entrusted their interests to a
Congress in which they vested dictatorial power. But Metacomet, chief
of this formidable coalition, was betrayed early the second year. The
death of this young hero, worthy of a better fate, brought on so many
tribal divisions and defeats, that these warriors did not accept the terms
of the peace offered them: one part withdrew to the interior of the continent; they persuaded another to settle at Chappoquidick, Nattick, Suck-
iang, Nantuket, etc., where they hoped that with the help of religion
and example these men would finally learn to cultivate the lands they
had reserved, and like the white men, they would multiply in the bosom
of abundance and peace.

These plans, these hopes, inspired by love of justice and humanity,
vanished after a few years; in ceasing to be hunters, they became in-
dolent, lazy, numb to the needle of desires and emulation, and as in the
woods, deaf to the advice of foresight.

Of so many families who became farmers, not one reached the point
of ease; all of them disintegrated, without anyone ever knowing why;
while the number of whites increased beyond anything that had ever been
seen in modern times. The same secret causes have produced the same
effects, in Jersey, Pensylvanie, Virginia, wherever people tried to bring
them together on their own lands. In 1763, they still counted nearly 800
Indians dwelling in the state of New-York: today there exist perhaps no
more than 50.

12 RAISE THEIR WIGWAMS ELSEWHERE. Whether it stems from a climatic factor or from some difference in their constitution, the northern nations are of a more wandering disposition, and much less attached to the places of their birth than are the nations of Georgia or of Florida. Although most of their villages are favorably situated on the banks of navigable rivers, and near alluvial lands, they consider their dwelling—especially the youth, self-styled soldiers—as the tent under which they camp. An epidemic, wretched dreams, the arrival of the bees in nearby trees, these among others are reasons that make them decide to leave their villages to raise their wigwams elsewhere.

One must admit, men who often have no belongings other than their bearskins, their kettle, and their rifle, and who find birch bark everywhere, can easily change dwelling place. Yet they are sometimes restrained by their respect for places long consecrated to the tombs of their fathers; the idea that after they abandon their village the plow of the white man will expose to the rain and dew these venerable remains sometimes prevents their emigration: this thought is one of the most crushing that confronts them. But since the neighboring tribes of the frontiers have lost, by example and association with the white men, these primitive differences which still distinguish the nations of the great lakes; since the irresistible bait of intoxicating liquors, they have been led to the most shameful moral depravity; these customs, these distinctive traits which once made them respectable to the observer, have entirely disappeared.

They are no longer the same men; today they sell their lands, without thinking of the ashes of their kinsmen and their friends, contenting themselves with reserving a few thousand acres which proximity to the white men, scarcity of game, and their eternal scorn for industry and culture will force them to abandon in a few years.

13 OCCUPATIONS WORTHY OF A NISHY-NORBAY. It is by this name in the Chippaway tongue that the Indians are distinguished; the race of hunters. It is opposed to the word Saganash (red man), by which the Indians designate the English, because of the uniform of their soldiers.

14 GREAT WINTER HUNTS. The Indians have two hunting seasons: summer and winter. The first, that of the roe, furnishes them with the meat they need, and whose preservation they understand by means of smoking; the second procures for them fine furs which they sell to the Europeans; these are skins from bears, foxes, elk, beavers, otter, muskrat, and sable, etc.

Since these wild beasts can be found only in the cold and solitary regions of the north, in order to get to them, the Indians are obliged to undertake long and hard journeys, going up rivers which, for the most part, are a series of falls, rapids, and portages; but, since it is impossible for them to provide themselves with enough provisions, because of the feebleness of their canoes, they are obliged to stop on the way often, in order to hunt and fish: since these hunting and fishing excursions are not always lucky, they are exposed to hardships to which it is not rare to see them succumb. Such is their manner of traveling, until they have reached the places which they imagine to be filled with wild beasts.

After building a wigwam whose size is proportionate to their number, each chooses his hunting region, often at considerable distances from the general quarter. There they stretch nets, dig ditches, set traps, and put into use every means experience suggests to them; the more severe the season, the happier their hunting. It is in the midst of the deep snows and mighty freezes of these icy climates that these nearly naked men spend three or four months, exposed to hardships of which one can have no idea, unless he has shared them with the Indians.

I knew a European filled with all the confidence which youth and the strength of Hercules inspire; he wished to follow along with a band of Indians during their winter hunting campaign; he needed two months of care, rest and good food before he recovered from the fatigues he had suffered, and especially the privations to which he had been exposed during this long and severe experience.

No sooner have the winter ices thawed, than the Indians hasten to reach the places where the traders await them with an assortment of merchandise to suit their tastes; for, quite different from the Europeans, their taste is invariable: they clad themselves in the same materials they were first introduced to. Beaverskins serve as basis for exchange; it is like money in trading.

At the trading posts, under pretext of relaxing from their fatigues, they drink to excess, and these excesses always bring on bloody brawls. Like the sailor returning from the Indies, squandering, in a few days of feasting and folly, the money he has so painfully earned, these careless hunters dissipate in drunkenness the fruits of their long and laborious hunts. Instead of resting, instead of eating nourishing food which they need, they expose themselves to the new dangers of inflammations, pleurisies which destroy a great many of them every year: iron bodies would not resist such a rugged régime.

15 REASONS FOR THEIR WARS. Like the plague and epidemic diseases, war is an inevitable evil, since it is the consequence of our passions which are, after all, the same in the forests of America as on the plains of Europe.

It is even reasonable to assume that the factor which united in hordes and tribes the first scattered families was that of attacking or of defending themselves. Such was the state in which the famous Cook found the inhabitants of the lands and islands he discovered, and such was the state of this continent at the time of the arrival of the first Europeans.

But, one will ask, what can then be the reasons which stimulated them to making war, separated as the tribes were, by forests, impenetrable swamps, swift rivers, or stormy lakes; knowing neither greed, nor desire for conquest? What reasons! A dream, a false rumor, the boiling impatience of a youth long lazy, the desire to elevate the glory of their nation and to boast about it, that of currying the approbation and admiration of the women while singing before them of their prowess and their victories.

Let the eagle or the vulture dare to defy the storms in pursuit of their prey, imperious necessity excites them: but, let men not yet emerged from this primitive state which the poets call the golden age, abandon their villages, where they lived in peace, to go great distances in order to exterminate other men, and, like starved wolves, feast on their carcasses, celebrate their barbarous triumphs by drinking the soup of their flesh!. !.. ! What an inconceivable destiny! Yet that is how they began.

As soon as war is decided on, the young people assemble, and elect a chief; they all paint their faces and bodies, hang the kettle, around which they dance while yowling their songs of Cannibals, and impose on themselves a rigorous fast; for, they say, to be inexorable, one must have been long sharpened by the pangs of hunger. Who taught them this new means of exciting their ferocity? Could it be instinct? Then it must be the instinct of demons!

Since the white men have directed their activity toward hunting, by making known to them the value of their merchandise, wars have become rarer among them; the hope of ransom has made them less cruel toward their white prisoners.

16 PONDIACK. Ancient chief of the Outawa nation, long celebrated for his bravery, his eloquence, the wisdom and vigor of his advice. It is to him that History attributes the coalition of the great nations of the Ohio and the lakes, after the conquest of Canada in 1763, to chase out the English from the lands "above" (to the north), and to seize their forts by treaty and by war. The persistence of the efforts of these nations, the rapidity of their movements, the astonishing exactitude of their attacks, although at considerable distances; the defeat of one of their units in the mountains of Pensylvanie, after a bloody and stubborn battle; the blockade they made of the town of Detroit and Fort Pitt; the treaty of peace concluded at the forks of the Muskinghum; all these details are recorded in History, and justly considered as the most formidable test of their strength that had taken place from the founding of the English colonies on this continent. These plans vanished at the death of the great chief who was assassinated, they say, on secret orders.

After the conquest of Canada, the English having seized everything that could be called Indian trade from the banks of the Mississippi to the arctic regions of the Hudson Bay, the Government spent annually in presents more than 20,000 pounds sterling. On the other hand, the traders, not being restrained, as in the time of the French, by the quantity of intoxicating liquor which they were permitted to send to the lands "above," the number of Indians diminishes with an astonishing rapidity. They say that three-fifths of their population has disappeared since the freedom of English trade succeeded the stricter régime of the French.

17 WHAT AN EDUCATION! WHAT A STATE OF THINGS! In order to convince the reader in greater detail of the strength of opinions on

which anthropophagy is founded, I think I should report here a conversation which took place at the camp at Fort George in 1758, between a Pootooatamy chief and a French officer serving under the Marquis de Montcalm, a few days after those ferocious Indians had attacked the English garrison, which, in accordance with the capitulation, concluded with Colonel Monroe, withdrew—minus their weapons—to Fort Edward, where the Indians had scalped a great number of soldiers, some of whom were cut up and put into the kettle. I heard this officer recount all the details of this frightful butchery.

The French officer: "You say that you are a man! Non! You are worse than the wolf and the panther."

Kanna-Satego: "I—worse than the wolf and the panther!!! You exaggerate, almighty chief of warriors that you are, do you hear me!"

F.O.: "Is it not true that you eat your equal, who, like you, is the son of woman, and consequently your brother?"

K.: "My brother! No! He is my enemy, since he would have eaten me, if he had been stronger or more skillful. What matters it to a dead man, whether he is digested in my stomach or in that of a wolf?"

F.O.: "In cutting up a body like yours, do you not feel something within you that is repugnant?"

K.: "I do not understand this word. And as for you, when you arrest a man, your equal and your brother, because the wind of misfortune has blown upon him and he can no longer pay what he owes you, and when, depriving him of his liberty, to cause his wife and children to die of hunger and chagrin, do you not likewise feel some repugnance?"

F.O.: "It is the law that dictates it, not I."

K.: "Yet, with this law, you kill this man, as I kill my enemy with my rifle or my tomahawk; and can you believe yourself as brave as Kanna-setego? No, since, like him, you do not risk your life."

F.O.: "Where did this custom of eating your prisoners come from?"

K.: "From the subterranean plea of our braves, who died while fighting; whose ghosts pursue our warriors until they have appeased them by covering their bodies, by wiping from the earth the traces of their blood, and putting their enemies into the kettle. Besides, shouldn't our wives and our children participate in our triumph? It is the best soup we can offer them. Would it not be in dancing around our kettles, when they are not filled with anything but bear or venison, that we could sing our songs of valor? No; it is the hunter's meal, and not the festival of victory. You, whose mind is at the end of your tongue, explain my words. As for my mind, it is at the end of my arm."

F.O.: "Why do you not cultivate as we do, these little seeds, with which one satisfies so easily the pangs of hunger when they strike?"

K.: "Why would we do what our ancestors have never done? In the long run, your little seeds would kill our braves, for renouncing the need to eat, they would spend their time smoking and sleeping: our young people, not being obliged to hunt and fish in order to live, where would they learn to become skillful, and patient in withstanding evil and hunger? Soon they would forget how to wield the tomahawk of war. Furthermore, who would furnish us with clothing? Could we say to the stag 'I need mokissons; come, let me skin you?' To the buffalo, the beaver, the otter: 'I am cold, my shoulders are bare; give me your fur?' "

F.O.: "Have you never known pity?"

K.: "Yes, toward the weak, the sick and toward women. If the eye of a man should always be dry, how could that of a warrior be wet?"

F.O.: "Everything you have just told me fills me with horror."
K.: "Very well, then, go back to your land and cultivate your little seeds; and let us live here as our ancestors have lived. The sun and the moon rise and set; winter follows summer; like them, nothing changes; why should we change?"

18 ARSACIDES AND DANDAMAN ISLANDS. Located northwest of Cape Achem, whose black inhabitants are cannibals. These islands were discovered by Captains Bougainville, Surville, and Shortland.

19 POOTOOATAMIS. A once powerful and mighty nation, traces of whom still inhabit the southern shores of Lake Michigan. The French founded a mission among them, on the banks of the Saint-Joseph River which has long been famous; there they constructed a small fort in whose environs many Canadian families have settled. This place, fallen into the power of the English after the conquest of Canada, was seized by Pondiack's people, and the garrison, as well as the one at Michillimackinack, entirely destroyed.

20 WIGWAM. This is the name which in many languages the Indians gave to the dwellings which they built before having known the use of iron; in some cantons, they are still in use. The frame is simple, light, and solid. It is a series of small pieces made of wood of the most durable type; they are six or seven feet high, but instead of joists, they mount at their tops semi-circular hoops, covered on the sides, too, with great sheets of black birch, artfully sewn together, and whose seams are smeared with turpentine. The opening, mounted on a little frame which flaps against the threshold and the lintel, is covered with the same bark. In the middle of the roof, they make a semi-circular opening to permit the smoke to escape, and from it they suspend a crooked stick, to which the kettle is attached.

If it is the wigwam of a warrior, one sees there some scalps whose skins have been carefully tanned and painted red, attached on a hoop; the hair is the same length as when its enemy-owner was killed. In the evening around the fire are unrolled the skins of beavers, buffalo, or bear; these serve as their beds. Their utensils are few in number. These smoke-filled wigwams are far from clean. Yet the Indians' attachment for this kind of life is so great that when they come among the whites, they prefer camping in the woods nearby, where they raise a little shelter, to staying in our houses and sleeping on our good bed.

21 OPPOYGAN. This is the name which they give to a special kind of pipe, whose bowl, artistically fashioned, is always of red or black marble, which they seek in the region around the Mississippi. They insert a stem made of light wood inside the bowl to which a little copper chain is always attached, to prevent its breaking. When it is a certain length, three or four feet, for example, and when it is covered over with speckled snake skin, and decorated with a special array of feathers, it is considered the symbol of peace; the envoy or ambassador who carries it enjoys the most perfect safety, and even in enemy villages, at the sight of him with the pipe, vengeances and hatreds hush.

This pipe is also used in adoption and marriage ceremonies, as well as in peace fests. It is also the signal for war, when the feathers with which it is ornamented are red: it always precedes or accompanies the dances destined to represent attack or victory. From all this spring the metaphors which they use so much. "Let us raise our war tomahawk, let's smoke the pipe of blood." Or, "Let's smoke the pipe of peace, of intelligence, of good memory; may our thoughts be as one, good and sweet, like the smoke of our peace pipes."

The quarries where they go to seek this marble are places which, since time immemorial, have been consecrated to peace; it was here where the earliest rumor about the presence of this marble spread: whoever says that he is going to or coming from there, is invariably respected. But since on journeys as well as everyday life, this pipe would be very inconvenient because of its length, they have some that are smaller, or rather, they attach to the end of their tomahawks a pipe bowl of iron or copper, which is held there by a screw whose hollow connects with the stem, at the other end of which they put an eagle's featherstem, so that they can smoke with greater ease.

It is their constant diversion when they are in their homes, and to this occupation they attach a great deal of dignity and importance; but they push further than we do the luxury of this enjoyment. Instead of tobacco, often bitter and disagreeable, they mix in their pipe some aromatic leaves, such as those of the segokemack, and the sumac. Nothing smells pleasanter than this mixture, a supply of which they always carry in a tanned otterskin, duck or opossum skin suspended from their waists.

22 BEES. Convinced that the bees came from Europe (very doubtful, by the way), the Indians look upon them with evil eye, and consider their progress into the interior of the continent as an omen of the white man's approach: thus, as they discover the bees, the news of this event, passing from mouth to mouth, spreads sadness and consternation in all minds. One day as I was going to the Osséwingo village, I met a Cayuga Indian whom I had known for several years; he was seated at the foot of a tree, his eyes fixed on the ground, gravely smoking the pipe end of his tomahawk.

Since he appeared little disposed to talk to me, I said to him:

"Is your tongue tied and your hand paralyzed?"

"My mind is in the shadows," he answered me, "and my eyes look without seeing, when I think of this evil spirit who never ceases turning his back on us."

"What do you mean? I can't seem to understand you."

"Don't you know that this evil spirit takes your people by the hand the very day of your arrival on this earth, and that since that day he has constantly cleared their paths, and covered ours with thorns, thickets, and stones. Is it not their flies that arrive in our midst, to frighten off our game?"

NOTES TO PAGE 16

"Well, in that case, do you know what you should do?"

"No."

"I shall tell you. Have one field, two even, if possible; cultivate them carefully; have your comrades follow your example: then these mosquitoes which frighten you today will bring you happiness, for they are a model of industry, good will, and good government."

"What you say is true but the evil spirit does not want us to cultivate fields as the white men do."

"Your evil spirit is merely a shadow, a phantom, and a phantom is nothing. If you scorn the industry of the whites, at least imitate the beaver's; may the sun of reason enlighten your village, and then you will see this phantom, this shadow, pass like the noise I hear, and which suddenly I don't hear any longer; like the wind which stirs the surface of the lake and is already far off."

"Take your words to the village, and may our people say 'Yes, Yes, Yes' then I shall consent to it."

23 SHAWANESE. This great and good nation lives in the plains irrigated by the Scioto and its branches, one of the largest of all rivers emptying into the Ohio. Its confluency with this river is 130 miles from Pittsburgh, and 266 from the Mississippi. At the time of William Penn, this nation was composed of seventeen tribes, of ten to twelve thousand warriors. But, like all those one knows, they disdain to attach themselves through farming to the rich soil belonging to them; they reject the ideas of civilization which this famous founder taught them through Kelappama, one of their most enlightened chiefs, who had come to Philadelphia to see William Penn. What can be the cause of this deluding prestige, this moral blindness?

Of all the nations on the continent, the Shawanese are the most advantageously situated to become farm-minded: mildness of climate, richness of soil, great number of small, navigable rivers, proximity to the Ohio and great lakes, and to the natural prairies on which they would have been able, as did the Muscogulgés and Seminoles of the two Floridas, to raise horses and cattle without much care or difficulty: for it is on the banks of this river that one begins to see these plains covered with grass or reeds, known in the southern states as savannahs; it is there, too, that one sees trees, plants, and flowers which are quite different from those in the North; as well as the beautiful birds peculiar to the South.

What a pity, too, that their harmonious, soft, and expressive language has not been cultivated, and that the zeal of the missionaries has not yet had printed, for the use of their Neophytes, some prayer books in their language, such as one sees in the language of the Mohawks and the ancient inhabitants of the Bay of Massachusetts! It is feared that soon there will be no traces of them. The losses suffered by the Shawanese in their last war with the United States, the treaty they have just made with them, finally made them determined to live peacefully on the immense reserves set aside for them. And I venture to say that in this last haven, even, they will not adopt the only remedy which might still preserve their existence: farming.

24 WYANDOTS OF THE SANDUSKY RIVER. The traces of this ancient nation, once vanquished and chased from the mountains of Ouasioto by the Cherokees, seized the banks of this river, from which they exterminated the former owners, the Sanduskys; one's eyes could scarcely light on any part of the land that was not covered with human blood. Just as were the great nations of Europe and Asia, the nations of this continent appear to have been always in a continual state of warfare. The tribes which perished, as victims of these vengeances, were replaced by new hordes whose hatreds, jealousies, and dissensions swiftly excited new combat. Just like the Shawanese, their neighbors, they suffered even greater losses, which they are slowly repairing among these nations of hunters.

The river on whose banks they live is one of the loveliest and most constantly navigable of all those that empty into Lake Erie; its mouth could easily become a fine port.

25 MUSKINGHUM. Large and beautiful river which empties into the Ohio, 58 leagues from Pittsbourg, and 339 from the Mississippi. It is very interesting because of its twistings, and the extent of its navigation as far as Tuskaraway, a confluency formed by the meeting of the Némenshéhélas and the Lamenshicola, and celebrated by the treaty of peace made by General Bouquet in 1764, with the nations of the Ohio. Like the Tuskarawa, the Muskinghum has regular swellings, but they never cause floods. The villages of the Delawares, situated on fertile terrain, reflected abundance and peace, which they would still be enjoying without this baleful war into which English policy dragged them. It was on this river that the Moravian brothers had established a good-sized colony of Indians, whom they civilized by education in religion and farming. Irritating events having scattered them unfortunately, the Government has just granted them 10,000 acres of land in a region far removed from the chance of war.

Some day the mouth of this river will become famous in history, by the first settlements of the new state of Washington, established there in 1786, as well as by the founding of the town of Adelphi, since renamed Marietta, on the ruins of the famous entrenched camp which was discovered in 1780; plan and details of this camp can be found in Chapter VIII of Volume III in this work.

26 WAR WHOOP. I believe this yell is the most piercing it is possible for a man to make; no other reverberates so far in the woods, nor on the waters. According to circumstances, the Indians can make its modulations more or less disagreeable or frightening, by clapping rapidly with the four fingers of the hand over the lips during periodic exhalations. It is the yell of victory, like the roaring of the lion, it is also the yell of ferocity, by which the Indians stimulate themselves to war: they often use it to end their war songs.

27 SIR WILLIAM JOHNSON. He was for a long time superintendent
general of Indian affairs for the colonies of the interior and he was
likewise dispenser of the presents which England showered every year on
the six nations and their allies. It is with these irresistible means that,
since the conquest of this colony of Dutch in 1663, this Power assured
them friendship and their assistance, every time they needed it in their
wars with the French of Canada. This alliance contributed a great deal
toward the progress of settlements, toward the peace and security of the
inhabitants of the colony of New-York, and facilitated the acquisition of
lands, in proportion to the greed of the Governors or companies of
speculators.

To assure himself a position of influence in the councils of this confederation, Sir William Johnson married a woman of one of the largest
Mohawk families (Owentawegan), whose native intelligence and deep
understanding were extremely useful to him in the administration of this
department. She told him their secrets, their schemes, their sources of
discontent. He owed to her a great deal of his success in governing and
conducting, during a great number of years, these children of nature,
who had no wish other than his, and who were very useful to him during
the war in Canada.

One must agree, the long duration of his government was for these Indians one of peace, quiet, and plenty. If ever any European could have
inspired them to farm, it was Sir William Johnson, and he did not succeed in doing it, although he had built a great and beautiful home in the
midst of what was then called Mohawk Castles, and carried on farming on
the very lands they had given him—right before their eyes!

His wealth permitting him to give way to his great liking for entertaining, his house was always open to foreigners and colonists, who were
attracted to him out of curiosity to see and study the customs and habits
of the Indians, and were assured a simple, sincere reception in his home.
Only occasionally was his simple table presided over by his wife, Agonetia,
who, speaking English imperfectly, feared that she would be out of place
surrounded by a great number of persons whom she barely knew.

Convinced through habit which binds us to ideas about conventions
which we have followed since our very infancy, she always thought it
would be ridiculous for a Mohawk woman to appear in European clothes,
and she never abandoned her tribal costume.

Some people perhaps might have wished her to be more demonstra-
tive, but the charm of her remarkable modesty impressed most people;
her generally mild and unaffected nature took people unawares before
they had time to see whether her manners needed a little more refining;
one could not ask for more elegance.

Born on the banks of the Oriskany (branch of the Mohawk) and under
a birch bark wigwam, she proved that nature, without the aid of civilization, without the aid of art, could endow her with lovely gifts. It was
always with delight that one watched her preside over Sir William

Johnson's table. This woman, good and generous toward the whites, just as she was toward her own comrades who had experienced misfortunes, was always loved and respected by the two different peoples. What might she have become, had she been born in London, or Edinbourg, and received the best education possible?

28 HENRIQUE NISSOOASSOO. This worthy Mohawk, hereditary sachem of the Garakontie (duck) tribe, died in 1775, at an advanced age. Speaking English as well as Dutch, he was always one of those Indians with whom the foreigners who came to see Sir William Johnson chatted most often, and the remarkable thing is that never did the delight slacken with which he answered questions. I myself chatted with him during long hours without observing the slightest manifestation of impatience.

Although born in the very midst of the white men, so to speak, his European "costume" was as little European as though he had been born on the banks of the Ouisconsing, or on the shores of Lake Superior. I recall in 1766, when the dowager Duchess of Gordon who had just arrived in New-York, having been informed that the deputies of various nations were to assemble at the home of Sir William Johnson, left immediately for this Congress. The very day of her arrival, Sir William Johnson was careful to put Henrique Nissooassoo next to her at the table, for he was very well acquainted with his charm and talents.

Nissooassoo, knowing as he did that this lady was from a distinguished family, wished to appear at his very best and, in order to accomplish this, they say he spent a great deal of time grooming himself. His head was shaved, with the exception of a little tuft of hair in back, to which he attached a piece of silver. To the cartilege of his ears, which, according to custom, had been cut and considerably lengthened in his youth, he attached a little brass wire twisted into very tight spirals which, indeed, hid the cartilege but did not shorten it. A girandole was hung from his nose. A wide neckpiece covered his chest. Over his crimson vest which was not buttoned (for that would have been too annoying), he had put on a blue cloak adorned with gold; its tailoring and measurements were not made for him. Yet, so far his toilette was somewhat European; what followed will appear less.

Since, of all our clothing, breeches are the ones the Indians find hardest to become accustomed to, he thought he had skillfully compensated for them by breechcloth fringed with glass beads, which covered the lower part of his thighs: the rest was hidden by the low part of a long and large shirt. One could see on his face, which he had painted the day before for a reception of various foreign chiefs, the various colors. On his feet were moccassins of tanned elk, elegantly embroidered with porcupine quills and decorated with tiny silver bells.

Thus bedecked, he dined beside the fascinated dowager, who overwhelmed him with questions to which he replied with all the charm possible. Every time she was present at the sessions of Congress, she beckoned him to her side, that he might serve as interpreter. Extremely pleased and full of affection for these Indians, she even ventured up the Mohawk River with the plan of seeing them in their very villages; and she reached Fort Stanwick. There, escorted by various hunters, she crossed the forests, then pathless, and arrived without mishap, after seven tiring days, at little Otsego Lake, where she set sail down the Susquehannah, more than 200 miles, to the mouth of the Juniata, whence she was taken by coach to Philadelphia.

The Indians were so impressed by her courage and so grateful for the presents she gave them, that they adopted her under the name of Cherry Moyamee (Woman of the East), and gave her five or six thousand acres of choice land, located near Anaquaga, on the Susquehannah, in order that she would have a place of her own where she could raise her wigwam, light her fire, and hang her kettle every time she came to see them. One must note that, at this time, the regions she traveled through (today covered with dwellings) were then merely boundless forests.

It is the first time since the founding of these colonies that people had seen among them a lady of such high rank and sizeable fortune, and such an advanced age, who, having crossed the Ocean, to travel in a country so new, dared to penetrate into trackless forests, crossed by creeks and rivers that had no bridges, accompanied by Indians who, despite their zeal, could prevent neither the inconveniences nor the inevitable fatigues of such a journey. What progress this country has made since that time! What has become of the Mohawk nation, who at the time described above, numbered nearly two thousand warriors?

29 MISSISAGÉS. A once numerous nation whose tongue was spoken as far as Hudson Bay. Some lived in the Moutouallin islands, the east shore of Lake Huron, as well as the winding waters which connect from there to Quinty Bay. The others had built their villages beyond, near the bays at Toronto, Katarakouy, Niagara, etc., whose western cape, formed by the mouth of this latter river in the Ontario, still bears the name Missisagé.

Shortly after their settling at Montreal, the French made an alliance which, as it turned out, was useless to them, when they were attacked by the English and the Mohawks. Since this ancient time, they have not ceased being their constant and faithful allies, until the conquest of Canada. It was from them that they received the first fine furs that were sent to France, furs which their tireless hunters sought in the neighborhood of lakes Nepissing, Témiskaming, and Abitbee. Although far from the white men, and living in a region that was too cold for the white men to settle in, this great nation became extinct and almost entirely disappeared. Of all the once numerous tribes, of all the warriors who loved to tell of the prowess of their ancestors, by helping the French repulse their enemies at Hotchelaga, Misiskouy, Tikonderoga, etc.; of that great number of hunters who went in pursuit of the beaver to the land of the Eskimo, today only a few families remain, degenerate, disgustingly unclean, going from time to time to Niagara, Katarakouy, to exchange the product of their feeble hunting and fishing for bread and brandy. Scarlet fever has destroyed them by the thousands in the course of a few years. Such is the lot to which all of these nations seem to be irrevocably destined.

30 MARVELOUS LITTLE SEEDS. Wheat, rye, and barley which the French, who settled in Canada, planted. Indeed, what must have been the surprise of the Indians the first time they saw horses, and these horses harnessed to a plow, and this plow working the earth, and the colonists confiding to the earth's bosom these marvelous little seeds, destined to produce abundant harvests from which they made excellent nourishment! Does it not seem astonishing that they have never wanted to imitate such a fine example, that they have never planted a few handfuls of these seeds on this alluvial soil, near which they generally build their villages? Not at all; the astonishment which accompanied the first accounts of Koreyhoosta, the tears which the anxiety of foresight wrested from his eyes, made no impression whatsoever on these hunters.

Could it be then that, different from the others, their imagination absolutely refused to contemplate the future, and that like animals, they were destined to think of their lives only in terms of the present? Is it possible that nature could have refused them the extent of comprehension necessary to perceive the utility of new things? Could it have been pre-ordained that they would never know farming, domestic cares, civilization, morality, and laws? That is very probable.

CHAPTER II

A COLLEGE OF FRANKLIN. This venerable person, having long observed how great was the attachment the Germans of Pensylvanie had for their language, plus the obstacles involved for young people in English schools, conceived the notion of founding a college where the sciences would be taught in German.

As soon as he was named Governor of this State, after his return from France in 1786, profiting by his influence on public opinion, he easily obtained from the legislative body the ground and appropriation necessary, and early the following year, the college was founded at Lancaster and incorporated as a large school.

Although originally from Boston, where he was born in 1705, he has lived in Philadelphia since 1723. Having little taste for the trade of his father, who was a candle-maker, he came to seek his fortune in this town, which at that time was merely a large market place. Not knowing how to procure books, he got a job as printer's assistant: during the day he worked; night was devoted to study. Soon there spurted from his pen sparks of genius that announced that one day he would become one of the most enlightened men of the continent.

The notables of almost all the colonies, being assembled at Albany in 1744, to agree among themselves on a pact of union, and to decide on their relationships with the mother country, as well as the sum total of subsidies it ought to give her, Franklin's plan was accepted. England refused it. What a difference today in the state of things between America and Europe, if England had been able to foresee that thirty-two years later she would uselessly spend one hundred million pounds sterling, and would sacrifice the lives of one hundred thousand men in opposing the freedom of the colonies, a plan directed by this same Franklin! On what, then, do the destinies of Empires and Nations hang?

It is to the happy genius of this famous man that we owe various important discoveries, among others, lightning rods, immortalized by the medal which was engraved in Paris in 1784, with this motto:

'Eripuit caelo fulmen, sceptrumque tyrannis.'

Possessing to an eminent degree the talent for making useful observations about everything he saw, nothing escaped his profound wisdom. The world will be generously convinced of this when his grandson, Mr. Temple Franklin, publishes the prolific *Memoirs* which he bequeathed to him.

Not content with having enriched the world through his discoveries, what services did he not render his country, long before the revolution, as agent of the colonies of Massachussetts and Pensylvanie, and since that time, as member of the first Continental Congress which launched, conducted, and ended the war for independence, with so much wisdom, steadfastness, and glory; and finally as ambassador to France! It is to this man that Philadelphia owes its finest buildings, the Public Library, the University, the Philosophical Society, whose president he was over twenty years, although absent.

Born of poor but honest parents, he owed to his genius alone the immeasurable knowledge he acquired, as well as the important role he played in the world: and a very rare thing: happiness, success, esteem, and public consideration have constantly accompanied him in the course of his long life. Few persons have acquired more rights to the eternal gratitude of one's compatriots.

He left a thousand guineas to the town of Philadelphia to be used for the construction of a fire pump which will raise the level of the water in the Schuyllkill, to bring it to Philadelphia, in the event that at a certain time, according to his calculations (written in his Bible) the well water becomes unhealthy. He left to his native town an equal amount, destined to give encouragement to wise and industrious young men who, at the end of their apprenticeships, would need help to begin their career.

Posterity will recall only with admiration the great things he did by the sheer force of his genius, without any of those resources which have accompanied the enterprises of so many others. Here is the epitaph which he made for himself, shortly before his death, which occurred on April 17, 1790. He was then 84 and three months.

"Here lies Benjamin Franklin, like an old abandoned book of poetry; but they will gnaw only the exterior; the work will remain intact, and will soon reappear in a new form, whose impression will be more correct and more lasting."

1 ESQUIMOS. This race seems to be extremely different from the natives of the continent, not only because of the complexion, the color of hair and eyes, but also because of the language, the habits, and customs which are infinitely more refined than those of their neighbors. One sees them in New Foundland, on the coasts of Labrador, on the banks of Hudson Bay, and as far as the 67th degree of latitude, the last boundaries of life and vegetation. They are all harpooners and fishermen. Without fixed places to live, they spend their lives wandering across these inhospitable deserts, or on the shores of bays, lakes, and rivers, covered with ice and eternal snows. It is difficult to conceive an idea of a more wretched existence; yet they are so attached to it that it is almost impossible to lure them from it. I saw one of them in Quebec a few years ago; despite all the attentions lavished on him, he never stopped lamenting; he died of regret and disappointment at the end of six months.

This everlasting series of misery and privations which they experience in these frightful climates is not by any means the only tragedy to which nature has condemned them; having ordained that man be the enemy of his equal in all lands, nature placed, since time immemorial, the most implacable hatred in the heart of their neighbors. These neighbors, known as Aratapeskow (after a lake in the interior of this part of the continent), occupy the region west and south of Hudson Bay and wage continual war with the Eskimos. They destroy mercilessly all those whom they overtake: old men, young men, women, children: whole tribes have been massacred in the same day. One cannot imagine how it is that this wretched race can still exist. According to the discoveries of Mr. Hearne (today Governor of the English trading post on Hudson Bay) who, in 1771 and 1772, went more than 4,000 leagues northwest of this Bay, one can find individuals of this race in the most remote and uninhabitable regions of this part of the continent, and further, their height decreases as one gets nearer the pole.

2 BERING STRAIT. This strait, which separates the continents of Asia and America, of which the Russian navigators spoke, and which the celebrated Cook crossed in 1778, is only six leagues wide. The cold there is extreme. What can be the cause of this rigorous climate which is felt in America in latitudes under which, in Europe, one enjoys benefits of farming—the latitude of this strait being only 66 degrees? What a difference in the mild temperatures of the old world at 45 degrees latitude and the rigorous winters of Canada under the same parallel!

3 SAINT-PIERRE RIVER. This river which rises in the mountains of California, known by the Indians as Wadappa-Ménésoter, is deep and is 300 feet wide at its mouth. The length of its course, as well as the vast land it waters, are still little known, but what makes it interesting is the proximity of Saint Anthony's Falls, which are only ten or twelve miles away.

This cataract, the only one known in the Mississippi course, is located under 44 degrees 50 minutes, 567 measured leagures from the sea and 790 if one follows the course of the river. Quite different from the others, this one is in the middle of a fertile country, covered with hills, plains, and natural prairies. How regrettable that the name of an obscure hermit from ancient Egypt has replaced the name under which the Indians knew it! This is not the only loss that occasioned this monkish mania. It is especially in the Catholic colonies that one finds irreparable losses: instead of conserving the Indian names of rivers, mountains, and lakes of this land, mostly charming and sonorous, their names have been replaced with Roman calendar characters. What absurdity, to give the name of a woman or a man to an island, to a great river, to a cataract! Even if these men had been navigators like Sir Francis Drake, Hudson, Cook, Bougainville, etc., or benefactors of mankind, gratitude would have made their memory hallowed.

The width of this beautiful cataract is from seven to eight hundred feet and its height, from 35 to 40: it is divided in the middle merely by an immense rock, estimated to be between forty and 50 feet high. In the middle of these rapids caused by this tremendous falls is an island covered with very high trees, which serves as an asylum to all the birds of prey in the vicinity. In the shelter from enemy invasion, they live from generation to generation on the debris of fish and animals which the Saint Pierre river drags down.

4 NADOOASSES AND PADOOCAS. Numerous nations, divided into various tribes, known under different names. Some live on the plains, others in the wooded sections of the vast regions located west of this great river: that is why they are distinguished by the name of Nadooasses, meaning "of the plains or woods." Born in a temperate climate, owning a fertile soil, a land extremely abundant in game, they have become more farm-minded than the northern nations, and they have much more refined customs, although, like the Nadooasses, they are fond of war and have waged it a long time with the Spanish of New Mexico. From there came the horses and cattle used by those nations; that is why it is not rare to come upon many herds of them, especially in northern Missouri, mounted on horses from Andalusia, which still have the fire and speed of their ancestors.

Like the Tartars, these nations pitch their camps in places having the most abundant pasture lands: they have slaves, whom they shanghai from among the neighboring nations in the California mountains. This region is known as Panis, and I have seen many people from there in Montreal. They exchange the results of their hunting for European merchandise at Pancore (Saint Louis), a town built by the French in upper Louisiana, at the confluency of the Missoury with the Mississippi, 402 measured leagues from the sea, and 54 leagues north of the mouth of the Ohio.

Their plains and their forests are filled with deer, buffalo, geese, pheasants, cranes, pelicans, curlews of various types, and their rivers abound in fish. Separated from savage Indians of the north by this great river, as well as by their vast plains, free, independent, several tribes lead a mild and pleasant life in the bosom of abundance. This intermediary state, likewise far from the inconveniences of life—wild like those of too great a civilization—is perhaps the happiest one imaginable.

5 LEXINGTON. Town of the new state of Kentukey, founded in 1780, at a little distance from the Elkhorn * in the heart of one of the most fertile plains of this land: it is the place where a great many roads join, and has so far been considered the capital of Kentukey. In 1796 there were 400 houses and 1,800 settlers; it is 346 leagues from Philadelphia, on a direct line, and eight from Frankford, in LaFayette county, and twenty-four from Louisville on the Ohio, seventeen from Washington, in the district of Limestone, ten from Danville, and 83 from Nashville on the Cumberland Road in the state of Tènézee. There one finds a printery, the first to be established west of the Alleghanies. There are also some cotton spinning mills whose ingenious mechanism was sent to Philadelphia in 1786 by Mr. Brown, today senator of the United States. It is in the neighborhood of this little town that one finds traces of two entrenched camps: the first covers a surface of three acres, the second six.

6 THE TWO MIAMIS. Two rivers by this name empty into the Ohio: the first at 172 leagues from Pittsbourg, the second 184: they are navigable only during the spring floods. The space separating them is the site of the colony made by Colonel Cleves-Symes in 1783. These federal lands, the first to have been sold by Congress (as well as those in Kentukey), are very productive; some day the colonists will cultivate silk, cotton, tobacco, and all the seeds of the north. There are three towns there: Colombia, Cinncinnatus, and Washington. The latter is estimated to be 507 leagues from New Orleans, by following the course of the Ohio and Mississippi. The first grant was of a million acres, but since then this colony has extended its boundary to the Little Myami, by making further purchases. Twenty miles from its mouth, traces of ancient fortifications made of earth have been found, not as large, but quite similar to those camps along the Muskinghum.

7 BIG-GRAVE-CREEK. This little river, which empties into the southwest bank of the Ohio, 30 leagues from Pittsbourg, in the Indiana country, took its name from a conically-shaped tomb, and like those which the ancient Caledonians called Kromlaeck, the Gauls Carneds, and the Bretons Barrows. There one finds human bones of an extraordinary size; but what makes this tomb worthier of attention is a series of entrenchments with their ditches, which begin four miles below the river; some are circular, others square. One sees also some redoubts raised at unequal distances from each other on a fairly wide plain; but such is the thickness of the forests and the great number of trees that cover it, that it is almost impossible, especially in the summer, to examine these works with success: one thinks he has seen everything and sometimes one learns through hunters that these works extend even further.

* Main branch of the Kentukey River.

8 TRACES OF ANCIENT MONUMENTS. See Volume III, Chapter VIII.

The note in which the author speaks of the remains of these ancient fortifications, discovered some years ago on the banks of the Muskinghum, Bald Eagle, and Big-Grave-Creek Rivers and elsewhere, is so long that the translator thought he should give it chapter status without changing the form: he thought he was further justified in this change by adding the sketch of the two entrenched camps which accompanied the footnote.

CHAPTER III

1 ONONDAGA. Former "capital" situated on a good-sized creek which empties into a salt lake, 40 miles from Fort Stanwick, twenty-five from Oneida, and 48 from Oswego on the Ontario. The newly cut road from this fort to the land of the Ténézées crosses it. This village is only a short distance from lakes Oxaruatetes, Ostiko, and Owasco, which, with eight or nine others, contribute a great deal toward enriching, linking, and embellishing this part of the beautiful State of New York. The number of Indians in this village, once famous, has considerably diminished: in a few more years, only the name Onondaga will remain, given perhaps to a little village or district nearby.

2 FORT STANWICK. Although this little fortress, which the English built during the war with Canada, no longer exists, and although even the name has been replaced by Schuyler, maps and custom still use the name of Stanwick. At this point begins the navigation of the Mohawk whose sources are twenty miles north in the region of Castorland, and the elevation of the lands in this part of the State of New-York. This site is only a mile from the waters of Wood-Creek, which runs in an opposite direction into Lake Oneida, and from there into Ontario, through the Onondaga River, 94 miles away.

The canal destined to open this important communication has just been completed. The same company is cutting many peninsulas in this winding river, so aptly named Wood-Creek; this will shorten the length and boredom of navigation through here considerably. This company was incorporated in 1792.

3 SHIPPENBOURG. This little town, located in Cumberland County, is 140 miles from Philadelphia and 21 from Carlisle. It is built on one of the branches of the Conédogwinet and on the great road that leads to Pitt'sbourg: the town has 200 houses and 1,100 inhabitants. There is nothing remarkable to see there, except for the happiness and peace enjoyed by the inhabitants; it is also the haven of its respectable founders who own much land and many mills in the region. This land produces only wheat, whose flour is sent to Philadelphia. It is hoped that the great road to Lancaster, which is to cross it, will be continued as far as the mountains. I knew this town in its early infancy; I have seen the forests of the neighborhood become fertile fields, and lowlands and beautiful

prairies. Never will my glances light on this place without feeling emotions of the very keenest sort.

4   DICKENSON. Member of the first Congress which founded the independence of these States, and one of the most esteemed persons on the continent. Long before necessity had put weapons in the hands of his compatriots, he reviewed their rights as colonists, as well as the unjust claims of Great Britain, in a work well known under the title of *Letters from a Pennsylvania Farmer*. While he was Governor of that state he got from the Legislative Body a charter and funds, to which he added a considerable amount, to establish a college at Carlisle. Public gratitude has given this college his name, long inscribed on the list of founders of the liberty and independence of his country.

5   LOG HOUSE. The name given to the colonists' dwellings—as opposed to framed-house; these tree trunks, joined at the corners, are placed on top of one another and the space in between is filled with wood and mortar. It is the first asylum of the man who ventures forth into the woods to settle: they are more or less modest, or finished, depending on the taste, or rather the state of mind of the owner. It is easy to judge the different degrees of prosperity and industry among the colonists, by the mere inspection of their farms, their poultry yards, and their dwellings; at first they are covered only with the bark of the first trees they uproot; it is not until five or six months after their settling that they are able to procure roofing board and shingle from the cedars, pines, or chestnut-trees of the neighborhood. Nothing is bleaker than these log houses, when they suggest neither the idea of industry nor of cleanliness.

6   MASHOPING. A large creek emptying into the Susquehanna a few miles below the pretty river of Wy-o-Lucing. It is navigable as far as twelve miles from its mouth. It is the route travelers take going to Albany, and this route is still nothing more than a poor path.

7   COLONISTS OF NEW ENGLAND. In colonial times this is the name by which the four northern states were known: New Hampshire, Massachussetts, Rhode Island, and Connecticut. There were 101 of the first colonists to embark at Plymouth, in Massachussetts Bay December 31, 1720 (sic). When one sees in the history of these states the innumerable obstacles they met, the difficulties of all kinds which the climate brought on, the jealousy of the Indians, one can scarcely imagine how they overcame such obstacles; but, aroused and inspired by the dauntless courage which religious fervor awakens, they succeeded in making respectable settlements in various places, and in resisting the fury of the Indians. It was not until four years after their arrival, that they received three cows and a bull from which are descended the countless cattle they have today.

It is perhaps to these painful beginnings that we owe the tireless industry, intelligence, and activity of which they are the most perfect model today. On the sea they have the reputation of being the leading whalers in the world, as well as very skillful cod fishermen. Their vessels reach all parts of the globe. On land they are model colonists; indefatigable, persevering: nothing discourages them. It is rare that you find a man who is not a combination of carpenter, weaver, cooper, and black-smith. During the early years of their settlement, most of these colonists know, like Robinson Crusoes, how to be sufficient unto themselves.

They are the only English stock on the continent. Their population, having always been large in proportion to their land area, they have had no need of foreigners: likewise, they have a religion, customs, habits, and a kind of national ingenuity. Although a great number of young people leave every year to settle in other States, New England population is estimated at one million, including the province of Maine.

This country is famous for its colleges, the most highly endowed and the oldest on the continent, as well as for the instruction, in which their inhabitants participate, by means of schools established according to the laws of the district. How much it is hoped that such a fine example will be followed by the other States, especially by those in the South! Thus, New England, more than any other region on the continent, is filled with enlightened and learned men. The appearance and culture of many regions resembles the finest one sees in Europe.

However, one must make an exception of Rhode Island whose Government, far too democratic, has always been agitated by political parties. Instead of working, the colonists lose a great deal of time in holding new elections all the time, in plotting in these elections of their magistrates and their deputies. What strange quirk prevented them from wanting to imitate the wisdom of their neighbors, in Massachussetts and Connecticut?

8 SEEDS OF INDUSTRY, RELIGION, AND CIVILIZATION. Wherever the colonists of New England settle, they take with them and manifest everywhere a spirit of order, industry, and religion which distinguishes them from all the colonists coming from Europe or from other states of the Union; these are precious fruits of the wisdom of the laws of their land, and of the system of education which they have established there for more than a century. Raised in the knowledge of these laws, accustomed to the municipal and religious institutions of their region, no sooner have they cleared their fields and overcome the early difficulties, than they feel the necessity of setting up a government, summoning a minister, building a church and schools. Eleven years before the great line of demarcation which today divides the states of New-York and Pensylvanie, running from the Delaware River to Lake Erie, seventeen families from Massachussetts came to settle on the banks of one of the Tiogo branches, without knowing under what jurisdiction they were. Soon after arriving, they elected three persons (selectmen) to judge differences and disagreements which might arise in the community.

These families lived for a long time in the shelter of the great tree of peace they had planted, when the rapid progress of the world outside them reached this little colony, lost so long to the remoteness and solitude of the forests. During this interval of time seventeen families, originally composed of 102 individuals, produced 41 marriages, and at the time of their incorporation into the new county of Tiogo, the total number of inhabitants was 274.

As soon as Governor Clinton, who gave me these details, was informed of it, he sent a peace commission to these worthy Magistrates. With what even greater speed, the clearings, the prosperity of the inland colonies, would they not increase, if the colonists coming from other states or from Europe would bring with them the industry, the activity, the customs, and the religious principles of the inhabitants of Massachussetts or of Connecticut!

9 SWATARA RIVER. A river in Pensylvania which empties into the Susquehanna, 12 miles from Harry's bourg, six miles from Conéwago Creek, and 45 miles from Lancaster, and whose mouth is designated on maps by the name Middletown-Creek. This pretty river is navigable for a space of thirty miles, whence a canal, which will soon be finished, is to open communication with the waters of the Tulpéhoken, a navigable branch of the Schuyllkill. This enterprise will assure Philadelphia the arrival of all the seeds and flour, as well as the other commodities which this vast country irrigated by the Susquehannah produces: they will reach Philadelphia with even greater ease when the canal is finished that is destined to unite the waters of the Schuyllkill with those of the Delaware. This will begin at Norristown (a little town located 17 miles from Philadelphia). Then this capital of Pennsylvania, the city of New-York, Washington (the federal capital), and Charlestown, which have become centers of a vast inland commerce, will grow and become beautiful, the equal of the capitals of Europe; they will become the center of sciences and the arts.

10 FALLING OF THE LEAVES. In order that the colonists can be rid of the bushes more easily, as well as the brambles and the branches of the trees they have cut, cleared, or piled together, it is necessary that this operation not be done until after the leaves have fallen; then more quickly dried and more combustible, the burning of this debris will be greatly expedited.

11 HARROWING THE EARTH. I have known some Europeans who were astonished to see the colonists plant their fields without working them, and content to harrow them with a tree stump of medium size, dragged by oxen. The reason for this practice is that after the soil has been cleared, the quantity of roots is so great that it would be impossible to bring in the plow, or even to harrow it properly; therefore, one must necessarily wait until the roots rot: it is the work of time. The same is true of the stumps which often last from twelve to fifteen years.

12 APPLE AND PEACH TREES. There are few farms between Pensylvania and New Hampshire that do not have a good-sized orchard of apple trees. Just as in the South, they have peach trees; but often, for lack of care, these trees which sometimes are not even grafted bear little fruit of any value. In the counties nearest the large towns, cider of an

excellent quality is made, such as the ciders of West-Chester, New-Ark, Wood-Bridge, etc. This cider is sent to the southern states.

The orchards of peach trees are daily becoming more common and more extensive in the southern States of the interior; besides the pleasure of eating their fruit, they fatten the pigs with it and make brandy from it. Color and a very toothsome taste is given this brandy by putting dried fruit and other ingredients into a great kettle. The State of Kentukey, as well as the new settlements west of the Alléghénies, have planted a great many peach trees, but in order that these trees, which grow very rapidly, will be more lasting, one must graft them with their own shoots; in this way they live a long time. It is by grafting them with the wild apple tree of the New Jersey forests that people succeeded in making a new type of apple, such as the spitzenberg, the newtownpeppin, a delicious fruit, great shipments of which are sent to Havana, Jamaica, etc., where they are sold very high.

13   FAIRFIELD. Pretty little place, chief town of Fairfield County, located not far from the Sound, in the midst of a very fertile country. Nothing is more blooming nor prosperous looking than its environs: fields covered with fine harvests, blooming orchards, and fields pied with daisies. Every week two packet-boats leave for New-York, laden with the commodities of the land, and the fruits of the colonists' industry. Like the young people of all the other towns in Connecticut, the young people from Fairfield leave every year to make new settlements in the heart of the continent, or to embark on long journeys. These little coastal towns are inexhaustible nurseries for enterprising, industrious, and active men. Like New-London, Norwalk, Grotton, Greenfield, and so many others, it was destroyed by Governor Tryon who would have ruthlessly destroyed the entire coast of this State if the commander in chief of the English army, Sir Henry Clinton, had not recalled him. One must admit, it was a shameful glory, that of burning small towns that were unguarded and unfortified, towns in which there were only old men, women and nary a cannon. What makes Fairfield's destruction even more shameful, is that this Governor, at the time they passed around the torches for the soldiers, promised to save the church, into which the women and children had withdrawn, and to which, notwithstanding all this, he set fire. However, he did have the generosity not to shut them up in it!

CHAPTER IV

1   INCORPORATION. See Volume Three, Chapter IX
2   USE OF SALT. See Volume Two, Chapter XIV
3   TREES. Far from admiring the beauty, the majesty of an oak or a pine tree, far from reflecting on the utility of these fine trees, on the state in which the surface of the continent would be, if nature had not covered it with dense forests, the common herd of colonists is so accustomed to destroying them, and this destruction is so rude, that one of them, sum-

moned to Ireland on business, exclaimed on disembarking on a bare beach: "Ah! a beautiful land! Yet I see not a single tree!"

4 STREAMS. The drying up of the streams which do not come from high terrain, the entire disappearance of a great number of them, are the effect of the drying up of the swamps and the clearing of lands. This decrease is even beginning to be felt in the large rivers, such as the Delaware, the Mohawk, and the Potawmack. I have seen ruins of mills in the midst of fields, where twenty years ago fat streams swelled. But even now, our water supply is greater than Europe's. But what will it be in a century or two?

5 HEMP. Cultivation of this has increased greatly since Congress offered substantial premia to its growers (in some States, it is one piastre 51.5 shillings per quintal) but manpower is still too scarce and too high. Nature sponsors its growth in many regions where the Indians used it. It is stronger and silkier than European hemp. Several years ago some was sent to London; the result of the experiments made by the rope-makers there was to encourage Americans to transplant it from the woods to their fields.

6 POTASH. The manufacture of this product, long known in the northern States, is increasing every year. The value of the shipment sent from New-York in 1797 to Scotland and Ireland was 4,037,500 pounds. Instead of spreading over the soil the ashes from the enormous piles of brush which the colonists were obliged to burn in order to clear their fields, they take them to the small factories nearby where they are washed in lye and converted into potash. It has been observed that the ashes coming from the thin, green branches produce a greater quantity of salt than the thicker branches near the trunks and roots. Five hundred bushels are needed to make a ton of potash weighing 2,200 pounds. This branch of exportation, and that of linseed, which amounts to 300 thousand bushels annually (a bushel contains 60 pounds of wheat), is extremely profitable for the United States.

7 MAPLE SUGAR. The misfortunes in Saint-Domingo have contributed immeasurably to increasing this new branch of industry, as well as the bounty of two "sols" per pound offered by the Society of Quakers in Philadelphia. The tree which produces this sap in such great abundance is found between the 34th and 45th degree of latitude, that is to say, from Ténézée as far as Canada; it is one of the most vigorous trees known. The stumps survive even those of the oaks. For two or three years, at the return of spring, one sees the ends of the trunks felled so that more sap and sugar can be made. Its branches make excellent fodder for cattle and sheep, especially during the winter. As soon as one of these trees is pruned, one sees the animals run toward it from every direction. Its wood is as combustible as hickory. The bark of the most sugar-producing trees is always black, caused by the green woodpeckers that attack only the best trees, leaving part of each tree exposed to the air which coagulates the sap and blackens it.

The astonishing fact is that the more these trees are tapped, the greater the quantity of sugar they produce! For example, one which has not been tapped will yield on its first tapping scarcely a half pound of sugar; on the other hand, those trees whose cuts are numerous, from two to two and a half pounds, often more, especially when one has been careful to expose them to the sun's rays, by felling nearby trees.

In Claverac, in the State of New-York, I have known some that have been tapped thirty-four years and still appear healthy and vigorous. It is true that the owner takes very good care of them: he has destroyed their neighbors and their rivals. Instead of stopping up with dry wood the gaps made in them or leaving them open, as do many lazy and careless colonists, he inserts a branch of the same tree, which soon unites and becomes part of the trunk.

The suitable season for making sugar depends on the climate. In Kentukey, trees are tapped early in February: in Pensylvania, this operation does not start until the early days of April. An augur one-half inch in diameter is inserted, which must not be penetrated more than one inch, then up to three, as soon as one sees that the sap supply is diminishing: it is always on the south side of the tree that one taps. The amount of sap they give depends on the state of the atmosphere, and there is no surer barometer. The sap flows more abundantly when the nights are cool and the days warm. I have seen one tree give in 24 hours 23 pots and a pint of sap from which 2 pounds seven ounces of sugar were made; others, on the contrary, gave only 5 or 6: it is estimated that each one of these trees will yield from one to two pounds per season; the one which doesn't start yielding until the end of April becomes so feeble that one must content oneself with making syrup and vinegar from its yield. What a fine present from nature!

If, with the little care the colonists have administered to this industry so far, they reap such advantage, what will it be eventually when skill and knowledge will direct the cultivation of these trees, and when one is more careful in his methods of tapping and extracting the sugar, the syrup, the vinegar and the rum? How much greater the yield will be when the trees are planted in orchards and exposed to the beneficence of the sun's rays! In less than a century one will see them maintained with as much care as apple and peach trees.

8 GINSENG. Panax. Since the vessels of the United States have been going to Canton, the root of this plant has become a new branch of exportation. During my stay in New-York, I saw 8,000 pounds loaded on board one ship; the return shipment represented as many piastres: that was in 1788.

9 SEINE. A net widely used in the United States; I have seen some 200 arms length long. During the aloe, bass, and herring season, each association takes in a certain amount of fish, proportionate to the money he has advanced; this custom is extremely advantageous to the colonists whose plantations are remote from the rivers.

CHAPTER V

1 SALT. The further one goes from the sea, the more frequent are the Salt-Licks which, before the European colonizations the buffalo, deer and all the former forest animals, stimulated by their need for it, came to lick it. These salt licks are even more common west of the mountains. For a long time, the colonists of Kentukey who discovered twelve very large ones in their territory, have been making all they need. During the early years they were obliged to evaporate 800 pots of water to obtain a bushel of it, but since that time when they dug wells 40 to 50 feet deep, they have succeeded in procuring a much finer brine.

2 STERLING. See Volume I, Chapter XVII

3 OLIVER EVANS. It is to this ingenious mechanic that we owe a new perfecting in the inside mechanism of flour mills which simplifies all the operations and consequently cuts down the cost of this manufacturing. This is an extremely important factor in a land where manpower is still so rare and dear.

Here is what the improvements consist of. The first is a cylinder 8 or 10 inches in diameter, placed horizontally and crossed by an axle to which are attached, spiral fashion, and at a very special angle, a great number of wooden valves three and a half inches long and two inches wide. This axle, moved by the wheel, transports the flour as it leaves the millstones in an adjacent space, which is its first stop. The second of these improvements, called the elevator, is a box eight or ten inches square which reaches from the floor of the storage space just mentioned to the top story, at the extremities of which are placed two wheels which rotate a chain pump with little buckets, as large as a cup of tea; the flour, raised in this fashion, is poured into a vast bin called the cooler: after being gently stirred by the pieces of wood that turn it horizontally, and like the rest, receive their movement from the motion of the mill, they come down through several holes into the various different sifting compartments, and from there to an inside space where they are put into barrels whose dimensions are prescribed by law, and which, consequently always weigh one quintal and three quarters: this same law requires that these barrels bear the name of the owner and his mill. Furthermore, this flour can never be exported until it has passed inspection. All the other processes of cleaning, cribbing, and airing the wheat before processing it through the mill-hoppers (funnels) have likewise been vastly simplified. From Pensylvanie this new perfection has spread throughout the continent. The Government rightfully has accorded Mr. Evans exclusive rights for fourteen years; never has a new invention been more quickly adopted.

CHAPTER VI

1 CHIPPAVAY. A half century ago this nation was the leader in this hemisphere; and although considerably diminished, it is still very nu-

merous in the region around Lake Superior, Lake of the Rains, Lake of the Woods, and Winipeg Lake. The Chippeway tongue is spoken as far as Hudson Bay. One of its tribes still existed 40 years ago, near the sources of a river which empties into Lake Erie. Today only the name which they gave to the river exists.

2 OUTAWAS. A nation which, like so many others, has experienced great losses. It occupies the great peninsula dividing Lakes Huron and Michigan, whose northern end forms the strait known as Michillimakinack, the common name for the fort which the French built there 70 years ago, to command this passage, as well as the strait of Sainte-Marie, through which the waters of Lake Superior flow into the Huron. This place was long the rendez-vous for the Indians of the North who came to exchange their furs for the European merchandise; but since the discoveries made by the English as far as the 60th degree, Lake Winnipeg, 300 leagues away, has become the center.

3 RAVAGES OF SMALLPOX. Of all the diseases the Europeans have introduced among the Indians, there is none that has been more disastrous: often it happens that villages are wiped out by it in the course of a few weeks; and even entire hunting parties have perished on their expeditions. It is almost always confluent smallpox. Thus, hordes of men were destined to be swept from the earth by an offshoot of a disease coming from Asia, to Europe in the twelfth century and carried to the Indians in this land five hundred years later by some inhabitants of ancient Albion.

4 ONEIDA. A nation once numerous, the second of the six which comprise the Mohawk league, long so formidable and famous. It owed to the wisdom of some of its chiefs survival from the torrent which swallowed up its neighbors, the Cayugas, Seneccas, Tuskaroras, and Onondagas. Many among them know cleanliness and farming, have horses and cattle; but unfortunately their young people consider the title of warrior infinitely superior and even incomparable to that of farmer.

This nation is the only one, of all those I have known, that has sincerely wanted to become agricultural. Brought together in general assembly in 1788 in the village of Skanondoé, aided by the enlightenment of the Ambassador from France, the chiefs agreed on a form of government, drawn up in twenty articles; they proposed to divide their lands, fix their boundaries; call into their midst the scattered debris of the neighboring nations; set up schools; send some of their own young men traveling. This act was sealed with twenty signatures, among which one could see those of the two women chiefs, Kononwayété and Gwartinda.

Whether, discontent with this measure, the Government of New-York may have fomented divisions among them, whether the chiefs did not find in the young people the deference they were expecting, this plan was never carried out: they experienced the plight of their neighbors and sold their lands, with the exception of a reserve of sixty thousand acres of which the great village of Oneida is the center. This former meeting place is located on a creek which empties into Lake Oneida, eight miles away, fifteen miles from Fort Stanwick and twenty miles from the mouth of the Oriskany River in the Mohawk.

5 LAND OF THE ONAS. This name, given by the Indians to the famous founder of Pensylvania in 1682, and which, like Penn, means feather, by which this land was designated and has been known among them ever since that time; and *Land of Onas* has become synonymous with Pensylvanie, as son of Onas, to a Pensylvanian.

6 CHERRYHUM-SAGAT. Man of the young sun, or man from the East.

7 TOCKSIKANÉYOU, THE ELDER. Name which the Canadians once upon a time gave to the Mohawk tribe, which, after having been converted to Christianity by their missionaries, came to settle on the banks of the Saint Lawrence, opposite Montreal. It is difficult to imagine how, from the word Caug-na-Wagas, the name of this tribe, they could form "Anier." The same is true of the names Huron, Sauteurs, Iroquois, etc., which exist in none of their languages except by approximation; is it not astonishing that their missionaries, who spoke these languages and who lived for a long time among these nations, did not rectify such errors on the maps, as well as in the histories they wrote of these lands?

8 OSSEWINGO. Old Oneida village, located on the Kanaséragé, which together with the Butternut empties into Lake Oneida, ten miles south, and eighteen miles from the village of Oneida. This name has been guarded in the reserve of sixty thousand acres.

9 THIRDS AND FIFTHS. If, to the instruction of the salutary precepts of the Gospel, the early missionaries had been able to unite those of music, I am convinced that, like Orpheus and Amphion, they would have succeeded in mitigating the ferocity of their young people, and in making known to them the advantages of a sedentary and agricultural life. In this respect, how superior the ancients were to the moderns! I often had the occasion to watch the sudden effect which the harmony of only two instruments produced on these faces, flat and imperturbable like the ripples that the path of a slight breeze produces on the water surface, on a calm day, these movements were obviously those of pleasure, the indications of an inner glow which they told me they had never before experienced. How much more far-reaching these effects would have been if the number of instruments had been greater and the music better!

CHAPTER VII

1 AGAN-MATCHEE-MANITOO. Literally, very evil jinn; he is their Ariman. Considering the scourges and calamities to which men are exposed, it is scarcely astonishing that from the beginning of societies, people have believed in the existence of two jinn: one to whom they owe the beautiful days, health, success, happiness; the other, storms, plague, war, and epidemics.

2 TO BLOW ON THE FIRE-BRAND. The first step which a young

warrior takes is to offer a flaming torch to the maiden he would like to marry; if she blows on it, it is to make him understand that she does not disapprove of his gesture, and that he can hope; then he begins to sing his war song; that is to say, in chanting the recital of his prowess, he tells of the dangers he has risked; the scalps he has taken: nothing stimulates more quickly the admiration of the maidens and leads them more promptly to interest and to love. That is why, before offering their fire-brand, the young men have such a great desire to distinguish themselves; this is what used to excite them to war in days of yore and even today stimulates them to undertake long, and arduous hunts.

"There is my fire-brand," says a young brave to the maiden he loves. "You know what it signifies: I took it from my fire, and from none other. Open your mouth, blow on it the breath of consent and you will make me happy. You are lowering your eyes; I continue. To convince you that I am a brave, look at the handle of this tomahawk: there are the marks of seven bloody scalps. But, lest, as a black cloud darkens the light of the sun, doubt overcast your spirit, follow me, I shall show these scalps to you; they are hanging in my wigwam. There you will also see the smoked meat, the cooked fish, the bearskins, and the great quantity of furs. Do you want a warrior for a husband? I am worth as much as another. Do you want a tireless hunter? Take me; you will see whether hunger invades your wigwam. Do you want a patient, subtle fisherman? Come with me in my canoe this evening by the light of the moon; you will see what I can do. If the water from the clouds or cold from the winter enters your wigwam, I shall know only too well how to chase them out: birch bark is abundant in the woods and there are my ten fingers. As to your kettle, it will always be full, and your fire will always be steady. You are silent; I say no more. May I return—bringing with me my fire-brand?"

3 DESTROY THE THRESHOLD OF THE WIGWAM. Of all the accidents, this is one of the most disastrous that can befall the Indians, for this item is considered the symbol of domestic happiness, security, and shelter. It is the only item in their dwellings to which they seem to attach any mystical notions. One could carry off the door to their wigwam, or break it, as long as the threshold remains intact; for they could build another wigwam—or another door—and with confidence: on the other hand, even if the threshold cracks without apparent cause, that would be sufficient to inspire baleful dreams and arouse in them the desire to raise their wigwam elsewhere. Since they have always refused to answer questions I have asked them about this, it is impossible for me to say anything that is more satisfactory.

4 CATAMOUNTS. Mountain cats; a kind of lynx which climbs trees, jumping from branch to branch with incredible nimbleness. Such is their cunning and their ferocity that the Indians never try to shoot at them unless there are many Indians present.

5 WOLVES, FOXES. This is the metaphor they ordinarily use when they

speak of their dealings with the white men, alluding on the one hand to their status as hunters, a condition which exacts courage, patience, and skill; on the other, to the guile and the art of lying in which they agree that the Europeans surpass them. Often, they say to each other that these men are cheats and liars, like the shadows of the setting sun.

6 MERGUM-MERGAT. This word arouses in their minds the same idea as that of the plague among us; and if this scourge were known among them, they would not invent any other name.

7 NOTHING LIVING EXCEPT THEIR DOGS. A few years ago, several canoes full of Indians were returning from Niagara, where they had gone to sell their furs; they were seized with smallpox near the great cape jutting out of Lake Erie. All of them perished; their dogs were still alive some time later when a boatload of white men stopped off near this cape. The white men found the bones of these ill-fated Indians whose bodies had been devoured by the wolves in the region.

8 PLAINTIVE CRIES OF THE BEAR. "My companion being with me, and having discovered two bears, fired and killed on the spot the bigger (bear). The other, appearing not the least bit frightened, approached the dead bear, sniffed around him, touched him and seeming to be very sad, began to moan, looking first up into the air, then in our direction, then he began to cry like a baby. The incessant cries of this animal, deprived of his protectress, affected me deeply; I was touched with compassion and reproached myself for having been an accomplice in the death of this bear. My intercession was useless, for my companion fired another shot and the baby bear fell dead on its mother." (*Journey of John Bartram into the two Floridas,* Volume I, page 16) TRANSLATOR'S NOTE.

9 TEARS OF THE BEAVERS. No one who has accompanied the Indians beaver hunting has not seen them wail and cry, especially when they see their children in the torments of the last agony. Often, with their eyes filled with tears and raised toward their aggressors, they seem to implore pity; but hunters are indifferent to this feeling, as well as to the emotions of these wretched animals.

10–11 TORONTO, NIAGARA. Good-sized ports on the Ontario: the former, situated west of this lake, is formed by a deep and convenient bay, where the English Government is building a dockyard, and a town to which they have given the name of York; the latter, located at the southwest, is formed by the mouth of the Niagara River, to the east of which is the fortress of the same name, and to the west, the Cape of the Missisagé, on which they are building a new town destined to be the chief town of Upper Canada.

12 HOTCHELAGA. Ancient name of the island called since then, Montreal, after having long been known as Sainte-Marie, which the priests of Saint Sulpice had given it when they became owners of it through a land grant from Louis XIV.

13 TO PLOW OVER THE BONES OF THEIR ANCESTORS. One of the most deeply rooted opinions among the Indians before we corrupted them

was their respect for the ashes of their ancestors and for the resting places of their ancestors, places often shared by various tribes. Never did they pass by them without stopping a few moments. One of the conditions of the first sale of land they made to the Europeans was that these places would be forever respected; and even today, they speak only with horror of the colonists' profanation of them. One of their most vigorous curses is to wish that the bones of their enemies be crushed 'neath the feet of passers-by, or bleached by the rains and the dew.

14   TOMAHAWK. This is a small axe of polished steel, appropriately helved, whose opposite end is a piece of iron, octagonal and hollow, through which they smoke. On the handle they mark the number of scalps they have taken, and the number of enemies they have killed.

15   CORLEAR. This was the name of one of the first interpreters whom the Dutch used in their trade with the six nations, then formidable. The fairmindedness of this man who never deceived them (as often happens) together with his kind deeds to them earned him their confidence and esteem for a great many years. When he became old and rich, he retired to New-York, then a mere marketplace, where he obtained grant of a cape at the eastern end of the city, still known today as Corlear's Hook. Every time the chiefs of the six nations came to negotiate with the Governor, the home and hospitality of this worthy interpreter was at their disposal: from this fact rose the custom of substituting his name for the one of the town and colony, and the expression "to go or return from the land of Corléar."

16   TOMAHAWKERAI. Because people say: I shall gun at, I shall draw saber at, why not use the substantive as a verb and express thus the action of killing one's enemy with this weapon?

17   TOOTH AND KETTLE OF THE ENEMY. This expression comes from the fact that once upon a time it was a very common practice for the victors to cut up their victims, put their limbs into a kettle, drink the soup that was cooked from them, and eat the flesh. Their ancient songs recall these very horrible and disgusting images.

18   CAWEN. Indian word meaning "no."

19   CAYUGAS, SÉNÈCCAS, TUSCARORAS. Names of ancient tribes, who, jointly with the Oneidas and the Onondagas, formed the Mohawk league, which was always considered the principal nation. This power disappeared almost entirely; scarcely 200 scattered families remain.

CHAPTER IX

1   WAMPAUM BELT. Belt or branches composed of little round circles made with the inside of clam shells, artistically shaped and polished and pierced lengthwise; they are about one half inch in diameter. Some are blue, others white. Taken separately, these little trinkets can be considered as money for Indians' use. Are they strung together at a certain length and various links sewn together? Then it is a belt. Worn across the chest, it is considered the most precious ornament: given after a promise, a bar-

gain, an act of adoption, a speech, these belts are considered as a guarantee; it is their official seal.

CHAPTER X

1 GROUSE OR DRUMMING PARTRIDGES. These fine birds, known in the United States as pheasants or grouse, are of a species peculiar to this continent. The feathers on the back and wings resemble those of pullets; those on the stomach and thighs resemble the winter thrush's feathers. They are feather-legged like pigeons, and have a beautiful tuft of feathers on their heads. The name drumming partridge comes from the muffled, rumbling sound which they make with their wings when they are perching; this noise can be heard more than a mile away, and resembles the rolling of a drum. These birds are very common and often furnish for travelers "daily bread."

2 NEW-HAVEN. Formerly known under the old Indian name of Quini-pack: it was founded in 1638, the time of the first colonization of Connect-icut. This town is located 45 miles from Hartford, 30 from New-London, on a bay whose lovely, cultivated shores offer a splendid view. This bay abounds in fish and communicates with the Sound, an arm of the sea which separates Long Island from the continent and leads to New-York. It is one of the most delightful and picturesque towns on the continent: it has been marked off into lots of 100 square rods, many of which are embellished with very high weeping willows. The center lot, likewise surrounded by trees, is occupied by the church, the college, and several public buildings. Although the streets are not paved at all, they are wide and clean; there are 500 framed houses, all nice looking and well painted—and 4,000 inhabitants. In order to make for greater depth of water, they have just built a jetty 2,000 feet long, without any doubt, the finest on the continent. Although light, the soil of the neighborhood is extremely productive, and covered by magnificent orchards. There one sees many mills, as well as a happy mixture of activity, both rural and commercial. Without being wealthy, the inhabitants there are very well off.

A stay in this town is made delightfully pleasant by daily connection with New-York, by land and sea, by means of fine, well-appointed boats and countless stagecoaches bound for the northern states, an abundance of food and the fine spirit of the inhabitants. The town was incorporated in 1782.

3 THE COLLEGE AT NEW-HAVEN. Known also as Yale, after its first benefactor, this college was founded in 1700 and incorporated one year later. Built of bricks, this building is 100 feet long, 40 wide and has three stories. Its library, which had suffered a great deal from the British occupation during the war, has just been considerably enlarged through the generosity of many persons, in gratitude for the excellent education which their children received there. The building known as the museum is still in its infancy. The Governor and the chief magistrates of the state, jointly with a certain number of ministers, are the administrators of this uni-

versity. It is before them and in the presence of nearly all the inhabitants of the town that the scholars are strictly examined twice a year. The course of education includes the ordinary cycle of literature, the three learned tongues, and as many special sciences as one can learn in four years.

The Government, protector of this college, has just added a great sum to its income; with it they are going to build another building, and finish the physics laboratory. Here are sent not only young men from the southern States, but also from the western islands and the Bermudas.

4 CHERRY WINE. This wine is made from a mixture of cherry juice, raspberries, currants, wild cherries, to which one adds a certain amount of sugar: after having been fermented and purified, it is put into a bottle. I have known many Europeans who, deceived by its color, its transparence, and its bouquet, believed that it came from Frontignan or from Provence.

5 PEACH BRANDY. Nothing has become more common today than this brandy, especially in the southern and trans-alleghanian states: that is why one sees such a great number of peach tree orchards. A full bushel of this fruit yields one gallon, or four bottles. Just as with all other brandies, it has to be aged in order to be really fine and smooth.

CHAPTER XI

1 SWAMPS WITH DIFFICULT CROSSINGS. Most of the wooded swamps, and even those known as Bog-Meadows, below the surface, are nothing but a web of trees uprooted no one knows when or how. Some day these reserves will offer great resources to posterity, when the clearings have yielded wood as rare as the wood of Europe. In the neighborhood of Baskind-Ridge, once the lovely estate of Lord Sterling, I know a swamp 5,000 acres, covered with beautiful water-ash, maple trees, hycoris, etc. To assure himself more positively of the quantity of wood located under a surface that is 10 square rods, he cut down the forest that covered this area, he dug it under four feet; and to his great astonishment, he observed that the quantity of wood underground exceeded by far that of the living trees.

2 PIAZZA. This is the name given in some States to the extension from the roof of houses that is supported by little columns of cedar; this is a device that shuts out the sun eight or nine feet during the summer, and during the winter, the snows and rain. I know some houses which are entirely surrounded by these piazzas, from a distance that gives them the appearance of a shelter and keeps the houses dry and cool.

3 BOLLAND ISLAND AND SIERRA-LEONA RIVER. Inspired by the desire to introduce to the coasts of Africa the cultivation of sugar, and to destroy gradually the godless trade of Negro slavery, a great number of persons in England, headed by Thomas Fothergill (that hero of humanity), after contributing the sum of 300,000 pounds sterling, sent agents to the coast of Africa in 1786; there they bought a beautiful and healthful

site between the Sierra-Leona and Sherbo Rivers; the purchase was fifteen miles long and ran twenty miles back from the shore. The center of this tract is a convenient, safe bay known as Saint-George. They also acquired Bolland Island, adjoining this coast.

Everything in readiness, a great number of freed Negroes were sent there from England, under the leadership of persons who were planning to settle in Africa. They were accompanied by skillful gardeners, botanists, farmers, and all necessary help. They were to cultivate sugar, cotton, indigo, copal rubber, etc. Despite several disasters and delays, this colony, free from its very start, began to prosper; when French vessels appeared off the coast and entered the bay, everything they could not take away was destroyed.

I have heard that these misfortunes scarcely cooled the zeal of these illustrious founders: that the losses were repaired promptly, and that this free colony (thus they called it) is finally beginning to gain ground. May these precious seeds bear fruit beyond their hopes, and the example of industry and success of these black colonists open the eyes of their fellow-countrymen and convince their princes, or rather their tyrants, that it would be much more advantageous for them to have their subjects cultivate their sugar cane than to sell these subjects as lowly herds.

CHAPTER XII

1 VERMONT. The early clearings of this territory, then dependent on New-Hampshire, began in 1762. For a long time, the families who came there under General Bayley and Colonel Johnson, isolated in the midst of these vast solitudes, found themselves more than 100 miles from any dwelling. Settled on fertile land, they prospered; gradually their number increased; but soon, as they emerged from this deep backwoods, these colonists became the subject of public talk and were known under the derisive name of Green Mountain Boys.

Soon after the conquest of Canada, the Governor of New-York, backed by the British ministers, claimed that the New-Hampshire government had wrongfully ceded some land west of the Connecticut river, and declared that, according to the new boundaries of his colony marked on the map, all the territory between Lake Champlain and the Connecticut river belonged to New-York. Indignant over a resolution as unjust as it was tyrannical, one that annulled their rights and relieved them of their property, these peaceful farmers, united for the first time, resolved to present a request to the king, and if he was deaf to their pleas, to put up vigorous resistance to the laws through the leading lawyers of the continent.

On the other hand, the Government of New-York, according to custom, divided their land into counties and districts, named magistrates, and established courts of justice.

However, whether the judges were convinced of the legitimacy of the rights of their compatriots, or whether they were intimidated by fear of their resentment, judicial opinion was almost entirely in favor of the plaintiffs. Irritated by this condescension, the Government of New-York sent some high judges of the Supreme Court, and some Scotch colonists, under conduct of their officers, to whom they had ceded lands.

Informed of this step, the young men took up arms and, preceded by some of their leaders, went forth to meet these strangers under pretext of escorting them and bringing them to their destination. The Courts of justice were opened with much dignity and calm; but toward the end of the session, these judges, having wished to influence the opinion of the jury, rose and after quickly reproaching them for the guilt of infracting the law, made them sign an agreement by which they promised never to come back into their land. As to the Scotch colonists, whose officers they sent away with much greater clemency, they confirmed the gift of lands promised to them and quickly inspired in them the same opinions, saying to them: *ubi benè, ibi patria.*

In New-York it was suggested that they be reduced by force, but in the fear of igniting a civil war, this plan never came off; things remained undecided until the time of the revolution. Renouncing then the jurisdiction claimed by New-York and New-Hampshire, they declared their territory independent, with the name of Vermont, and themselves invested with all the powers of legislation. Shortly afterward, they sent two fine regiments to General Washington, to whom they wrote a justifying letter; they made a constitution like Connecticut's, with the exception of the council of censors renewed every seven years, and were finally recognized as the fourteenth member of the Confederation, March 4, 1791, thirty-one years after the first tree of this vast clearing was uprooted. Since that time, they have founded a college on the shores of Lake Champlain, opened roads, built bridges, endowed churches and schools in sections formerly cultivated. By a law which the legislative Body has just passed, it is ruled that two lots of 350 acres will be reserved in each of the two hundred districts of which this State is composed; one destined for the maintenance of the ministers of the gospel, and the other, for the schools in the region.

This region, very abundant in pasture land, furnishes the finest cattle on the continent, horses, lard, peas, linen, potash, and a great quantity of maple sugar. It has 130 souls.

2 UNKNOWN TYRANNY. As soon as the measures taken by the Government of New-York to incorporate in its own vast territory the territory known as Green Mountains were sent to England, everyone hastened to seek grants, not of wooded lands, but of cleared districts, long under cultivation. Indeed, nothing was more convenient than to obtain, by a stroke of the pen, fine pasture lands, fields, orchards, and mills and to oust the owners of them. Astonishing thing! This last excess of injustice, unknown until today, infuriated people in Europe, where landownership is supremely respected.

Some officers having obtained a grant of two of the oldest districts, containing, according to custom, 23,400 acres each, set sail to take possession of it. Their arrival in New-York, as well as the aim of their journey, having been announced in the gazettes, the owners sent several persons to Benington, which these foreigners would obviously pass through on their way to "their" lands. These representatives were bearers of a memorandum in which, after exposing the horrible injustice of despoiling them of their property, the owners announced the firm resolution they had taken to resist property seizure on peril of their lives.

"What would you do," they said to them, "if your Parliament passed a law taking from you your estate, your parks, and your forests? Well, our fields and our hearths are even dearer to us, since it is by the sweat of our brows that we have cleared the fields and built our homes."

Impressed with the justice of these utterances, as well as the fairness of their methods, the officers withdrew the claims which the orders whose bearers they were could not justify; they signed an act of renunication and asked only permission to visit a land inhabited by such worthy men. They were received and treated with great kindness and hospitality. Since their return to England, no one has heard any talk of concessions.

3 LAKE CHAMPLAIN. Quite different from the Great Lakes, whose immensity awakens only astonishment and awe, this lake, covering a smaller area, stimulates delightful and agreeable emotions; the eye, in roving over it, almost always sees parts of its shores, or lights on the numerous islands which dot it; these shores, often virtual cliffs, always picturesque, are composed of rocks, whose sharpness, form, and height make a myriad of bizarre and fantastic objects for the imagination.

This beautiful lake is 120 miles long, from South-Bay to Pointe-aux-Fers, at the entrance to Canada; its width is only two miles as far as Ticonderoga, at a distance of 30 miles; it is rather like a deep, quiet river, whose banks are beginning to be well cultivated. The environs of this natural fortress consist of a vast stretch of pasture lands: beyond at Crown Point, at a distance of 15 miles, the width of the lake is greater; it is a majestic river whose fertile banks are covered with houses built close together. On the first falls at Fair-Haven Creek, which empties into this first part, the largest forges on the continent were built twenty years ago; there one also sees a nail factory and a blast furnace. The owner (Colonel Lyons) extracts all the mineral he needs from a chain of rocks which forms the west shore of the lake, from Crown-Point to Will's-borough. Here is a collection of ferruginous deposits that are the richest and most extraordinary known: here one also finds copper and lead. At this place the width of the lake is five to six miles; but farther north, it is 18; about here one begins to notice numerous islands which occupy part of this space for fifty miles.

The largest island (South Hero) is 16 miles long and 14 wide, and is inhabited by five hundred Vermont families. Gradually the lake boundaries narrow as far as Pointe-aux-Fers, from which point, like a beautiful river, it rolls its waters toward Saint John, Chambly, and Sorrel, before uniting with the waters of the St. Lawrence River.

One of the most impressive points of the west shore is this long and wide peninsula, once known as Skenonton (roe), today as Cumberland Head. One will see few locations more beautiful and more imposing and whose soil is more fertile. Two miles from the line of demarcation separating the States of Vermont and New-York from Canada (45th parallel), one finds on the east side a windmill of very remarkable construction, the first one built in these remote cantons. The counties of Washington and Clinton, which occupy the west side, founded in 1783, contained in 1797, 22,473 inhabitants. The surface of this lake is estimated to be about 500,000 acres.

4 BRIDGE AT COHOS. This fine bridge, built on the Mohawk, five years ago, is located three quarters of a mile from Cohos and three miles from the junction of this river with the Hudson. Its construction, having raised unforeseen difficulties, the Government, in order to encourage the association which had undertaken it, gave it 7,500 piastres (nearly 40,000 pounds). It is 900 feet long, 40 feet wide. The frame, which is very beautiful, reposes on 27 piles built of stones.

5 MARITIME TOWN, PRESQU'ILE. Peninsula located on the southern shore of Lake Erie, sixty miles from Niagara, which, like the mouth of the Cuyahoga, forms a harbor that is extremely useful to navigators, this coast being merely a series of very high rocks. It is situated in the territory of Pensylvanie; its width is only 40 miles, being very much limited by the western boundaries of New-York on one side and on the other, by the Connecticut reserve. A town has just been marked off in the environs of that harbor.

6 NAVIGATION OF THE POTOWMACK. This river, whose sources spring from the Alleghany chain, empties into the Chespeake Bay, after meandering through a fertile land for more than 400 miles: its confluency in this bay is seven and one-half miles long and seven fathoms deep, four at the quays of Alexandria, and three at those of Washington (the federal town), seven miles beyond at the last terminus of coastal navigation, located 150 miles from this great bay and 438 from the capes of Virginia.

This river has become much more interesting since the canals and sluiceways, built to avoid the falls, have been finished. The first is 1,320 toises long, four sluiceways are 10 feet high at a slope of 76 feet; the second, 2,200 toises and 10 sluiceways, at a slope of 168 feet, including that of the terrain 90 feet, and that of the falls, which are 78 feet high.

From this point its course is gentle and quiet as far as Will's-Creek, and at Shawanèse-Fields, where there are three rapids, on which they have been working for several months; beyond, they plan to improve the road which was blazed through the mountains in 1755 for Braddock's expedition against Fort Du-Quesne: then 37 miles nearer, the waters of the Atlantic will communicate with those of the Ohio through the *Cheat*, a navigable branch of the Monongahéla, an objective of great importance, considered in all political and commercial respects: perhaps even in time to come, they will succeed in shortening this distance, by uniting the waters of the mountains, by making navigable canals of them.

7 CANAL AT NORFOLK. This canal, in a distance of 28 miles, is to cross Dismal Swamp. Quite different from the other swamps, this one is a strange mixture of dry, wet, miry lands or those entirely covered by water. On the former grow the most beautiful oaks that one can see; the second offers only forests of very high reeds, which, seen from afar, when the wind stirs them, resemble the slow and long undulations of the sea on a calm day: thus does one speak of these great glades (green seas). The third is covered only by cedars, cypress, and pines of tremendous height.

In the midst of this vast swamp is a little lake (Drummond's Pond), whose waters, blackened by the reflection of the evergreen trees of the region, resemble those of Averne; these forests are so thick, so somber and so gloomy, that the sun never penetrates; yet, one sees there neither snakes, nor insects, nor birds.

This swamp, which begins nine miles from Norfolk, is thirty miles from north to south, and twelve from east to west; it contains 192,000 acres. One part belongs to Virginia, and the other to Carolina. Five rivers emerge from its vast reservoirs; to wit, the southern branches of the Elisabeth and the Nausémond, which empty into the Chésapeak Bay; the North, the North-west, and the Perquimons, which empty into the Sound at Albemarle.

A great part of the surface of this swamp appears to be merely a crust, supported by an immense accumulation of water; for scarcely has one dug a ditch, even in the dryest parts, when it is immediately filled. Almost anywhere one can sink a pole, however long, without feeling any resistance; nowhere can one see trees of greater diameter, nor greater height; but because the bottom on which they grow is very miry, the trees are often overturned by winds; this makes the swamps absolutely impenetrable to man, as well as to wild beasts. Other places, whose ground is dryer, are no less difficult to cross because of thorny and trailing vines, and especially bamboo thorns, with which the surface is entirely covered.

Long before the revolution, the Government of Virginia, wishing to open a canal from Elisabeth to Paskotang in Carolina, had chartered a large company who were to undertake this fine and useful enterprise, and to encourage them, had given them 80,000 acres of this swamp; they were working there with success when the English, in their first invasion of this land, shanghaied the Negroes, destroyed the tools and the houses. It is only since 1793, encouraged by the legislators of Carolina and Virginia, that this company resumed its work.

Including the length of the little lake, that of this canal will be 28 miles. In 1796 there were already twelve of the ditches dug. From the beginning of this project General Washington has been one of the associates in this numerous company; he contributed a great deal to it. I understood that it was to be finished in 1800.

8 CANAL AT RICHMONT. Since the time when, by legislative act, the seat of Government was transferred from Williamsbourg to Richmont, and consequently the latter town has been considered as the capital of this State, they have been busy perfecting navigation on the James River, at the foot of whose falls this town was founded. The greatest obstacle were these very falls or rather, rapids, which, in the space of six miles, fall 80 feet. A canal was planned at that time; it has just been finished; today commodities from the interior arrive at Richmont, from the foot of the Blue Mountains, 200 miles away, as well as from Rivanna. With slight expense the latter town can be made navigable as far as Carpenter's Creek, located 25 miles from one of the branches of Green-Bryar.

9 FOUNDING OF THE NEW STATE OF WASHINGTON ON THE BANKS OF THE MUSKINGHUM. Among the officers of the continental army, who found themselves bereft of fortune after the demobilization of this army, some resumed the professions and business which they had abandoned at the beginning of the revolution, in order to hasten to help their country, invaded by an army of 70,000 men. A greater number united in societies, in order to settle the new lands which Congress and the States had given them (as reward for their service) on the banks of the Ohio and elsewhere. These leaders united with those of their former soldiers who wished to follow them, and having brought to the formation of these new colonies a great spirit of order, much wisdom and foresight, they all succeeded and became in a few years flourishing regions, where in the shade of their laurel trees, these worthy soldiers cultivated their fields.

The principles on which the colony at Muskinghum, for example, or as it was called, the new State of Washington, was founded, could serve as a model to those who eventually would like to carry out a similar enterprise. The lands which these founders had received from the Government, as well as those which they received with their certificates, having been surveyed and subdivided with great care, at first they sent forth a certain number of workers to clear, plant corn, and build log houses. Everything in readiness, the families arrived without incident, accompanied by a minister of the gospel and a schoolmaster, bringing with them a town clock, even, for the use of the church which they planned to build; it was the first clock heard west of the Alléghény mountains.

The division of lands, the drying of the swamps, the mutual aid which they were to practice—everything—to the nomenclature of their town, its streets, its squares, and the districts of their territory, had been so thought out and planned that nothing delayed the clearings and the progress of this fine little colony of former soldiers, despite the war with the Indians. These soldiers, raised on the religious principles of their country, accustomed to municipal forms, to subordination, have become suddenly hard-working colonists, and fathers of fine families. One must admit, their progress would not have been so rapid, if part of them had been foreigners with neither customs nor religious principles.

CHAPTER XIII

1 JOURNEY TO ALBANY IN 54 HOURS. It happens quite frequently during the summer that in journeying to Albany in a south wind and the beginning of the tide, one can go up the river to Albany (although 66 miles distance) in very little time, especially if this wind is not checked by the wind from the north, which almost always prevails over the chain of mountains; because the progress of the vessel is equal to that of the tide, one finds the sailing constantly favorable.

What sight is more interesting to see than that of the banks of this beautiful river, now raw and lofty, shaded by ancient trees; now more pleasant, covered with orchards and dwellings; what sight is more interesting than that of vessels, which ceaselessly ply up and down the river; and especially the sight of those landings that one sees on both banks, with their piers, their shops, and their cranes. It is especially during the beautiful season of summer when the various views of this river would merit all the attention of the poet, naturalist, and painter. One never tires of admiring the varied, picturesque beauty, or the still, deep waters, when crossing this long and winding strait, known as the passage of the Highlands. The astonishing thing is that the tide flows forty miles beyond!

2 THREE ERSE FAMILIES. Ancient name by which the inhabitants of the mountains of Scotland are known; the Romans designated them by the name Picts or Picti. The language they speak is the same written 1,600 years ago by their celebrated bards Ossian, Fingal, etc. They still preserve some of the customs of bygone days. This is one of the aboriginal races of the most respectable ilk in Europe, and the country where education is most generally common among all the classes.

3 SILVER-EELS. A species of eel which, at the beginning of autumn, comes down the river to the sea; its stomach is of a remarkable whiteness. These eels are fat, delicate, and very much sought after, especially after being smoked for some time.

4 GROWTH OF PEACH-TREES. In this country there are no peach trees known whose growth is so rapid; it is not rare to see some which bear fruit early in the third year from the time of the planting of the pit; yet their existence is very short, and subject to many accidents and much sickness. Insects devour them; they become gummy; their tender wood easily breaks and their fruit is not good. To remedy these inconveniences, one must bud them; this art is as yet only slightly known to the colonists. Introducing a little mercury into the trunk, according to Doctor Franklin's experiments, keeps off the insects without destroying the fruit.

The cultivation of this tree has become much more common since the establishment of the colonies beyond the mountains, the peaches being equally good for fattening pigs and making brandy, to which they know how to give a special taste and color, by infusing the wild grape, apples, and dry peaches.

5 THE LAST CULTIVATABLE BOUNDARIES OF THE UNITED STATES. According to treaties, these boundaries are fixed at a line which is supposed to divide the St. Lawrence river, lakes Ontario, Erie, Sainte-Claire, Superior, etc., as far as the Lake of the Woods, from which place another line runs west, as far as the Mississippi; from this point, the middle of this great river separates the United States from the Spanish possessions as far as the 31st degree, somewhat below the Land of the Natchees, where the boundaries of Georgia begin. But although under such temperate latitudes, all the land bordering lake Superior, the shores of lake Michigan and Green Bay, as well as the cataract of the Mississippi (St. Anthony's Falls) is in such a rugged climate, it is scarcely probable that American plows will ever go farther than Ouisconsing, or than that very cataract, located 566 measured leagues from the sea, unless the clearing of the rest of the continent causes a great change in temperature. The surface of the land included between these boundaries and the riverbanks bordering the Atlantic States is estimated at a million square miles, equal to 650,000,000 acres, from which one must deduct 51 million for the lakes and rivers; this leaves 589 million; the Indians still own 220 million acres of it; that leaves 329 million, to which one must add 23 ceded by the treaty with England; this gives 380 million, for the surface which is today owned by the United States.

CHAPTER XIV

1 NARROWS. This strait, which is only two leagues from New-York, is formed by the meeting of the western part of the islands of Nassau (actually Long Island) and the States. It is about a thousand toises wide and has a great depth of water. This is the route of all the vessels that leave the town or arrive from abroad, after having dropped anchor at Sandy-Hook, 9 miles farther. This is perhaps the only place from which one can prevent the approach of a small enemy fleet. By means of a vast cone sunk in the middle of this strait, whose fire would be kept going, and, crossed by broadsides of red bullets, placed on the nearest banks, it would be easy to close the entry to the port on this side. Nature has adequately defended the port at Hellgate, whose dangers are well known to navigators.

2 HERSCHEL'S SATELLITES. This great astronomer has just discovered four new ones, which, added to the first two and the two others which Doctor Wurm has also discovered, form a group of eight moons by which this last planet of our system is accompanied. Its year is equivalent to 83 of ours, plus 33 days.

3 EXTENT OF THE OHIO. This trans-Alleghanian part of the continent is destined some day to become its glory. This beautiful river, into which more than twenty good-sized rivers empty, crosses this area for 396 leagues, from Pitt'sbourg, under 40° 31' 44", to confluency of the Ohio with the Mississippi, under 36° 43', and extends over an area covered by ten degrees of longitude. There are few countries on earth whose fertility

and location promise industry more assured rewards. In order to get some idea of the extent of this region, imagine a parallelogram whose length would be 300 leagues (subtracting 96 for the twistings of the river); let one suppose that the rivers flowing from the north and the south, contributing their waters, are only 25 leagues long; this would give 50 leagues of width to this parallelogram, and consequently 15,000 square leagues, 7/10 of which are estimated to be cultivatable. If to the products of agricultural industry, one adds those of the forests of cedars, pines, mulberry trees, maple, quarries and mines, then one will have a slight notion of what this vast land will furnish some day. And if, on the other hand, one considers the Ohio only as one of the branches of the Mississippi, it is easy to imagine that New Orleans is destined to become the center of an immense trade.

4 INDIANA. See Volume Two, Chapter XV

5 LIMESTONE. This little river falls over the southwest bank of the Ohio, 167 leagues from Pitt'sbourg, and crosses one of the most fertile and delightful regions of Kentukey, of which Washington, located on the route to Balchutta, is the principal place. The mouth of this river is where the colonists disembark who are going down the Ohio to settle along the southern parts of the Limestone. But what makes it more remarkable in the eyes of travelers is the difference they observe between the climate of Pitt'sbourg, where they embarked, and that of Limestone. Indeed, nothing is more striking, especially in the spring, than this sudden transition from the bareness and melancholy of winter to the burst of sunshine and beauty of vegetation. After disembarking, one climbs a steep but gradual incline and instead of arriving at the summit of a mountain, one finds himself in a flat country, enriched by all nature's treasures, well cultivated and covered with dwellings; there one sees sweet-smelling bushes and flowers unknown to the North. It is here that one begins to hear the warble of the birds of the South. This fertility continues as far as Washington, Johnson, Bourbon, Lexington: everything that is not wooded is covered with reeds, with ray, and buffalo grass, as well as three kinds of clover. It is estimated that during the years 1787 and 1788 more than 12 thousand colonists coming from Europe as well as the different states of the Union passed through there.

6 GRAND KANHAWA. This river rises in the mountains around North Carolina known as the Iron Hills, from the vast bosom of which the principal rivers of Virginia and Ténézée rise. It empties into the Ohio, 76 leagues from Pitt'sbourg and 320 leagues above the confluency of the Ohio with the Mississippi, after meandering 133 to 160 leagues. Some of its branches, such as the Green-briar, Louisa, etc., have deep and navigable intervals; but with the exception of four or five leagues, from the beginning of the rapids as far as the Ohio, all the rest of the course of the Kanhawa is merely a long and tortuous torrent, especially in its descent from the mountains of Ouasioto and in its passage through the Laurier chain. This vast space is only a deep and useless solitude, composed of

masses of sharp, bare rocks, and narrow, sterile valleys which the sunlight has never penetrated and on which the mighty power of nature and of time has been able to make grow only a few isolated cedars or juniper bushes. How regrettable that the celebrated poets of Europe, those great interpreters of nature who have described everything great, beautiful, and majestic in the Pyrénées and the Alps, cannot be transported here! How many sights worthy of their brushes and of their whole range of poetic expression I could point out to them! There are no lands more fertile than those near the Kanhawa, four or five leagues before it empties into the Ohio; they belong to General Washington, who sent 53 families, a number which has since increased greatly. Here there is no outlet, other than the Ohio.

7 GALLIPOLIS. A little French colony which was to settle originally along the banks of the Scioto, 38 leagues south, but to which, according to new arrangements, lands have been granted on the Ohio, opposite the mouth of the great Kanhawa. This colony is beginning to prosper, after languishing, because of the war with the Indians. It is estimated that Gallipolis has between seven and eight hundred families.

8 SCIOTO. Wide and beautiful river which empties into the Ohio 130 leagues from Pitt'sbourg, and 266 leagues from the junction of this river with the Mississippi. It is navigable for a distance of 66 leagues; the lands which it waters, the plains which its numerous branches cross, are of a great fertility, and were inhabited by the Shawanèse nation until the last treaty of peace with the United States, by which the Shawanèse were forced to abandon the plains and to withdraw farther west. The floods of the Ohio are felt at a considerable distance from its mouth.

9 KENTUKEY. A land whose richness of soil, mildness of climate, astonishing growth in population, and cosmopolitan nature have made quite famous. It is a part of Virginia, located on the Ohio river, 209 leagues from Pitt'sbourg. The Government of Virginia freed this land as soon as the colonists had become numerous enough and were capable of self-government and of providing for their own needs. Kentukey was admitted as the 14th State in the union on February 4, 1791, only 17 years after its first colonization.

The climate and soil are adapted to the cultivation of tobacco, cotton, silk, and wine, as well as beans. In no part of the United States does one see as fine sheep—nor wool so elegant. The first horses, having come from Virginia, have produced an excellent breed. Hemp and flax are also grown in Kentukey.

From their salt springs, the colonists take all the salt they need; from their forests, all the sugar they need; from the peaches of the peach trees and from the grapes of wild vines which grow with extraordinary lushness, they are beginning to make brandy and vinegar. Iron has been discovered in the mountains around Belachutta and Cumberland, where it is probable they have built great foundries. In 1784 there were 30,000 inhabitants; in 1790, 70,000; and today nearly 167,000. In the course of the year 1787, nearly 20,000 colonists arrived in Kentukey, as many from the two Carolinas and Virginia, as from the northern States and Europe. It is in the county of Woodfort, several miles from the Ohio River, that big bones lick was discovered on the surface of a terrain that was very salty; likewise, enormous remains of the mammoth; in many other places, cone-shaped tombs whose inner layers are of stone; remains of entrenched camps, as well as fragments of pottery, which suggest certain elegance in form.

The natural history of this country is no less interesting: almost all the rivers flow in beds of great depth. In many places, the waters are 300 feet lower than the ground they cross; this makes the passage very difficult. The rocks of these escarpments are of marble or calcareous stone, pierced by caves and grottoes whose walls abound in nitrate of potassium. All the lesser rivers dry up early in the month of July and do not fill up again until mid-October. In following the tracks, or rather pits made by the buffaloes and other wild animals, twelve or fifteen little salt swamps were discovered whose surfaces the animals came to lick; from this originated the word "licks," so frequent on the maps of this land. By means of wells, people have succeeded in obtaining in abundance the water from which they make very fine salt: also many bituminous and sulfurous springs were discovered.

I think it would be difficult to imagine a mixture more astonishing than that of the population of this new State. There is perhaps no nation in Europe and no State in the Union in which one would find so great a melting pot of individuals. It is doubtless to this cause as well as to the arrival of many wealthy and educated families that are due not only the tranquility and good order one observes, but also the progress of industry, the cosmopolitanism of customs, the establishment of a great number of churches, schools, and the founding of a college (Salem) to which the new Government has given ten thousand acres of land and considerable funds. Early in 1783 there was a printery, the first one to set up a gazette west of the Alléghénies and more than 300 leagues from Philadelphia.

From this new stock of settlers, already many swarms have sprung who have ventured forth to settle on the Mississippi, the Wabash, the Illinois, etc. The militia is composed of 17,000 men. The federal constitution served as model to the one which they made and adopted in 1792. The wool, cotton, silk, and wine will some day be the principal branches of their exportation. Already they ship great tobacco crops and meal to New-Orleans.

10 LAKE PEPPIN. Located 547 geographical leagues from the sea, and a little distance from the confluency of the great Chippaway River. There the Mississippi suddenly widens; this extension, to which the name Lake Peppin was given, is twenty miles long and six miles wide. This surface is perennially covered with water birds such as ducks, swans, geese, and cranes. Once upon a time a Canadian family had settled on the banks in

order to make a treaty with the Nadooassés nations. It is on the east coast that Carver discovered traces of a retrenched camp in 1766; its platform was four feet high and one mile long. This lake is only twenty leagues below Saint Anthony's Falls.

11 NADOOASSES AND PADOOKAS. See Note 4 Chapter II

12 MISSOURI. A river which by the great length of its course and the volume of its waters should be considered as a river, and not as one of the branches of the Mississippi. Many of these branches come from the mountains of California and from the kingdom of Santa Fé in New Mexico. They cross the vast plains that have not yet been exposed to any geographical observations. It is from its confluent in the Mississippi that the clear waters of the Missouri river suddenly become thick and muddy. The numerous Nadooassés tribes that inhabit the banks and hunt on horse through the vast grassy plains sell their skins to the traders at Pancor (Saint-Louis) and Missire, pretty little towns built by the French in Upper Louisiana, on the banks of the Mississippi, 410 measured miles from the gulf of Mexico.

13 CHIKAGO. Quiet little river which empties into the southwestern part of Lake Michigan, and through which, by means of a short portage of four miles, one arrives at Theakiky, a branch of the Illinois which runs into the Mississippi. From the time of the Canadians, this passage into upper Louisiana was very much frequented.

14 MICHILLIMAKINACK. Fort formerly built by the French on the northern extremity of the great peninsula which divides the waters of Michigan and Huron. This fort has just been ceded by England to the United States, in accordance with the treaties. This place was formerly the center of a great Indian trade, which today has moved to Lake Winipeg, almost 400 leagues farther north.

15 LAKE SUPERIOR. According to French maps, this vast sea is between the 46th and 50th degree of latitude, and about 500 leagues in circumference. It contains several islands, of which the so-called Royale is 40 leagues long. This lake receives the waters of a great number of rivers, and empties into Lake Huron through the strait at Saint-Mary. Its surface is estimated to equal 21,952,780 acres. Like the ocean, it is subject to storms and its waves rise very high. It abounds in fish of various species. In the southern direction one meets the Chigomégan peninsula which is more than 20 leagues long, in the neighborhood of which one finds virgin copper in considerable deposits. Its shores in some places are but a series of extremely escarped rocks. Although in such mild latitude, the climate is cold and the soil not very fertile.

16 DETROIT. Town built by the French nearly a century ago, on the fertile banks of the strait or Détroit river which carries the waters of the great lakes Superior, Michigan, and Huron to Lake Erie. It has 300 houses; streets that intersect at right angles, align in a parallel fashion with the river. Since the conquest of Canada, the English have surrounded it by strong palisades, flanked by four redoubts. The environs, as well as the

banks of the Detroit river, offer rich and beautiful countrysides, covered with respectable homes, surrounded by cherry trees, peach trees, and orchards; nowhere can one eat better fruits; the caille kind of apple is the best there is. The interest aroused by this fine farming is increased by the thought of the great distance from this region to the last outposts of Canada, from which it is more than 150 leagues into the heart of the continent. The Indians one sees there in great number are the remains of the ancient and war-like nation of Hurons, for whom the French had built a church on the other side of the river.

Although 400 leagues from the St. Lawrence Gulf, the trade of this town is considerable; the beauty of the wharves, the number of vessels arriving and leaving are indicative of the activity and movement of a seaport. It has 12 vessels of 50 to 100 tons; one is no less astonished by this, when one considers the extent of inland navigation Detroit enjoys. On one hand, Lake Erie, which is more than 100 leagues long; on the other, Lake Huron; Michigan, and Green Bay, still farther. From the time of the surrender of the forts, this town has become the general quarters for the American forces in remote regions. It is located under 42° 43′ latitude.

CHAPTER XV

1 PASSAGE OF THE POTOWMACK. The winding of this river through the Alléghénies' chain known as the Blue-Ridge is quite an imposing spectacle. The Shénando, after bathing the foot of this mountain for more than thirty leagues, appears on the right; on the left the Potowmack appears, and the very moment these two waters unite, they cross this chain, estimated to be 3,140 toises wide. For whoever has considered attentively this great and interesting phenomenon, it is obvious the rivers began to flow only long after the formation of the mountains; that, after having been able to cut a passage, they filled all the valleys, until, arriving at the summit of the Blue-Ridge, they uprooted and overturned these obstacles in their path. The fragments, the blocks of scattered rocks on the banks and in the middle of the rivers, attest to a break, a passage obtained by the slow but uninterrupted efforts of the course of centuries, of time, one of the most powerful agents of nature.

2 PASSAGE OF THE KANHAWA. Like the winding of the Potowmack through the Blue-Ridge, after having been swelled by the Shenando, the great Kanhawa crosses the chain of the Laurier and Ouasioto only after receiving in its bosom the waters of the Green-Briar; but, whether the the volume of water is not large enough, or whether the mass of rocks of which it is composed has offered them invincible resistance, the opening is not as deep as the one through which the Potowmack flows. This spectacle is no less interesting to watch when, seated on the crest of one of the promontories of these hideous riverbanks, one sees this immense volume of water, whose width is five to six miles, falling from precipice to

precipice with a sharp, whistling noise; it is more an impetuous torrent than a great river, and this torrent is more than 14 leagues long. In several places, it is divided by islands, or arrested by rocks against which it dashes with an incalculable violence; in still others, raised by inner layers, these currents suddenly become whirlpools of foam, falling in opposite directions. Morning and night, this eternal conflict fills the atmosphere with vapors that obscure the light of the sun.

Whatever the population and industry of the inhabitants of these regions, the land which this river crosses from its junction with the Green-Briar as far as ten or twelve leagues of the Ohio will never be suitable for any farming, so bare, harsh, and broken is this chain of the Ouasioto. These dismal solitudes, a most striking picture of brute and ignorant nature, will never be the abode either of vegetation or of life.

3   HADLEY'S CANAL. The peninsula located 8 miles from Springfield on which this two-mile canal has just been built, being too high for it to communicate with those of the Connecticut River, the boats, loaded and placed on a form or canal, go upstream and downstream with the aid of an inclined plane made of wood; they are drawn by a cable and capstan which a wheel rigged on the riverbank causes to turn. Sixty or eighty miles beyond, are the falls of Bellones, in the State of Vermont, near which the same company has just dug a canal that is far more convenient, since by means of sluiceways, the boats enter and leave there at the level of the river whose inland navigation today extends even beyond the college at Dartmouth.

4   CANAL AT SOUTH-BAY. Toward the southern extremity of Lake Champlain, narrow and deep, known as South Bay, falls Wood-Creek river, navigable for fifteen miles, as far as old Fort Anne: a company incorporated in 1792 is deciding to clear obstructions from the upper part and to dig a canal which would lead to King'sbury, on the Hudson. The advantages which would result from it are so considerable, that however great the expense, it would be wise for the Government of New-York, the wealthiest of any in the Union, to advance money for it; then the commodities from Vermont and from the counties of Washington and Clinton, located on the shores of Lake Champlain, instead of going to Canada through Saint John and Chambly, would be easily transported to Albany, and from there to New-York. This important enterprise will not take a long time.

5   POUGHÉPSIE. Chief town of Duchess county, in the State of New-York, located a quarter of a league from the Hudson, on the main route to Albany, and also on the route from Litchfields in Connecticut. Being extremely modern, the houses of this town are well built, the streets well planned and embellished with trees: there are 350 houses and nearly 1,800 inhabitants. Before the Revolution it was only a little straggling village where the Governor of the State of New-York lived, as long as the English were masters of the capital. The county whose center it is can be considered one of the most fertile and best cultivated in this State. Wheat is

one of the main products. This young town boasts six vessels continually occupied in transporting the commodities of the land to New-York.

6 ISLAND OF MANHATTAN. This is the Indian name of the island at the western end of which the city of New-York is built; it is fifteen miles long and a mile and a half wide. Although the soil is extremely poor and covered with rocks, the wealthy inhabitants of this town have succeeded in overcoming nature by virtue of labor and expenditures. On all sides one sees houses of pretty shapes, surrounded by productive gardens, fruit trees, acacias, tulip trees, especially on the banks of the east and west. This bare and sterile surface no longer resembles what it was before the revolution: the property has become as expensive as in the neighborhood of London and Dublin. There are few foreigners who have not shared 'neath its elegant roofs the charms of its hospitality. Not far from these picturesque places lives Horatio Gates (Burgoyne's victor) in an attractive house located in the region of the shores of the Sound, whose waters, abundant in fish, are ceaselessly covered with vessels going to and coming from the northern States.

7 ECHOES. Mr. John Watts, member of the New-York council in 1764, speaking to General Gage, then commander in chief in the colonies, and residing in New-York, about the echoes that inhabit this chain of mountains, invited him one day to come by water to dine in a house which he had had built. In order to convince him of the fidelity with which these hamadriads transmitted whatever one said over a considerable distance, he located the military music of the general 3,145 toises away, in the midst of woods on the banks of the river. Everything was favorable; the tide was coming in; the sky was cloudless and the atmosphere calm. In accordance with what Mr. Watts said, the General distinctly heard the music whose playing he had ordered. The instruments were a mixture of horns, clarinettes, flutes, hautboys, and cymbals; one moment they were playing together, another there were solos, according to the orders which had been given in writing to the musicians, one copy of which each guest had.

"Of all the concerts I have ever been present at," said General Gage, "I have never heard any so impressive, so touching, nor so smooth; these chords, soft and trembling, produce a harmonic effect which lifts me up and yet saddens me. That is how we should have it at concerts and in the churches. This outdoor concert has all the charms of illusion, something our hearts and imaginations often need."

According to the most exact research, it was the voice of the fifth echo one heard. I speak of this little experiment with all the more confidence since I was one of the guests!

8 "We had embarked on the General's barge in order to cross the river, which is nearly a mile wide. As we approached the opposite bank, Fort Westpoint which, seen from the east bank appeared meekly located at the foot of mountains, stood before our eyes and seemed itself to be the top of an escarped rock; yet this was nothing more than the bank of the river. Had I noticed that the crevices which divided it in different places were

merely embrasures for cannon and formidable batteries, I would have been prepared for the 13 successive volleys of 24 cannon. It was a military salute with which General Heath wished to honor me in the name of the thirteen States. Never was an honor more imposing or majestic; each volley from the cannon, after a long interval, was echoed by the opposite bank with a noise almost equal to that of the very discharge itself." (*Voyage de Chastellux*, Tome 1, page 70) Note inserted by the translator.

9 FISHING EAGLE. I was visiting Mr. Verplanck whose farm is only a short distance from Fish-Kill (located on the banks of the Hudson), when he said to me: "Follow me, I wish to show you with how much skill my purveyors can catch the fish we are to eat tonight." Reaching the last escarpment of the bank in the greatest silence, and hiding under thick bushes, we were watching carefully the part of the river before us when at some distance from behind, a vessel which was sailing full speed, I saw a considerable movement in the midst of the channel, as though someone had thrown a great stone; from this point, soon after, I saw a fishing eagle emerging with difficulty from the waters' depth, holding in his beak a fish whose length and tortuous movements seemed to slow down the eagle's flight; by turns he would rise, swoop down, almost sink and then rise again; finally, after many efforts, profiting by a puff of favorable wind, he was heading slowly toward his eyrie, located not far from the place where we were hidden, when Mr. Verplanck called my attention to his proud antagonist above our heads, the bald eagle which, to judge by the flapping of his wings and his excited look was preparing himself for combat, or rather to exercise the right of the mightiest. Overloaded, the fishing eagle made no resistance and abandoned his prey; the prey was about to escape the avidity of his enemy when the bald eagle, by an effort of skill and incredible redoubling of speed, seized it at the very moment when it reached the river. He was approaching his nest when surprised, perhaps intimidated by the noise made by Mr. Verplanck, he let it fall. It was a sea bass weighing 21 pounds. "In this fashion," he told me, "often the prey of the weakest becomes the property of the strongest. Nevertheless," he continued, "for fear of scaring away these birds whose flight, skill, and fights are so interesting to watch, I rarely disturb them; I committed this indiscretion today only to let you enjoy one of the most curious spectacles of natural history presented by this beautiful river.

"In the same way," he added, "the pirate from whom an enemy snatches his prize at the sight of port undertakes a new expedition in the hope of being luckier; thus does the fishing eagle rise anew in the air, when with the speed of lightning, he rushes toward the water and reappears holding in his claws a new prey which he finally succeeds in keeping from the violence of his enemy, especially when it is lighter. These birds stay here until the time when the bass return to the sea; then the bald eagle leaves for the mountains and the fishing eagle for the shores of the Ocean, where he has no more tribute to pay."

This *talco piscatorius* is large, and his flight is lofty and speedy: his wings, long and pointed, give him a considerable spread, proportionate to the largeness of his body. He lives only by the fish he catches, scorning any fish cast up by the ocean on its shores.

10 POOPLO'SKILL. Only after putting into motion the hammers of the two great forges and the bellows of the two furnaces does this little river join the Hudson, falling from the height of rocks on the west bank. In calm weather, the noise of this pretty cascade resounds afar.

11 CANNON OF RETREAT. Fort Westpoint, considered as a military installation in which the Government has deposited some of its heavy artillery, as well as the artillery taken at Yorktown, maintains a garrison of 200 men; that is why, morning and night, a volley of cannon is fired there.

12 DUCHESS AND COLUMBIA. Bordering counties located on the east bank of the Hudson. They occupy all the space included between the mountains and Albany for thirty-five leagues. This part of the state of New-York is extremely fertile, populated, and as well cultivated as it can be. The art of irrigation has been known for a long time there, not only for the irrigation of meadows but also for orchards. Nowhere can one see as beautiful meadows as the district of Nine-Partners, Oswégo, and Oblong, where one is astonished at the sight of magnificent meadows which decorate the heights as well as the valleys of the hills. These districts are inhabited by a great number of wealthy families who unite travel with education and a taste for farming.

CHAPTER XVI

1 HESSIAN FLY. The colonists of Long Island, noticing that an insect, then unknown, was destroying their wheat in the neighborhood of the camp of the Hessian troops, gave the insect this name; indeed, it is a mosquito. As soon as the stalk and the ear are formed, it wounds with its needle the upper and lower parts of the first joint on the stalk in which it deposits its microscopic eggs. No sooner are the eggs hatched than they intercept the sap and feed off it and the plant dies. From Long Island this new scourge has spread into several States; but as it advances into the interior, it is observed that this fly abandons the first places it has ravaged.

It is very doubtful that this insect came from Europe. The wheat growing in poor or badly cultivated soil is more exposed to its destruction than the wheat growing in fine or well-smoked land.

2 SHELLINGS AND PIASTRES. The piastre, which has become the standard exchange, is divided, according to the new decimal calculation, into one hundred parts, represented by as many pieces of copper, called pence (sols). Before the revolution, this same piastre was divided into shellings, whose number varied in different colonies from four and a half to eight; from this it resulted that the pound, always composed of twenty shellings, had no uniform value. In order to remedy this great inconvenience, Congress introduced the method of counting by piastres (dollars) and decimal parts of dollars.

3 TO BUY LANDS FOR HIS CHILDREN. The lands which the general Government or the States acquired from the Indians have become a great object of speculation; people sell or acquire 10, 20, 30,000 acres with as much ease as buying a small farm. But this land speculation is felt only near the towns. More timid, or wiser, farmers content themselves with buying select parcels which they keep up as a precious reserve for their children. If these acquisitions are made during their minority, the children are assured, on reaching majority, that the progress of population will double the land value. The purchase of these lands is much more profitable than investment in Government bonds.

4 SURINAM. HORSES. Before the revolution the colonies of Dutch Guiana admitted to their ports vessels from Connecticut, New-York, and Pensylvanie only if they carried a certain number of horses, in addition to their other merchandise; but it sometimes happened that in storms, horses had to be pushed overboard. In order to prove that they had conformed with the colonists' stipulation, the tails were cut off; from this sprang the custom of always having some on board.

5 BERMUDA. The latitude of this little archipelago, located 300 leagues from the continent, as well as from Cape Hatteras, on the coast of North Carolina, being the distance separating the variable winds from the trade winds, is very subject to storms; from this fact springs the sea proverb: "If Cape Hatteras tells you nothing, watch out for Bermuda."

6 SURINAM. Large river in Dutch Guiana on the banks of which the town of Paramaraibo has been built; it is considered the capital. One cannot watch without a mixture of astonishment and admiration what perseverance and industry have done in this marshy land in one century. The grandeur of the canals, the richness of the farms, the elegance of the homes built on their banks—everything there is impressive.

7 ESSÉQUIBO. Another river west of the one just mentioned above; a town by the same name has been built on it, belonging likewise to Holland.

8 NASSAU. Legal name of Long Island, that is to say, the name people are obliged to use in all public and private acts.

9 MAPLE VINEGAR. It can be made only with the last sap in the month of April. Its strength depends more or less on the degree of evaporation permitted it.

10 GREEN WAX. The bushes (*myrica cerifera*) from the berries of which this wax is made are so common from Carolina to Massachussetts, that they are used for different purposes. By mixing an equal quantity of tallow, wicks and candles can be made with it; it is also put into the mixture with which one varnishes boats. I am astonished that these bushes have not yet been cultivated in Europe.

11 CRANBERRY. Because of the color and acidity of its juice, the fruit of this beautiful shrub resembles very closely the swamp berry, known in this land as cranberry and what, in Georgia, are called lemons from Ogeechée.

12 GOSHEM. Pretty little market place, center of Orange County, in the

state of New-York, surrounded by meadows and well-cultivated fields. Instead of being contiguous, the houses are separated from each other by fences, gardens or fine orchards. The inhabitants there have founded an incorporated academy at which a great number of young men are instructed and prepared for admission to a university.

CHAPTER XVII

1 MONT-VERNON. This home, to which the illustrious Washington has given great renown, is located on the west bank of the Potomac, a bank that stands 200 feet above the level of its waters and whose width is more than a league. On the left the river drops out of sight; on the right, one can watch its course for more than five leagues; opposite, this great vista ends in far-off hills, with the forests and plantations of Maryland. The house is paneled with painted cedar planks and has a stone foundation. The approach is by a beautiful lawn, surrounded by gravelled paths, planted with trees. The rear of the dwelling is embellished by a portico 96 feet long, supported by eight columns. On taking leave, one finds oneself on a second lawn which stretches half way up the hill. There begins the fence of a great wooded park where one can see buck and roe-deer leaping; the former were sent to the General from Europe; the roe-deer came from the inland forests.

Two semi-circular galleries lead to the wings, lower courts, and garden, in which one notices with pleasure the nursery of useful trees, some of which are imported from Europe. The surrounding grounds are well cultivated; but the large farms are 3 or 4 miles away. The barn is an immense brick building more than one hundred feet long and almost as wide, in which the General has combined stables, cattle-sheds, and all the conveniences necessary to so large a farm project. He owns 16,000 acres in this region and perhaps 200,000 in the State of Virginia. Before the Revolution, he was regarded as the foremost farmer on the continent. He had forty plows and sold annually from ten to fourteen bushels of wheat. Like a second Cincinnatus, he was busying himself with pastoral pursuits, when in 1789, the voice of his country forced him to leave his hearth to take the helm and fill the duties of the presidency, which he has just left— to return once more to the gentle, peaceful business of farming. May Heaven prolong to the last limit possible the days of a man, the first, without contradiction the greatest in this new hemisphere, for his example is as useful to his country during peace as his wisdom and courage were when he commanded the armies!

2 DROWNED LANDS. Natural meadow, estimated to be 70,000 acres, located partly in the state of New-Jersey and partly in New-York. It includes several large islands covered with hemp. The law which the two states have just promulgated offers hope that the work to clear the eastern part, begun a long time ago, will soon be completed. Then this vast expanse, being completely drained, will become the chief source of wealth of these districts.

3 BUTTER, CHEESE. Long before the owners of this vast prairie land had joined their efforts to drain off the waters, its land was cultivated; covered with cattle and hemp. The quantity of butter and cheese exported from this region was tremendous and is increasing every year. Last year nearly ninety thousand barrels of butter and cheese were exported.

4 HIGHLANDS. Name of that chain of mountains crossing the State of New-York, twenty leagues from the sea; there are only seven sizeable mountains in the chain. In Pensylvania the chain continues under the name of Kittaling Mountains.

END OF FIRST VOLUME

VOLUME TWO

CHAPTER SUMMARIES

VOLUME TWO
---

reactions produced by this idea.—The first traveler discovers a branch of groundnuts.—Return of hope.—Origin of anthropophagy.—The travelers hear the sound of a bell.—Act of gratitude.—They encounter a herd of cattle.— Have the good fortune to obtain milk from three cows; follow the herd; arrive at a dwelling.—Humanitarianism of the mistress of the household.—A corn concoction.—Conversation with the master of this farm.—His story.— Gratitude of Mr. Herman.—Return to Mr. ———'s dwelling.—Departure for Shippenbourg.

Here there appears to be a lapse of time, or else several chapters have been lost.

Ténézée.—What these people say.—Meeting with a colonist coming from the region around Orangebourg in South Carolina.—Details on the wandering and patriarchal life he led for four years at the foot of the Alléghény mountains, from the frontiers of Georgia, to Virginia.—He tells the story of his life.

Criticism of the conduct of almost all members of the administration.—Attack on the execution of the political principles of the President of the United States.—Long and interesting reply made to him by one of the passengers.— The New Yorker considers the unlimited freedom of the press incompatible with the peace and quiet of societies.

CHAPTER XVII 373

Arrival of Mr. Herman in the bay of New-Haven.—Excursion into the town. —Curious and interesting encounters.—Visits to Mr. H. H., member of Congress.—His taste for agriculture.—Knotty oak.—Its strength and durability. —Details about the first mulberry bush nurseries in this State.—Ingenious means used to spread knowledge of its growing.—Manufacture of silk in Mans'field.—Charter of incorporation granted to the owners of mulberry trees. —Reason for this charter.—Historical sketch of Connecticut.—Commencement exercises at Yale.—The Governor and the chief State administrators are present.—Address of the President to the students whose education is terminated.—Reflections of Mr. H. H. on the utility of annual speeches.—Visit to this colonist.—Beauty and fertility of his farm.—Reflections of this colonist on the inconveniences of pastoral life and farming.—Objects of his poetry, if he were a poet.—Reflections on the beauty of nature's works.—Difference between the plight of a European farmer and that of a colonist.—What happens to Mr. Herman in his inn.—Fainting spell of a traveler.—Favors done him by Mr. Herman.—Scene of sadness.—Touching thoughts of the traveler on his losses.—His life.—Thoughts on death.—Mr. H. H. leaves for Hartford. —Visit to Colonel Wadsworth.—Happiness and reunion of this family.— Fine use he makes of his fortune.

CHAPTER I

THE CHEROKEE TRADITION *

From generation to generation this tale has been passed on by our ancestors.

From the earliest days Agan-Kitchee-Manitou, the Great Animator of Matter, was known to have magic powers. One day he decided to come to earth to see how things were getting along.

He turned himself into a wolf and joined the first pack he met. Surprised at the arrival of a stranger, the chiefs surrounded and questioned him, took him in only after ascertaining that he was of ancient stock.

"I note with pleasure," he mused while hunting with them, "that they always use the same weapons I gave them; that they are just as crafty and nimble in mind and body as of yore. In dire need they are clever enough to unite under chiefs when it is a question of attacking or defending. Each is satisfied with his share of the spoils. It is true that misfortune and famine occasionally shrink their number, but then, somehow, a more favorable turn of events retrieves their losses. The fate of the individual is of little importance to me. I am interested only in the species. For the latter will not be held in check until the time when destiny brings to this land a race of farming men. That time is still far off."

Satisfied with his findings, Manitou left them five days later while they were pursuing a stag, and this time turned into a bear.

"What are you doing in my den?" said the first bear he met. "I dug it out myself, as you can see; there's room only for me, my wife, and my little ones."

"Don't your friends ever come to visit you?"

"I don't know whom you mean. Get out or I'll show you who's master here!"

"You are just like your ancestors: wild and unsociable, but I am not the least bit annoyed with you."

Whereupon, he left, this time to become a fox.

"Aha!" said the first fox he met. "You have a foreign and suspicious look. It seems to me you smell like a bear. Who are you, and where do you come from? Start talking!"

---

* This account of an ancient tradition was translated in 1774 by order of the mighty war chief, Attacul-Culla (the little carpenter), to be sent to the Governor of South Carolina, William Campbell, whose secretary, M. Atkins, permitted me to copy it several years later.

"I am a fox of good stock. I have come from the Cheryhum [1] country; I'm hungry."

"You've got a lot of nerve: begging from people who live only by dint of scheming and craftiness. Why don't you hunt as we do? Where were you brought up anyway?"

"In the Noyawanda country which is rich in big game."

"Nothing like that here," replied the fox. You should see how far we have to travel to trap any prey! What a miserable lot is ours! Racked by fear and famine, risks and gnawing need, forever surrounded by trap or ambush. Judge for yourself whether we have any food to give you! Get out of here! Back to your Cheryhum country among your Noyawandas!"

"Gladly," Manitou replied, "but come with me. You will fare sumptuously."

"What is this! You think you can betray us, then?"

"How can you conceive of one fox wanting to betray another! One would think that you had lived among men."

"True, we have, but unbeknownst to them. They are our best providers."

"How does that happen?"

"When they are at war with one another—and that happens often—we devour the carcasses of those whom the conquerors do not want to eat."

"What! Is it possible that man eats man?"

"Does he! Alas, yes, to our great regret. Were it not for that, we would be fat and sleek all year long. Why aren't men more numerous on earth! What a good time we would have!"

"Perhaps that will happen some day," concluded Manitou. And suddenly he transformed himself into a buffalo beyond the Alleghanies. [2]

"Ah, what a fine rich country," he said to the first buffalo he met. "Wide open prairies, always lush with tender, sweet rush. [3] What superb pasture land!"

"All very true," replied the trans-Alleghanian. "Yet we are an unhappy people."

"Why? Don't you get along with each other?"

"Yes, we live in peace and harmony among ourselves but this Mammoth [4] who swoops down from the mountains onto the plains uprooting the trees, forever pursuing and devouring us! Why did Agan-Kitchee-Manitou give life to such a monster?"

"Because, your people would have multipled so in this fair land that they would have died of hunger. He has done what he could to please everyone, but that was impossible. Some day Manitou will strike his forked thunder between the horns of this Mammoth, and pfft!— his bones will then be but a source of astonishment to posterity.[5] Why don't you urge your friends to cross the Mississippi? They would find on the west bank of that beautiful river, meadows that would take more than a week to cross." [6]

"Everyone loves his own land," replied the buffalo. "To persuade one to leave his country, things must be very bad, or else the power of the Mammoth destructive and horrible. And perhaps the Mammoth would follow beyond this river. That isn't all: we still have another enemy to combat: none the less cruel, and threatening our entire breed with total extinction."

"What could this second enemy be?"

"A puny, hairless animal that has only two feet. After taking his fill of our flesh, he sleeps in the shade of a great tree. All his strength and will comes from his knowledge of lighting a fire. Where could such extraordinary knowledge come from?"

"He has to have this knowledge to compensate for his nudity and feebleness. Otherwise what would he do on earth? Besides, he's not much happier than you. But how does he use this fire to destroy you?"

"He lights the cane and the dry reeds of the prairies in the heat of the summer and traps us in the midst of the big conflagration that follows." [7]

"Well, why don't you flee? You have four good legs and your enemy has but two."

"Fright seizes us and checks us."

"Perhaps things had to be so. . . ." And suddenly Manitou vanished, to reappear as a dog.

"Ah, my friend," he said to the first dog he met, "give me something to eat. I'm hungry."

"Ask my master, sleeping yonder in the sun," the dog replied. "As for me, I have nothing, for instead of being his friend, I am his slave. Often he hasn't enough for himself. Then I suffer, I fast. The man with whom I live is ungrateful, brutal even. Though unfailingly busy in trying to please him, my efforts are mostly futile. But why should I complain? He has no more respect for his wife than for me. I don't think I'd enjoy changing places with her. Why must a free man have two slaves? I want to leave this tyrant and live on my own, for even though I don't express myself as easily as he does, I think nevertheless and my ideas are more just than his. I have accomplished and predicted a thousand times what he could neither have accomplished nor predicted. I should like to become a wolf; they say we are descended from the same stock. Then I would be dependent on no one. I would have a wife and children who will help me in my old age and—for the first time in my life—I would enjoy freedom."

"See that you don't carry out this plan; the wolves would scorn you because you have been a slave; they would put you through a terrible apprenticeship. Believe what I tell you, for I have just been among them. Just as calm is preferable to tempest, repose to work, sleep to nerve-wracking insomnia, a mild and fair servitude is far better than limitless liberty. Man cannot do without your service anymore than you can do without his help. All men are not like your master."

And Manitou changed into an otter.

"Look how you are fitted out, wretched creature! You seem to me to be perishing with cold," he said to the first otter he met. "You are trembling despite your fine fur coat."

"Yes," she answered, "the season is severe; the ice covers the water; but I must live."

"Are you alone?"

"Yes, almost always: that is my fate; quite sad, too, I admit, but I am used to it; and as long as I can catch some fish, I am happy."

"And your little ones?"

"I hide them as best I can, for I have so many enemies and among these enemies there is always one who begrudges me my fine coat."

Just as she was saying that, an arrow shot from afar, pierced her side. Manitou, in order to talk with the hunter, suddenly changed into a man.

"What do you plan to do with this otter?" he asked him.

"I shall cover my bare shoulders with her skin and cook her flesh in my kettle."

"Is your kettle big?"

"Yes, for I have five mouths to feed. Follow me if you are hungry, and I will feast you."

Manitou followed him, and on entering his wigwam great was his surprise to see five persons busy cutting a human body to pieces.

"Is that the flesh you promised me?"

"Yes, it's the best I can offer you."

"Why do you eat this man?"

"Because he was my enemy."

"But why was that?"

"Because he and his people live on the other shore of the Wenowee River and for years we have hated and fought one another. They eat us, too, when they catch us."

"Then there is neither game in the forests, nor fish in the river?"

"Sometimes they are hard to find."

"But why do you eat your fellow-man?"

"Because his flesh is tastier than buffalo meat or venison, and because it would be absurd to abandon the carcass of one's enemy to the wolves. Otherwise, what would be the use of killing him? And would I deserve to have another victory? Then, too, how proud and happy one is to think of eating one's fill of someone he hates, to satisfy thus hunger and revenge. How proud our war chant shouts! How our women, children, and neighbors admire us! And after all, hunting is not always lucky."

"What do you do when luck is at a low ebb?"

"Oh, I starve and suffer. Everyone in my wigwam suffers. Then when need exerts its irresistible force upon me, I go away, far from here, and sate it. I kill the first man or woman I meet. Ah, I can readily see that you are not a warrior; you don't know even what it is to be hungry. Let me tell you, if ever hunger pursues you and ensnares you, you will find out."

Horror-stricken, Manitou left this cannibal, not without regretting that he had created such a man. As he made his way slowly, musing over what he had just seen and heard, he changed himself into an opossum [8] to banish his ugly impressions.

"Well, Gossip, how is it with you?"

"Fairly well. I am able to hide easily because I am small. I have more wisdom than courage because I know my weakness. Because of this, I escape the pursuit of man, my cruelest enemy. I compensate for the distresses of my life in hiding and by the care I take of my family. The longer we live together the happier we are. You see around me here three generations, all in good health. I am the great-grandmother and still loved by my family."

"But when the enemy approaches your hideout, how do you manage to escape with all your brood?"

"We have a bag under our bellies, in which the young ones take refuge as soon as danger approaches. Only observe...." She gives the alarm and immediately the little ones respond. Their sacks full, each mother takes flight and disappears.

Impressed with his happy expedient, Manitou smilingly approved his work.

Changing into a man again in order to travel more conveniently, Manitou was suddenly caught in a frightful storm. The echoes of the forest could scarcely keep up with the thunderclaps. Lightning flashed. The rain which fell in torrents began to inundate the land. Not knowing what to do, Manitou leaned against a great tree on which he had seen some squirrels. Shortly after, he turned into one and climbed among them.

"May health, happiness, and swiftness be yours!" he said to the first squirrel he saw. "Although I am a stranger, I seek shelter among you."

"Make yourself snug in this branch and curl your fine tail above your back!"

"How is the living in this region?"

"Wonderful: we have an abundance of nuts, especially beechnuts. During the summer we play, we frolic, we make love. We are happy and content. As soon as winter comes, we retire to the hollow of big trees, where we have stored our provisions. There, united with our families, we await the return of spring 'mid the most perfect peace and harmony."

"Don't you have any enemies?"

"Some. Man is the cruelest of all and especially his accursed children. It is on us that they learn to let fly their first arrow. But our legs are so nimble, our eyes so quick, and our judgment so sure, that rarely do they reach us. We are happy with our lot and wouldn't change it for that of the buffalo, giant though he appears to us."

"Some day your people will have great dangers to encounter."

"What kind?"

"These magnificent trees will be uprooted. These fine forests will disappear."

"Who could ever uproot these mighty trees?"

"Bearded men, coming from beyond the rising sun, will invade this continent, sharp tools in their hands. They will multiply like fish in the waters. Then, everything will change in this land. They will replace these forests with harvests, these marshes with meadows. Strength, wisdom, and good luck will be theirs. As their number increases, yours will decrease. The bow and arrow will be replaced by deadly fire-arms."

"Is this day far off?"

"Oh, yes, quite far. You will not live to see it, for from now till then there are still more than a thousand solar revolutions."

"Well, then, let's live as we have, for too much foresight is folly."

"You reason well for a squirrel. You are the first happy creature I have met on my journey."

"Who are you, my friend? And where did you come from?"

"You would die this very hour if I were to answer your question.

Suffice it for you to know that the universe and all its wonder are the work of my supple hands, the overflowing of my lifegiving bounty, the pouring forth of my creative power.''

''What! You, a squirrel like me! What are you talking about anyway! Well, if you did make the world, why don't you stop the bearded men of the East from coming some day to destroy these beautiful forests which are rightfully ours?''

''There is a power which exceeds mine.''

''Who is that power, then?''

''Tibarimaw (destiny). She often does strange things.''

''Why don't you reason with her?''

''She is unalterable and unrelenting.''

Manitou, once again a man, after the storm had ceased, resumed his journey and was still thinking of the squirrel's contentment, when inadvertently he fell into a hole which had been lightly covered over with underbrush and moss. At the bottom he found a panther, two wolves, a fox, and Wabémat.*

''You seem to be quite chilled,'' Manitou said to him. ''Are you suffering?''

''Do I suffer! Suffering is all I know, for my life has been a perpetual maze of misfortunes. Why was breath given me, since I breathe only to suffer? Every day I feel the sting of need. And as for my family.....their plight breaks my heart. Ah, if only I were a wolf or an eagle! How well I would fare! When I hunt, either my arrow does not pierce my prey, or a wild cat makes off with what I manage to shoot. When I fish, the fish knowing the fishhook of the unhappy Wabémat, nibbles at the hook only to carry it off. The other day I was sleeping under a tree. What do you think? A branch, snapped off by the wind, fell and broke my leg. Four times fire has destroyed my wigwam. My wife is nearly always sick. Yesterday my eldest son drowned in the river, although he could swim like a fish. In the winter, I freeze. In the summer, I suffocate. Here I am, at the bottom of this pit. A thousand times I have cursed life and all the evils it engenders. Why doesn't the mighty Manitou, who lives above the clouds, they say, come to earth occasionally? Perhaps his benevolence would be touched by the sight of man's struggle. Perhaps he is not aware of all the evil that men take such pleasure in fomenting; perhaps he does not know, either, the harshness of the elements, to which he has exposed us unclad. Why has he subjected us to gnawing hunger, and given us so many other needs, without some means of satisfying them, and with no instruments other than our wretched, helpless ten fingers? Al-

* One of the Indians of the neighboring village.

though weak, why are we more evil than the panther, and more ferocious than the wolf who never eats his fellows? Whence comes this state of mind which arouses us unceasingly to hate, to tear in pieces our neighbor, and whence this fury that urges us ever to war? Why are we unable to live 'mid plenty, with peace and understanding? Why..."

He was interrupted by the arrival of the man who had laid the trap. When he missed the wild animals, which the Great Spirit had set free, he became angry and was about to strike the two men down when the great animator spoke:

"Tireless hunter, brave warrior, spare our lives."

"What do I care about saving *your* life? I have lost my quarry, and it's your fault. I shall eat you since I am hungry and I am the strongest."

"Don't eat us," replied Manitou. "Before the sun sets this very day, I shall present you with a fine fat buffalo, whose skin will serve to cover the nudity of my hapless friend here!"

"Why doesn't he hunt for himself, this hapless friend of yours? I want the whole buffalo—or your lives."

"Agreed."

And off he went to look for a liana which would help them climb out of the pit.

"What a scurvy creature!" said Manitou to Wabémat.

"But that's the way men treat each other here. When they are hungry, a frequent occurrence, they make no exception of brother or friend. The weak succumb to the strong, trickery triumphs over innocence. Can it be thus throughout all the land lighted by the great sun?"

"Just about," replied Manitou.

"What a destiny, to be born without weapons, without any covering, and with only two legs, doomed to an existence in a climate like this one, and to live only on the flesh of animals, who have four legs and are every bit as intelligent as we are."

"Ungrateful wretch," said Manitou, "these ten fingers that you scorn so are nevertheless far superior to the wolf's or tiger's claw. The fine sense of touch of which they are the instruments, together with their flexibility, has made them the sceptre of man's almost magic power. They are responsible for man's good fortune in being able to light and propagate fire; they are his means of having weapons, his canoe, his dwelling, his clothes. True, he has only two legs, but of all creatures, he is the most majestic, he alone commands all nature with his gaze, only he can admire the splendor of the heavens, the beauty of nature in all her glory * and elevate himself through his power of thinking toward an understanding of his inscrutable author.

"The amazing perfectibility with which the Creator has endowed man's intelligence, the sublime feelings that he has put in his heart, all masterpieces of his bounty and his power, are the most precious present a father could give to his children. And after all, what is man, this vain and presumptuous being? A living atom whose generations succeed each other on earth like the shadows of clouds chased by the wind. And what of this world? A mere dot in the infinity of the universe, one of the smallest spheres in the millions of which the universe is composed.

"Yet, far superior to other creatures, who are forever bound within the narrow limits of their sphere, although, like them, he is abandoned to the rule of chance, some day he will rise to an understanding of the greatest concepts through his own might. He will subdue the elements, cross the seas, whose storms he will learn how to brave, he will improve the land and make of it a delightful home. It will depend only on him to become the artisan of his own glory and happiness.

"If his lifetime seems short, if his days seem filled with hazards and hardships, inseparable companions of life, the unquenchable spark which inspires man to act, to feel, and to think will survive till his death, will bring him, in the realm of spirits, a reward from his suffering and his virtues, or punishment for his crimes. If this law of compensation did not exist, it would be a thousand times better not to have seen the light of day, for, if he were endowed with reasoning powers, and deprived of the consolations of hope, he would be the unhappiest of creatures."

"These are strange things you are telling me," Wabémat replied. "Where did you learn all this? It seems so new."

"In the land I came from."

"Where is this land anyway? I have never heard of it. Does one have to hunt and fish in order to live, as we do in this country?"

"It rests only with you whether you will come to know it some day," answered Manitou, "and that day will be one of eternal joy and happiness, for troubles and needs are unknown in that land."

Finally the promised buffalo arrived and on leaving the pit, Wabémat said to Manitou:

"Don't go to this devourer of men; come with me."

Manitou followed him; the fire of his hearth was well kindled, but

* Ovid said:

> Os homini sublime dedit, coelumque tueri
> Jussit, et erectos ad sidera tollere vultus
> (Note written to the author by Citizen Bilocq.)

there was no kettle, for someone had put it aside. Some roots cooked under the ashes were the only food, offered to the guest.

"Why is your kettle empty and your family so naked?" Manitou asked him.

"Because the Evil Spirit always follows or precedes me, and nothing I undertake ever succeeds. Yet I never forget to offer up to him the smoke of my first pipe every day just as the sun rises."

"Have you ever seen the Evil Spirit?"

"No, never."

"Well, then, what makes you think he exists?"

"Who could ever doubt his existence when for forty-two times winter snows have squashed our wigwams; for forty-two winters the ice has carried away our canoes; packs of wolves have carried off our women and our children, while we were off hunting. Deadly epidemics have poisoned half of our villages, tempests have uprooted our forest, and the fire from on high has destroyed all. Why did there have to be men created on earth since they were born to meet nothing but misfortune in all their ways?"

"Just what is this misfortune? Have you ever seen it in your life?"

"No, I really don't know what it is like. As cunning as a squirrel, it hides itself behind the trees that I pass. But if I can see it ever, I shall certainly kill it. It is the only enemy that I should like to eat. It has made me starve so much!"

"Is it possible that you do not eat what you kill by tomahawk in war, as do your fellow men?"

"No."

"Why not?"

"Fear that you will poke fun at me prevents my knowing what to say."

"Speak freely. I am not one of your countrymen, as you know."

"Very well, I shall. Here is what my reasoning tells me every time I am gnawed by hunger and inclined to follow my neighbor's example. How can you eat your fill of a person whose tongue, like your own, might have spoken? Or of a person whose heart, like yours, could have loved wife and children. How can you bring yourself to drink the brewed flesh of a man who, had he been born on this bank of the river, would have been your neighbor, aye, your friend mayhap. Wolf never eats wolf, a fox would sooner die than eat one of his own species. And you, a man, would eat, and ravenously, too, one of your fellow men! Aren't your hate and revenge sufficiently appeased when you have spilled the blood which gave life to his body to be food for the flies? When you are starved, why don't you go into the woods and seek the

orikomah, the wotta-towah, or the wennasimah? If you boil or cook
them over embers, they will nourish your family.

"That is what my reasoning tells me every time my comrades start
cutting up a corpse, after killing an enemy. They turn my repugnance
into ridicule, call me a weak, faint-hearted Nishy-norbay, who doesn't
know how to enjoy the spoils of victory. These reproaches uttered by
my neighbors increase my unhappiness."

"Then you aren't a warrior?" Manitou inquired.

"Why, yes, just as good a warrior as the others: when our enemies
cross the Wenowee River to attack the village, at the risk of my life, I
defend the honor of my family and tribe; but when *we* must cross the
river to attack *them*...that's different. I stay right here, with no
desire to entangle myself in a quarrel which doesn't interest me. Again
I am ridiculed, again they insult me in my very wigwam, but I am as
unyielding as a huge rock in the river."

"Then you have never tasted human flesh, no matter how gnawing
your hunger was?" asked Manitou.

"No, never. When I have been unable to catch either fish or game, I
eat roots, as you notice. As long as my family likes them, I am satisfied."

"Wabémat, bless the moment when I fell into the pit, for the roots
that nourish you will soon bear fruit. The time for retribution is at
hand. Now which do you prefer: to wait until death, whose date is
uncertain, comes to deliver you from the burden of life to enjoy the
unalterable, eternal pure happiness of the spirits—or—would you
rather revel in all the fullness of the happiness one can enjoy on earth
beginning now?"

"Alas!" Wabémat replied, "what can you do about it, since like me,
you are only the son of a mortal woman?"

"I can answer your questions," Manitou said.

"The happiness of the spirits! I've never heard of that! Is such a
land far away?"

"Yes, quite far."

"Why can't I go there right away?"

"The time is not yet ripe and the other land, why it's fairly near
yours!"

"Do people there die of hunger as they do here, when hunting and
fishing are poor? Do men war against one another?"

"People there live in peace and plenty."

"Ah, what a fine country."

Those words made Wabémat's heart leap with joy.

"Well, then," he said, "if you can accomplish what you wanted to, make good your promise. I am so tired of my diet of herbs and my misery that I can scarcely wait to get there.''

"I know an island in the Lake of Tempests (Michigan) where I shall take you and your whole family. But, before hearing my last words, bow down.''

"What! Bow down before my equal!''

"Oh, I only appear to be your equal.''

"Who are you anyway?''

"In the silence of the night, haven't you ever watched the glory of the heaven, and the twinkling stars which brighten and give life to the thousands of worlds just like this one which, although invisible to your eyes, move about through space? Haven't you ever admired the radiant sun in the magnificence of dawn and in the glory of her daily sunset over the lake waters? In casting your eyes over the beauty of living nature, haven't you ever felt an involuntary impulse of respect and admiration? Haven't you ever asked yourself what was the life-giving principle which animates all earthly things of the land as well as those under the water and in the atmosphere? Who is responsible for maintaining everlasting freshness and eternal youth? Who, from the most contemptible refuse, makes the elements of new reproduction? Well, Wabémat, it is I who am the life-giving universal spirit. Now judge of my power and my bounty. Without me, the order on which the very existence of the universe depends, the stability of its intricate counterbalances would soon be upset. Long since the light of the sun and moon would have been extinguished and matter would have returned to the chaos of the void and of eternal darkness whence I freed it many moons ago.''

Seized with awe and respect, Wabémat bowed quaking before Agan-Kitchee-Manitou. Scarcely had his face touched the earth when the dark clouds which hid the majesty of the sun dispersed. The whistle of the wind ceased, the cry of the animals, the buzzing of insects, even the song of the birds could no longer be heard and the primeval silence of nature returned to the earth, and the great life-giving power continued:

"Since you prefer to hasten the moment of your happiness, rather than await the great day of retribution, you must cease being a man. Do you consent to that?''

"What! Cease to be what I am! What are you going to do with me anyway?''

"Do you consent, I ask you?''

"May your will be done.''

"So that you will not be distracted by futile thoughts, source of the greatest part of your unhappiness, you must lose your power of speech. Do you consent?"

"Lose my power of speech? But how could I chat with my neighbors, with my wife and my children who are so dear to me?"

"Do you consent to this, I ask you?"

"All right, since your benevolence, which is a necessary companion to your power, would wish only for my happiness."

"This gift will be replaced by a series of sounds simpler but every bit as useful as speech, and although less varied, just as expressive. With these, you and yours will be able to carry on all undertakings. Just as before, you will know love, conjugal and paternal happiness, as well as sobriety, temperance, and chastity. Your children will respect you, and love you and succor you when you are old. The absence of mental anguish will take the place of enjoyment and happiness for you. You will be able to conceive, and execute intelligently, all the plans necessary to the well-being of your family and for that I will permit you to retain your memory, your foresight, and your judgment.

"You will enjoy social privileges whence come peace and repose. Misfortune will never follow nor precede your every step as it has in the past. You will love life and you will enjoy it long with neither sickness nor infirmity. Your appetites, your wants, and your tastes will always be simple and moderate. Looting and warring will always horrify you. Your pure hands will nevermore cause blood to be spilled. You will have no more enemies, nor will your descendants, as long as they stay on this island, unknown to man.

"You will be a fine architect. You will understand the principles of water power. With the help of your family, you will construct a spacious, comfortable, clean home on the water. You will have sharp words with which to defend yourself, without ever having any desire to be the aggressor. For you will love peace, retreat, and silence. You will be able to live under water as well as on land, and for that purpose I shall give you the most beautiful of furs.

"A soft, quiet light will soon replace the flaming torch of your reason, which has served only to dazzle and distract you up till now. Guided by this new light which never wavers, you will be happy, with no anxieties, wise, with no sadness, provident, without futile desires, thoughtful though sated in spirit. Only the darkness of death will extinguish this light.

"If ever you come to regret the loss of your reason, you will be able to console yourself in the thought that you have been freed forever from its errors, its illusions as well as its aberrations, for paroxysms of abysmal despair will no longer seize your soul, since you will nevermore know the frightening outbursts of delirium and revenge, the shameful fits of frenzy, nor the degrading errors of anger and madness.

"These are the foundations of the happiness which you shall enjoy, Wabémat; that happiness which your privations, your sufferings, and your abstinence from human flesh have so justly deserved. What does your heart tell you?.... Speak."

"Powerful as you are, why, in order to achieve happiness, must I lose my identity as a human being? Is it possible that your eternal decrees have ordered that man should never know happiness! You, the creator, the organizer of all matter, the soul and the support of the universe! Give heed to your own goodness and Wabémat and his brethren will be happy. Since before calling man from the void of life, you necessarily foresaw his destiny on earth, why didn't you provide him with..."

Scarcely had these words been uttered when by a sudden metamorphosis, there appeared the first family of beavers that had ever been known on earth.

After watching this new and last example of his creative power, this masterpiece of his strength and generosity, Agan-Kitchee-Manitou disappeared and has not revealed himself since.

And, in accordance with his words, this family of beavers lost no time in constructing a dam to swell the waters of the first stream that it met on the island of the Tempests (Michigan) where the beavers were suddenly transported. And on this dam, they built a spacious home, clean and comfortable, where after many vicissitudes, they finally found peace and plenty. For this island, unknown to man, was covered with many alders, birches, and willows. The family shed tears occasionally but they were tears of joy, pleasure, and gratitude when, united on the river bank, papa told of the old days of war, of want, and of misfortune. (For, by a very special favor which was limited to the first generation, the mighty Manitou wished to preserve in him the memory of man's former state.)

After many snows had passed over his head, the old beaver Wabémat succumbed in the arms of his children and in accordance with Manitou's prediction, his family was everlastingly happy, to the point where the happiness they enjoyed so long increased their number, that several families were obliged to settle on new sites of Lake Michigan's shores. From there by slow degrees, they spread throughout the northern region of the continent. Then man, enemy of all living creatures, declared war on them to cover his nudity with their fine furs, but still with some compassion and some regard for their divine origin. The result is that even today when hunters come upon a beaver colony, they always permit a certain number to escape.

Translated by the undersigned interpreter of the king for Cherokee, residing at Sinica, on the Keowee River.[9]

June 17, 1774

Adrien O'Harrah

(The chapter following was found to be so defaced that the translator, to his deep regret, could decipher only a very small part. It contained a lengthy and detailed account of the population and culture of the provinces of Pennsylvania located beyond the Alleghanies as far west as the junction of the Ohio and Monongahela.)

CHAPTER II

After having explored the region beyond the mountains in Pennsylvania, where we had spent the greater part of a year [1] we returned toward autumn to find rest and to enjoy the comforts of hospitality in the home of Mr. M., former officer in the Continental Army who, like a true Cincinnatus, cultivated his fields with as much intelligence as ingenuity. Among all the valleys of the Alleghanies (the Cordillières of the Western Hemisphere), the Juniata, in which this esteemed military gentleman lives, is one of the largest and most productive. The west branch of this river, fed in its course by numerous creeks, which rise in neighboring heights, winds through the entire valley. It is beginning to be tolerably well cultivated, furnishing the settlers with pasture land, wheat, corn, and flax. But so recently have these settlements been made, that the soil, scarcely cleared of its superfluity of trees and useless growth, has not yet given its full measure of fertility. Many years will necessarily elapse before man's labor will have achieved the picturesque beauty that one admires in so many regions of Switzerland.

Watching us observe with interest the clever irrigation system used by our host for the improvement of his land, Mr. M. said:

"There is no end to the vast productibility of the land if it is properly irrigated. One can force prodigality from it just as the sun of springtime makes buds sprout and flowers bloom. The quantity of water which is available because of this dam is a source of wealth and abundance. Not only have I tripled the amount of hay that I harvest, but I have also improved the productivity of my two orchards. These are peach trees and although first planted three years ago, already they bear fruit. That, my friends, is why I prefer living in the mountains, rather than on the plains. That explains also why I would not trade my four hundred acres here for double the amount in either Washington or LaFayette counties from which you have just come."

"Why is the thin trickle of water that turns your windmill so feeble?" asked Mr. Herman.

"A greater flow would be wasted, for by introducing cylinders,[2] I have lessened the rubbing and hence decreased the friction. The cylinder is a new invention from Boston where it was first tried in 1784. It can be used with equal success in horizontal as well as perpendicular motion: in the shaft of a sawmill, on pulleys, as well as in ship capstans. What a triumph over resisting forces!.... But let's go into the house. This evening I expect two friends from Philadelphia. They are engaged in research on gypsum and millstones similar to the kind we import from France.''

Sure enough, they arrived and seemed to us far more conversant with matters of natural history than anyone we had yet met in this country, still so young. They told us of evidences of diorite sand and coal deposits that they had discovered in many regions; of the efforts by the farming society to introduce sainfoin and alfalfa; they showed us an orographic map of the various mountains in Pennsylvania on which were marked their mineral strata, their height, as well as the breadth of the valleys which separated them.

''It is high time,'' said Mr. Finley, one of the visitors, ''that we sought the useful elements concealed beneath the surface of this continent. It is highly probable that we will find just what has been found in the same latitude in Europe. Until now, on this continent, man has been too busy clearing the land and building homes, blazing trails and building bridges.''

''What kind of millstones have you been using in the construction of your ordinary mills?'' my companion asked him.

''A kind of sandstone, made of very fine infusorial earth, like that at Eusopus (Kingston) in the state of New York. But experts prefer the millstone from France to the kind which we have been using up till now.''

''Since this land contains so much calcareous stone, why do you need plaster?''

''Have you never heard discussion of the experiments that our agricultural society made in the past two years?''

''I am not acquainted with them.''

''I am even more astonished since they were written up in the newspapers and magazines and since already crude and ground plaster is being used as fertilizer in farming. This powder is put into large barrels and transported wherever it is needed; farmers spread a certain amount of it on grass and on wheat; it is also used on the corn and everywhere it works wonders. I am convinced that these experiments cost more than 1,500 piastres.''

''Where did the money come from?''

''From the annual dues of the members, as well as donations given by lovers of the venerable science of agriculture.''

''Has the Government done nothing for a society as interesting and respectable as that one?''

''It granted a fine site in Philadelphia and gave it a charter for incorporation.''

''That does not seem extraordinarily generous to me.''

"Every bit as generous as it can afford to be; it enforces laws, that is all we ask. The best Government is not that one which interferes with its everlasting law-making, but one which, on the contrary, practices laws while protecting. Private interest, stimulated and encouraged by this steady protection, busies itself with enterprises and plans useful both to speculators and the public. It is thus that almost everything you have seen in this state has been accomplished: the Great Hospital at Philadelphia,[3] the House of Correction (Bettering House),[4] the libraries, the canals, the bridges, and the schools, known as academies, as well as the great number of private companies; all that has been the work of individuals, whose subscriptions and ideas have been consolidated by corporation charters that give them legal existence and indefinite term. Among the various projects coming under this legal sanction, there have been some inspired only by the ardent desire for well doing; such are those to which we owe the establishment of hospitals, schools, libraries, public dispensaries;[5] others, by private interest: such are the construction of bridges, canals, dams, great highways, etc. Of the latter, some are chartered by the Government at life interest, others become public property at the expiration of a certain number of years.

"In the words of one of our most illustrious citizens, Tench Coxe,[6] I tell you that there are few countries where one finds a greater number of charitable institutions, nor any more famous for that public spirit which has already produced so many advantages. Perhaps you will not believe it; nevertheless, it is true that in the span of a year, more than eleven hundred thousand piastres have been offered and given in Philadelphia for the repair and building of roads and canals, for the perfection of inland navigation, and the encouragement of the maple sugar industry. All that is the work of the confidence inspired by these charters. Owners of new inventions and authors of literary works enjoy exclusive privileges whose term has been fixed by law.

"The same is true with the churches: the Government, respecting all cults, protects them equally and encourages religious groups who keep building new ones by incorporating them with a legislative act, without whose sanction they would not be entitled to possess any real estate nor have any political existence in the eyes of the law.

"In this state such is the spirit of the Government and the state of things: this progress would be even more rapid if we were more populous; but no sooner does the population increase in certain cantons than the desire (or rather the restlessness for self-betterment, although this is so often illusory) and the ambition to possess a great quantity of land cause young people to settle on the Ohio, in Kentucky, Tennessee, or northern Virginia. This fever of emigration is a craze that, although very fortunate with respect to the general welfare of the Union, does great wrong to this state. That is what delays now and will continue for a long time to delay the organization, the consolidation of our manufactures, the improvement of our roads, the building of bridges, canals, and above all the perfection of agriculture, the foundation of all prosperity. There is quite a span between the state of infancy we are in and that of the European nations who have reached a plenitude of things; who are surrounded by fortified sites, possessing all means of attack which the experience of centuries has perfected; nations whose dependents, unfortunately we are, for a multitude of items which we would be able to manufacture if there were more of us!

"On the other hand, our venerable and esteemed leaders, who, after steering us so skillfully to independence, have guided our convention like beacons lighting sailors through reefs, imperceptibly disappearing and extinguishing. How many losses we have already suffered! One trembles when one thinks of the even greater one that we are destined to suffer: what an emptiness it will leave on this earth, as well as in the heart and soul of men! May Heaven postpone it beyond the century which is about to finish!

"We are not far enough from Europe to prevent a volcanic explosion of new opinions which are spreading there; to prevent the impact of a background of cannon and victories from reaching our shores. The arrival in this country of so great a number of foreigners of all shades of political opinion, the secret and treacherous intrigues of our enemies, as well as those who are jealous of our good fortune, the political parties that have arisen among us; such are in part the dangers in the midst of which we find ourselves in the twentieth year of our political existence.

"Furthermore the territory of the United States is so vast, the sea-coasts so far-reaching, so accessible, the times we are facing (and which the union of so many causes seems to have brought together from afar) are so formidable and so new, and our Government still so young, that only it could pierce the impenetrable clouds which hide the future from us: only such a government would be able to herald difficulties, obstacles, and perhaps even the storms that await us. The existence of nations is like that of individuals: merely a perpetual struggle, a series of efforts and resistances, a mixture of wisdom and errors, of good and bad fortune. Ten more years of peace and our tree of life, as the Indians say, will have grown strong roots and our first crucial epoch will have passed."

"At so great a distance from the capital," my companion said to me as we were going to bed, "to the center of the state whose first settlement dates only from 1682, to the heart of the Alleghanies, think of hearing details and such an interesting conversation; think of finding oneself under the hospitable roof of a learned man, who, after serving his country, works and cultivates his fields! What a rich source for reflection!''

''None of the states of the Union,'' I told him, ''is so advanced as this one. In those states of the South and in Rhode Island, the customs, the instruction, the culture are quite inferior; they are children of the same family, it is true, but the climate in which they have lived and the circumstances of their lives have corrupted and retarded education and progress. Time and necessity will soon cause these original clouds to disappear. How many changes we will see there in less than a half-century!''

The next day we accompanied our host to his mill for the second time. I confess, in seeing the ingenious use he had made of these little cylinders of copper mounted on boxes of metal, and placed on trunnions, I was amazed, unable to fathom why such a simple idea inexpensively put to work had not sooner entered man's head. Thus very inexpensively could the friction of machines be diminished and consequently their driving power increased. From there he took us to his barn; it was located not far from a lively stream, one branch of which flowed under the turbines. This little mystery was soon revealed, when I noticed that this current of water was designed to propel a wooden roller in the shape of a sugar loaf reinforced with rows of pins, turning of its own accord around an iron axle placed in the center of this turbine.

''This,'' he told us, ''is an invention which is new, I'll have you know, and saves us much time and expense, for here manpower is dear and hard to obtain: in one day I can separate the wheat from the chaff of 25 to 30 bushels, whereupon I pour it into the millhopper of this little windmill which, propelled by this same current, winnows it and sifts it. All this is more useful than ingenious. Here is another machine for cutting the hay which I feed my horses and which I also operate by means of waterpower when I wish.''

From his barn, he took us to his dairy; the floor was paved; one could see a little trough around it.

''Of what use is this little trough?'' Mr. Herman asked.

''During the summer heat,'' he replied, ''we let water in on the floor as far as the height of the receptacles that contain the milk; the cream which is separated by the coolness in short order, gives the butter a quality far superior to that processed in an ordinary fashion: that is why these dairies have become so common.''

"What!" I remarked, "a herd as large as this in these mountains! Have you no fear at all of wolves?"

"They have been terrifying, but the premium paid by the Government and the districts for each head [7] has been instrumental in decreasing their number; anyway, my sheep come back into my backyard every evening."

"How white their wool seems to me!"

"That comes from the fact that during the summer they are always outdoors, and during the winter they are sheltered only by a simple shed."

From there he took us to a very high and almost inaccessible promontory, covered with beautiful cedars whence one could see the entire stretch of this valley; it was what he smilingly called his Belvedere.

"If we had a good telescope," he told us, "from this midland point I could show you nearly all the region beyond the maritime provinces of Pennsylvania; you would see, and with astonishment no doubt, what has been done hereabouts in the last one hundred eleven years. How many towns and villages, houses, barns, and mills have been built! What a great number of swamp lands and lowlands, once submerged, have been reclaimed and cleared and are now fine pasture lands! How many cleared and cultivated lands, covered with crops and cattle, were formerly bogged down with trees, stumps, brambles, a veritable den for wild animals! And fancy! This has been accomplished in the short span of time I mentioned, by men who had been forced by disorders, wars, misfortunes, the oppressive yoke of laws to abandon their countries!

"Would you believe that a man who saw the first tree uprooted, cleared the first field in this state, and built the first home in this town, who often told me that on the site of one of our finest churches he had heard the croaking of frogs, who knew personally the famous founder of Pennsylvania; who, on that very river where during his boyhood Indian canoes plied up and down, has lived to see the coming of vessels from all over the world; would you believe, I say, that a man who saw the birth and progress of a state today so flourishing, did not die until 1782? [8] If, during this short span of time, we have been able through all the difficulties of our colonial infancy, those of the war to which we owe our emancipation, to raise ourselves to our present peak of progress, today when we possess so many resources and wealth, who can tell where we will be headed in the same number of years!

"As you see, we have enough space; we need more manpower; new strength is born daily. We lack easier communication with our capital; already they have constructed a great road from Philadelphia to

Lancaster which will be continued as far as the mountains; there is talk of opening another route to Stockport on the Delaware [9] from there to the mouth of the Tiogo; [10] a third toward the west branch of the Susquehannah; still another toward the Juniata and the Alleghany, and finally from Sunbury to Toby's Creek, beyond the mountains. Then the value of the land, the price of commodities will rise here and agriculture will prosper rapidly. Then the colonists, no longer reduced to the necessity of sacrificing half of their crops in order to pay for the transporting of the other half, will become prosperous and well-to-do. This opulence will procure for them the means of increasing their clearings, building better homes, planting and caring for their orchards. From this time will date the growth and real prosperity of Pennsylvania, which, not being crossed, as is New York, by a navigable river, has greater need of fine roads and canals. The canal at Swatara [11] is already finished, as well as that of Conewago. [12] They are at work on a new one which will unite the waters of the Skullkill with those of the Delaware. The Government is also thinking of perfecting navigation of the Susquehanna, from Middleton Creek to the mouth of the Juniata. [13] The fine attitude of our Legislature that has had made a map of all our rivers guarantees to us that this project will soon be realized.''

The next day, while walking on the slope of a very high mountain, we saw its summit whose surface reflected the sun's rays. I asked what was the cause of this phenomenon.

''Amazed, just as you were, by this phenomenon, I climbed to the top to remove some samples of soil which I sent to the secretary of our philosophical society in Philadelphia. But after several attempts, I found that these stones contained only a little sulphur and mica leave, at the most; if this summit is not interesting to mineralogists, its base has great interest for colonists. Almost all the trees covering it are hollow and filled with bees: it is our Mount Hymette. These bees love liberty and independence so much that despite our cares, they often abandon the fine beehives which we build for them to settle in the hollows of these old trees. We console ourselves over their flight, since we have discovered those habitats in which they live and have found the secret of getting their honey.''

This hunt, all the details of which he furnished us, seemed to Mr. Herman and me to be such a novel enterprise, that we resolved to undertake the next day a little excursion into the woods. It was to be very simple, since this mountain was merely 6 or 7 miles away, and Mr. ——— himself had cut the path, marking all the trees. [14] With the intention of leaving at dawn the next day, we retired early.

CHAPTER III

In accordance with our plan, the next day toward noon we departed in high spirits, supplied with a tinder-box, flint, and steel, various items necessary for discovering bee trees,[1] an activity that precludes our toting guns along. Indeed nothing could have been more convenient than the direction mapped out for us by Mr. ——— by which we could have cut through and beyond the Alleghanies. In less than a half hour our route led us to the banks of a wide and deep ravine that appeared to serve as an outlet for torrents caused by the melting of snow. In all our travels we had never seen such an impressive sight; it was the reflection of destruction and ravage. On one side one could see pools of stagnant water, filled with snakes, isolated rocks against which the waters must have dashed with a great violence; on the other, accumulations of mud, sand, and gravel, multitudes of inter-twined trees, forming virtual dikes which, to judge by the considerable piles of dry leaves and clay, appeared to have resisted their impetuos-ity; there were stumps and branches heaped against the river banks making approach well nigh impossible.

In view of how difficult it would be for novices like us to cross so many obstacles, we were surprised that Mr. ——— had not spoken to us about them. We decided to follow the banks of the ravine until we could find a place that was narrower and would enable us to cross with greater ease. This was just a little over two or three miles away. But, preoccupied and absent-minded as we were, we continued walking straight ahead, after passing right by the ravine, instead of going through it. Fatal forgetfulness! We had gone deeper into the woods, I know not how far, when Mr. Herman, stopping suddenly, said:

"And our trail! Where is it! We have strayed and we are lost!"

As a lightning flash reveals to the traveler's eyes the edge of the precipice which he has approached unknowingly in the dark, these words opened my eyes and made me see the danger in which this absorption had thrown us.

"Let's retrace our steps," I said, "since thus far we have kept the moss under the trees on our left as we made our way in a westerly direction, now if we keep it on our right, we will find the ravine again for it runs in a north-south direction;" but, not having, as do the Indians, the knack of retracing our steps by watching the position of the trees' leaves and being disturbed and upset, we were led further astray. Nightfall took us by surprise, without our discovery of anything that could reassure us. In the woods as on the sea and elsewhere, one error leads to another; the greater the space one covers seeking to find his way, the more lost one becomes: that is what happened to us.

Although seven months have already elapsed since this unhappy incident, I still recall frightful images of that day when we left the woods. Never will time, with its file and its sponge, erase from my memory the mournful recollection of that moment when I caught a glimpse of death through the horrors of despair and hunger. As night had fallen, I was busying myself in fetching wood dry enough to light a fire, when Mr. Herman, who was a little way off, cried out:

"What are we going to do? What will become of us?"

"What's the matter?" I asked him.

"I have lost the flint I was carrying, probably in the fall that I took crossing the ravine; would we ever be able to find it in these woods now?"

"Unlikely," I told him, "besides, we can scarcely see. It is certainly true: misfortunes never happen singly. Give me the piece of steel, I shall try it on the first stones we come upon."

Our attempts were fruitless.

"What!" said my companion to me sadly, "does one have to be exposed to the fury of wolves and panthers for lack of flint when there are so many useless things on earth! Of all possible combinations of misfortune, this one seems to me to be the most fatal. On what, then, do happiness and life depend? Elsewhere these stones are squandered in the repair of roads; here a single one would suffice—aye, would console us—would recall our confidence and courage, procuring for us the aid of fire and light."

"For one night spent without fire at the foot of a tree," I told him, "let us not abandon ourselves to utter despair; if we do, we are lost. Give me your shoes, I shall put them with mine, at some distance from us;[2] rest assured that in the shelter of this feeble little rampart, we shall spend the night peacefully, and tomorrow we shall leave this labyrinth."

Weakened by fatigue, overcome as we were by the pressure of anxious thoughts and sad and gloomy presentiments, how long the hours of this night appeared to us! Our eyes would close for a few moments; the more or less far away yowls of the wolves, the screeching voices of the owl[3] and osprey emulated by the nocturnal echoes of this forest, the noise, the suspicion of the slightest movement, even the sighs of the breeze, awakened a thousand conjectures in the disturbed mind of my companion. His imagination exerted all its power in the creation of the most sinister omens, completely shutting out sleep from his tired eyes. Whence came this effect of darkness on the minds of the majority of men?

After busying myself for a long time in recalling the little I knew of the geography of this part of the mountains, the course of the ravine, the direction of the route which we had followed since we crossed the ravine, I resolved as soon as day dawned, to climb to the top of a tall tree to watch the sun rise. I was telling Mr. Herman of this plan when, with a tinge of anger in his voice, he said:

"You are the one who led me to this precipice talking to me about hunting bee trees!"

"Well," I replied, "am I not affected by it, too? Is bitter rancor going to replace friendship and confidence? That is typical of men; circumstances alone decide their relationships."

Finally this eternal night ended and as soon as day dawned, I carried out my plan: then, certain of the point on the horizon whence I had seen the sun rise, and convinced that our route should be northeast, we struck off in that direction. We would probably have found the banks of the ravine again had we not been obliged to cross several good-sized valleys covered with high bushes in the midst of which we strayed again. How were we to get through these forests when the objects that met our eyes resembled so perfectly those we had just left behind us? On what should the indications and knowledge necessary for travel in the lonely woods depend? Is it the result of study or of inspiration? How do the Indians manage? In talking to my companion about what I knew of the inconceivable wisdom of animals that never get lost in these woods, he remarked:

"It is enough to make one blush with shame: when one thinks that two men with reason and judgment are less capable in this moment of crisis in getting out of difficulties, than two cows with instinct would be!"

We walked, or rather, we roamed all day long without seeing the slightest indication that would announce proximity to a plantation or ravine; nor did we come on a single fruit, a single bush on which we could appease the hunger that gnawed at our vitals. How many times in the course of this unending day did we prick up our ears at the slightest noise, unable to hear anything but gloomy tones of forest birds and that vague, indistinct murmur, which in happier moments, would have seemed to us like the voice of Nature! How many times we called out, to be answered only by far-off echoes whose responses made us tremble more than once because we believed them to be those of a man. Why does time, which in ordinary moments of life passes like a shadow of the sun with almost imperceptible progress, let moments of happiness slip by so quickly, yet prolongs those of misfortune as though to make us feel bitterness more keenly? It was in the midst of torments of hunger, irritation, and despair, that the second and cruelest of any night I have ever known finally ended. Such were the tragic auspices under which I began the third day of this fatal excursion in the woods.

We were no longer talking; absorbed, plunged in the last degree of consternation and feebleness, we were walking slowly toward what we believed to be northeast, when Mr. Herman suddenly called:

"We are not far from a farm; we are saved. There are some leaves recently nibbled at; that can be only the work of pigs."

"Alas, would to God it were," I told him, "it was but the work of a flock of wild turkeys [4] which fill these forests."

Again we thought, if only we had brought our guns along! One of those fine birds would have sustained our hunger for a long time, since nature has not fostered here the growth of any fruit on which man can feed. Never have I seen such sterile forests!

As if somber despair, the piercing and inexpressible gnawings of hunger had not sufficed to overcome our pains, toward the middle of this day, fury seized our hearts: [5] if we opened our mouths, it was only to heap on each other insult and reproach about the journey; if by chance, our eyes met, though spiritless and feeble, they became immediately inflamed with the fire of anger and indignation. These passions, which until that moment we had never known, manifested themselves suddenly with the greatest violence, as if some evil jinn had suddenly blown them into our hearts. But no, the seeds that Nature had hidden there, were awaiting the distressing circumstance to which we had been reduced for full fruition before maturation. Ah! if in these dreadful moments, we had had weapons, or even the strength to seize one another, frantic as we were, one of us would certainly have killed the other.

These upsets, whose memory I recall only with shame and fright, gave way to the calm of extreme feebleness and annihilation; we seated ourselves at the foot of a tree and soon afterward we were seized with a burning feeling which at every moment gave us a craving for drink. Thus, to the torments, to the perpetual irritations of extreme lifelessness, was added the devouring fever from thirst, the most unbearable of the needs to which mankind can be subjected. Fortunately, after a change of wind brought us the noise of a falls nearby, we followed it, leaning from time to time against trees, finally arriving at nightfall on the banks of a river, which I learned since was one of the branches of the Alleghany. Here we extinguished the burning heat of thirst.

Mr. Herman spent almost the entire third night in the most frightful delirium. He cursed the day when he had been born, his crossing of the

Atlantic, and especially his companion whom he wished to see seized by final torture before dying himself! But, although the passing of this fever seemed to give him new strength, I feared that he could not survive another violent seizure. The great quantity of water I had drunk produced an opposite effect: it calmed the fever and the sharp pains, but for a long time inundated my body and face with a cold sweat; my faculties being more dulled, more weakened than those of my unfortunate companion, perhaps, I was suffering less, although I was just as miserable. My eyes closed and the last idea that I can remember today was the one concerning the state of resignation in which I found myself and the feeling of the rapid decline of life. However, I deplored dying alone, abandoned at the foot of a tree. The prospect of being devoured, after my death, by flesh-eating animals pervaded me with the deepest horror.

Nevertheless, nature was again vigilant over our preservation. The cessation of thought in us was but the beginning of drowsiness. We thought we had slept several hours, when despite all probabilities and the feeling of our gloomy premonitions, we saw the light of the fourth day; but like a funeral torch, it served only to increase the horror of our situation in making us see the gates of the tomb which we were touching.

Our eyes, covered with the shadow of death, instead of seeing real objects, no longer saw anything but fantastic shapes as we lay agitated and trembling. Now the shadows that surrounded us would suddenly disperse by glimmers of moving, fleeting light; now they would appear to us as phantoms which, having approached us in flight, grazed the surface of the ground, touched the tops of the bushes and would perch on trees above our heads. Often our eyes, almost closed, would still see some sort of transparent fog, yet be unable to distinguish anything.

"It is often when the measure of misfortune is at its height," I could still say to my companion while we dragged ourselves along the river edge, "that reassuring thoughts and rays of light appear.

"Have you never observed on the sea those consoling lulls during the most frightful tempests? Here we are at the lowest ebb of misfortune. Let us continue to hope."

"How do you dare utter this word?" he said to me with the tone and gesture of one enraged. "Despair and death have dispelled our last illusions. Since you are a coward, hope; as for me, I am going to throw myself in that river at the bottom of which peace and quiet sleep await me. Who would want to endure any longer these bitter circumstances when, from the midst of hell to the bosom of repose, there is but twenty feet distance?"

"Let us see this day through," I said to him, "if that is possible;

let us drink more water and if no favorable indication presents itself, this evening we will drown ourselves together.''

''For one who suffers as I do, this evening is one hundred leagues off.

''Well, then, since you have become my enemy, wishing to persuade me to live a few more hours, kill your dog; give me my share, so that I may sate my appetite. If you are savage enough to refuse me this gift, permit me to die now.''

The idea of killing this animal, an idea that as pressing a need had not yet provoked, suddenly recalled hope and life.

Far from listening to the voice of affection and remorse at the sight of this dog, who was as enfeebled and as languishing as we were, I was seized by a feeling more violent even than anger. It was the inflammation of fury. I trembled before it. My shaking hands were hastily seeking the knife that I had let fall among the leaves, when my companion, revived by the hope of appeasing his hunger, accused me of delay and reviled me once again. As I approached my resigned victim, that invisible power that presides over all our destinies directed my eyes toward a branch of groundnuts.[6]

''We are saved!'' I cried. ''We are saved! The ground on which we have spent the night and on which we thought we would die yields a life-giving substance, for there where this branch grows, we are certain to find a thousand like it—and we did not even suspect it!''

''Merciful God our benefactor!'' he cried; ''are you not deceiving me perchance?''

Immediately I offered him the first of those roots that I had just snatched, but we were both so weak that it cost us much sweat and effort before we were able to obtain a large enough quantity to satisfy our gnawing need. Ah! if only we had had the means to light a fire, what a sumptuous meal we might have had!

But how can we express the effect produced on our morale by the certainty that we could procure a greater quantity of these groundnuts? How can we describe this exquisite new feeling, this incredible delight that suddenly gave new strength to our beaten spirits, seized our downcast hearts, recalling to them the delightful and divine consolations of hope? The sudden passing from extreme need to the possession of some nourishment cooked, one might say, by the light of a feeble ray of hope, that of a desperate state to one much calmer, the change from the banks of the gloomy Cocyte to the fields of life itself?

No doubt that is how in the beginning of societies, anthropophagy began among men after several days of fruitless hunting; for the span is not as great as one thinks between killing one's dog and killing one's friend in order to give life to one's dying frame: like us, after having long struggled against hunger, incensed to the point of frenzy for lack of a dog, the strongest will kill the weakest. Sad and deplorable consequence of a situation at the mercy of necessity! But stay! This same necessity has never goaded the most ferocious and the most cannibalistic animal to destroying his equal and to devouring his carcass. Consequently, war having bred the same needs, starved conquerors will eat the conquered, just as it still happens today among the nations of the interior of the continent, among those of Brazil, and wherever Cook disembarked. Anthropophagy must have ceased only because of the knowledge of means for breeding and raising cattle; but how many centuries preceded this happy discovery! Without this benefit of nature, where would we still be? And what about me? Have I not touched the moment of becoming a man-eating being? Most certainly, since I was on the point of seizing on the flesh of someone whom I loved, killing a companion who for so many years had done so many fine things for me, had saved my life during the crossing of a river; a friend, I dare say, whose experience, wisdom, and affection had often impressed me with respect and admiration. Ah, poor Ontario, what good fortune for you, even more so for me, that you may never know that I was on the point of raising over you my fratricidal hand! But even if you found out, either you would not believe it, or you would pardon me.

Meanwhile, after satisfying our urgent needs and enjoying several busy hours in looking for these groundnuts of which we wished to make an abundant store, we were becoming calmer. Suddenly I thought I heard the noise of one of those bells which the colonists customarily attached to the collar of the strongest beast in their flock. My ears . . . what am I saying! My whole soul was recalled from its depression by the mere suspicion of this consoling noise; I stood in the lee of the tree in the direction of which I thought I had heard it. How long and cruel were these minutes ticking in the torment of doubt, inquietude, and fear of being mistaken. I was going to speak of it to my companion, when this hope for sound burst out again and so distinctly that with my eyes suddenly dimmed by tears, my heart swollen and pounding, I could scarcely say to him:

"Yes, it is the noise of a bell. I am sure we shall not perish in these somber and solitary depths; the Alleghanies will not be our tomb after all. Can you hear this consoling and marvelous sound?"

"Blessed be the breeze that brings it to us on its wings! . . . Yes, it is Heaven who sends hope to our rescue; rise and obey lady hope!"

But, still moved and trembling, eye dazed, ear tuned to the wind, it was not until we had heard the noise of this bell several times that we were gradually revived, summoned to live again. Then we found the strength to follow this sound which became more distinct as we advanced, until toward five o'clock we finally discovered through the woods that guardian flock which was passing through a bog meadow.

"Let us pray," I said to Mr. Herman, "to this unexpected boon, this resuscitation to life, to society and to our friends through emotions as well as by thoughts of keenest gratitude."

And at that moment, we knelt at the foot of a tree to address to Heaven words that our agitated hearts inspired in us and that our feeble mouths could scarcely utter.

This herd, to whose wisdom and instinct we owed our return to civilization, comprised 42 head among which we counted 8 cows.

"I recognize these good mothers," my companion said to me, "but how can we get milk from their teats?"

"With patience and gentleness," I replied.

Indeed, after several attempts, we succeeded in milking three hatfuls. How magnificent this nectar, heaven sent, seemed to us! It seemed like the restorative balm of life and I did not forget to give some to this humble, faithful friend that I had planned to sacrifice to the delirium of hunger only the day before.

While we were awaiting impatiently the time of the flock's return, Mr. Herman, recalling all that he had said in his fit of frenzy, implored me to forget.

"These vilifications," I told him, "sprang from the deplorable situation to which we were reduced. Alas! they were the least of our misfortunes! We have surmounted them; we are on the point of leaving these woods; of seeing the light of the sun again, some cultivated fields, human beings who will be our friends, since we are unfortunate; for could man hate his equal, when neither his passions nor his interest order it thus? Let us unleash our hearts, so long caged, to the feelings of joy and tenderness; let us return to the warm emotions of friendship and good fellowship; may these sad and painful memories be forever erased from our mind and be consigned to the deepest oblivion."

Finally, the bell-bearing bull stopped grazing, and as I had foreseen, started plodding toward the northeast. Slowly we followed this herd of guides as Mr. Herman, who was now walking with obvious effort, said:

"Night is approaching, as you see; I am still not sufficiently convinced; I fear lest these beasts might be straying and may not be able to find their abode!"

"Never fear," I told him. "Trust the infallibility of the instinct which leads them; this neverfailing light appears to be much more certain in everything that is useful to them—more certain even than our own reasoning power. I am well acquainted with traits of sagacity and foresight among animals raised in the woods which would do honor to the intelligence of the proudest man. Quite different are those animals that are always kept fenced on pasture lands."

Meanwhile our eager, impatient eyes, focused in the direction of the forest toward which this herd was making its way, finally saw the faint light of a clearing,[7] and filled with tears. We were smitten with a feeling so extraordinary, so nigh to suffocation, that we sat at the foot of a tree: sweat ran off our faces; our hearts pounded as they are wont to do in the first moments of fright; we were both near that state of consciousness in which we could foresee neither the consequences nor the end. Joy and happiness, it seems, also have their anguish and their dangers! During all this time we were becoming calmer, and we could rejoin the herd. "O memorable day!" I said to myself. "O day of my second birth! Thy memory will never be erased from my mind. If ever misfortune, unhappiness or worry besiege me, I shall mitigate their wounds by thinking of the wounds, so much more profound that you are soon going to heal."

If the sudden transition from darkness of the woods to light is ever a striking contrast to those who have lived there long, how much more it is for us who were emerging from the very shadows of a tomb! Meanwhile the horizon was brightening gradually; already we could see a field, apple trees, cherry trees.

"I can really see these interesting objects," said Mr. Herman; "but no dwelling yet."

"A little patience," I said to him, "the roof belonging to the family who undertook this great clearing is not far off."

And a few moments later we saw a column of smoke that rose perpendicularly, for the wind had gone down with the sun.

He who, dragged down by the violence of the torrent, is rescued from it at the time when the waves are about to engulf him; the sailor who, uncertain of latitude, discovers in the midst of fog a cape of land, does not experience a keener joy, profounder than was ours at the sight of this smoke, which was the torch of our greeting. We finally reached the house. It was high time; the state of feebleness and trembling in which we were would not have permitted us to go two miles further.

"Today you will have considerably less milk than you had yesterday," I said to the mistress of the house, who at the sound of the bell, had left the house, accompanied by her two daughters, to greet us. "Almost dying of hunger for four days, we had the good fortune to come upon your cows and to milk three to give us strength, then by following them, to come here to beg hospitality of you.''

"Judging from the sad state you seem to be in, Gentlemen, even enemies would have the right to hospitality,'' she answered; "give us your arm; let us go in.''

Never were words uttered more distinctly, nor heard with greater attention and gratitude. The first favor this generous woman performed for us was to perfume with maple sugar the beds she indicated for us; the second was to bring us a plate of corn [8] cooked in soup, only a small part of which she permitted us to eat at first. When we reproached her with some bitterness for giving us such small portions, the softness of her voice, one of humanity and reason, repressed our desires and imposed silence on us. What nutritive power this preparation of corn contains! Since that time I have often heard it prescribed by doctors for use by convalescents. This fine woman or one of her daughters stayed with us until this restorative had subtly lulled us to sleep ... what am I saying ... to the profoundest kind of repose, the greatest balm that ever nature in all her bounty has deigned to give to unfortunate beings. The sun of the following day had reached its zenith before we opened our eyes to its light.

Then the master of the house appeared; business had obliged him to go to Bedford [9] the day before. He brought us a fine salmon trout which he permitted us to eat abundantly and he gave us some gooseberry wine, five years old; wine that one finds more commonly in the homes of the worthy colonists of Pennsylvania than in the other states. What time in our lives ever matched the festivity of this meal! What a contrast between the delightful, comforting ideas that were reviving our spirits and those which had ravaged them the day before! We enjoyed the calm and wonderful immobility to the fullest measure.

After thanking the master of the house with all the effusion of our hearts, for the favors we had received from his wife, we told him our long, sad story.

"It is hardly extraordinary,'' he told us, "that people who know neither the course of the waters, nor the way of the mountains, nor the tracks, occasioned by the displacement of leaves, may have wandered, become lost, and have been at a starvation point. You are not the first who have experienced this misfortune. I congratulate myself that it is to our cows that you owe your safety, and to me the pleasure of receiving you in my home. I will conduct you to my neighbor's house, when you are entirely recovered. His house is only seven miles from here. Rest assured; we will take care of you as though you were our relatives or our friends.''

"May destiny some day permit us to be able to convince you that you have not given favors to ungrateful people!" Mr. Herman told him. "To cap your kindness, would you mind sending one of your men to Mr. ———? Perhaps he is worried about us and believes us to be lost."

"Write him," he replied. "A letter to him will not take long."

Sure enough, early the next day this fine old soldier arrived; he was deeply moved with pleasure and astonishment and could not imagine how we had strayed so far as the banks of the Alleguipy. He told us that he and his companions had looked for us in the woods, to the north and to the south of the dividing line. They had gone as far as the shiny mountain and had not abandoned their search until the third day.

How comforting it is to recall such essential favors performed with as much speed as good fellowship! No, never will I forget what I owe to the good and saint-like hospitality of the Forbes family in Bedford district in the Alleghany mountains. Finally after four days of rest, we were permitted to regain our strength through exercise and walking and, accompanied by our host, we explored his entire farm.

"For fifteen years I have been here," he told us. "Two of my compatriots from the Scottish Highlands have helped me clear these fields. I helped build their settlement and they are now very happy there, just as I am here. As you see, I have a fine wife who unites wonderful gentleness of character with high intelligence, industry, and cleanliness. Since I have been here, I have not bought a single ell of cloth nor any European merchandise, so well does she know how to use the linen from our fields, the wool from our sheep, and the cotton that comes from Virginia. Soon my children will be old enough to help me. So far the Government has protected us without taxation."

"By what chance did you come to settle in these mountains?" I asked him. "In crossing them you would have found in the counties beyond and through which we came land more agreeably situated."

"Very true, but what I own here is a military concession that I became entitled to as son of a sergeant killed in 1755 under Colonel Washington at Braddock's defeat in the vicinity of Fort Duquesne, today Pittsburgh. The lowlands hereabouts are highly desirable; moreover, I enjoy the inappreciable advantage of being surrounded by forests which will never be conceded, the soil being ill suited to farming. Every year I sell 150 to 200 bushels of wheat and a great deal of lard to the colonists who come to settle along the Ohio or one of its branches. All we need for our comfort is a great highway from here to Philadelphia. They say the Government is busy constructing this highway, as well as others. But can I complain—above all when I stop to think that it is not yet twenty years since these regions have been settled? Am I not happier here than if destiny had detained me in the cold, sterile highlands of Scotland? There are so many others, I would have been crushed or lost in the crowd for lack of space; here, as you see, I have plenty.

"Only one misfortune has befallen me since my arrival here: the fifth year lightning struck my barn a few days after I had filled it with a full harvest. Inattentive, like so many others, to the use of lightning rods, I had ignored helpful advice that the venerable Franklin often used to insert in his famous *Poor Richard's Almanach,* as well as his urgent solicitations to protect our barns and houses. I know not why, but the former are much more subject to being struck by lightning when they are filled than when they are empty. In order to save two guineas, or rather, through indifference, I lost more than two hundred guineas. That is the nature of most men: they close their eyes to the evidence of useful truths; it is never in the lifetime of those who have discovered these truths that they begin to sense the importance."

Finally, after ten days of rest we left this good and industrious family to whom we had so many obligations, not without regret. We took with us one of the sons whom Mr. Herman undertook to raise at his own expense at Franklin Marshall College.[10] Toward evening of the same day we arrived at the home of Mr. ———, where we stayed a week. Then finally, refreshed from our fatigue, we left the banks of the Juniata, to return to Shippenbourg, where already our friends were acquainted with the details of our adventure * and were awaiting us impatiently.

(Here there appears to be a lapse of time, or else several chapters were lost.)

* This adventure, whose details make one shiver, recalls the more tragic tale of the two unfortunate, wretched creatures who had strayed in the vast subterranean depths of the Observatory in Paris, and were found long afterward in such a state that one could not doubt but that the need for food had reduced them to the horrible extremity of eating one another. (Note communicated to the editor by Citizen B.)

CHAPTER IV

Although I had twice seen the celebrated Niagara Falls, the season being favorable for travel, I decided to accompany Mr. Herman whose enthusiastic invitation I could not refuse. From Schenectady, where we were located at the time, we left in a light skiff to go up the Mohawk, and arrived in seven days at Whiteston, a town recently founded at the end of the navigable part of this river. From here on, a very short canal on which they are still working is soon going to make a link with the waters of Wood Creek. They told us that the same company which had undertaken this enterprise was also to cut through the bends, for it is one of the most tortuous rivers that I have ever seen. Our former host, old Keskétomah, whom we had the good fortune to meet on the shores of the lovely Oneida, took us in his canoe to the other end, thirty-six miles away, where we hired a boat in which we went down the Oneida River,[1] at the time overflowing its riverbanks, as far as Oswego, on the shores of the great Lake Ontario.[2]

During this last part of the trip, we experienced only a little inconvenience from the narrows[3] through which, we were told, the Government is planning to build canals. When finished, this canal, long planned, will unite the waters of the Mohawk with those of the Hudson;[4] then, one will be able to go by water from New York, as far as nine miles from Niagara Falls, an estimated distance of 200 leagues from this capital. Then all the produce from the land of the Mohawk, Genessee, Onondaga, and Beaver Swamp will easily be transported to Albany and thence to Europe. What incalculable advantages for that great and wonderful state!

The harbor at Oswego, just as safe, although less spacious than those at Toronto, Katarakouy, and Niagara, has the disadvantage of having only fourteen feet of water on the bar; this prevented the English during the war with Canada from being able to construct frigates as strong as those belonging to the French who had a depth of 18 feet in their ports. A lieutenant was in command there. The uncertainty in which they had existed since the independence of these states, regarding the possession of a land and region which, in accordance with the treaty of peace, sooner or later was to be given to them, has prevented colonists from making settlements there. We noticed in this region some well-cultivated gardens. A tanker of 90 tons being ready to sail for Niagara, we easily obtained permission to embark. It was commanded by Mr. B., a Canadian by birth, and a well-educated man whose father had been pilot to the king of France at Katarakouy. His son, who had traded with the tribes of the great lakes long ago, had become a lieutenant. He showed us an interesting hand-drawn map of those remote lands whose geography is so little known.

We had scarcely put the port of Oswego behind us when the wind came up and the wash of the great lake made us feel as though we were out on the open sea. Looking south at sunset we saw several columns of smoke. These, the captain informed us, were emanating from clearings of an American settlement, established a year ago near the mouth of the Assedorus [5] which empties into this (Ontario) lake forty-five miles away at Oswego, making a very generous and convenient harbor there.

Mr. Herman, astonished to find himself so far from the sea, on a body that resembled it by its immensity, its depth, and the height of its waves, was chatting with the captain, asking him many questions.

"My father and I have seen six frigates of 26 cannon each on this beautiful lake; three of which, out of Katarakouy, belonged to the French; three others, out of Oswego, to the English. But how things have changed since that time! Some years after the English ships were seized by Canada, the colonies (to which the ships belonged), became independent states whose population, since that famous epoch, has increased with astonishing rapidity; already people have crossed the Alleghanies, founded settlements on the banks of the Ohio and on those rivers that flow into it.[6] And, as you see, their plows have already arrived on these shores.

"While exploring with the aid of this map the immense extent of this continent," he continued, "one is impressed by the layout of these mediterranean seas, that from the lakes of Winnipeg, Pluyes, Lake of the Woods, and that long chain of little lakes, which lead to Lake Superior, open an easy communication to the sea in a space of perhaps 800 leagues. One is no less astonished when one considers that these lakes receive in their bosom navigable rivers coming from almost every direction, the principal ones of which will open by means of canals to even more remote communications.

"What an impetus inland trade, industry, sciences, and the arts will take on then when men become numerous enough to appropriate all the treasures that cultivation promised to them in a land so vast and situated in such a variety of climates; not to mention the advantages offered to them by nature! And the 400 leagues of shore line sprinkled with bays, harbors, rivers—what an opportunity for navigation! If my son lives to my age, he will see the plow of American colonists break ground on the banks of the upper Mississippi, and their cattle graze on the vast natural prairies which water the Illinois and Wabash Rivers.

"The population of Canada," he continued, "has tripled since the conquest, because every man who knows how to fell a tree, whatever his religion, can come settle there. Under the French domination, it was mandatory that one be Catholic. But soon on this beautiful lake we will also have Toronto and Katarakouy, for they say that in accordance with the treaty of 1783, England will cede to the United States the ports of Niagara and Oswego, as well as the ports of Détroit and Michillimackinac. The former, built in 1687 by the French, was for a long time the general council place of the Indians; they came there from far-off regions to exchange their pelts for things they needed; today it is merely a portage. In a few years the riches of farming and fishing will replace those of trade; perhaps even the new town of Niagara, built by the English on the Missisages [7] on the other side of the roadstead, is destined to become the capital of upper Canada."

Thereupon he told us about the salmon and sturgeon fishing, as well as the attempts that had already been made to extract oil; of the copper mines of virgin ore that had been discovered in the neighboring regions of the lake. But the wind had freshened in the night, and the next day we found ourselves out of sight of land. The same was true on the ocean: here too, we were only a speck 'mid immensity and a line of 200 fathoms would not have reached the bottom.

"What do I see on the horizon which seems like a pyramid of snow and appears to rise as far as the clouds?" [8] asked Mr. Herman.

"That," replied the captain, "is a column of vapors formed by condensation of the waters of the cataract. Moreover, we are, in my estimation at least 50 miles away. As you see, it is the torch of navigators. Tomorrow if the wind keeps up, we shall see the peninsula on which the fort was built."

In fact, by sun-up, the dwellings situated to the east and west of the mouth of the river, as well as some of the houses of the new town of Niagara seemed to be all island in the middle of the sea. After crossing the bar and passing the roadstead where two vessels of war, several brigantines, skiffs, and dug-out canoes were at anchor, our vessel was made fast to a pier.

"Everything we see here," my companion remarked, "resembles a veritable seaport, and mark you, we are 320 leagues from the St. Lawrence gulf and 206 leagues from New York."

"What will it be like when some day the shores of the two lakes are covered with colonies?" I queried.

As soon as we had disembarked on this famous isthmus, we hastened to present our letters of introduction to Colonel Hunter, commandant, who received us with cordiality and even urged us to stay in the fort and use his horses any time we wished to go to old Fort Erie [9] to see the falls.

"Gentlemen," he admonished us, "do not regret the fatigues of the journey you have just made; you will be more than amply recompensed by watching this great phenomenon. However cold the imagination of travelers, this spectacle, at once astonishing and exciting, stimulates the imagination to an extraordinary degree. Everything about the cataract is vast, majestic, impressive, and sublime, like the immensity of the sea, the rising and the setting of the sun in the tropics, or the eruption of a volcano. But it is only after returning from the kind of weariness that robs us of our faculties and senses, that we are permitted, refreshed of mind, to examine the main details. Captain Irwine, engineer of the garrison, estimates at 1,890 feet the width of the west branch including the part that doubles back from the center (Horseshoe Falls); the east branch he puts at 900, and the island dividing these two sheets of water, the height of the first at 172, the second 182, and the elevation of the column of vapors when the weather is calm at more than 2,000 feet.

"The noise that strikes the ears," he continued, "resembles the wrackings of a tempest during its most violent moments; it is more than noise, it is a reverberation that wracks and rends both body and mind alike; it is impossible either to conceive or transmit a precise idea of it. Animals, especially birds, rarely inhabit this region, for they love the peace of retreat and the pleasures of love; yonder they would hear only the movement and din of destruction.

"But although fortunately for the inhabitants of the region, the reverberation never rises above the vast gorge of this great abyss, silence and terror appear to reign in the region; everything is quiet— to the very echoes, which, from the beginning of this cataract, did not dare to inhabit places as noisy and as savage as these.

"Yet, in the midst of so many features, the first view of which provokes only an idea of chaos, what harmony one observes in this great and sublime aggregation! How effectively nature understands how to stamp its works with a majesty that summons both respect and admiration, condemning reason to silence! Indeed, what worthier spectacle exists to inspire this dual sentiment! And what is there more difficult to paint, to conceive, than the immensity of waters, the strength, the weight, the speed with which they precipitate after having formed these two water sheds?

"Nothing more is needed than the irresistible impulse of the most avid curiosity to have the courage to surmount the difficulties and obstacles which beset those travelers who wish to see everything. Yes, indeed, all this is necessary to go from rock to rock, or to descend with the aid of shaking ladders [10] either into the depth of the gorge of the east branch, or to cross the precipitous and hideous banks of the west branch, leading to the edge of the whirlpool; to manage to see the falls, to avoid the dangers, to hang in midair sometimes clinging to branches, to climb, slide until one has finally reached that mobile unit, the cave of the winds (something few travelers have dared undertake), which ceaselessly pushes forth torrents with a deafening din, into an abyss of from four to five thousand feet diameter, whose waves, ever foaming and frothing, relentlessly roused by the enormous weight of the falls, would swallow up the largest vessels, and make the most fearless man shudder; it is then that, plunged in the stupor of astonishment, and appearing to be no more than a feeble atom, one recognizes the hand of the Creator, and one becomes humble, worshipping His power.

"But," he continued, "such is the feebleness of the human organism, that soon, tired of seeing, hearing, and even admiring, the traveler hurriedly leaves these somber and watery places to seek daylight and the sun. Among the great number of strangers whom I have seen here, how few were in a position to articulate clearly the impressions that the contemplation of so many extraordinary sights awakened in them! Indeed, when curiosity is stripped of knowledge, memory recalls only imperfect images, doubtful or dark; only the main outlines remain distinct.

"It is during the vagueness of early twilight or when the first shadows of night have partially veiled the principal points of view and annihilated distances, or when, enveloped in the shadow of one of the great rocks of the bank, that the traveler watches the cataract by the light of the moon and believes himself in a suspended state of enchantment and marvels. Like the cave of Trophonius, it can be forgotten only when one has seen it.

"But," he continued, "before leaving this place for old Erie, customarily people like you, Gentlemen, come to see an old Indian who for several years has lived alone in a cabin which he built in the middle of rocks on the bank of the river. What misfortune, as a Spanish monk would say, that he is not Christian; he would be a true father of the desert. Yet, he is neither hermit nor recluse, but a free, independent man; his advanced age, his benign face, his manner of expressing himself, make him very interesting. Like the last rays of a setting sun, which has vivified everything in its course and now becomes feeble, imperceptibly, leaving at dusk a soft memory of its splendor, his imagination still has preserved some sparkle of the fire that it lit in the age of his vigor. He speaks our language moderately well, a rare accomplishment among these Indians, and he has long been one of the eminent chiefs of an important tribe of the Chippeway, today reduced to nothing.

"This man is the Nestor of northern Canada, and beyond any doubt the phenomenon of his race, for rarely does one see any of his tribe reach such an advanced age. Although born healthy and vigorous, and raised in a tradition of daring that teaches resistance to nature and the elements, their winter hunts are so long and tiring, their manner of travel so arduous, the abstinences to which their guilty lack of foresight exposes them so cruel (not to mention the abuse they make of brandy), that this terrible regimen wears away their stamina and shortens their days. So far as I am able to judge by the turn of events and the succession of Governors of Canada whom he claims he has known, he must be seventy.

"As long as he is able to fish," continued Colonel Hunter, "and satisfy his principal needs, I shall leave him where he is, for I know how much these men of nature prefer to depend on no one. They consider as the lowest degree of laziness relying on others for their subsistence, and, to borrow one of their expressions, "filling their kettles." Until now, I have contented myself from time to time with sending him bread, salt, and some bottles of old wine. For, quite different from his compatriots, he detests brandy. What a man he must have been in the full vigor of manhood! How effectively he must have expressed himself when he was chief of his tribe!

"What more shall I tell you, Gentlemen? If ever your friends request you to tell the story of your travels in these regions, the little excursion that I suggest to you would perhaps become a very interesting episode. Were it not for some business at the garrison detaining me, I would accompany you with great pleasure."

CHAPTER V

In accordance with Colonel Hunter's suggestions, the next day we crossed the roadstead at Niagara in his six-man canoe and, guided by the soldier who cooked for us on the way, we followed an extremely picturesque, wild trail, and arrived at the wigwam, or rather hermitage, of old Agoueghon.

"We have come from New York, brother," I told him, "especially to see the falls, but the commandant of the fort who is our friend and yours spoke so inspiringly of your wisdom, of your long span of experience, and of your solitary existence, that we wanted to shake your hand and spend the day with you before leaving for Erie."

"Welcome," he replied.

After telling him of my adoption into the Oneidas, as well as my travels among the tribes of the Ohio River Valley, I said to him:

"Here is some wine we have brought you, worthy and esteemed Agoueghon; let us drink some of it so that you will remember your meeting with us; this young European is my friend."

"Give me your hand, Kayo," he answered. "And you too, Cherry-hum-Segat; sit down on this bearskin and let us smoke together; among our people, that is the symbol of friendship and good will. As for your wine, wait until we have eaten together. I have been among the whites enough to know that it is not poison, like their scarat [1] which burns and leaves a craving for more; wine, on the contrary, animates and strengthens. In the wake of firewater come, like an unleashed torrent, irritation, anger, fever, frenzy, and wrath. Wine summons only joy; inspires only peace; it is the balm of life and the blood of old men. But before resting yourselves, I want to show you the plots of land in which I plant my corn, potatoes, and tobacco; from there we shall proceed to the banks of the river where you will observe with what ease I catch all the fish I need, and even more. As for the tube-like pieces of bark, they keep me well supplied with the clearest water in the land. What more does a man need during his journey on earth, especially when he is free and independent as I am? As to winter wear, my little harvest of tobacco, procures (by trade) such covering as I need. That is all that I ask from nature."

"How happy I am," said my companion to me in a low tone, "to have come to see this Indian! How interesting he is! Colonel Hunter certainly did not deceive us!

"Why do you live alone, esteemed Agoueghon," he inquired. "Why in such solitude, do you not have a companion who would keep your

fire going and refill your kettle? One who would light your pipe when
you cannot lean over, who would help catch the fish from your streams.
One who would guard the opening of your wigwam from the violent
winds of winter: Do you not know that old age without a companion
is like the old oak without its covering of moss—like a traveler who has
lost his dog?''

"I shall tell you, brother," he answered, "how it happened and
then you will see that the same secret and powerful cause that directs
the great destinies of the whites also directs ours. If the Ocean tempests destroy and unmast vessels, causing shipwrecks, do not imagine
for a moment that we, too, on our lakes, do not experience similar
things that upset and swallow our frail craft! Have you never heard
talk of the plan that the chiefs of the tribes up yonder formed many
moons ago as soon after Corlear's people had chased those of Ononthyo from Canada?[2] Ashamed of the servitude in which they had
been held, as well as of their folly in spilling blood, sometimes in
behalf of one group, sometimes of another, they resolved to free themselves from this shameful bondage. You are perhaps well acquainted
with what happened to our people at Bushy-Run,[3] despite their efforts
and their courage. Perhaps you have also heard of our misfortunes at
the battle of the strait; when we realized that for lack of cannon it
was impossible to take it, we besieged it for two months. I do not
know what happened, but despite our vigilance, the vessels from Erie
arrived; we killed a great number of soldiers on their disembarkation
and the rest entered the town. Then we were obliged to abandon this
glorious undertaking. But scarcely had we returned to our villages,
when those among our warriors who had brought some English clothes
with them[4] were attacked by scarlet fever. Like those foul fogs that
neither wind nor sun can dispel, this cruel malady spread beyond the
banks of our river, penetrated all our wigwams, bringing terror,
desolation, and death. Like the feathered seed of the thistle on the
riverbanks, it became a pawn for the winds; as the trees of the valleys
are uprooted and dragged down by spring torrents, these men, so
proud, so strong, so brave, were stricken, crushed by the power of this
murderous poison, and disappeared from the earth, leaving behind
them only the sad memory of their number and worth. Even this recollection will soon lose itself in the misty remoteness of bygone days.
In a few more moons, the existence of our tribe and that of so many
others, who, like shining fireflies, so often light up during tempests,[5]
will be no more than a forgotten dream. Indeed, how long does a
warrior, a family, a nation last, compared with this rapid river, which
flows forever without tarrying?

"This deplorable catastrophe is not the only source of regret that has flooded my heart with sadness. After the gloomy eclipses, the sun, as though to dissipate the fright of men and console them, reappears as brilliant as the day before; but never will the children of my youth who died so prematurely reappear again: never will my eyes see Néhan, Néhiou, Kayoulah, and Cog-na-Wassy. Their mother, Agonethya, crushed under the weight of the tragedy, like the ices of winter under the feet of the traveler, followed. Instead of six happy and gay people, my roof no longer sheltered, my fire no longer lit any thing but the solitude of a man broken by his sorrows. This fire I abandoned—as well as hunting and fishing—and I lived in tears and torment: like the birds of the night, I would shun the light of day, and like the reclusive marten, live in spots most removed from the view of hunters. Why does the Great Spirit, instead of protecting men to whom he denied the beaver's fur, the eagle's speed, and the moose's strength, permit the evil ones to cover their paths with leaves, traps, and precipices? If, as people say, our breathing is but an emanation of his living breath, why, when his children suffer and starve, is he deaf to their cries, as the captious northwest wind is to the little cries of autumn insects, when it precipitates them by the thousands into the lake waters, like the inexorable worker to the timid pleas of the summer ants, when he crushes their hills under the feet of horses? How can one conceive the idea of his omnipotence separated from goodness?

"Like the tenacious mercury,* this companion of old oaks, which grows despite the thunder that often strikes these trees, I exist despite all the misfortunes that this homicidal arrow has so many times aimed at me, and I even seemed to enjoy some moments of calm: it is that of a concentrated pain, which too often thought revives, as the breeze of the night revives the dying echo that one could scarcely hear, or the fire of a hunter fallen asleep; it is like the evening of a day that has been too long, since life and the future no longer hold anything for me. And why would I want to see tomorrow? And, if I continue to live to see tomorrow, so futile for me, why do I care to see the day after, even more futile? The moons, those daughters of ancient times, that sometimes, through pity, erase from man's mind the memory of his pains, and have not been able to mitigate those of the unfortunate Agoueghon, will they bring back on their way the companions, the wife, the children whom he has lost? No! Just as before, they will follow their eternal roads and will leave him just as they found him, alone, 'mid these lonely rocks, prey to his pain, reduced to

* Ecomanthus.

neither feeling nor desiring anything other than the need to go rejoin them in the land of our ancestors: like the old cedar on the promontory that has long braved the winds and the storms, whose sap is dried up and whose shoots are dead and which the first breeze from the lake knocks down.

"The Great Being loaned me life and breathing, why did he not take it from me and let my children keep it? For my part, I had lived long enough and they had just begun. What remains of me belongs only to the past, and this past is no more than the imprint of memories remote but still bitter. That is all I have gained for having lived this long.

"Somber and sad, old and decrepit, as you see me today, once I was strong and vigorous, brave and fearless, chief of a great tribe and renowned among the Nishy-Norbay. But of what use is a hunter when he begins to bend under the weight of years? When time has dried up the marrow of his bones and imprinted on his brow the furrows of old age? Having left the heights of youth and life, for in the valley of silence, shadows, and death never will he see the light of spring, never will his bowed head raise itself and grow young again like the branches of the willow under the weight of snows and cold weather of his last winter. His step, not so long ago proud and fast like that of the deer, now resembles the slow pace and winding trail of a snail, and like that reptile, he is crushed under the feet of passers-by. His feeble hands slip from the paddle in a moment of danger and soon the current drags him down from the crest of the cataract to the abyss of destruction and eternal oblivion; it is as though he might never have been born.

"Of what worth is a hunter and warrior through whom the shiver of decrepitude creeps, making his hands tremble and his feet stagger? Incapable of bending his bow, wielding his tomahawk, or filling his kettle, he is no more than a meteor, whose traces once shining, now extinguished, are but smoke; like a cloud that has burst its thunder and is nothing more than a light and humid vapor, toy of the breeze and the winds. The feeling of respect which his bravery in war, his prowess in the hunt, and his words at the council fire had inspired, that of cold and useless pity, companion and neighbor of disgust and scorn: and if, like me, he has lost the consolation and support of his children in his old age, a thousand times better off would he be if he had never lived. He lives, true, and yet is no more; sadness and chagrin assail him; his ears are closed. He becomes deaf to the voice of friendship as to that of nature who speaks so melodiously in the song of the birds, the fogs, precursors of death, surround him; his eyes dim; he does not recognize his kin and his neighbors until he has shaken their hands; his memory imperceptibly dies out, like the rays of the sun, when at twilight they plunge into the mists of the lake. Hunting and fishing, the elapse of time and seasons, the arrival of the fish and birds no longer mean anything to him; and soon the sad remaining sparks of his mind, his courage, his soul, sink in the shadows of death, as the light of day loses itself when night falls.

"Once upon a time when I was surrounded by my children, I lived only with pleasures and hopes; I enjoyed less the happiness of seeing them as they were then, than as they would be some day. Their departure has blighted my hopes, like the grass on which warriors have long camped; like the sweet rush, blighted by summer heat. I dreaded at that time the mighty arrow of Agan-Matchee-Manitou, who appears and strikes without being either seen or heard; but today, what do I have to fear since I have lost everything? What can I tell you, brother? What remains to me of life no more deserves that name than the moonbeams, enfeebled by the clouds and reflected by the agitated surface of the lake, deserve the name of light.

"But I feel that this wine is arousing me and stirring me, just as after a prolonged calm, the wind fills the sails of our dugouts, pirogues, and canoes. Of all the futile riches of the white men, it is the only one I envy them. Come! Put your hand to my heart; do you feel how it beats? Do you see how my old veins swell? How my narrow eyes dilate? That comes neither from anger nor pleasure, but from the wine that you had me drink. Whence comes this wine? Of what is it made? Is it the sun spirit or the juices of the land that produce it? Could it be the fruit of the white man's industry or a present from the Great Spirit? If it were, why would he have denied us this thing, since, like the white men, we are his children? Yes, he gave them odzizia [6] (Mohawk for 'wine') during his charitable moods and scarlet fever during his moods of anger, but the whites have acquainted us only with this murderous poison."

"Both are useful," Mr. Herman told him. "Only abuse of them can be harmful."

"How can we separate use from abuse?" retorted the venerable Agoueghon.

"With the help of reason."

"And supposing our young people do not wish to listen to the voice of reason?"

"There is no other remedy, for man bereft of reason is inferior to the elk or stag of the forests. Why did you not repress intemperance when you were chief?"

"What could I do, since obedience to command was not respected?"

"What, then, did you do to command obedience?"

"I commanded them only during war."

"How then?"

"By example and persuasion, that is to say, by bravery and eloquence. Once back in the village, only the voice of exhortation was left to me, but as soon as the effects of drunkenness and frenzy made themselves heard, our young people were deaf to my voice. It was as if I had spoken to the waters of the torrent or to the wind over the lake!

"However, after the ravages of the mergum-megat were passed, I continued to live for a while longer in the village, trying to make some order out of the chaos, and find a place elsewhere to raise our wigwams: my efforts were futile; our old men were no longer alive and the survivors remained uncounseled; some were to join the Oneidas; others followed their fancy and scattered. Thus disappeared the remains of a Tribe, which in my greatest peak of glory counted three thousand warriors. Unable to find happiness in this land of unrest, I covered the bones of our venerable ancestors with stones and retired to Sandusky with the Wyandottes. There I lived peacefully enough, although my mind was stirred by my sad memories, like the lake waters after a tempest. Seven times the snows of winter had swollen the rivers; seven times the ears of corn had yellowed, when one day a canoe of whites, coming from Erie on their way to Détroit, were forced by contrary winds to put in at our bay. Unfortunately there was some brandy on board which they traded in the village. Like the consuming conflagrations which our hunters lighted in the midst of the savannahs,[7] these waters of fury and war spread in all directions the germ of quarrels and dissension; no longer could one hear anything but shouts of anger, fits of violence; not a single wigwam of young people was excluded. The hunters' wives, running hither and thither, could scarcely prevent them from selling their very bearskins. Here, I deplored, beating my chest, is bewilderment, craziness, and desolation; that was the cause of the destruction and annihilation of so many nations, of so many ravages and bloody scenes; that is how the foxes at daybreak[8] have learned how to seduce the mighty wolves of this great land.[9] For my part, as one of the old people, I wanted to speak forth, to plea, to urge, to restrain these blind young people; but they flung afar my advice as well as that of their own chiefs. Foreseeing that peace and good will of the village would be troubled for a long time, that hunger would soon knock at the door of these drunkards, and finally feeling my sight begin to fail, I left for the land of the Jenezees whose sachems Kayaderossera and Koronkiagoa I knew. I returned by the Cayahoga[10] as far as the portage at Grand Castor, where I was obliged to leave my canoe, being alone. Finally after several days journey, I arrived at

Shenandoah, where I found old Poopoko, who welcomed me warmly and invited me to share his fire and receive his hospitality. During the good season, I hunted again, but as soon as winter snows arrived, my eyes grew dim; I found myself reduced to fishing in the lake on whose shores we lived. One day, surprised by a squall which the weakness of my eyes had prevented me from seeing, I capsized. I could swim, but Poopoko's canoe sank to the bottom. Imagine my chagrin! On the very next day I took to the woods to obtain the bark of the black birch and cedar, which I would need. For several days I worked quite hard, but when it came to the work on the seams, my eyes failed me. Full of anguish and despair, I said to myself:

"Agoueghon is still living and he is no longer good for anything! He lives, aye, and he has ceased to be a man! He has fathered four fine boys, and not a living being of his own blood is at his side now to help him in his old age!

"I went to bed, wanting very much to die and follow my loved ones, but ere long help came to me. I was consoled and the canoe was finished. Fearing, however, that I could no longer maneuver the canoe, I built myself a raft of white cedar from which I continued to fish, until threatened with complete blindness when I was obliged to abandon that.

"So humiliated was I at being unable to fill Poopoko's kettle any longer, that I determined to come live on these rocks whose location I had known for a long time. After giving my rifle to my host's son, I came among the Cayugas whose old chief Nagooas-Missey conducted me to the Onondagas of the lake whence Ashamit, the story-teller, took me as far as Oswego; there I embarked in the pirogue of a white man who was going to Niagara. I was quite sure that once my fire was lighted here, I could easily catch all the fish I needed, with neither canoe nor raft, because every morning the fish arrive from the lake to swim to the foot of the torrent where they feed on the assorted debris that the falls bring down. My hopes have not been deceived, for with the aid of these two rocks and the bark which some travelers helped me peel, I made myself a shelter against the wind and rain. I have plenty of wood, cutting and carrying it is almost the only occupation of my remaining strength. What I do not eat of my fish during the summer, I dry out to store for winter.

"From time to time I go to Niagara where I am always well received. Some say: 'Agoueghon, do you need a kettle? Speak!' Others: 'Do you need a blanket? Speak!' 'Would you like a hatchet already helved? You have only to say yes.'

"We smoke together, these friends of mine at Niagara and I, after clasping their hand, return here, heavy-hearted and moist-eyed, saying to myself: After all, one finds some good people among these whites.

"Here, as you see, I bother no one and no one bothers me; I can go here or there, rest, smoke, sleep, or fish, according to my caprice or my will. I breathe a great and good air. On my left, I have Ontario, that beautiful, blue sea that I am still able to see; on my right, the turbulent waters of the falls whose din, when the wind rises from Erie, is the only thing that displeases me. Almost opposite I see Niagara, as well as the vessels which come there from all parts of the lake.

"Alas! where is the time of my youth when these waters were covered only by canoes, when the tomahawk of war glistened in the hands of all nations, like the ices of winter 'neath the sun's rays. What has become of these nations?

"I sleep a long time and that is a great consolation because time is nothing during sleep. Every morning I go down to the bank of the river and never do I return empty-handed. In the past, I wanted death as a sick man wants his cure; today I await it like a tired hunter who awaits the peace of sleep after making a shelter for the night. However, I still enjoy some moments of involuntary ease: for example, I love the sun of our land. It is my only remaining friend; he says nothing to me, it is true, and yet his presence consoles me. I do not know how it happens but his splendor takes the place of clothing and food for me; often even, it breathes into me something that grows and revives me. Suddenly I feel as though I have my rifle and that I can kill ducks and geese. . . . Old fool that I am! Who would go fetch them for me, since no longer have I my canoe or my dog?

"Oh, how good and kind the smoke of my peace pipe seems when I inhale it—exposed to the rays of the sun! What I experience then is not sleep, nor intoxication, but bewilderment, absence, happy oblivion of myself. Sometimes, wishing to know how much I have been able to quicken the thorny passing of time, I raise a little stick on a flat stone; then when I open my eyes to the light, I can easily guess the span during which I ceased being its victim.

"Almost all those who come to see the falls, stop here on their way to shake my hand and smoke with me; like you, some call me Agoue-ghon; others brother; others Coohassa-Onas, Father of the Falls. They come to me; they leave with the hand and words of friendship. That is all I need. During the winter, like an old fox in his hole, a bear in his den, or a squirrel in the hollow of a tree, half of me goes, I know not where, and does not return until spring. My fire warms me, it is true; but it is no longer father of nature and friend of old men.

"As for the passing of the moons; I have lost track; they pass without my notice, like the wind that blows, like the water that flows. Such is the story of the last part of my long life, but will it be of any interest to the men who live in the region of the great sea, the land of iron and houses, where there is no need to fish, as I do, in order to fill one's kettle?''

"Then have you forgotten, brother, my first conversation? I told you that during my youth I had been at the great port of Wabash among the Ouyatanons; to the forks of the Muskinghum, among the Delawares. Have you forgotten, as you shook my hand, when I told you about my long journeys with them, of the promptness with which I would throw myself into the water, when I had to help take the canoe over the rapids or how I would lend my shoulder to transport it across the great and little portages? Yes, like you, I have walked on the snow, slept on the leaves at the foot of a tree: like you, I have known the height of mountains and I have come down over the rapids and crossed the lakes in rain and wind.''

"Your reproaches pierce my heart like an arrow," he answered me. "Give me your hand, Kayo. I feel it; it is that of a man who has known and loved the children of this land; I am old and memory, you know, turns its back on old men. Let us continue: where were we? At the point, I believe, where you mentioned life no longer holds anything for me.''

"I remember," I told him. "You were speaking to me of the moons whose number you have forgotten, and I was about to tell you that I noticed with pleasure how much the advantages of your situation would soften your solitude. It is less enjoyment than rest; less pleasure than absence of difficulties and sufferings. The river and your land provide you abundantly. Perhaps you are richer than you think. You need so little, and of this little quantity you are assured; and to obtain it, you are not obliged to ask for it; you depend on no one; it is nature that offers and gives it to you; you live no more except by obedience to her laws; your heart beats no more except as an organ of circulation: in Niagara at Erie, they respect your advanced age: travelers come to warm themselves at your fire, to converse with the wisdom that is yours. Indeed, next to this great waterfall, what in these regions is more worthwhile meeting than a man who, like you, has seen the sun of spring make the forests green again almost 70 times; one who has been witness to so many things; one whom experience has taught so much and who, like a rock, has resisted the violence of the torrent in which your nation has been embroiled? You live; you exist without pain or any infirmity other than the feebleness of your eyes; you neither think of nor foresee your end; except as the tired hunter dreams beside the stream near which he is to pass the night.

"We had come here to deplore your plight, to sympathize with your solitude, and mingle with your tears the warm tears of our sympathy; and here we are: congratulating you on the advantages of your situation; on the peace that you enjoy, treasure of old men; on the consideration that the white men, your neighbors, have for you; on the happiness of being free and independent to the last day of your life. Your solitude has no element of sadness in it since you know how to be sufficient unto yourself. I know some among the white men whom people call rich, and who are more to be pitied; like you, they have grown old, but overcome with infirmities, unknown to your race, accustomed to what they call enjoyments, they suffer at being unable to enjoy any longer. Languor repels them; pusillanimity assails them; remorse, fears of the future, and the terrors of superstition, ambition, and avarice, the sort of pain that you ignore, pursue them night and day and torment them. Often in making their way toward the last period of their lives, they encounter only the oblivion, indifference, or ingratitude of their neighbors; they die a death much more frightening than yours will be, since it is not a quiet departure, but a cruel heart break.''

''I do not complain, brother,'' he told me. ''I know what it is to suffer, for I am a man. I do not know how the white people of your town end their lives. Is it not necessary that, like us, they give up the breath that has been given them?''

''You are right; they fear so much at being what they call miserable in what they call the other world; as if it had not been enough for them to have been miserable in this one; so much do they love money, houses, and things of the land, that they must leave it with much more regret than we do, who return to it as we arrived. For this reason our end is far milder and quieter since death for us is not a chain that breaks, but a knot that unties.''

''At Michimillmakinac I knew white men whom I believed to be brave and just imagine! They needed a soothsayer to help them die. That reminds me of a young bearded man whose name I have forgotten: every time that some of our people 'went West,' he always visited their wigwams.

'' 'What are you doing here?' I asked him one day.

'' 'What am I doing?' he replied. 'I have come to admire the calm and quiet patience of your sick ones, and the courage with which they die, with neither regrets nor wailing. I have come to learn to imitate them. You are not angry, I hope?' That is what he told me.

''But when the last rays of my last sun have ceased to shine on my tree of life and when the breeze of the night has upset it, who will cover with earth the sad remains and put them in the shelter beyond the reach of the teeth of wolves? No one! Just think! And I have had five fine sons.''

"Give me your hand, venerable Chippeway, old man of the old men of the region!'' I said to him. "How many days of journey we would have to make before meeting a man like you, a Nishy-norbay who would tell us such interesting things! Be sure that I shall never forget them: the spirit from on high who inspires them in you has also engraved them on my memory. You are striking proof of the great height which natural instinct alone can achieve without the help of our education. I have known in my day a great number of people among your race. Well, everything they told me compared with what I have just heard were but light feathers windswept through the air. Go! I am happier for having seen you and heard you than if, being hungry, I might have killed a moose or a stag.''

"And I, too,'' Mr. Herman told him. "You can be assured of that: I shall not leave this country without seeing you again and leaving you some token of my happy memory of you.''

"As to your fears,'' I replied, "relative to the last moments of your life; be assured that the people of Niagara and of Erie will not forget you. You know their chief. I know what he thinks of you; he is as generous as he is brave. You will smoke your last peace pipe surrounded, succored, if not by your own people, at least by whites who are compassionate and sympathetic and have respected you for a long time, as you deserve.

"But night is approaching; we have come today from the fort; tomorrow we return there to take the route of the portage that leads to the falls; fatigue and sleep win out over the desire to listen to you longer.''

Thus finished our conversation. The next day after accompanying him to the edge of the river, and helping him to bring back the fish from his little streams, we ate the finest of them which he preferred to dress in his own way. Finally after having drunk some glasses of wine, and smoked a long pipe of friendship and good memory, we shook hands with this great old man and started back with the soldier as guide.

CHAPTER VI

"Well!" said Colonel Hunter on our return. "Did I not predict rightly that this little excursion would interest you? I have another to propose to you, of a little different kind: it is a fishing party that some officers in the garrison are going to make several miles from here. You will go by water to the mouth of the Prideaux River on the east bank. During this season the most delicate fish in the lake can be found; the Indians have taught us to preserve the fish by means of smoking them." [1]

Everything contributed toward making this excursion a delightful one: the beauty of the lake, the favorable wind, the mildness of the temperature, the abundance of fish, and the delightful gaiety of the company. In the evening it was decided that we would return by land to avoid the monotony of the long tacks that we would have been obliged to make. We had not gone more than two miles through the woods when we saw a fire around which fourteen Indians were squatted, peace pipes in mouths, heads bent, eyes fixed on the ground.

Mr. Herman, who had not seen any Indians, except at Onondaga, wanted to meet them. The officers consented; the group turned out to be a mixture of young Mohawks and Cayugas, who, like us, had spent the day fishing and were entertaining themselves by telling stories. Next to courage in war and skill in hunting, there is nothing among these people which yields greater prestige than the talent for story-telling. The attention with which one listens in Europe to a sermon, tragedy, or an academic lecture cannot be compared to that with which these idle, unoccupied men listen to the recountings of their story-tellers. They have gay and serious ones: the former are almost invariably based on the ridiculous quality that appears to the Indians in some of our customs; the others are adventures of hunting, traveling, or various military exploits.

The last Indian to have finished his story was on my left, so I nudged the one on my right, saying:

"Do you not realize that it is your turn? Get up, then, and tell us something."

"I would rather receive than give," he answered brusquely; "to listen rather than to speak."

"For a Cayuga, I do not find you very generous; or else you are poor."

"What do you mean poor? Am I not as rich as the others? Although less given to prating, like them, I have ears which during the night tell me what is going on around me and eyes which during the day see game at great distance, good legs to pursue this game and something there (putting his hand to his breast) that makes me proud. Do you understand me?''

''If you are proud,'' I replied, ''then you should answer me; I am no less than you, when I ask you a question. Do you understand me, too?''

But, in order to quell in its infancy this germ of a quarrel, I said to him:

''Do you want some wine?''

''I would prefer what is worth wine six times [2] (brandy); do you have any?''

''No.''

And at this moment everyone ceased talking as another storyteller volunteered to speak:

''Massatowama, son of Wapanome, of the village of Niskotowassee of the Chikassaw nation, was a warrior and hunter who for a long time had shown proof of courage and skill. He had built himself a large and beautiful wigwam in which his fire burned and his kettle hung. He had an abundance of beaver, buffalo, fox, and bearskins. In fishing he was as lucky as he was in hunting; in war as brave as the bravest among us. One day as he was repairing his canoe on the banks of the Caspetowagan River, he saw Napotelima, daughter of Tatoba-mico, who had come there to fetch water. Inwardly struck by something he had never before felt, he approached her and said:

'' 'Would you blow upon my torch?'

'' 'Speak to my father,' she replied.

''And early the next day he sought out Tatoba-mico at his fire and said:

'' 'Would you give me your daughter Napotelima for wife?'

'' 'Tomorrow,' said the old man, 'I am leaving for far-off hunts. Will you accompany me?'

'' 'Yes,' replied Massotawana.

''And they left. The navigation of the rivers was difficult because of the rapids and falls with which they were filled, and they found it necessary to cross some by punt; and to avoid others, they had to carry the canoe on their shoulders until they came upon calmer waters. Reaching the hunting lands, each settled in his own region. Massotawana caught a great number of stoats in his traps, wolves in ditches, beavers under the ice, foxes trapped, and elk on the snow. After smoking the skins and meat, he took everything to Tatabo-mico's hut. The old man said:

" 'Ah! Ah! I am glad to see that you are skillful and subtle. Tomorrow I leave for the village. Do you wish to return with me?'

" 'Yes,' replied Massotawana.

"And they left.

"But in coming down the Nistotowa River, the canoe grazed the branch of a tree and sprang a leak. Massotawana unloaded it and carried it to the foot of a tree and spent a day fixing it with neither help nor advice from Tatoba-mico. The next day after carrying it back to the river and replacing the load of pelts, he sought him at his fire and said:

" 'Everything is in readiness; as soon as you have smoked your pipe, you can embark; there is your paddle.'

"They set out.

"On their return to the village, Tatabo-mico said to Massotawana:

" 'I need a four-man canoe; can you build me one?'

" 'You will see,' replied the other.

"And early the next day, he dug the ditch that served him as mold; he went to the woods to find bark of the black birch for the lining; white cedar for the sides; marshy ash for the floor; tropical creeper for the seams, and sap gum to cover them all. In a half moon the canoe was finished.

" 'Here,' said Massotawana to Tatabo-mico, 'here is what you asked of me. See if it is water-tight.'

" 'It is dry and well made.'

" 'Are you satisfied?' the young hunter asked him.

" 'Not yet. This evening I was planning to fish by torch; but during my absence, they burned the torches I had left. Can you make me some?'

" 'You shall see.'

"And soon afterward he brought him six torches four palms long.

" 'Here are some elk and buffalo skins. Can you smoke them and cure them?'

" 'You shall see.'

"And a few days later he brought them back, supple and well prepared.

" 'Do you know how to fish by torch?'

" 'You shall see,' replied the young man.

"And they left together, each in his own canoe. Massotawana speared a great number of sturgeons.[3]

"When the fishing was over, Tatabo-mico said to him:

" 'Come, warm yourself at my fire.'

"Massotawana followed him.

" 'Fill your pipe and let us smoke together. I see that you are a skillful, patient, and tireless hunter; that you know how to repair and construct canoes, fish by torch and through the ice by day as well as by night; I am told that you are alert and of great prowess in all exercise; that you are as brave a warrior as you are a good hunter; that you bear hunger, fatigue, and pain without complaint; that you consider death as the path that takes the brave to a land which our ancestors inhabit; that you are disposed to sacrifice your life for the honor of our nation and of our tribe; that you built your own wigwam; that you keep your own fire; and that you take care to keep filled the kettle of your old father; that you respect old age; that you prefer to listen rather than speak; and above all, that you scorn the white man's firewater. Since all this is true, you are a man worthy of being a husband. Go, find my daughter Napotelima. Repeat to her what I have just told you; sing her your war song and if she consents to become your wife, let her blow on your torch. Be happy with her and may she be happy with you. Never forget what a brave owes to the frailty of women; without them, there would be only bears and wolves in the land.' "

As soon as this little story was finished, another speaker rose and said:

"Having recently returned from Hoppajewot (Land of Dreams), I shall recount how things are going there and what I have seen. If anyone says to me: 'You are dreaming, as sick men do,' or 'you exaggerate as drunkards do,' I shall say to them: 'go and see for yourself.'

"In that land there is neither night nor day; the sun neither rises nor sets; it is neither hot nor cold; there neither spring nor winter is known; there neither bow nor arrow has ever been seen, nor tomahawk. They do not even have in their language a word for hunter and warrior. Gnawing hunger and burning thirst once came there in ancient times, they say, but the chiefs flung them to the bottom of the river where they have remained.

"Ah! What good country! Does one want to smoke? One has only to open his mouth, and raise his pipe to it. Does one want to rest at the foot of a tree? One has only to stretch his arm out, one is sure to encounter the hand of friendship. The earth being ever green and the trees always leaf-bearing, one needs neither bearskin nor wigwam. Does one want to travel? The river current carries him wherever he wishes to go, without the help of either oars or paddles. Ah! how good, that country!

" 'Do you wish to eat?' the elk says to those who are hungry. 'Only take my right shoulder and let me go into the woods of the Ninner-

Wind; it will grow back in again soon and next year I shall return to offer you the left shoulder; but take care lest you destroy too much, because in the end you would have nothing!'

" 'Come come,' says the beaver, 'cut my beautiful tail, I can do without it until another grows, since I have just finished building my home; but take care not to be too voracious, for it is said, 'Four beavers you will take and the fifth you will permit to go free!'

"Ah! what a good country. One has only to drink, eat, smoke, and sleep in such a country!

" 'Do you wish to restock your supply?' says the fat fish of the lake. 'My task is finished; I have just laid 10,000 eggs: cook me as you like: but take care not to be too greedy, for it is said: Eighteen fish you will catch; and the nineteenth you will let escape.'

"Ah! what a good country! Not being obliged to anoint themselves with bearfat, women there are always beautiful and sleek; they need only keep the kettle boiling and teach the children how to swim.

"One day when I was present at the Council fire, on hearing an extraordinary noise, the mighty Okemaw who presided, ordered that someone investigate what it was.

"It comes from a great fleet of dug-outs, which, like sea birds chased by the wind, are approaching the riverbank. Our people are amazed and do not know what to think or say.

" 'Can you see men in these dug-outs?'

" 'Yes, they are white men with beards, tired from their long voyage, for they have come from the land of Cherryhum. They humbly beg permission to disembark and rest on our shores. What does the mighty Okemaw say?'

" 'Although white and bearded,' he replied, 'and coming from a land where I did not believe there might be any inhabitants, they are unhappy and suffering; let them disembark and rest here for a few days.'

"I do not know how much time elapsed after the arrival of these strangers before they met the great chief Hoppajewot, whom they asked for a little land to the right and left of the site where they were encamped. Surprised at such a curious request, he said to them:

" 'What do you plan to do with it?'

"They replied: 'Plant some seeds which we have brought with us; their yield is one hundred to one, and when one has neither fish nor game, one can eat their yield.'

"Scarcely had the chief granted their request, when they all began to scratch the land, pull up the weeds, to the great astonishment of Hoppajewot's people, who had never seen anything like that. Several moons later, perceiving that their seeds had sprouted, they addressed

Okemaw again and asked him for the peninsula that formed the bay entry; seeing nothing untoward about that, he granted them the land; and immediately they saw them felling trees, with a piece of very hard metal, dig the earth, erect a little mountain of wood whence morning and night fire leaped and a noise such as had never before been heard in the land of Hoppajewot.

"Then Awakesh, the great elk of the woods appeared before Okemaw, saying:

" 'Woe unto you, chief of this nation, and woe unto your people; woe unto us and the other fur-bearing animals; if you permit these bearded men to uproot and burn the forests which the great spirit has given us. Soon there will be no more on earth; neither vegetation nor shade; then we will be obliged to abandon your land. Take care: these white men, so humble and ingratiating, who call you brother when they disembark, will chase you from here when they begin outnumbering you. Do you not see how they already behave behind their mountain of fire, smoke, and noise?'

"These words produced a great effect on the minds of the group, and each one began to reflect over it. But while they were reflecting thus, someone came to tell them that bearded men in the villages had begun to entertain the women and children, telling them stories, which they said were worth more than the legends of the land. Indignant over these proceedings, the messengers addressed the mighty chiefs, saying:

" 'Peace among the families, good feeling in the villages no longer exists; these whites have turned the heads of our womenfolk; our witch doctors have lost their influence. By what right do these foreigners from Cherryhum come to talk to our people of the God of their land? Does not each country have its own, as it has its lakes and rivers? And after all, that one of the land on which the warm and radiant sun shines ceaselessly, is it not better than the God of the earth on which it rises pale and without warmth? What must we do, wise and powerful Okemaw?'

" 'May the tricksters, bearded and beardless, assemble here tomorrow,' he replied, 'and we shall see.'

"They assembled, and according to Hoppajewot's custom, the foreigners were permitted to speak first. Among them were four speakers whose speeches were so long that the old men had time to smoke two pipes. The first spoke of a land where one could go only after death, a fact that astonished the entire gathering very much. This country, he said, is situated beyond the sun; it is neither warm nor cold there; and there one is happy and satisfied, needing nothing, and this happiness never ends once it has begun. The second speaker explained everything that one had to do and not do in this land to obtain permission to be admitted there, in a land of spirits. The third spoke of a lake which burns whatever one throws upon it, without consuming it. In this lake are drowned all those who are not admitted to the land beyond. The fourth man entertained them with stories of a tribunal before which appeared the spirits of all those whose sentences are irrevocable and assured them that in following his advice, they were certain of making the great judge favorable toward them.

" 'There are four good and long stories,' said Okemaw. 'It is our turn to speak. Beardless tricksters, rise and tell some of our stories. Begin with the one about the manifestations of the great spirit on the mountain of Aratapeskow, accompanied by two faces of potters' earth which he dried and animated with his breath; to the first of these he gave the name Pegick-Sagat (first man) and to the second Sanna Tella (companion). Talk to them about Nassanicomy who descended from the clouds on the island of Allisinape and caused corn, rice, squash, and tobacco to grow there while he busied himself spitting to the north, south, east, and west.'

" 'These are merely lies, impostors,' said the bearded speakers; 'we don't want to listen to them.'

" 'Since we have heard you patiently and faithfully,' replied Okemaw, 'you should listen to our people in the same manner. Why would you scorn our traditions, as well as yours? They are respectable by their very antiquity. Why did you cut down the beautiful trees which covered the earth that I lent you? You are deserving of the Creator's indignation as well as ours, since, like us, these trees are the work of His hands. Why do you drive us from your little mountain with the fire, the smoke and noise of death, we who have received you like a brother? Is that what we should expect as hospitality? If it is in such a manner that men conduct themselves in your land of Cherry-hum, your great spirit is unworthy of ours, for here you have found peace and good will and you have introduced us to strife and unrest by means of your stories. Go, return there, and leave us to think and live as our ancestors have thought and lived.'

"Instead of replying civilly, the white men rose, made a great deal of noise, and left the group saying things no one could understand; and from that moment on, the two races swore an implacable hatred.

"Some time later, having discovered that by means of brandy the same white deceivers had come to introduce themselves again into the village, and to make the women believe everything that was told them, the mighty Okemaw summoned them a second time and said to them, raising his voice:

" 'Stubborn bearded one: you are mistaken if you think you can do here what your people have done in the land of the Nishynorbays; you will not seduce us with your waters of fire and folly, to invade our lands as your compatriots have seduced those unfortunate ones; for we are neither as easily deceived nor as blind. Drink these waters yourselves; and may they consume you as they have destroyed so many fine tribes. May these bottles of poison be broken!'

"At the moment when they carried out his orders, one of the bearded tricksters, of black brow and searching eye, proud step, bolder than the others, dared to take hold of the great chief who, in telling him haughtily, 'you have been poorly educated in your land,' upsets him with his mighty muscle arm and scalps him; but what was his astonishment on seeing that his hair did not grow on his head, but that he was wearing a wig!

"Okemaw, as well as the spectators, never having seen anything quite like it, burst involuntarily into uncontrollable laughter: this laughter made possible a distraction which the trickster and his companions seized adroitly to make their escape, leaving the astonished chief with the false hair in his hands. When they had arrived among their compatriots, one could easily see that they had spread the alarm throughout their dwellings and that already there was great activity among them.

"Then Okemaw summoned a herd of deer, preceded by Awakesh. He instructed each brave to take a flaming torch and to set fire to the fields of grain located around the little mountain. This they did so skillfully that despite the noise, the fire, and smoke which resulted, everything was burned before daylight. As soon as the sun appeared, they saw the white men embark in their dugouts and leave with a favorable wind. Since that time, no one has ever heard of the bearded whites in the land of Hoppajewot. That is my story."

The speaker, who had been enthusiastically applauded, was going to begin another story, when some officers, observing that we still had several miles to go before reaching Niagara, informed us that it was time to leave.

CHAPTER VII

The day after this pleasure party, various persons with whom we had become acquainted at the garrison invited us to see their plantations situated on the east river whose land grant, they told us, had just been confirmed by the Government of New York. These concessions, originally Canadian, extend well beyond Prideaus Creek at the mouth of which one can see a small harbor, extremely useful to fishermen in the neighborhood. These new settlements are situated at some distance from the shores of the lake whose slope barely reaches the level of the isthmus. Although somewhat sandy, the soil, irrigated by several streams, appeared to us very favorable for the cultivation of crops, as well as that of apple trees, and especially peach trees, from whose fruit they had already begun to make brandy.

Seen from the lake at some distance, this mixture of young orchards, prairies, and fields, were heaped high with healthy harvest, like pieces of mosaic, in the middle of which are great masses of primeval forests. These surfaces were still filled with stumps or withered trees. The various colors of the different crops covering them, the fires and smoke which catapulted into vortexes made this entire scene one of industry that was as interesting as it was picturesque.

"What we see," said Mr. Herman, "is really the scene of the first efforts toward a budding colony, and never was a location more favorable to the progress of farmers. On one side they have this beautiful inland sea which furnishes them an abundance of fish and offers them easy communication; on the other, neighboring forests whence they draw the wood they need. For them Niagara is a market place where some day they will be able to dispose of the products of their soil. Exempt from all kinds of obligations and taxes, all they need to ask from heaven are health and favorable seasons."

"Thus," I replied, "on all points, the deserts of this continent, unknown for so long to the Europeans' curiosity, covered during so many centuries by darkness, and the silence of the forests, are slowly converted into fertile fields. In these places, recently uncultivated and wild, we enjoy the charms of hospitality and hear interesting conversation, although we are under roofs that are still so rustic. What will it be like in twenty years?"

The next day, as we were on the point of leaving, Colonel Hunter handed us a letter for Mr. E., saying:

"This colonist owns all the land which borders on the east branch of the Falls as far as the Tonnawanda River.[1] You will be astonished to find in the midst of these woods a very decent dwelling, a garden, and fields that are well cultivated. He is rich, learned, and very industrious; no one in this region knows better than he the accessible parts of the falls; no one has made more observations to determine the height and width of its two branches as well as the quantity of water it shoots in a given length of time. Moreover, you will find under his roof everything of interest to a man and to a traveler."

In less than two hours we arrived at the old landing stage E located on the east branch of the Niagara River, nine miles from this fort. It is the last terminus of navigation for vessels which come from the lake and here begins the overland haul.[2] The road, although somewhat neglected, since they have been busy in building one the other side of the river, is nevertheless fairly well kept up. It was formerly laid out and made by the French, parallel and at a little distance from this same river whose width, they say, was 1,836 feet and whose current was six miles an hour. The landing stage there is composed of several stores where the skins from the north country are collected, as well as merchandise from Europe coming by way of Katarkoui. We had gone scarcely a mile beyond this wharf, when we began climbing a very long slope whose declivity had been artfully contrived. It is the lowest base of the heights of this isthmus: at this point starts the immense ravine at the bottom of which flows the impetuous torrent that comes from the falls; the great collection of rocks piled up to the topmost heights of these formidable but imposing riverbanks are covered with black spruce, somber hemlocks, cedars, and saplings, as well as thick brush and trailing vine, making them impenetrable.

After an hour and a half walk, still climbing, we arrived at plantation F, called the Lookout (le Coup d'oeil), because from the orchard which the owner planted on the right side of the road, the traveler can see Lake Ontario and the Falls at the same time, though its incredible din is still faint. Noticing an isolated tree near the escarpment, my impatient and eager companion had soon climbed to its top. From here he could view to his heart's content the magnificent spectacle he had wanted to contemplate for such a long time.

"On what a great scale," he said to me after climbing down from his observatory, "has the creative power formed and worked these places, these riverbanks, this cataract! The width of the ravine, the incalculable impetuosity of the torrent whose speed one can scarcely measure, the breaking of these foaming waves, irritated by so much resistance and so many obstacles, these moss-covered rocks bearing the imprint of centuries; these rocks, witnesses of the ravages and upsets that occurred in an unknown epoch, all these objects which at first glance appeared so hideous and so repulsive, are, I realize, necessary accessories to prepare the mind and eyes for great impressions. And by virtue of their immensity, they are worthy of preceding and heralding this cataract 5,000 feet steep which makes the background of this sublime scene. Everything blends with perfect harmony.

"What an admirable contrast between the peace and calm of the island crowning this awe-inspiring precipice and the force, the noise, the foaming whiteness of the currents which almost seem to swallow up its banks! What a contrast between this quiet sojourn of spring and the wild and savage appearance of the surrounding terrain. And that column of vapors, so majestic, which from the depths of this pit rises to so great a height, where I saw three rainbows: how it embellishes the objects veiling its light transparence! And this noise, this commotion which nature's destruction seems to announce—who could give any idea of it? As the commandant of Niagara told us, one must content oneself with admiring these sublime efforts of nature in respectful silence of meditation and contemplation."

Believing that he felt a shaking similar to that of an earthquake while he was atop the tree, Mr. Herman spoke of it to the settler, in whose shed we had put our horses. The latter replied:

"You were not mistaken; I shall show you."

Whereupon he placed on a drum that he brought into the living room of his home a lead bullet whose quivering was very obvious.

From this dwelling the road rambles so considerably from the banks of the stream, to avoid a sharp slope, that soon the noise of the falls seemed to us like a remote humming. This long and difficult climb is the last one takes before reaching the summit of the isthmus whose height is estimated at 1,380 feet above the level of Lake Ontario.

Toward mid-day we arrived at Mr. E's dwelling, "G." Built on a fairly high knoll, it commands a view of Rapid Lake, although it is quite a distance from its shores, as well as that of the east branch of the R cataract, the island in the middle, which is the anchorage of the vessels from Erie,[3] and even some part of the amphitheatre of the Alleghany mountains whose peaks were shining in the noonday sun. The regularity of the fences, the height of the barn, the vigor of the trees in the orchards, the fertility of the soil—everything heralded care, industry, and opulence on the part of the owner. After a hasty glance at the letter of introduction we gave him, he presented us to his wife, young and sparkling. He bade her serve dinner.

"You have come to see this cataract," he observed. "I believe it is the largest in this hemisphere, as much by its perpendicular height as by its great volume of water. You could not ask anyone around here who would be better acquainted with its accessible parts, nor who would take greater pleasure in showing them to you. I hope I can satisfy your curiosity.''

After we had chatted with him about the extent of his clearings, the vigor of his fields, and the unique location of his farm, he said to us:

''This site, perhaps one of the most remarkable in the civilized world, since—as from the height of the isthmus of Panama—one will some day be able to see two seas—is not however without its inconveniencies. The noise of the falls, although 242 feet below the level of this house, and a mile and a half from here, is nevertheless loud enough to disturb conversation, above all during a west wind. Often the vapors rising from it cause much humidity; my wife complains at not hearing the warbling of the birds, whom the violence of the waters and its noise frighten from this neighborhood; but on the one hand, these vapors, like a beneficent sun-dew, fertilize our fields, without destroying the growth of the seeds. Here we eat cherries and peaches long before they are ripe in Katarakoui and Montreal. Situated in the middle of the continent, we can easily get to Quebec and the St. Lawrence Gulf, 330 leagues distant, as well as to the great lakes and the Mississippi, 470 leagues away, and even to New Orleans, 750 leagues.

''What activity one will see here some day when the population, the prosperity of farming, the resources of intelligent industry will embellish and vivify the vast regions watered by these inland seas and the rivers which empty their waters. Then this isthmus will become perhaps as celebrated and interesting as those at Corinth and Suez have become. It appears that the height of this falls was at one time much greater than it is today, and nearer Lake Ontario. That is even a tradition among the Indians. Indeed, the mass and debris of rocks, with which the bottom and shores are glutted, the height of the banks of the ravine, to the bottom of which it precipitates with a roar, are unexceptionable witnesses which attest to the ravages of the waters. As to the fertility of the soil which I cultivate, and the beauty and the height of the trees, and the riches of my pasture lands, all that comes from the long sojourn of the waters of the Erie in the Tonnawanda valley, crossed by the pretty river of the same name.

''Is it not fair that the early colonists, who were to undergo so many privations, hardships, and inconveniencies, were rewarded by the beauty of their site, as well as by the ease with which they obtained abundant harvests, despite the imperfections of their farming methods. As to the speed of my land clearings and the improved state in which you see this plantation, I owe it to my friendships with Colonel Hunter who permitted me to use soldiers in the garrison. I have had as many as thirty; that is why I have been able to do so many things in such a short time. All this cost me nearly 3,000 guineas and never before had I invested money at such high interest. The quantity of provender and provisions I send to Niagara is already considerable.''

After dinner he led us to the second story of his house to show us the Lake of the Rapids [4] which is 5 miles long and three miles wide. It is formed by the junction of the two rivers or canals which feed it water from Lake Erie. This lake is remarkable, not only because of the extraordinary swiftness of the current, but also because of the rocks surrounding and filling it, their peaks jagging upward at various heights. The violence and noise with which its waters break against this multitude of obstacles, the impetuous eddies and cross-currents produce a kind of dizziness that is extremely tiring. Scarcely has one glanced at this vast torrent when, in spite of himself, one gets the illusion that he has seen these tops of rocks, like animated creatures, come back up the lake with the same degree of swiftness as that of the waters approaching the falls. It seems as though everything preceding and accompanying it borders on the extraordinary. You can well imagine that water birds never come to populate, animate, and flutter across this great surface of water whose swiftness would not permit them to plunge beneath in order to seek their pasture land. It is even very doubtful that there are any fish in these depths.

After supper Mr. E. showed us his library, small but well chosen.

''Here,'' he remarked to us, ''are friends of every moment, every day, united in the same place, although speaking such different tongues, and living in such different epochs. It is here that my wife and I come to relax from our labors: these friends tell us nothing, it is true, before we consult them; but then their voices, although quiet for so many centuries, make themselves distinctly heard—just as distinctly as though we were in the midst of the schools of Greece and of Rome. They speak to us, instructing us as though we were contemporaries. The divine art of writing has transmitted to us their sublime knowledge through the innumerable revolutions of time just as that of printing will transmit them in centuries to come. These works and those of the moderns are beacons which nothing can extinguish. Without the instructive pages of history, what would be the accounts of travelers, the experiments of chemistry, the lessons of morality and those of so many others that embellish life?''

''Among all those books,'' observed Mr. Herman, ''I see books in six languages. Do you understand them all?''

''Yes,'' he replied. ''Fairly well. I speak three.''

''What! With such a fine education, you come to live on the heights of this isthmus, deliberately resigning yourself to endure the discomforts, fatigues, and boredoms of crude colonizing? Of all the habitable places in North America, how does it happen that you chose this one?"

"Do you not realize that despite our pride, we are mere agents motivated and stimulated by unknown causes, which, as though to mortify this pride, the immensity of effects is generally in inverse proportion to that of the causes. It is especially during the early years that youth really appears to navigate on the ocean of chances and risks. Old age, the port of life, is less exposed to their caprices. My stay here is a striking example of this incongruity, as well as that natural chain of human events which it is impossible to escape.

"I was born in London; reaching the age of twenty, ten of which were spent at the University of Oxford, my father sent me to Russia with an uncle who was in charge of the English factory at Archangel."

"What," said Mr. Herman, "from White Russia to Canada! From business to the woods! How powerful the motives behind such an uprooting must have been!"

"Not at all; it happened just like the chain of events in the story of for-want-of-a-nail-the-shoe-was-lost."

"You are jesting!"

"Far from it; but in order that this oddity of destiny appear less astonishing to you, recall some of the principal epochs in your life: go back to the origin of the circumstances on which they have hung; then you will see that they were every bit as insignificant and capricious as those which led me here. There are no men on earth who can't say just as much: the same is true about the great events on which depend the destiny of families and nations; each page of history proves that everything is linked, chained together, that is to say, that everything that happens emanates from what has preceded it. But it is late; you are tired: tomorrow I shall tell you my story."

CHAPTER VIII

The next day Mr. E. kept his promise.

"I was invited to the wedding of a young Boyard in the vicinity of Archangel, and asked to take in my party seven people from the village. The cold being very severe at that time, I had my horses shod for the occasion; but we had gone hardly two miles when I noticed traces of blood: one of the horses had been cut. However, impatient to get there, I was continuing on my way when, in order to avoid a snow bank which the wind had piled up at the foot of a rock on the right side of the road, I forgot that on the left there was a steep decline also covered with snow. The wounded horse fell and the carriage overturned. As a result of this, I received a chest contusion which made me spit blood. My uncle, disturbed over the possible complications of such a wound, sent me to St. Petersburg, with instructions to sail on the first ship that would leave for France or Spain after the breaking up of the ice. I lingered at Le Havre until I received the letters of introduction I would need. Among the people from whom I received these was a Monsieur Marmontel, member of the French Academy, with whose works I was acquainted. One day as we were going to his little estate at Gri..., he said to me:

" 'Today you will dine with an ecclesiastic, interesting because of his advanced years and his fine and vigorous health, and because of his knowledge of North America, and the fertility of a memory which the years have not mitigated in the least. But one must be well acquainted with the geography of this new continent to know precisely in what part he was born.'

"Shortly after our arrival, this venerable American was introduced, and appeared to me just as Monsieur Marmontel had described him: his eyes still sparkled with a glow which contrasted with the color of his hair, white like the snows of his native land.

" 'Here is a young man,' Monsieur Marmontel told him, 'who has come from White Russia, and has lived a long time on the banks of the Dwina. If you had both been some degrees north, it seems to me that you might have met. Mr. E., from the point of Kamschatka, and you from the promontory of Alaska.[1] Would you like to give us some details about the interior of the continent, as well as about the Indians among whom you were born?'

" 'With pleasure,' he replied. 'Do you see at the foot of Lake Michigan a bay formed by the mouth of the Chicago River, on the banks of which the Pootooatamis [2] have long had one of their principal

villages? That is where I was born. My father, an agent in a house at
Quebec, had been living there several years; yet I doubt that I am
Canadian, having been born nearly 400 leagues from that town and
only 170 from the Mississippi. But the thing that makes the bay of
Chicago important is the easy, uncomplicated navigation of its river
which one can travel as far as four miles from Theakiky, one of the
branches of the Illinois, emptying into this great river a little north
of the Missouri. This passage, much traveled by those who go into upper
Louisiana, will be even more so when a connecting canal is opened between the two rivers. The first language I spoke was that of the Indians
among whom I was born. At the age of twelve, my father sent me to
Michillimakinac, a fort built, as you see, on the peninsula separating
Lake Huron from Lake Michigan. An uncle who was missionary there
among the Outawas taught me until I was fifteen and then sent me to
Quebec. Having become a priest, I was appointed by the bishop of that
town to the mission of the Winébagos [3] and some time later, to that of
my native land, known under the name of St. Joseph. After the conquest of Canada, I obtained one of the canonships of the cathedral at
Quebec, where I would be now were it not for the necessity of crossing
the Ocean to come here and finish the business of an unexpected inheritance. Out of consideration for my advanced age, the King of
England has the goodness to permit me to receive my salary here until
I am able to return to my native land.'

"Whereupon, finger on the map, he showed us the rivers, the
portages, as well as that long chain of great and small lakes which,
from the shores of Lake Superior, stretch to 65 degrees latitude; such
as (among the principal ones) the Lake of the Rains, the Lake of the
Woods, Red Lake, Winipeg Lake,[4] Aratapeskow Lake.[5] By means of
these lakes, European merchandise is transported great distances.

"The furs and skins which the Indians get in their hunts, taken to
the great portage,[6] are put on board vessels which transport them as
far north as Niagara Falls, almost 400 leagues away.

"He also told us about the native copper which could be found in
abundance around Chigomegan Bay, located on the northern shore of
Lake Superior, through which the waters of this Caspian Sea run into
Huron; and about the navigation of these lakes, often dangerous because of the violence of the winds and the frequent storms that come
up in the area during certain seasons of the year.

"Such," Mr. E. told us, "is the progress; such are the subdivisions
of this trade, sometimes exposed to great reverses by the death of the
Indians, by the increasing rarity of wild game, and by the shipwrecks
in crossing the rapids of these rivers. As to the good faith of these

Indians, it is seldom that they seek to deceive, unless they have been very unhappy. Imagine! Although perhaps 15,000 hunters are busy for four months each winter pursuing their prey, the returns barely amount to 250,000 pounds sterling.* If this business has eliminated the causes of their wars, it has acquainted them with the poison of strong liquors, and that of scarlet fever, diminishing their number with frightful rapidity."

"What a country!" I said to him, "for extent and ease of communications! What will it become some day when the Europeans have brought their plows and their industries to the most remote regions arable in the U.S.? This knowledge acquired on the spot is tremendously interesting, above all for one like me who comes from the heart of Russia, and had almost no idea at all of this new continent."

"Indeed," Mr. E. mused, "there is quite a distance from Archangel to Paris, but to young people as well as to the birds, journeys cost nothing: the pleasure of change, the enjoyments of curiosity, compensate for the fatigues. Could I ask you what the reasons are which have made you decide on such a great move?"

"I came here," I replied, "to seek health, to see a country so worthy of foreigners' curiosity, to admire these marvels that art and ingenuity bring to bear every year, and to converse with those writers whose works make the delight of Europe." (This was in 1783.)

"When you came from Michillimakinack to Quebec," I continued, "what route did you follow?

" 'I crossed Lake Huron and Lake Otsiketa (Saint Claire) in a schooner of 160 tons which was going to Détroit: from this town I embarked on an armed brigantine destined for Erie whence I went on foot as far as Niagara, 18 miles distant. After a delay of several days, I took passage from Lake Ontario on a vessel loaded with leather and maple sugar [7] going to Katarakouy, where the river of the same name begins. From this port, a ship took me to Montreal in five days: from there by stagecoach to Quebec, estimated to be 422 leagues from Michillimackinack. Including 2 weeks wait, it took me only 47 days to make this great voyage, during which time I changed vessel three times.'

"Then you have seen that famous cataract?"

" 'Oh, yes, four times in my life, and always with the same degree of astonishment and admiration.'

"Is it really true what geographers have said of it regarding its perpendicular height and to the volume of water it drops?

" 'I am not acquainted with what they said about it; but it seems

* Since the discoveries of M. Makensie, it has increased considerably.

impossible for me to conceive a precise idea of it, without seeing it on several different occasions. Everything about it is so big, so disproportionate to the feebleness of our perceptions and to our articulation, that I have in vain tried to give a description of it, and nevertheless I am well acquainted with all parts of it. The last time I passed by there, I was obliged to stay on the east side with a group of my old fellow-countrymen whom I found camped some distance from the banks of the river Tonnawanda to fish and hunt. It is one of the most fertile regions I know. What superb meadows one will some day see blooming there as well as on the island which fills the space between Rapid Lake and Lake Erie! What magnificent harvests of wheat the industrious colonist will obtain from this fertile soil! In a few years, the entire isthmus will be covered with rich dwellings and perhaps even Niagara will become a city! If I had been destined to become a farmer, it is here where I would have sought a concession, assured of realizing a hundredfold on the investment which I would have in clearing these beautiful lands!

" 'Never do I think of Canada without wishing I had a second life to spend there! Canada—with its unlimited forests, whose deep solitude is so impressive; the inland seas, often tempestuous as the ocean, this Katarakouy River, called, I know not why, St. Lawrence, which, from the vast basin of the Ontario, rolls majestically as far as the sea over a space of 251 leagues! Never do I think of the Mississippi, the foremost river in this hemisphere of whose course only 1,000 leagues is yet known, of those rapids, those raging, foaming, foggy cataracts, which excite simultaneously terror and admiration. My octogenarian imagination still soars with pleasure over the great spaces which I crossed in my youth; it still sees with paternal tenderness those Indians, whose candor and mildness of temperament make them very interesting to those who, like me, have lived long among them. If in war they are ferocious and cruel, it is from their injurious education that they derive these disastrous dispositions. For, like other men, they are born good, and of mild temperament. I know of nothing more edifying than to observe the calm of their villages, the calm of the bosom of their families, and that happy disposition to help one another.

" 'A great number of these men, it is true, dragged down by their irresistible craving for intoxicating liquors, often commit excesses that brutalize them, degrade them, causing them to lose their independence, that noble pride which some still possess whom chance has placed far from this baleful danger. But these excesses are due to the white men who, in order to wrest from them their last bearskin, arouse them to drink or rather to plunge into the delirium of drunkenness. The old men feel keenly all the horrors of these carryings-on; but how are they going to do without the iron, the ammunition, and so many other objects that we have introduced to them?'

"Such was the conversation to which I owed the first idea of coming here to settle. Yet it is probable that I would never have carried out this plan were it not for the chance meeting with an aide-de-camp of Lord Carleton's (Lord Dorchester), Governor of Canada who had lived for a year in Détroit and Niagara. I was encouraged by what he told me relative to obtaining a concession and founding a settlement, and of becoming the creator of a great land; the ease and good fortune attached to this manner of living. Moreover, excited by other motives no less powerful, I resolved to carry out my plan. It cost me many efforts before being able to obtain the consent of my family and that of my wife. She was young, wealthy, raised in the capital, and the idea of crossing the ocean and living in the woods, horrified her.

"Some time after my arrival in Quebec, I had the good luck to make the acquaintance of a M. Stedman, the contractor of the portage who, in accordance with the treaties, before being transferred to the west coast of the isthmus, sought to negotiate for a concession of 1,700 acres located on the east coast, a tenth of which was almost cleared and on which there was a fine barn, a house in poor condition, a sawmill, and a newly planted, well-fenced orchard of 1,200 apple trees; the title to all this had just been confirmed by the Government of New York. We agreed on the price and closed the transaction. That, Gentlemen, is how the merchant of Archangel became a settler in upper Canada; or rather a freeholder of Ontario county and a citizen of the state of New York whose northern boundaries begin at Oswegatchee on the St. Lawrence River at the 45th parallel and extend on Lake Erie as far as the eastern boundaries of Pennsylvania.

"But how things have changed since my arrival here! With what speed everything grows and improves. From one side the population of Canada has penetrated as far as Katarakouy where several years ago the English built a town which they named Kingston. They speak of founding another such town among the lakes of Huron, Erie, and Ontario.[8] Upper Canada, of which Ottawa is the capital, has just received a special government. On the other side, the inhabitants of the United States are beginning to make settlements on borderlands known under the name of Genessee.[9] Instead of being isolated in the middle of the continent we are going to enjoy the advantages of high society; workers and artisans will no longer be so rare. In a little while commerce and industry will be flourishing, for until now people have been busy building shelters for themselves and making a living from the earth. Communications will be perfected; bridges will be built, swamps reclaimed, the countryside cleared.

"This is the seventh year that I have been busy clearing this wild ground, uprooting and burning the trees and bushes that choke it, adding to my pasture land whose extent would astonish you. I dare say busy, too, in beautifying this place, although, it is true, I am much less attached to that which is decorative than that which is utilitarian; since labor is so dear, today's hand-wrought things will be prized by future generations. Some day when the forests of the surrounding region are replaced by meadows and fertile fields, from this house people will also enjoy the scenery surrounding the falls, some of which offer extremely bizarre and capricious masses. Eyes will rove with interest over the great stretch of Rapid Lake on both Erie rivers, over vessels anchored on this lake, over the mills, the dwellings, the orchards; they will contemplate with delight the beauties of a countryside as wide as it is varied, enriched on one side by the beauties of agriculture; on the other by the noise, the vapors, and some parts of the cataract. Few sights on land will offer a scene as striking as it is picturesque."

Hoping that the next day would be a favorable one, and that, in accordance with his promise, Mr. E. would take us to the falls, we spent the rest of this long and interesting evening in chatting about various things. We talked of the dark clouds that seemed to be looming over the horizon of Europe in the near future and whose mysteries we were trying to penetrate; of the hope that the turmoils of Europe would never reach our shores. We spoke of many things: of the principles on which the Greeks had founded their colonies in Asia Minor, Calabria, and Sicily; of the inland navigation on the continent; of the fishing industry that would some day be established on the lakes; of the recently discovered mines—and what not!

It was midnight when Mr. Herman and I entered our quarters: the air, the sky, nature—everything was calm and serene, the moon hovering over the forests of Erie bathed in soft and timid splendor the different objects that rose in sight. The rocks with which Rapid Lake is scattered, the island that divides the falls, the column of vapors, the two Erie rivers overflowing their banks, the mills and the shores of the west side—everything was moonlit.

"What a fertile source of illusions," he remarked to me, "the uncertain appearance of everything we see! It is a fairy-like spectacle in which what I see now does not resemble one bit what I saw before, deprived as I am of the power to make comparisons, of the resources of sight, and judgment of distances which light alone can give us. As

though to embellish the nudity of this lake and make the approaches
to the cataract even more impressive, nature has adorned it with this
great number of rocks, some sharp, others rounding, varying in height
and having different shapes. Illuminated by this vaporous light that
veils more objects than it hides, the projection of their shimmering
shadows on the rippling surface of the lake awakens the idea of a
troop of giants fighting against the violence of its current. And these
streams of silvery light! And those thousands of reflections that the
rippling of the waves and their innumerable facets modify as far as
the eye can see. How to seize these fleeting images, so readily defaced
by those that have succeeded them! How impressive is that island,
situated at the foot of the precipice! Inaccessible as it is, its silence
and solitude have never been disturbed by the presence of man, nay—
nor by the song of the birds. Who can tell us for how many centuries it
has resisted the efforts and violence of a stream that is estimated to be
six or seven thousand feet wide, whose depth and velocity will never
be known? And that pyramidical cloud which arises from the bottom
to such a great height; source of fertile streams, beacon of the pilots
who navigate the Erie and Ontario! How much more imposing it is in
the midst of the calm and deep blue of this beautiful night, than during
the dazzling splendor of daylight. And these mysterious shadows that
envelop the island from the middle, lighted partially by this midnight
moon, do you see how streaked they are by these bands, by turns
luminous, transparent, or dark? For nature is sublime even in the
combination of its shifting tints and modifications of its shadows.

"Do you hear the murmur which the breeze brings us from the lake?
What a contrast with that of the fuller and more solemn sound of the
falls which at one moment resembles the great rumblings of thunder in
the midst of mountains, at another, the somber tones of a bellowing
from the bowels of the earth."

"Let us wait, shall we, until the return of daylight," I suggested,
"to complete the elegant tableau which you have just sketched; for in
the midst of the effervescence of so many ideas, how are we to induce
and obtain the benefits of sleep? Let us turn our eyes from what we
have seen and what we look forward to seeing, so that we may enjoy
the healthful sleep of night time."

CHAPTER IX

The next day a violent storm prevented us from seeing the falls. Mr. E., by way of consolation, read us the following item, which he permitted me to copy.

"It is during the beautiful days of winter when the sun, appearing at its zenith, covers these falls with its rays, that the eyes and imagination of the spectator are offered one of the rarest and, I believe, most magnificent spectacles that it is possible to see on earth. The trees, bushes, rocks, and copses of the riverbanks, the giants of the lake, everything one sees during the summer disappears and is replaced by objects whose forms and appearances are entirely different. It is like a new creation. The exhalations of the falls which the winds disperse afar, condensed by the vigorous cold, attach themselves to all these surfaces, covering them with gowns of resplendent whiteness, crystals and elegant sculpture, icicles and glazed frost whose innumerable and bizarre collections are indescribable, like those beautiful dreams of children of health, youth, and happiness. Sometimes one imagines he sees Gothic buildings, columns placed according to the principles of aerial perspective, ancient castles, ruins or heaps of stone cut with a marvelous artistry and precision.

"The walls of the promontories, so gloomy and somber during the summer, are then reclad with brilliant blades and the trees atop their peaks, converted into transparent obelisks; the rocks of the lake resemble pedestals mounted on blocks of alabaster, from which a skilled sculptor would have made statues, supernatural beings, or gigantic birds. The debris and rocks which surround the basin within 15,000 feet are like a wall of ice, formed by the gushing of waters which the cold quickly freezes. Here stalagmites seem to rise 40 feet high; there fluted or truncated columns; farther on caryatids, busts or everything of the richest and most sumptuous to which a keen and fertile imagination can give birth.

"The venerable cedars, old, mossy spruces, ancient larch trees, gigantic pines, all these trees and ice-laden bushes that grow in the midst of rocks or on the north of river banks, like candelabra of a vast sanctuary, still embellish this magnificent hyperborean scene. Often, too, succumbing to the weight of their ornament, they fall to disappear into the abyss.

"The island from the middle, whose width on the crest is estimated at one mile; this island, so cool and green during the summer, like all the objects around it, takes on an entirely new aspect; the trunks, the branches and the tops of trees covering it, the bushes, and even the soil —everything has changed; the rigors of the season have reclad them, decorated them with efflorescent icicles as varied in their form as in their grandeur. The trees resemble enormous pyramids whose brilliant and silvered summits contrast marvelously with the blue of the skies. The richness of the jewel-box, the sparkling lustre of light suspended from almost all the extremities of their branches, produces on the imagination a magic effect, especially when they balance themselves lightly at the whim of the breeze. However regretful one may feel in watching these overburdened branches lose their icicles and detach themselves from the trees, one cannot help but be fascinated.

"Nothing can compare with this island, fully resplendent with glory, light, and transparence. Sometimes it would recall those magic imaginings of the Arabs, that of the enchanted palaces, works of the most ingenious fairies, or the idea of an earthly visit of some unknown divinity who, to avoid the flattery of mankind, would have chosen the crest of this frightful precipice because it is inaccessible to them.

"This column during the summer is a great mass of mists and would appear to be a vast vortex of winged crystals, of microscopic meteors and scintillating atoms; as light as air, they obey these impulses, kneel, rise, or disperse afar following the force and direction of the winds. Such is the inexhaustible source of all the northern rivers in the region.

"It is neither from the strayings nor from illusions of the imagination that these objects borrow their beauty; no, this beauty is the real effect which results from the size, magnificence, and brilliance of this vast ensemble of obelisks, pyramids, and accessories, brilliant, wild, and picturesque, from whose center two sheets of water fall. Their surfaces are estimated at 491,400 square feet. How can we describe the deep impression made by the immensity and variety of so many streams? The size of these streams whose volume of tidal flood forms two great whirlpools, the height from which they fall, the tumult, the circular and impetuous movement, as well as the flow, the steaming waves which fill this vast fortress? How can I express the terror and fright which the terrifying noise of this overwhelming chaos inspires in the midst of which one often sees floating on the surface trees or fragments of icicles?

"Watching these objects so numerous and so fragile, one would think that nature has stored here a supply of molds, weights, and types of infinite variety which she uses only at this time of year to imprint these crystallizations with all richness of carving and sculpture and make of them masterpieces which have the appearance and merit of works of art.

"It is here that imagination becomes creative, grows, rises, and soars in a wave of new objects that it decorates in its most brilliant colors. How this striking and magnificent scene is set off by the nudity of forests and the harshness of the season; by the somber sadness of these steep riverbanks between which the Niagara River rushes in with it wild waters. For the keener the cold, the more numerous are these crystallizations and these vast sheets of ice, resplendent above all when the sun floods them with its rays."

"Since you speak of these contrasts," I told him, "can we forget how many contrasts your family, your house, and everything surrounding it offers? Here everything is quiet and peaceful. It is the haven of repose and peace; three miles toward the North, on the contrary, everything is tumult and chaos; even the night scarcely knows quiet. Here nature is smiling, animated; under this roof, as in the neighboring fields, everything grows and ripens; scarcely can the eye absorb the richness of fertility; farther down everything coming from the lakes and abandoning itself to the Erie is irresistibly dragged down and reduced to atoms in this vast abyss of destruction. Here everything is the reflection of order, of life, of progress; there, on the contrary, everything paints chaos and death. Here breathes rest, ease, and happiness; there everything summons and excites astonishment, terror, and fright. The poet and the painter will never be able to bring together as eloquently in the same painting the two periods of existence: the contrast of birth and death." *

* This rich description which one would believe to be the product of the author's imagination, if the tales of travelers did not verify the magnificence of the spectacle, gives a sublime notion of the majesty of Nature and the power of the Creator. Who will tell us why such a monument of greatness entered into the plan of his creations? Why it has been placed somehow, far from the glances of civilized nations, that is to say, of those whose religion and philosophy have made them worthy of the admiration and respect of the Creator? O altitudo!
(Note communicated to the editor by Citizen Bilecocq.)

CHAPTER X

As we were leaving to see the Falls, a fog coming from Erie having suddenly obscured the sun, our host, who wanted us to see this great spectacle on a beautiful day, suggested an excursion through the fields to his sawmill, situated on Beaver Creek, the west branch of the Tonnawanda which crosses White Cedar Swamp.[1]

"Here," said Mr. Herman, "is the thickest and gloomiest forest that I have seen since I arrived on the continent; it is only noon and one can scarcely see."

"It is also one of the most valuable," replied Mr. E.; "the fences made of this wood are everlasting: this same wood serves to cover our homes and our barns as well as the fine cooperage in which we make all the pails used in our dairies. The wood is as light as it is durable. I owe this fine acquisition to the information that an old Indian gave me shortly after my arrival in this country on returning from the Upper Chippaway where I had taken him in my canoe so that I could see once again the site of his old village."

"Are you referring to old Agueghon?" I asked him.

"Yes, and how does it happen that you gentlemen, coming from New York, know this old man?"

"Excited by what the commandant at Niagara had said, we went to spend twenty-four hours with him on the banks of the stream, and never have we had a more interesting visit, nor one that seemed so short."

"That does not amaze me at all! When one realizes that his education was only that of a simple Indian, one can scarcely refrain from admiring him and wanting to have known him in the full vigor of his youth.

"Like the last moments of a beautiful day," continued Mr. E., "his imagination during his declining years, still radiates some of his old splendor. What beautiful flowers this imagination would have produced if from his youth a skillful hand had given this vigorous savage some of our knowledge! Perhaps he might have become the poet of these nations. Here is what he would tell me while we explored together the haunts of his village, of which only traces remain.

" 'Why do years soften the memory of our losses and our misfortune, without ever permitting them to lapse completely into oblivion; just as great distances soften the wild appearance of mountains and rocks which one cannot approach. That is what I have never been able to understand in my long life. The memories which I recall of these places today, so sad and lonely, formerly covered with wigwams and enlivened by a fairly numerous population, fill my eyes with tears, but they are less burning. The crushing and heart-breaking anguish of bygone days, although still bitter, are no longer deep, silent sighs: my heart is swollen with them.

" 'How changed—all that! The bushes that I tramped through have become trees with high peaks, and among the old oaks, once superb, in whose shadow I would romp in my early years, some are broken by decay, others, like our warriors, reduced to dust, covered with earth and leaves. Do you see those young branches growing over the debris from these old trees? Well, the strongest, after overcoming the weakest, will grow to the height of their predecessors and in their turn, will perish. And, so it is with human generations; they come to life, they hurt each other and they die.

" 'And that mutilated old cedar! Old from my tender youth; the tree against which I learned to throw my tomahawk, and let fly my arrow: like me, it has survived its innumerable wounds; thus, like me, it has lost its plumage; like mine, its mossy head will never produce another growth, the source from which it pumped its vigor is dried up.'

"Then suddenly becoming motionless, like someone who thinks he sees a phantom, he told me in a tone of the deepest sadness:

" 'Look, brother, here is the place where I raised my wigwam; my trembling feet under the thick weeds have just touched the debris of the fireplace where my fire used to burn and by the heat of which in joy and pleasure, I saw my children grow. Winter has fifty-three times whitened the land and frozen the surface of our lakes since these times of happiness; and this vast interval seems to me like a long day whose sun has just set: yet these stones and the hands which put them there still exist on earth! But let us go on further. My face is covered with a cold sweat; an emotion similar to the shiver of death during the shadows of the night chills and stirs me. My heart would break if I lingered here any longer. You would have to cover my body with earth to keep off the mosquitoes.

" 'Do you see this foaming falls into whose dangerous current the young people of our village used to let themselves be dragged? Its water still gushes forth with the same din, and of all the old swimmers, I am the only one still alive! The leaves of spring replace those of autumn; birds of passage leave and return; seasons follow; and are gone, disappeared forever! The progeny of wild beasts hunted by the Chippeways still crosses these woods; yet that of our hunters has been uprooted from the earth like the weeds on our savannahs before the mighty breath of a storm, like the trees of the forests struck by the fire and hatchet of the white men. The echoes from these places, which so often reiterate the yells of the Warwhoop and the songs of victory, are still perched on the same trees (do you hear how they answer me now?) and the voice of our warriors is lost in the wave of eternal silence, the breath of their life mingled with the air of nature!

" 'The bird that flies through the air, the gleaming fish that swims 'neath the waters, the mosquito that bites me, the cicada that sings, still exists: and these men, once so strong, so brave, are no longer anything. What is life anyway? Coming I know not from where, loaned to us I know not why; whom the tooth of a snake, the branch of a tree, the water of a stream can take from us? What, then, is this life, I asked one day of Kouetategen, ancient war chief of the Nassakoohasset tribe?

" 'Life,' he replied, 'is merely a succession of hardships and fatigues, of vigorous and burning seasons. It is like a journey through a feebly lighted forest, 'mid whose paths men meander, arguing about the objects around them: it is only after having left them, they will feel how very deceiving the lights and shadows of this forest were, that they will be able to walk, heads high, watching the sun in its full glory.

" 'What does it matter what life is,' he continued, 'since yours does not belong to you? You owe it to your tribe, to your nation who, for you, is like the sun-dew on plants every time its honor or independence demands it.'

" 'Whence came these forests and these men?' I asked him.

" 'Can the insect know from what country comes the swallow which pursues and devours him? Or the reeds of our meadows, can they know the origin of the first sparkle of fire which consumes them, reducing them to ashes? Or the oak, can it ever know the origin of the storms?'

" 'You are right,' I told him; 'these questions are like a mountain or a precipice which one meets on his way; it is wiser to make a detour than to cross them.'

" 'Do you see these piles of stones?' continued old Agoueghon, 'under whose weight, in whose shadow of the wolves' teeth lie the bones of so many generations of Chippaways? If ever the feet of the white men trample on these hallowed remains; if ever your plows expose them to be whitened by the rain or dew, may health, peace, and happiness flee from their dwellings, as the arrows spin from the warrior's bow, as the waters rush from the height of this fall, may their skins become the pasture lands of carnivorous animals!

" 'Would that, then, be all that remains of these fearless chiefs, these bold warriors who made the mighty Mohawk league tremble, subjugated the tribes of the Hopponiare, the Yamanee, the Tawatongo, and so many others and carried the tomahawk of war to the ends of the Cayung Gamineck (great lake or lake Superior)? How short and transitory was the duration of these triumphs, of this glory! I saw it pass like the shadow of the clouds chased by the tempest, like the days of spring at the approach of the Dog Days in August.

" 'What has remained of these bloody combats, these destructive undertakings so long meditated and discussed around their council fires? Nothing! Of so many chances, losses, and dangers? Nothing! What is this nothing, I have often wondered. Could it be only the beginning and the end of life and of everything? And this dream of only a few moments only an interim between these two nothings? This present of the mighty Manitou would not be worth the hardships and difficulties, the anguish, worries, and misfortunes that one experiences dreaming.

" 'But perhaps our warriors are sleeping; perhaps their sleep will not be eternal; perhaps, as Kouetategen once said, another land exists west of this one; one where forests abound in game and rivers abound in fish; one where the sun is less capricious than ours, and where in the shelter of the great tree of peace we shall be able to go live by our hunting and fishing and enjoy a well-earned rest. If I could not hope thus, I would rather be a wolf, a beaver, elk, or vulture, than a Nishynorbay.

" 'When I see canoes paddled on our lakes, I think less of the men who paddle them than of those who have built them; by the same token, when I see the sun appear, and set, rise to reappear again; the moon at once so constant and regular in its journeys; the unalterable succession of seasons, of creatures of plant life, and of so many other phenomena which surround me; as the sun of the morning absorbs the night dew into the clouds, in the same way does the sight of these magnificent works raise my feeble thoughts unto the worker who has been able to execute such great things. Where does he live? Why are we unable to know him and lavish on him our admiration as well as our gratitude? Is he interested in our fate? Is he unconcerned or does he know what pity is? Blind as I am! I seek, I grope, but my stick, as blind as I, leads me nowhere in his direction.'

"Thus he would speak of these places as we explored them, today covered with bushes, reeds, thick growths of herbs, symbols of abandon and solitude.

" 'After treading over my native land for the last time, and breathing that air which gave life to so many generations, and which, perhaps still holds the germs of a great many others, like the snail, which, at the approach of winter, attaches itself to the ledges of a rock and coiled thus, awaits with indifference the events of the future. I am going back to my solitude and await there with gentle patience the time for leaving the forest, and finally rejoin my wife, my children, and my ancestors.'

"After placing rocks on old tombs, a sacred duty that I hastened to join him in, he led me four miles further, to show me one of the most beautiful fountains in this land. It gushes with great gusto from a deep and vast cavern formed by limestone under whose roof one can easily enter and sit down. Its clear waters, after forming 400 feet beyond a falls eleven feet high, fall and flow into a little river which is one of the branches of the Chippeway, called Canawasco by the old Indians.

"The forests of this neighborhood were composed principally of oak, chestnut trees and black birch trees, whose bushy tops made a shadow which the sun could scarcely penetrate. Like the powers on earth, these trees had smothered their neighbors; one could see there neither shrubs nor bushes. In vain did I call forth nymphs from gloomy, desolate coppices and the water nymphs from this magnificent fountain; no noise could be heard other than the reverberation of the falls. These Elysian Gods will come to live here only at the time when work and industry have converted these places today uncultivated and solitary into prosperous countrysides rich in harvests. Then perhaps will be born the troubadours who will sing of its poetry; then perhaps a new Petrarch will appear, whose loves and verse will make this fountain as celebrated as that of old Vaucluse, a name which I gave it in a report to a surveyor-general of Canada, as being the first European who had seen it and who might know something about it." [2]

CHAPTER XI

Eager to be in the neighborhood of the falls before sunrise in order to enjoy fully the effect of its first rays on the stirred-up surface of a great body of water, we left early, with our guide, Mr. E., and entered the forests. How impressive they are when one crosses through them during the coolness and 'mid the half-obscure shadings of a beautiful summer's night! Like the voices, the steps of a traveler, the throwing of a stone, the crackling of the smallest branch, or the reverberations of the slightest sound, before the light breeze which precedes and accompanies the dawn can be felt. Everything was still asleep, the lonely echoes, the humming insects, the forest animals and birds; this universal silence was interrupted from time to time only by a vague noise, almost indistinct, like the roaring of the sea on a far-off beach, it came from the cataract, which during the night rarely rises above its deep embankment.

But soon we arrived at Mr. E.'s sawmill. Its power, he told us, he had just increased by the introduction of copper cylinders in all its turnings, in order to lessen the friction. What better location could there be for this mill than on this beautiful falls 19 feet high, 'mid these primeval forests of chestnut, oak, hickory, and plane trees?

After walking three quarters of an hour, we finally came upon the tumultuous currents of Rapid Lake, and the immense column of vapors which rises to a great height, making the noise of the falls more audible.

"It must be as old as Saturn," Mr. E. said, "since the heights of this isthmus are a part of the Alleghanies, which, after stretching along the southern coast of the Ontario as far as Toronto, cross the land of the Mississages, and cut across the swirling river of the Outawas [1] and join the snow-covered mountains of Hudson Bay. It is to this arrangement old as creation that we owe what is perhaps the greatest supply of water on earth and the inestimable advantage of inland navigation on this continent; for it is not rare to see at the roadstead of the Erie schooners and brigantines coming from Chicago, which is situated at the other end of Lake Michillimakinack more than 240 leagues away, as well as the land of the Winebago, Green Bay, Detroit, and Michillimakinack. Without these waterways, what would the interior of this continent be? Like that of Africa, it is reasonable to assume that it would be uncultivated, or would be inhabited only by tribes whom the civilization of the Atlantic nations would reach only with great difficulty; for navigable waters are one of the prime causes not only of prosperity but also of civilization. Far from complaining, like so many others, of the inconveniencies of this portage, I consider it a great benefit. Although if one is prudent, one can examine these falls at close range and even go down into the gorge, however, I warn you, one must have courage to conquer the great repugnance and fright that involuntarily seize one in approaching the cliff. Furthermore, you will soon discover how much the ladders I put there two years ago lessen the danger in approaching.''

We arrived at point O. It is merely a mass of rocks piled atop each other, covered with high cedars that grow in its crevices, plus thorny bushes. Mr. Herman, impatient and eager, had soon climbed to the highest tree, whence, after a moment spent in that speechless astonishment and admiration, which great sights such as these inspire, he climbed down, and said to us:

''What are the falls of which travelers speak, compared with what I see here? What is the Passaick of Jersey,[2] the falls of the Jenezee,[3] the cohos of the Mohawk,[4] the waterfalls of the Montmorenci and the Chaudiere in Canada,[5] the passage of the Tenezee through the Cumberland mountains? [6] This magnificent scene with its regularities hardly seems the work of chance. How this superb sheet of water 1,000 feet wide, formed by the foaming, rushing waters of Rapid Lake, suddenly becomes by its great power a solid, uniform arch, without any check or let-up! I thought I was looking down on a crystal vault, suspended in the air: if the deafening din did not prohibit meditation, it is here, in the shelter of these beautiful cedars that it would remain. How regrettable that because of the position of the island separating the two branches of this cataract, one is prevented from seeing it in its entirety, which is estimated to be 4,500 feet! And these magnificent approaches and mossy rocks, witnesses of earlier upheavals, whose fantastic forms present imitations of what one is sure he has seen elsewhere; and the gloomy forests surrounding; and that column, which from the depths of the abyss, rises above our heads! The ensemble of all these features bears the imprint of a grandeur both imposing and sublime. But let us come as close as possible to this cataract of which Hontan and Charlevoix had given me only a very imperfect notion.''

After making our way with difficulty through these thick bushes, laden with creepers and trailing vines, after climbing down or sliding over wet surfaces covered with moss, we finally reached a level place covered with debris and hemlock, spruce, veined maple, and water ash, on which grow young trees of the same kind. Elsewhere, our attention might have been caught only a few moments by this odd sight; but so near this cataract, it was entirely absorbed by objects otherwise quite interesting.

In this moment the sun rose and dispelled the shadows of the night. Its rays, after bathing the hills and the surrounding objects, fell upon this column at different angles, which made them transparent; embellished with their splendor, the whirling waves of Rapid Lake, and gave this great sheet of water the crystal clarity of glass. It was then that we discovered three rainbows: the first, on the waters of the abyss; the second nearer us; and the third above our heads.

"What magnificence!" said Mr. Herman. "How can these clusters of radiant colors seem motionless although refracted by light that falls with such speed."

On our left, we were only a little distance from the forests of Tonnawanda, whose trees, constantly moistened from the vapors of the falls, grow with an extraordinary vigor, to the very ledges of the highest rocks along the escarpment. On the right (200 feet below), the immense basin or rather the abyss whose waters, raging like the waters of tempest-tossed sea, washed over the circumference several times before escaping to form the rapids and the whirling cascades of the Niagara River. Conversation was well nigh impossible because of the ceaseless noise re-echoing from these great falls and these swirling currents.

Mr. Herman, absorbed, could scarcely understand the signs we were making. Finally, after fortifying ourselves with a glass of rum, we followed our guide, and with the aid of ladders, we climbed down from resting place to resting place on to the very last ledge where it was safe to venture. There, seated, holding on to a cedar branch, we watched with awe this tremendous volume of water, falling with incredible speed from a point 142 feet above. Its volume is estimated to pour forth 982,800 cubic feet of water a minute. Seven fathoms below was vast confusion of waves ceaselessly rolling, swirling, bubbling through the debris which filled the bottom of the abyss. The gushing occasionally threatened to drag us down, but repulsed by the slant of the rocks, these waves would fall back into the abyss with a din which one can scarcely conceive, only to rise again to the same height. I do not believe that there is on earth another phenomenon as soul-stirring as this.

But how can one describe the impact which the prolonged contemplation of the perpetual motion of this eternal struggle leaves on the mind and on the senses, that of the continuity of a resounding as violent as utter chaos? How can one analyze the impressions that result from the sight of these gigantic and threatening objects whose immensity is so disproportionate to the feebleness of our senses? It is only in the quiet of one's study, and not in these places, that it is possible to capture some notion; but even then one would need the brush of Vernet or Thompson or the pen of Rousseau. Why, even the most skillful painter could offer us but a mute and sterile representation of relative grandeur, and not a merit of the living and sublime image of the motion, the glory and the noise of this majestic scene.

However vivid the imagery, however magic the beauty of a poet's description of these scenes, could it possibly communicate to the soul of the reader, seated on his sofa, the numerous, profound impressions the spectator experiences, especially that involuntary feeling of respect and humility which seizes him irresistibly? When from the top of a tree or an elevated rock, or suspended between existence and eternity on the banks of Table Rock (B), he watches, shivering with fright and admiration, the different parts of this great phenomenon and particularly this vast elliptical and crystal-like sheet less than three feet away, and which, since the creation, has been falling, while roaring its incalculable torrents in abysmal waters which its enormous weight raises ceaselessly to a great height.

Finally, tired of watching, hearing, and admiring, even more tired from having tried futilely one hundred times to articulate our reactions, we wanted to return once again to the light of day pure and free from the mists by which we were surrounded, and to leave this deep, gloomy, and damp abyss. It was noon when we reached Point O, safe and sound; there we changed our clothes, and, seated in the shade of a leaning rock, we enjoyed with delight the rest and meditation which we needed so urgently. Unique indeed are these precious moments, when one comes back as in a re-birth to self-consciousness after being overwhelmed and worn out by the impact of striking experiences and new ideas.

We resumed our way toward the forest of Tonnawanda; but instead of following the route we had taken in the morning, Mr. E. led us to a bridge and a cabin built a mile beyond his sawmill. The bridge was nothing more than an uprooted tree, to which a railing had been attached; the dwelling was as simple in construction. There we found to our great astonishment, his wife, Mr. Stedman, Captains Goldworthy and Delancey who had come from Niagara, and M. de Beaubassin, a young man from Quebec who had come to see the falls.

"What a contrast," my companion said to me, "between the peace, the coolness, and the calm of this haven on the banks of this lovely stream and the din, the danger, and the dampness, the stultifying heat of the abyss from which we have come! What a contrast between the spectacle which those great and terrible images offered and this mild, peaceful scene of happiness, hospitality, and prosperous industry! I confess, my soul, tired of those kaleidoscopic scenes, needed repose;

I am grateful no end to this charming American lady for having surprised us so delightfully. What gratitude we owe Colonel Hunter, who
made possible the friendship of a family in whose home one finds so
much kindness, enlightenment, and comfort in spite of such a rustic
surrounding. From here to Fort Stanwix, one would not find another
like this."

"That is very likely," I replied.

"Tell me," Mrs. E. asked my companion, "did my husband guide
you well? Are you satisfied with your journey? Were you disappointed
in what you saw? Did this spectacle compensate for the fatigues and
dangers to which you were exposed? For here, as elsewhere, nature
exacts some compensation for the pleasures and enjoyments she gives
us."

"If I had been able first to watch this great marvel without a guide,
in order to take the edge off my early impatience, I would be in a
better state to answer you. I was much too moved, my eyes were lost
in the variety, my imagination was bewildered by the extent and
grandeur of the objects: everything is so awe-inspiring and so sublime,
so imposing and so new that I feel the need to meditate on what I
have seen and even see it again. The impressions which linger resemble the ones of those gigantic and fantastic dreams whose memory
at the time of awakening requires some moments of quiet concentra-
tion, or whose features and nuances escape one when he wishes to revive them. Perhaps after dinner I shall be able to reply with greater
ease to your question."

"I cannot see," said Captain Delancey, "how these rocks and fragments have until now triumphed over time and centuries and resisted
the continual weight of these two torrents whose flow is estimated per
minute at 2,948,400 cubic feet of water weighing 206,388,000 pounds.
How does it happen that this enormous volume of water has not dug
through to the bottom of the abyss to the very center of the earth?
Did these rocks exist before the cataract had begun pouring forth its
waters? Could there have been a geological epoch prior to the time
of the formation of the Great Lakes? Nothing seems more obvious
when one considers at close range the indelible marks of breaks which
all the rocks in this region present, as well as the deep and frightening
banks of the Niagara River. Perhaps even before flowing into the
Ontario, the waters of the Great Lakes would join the sea through the
passage of the Mississippi whose immense plains and savannahs attest
to its traces."

"Quite right," replied Mr. Stedman, "everything indicates that
the surface of this continent has undergone great changes in the long

course of centuries: it would be quite interesting to know what the condition of this surface was before the Potawmack and the Shenando had pierced the Blue Mountains and the Tenesee, those of Cumberland; before the great Kanhawa had crossed the chain of the Laurier and the Ouasioto; the Delaware and the Hudson, and the Kittatiny.[7] Unfortunately, the remains of this primitive state, these records of time, like Egyptian hieroglyphics, became unintelligible. It is very probable that before the break-through of the strait of Sainte-Marie,[8] the waters of Lake Superior might have flowed into the Mississippi, several branches of which are not far away, and those of Lake Michigan communicated at the same time with the Illinois through the Chicago and the Théakiky. Oh well! Let us bless the present order of things to which we owe the advantages of an inland navigation of more than 500 leagues, from the Gulf of St. Lawrence to the extremity of Green Bay, and in the course of which one meets no interruption other than this portage. In twenty years more, the population of upper Canada and the colonies, which the United States annually set up in bordering regions, will have cultivated these new regions as well as the banks of the Erie and the Ontario. Then, from all parts of the Atlantic States, travelers will be able to visit and admire this famous cataract, with as much ease as one goes today to Virginia in order to see Natural Bridge of Rock-Bridge County.''[9]

''Are the approaches of the west branch as difficult and inaccessible as those here?'' my companion inquired.

''Much less,'' replied Mr. Stedman. ''One can, not without difficulty, however, reach the foot and even the watery and gloomy cavern of the falls. From this location, which the heat and suffocation make extremely unbearable, is, I believe, one of the most imposing spectacles anyone could picture. Imagine yourself leaning against a wall estimated at 172–180 feet high, from whose crest gushes forth with the greatest speed and without interruption a sheet of water 356 fathoms wide flowing at the rate of 1,965,600 cubic feet a minute and which, curving into a majestic arc, falls and swirls into a vast abyss of roaring waves; imagine these waves in a perpetual turmoil, broken, repulsed, dispersed, or converted into vapors, and leaving this violent state to form the Niagara River only after running through a multitude of rock fragments, reeking and foaming with froth!

''In this enormous mass, every drop of water contributes to the uproar and racket; day and night the constant whistling and the deafening din of this eternal deluge pierces the ear, often occasioning in the sudden and shifting air pockets, sudden commotions which threaten to drag down the terror-stricken spectator.

''To contemplate nature in all its pomp and splendor, or rather in the exercise of its greatest efforts, one should come here to admire it in its totality, examining and studying at leisure the details of this cataract. It is probably the greatest of any on earth. The waters of 38,881 leagues of lakes and rivers run into it.[10]

"To be sure, the descent from point N called the Indian Ladders, to the edge of the swift stream, requires perhaps much less courage; but it is a far more strenuous undertaking. One must walk upstream, climbing over or scaling endless debris and rocks, before arriving at the foot of the falls. And one must pay dearly for this curiosity and this pleasure of being able to say that he has reached the Cave of the Winds.

"Quite different from the east branch which forms an almost straight line, the west branch toward the center tapers gently here and the quantity of water that it pours in at this point is beyond all conception. The contact, the terrifying conflict of a part of these two sheets of water, breaking and intermingling before reaching the bottom of the pit; the whirling, the foaming froth of their waves, the column of vapors which from this point rises often to a prodigious height; the resplendency of the rainbow, which, according to the position of the sun, appears to make the colors flash; the eternal din, the re-echoing so tiring to the ears—in short, this entire tableau is one of the most astonishing ever seen by man. Of all the parts of the cataract, this east branch is the one which particularly seems to hold and attract travelers' eyes. I have seen some spectators who had to be pulled away. Pale from fright, struck with astonishment, absorbed in deep reverie, they would emerge only with the greatest effort from the almost supernatural ecstasy in which the contemplation of these great and magnificent objects had plunged them.

"Tomorrow, instead of crossing the Erie River at Fort Chippeway,[11] you will go to the old fortress, from that point my canoe will take you to Queenstown.[12] After resting there on your return from the falls, you will spend the night in my home at New-Arrk,[13] and the next day you will spend with the commandant of the fort who has invited you on a hunting party. You will also see a Swiss officer, who has recently come from France, where he was witness of bloody scenes whose telling makes one shiver. I hope the sun is as bright as it is today, for if the day is not clear, one cannot enjoy the beauties of the falls."

After dinner, the group went trout fishing near the sawmill, Mr. E. and I talked of the Government that Great Britain had just granted to the inhabitants of Northern Canada; of the causes which had retarded and would probably continue to retard for a long time the population of that land; of the foolhardy project of founding a town between lakes Erie, Huron, and Ontario; of the port for the construction of vessels recently established at Toronto on the west shore of that lake; of the various enterprises undertaken to facilitate navigation on the St. Lawrence River from Ottawa to Montreal; of the forthcoming cession of forts Oswego, Niagara, Detroit and Michillimakinack to the United States in accordance with the treaty. Mr. Herman, having returned meanwhile, said to our host:

"Since you own such a spacious and commodious house, why have you built a cabin on the banks of this stream?"

"It belongs to my brother-in-law, Captain Goldworthy," he replied. "He built it in the middle of 300 acres of land which I sold him last year. Although he is still wealthy and young, the retreat, the silence, the solitude in the woods hold charms for him that he often prefers to those of society or to dissipation. He is very fond of fishing, natural history, and botany: his imagination, rich in riotous colors, paints charming perspectives. In this, he differs greatly from so many other people, who in considering the events and the germs of explosion recounted in gazettes from Europe, would like to chain their imagination, as if it were a redoubtable enemy, because it anticipates all evils, and prevents none.

"He never enters these woods without thinking that he hears harmony whose modulations vary at the will of the wind and breeze; he says it is nature who speaks to us and invites us to meditate. These rocks summon to his mind the same impression as those of old medals to that of an antiquarian; these everlasting witnesses of all times are indeed the most ancient things on earth; he examines their grain, as well as the mosses, the plants, and the cedars whose active roots dig deep into their crevices with a strength that seems inconceivable, often bursting the rocks with the very strength they derive from these rocks. For him everything is an object of instructive observation; the gnat that pursues the swallow, like the Kewass of the woods,[14] this phoenix among insects, which, in order to give life to its young ones, brings speedy death to itself; the humble bug that crawls on the ground, as well as the majestic tree of the forests; the petrified formations one finds on the bottom of the lakes, as well as the pebbles of their river banks. He is both painter and poet, when he describes the magnificence of nature on a beautiful spring day, when he speaks to us of the canvasses of the industrious Progné embellished, with trembling tears of the Dawn; of the battle and triumph of nascent Light on the Shadows of the night, of the imperceptible gradations of the light and shade of evening, the moment of peaceful contemplation and silence.

"The sight of a stream flowing and meandering under the mysterious shadow of older trees and leaning maples absorbs his mind, often whole hours: the murmur and motion of their clear waves through the roots of the trees which they refresh in their course, the passage of the leaves and debris that they drag down, the fluttering, ephemeral groups whose existence lasts only from dawn til dusk,[15] the moist herbs whose slow and gracious undulations recall the movements of sensitivity; all these objects are for him a fertile source of dreams and thoughts which, he has often told me, are the result of neither special will nor study, but the effect of a kind of irresistible prey similar to the gradual charm and subtle approaches of sleep.

"Impressed with the pleasant ease, the independence enjoyed in the United States by a colonist who has the means to make the necessary investment to lodge himself, clear his land well, and convert the swamps into prairie lands, he has decided to resign his commission, when his regiment is recalled to Europe. Moreover, his wife, for whom he has the tenderest affection, does not have the slightest desire to return to Europe until the storms threatening that part of the world are dissipated. He hired for a five-year period four soldiers in his company, excellent workers: helped by my experience, my advice and my sawmill, his progress will be rapid.

"Like me, he is convinced that more remote from the source of these revolutions and wars, which, so often, desolate the Old World, living here under the most paternal Government in the land, in the shelter from burdensome and arbitrary impositions, enjoying all the liberty that is compatible with a social state, the happiness of man is more assured here than elsewhere, I mean less exposed to the caprices of destiny. Indeed, a prosperous colonist, free from boredom by steady occupations and creative works, need fear only the intemperance of the seasons and the outrages of nature and should find himself happy, if he is wise enough to prefer an industrious, frugal, and modest life, to futile dissipations, to the dangers of ambition and laziness.

"What an inestimable advantage for our two families! Already we have formed a plan of union which will increase our power as farmers and our happiness as relatives, neighbors and friends."

Mr. E. was still talking to me of this wonderful plan when the group returned from fishing with seventeen trout. After spending an evening that was as pleasant as it was instructive, we separated with the intention of visiting the west branch the next day, and if the weather was not favorable, to go on to Niagara.

(The two chapters following were discovered to be so spotted that the translator could not read four lines in succession. It appears that long after seeing the west branch, the travelers embarked on Lake Erie, to go to Détroit and Michillimakinack.) Note by the translator.

CHAPTER XII

"The safety and ease with which you saw the east branch of the Falls last year is due to the result of a long visit made three years ago by two Russian travelers, one of whom had already traveled through the interior of the continent. It was for them that I built the Indian Ladders, which lead to the first ledge and beyond, to the last accessible point of the abyss. They disembarked at New Orleans, whence they came up the Mississippi and the Ohio as far as Louis-Ville, located 508 leagues from New Orleans. After spending three months traveling through the chief settlements of Kentucky, they arrived in Washington, county seat of Limestone District, beyond to the mouth of the great Kanhawa, where a colony of 53 families had just arrived; finally to the town of Marietta [1] on the Muskinghum, where the founders of this new state, generals Parsons, Putnam, and Varnom,[2] showed them the famous entrenched camp which, judging from the size and elevation of the trees covering it, must be very old. From the sources of this river, they easily reached those of the Cayahoga, only four miles away, whence a canoe of Wyandots took them to Lake Erie.[3] After staying a few days in their village and amusing themselves by hunting and fishing with the Indians, they went on to spend the winter in Détroit whose surrounding regions they explored as far as Sainte Claire. Toward spring, they embarked on a vessel belonging to that town, laden with pelts, maple sugar, and copper ore destined for Fort Erie where they arrived safely after having traveled from New Orleans, 912 leagues into the interior of the continent.

"Both of them were as accomplished geographers as they were artists and I believe they were sent by the Empress of Russia. It is from them that I received these beautiful sketches of the rapids and the picturesque banks of the great Kanhawa, that of the two branches of this cataract, as well as the sketch of the land between the peninsula of the Erie and the Genessee River, including the three falls that have a combined height of 212 feet. During their stay at Marietta, the secretary of this new Government gave them the plan of the former entrenched camp, on a part of which this new town was built. If one judges it by the names which milords the founders have given to the squares and streets, it will resemble a Roman town.

"During the travelers' visit, there was living in the woods, on the banks of the Prideaux River which empties into the Ontario, a family of Indians, whose chief died soon after their departure. The story of this man, once a European who had turned Winnebago, as well as his frequent conversations with these gentlemen, seemed so interesting to me that I wrote it down. Although badly written (for you see I am but a simple colonist) I think it contains some original thoughts. If you don't mind, my wife will read it."

"Delighted," we replied; "it will be adding something more to the numerous obligations we have already incurred."

"M.———, head of this family, was taken prisoner by the Winnebagos, during Braddock's campaign in 1755 and led to their main village located on an island, in the little lake which bears their name, more than 250 leagues from here. His family, hearing nothing from him, believed him dead. A long time afterward, his son came to Niagara on business; I do not know how it happened, but he learned that in this remote village there was a white man who had been kidnapped in the siege at Fort Duquesne, had been adopted and had remarried there. Although far from thinking this person might be his father, he decided to make certain and immediately he made the generous resolution to undertake this long and difficult journey, paddled by four Indians of that tribe whose language and customs he did not know.

"Having arrived in the village, they showed him the wigwam where lived the man of whom they had spoken at Niagara. Although clad in beaverskin and considerably aged, he recognized him after listening carefully and embraced him, calling him father. The latter, who had almost forgotten his native tongue, surprised at feeling himself embraced in the arms of a stranger, recoiled, stammering some words, but soon, recovering from his astonishment, he could articulate clearly enough to ask him questions concerning this curious mystery. Scarcely had his son spoken of his mother, before that name appeared to awaken something in the old man's heart, and recall to it the force of a feeling which years had not weakened. Stirred up, almost incapable of bearing up under this first confusion of a happiness so unlooked for, this conflict of emotions so sudden, eye so haggard and eager, he leaned over him and said in a trembling voice:

" 'Yes, you are the child of a woman whose memory I have always cherished; your features recall to me those of her face which neither time nor absence has been able to erase. By what inconceivable chance have you heard my name mentioned, and have you learned that I was living in this village situated in the heart of the continent, 600 leagues from the sea? How, without knowing the language of your guides, could you find your way here? Brave and inestimable young man, let me embrace you once again before my strength is spent. And tell me, is your mother still alive?'

311

" 'The Mighty One,' he replied, 'called her to his bosom three years after the time when the newspapers announced your death; she thought, as we did, that she was going to join the one of whom she spoke ceaselessly.'

"This old man, after lifting his tearful eyes toward the heaven, without uttering a word, withdrew to his bearskin.

"The next day, the Indians, whom the oddity, and the novelty of this event had united, hastened to congratulate this happy father and his noble son, shaking their hands frequently, and offering them the pipe of friendship. Such, they say, was the effect of this touching scene, that their dry eyelids were wet from it and their hearts of bronze deeply saddened: a triumph which nature rarely obtains over stubborn people who are prejudiced by their education.

"Nevertheless, humiliated by the appearance and garb of his father, dwelling like the others 'neath a smoky wigwam, this young man made every effort to persuade him to resume his European garb and to abandon his Indian family: he solemnly promised to place him comfortably among the whites and to take the finest care of him in his old age. It was all in vain.

" 'However great my happiness at having been found so miraculously by the child of my youth, never will I leave the one who cut my bonds when I was prisoner, and to whom, through adoption, I owe my life, nor from those by whom she made me a father. I feel all the strength of the prejudices which guide you, all the respect that I owe to the memory of your mother; but what would Nature say if I dared outrage her at this point as well as that inner feeling, that deaf but distinct voice which sounds off in the shadows of the night as during the light of day? I implore you, have some indulgence for an act of gratitude of which oblivion would tarnish the happiness which I owe you and for the customs that I can no longer shed. I will be no less your father, your tender father; you will be no less respected, nor less respectable in the eyes of the whole world.'

"They left, but as this old man had foreseen, no longer able to live in a closed house, nor sleep in a bed, he obtained permission to settle with his family not far from Niagara, in the direction of the springs of the Prideaux River, a region favorably located for fishing and hunting. He received his friends with all the simplicity of a true Indian, with neither chairs nor tables, offering them only a bearskin and a blanket, every time bad weather or some other reason obliged them to spend the night there. His dwelling was only a wigwam, built with a little more care than the one in which he had previously lived in the Winnebago village.

"Before leaving to make our first visit, I said to these Russians:

"Do not expect this European to be plunged in his old state of ignorance; he has become extraordinarily interesting since he re-learned his native tongue, and spends his time reading, while his children hunt and fish in order to feed him. I assure you that his clothing, his appearance, and his manners do not arouse any astonishment; that would humiliate him and would make our visit to him awkward. Never has it been demonstrated more obviously, as you will see, that one's physiognomy depends a great deal on one's kind of life; for, with the exception of the whites of his eyes in which there is no mixture of yellow whatsoever, as among the Indians, he is otherwise completely Indian.

" 'This attachment for a life as uncertain and as remote from his former ways,' Mr. Worsloff, one of the travelers told me, 'is quite strange; if it were not Mr. E. who told me about it, very certainly I should not have believed it.'

"Here," I said to the chief, "are the two travelers whom I present to you. They are Russians who, from New Orleans where they landed last year, have reached here by coming up the Mississippi and the Ohio.

" 'Little does it matter to me whence they come' he replied, 'since they are your friends. What motives,' he added, addressing the travelers, 'prompted you to undertake such a long trip?'

" 'Curiosity.'

" 'Did your own country not offer you a field vast enough to satisfy it?'

" 'There, as here, the earth is covered with snow six months of the year; there, as here, one seeks thick forests frequented by hordes who live only from the produce of their hunting and fishing.'

" 'That is true, but often one prefers things far off, because one believes them to be more interesting than those which are within reach: moreover, we obey the orders of our superiors.'

"After answering with kindness all the questions they asked him, he said to us:

" 'Since the time when the conversation of learned persons and reading of books reawakened me, and freed me from a nonthinking state, from that drowsiness of mind in which I had vegetated for so long, I feel like a man who sees his friends and the light of day again after a long lethargy. What events have taken place since 1755, the time of my departure from Scotland! How changed everything is in the Old and New World! What is this power that ceaselessly upsets nations and directs destinies of mankind? The English colonies which General Braddock had come to protect from Canadian invasion have become independent states, and their former government, England, has taken possession of Canada. The population of these colonies which then extended inland only 200 miles, has infiltrated as far as here and even beyond the Ohio; but the thing that caps my astonishment is the revolution in political and religious philosophy of one of the leading European nations, which, like a volcano, has just manifested itself in such a violent manner. Is it not to be feared that this explosion may be the prelude to long and bloody crises? Can the moment be far away when these convulsions crossing the Ocean will come to shake this Government, founded truthfully speaking, on the bases of justice and liberty, yet young and feeble? If ever this misfortune should befall, the simple, natural life I lead would repel less those who know nothing of its charms; the retreat of the woods would be considered a tranquil port in the shelter of storms. What a haven, indeed, for the victims of political dissensions would the stretch of these forests be for the independence and means of livelihood which they offer to those who inhabit them!'

" 'However violent the effects of a change which seems to me far off and doubtful,' replied Mr. Worsloff, 'can one believe that they will make themselves heard at 76° longitude?'

" 'Yes,' replied the Winnebago, 'because these new principles are extremely attractive to the multitude; because men, always discontent with their lot, hope to better it in the midst of tumult and upsets; because, like the surface of the sea, whose waves do not slacken until long after the tempest, it is impossible to foresee when the movement impressed on such a great mass will entirely cease; finally, because nations, like individuals, need discoveries that result from long testing as well as lessons in misfortune, before acquiring wisdom and experience.'

" 'After having known up to eighteen years the advantages of civilized life,' replied Mr. Worsloff, 'how can you still prefer a bark cabin to a well-furnished home, a bearskin to a bed, rather than this secure and quiet life, this uncertain, difficult one where isolated man, not knowing any of the tender principles of union and humanity, seeks his happiness in his sad and wretched independence?'

" 'Young man,' said the old man, 'learn that it takes greater strength and real courage and that there is perhaps more dignity than you think in being self-sufficient, in knowing only a few needs and in knowing how to stand sickness, hunger, and death with neither help nor consolation. It is the first state of man, the only one in which, being able to live without possessing anything, he enjoys security without the oppressive succor of laws and of independence and liberty which are restricted, without hurting anyone.'

" 'This liberty pushed to excess,' replied Mr. Worsloff, 'appears to me, on the contrary, to be a great evil, since it sterilizes the seeds of reproduction, while inspiring in these nations an invincible aversion to a sedentary life of cultivation which would increase their strength and multiply their number.'

" 'The rapid annihilation of these tribes,' said the old man, 'has come only with their trade with the whites, a trade which introduced among them a twofold poison: smallpox and intoxicating liquors. The first has already destroyed more than half the population; the second is lowering and brutalizing the rest daily. Before the discovery of the continent, there were no rivers known, on whose bank there did not live some small tribe—and they lived abundantly. Civilization is necessary only at the time when men, becoming too numerous to live by the product of their hunting and fishing, are obliged to bend to the earth, and to draw from it their livelihood. It is then when laws, subordination, the prestige of Government become indispensable. Here, each individual, like wild animals and birds, finding in his skill the means to live at the expense of nature, knows no other sacrifices but those of imperious necessity.'

" 'Yet you will agree,' replied Mr. Worsloff, 'that in this first state, man, although vigorous, is merely a wild and savage plant whose branches, for lack of cultivation, are often without flowers, and whose flowers rarely bear fruit.'

" 'What are you calling flowers without fruit?' asked the old man quickly. 'What name are you giving to this sublime sentiment which stirs them to risk their lives for the preservation of those to whom they have given life? To the attachment they have for their tribe? To their tender affection for their wives and children? To their bitter and poignant regrets when they lose them—regrets that their efforts to rise above their destinies cannot surmount? To their respect for the rights of men, for old age, for the bonds of adoption, as well as for the ashes and the memory of their ancestors?

" 'In no other people, can one find more steadfast, more faithful, nor more generous friends. Although they do not know this sensitivity which is the fruit of civilization, how many striking examples of affection, devotion, and gratitude I could cite! Strangers to the deceptive illusions of the future, to the anxieties of caution, they bear with much greater courage than the whites misfortunes, reverses, and privations; a state which seems to be that of nature, like trees, constantly exposed to storms, growing roots that are deeper than those which grow in the valleys.

" 'Do not be deceived; although plunged in what you call a state of ignorance and barbarism, how much superior they are to the common herd of Europeans! What a gap there is between the noble pride, independence, steadfastness, courage of these war-like hunters, and the baseness and vice of most of the inhabitants of the frontiers! Between the good faith, candor, self-denial of the former and the avarice, treachery, crafty deceit of the latter! Although they are not familiar with what you call social and religious virtues, go into the villages most removed from the dangerous proximity of the whites, such as the Outagami, Menomoni, and Chippeway, situated between the Mississippi* and Lake Superior; you will see there everlasting peace, and, in their families, that mild tranquility which makes the principal characteristic of their nature, although, it is true, once they are far from their villages, they are active, bold, and sometimes even wild. They are tall and agile; their limbs are muscular, robust, and well proportioned; they have the hearing, the sense of smell, and the sight of wolves. If the turn of their minds is more somber and sad than that of the white men, it comes from the forest which they inhabit, and for which they seem to have been made; yet, the young people are very fond of war dances.[4]

" 'But on the other hand,' he continued, 'they are not without their faults: from what mine can one extract a pure mineral? I know how fatal is their passion for far-off hunts and wars; how implacable their vengeance is; how atrocious their barbarism is toward prisoners whom they do not adopt. I know that their imagination is more quickly excited by the desire to destroy than by that of creating; that they attach no idea of grandeur and importance, except to their war plans and killings; that, incapable of cultivating the soil or of raising lasting monuments, their existence and their passage on earth will leave no instructive traces; that their way of life is as futile as an arrow that does not reach its target.

" 'Their mind seems empty and indeed it is, all the time when they are not busy with either hunting or fishing or war. From this springs the lack of foresight, the fickleness, and the thoughtlessness for which people reproach them; from that springs their inferiority in all the treaties they make with the white men whose dupes and victims they have been for more than a century, as if the experience of the past had had no hold on their mind, nor had ever deigned to instruct them. I also know how fatal is their insurmountable propensity for intoxicating liquors, as well as their inconceivable blindness to the tragic consequences of drunkenness, source of so many dissensions, murders, maladies, appearing to emanate from destiny.'

" 'Unless we admit,' replied Mr. Worsloff, 'that these Indians do

---

* Every time the Indians speak of the Mississippi, they designate it by the name of Cayung-Gawana—great river; in like manner, Lake Superior, Cayung-Gamineck, great lake.

not have the same degree of perfectibility as the nations of the Old World, how can we conceive that the example and the company of the white men have not taught them yet; that they scorn everything suggestive of creation and industry, as before the arrival of the whites; that they prefer exposing themselves to the fatigues of their far-off hunts, to the dangers of deadly dearth, rather than cultivating the earth, and forging iron as do their neighbors.'

" 'There is nothing more shameful,' replied the old man, "nor more dishonorable among them, than the sedentary and agricultural life. A young man who, like the others, would not spend his winters in pursuing wild deer on the snow, in trapping beavers [5] and martens, would never find a maiden who might want to blow on his torch, nor one before whom he might sing his song, however abundant his harvest of corn; he could never participate in the games in the village, nor even be present at the tribal council fires, without being exposed to the sarcasm and scorn of the warriors; his life would be filled only with disgusts and bitternesses; he would be obliged to leave the village. As to the inferiority of their intelligence and reason, perhaps it comes only from their lack of culture. It is a germ, a bud, which for lack of warmth can neither sprout nor develop. But what need do they have of this perfection? The distressing use which the great make of their knowledge daily—does it not attest to its futility?'

" 'And their wars,' replied Mr. Worsloff, 'what can be their motives, since they know neither greed nor thirst for conquest? For if peace could exist among men, it is in their isolated villages, in the heart of the forests, that, for centuries, it would have remained.'

" 'The causes of these wars,' the old man replied, 'are the eternal hatreds, vengeances, whose wounds never heal; sometimes retaliations, dreams, or even the simple desire to exercise courage, too long idle, of youth. Does history not teach us that in all times, in all countries, the first use the little as well as big countries made of their strength was to destroy one another? This deadly and inconceivable disposition which seemed to hearken back to instinct, is then the work of nature, an inevitable evil. At the time of the establishment of the Massachusetts colony in 1621, the Isle of Nantucket, in the vicinity of Cape Cod, had scarcely 200 fishing Indians! Well, this little nation was divided into two parts which carried on implacable war, the motive of which no one was ever able to discover, so frivolous was it. Every place on this planet life is, like the Ocean, exposed to the fury and ravages of storms: just like the nations of Europe and Asia, these tribes are dragged down by the sway of their passions, by the stream of chance and events.

" 'When reading history,' he continued, 'one comes on only a few intervals from time to time, when civilization may have contributed to the happiness of mankind, and these epochs passed quick as lightning. What was the plight of the human race under the long tyranny of the Caesars (two or three excepted) and under that of their successors as late as 1453? What was that of Europe during so many centuries of ignorance and servitude? How much Asia suffered under the destructive sword of the fierce Tamberlane! Which would it have been better to be then: Tartar or European, Mohawk or Shawanese?

" 'As long as these Indians can live from their hunting and fishing, never will they submit to culture; their invincible prejudices constantly contradict each other; the tribes which still exist will disappear like those that lived along the sea coasts, or will withdraw into the heart of the continent as the European colonies approach their regions— quite different in that respect from men of the Old World. Without any taste for work and sedentary occupations, the march of time is nothing for them, and yet they know how to divide it.⁶ Returning from their great hunts, they often spend days, whole weeks, peace pipes in their mouths, eyes on the ground, in a state of empty gazing and silence. Yet they know no boredom, an evil so common among civilized nations. To the fatigues of these hunts, which they make a point of honor at bearing up under, succeeds the most absolute repose; the privations, which a little caution would lessen, are followed by abundance. Such is the narrow circle of their activity, their desires, their happiness, founded as you see, on their aversion to everything which represents anxiety, or disturbance over the future.'

" 'One must admit,' said Mr. Worsloff, 'they are happy with little; nevertheless it is difficult to conceive how so many generations of human beings endowed with intelligence and will power have been able to exist for centuries without there having appeared in the midst of some a superior genius who, instructed by experience or chance, may have sought to enlighten them, give them some habits, some new ideas. Those, for example, of taming the buffalo in their savannahs, cultivating rice which grows right under their eyes, of forging the iron over which they walk, of looking cautiously during the abundance of summer to the dearth of winter, a forethought which the beavers, the squirrels, the bees, and the ants know; someone who might have made known to them some of the illusions of hope. What then is life among your compatriots? A night without the slightest twilight, a sleep without dreams, a river which neither ebbs nor flows, whose stagnant waters never quench the thirst.'

" 'Quite different from the animals,' replied the old man, 'who invariably are born without hope of any change, man, you know, is nothing until he has been shaped, fashioned by environment, example, and education. According to the kind of life of which I have just given you a slight idea, what can be the active faculties of these hunters, their habitual dispositions, as well as the exercise of their intelligence? Have I myself not experienced how much their energy becomes feeble and slackens in this state of numbness?'

" 'Ah well,' replied Mr. Worsloff, 'how can it happen, then, that in the midst of this numbness, the same individual, so mild and quiet in his village, can be so active and ferocious in war, as well as in the pursuit of his revenge?'

" 'Perhaps,' replied the Indian, 'man was born vindictive and ferocious, or perhaps he became like that through necessity and habit. But how can one analyze a creature as self-contradictory, who now raises himself to the sublimity of the highest virtues, and now descends to the lowest degree of vice—to the most atrocious crime; a being, a creature whose nature takes pleasure in being an Attila or a Marcus Aurelius, an imbecile or a Newton?'

" 'What means,' asked Mr. Worsloff, 'can old men and chiefs use to inspire in their warriors the astonishing courage with which they withstand torments when they have the misfortune to fall into the hands of their enemies?'

" 'By education and example,' replied the Winnebago: 'it is in this way that Brahmins are made, and here tigers and cannibals; they show their children how to make nets, and harpoon fish, to set a snare, make war on their enemies, as the spider does on the flies; to consider as a sacred duty astonishing their enemies by their steadfastness and courage, and give them thus a great conception of the heroism of the nation. This prejudice is so deeply rooted, that they regard as dishonorable those who have let themselves be adopted. That is why they no longer dare return to their villages where they would experience only shame and scorn. A warrior, they say, must consider adoption as a weakness; he must refuse it with disdain and prefer to die singing his song of death.'

" 'How powerful must this education be when it stifles the voice of nature and of instinct!' said Mr. Worsloff.

" 'The old martyrs—have they not given us a lot of similar samples?' answered the Winnebago.

" 'Speaking of adoption,' the traveler told him, 'how can it happen that an enemy whom one is about to devour may suddenly become a parent, a friend, and that this adopted one might fill with so much faith his new duties? Whence comes this astonishing contradiction between the mildness with which they treat the prisoners destined for the kettle and the hellish cruelty they make them endure? [7] What is the source of pleasure which they appear to experience when the voice of their wretched captives, stifled by the excesses of pain, can no longer make itself heard; [8] and that of their yelpings of triumph at the sight of the convulsive movements and of the last agonies of their victims? Such an excess of blindness and ferocity, worthy of Milton's demons— can it emanate from the heart of human beings? On the other hand, whence comes the inflexible courage which these wretched beings exhibit, and the perseverance with which they excite the rage of their executioners to their last sigh? [9] This astonishing mixture of magnanimity and barbarism, of mildness and inhumanity, would it be an attribute necessary to the primitive life, of that state of the hunter? The mind loses itself amid the ideas which these gloomy meditations provoke.'

" 'I am scarcely learned enough,' replied the old man, 'to answer these questions: I think that if you proposed them to the philosophers of the Old World, they would be as puzzled as I: for it is neither in books nor in the midst of society so ancient in origin that one can know man as he was when he sprang from the hands of nature. In books, it happens that truth was often sacrificed for theories, or else authors did not have enough experience to see things clearly. As to civilized man, like a river once impetuous, held in for centuries by strong dikes, he is merely the work of laws of the Government and a thousand other forces. It is to New Holland they should go, it is there that they must come to study him in all his primitive instincts; then their reason, or perhaps their self-love, would stiffen less against the form of institutions; obstacles without whose help great societies, like a torrent without dikes, would fall again into the chaos of anarchy toward which they have a continual tendency.'

" 'Do you believe them,' asked Mr. Worsloff, 'as happy in that primitive state as if they were in a more advanced stage of civilization?'

" 'Yes, I think so; perhaps they are even happier; for if on the one hand, they know only a small number of needs, pleasures, enjoyments, on the other, they are much less exposed to the disturbances of caution, to the worries of foresight, reverses and real misfortunes as well as those of imagination, whose illusions and prestiges, often agreeable, never so much as occurred to them. Contact with the white man produced no effect. In vain, missionaries have tried to urge them to agricultural pursuits through hope of abundance and repose. In vain, they raised some of their children to the age of 15 or 16: on returning to their villages, they soon forgot everything they had learned and denounced the opinions in which they had been raised.' [10]

" 'And cannibalism,' replied Mr. Worsloff, 'where did these Indians get their first notion of it? How does it happen that their notion of devouring their fellow men did not inspire in them an insurmountable horror?'

" 'The source of this inclination which one cannot realize,' replied the old man, 'springs no doubt from our organization, since it has been known in all nations, and they have not ceased being cannibalistic until after domesticating the animals and cultivating the land. Some attribute it to the furies of vengeance: others more reasonably to the gnaw of hunger. Indeed, when one considers that dissensions of war must have preceded the discovery and cultivation of rice, fruit of a slow process, one imagines that the starved conquerors must have devoured the victims, as the flesh-eating animals eat their prey. Yet the tribal chants [11] bear witness that this horrible custom was founded only on the pride of victory, whose reward consisted in devouring and swallowing his enemy.'

" 'Would not man,' replied Mr. Worsloff, 'have been destined only for brigandage then and war? Alas! That appears to be too reasonable. Let him whose conceit refuses to believe consult the ancient archives of the world, let him read the history of these Colonies and if he is still unconvinced, let him go to Botany Bay, to New Zealand, to the land of the Papous; he will see what has been the clumsy origin of the Papous; he will see what has been the clumsy origin of nations today so learned and so refined. Like the crude diamond, opaque and uncut, that cannot give forth its light, and sparkles only after being shaped, cut, and polished, it is only at the time when man became civilized that he merited this name, that he came to know fear and hope, that he began to lift his eyes toward the heavens, beautify the land, and by means of grafting, make the trees of the forest bear wild, delicious fruits and make the plants sprout the seeds which give us food; it is at this time, forever memorable, that he learned to taste the sweetness of peace, to feel the usefulness of laws and subordination, and finally to know morality, honor and integrity.'

" 'I do not see,' replied the old man, 'what he has gained in this new state, since, despite the help of science and the arts, despite the knowledge of what one calls philosophy, he has been unable to repress his leanings and his baleful passions, eternal source of wars and of jealousy. Has he enjoyed peace and abundance during long intervals? The population is greatly increased; and as a result, man's food was difficult to obtain, he saw himself more exposed to the ravages of epidemics and famines, and to the dangers of revolutions. I doubt that the common herd of civilized nations is as happy as the inhabitants of the forests: look at the unhappy plight of the Chinese people!'

" 'What are we to think of human nature?' queried Mr. Worsloff.

" 'It is an unexplainable problem,' replied the Winnebago, 'as well as so many others which confront us. Well, despite the disasters caused by wars, cannibalism, and want, these nations were much more numerous at the time of the discovery of the continent than they are today. Armed with a tomahawk, these men were, it is true, bloodthirsty tigers, hungry for the flesh of their enemies; but returned to their villages, they resumed their mildness, that peace of mind which is natural to them. If, on the one hand, the settlement of the white men caused the disappearance of their sources of war; on the other hand, it introduced among them the scourge of smallpox and that of intoxicating liquors whose ravages are so frightful to the persons interested in their plight. Rarely today does one see any of them reach an advanced age; they experience sickness, infirmities which had been unknown to them previously; that is what these nations gained by mingling with the white men.'

" 'Finally,' said Mr. Worsloff, 'since they have continually closed their eyes and ears to so many examples and so much advice, would it not be better if they were replaced by a population of intelligent, hardworking men, who busied themselves in clearing, in beautifying this continent so long unproductive?'

" 'And by what right have the white men come to poison these tribes of hunters, to seize their heritage? Were they not separated from it by a vast sea?'

" 'By what right, you ask. By that one which directs everything on earth and in the universe: by that of the strongest. This new part of the world, is it not destined to become one-fourth of the theatre on which will appear the same consequences of wars, revolutions, happiness, calamities, and glory that took place in the old world? When civilization of the latter and that of New Holland is complete, the plenitude of things will have been reached; catastrophes like those that preceded history and of which there remains to us only an obscure tradition, will upset the seas, will tear the surface of continents, and will bury under their debris the greater portion of the human race.

" 'To some families who have escaped this universal shipwreck will be born new nations, who, after stagnating in ignorance and barbarism for a great number of centuries, will, in their turn, become refined, learned, and aggressive. Such is perhaps the eternal chain of our destinies, and the succession of the great epochs of nature, which needs these long intervals of rest in order to form a new soil, conceive and develop new seeds.' "

CHAPTER XIII

During my long stay in Virginia in the inland counties of Bath and Botetour, located between the chain of mountains known as the Blue Ridge and those of Alleghany, where several years ago were discovered salutary salt baths, I made the acquaintance of several officers of the continental army whom honorable wounds, received while fighting for the independence of their country, obliged to visit these baths every year. These regions, far from the sea, so interesting because of the abundance of different minerals, the beauty of natural flowers, as well as the fertility of the soil and the gigantic stature of the inhabitants, will some day be the most beautiful part of this state. One can easily believe that in a country still so new, communications are very imperfect, lodgings crude: but when one considers the extent of Virginia in relation to its present population and the time of its first colonization, one is invariably less surprised at what has not been done than at what has already been accomplished.[1]

These baths are only 50 miles from Natural Bridge, a marvel, seen and admired only by a small number of Europeans, and 70 miles from the town of Fincastle, county seat of Botetour, founded in 1790. It is advantageously situated on the road which goes from Virginia to Tennessee by way of the Holston River and to Kentucky through the valley of the Powel and the Cumberland. Not even six years ago, this route, scarcely tracked, was extremely dangerous; no one could undertake this journey except in well-armed caravans, because of the bandits of Ouasioto and those of the valleys of Cowee and Chota, who were much to be feared at the time. Since then, progress of settlements has been so rapid that today mail goes through there regularly; it is the third route from the seaboard states to the trans-Alleghanian countryside.

It is also the one used by the numerous immigrants who arrive every year from the shores of the sea, as well as from the different states of the Union. During my stay at Fincastle, I talked with several heads of families who told me they had left Europe with the intention of settling there: they had disembarked at Alexandria on the Potawmack, and, guided by hope, they traveled with gaiety, a fact that surprised me a little considering that, as foreigners, they knew no one in the countryside where they were going. I told them my impression.

"It is true," they replied, "but is it not everyone's country since there is still so much room, and since nine-tenths of the land is not even inhabited yet? Moreover, knowing how rare craftsmen are, we are sure to obtain through our industry what we could not hope for in Europe, where every job is taken; a place of our own with a hearth, and land that will belong to us and will be taken from us only by the Government and law; this is what caused us to abandon the village in which we were born, our relatives, our friends, and the companions of our childhood. Consider the power of such a motive; for however wretched one is, it is impossible to leave forever one's native land and neighbors, without a great and deep wrench; but when one has a wife and children, when absolute necessity orders it, one would go to Botany Bay in order to get for them bread and the comforts of life. So far, divine providence has been very kind to us.

"In one of our morning excursions, General Howe said to me, 'Do you see that old man, accompanied by two young men whose carriage passed us going down the mountains? Well, he is the patriarch of Orange County in the northern part of South Carolina; he comes here every year, not to seek youth, as at the fountain of Jouvence, but to mitigate the approach of his decline. Yesterday in speaking about the Cherokees, I gave you some details about their manner of living, and about the abundant resources which they find in the woods; well, this old man, in order to avoid the fury and the plunder of the English during the war, had the courage to leave his fine farm and to live in the forests in the company of one of his Negroes who had long been prisoner with these Indians, and he had the good fortune to find there the same resources. Like the patriarchs of ancient times, he abandoned his home, his fields and, accompanied by all his animals and his people, he wandered to the foot of the great Alleghany mountains, from the frontiers of Georgia to those of Virginia. This long and odd pilgrimage from North Carolina was crowned with success for neither he nor any member of his family experienced any accidents during these four long years.[2] The young men with him are his grandsons, born beneath a tree in one of their winter camping places.

" 'Let us meet him,' he continued, 'ere long you will discover how interesting he is and how delighted he will be to answer the questions you ask him, especially those relating to what he calls his patriarchal life. What a pity that he refused to have printed the interesting diary of this long journey which, they say, is filled with botanical observations, of certain insects that are found nowhere else, and of several other extremely new matters: they say he is going to make a copy of it and send it to General Washington. The face of this elderly colonist inspires respect; the harmony of his voice, the smoothness of his speech awaken the keenest interest. I know of no one who tells stories with so much style, a talent that he owes to his excellent education and to his former travels in Europe.'

" 'Here,' General Howe said to him, 'is a stranger whom I present to you. He comes from the states in the north where he lived several years before the Revolution. Delighted at the happy opportunity that brings him the pleasure of knowing you, he would like you to tell him how you succeeded in feeding your family and your cattle during four years in the midsts of these forests. Being a European, he has only a faint inkling of such a way of life.'

" 'Gladly,' he replied, 'but here we are; let us dine together. I need some relaxation; my old memory will be refreshed by it; besides, nothing brings men closer together than drinking and eating together. And then, shall I confess it to you? I need everything that can contribute toward making my modest little story interesting from a stranger's viewpoint.

" 'Despite my advanced age and the infirmities that prohibited me from uniting my efforts with those of my compatriots in helping them to repel the unjust pretentions of our haughty Mother Country, I confess, I saw with a mixture of satisfaction and fright the moment of the bloody struggle which was to decide our destiny, because I was convinced that being united, and 1,200 leagues from Europe, we would be invincible, and that the independence of these states, however dearly bought, would reward us for our sacrifices. Aided by the generous help of France, we succeeded, and praise God! I lived to see the day! I had two sons old enough to bear arms; they were among the first to serve under the continental flag; I assumed the care of their wives. War broke out; you must know with what furor and animosity the enemy waged it in this state, as well as in Georgia. In the second year, frightened by the stories of their cruel plunderings, I resolved to abandon my plantation, and go live at the foothills of the Alleghanies, a region whose topography was well known to one of my slaves. For this undertaking I had four wagons built, filled with provisions, wearing apparel, linen, salt, iron, farming implements, a portable smithy, everything, in a word, that wisdom and foresight suggested to me. Aware that even in the most remote wilderness, one would sometimes meet isolated families, rich in corn and pork, but in great want of clothing, I supplied myself with everything I could think of which would serve as items of exchange.

" 'Finally after entrusting ourselves to the protection of Heaven, accompanied by my household, black and white, numbering nineteen persons, with four mules fully packed, as many colts, eighteen cows, one bull, four heifers, and five yoke of oxen, I left on April 15, 1778.

My departure was not without the bitterest regrets for my fine paternal heritage, located on the banks of the upper Saluda, and I plotted my route toward the sources of the Pacolet, a good-sized creek which springs from one of the main passes of the chain of mountains known as White Oak, where I hoped to arrive before the season for planting corn was over. We journeyed in easy stages, following as closely as possible the beds of the rivers, then very low, whose banks were almost always grassy, good grazing for our cattle. The wagons never left the forests, where we met no difficulties other than those of crossing creeks and streams; but with the help of our axes, our oxen, and our horses, we easily forded them. When the slope of their banks was too steep, we built bridges or rafts. After fourteen days' journey we arrived without mishap on the banks of the Pacolet, where we found in abundance "Bottom Lands," the very best for the cultivation of corn. While we busied ourselves planting, our cattle grazed on nearby slopes, where they found grassy shoots and succulent weeds in great abundance. The milk and butter we made seemed to me to surpass what we had made back home. What a magnificent settlement could have been made in this valley—so cool, so fertile, and so well watered! They say that since the end of the war our people have gone beyond these mountains. This does not astonish me in the slightest.

" 'But scarcely had we planted our corn, potatoes, and beans when extremely alarming circumstances obliged us to abandon this haven hastily. I thought I was lost—with no resources: yet the danger waned and we were able to return in the autumn and peacefully harvest our crops which the abundance of weeds and the deer had considerably damaged. We spent that summer, ever-memorable for us, near the sources of the Catawbaw, at the foot of the mountains of Monttigu, where we found natural prairies: [2A] they are located 126 miles from the Pacolet, in a northeasterly direction.

" 'Alone, isolated amid these vast solitudes, as witnesses to our labors, we had only the mild and harmonious meadow lark, the jay, the frolicsome boblink, the striped starling, the bold Kingfish,[3] the catbird with his piercing shriek, and the thrushes with their soft and melodious tones.[4] As to the mockingbird or rather the imitator[5] in order to get him to sing, all we had to do was to stop our work and heap our admiration on him. These birds, knowing nothing of man's destructive powers, were always around us and appeared to regard us more as objects of curiosity than of terror. Every evening, as soon as the sun had set, great flocks of cranes, with eyes as piercing as those of the eagle, slowly rose in regular and majestic spirals, as though to catch another glimpse of that luminary whose reflected rays through their whitish wings seemed to reach us sometimes. They swooped down again, in the same order and in the same silence over the places they had left. This interesting and almost daily spectacle lasted more than a half hour (when the weather was calm).[6] It was in this beautiful solitude that we spent our first winter. I had a spacious and attractive cabin built near one of the largest oaks I had ever seen; there my two daughters bore the children who wanted to accompany me here and to whom, in memory of their birth place, I gave the names Pacolet and Nawassa, names of the branches at the confluence of which I had built the cabin.

" 'I must admit, under a more disturbing sky, on a soil less abundant than Bottom Lands and savannahs, I would never have dared to undertake such a pilgrimage, because we would have had to have what we plainly could not have in another place; warmer houses and warmer wearing apparel, and our cattle we would have exposed to many more needs, sufferings, and miseries. Yet do not imagine that we did not often experience great difficulties; but what can one not conquer with firm and courageous resolution, inspired by the most powerful motive in the heart of a good father, that of contributing to the safety and happiness of his family! For everyone, except my two eldest sons, had accompanied me. Our life was simple and frugal; we knew no nourishment other than pork, corn prepared in divers manners, and whatever fishing and hunting brought us, which was sometimes a superabundance. The stream water that quenched the animals' thirst also quenched ours. How agreeably surprised was I when, instead of somber and savage outlooks, I noticed that the ledges of this vast amphitheatre offered, on the contrary, a fertile soil, to judge by the plants and high trees covering it, and the mild, cool retreats in which I would settle with pleasure! How I felt my imagination soar when my eyes roved over these vast savannahs, filled with beautiful reeds, surrounded by majestic forests; and these innumerable streams, the source of the rivers which water the southern states with their slopes, meanderings, and cascades, presenting at every moment the most bizarre and picturesque sights! Ah, if I had been a painter or a poet, what scenes I could have captured from this enchanting nature! Some day—and it is not far off—this superb region that borders the foothills of the mountains and whose length is more than nine hundred miles will become the richest country in this hemisphere: under such a soft sky, it enjoys the most beautiful gift that nature has been able to lavish on it, being equally remote from the burning plains of the coastal section of these states and the rigorous winters one experiences in the north.

" 'After planting our corn in the spring on the lowlands whose weeds we destroyed during the winter, abandoning our fields to nature until autumn, we left for the regions that I knew to be abundant in pasture land: rarely did we travel more than four miles a day.

" 'While one part of my family went ahead with the wagons to choose a suitable site and set up camp, the other was busy hunting or fishing, often at considerable distance. In the evening, after arriving at a pre-arranged spot, which was always on the bank of a stream, at the sound of the horn, my cattle returned to our fire and spent the night there as though they were being shut up in a park; from hour to hour two of my people, accompanied by some dogs, made the rounds. Such was the safeguard under which we slept a sleep so peaceful that we might have been in the bosom of the best-policed city.

" 'Well, this errant life, though exposed to so many inconveniences, has its charms nevertheless, not only for the Indians, but also for a great number of inhabitants of our frontier. The absolute independence from all manner of restraint; the small number of desires, rarely carried beyond our prime needs; the foresight, source of instinctive happiness that this way of life brings, and which, moreover, appears to be that for which nature had destined us; the custom of finding in the immensity of the forests, and in our own skill, inexhaustible resources: such are, I believe, some of the causes of this irresistible attraction that I had scarcely been able to foresee, but of which I had often heard. The Indians are so strongly attached to this way of life that, for more than a century, the example of our industry has been futile to them and it has been impossible for us to persuade them that cultivation was preferable to hunting.

" 'This primitive state is not less attractive to the Europeans who have lived for a long time among them. The subjection that our customs and laws exacts, that dependence which necessarily exists among all members of the social world, seems to them to be fetters that they cannot bear. They are irrevocably lost for their region and family. I have heard tell of a young Scottish officer, who was made prisoner by the Indians in 1755, and not freed until 1763; not having found in Europe the fortune that he flattered himself was there, he returned here, rejoined his new compatriots, and has lived since that time among them. I got this story from one of the judges of the Supreme Court of New York, Mr. George Ludlow, in whose home this officer had twice found lodgings. I would be curious to know what the savants and philosophers of Europe would think of this retrogression.

" 'But for fear of boring you with more specific details, I will content myself with telling you that I spent my second year near the headwaters of the Yadkin, not far from the boundary line, traced in 1749, separating Virginia from North Carolina, where I never walked 500 steps without coming upon a beautiful stream; the third year I spent near the sources of the Dan, located between the Ararat mountains and those of the Prairie mountain, named thus because of the vast savannahs surrounding them.

" 'This region is well known to our geographers, because of the celebrated passage of the great Kanhawa, swollen from the waters of the Green Briar, through the chain of Alleghanies and Ouasioto. On what an immense scale has nature worked these chasms! What efforts! what power, to speak in mortal terms. How small and helpless one seems when, in the shadow of the cedars that crown the promontories of the neighborhood, one contemplates at leisure these vast and sublime works! By how many different thoughts one's mind is besieged! Niagara Falls, Natural Bridge, the passage of the Potawmack and the Shenandoah through the Blue Mountains, that of the Delaware through the mountains of Kittatiny, the fall of the Potawmack from the top of the Ouasioto chain over a space of 30 miles, are monuments that attest to a great power and whose sight alone commands admiration and respect. When population and agriculture have reached this beautiful region, the philosopher, the geologist, tired from the tumult of the towns, will come to relax in these remote retreats, to contemplate at leisure these great marvels of earthly nature.

" 'A great many rivers spring from the bosom of these heights, so beautiful because of the majestic forests with which they are covered, so imposing because of their mass, neither desert-like nor sterile. Some of them, such as the Holston, the Clink, the Kallamako, the Tenezee, the two Kanhawa, etc., empty into the Gulf of Mexico, 800 leagues away. Others, such as the Catawba, the Yadkin, the Hawe, the Staunton, the Roanoke, the Fluvana, the Potawmack, etc., flow into the ocean along Carolina and the Chesapeake Bay. This fine region is the Tartarie of the northern states.

" 'Our walks and our encampments were regulated according to the seasons and according to the knowledge we had of the land and the position of the enemy. When we learned that they had reached Guilford, we withdrew to the peace of Mount Ararat. It was then that we experienced among the Moravian Brothers of Wachovia [7] the most touching wave of generosity and hospitality; without this unexpected help, we would have been obliged, in order to live, to kill some of our cattle, to which we had become extremely attached, from the time when the experience and dangers we had shared had made them infinitely more interesting than when they were in my fields at Saluda.

" 'I learned sometime after my return that during this campaign we had often been surrounded by dangers; but as we were then un- aware of it, we had been spared any worry. In my home I was supreme head; but as soon as I became a dweller in the forest, I established democratic government; each had his voice: the black as well as the white. I was merely the executor of the will of the majority, and every- one submitting to it believed he was having his own way! But I must confess, had my family been more numerous, I would have modified this form a bit, having had the opportunity to observe that wisdom does not always come from the greatest number of voters. If I had not been prey to the cruelest anxieties for the success of our weapons, on which hung the liberty and independence of our country, I would have enjoyed perpetual happiness, by securing that of my people who were so dear to me. Yet in the midst of these alarms, these almost daily raids, serenity, union, and sometimes even gaiety reigned under our roof.

" 'I had brought along books of history, travel, and botany. These we read during our winter evenings, by the light of bear tallow tapers. There are few bushes and plants in these regions that I do not know. What a study they will offer some day to learned men and to botanists! My teacher was one of my Negro slaves who had lived for a long time among the Cherokees of Chota. I made a great collection of plants and a good-sized collection of minerals, stones, and—would you believe it? —sea life. There exists a mass of evidence that all the lands, especially in the northern states, from the mountains to the sea, emerged from the sea; everywhere at 20 or 30 feet depth, one finds a soil whose odor alone betrays its origin; and above this soil, branches, tree trunks, and even leaves. One of my neighbors saves acorns in their pods, which he found while digging a well; but the most convincing proof of the long sojourn of the sea as far inland as 200 miles from its present shores is an elevation estimated at 70 feet and 7 or 8 miles wide, stretch- ing 60 miles, entirely formed with oyster shells. Whence came this immense deposit? What is even more astonishing is the shape and dimensions of these oysters: they are 15 or 20 inches long, 6 or 8 wide, and 2 to 3 inches thick. The lime that one makes from them is of an excellent quality. This plateau is found in Georgia, not far from Augusta.

" 'I knew very well that without a flourishing agriculture, there could never be any trade, but never before had I observed in as obvious a manner how necessary a free tariff is to arouse and stimulate agri- cultural activity and how much the rapid progress of our settlements is due in part to the prosperous state of our coastal trade. As I had foreseen, we often met families who were entirely isolated, whom backward customs, chance, or insatiable desire to better themselves had led into the depths of the woods. Although settled on the most fertile soil, although surrounded by cattle, enjoying at once the treasures of nature and the resources of agriculture, they offered only the reflection of discouragement, misery, and abandon, because it was impossible for them to trade what they had in excess for the things they needed most. Of all the items we had fetched with us, some empty bottles excited their interest and desires most quickly. Indeed, a thing is precious only when one has a pressing need of it, and when it is difficult to procure. I exchanged them as well as other objects for corn and pork. I dare not tell you what I received in exchange for a single bottle or a pin; yet we profited reciprocally.

" 'During the four years of my pilgrimage, I think I traveled nearly 600 miles, without anyone in my family being sick for a moment, so healthful are the mountains! Nevertheless it was time for peace negotiations; our patience, our courage, and our provisions were exhausted. Finally in May 1782 with unutterable pleasure, I returned to my home whose devastation and plunder two old servants had been unable to prevent. What joy was theirs at seeing us again, and finding us healthy, and noting that the family had increased by seven, two whites and five Negroes as well as 54 new beasts!'

"But what did you do to prevent your cattle from straying off during the night?" I asked. "Were they under the safeguard of your dogs?"

" 'Not at all,' he replied. 'They were safeguarded by their own instincts, which, in the woods, acquires a degree of perfection that is really extraordinary. At the first sound of the horn, all of them return to the "headquarters." The same is true of animals as of mankind: they are formed at the school of danger and experience.'

"I cannot imagine," I remarked, "how animals who graze night and day in immense forests, can fail to wander, however perfect their instinct.

" 'We have a special means of attaching them to us, causing them to love us and follow us.'

"What is it?

" 'Making them happy.'

"What can you do beyond turning them out to pasture?

" 'Give them something that acts on them like a charm.'

"Are you the only person who is acquainted with this charm?

" 'There is no colonist who does not know it.'

"Since every colonist knows it, there will be no indiscretion in asking you what it is, I suppose.

" 'Assuredly not; it will give me great pleasure to explain it to you; but, in order to be more precise; and to be able to tell you everything; tomorrow I will tell you what I wrote on that subject in the course of my nomadic existence; for it was then that experience put the seal to the instruction it gave me. If this little collection of observations appeared interesting enough so that you think you would like to bother making a copy, I have no objection; but in reading it, remember that a chief shepherd is not a writer.' "

CHAPTER XIV

(From my camp on the southern branch of the Roanoke May 24, 1779)

"The custom of giving salt to animals from time to time, practiced from Nova Scotia to the Mississippi, is as old as the settling of these states. The need, the desire of others to eat salt appears to be irresistible. It is with this bait that the colonists lead into the pasture lands the horses and the oxen necessary to them. With this very bait, they lead them out of the woods, taming those that have lived there for a long time, to a point where the animals become attached to them, follow them, and finally obey their every wish.

"In the midst of forests, in the bosom of mountains, the colonists build fences, attracting these animals gradually toward inhabited places. Not only does the salt preserve their health, but it raises their spirits when they are sad or downcast. However far away they may be, as soon as this driving desire, or rather this thirst seizes them, guided by infallible instinct, they know how to find their way back to the dwelling they left, and that way is always the shortest. That fact is so true that a great number of the routes that cross and link the different districts of the county in which I live were originally (that is, 40 years ago) mere paths blazed by animals that filled the forests then.

"This need is common to animals of European origin, as well as to the animals of our forests. A short time after their arrival, the early colonists discovered salt licks whose surfaces the stags and the bears, the moose and the elk often came to lick. They noticed also that in satisfying this common need, the animals would forget their natural antipathy, as often happens among the different species of fish and crocodiles, every time they met one another in the transparent waters off eastern Florida.[1] It is to their wisdom on this score that we owe the discovery of various sources [2] from which today is made the salt necessary to the inhabitants of the new trans-Alleghanian states.

"This appetite for salt does not manifest itself only among the four-footed creatures; countless flocks of wood-pigeons come twice yearly to swarm our countrysides and fill our forests, in their flight from the interior of the continent to the shores of the sea, where they go to sate their appetites. Let anyone judge of the power of the attraction which causes them to undertake a journey of more than a thousand miles!

"Although our cattle who live nearly all year at liberty are rarely sick, they are sometimes subject to upsets and to what we call melancholy: at such a time we must often give them a little more salt than usual, and mix with it some sulphur pulverized with antimony. My favorite panacea for my horses is assafoetida which long experience has taught me is very healthful for them. It is to the owner of the huge iron works at Ringwood, who used a great deal of it, that I owe this remedy.

"In order to judge of the indispensable necessity of giving salt to cattle, one must watch how their dispositions change when they have been deprived of it for a long time. It is astonishing. I have seen mild, peaceful cows, that at one time no fences could restrain; like bulls, they roared, crossed fences and ditches, appeared to have lost all idea of obedience and submission; and the remarkable thing is that their milk no longer gave any butter, that is to say, it was impossible to make, however long one churned.

"As far as the horses were concerned, they often stop in the middle of their work, with restive air, excited, watching their leader with intent eyes; it is impossible not to guess what they want. The most timid, feeble sheep bleat in plaintive tones, refuse to go in the fields, and even lose their fleece. Nothing is more pitiful than to see a flock that has been deprived a long time of its salt.

"The pig is the only animal which is insensitive to this attraction; yet, during the period of his fattening, salt is indispensable in flavoring his swill; without salt, he becomes bored with what he eats, eats less and consequently fattens slowly.

"Saturday is ordinarily the day of feeding salt to the pigs. No matter how far off the animals are in the woods, it is rare when they do not appear on that day. Some colonists scatter salt by hand at intervals over grassy terrain; others on flat stones. The best method is to have squared timber, on whose upper surfaces holes are dug out one or two feet apart, and filled with salt; but one must take care to put these trees or stones in a spacious place, because at the time of sating their appetites, it might happen that the stronger would wound the weaker. So keen is this appetite, which, despite the instinct by which each member of a herd knows his own strength, and consequently the precedence he must accord his superiors, the youngest, who are also the lightest, dare to arrive at the salt first; it is then when the right of the strongest, arbiter of small as well as great events, exercises itself in full force. As to the salting of sheep, that must always be done in a separate place, unless, having chased away the larger animals, what is left of their supply is sufficient for the sheep. Happy and content, the latter spend whole hours before feeling any desire to go out to pasture.

"Salt, especially during the warm seasons, seems to be necessary to all breathing life. One day, having noticed that my bees would often light at places where some old pickled brine had been laid out, I put a few morsels in front of their bee-hives, and what was my astonishment on discovering that they swarmed around it several times and then took it off with them! I would never have been able to believe, before this observation, that the manufacturers of honey would have tasted with pleasure an ingredient so different from the stamen of flowers.

"One must have lived longer than I, isolated in the midst of forests, surrounded by a great number of cattle of all ages, as their master and their friend, in order to know the changes of character resulting from the habit or deprivation of salt; it is then that animals show their true character, and then when it is easy to study them. Words fail me in trying to describe how amusing and instructive it is to watch them every day, to live and, one might say, converse with them, to govern them by making oneself loved, yet feared by them. The slavery, the solitude, the harshness with which the Europeans treat them, have abused them, degraded them, to the extent where they are not even the same interesting creatures, where they do not even have the same intelligence. They have lost those original characteristics, and that perfectibility so strikingly theirs. One must see them free in the fields, even freer in our forests, where they spend a part of their lives; it is there where experience develops their faculties, and where in several circumstances, instinct has appeared to me to raise them to the level of reason.

"Just as with us, creatures endowed with this prime faculty of reason, they have passions, that is to say, appetites which arouse these passions, desires, understanding among themselves, above all in great flocks; as a result there are nuances of character; just as with men, they experience rancor, jealousy, the pleasure of domination; the strongest feel their superiority and abuse it; the weaker are duped, timid, fearful; the former are imperious, arrogant; the others, slow, foxy, continually on their guard. Without a special surveillance, or the use of subdivisions in their yards, the latter would die of hunger. Horses, more susceptible to reason and more generous, are much less prone to invade the property of their neighbors: moreover, each of them, knowing his name, makes restraint of them easier by talking.

"Six dogs accompanied me in my wanderings. One would doubt my veracity, if I dared tell the degree of perfection to which this new way of life had raised their intelligence. Taking turns, two of them kept watch every night with one of my men. When my children ventured into the woods, my dogs never failed to accompany them, in the fear that they might wander. A stag which we had wounded went 17 miles from our camp to die; they followed him, came to tell us about his death and led us to the place where he had fallen.[3] Is an animal as respectable as a wicked man? Is not the gift of an intelligence so sure, so infallible, a more striking proof of goodness and creative power, than reason which has so often occasioned evil on earth, through the horrible abuse that has been made of it?

"Salt is an absolute necessity for governing cattle. But what of the colonist who, for lack of fenced pasture land, entrusts his horses and cattle to the vast stretch of neighboring woods at night? Guided by their tracks, he listens attentively until he hears the noise of the bell on the leader. As soon as he sees them, he calls them, hand outstretched; aroused by the stimulus of salt, they obey his voice, approach and follow him to his dwelling, where, while they lick the salt through, some are harnessed, others yoked. And some years later, when this same colonist has succeeded in fencing some fields, how, among a great number of cattle and heifers, will he be able to catch the ones he needs? For often it takes only one, either less trusting, or less docile than the others, to give the alarm and put them all to flight. Will he be obliged to call his family for help? No. Supplied with a handful of salt or an ear of corn, he enters his field, stands still and calls them; quickly they surround him; then he directs his bait toward the one he needs, gets a hold on him gently while the animal feeds; what will appear perhaps more extraordinary to you is that children all alone are often given this responsibility.

"Nevertheless it sometimes happens that, having learned by experience, the old horses and oxen are not duped by all this—especially when they see the yoke or the bridle; then, it behooves the master to command them, and not speak to them as a friend, who entreats. If that is not enough, they bring to the knees the most obstinate with leather reins. Therefore, it is to the use of salt that we owe both the good fortune of experiencing no epidemics and the means of keeping animals near us, without fences and commanding their wills. The following details will prove it in a manner that is even more striking."

The Mountains

"In the beginning of this settlement, that is to say, toward the year 1745, our predecessors, in buying from the colonial Government or the Indians arable lands of the province I live in, also acquired the mountains that cross toward the north, in order to make a reserve, which was to remain forever undivided. Here, during the summer heat, their cattle would find the shade, coolness, of the waters and abundant pasture land.[4] The inhabitants of each district of this county built together, out of common funds, several houses on the banks of these streams, in the neighborhood of which one would find enough irrigable pasture land that they could clear and surround by fences. As a consequence, these rights of reserve reached a great number of people; but this chain, which is 64 miles long by 30 miles wide, offers pasture land for six months of the summer to more than 20,000 head of cattle. Every year each of these associations hires a shepherd to whom, besides the privilege of cultivating this field and receiving a supply of necessary provisions, they give one piastro for each head of cattle, not for watching them, which would be impossible, but for giving them salt once a week.

"The dispositions of these men, who cling both to civilized and primitive life, form a very special class. Although they do not have sufficient ambition to undertake a lucrative trade, or cultivate the earth, they know how to trap wolves, panthers, lynxes, whose destruction the Government amply rewards. Would you believe it? They are almost all Europeans.

"The sudden change from a land extremely populous to a vast desert; from a state of dependence and oppression to the most unlimited freedom; from penury to the ease of life without any work; from the confines of the village to the immensity of forests; the air that they breathe; and above all the life in the forest, so natural to man, all these causes produce on the minds of these new inhabitants, especially in the first year, a kind of exaltation that I cannot define.

"Such are the men whom we employ commonly in our province to watch over our cattle, while they are in the woods, and feed them salt. Some weeks before taking the cattle to the woods, it is necessary to deprive them of salt, and to put a bell around the neck of the strongest and most intelligent animal of the herd. Soon, accustomed to this sound, they know how to distinguish it from all those they meet daily in the woods. From this moment on, the bell-wearing animal becomes the chief of the flock for the entire season.

"The day of departure decided on, generally during the month of April, the colonist, on horseback, offers salt to the leader, careful to retreat as the animal approaches, and he continues this manoeuvre until he has reached a considerable distance from his dwelling; then the herd follows with no difficulty. Once having arrived at his cabin in the woods, he leaves them to themselves, after giving each one of them a handful.

"Rarely do they wander off from this dwelling during the first few days; the abundance of pasture lands, the timidity caused by unfamiliarity, keeps them in the vicinity a long time. Until finally when reassured by habit and the knowledge of these places, they venture forth into the valleys, into the ravines, often at great distances from the shepherd's cabin. They lack nothing—shade, coolness, extremely nutritive plants, buds, and clear, cool water. Provided they have salt every 8 or 10 days, they are happy and before long they become very sleek.

"In the autumn, they are brought back to the farm, by this same bait, and during this long pasturage, very rarely do they get lost. A shepherd can give salt to as many as 1,500, provided they are divided into several herds. However numerous, each of them invariably follows his own leader, without ever mixing with the others. These nomadic tribes, peaceful and happy, meet without any rancor or jealousy, without ever wishing to do one another any harm. As to the accidents to be feared from wolves and panthers, they have become extremely rare; the strong protect the weak with a courage and intelligence worthy of admiration. The bounty of 10 piastros a head (52 pounds 10 sterling) that the government pays them excites the emulation of shepherds and hunters who have almost entirely freed the mountains of Tugeloo from flesh-eating animals.

"Eight or ten days before the time fixed for the return of my cattle, I never fail to spend some time in the woods. In addition to the pleasure of seeing them again, safe, fat, sleek, I love to wander alone in these vast and deep solitudes, nature's sanctuary, which the destructive fire and iron of man has not yet profaned. I love to watch the surface of the earth in its primitive state, so wild to ordinary eyes, but so interesting and instructive to the sensitive observer. I like to pass suddenly from the dazzle of light into a somber, obscure region; from a cultivated land, into forests, majestic and imposing by their limitless extent, as well as by the number, the size, and the magnificent appearance of the trees; from observation of the works of art and industry, to that of this new order of things. I like to watch these peaks on the very tops of which vegetation exercises its sway. Life in the mountains for me has a charm which it is impossible for me to analyze; never do I wander in these venerable retreats without being involuntarily moved, seized with respect and admiration; my ordinary gaiety is replaced by a kind of melancholy that is soft and dream-like, which I never experience in cultivated fields; moreover it is for me a necessary release to spend a few days free from the cares and work demanded by a large family and supervision of a large farm.

"During the night a bearskin laid out beside my shepherd serves me as a bed. Having become my companion, this man tells me a story of his former miseries, of the days when privation, misfortune, and misery seemed locked to his step. To the telling of his miseries, he adds the detail of circumstances, of the chances which, from the populated villages of the Old World, led him into the forests of America, to become there, if not a prosperous colonist, at least a free and independent being, obtaining necessities without undue fatigue and without being exposed to the worries of caution. I share with him his simple, frugal repast; knowing the art of making artificial flies, we amuse ourselves by deceiving the keenest fish (salmon trout) with which the streams and rushing creeks abound.

"When this exercise bores me, I climb to the top of the most accessible peaks in the region, most of them covered with cedars, emblems of vegetable immortality, or with chestnut trees, no less ancient, whose roots, as if they were endowed with special intelligence, run for considerable space over bare rocks, to reach the earth and water with which their cracks and crevices are filled. From there, I look over the valleys, the slopes that surround me, shaded with hemlocks venerable by virtue of the long moss; symbol of old age and decrepitude; of pines of prodigious height, of old oaks, whose thick branches and heavy shade have stifled everything that grew around them.

"Of all the moments I spend in the woods, it is those preceding the dawn that I enjoy with the most enthusiasm, when the weather is calm and serene. It is then when I dare rise in my thought to the everlasting guide of things, conservator of this universe, of which I am merely a speck, and address my humble prayers.

"How imposing and solemn the silence, how mysterious the darkness of the forests, during this struggle between the shadows of the night and the newborn light! It is that of a temple whose august divinity through pity at my weakness is hidden from my eyes, but whose magnificent works announce power and goodness, since everything around me breathes existence and life.

"But the light of dawn increases gradually; the stars disappear; the shadings of the horizon change; the eye begins to distinguish objects; the horizon brightens; dawn appears; it is then when the morning breeze, enchained by the shadows of the night, rises and blows through the branches and cone leaves of the pines and cedars. It is the hymn of nature greeting her Father and King at the time when the rays emblazon the mountainsides and extend into the valleys. It is also the hymn sung when those creatures whom his light recalls to life express their happiness and their pleasure in universal concert.

"Another object of my solitary walks is the contemplation of the falls and the cascades whose reverberations grow near or dissipate at the will of the wind that stirs them, or the whimsy of the echoes which repeat them. What a variety in their appearance as well as in the bizarreness of the accompanying background! For the elegance and the variety of the forms of nature are inexhaustible: some of these cascades fall with a deafening sound or roar through the crevices of the rocks, whose blackness makes a striking contrast with the white foam; others, after long combatting and surmounting a thousand obstacles, seem like smooth silvery sheets without eddies, in the midst of which one can occasionally distinguish isolated points, covered with green. Often one meets torrents which, roaring from the ravines whose tufted trees bend over their sides, hide the depths and the rushing waters; one guesses at their existence; one hears them. One follows them without seeing them until the time when, beaten, exhausted, they finally come to rest in the bed of little rivers that are sometimes navigable for the space of several miles.

"Several of these little rivers enclose islands whose vegetation, coolness, and beauty contrast marvelously with the sterility, the crudeness, and the harshness of the river banks. I know some of 8 or 10 acres, on which one could have gardens and cultivate the rarest fruits; for during the summer, the sun's rays have great power there; some are covered with weeping willows,[5] water ash,[6] white and black maple,[7] whose delicate textures and inimitable variability offer one of the most beautiful scenes of autumn; others are black oak,[8] sassafras, plane trees, and all varieties of willows and alder trees. I recall one of these islands, located at the foot of a very long cascade, which comes down from the side of a mountain; seeing it, one could not help believing that it might have been made and planted by cultivated hands; this area, like a beautiful green tapestry, was studded with flowers, without any odor, but with vivid colors, decorated with high cedars, in the midst of which one saw growing these beautiful bushes, known as Kalmias—Pourpris. A European, whom chance had brought into the mountains, impressed, as I was, with the beauty, the fertility of this almost inaccessible place, appropriated it for himself and has built there a fine little cabin. Although still young, and apparently having received a fine education, rarely does one see him leave this deserted place; in the summer, he cultivates vegetables and corn; in the winter he hunts. Nowhere beyond his little garden have I seen such fine melons; his vines are beginning to spread; the two branches of the river which surround his island furnish him with fish; the skin of animals as well as the bounties of the Government procure for him what he needs to wear. Like Robinson Crusoe, he is sufficient unto himself and is never idle.

" 'Young as you are, why do you live alone,' I asked him one day. 'Why do you prefer this gloomy retreat to all the other sections of Carolina?'

" 'Men are tigers,' he answered me, with an intent look. 'I have seen human nature in all its hideous colors; I have seen virtue proscribed and crime triumphant; perhaps even the reign of the latter is not yet over.* After losing my friends and my fortune, amid convulsive storms of a disorganized society, I can no longer find repose except in the solitude of these mountains. I hope that your Government, so mild, and so just, will not take from me this little island, from which I get my living.'

"Among this variety, this great number of trees with which our forests are so filled, the oaks attract me especially; nothing indeed is more striking than some of these giants of the earth, whose existence antedates by several centuries the discovery of the continent; their colossal size, the extent of their foliage, their durability, everything about them is imposing, everything, to the very cuts from the thunderbolts, which, like mortal creatures, they have resisted, and often when the weak sap can no longer stir their last branches, nature, as though to render their decadence more venerable, causes to grow there these enormous garlands of moss which wave at the will of the wind: I have seen some of them that were more than thirty feet long.[9]

"One of the most interesting features of these annual excursions is that they soften the wild character that my young colts have developed in the woods. It is difficult to depict their fright at the first sight of man: restless and ferocious, they follow their mothers only at considerable distance, and often even refuse to obey their mother's neighings: in vain would one call them; these strangers still do not know the voice that some day is to command them and inspire confidence in them. Yet, after several attempts, they finally follow them: it is at the salt-feeding time of the others. I do not know how or by what magic they have the art of communicating the pleasure or rather the happiness that they feel. If their colts are not deaf to their first invitations, it is a favorable sign; but one must be as still as a stump, for the slightest movement of the hand would make them take flight, and one would be obliged to postpone this experiment until the next day. Gradually encouraged by renewed neighings, emboldened by conditioned startings, they advance a step and then halt, legs bowed, like springs ready to snap. They do this a second time and stop again. Finally after a more or less long interval, spent in fright and fear, suddenly appearing to ask what they do not yet understand, they approach trembling, stopping again, until, reassured by the motionlessness of the hand offering them their salt, as well as by the presence and the invitations of their mothers, they stretch their necks and heads, their protruding eyes shining and flaming, they stick out their tongues and gradually lick

* This was written in 1796.

the salt. It is then when one sees the expression of enjoyment and pleasure: how they devour this new food! How the saliva mounts in their mouths! From this moment on, their wild and savage character softens, and the sight of man scares them less.

"Such are their first steps toward a civilized state: once this process is completed (often it takes several days), the herd is taken back to the farm by the same means that they were brought into the mountains. On their arrival, they are rewarded with the promised relish and the next day they are turned out to pasture again. Such are the resources offered us by the mountains of Tugeloo and the means which are used to lead there, hold and bring back from there our numerous cattle: what would we do without this help from salt?''

Fire in the Mountains

"In order that the pasture lands in these mountains may become more abundant and more nutritive, it is necessary to burn some of the leaves every year toward the end of March: this fire revives and stimulates vegetation, destroys the dried-up branches, creates new ones, whose buds give to the butter and to the cheese a quality quite superior to that which the best grass lands procure for them.

"In order not to damage the fences of the farms bordering the mountains, the owners assemble on a day appointed by law: after dividing themselves into companies to which are assigned certain areas, they set fire to the leaves which the wind has accumulated along the fences. At first, they burn slowly; this light fire in its rapid passage touches only the surface. As soon as the exterior skirt is dry, and there is no danger of its returning, they carry off sparks from it into different places in the mountains; soon after, these separated fires unite in sheets of great stretches, that roll over one another following different directions, and in a short span of time, the sides of the mountains, the valleys, and the highest peaks are covered with them; in less than 12 to 15 hours, this great chain appears to be no more than a black and burned surface; but these leaves have so little substance, the speed of the fire is so rapid, that not only are the ordinary trees, but even the bushes, the cedar trees, and the bayberry trees left undamaged.

"It is especially during the night when the short-lived fires offer a spectacle that is really interesting and curious, seen through the trees a few miles distant; now they appear stationary, now moving backward; now covering great spaces in the wink of an eye, according to the strength or direction of the wind. This operation, prescribed by the laws, procures for us the means of feeding during the heat of the summers a great number of cattle, and has rendered this chain infinitely useful to all the regions of the neighborhood. Who knows how useful the beautiful river, the falls, and the fine forests by which some of them are covered from their peaks to their bases will become some day to our posterity?

"We also use salt to improve our fertilizer and our land. If during the hay harvest, rains come and the hay is damaged, one puts several handfuls on all the beds where the haystacks are: soon it penetrates and mixes with the whole mass, gives it part of its original color, and for the cattle becomes a food that they prefer often to the one that has not been wet: the same thing is true of the straw: when they refuse to eat it, one flavors it with a little pickled brine.

"Such are the different uses one makes of salt in the United States."

CHAPTER XV

The date, as well as several of the first pages from this chapter, were entirely illegible.

"After this cruel shipwreck, I found myself without any resources; however, I still had one friend; he was a gardener living near Rotterdam. I owed to this man the happiness of finding at Lisbon in 1763 a father of whom I had never heard, and whom circumstances of the most extraordinary kind had obliged to become a monk. Thus do the whims of destiny play with us.

"Provided with an assortment of bulbs and seeds from the most beautiful flowers cultivated in Holland at that time, and recommended to the House of Guildemeister, I set sail for Lisbon. What a contrast between the two climates! Between the rosy complexion, the dress, the physiognomy of the men whom I had just left and the haggard, sunburnt, and even black faces of the inhabitants of this capital! On the day of my arrival, it was extremely warm, the sky cloudless; in the evening, the stars shone with a luster that I had never seen in them; the heavens resembled an arch of blue sprinkled with rubies, diamonds, and sapphires whose splendor was the same from the zenith to the horizon. It was the first time in my life that I had seen a sky as rich and as pure; seated on the balcony of my window, I admired the sparkling glory of these suns that give life and movement to the planetary systems whose center they are; the air I breathed was balmy. It was midnight before I could abandon a spectacle so new and so enchanting.

"The first person to whom I was referred for the sale of my flowers was Prince Don Emanuel, uncle of King Joseph. He had long been in his Majesty's service. Quite different from the other Portuguese lords, he had traveled afar and loved foreigners. I found him in his garden. He looked over the sketches of flowers I had made and was pleased with those I offered him. He ordered what he needed and paid me generously. I was about to withdraw when he said to me:

"'Come and dine with me; I wish to hear about the country whence you come.'

"One must know all the energy of which vegetation is susceptible under a climate as warm as this one; the perfection which the sun gives to the coloring of the flowers and to the flavor of the fruits; the marvels which the beneficent sun produces, in order to get an idea of the impression which the sight of this beautiful garden made on me.

This aspect convinced me more firmly than did the foggy regions of the North whence I came that the sun is the mainstay of nature and the soul of all beings. The day was scorching; but no sooner had I withdrawn within the grove when my eyes, tired from the dazzle of the sun, could open and focus, and I no longer feared letting them rove afar; the superb lattice-works under which I strolled, like protective clouds, tempered abruptly the heat of the day; the keener the heat, the cooler and more delightful this contrast of shade seemed to me, and the more refreshed I felt. Never before had the power of contrasts impressed me so much. It is then when one appreciates the advantage of a fully leafed tree; seated under its beneficial shade, how content one is to breathe, how revived one feels, as though to a new existence! With what pleasure one contemplates a pool, a cascade, whose murmur and appearance alone refresh and slake one's thirst. In cold, dismal climes one flees from the shade and the humidity; in those of the South, one seeks them as the source of happiness and of life. The orange, the palm, and almond trees and thousands of others were all at once covered with flowers and fruit. In Holland, Nature, greedy with its gifts, presents only once a year the symbol of hopes often deceptive: here more generous and far richer, it lavishes flowers and fruits nine months of the year. All it asks of men is that they keep the roots of the trees and plants watered.

"Dinner hour having come, I followed the prince. After climbing a wondrous staircase and crossing through several large apartments, we entered a dining room, cool like the shade of the grove which I had just left: the floor was of marble as were the walls, up to one's elbows; the rest above of highly polished stucco. No sooner had the prince brought the first spoonful to his mouth, when suddenly my ears, or rather my whole soul was assailed with a new and unexpected pleasure: it was a concert performed by a group of musicians he had brought from Vienna. Impressed for the first time by the effect and the power of these blended sounds, I felt transported beyond the ordinary limits of my enjoyment; I no longer breathed; I was all ears. Whence came this astonishing domain that music exerts on our souls? What added further to the charms of this concert was the illusion caused by remoteness, as well as by the repetition of the timid echoes of this vast palace. This angelic harmony seemed to me to be like a choir of celestial instruments blown on or touched by the angels. At the same time I enjoyed the pleasure of staying during the most scorching hour of the day, in an apartment as cool as though it might have been 500 feet above the ground, of hearing the murmuring of the clear waters falling from pool to pool, of feeling the spray, and, finally, of enjoying a delightful concert in the midst of such a resonant palace. At a signal it ceased; then the prince, behind whom I continued to walk, asked me several questions relative to education, Government, and trade in Holland.

"The next day I was invited to spend the night on the Tage, in the midst of that great fleet of vessels with which the harbor is always filled; this is a very common amusement in a country where there are scarcely any public walks and where heat is sometimes overwhelming. In cold, cloudy climes, night offers only the image of nothingness, silence, and inspires only sadness; at Lisbon, it has charms that one often prefers to those of daylight. How beautiful and resplendent the moon seemed to me! Its light, more analogous to the feebleness of our sight, illuminates perfectly all objects, without dazzling. But how can one paint the magic and graceful effect of its reflections, when the gentle wash of the light boat and the light breath of refreshing breezes, imprinted on the surface of these waters, slow and soft waves, faintly suggesting ocean waves which ceaselessly follow one another without ever meeting, and expire one by one on the shore. While the heat of the day is sometimes painful to bear, the nights are always delightful and cool; as long as the sun shines on the horizon, one languishes; as soon as it has disappeared, one is revived.

"Before 1701 it was much easier for the Protestants to live than die in Lisbon. The haven for their dead ones had been exposed to the plunder of a superstitious, ignorant people who believed that the ashes of heretics prevented the harvests from ripening; their remains could be covered with earth only with the greatest difficulty and protection; this first right of nature was refused to respectable men, who, during the course of their lives, had assisted the great number of indigent people who filled the streets of this town. A plot was given them: but who would believe it! Despite the orders from the court, the patriarch dared oppose his will to a concession as wise as it was politic, and for a long time, the Protestants were obliged to have their dead ones escorted in order to shelter them from these insults. This reminds me of the deplorable story of Doctor Young, minister of the Anglican church, whose daughter died in Montpellier; the priests of this town, as intolerant as those in Lisbon, having had the cruelty to refuse this wretched father permission to have her buried in this cemetery, was himself reduced to the horrible necessity of breaking the earth in the garden and burying the remains of his beloved daughter there.

"The ground once given over to foreign trading depots has since become not only the peaceful retreat of the dead, but also a promenade where the living come to learn how to bear up under and often even pardon the injustices and crimes of mankind, since, after all, evil is an inevitable attribute of human nature. It is divided by alleys planted with trees of great height, in the shadow of which repose non-Catholics who have died since 1701. Almost all the monuments one sees there are of white marble and of a touching simplicity. How eloquent they are, these plaintive tokens of affection, regret, and gratitude! How useful and edifying this esteem for the remains of our ancestors! May this beautiful area long be in the shelter from revolutions which, in upsetting the earth, carry their blind furies to the haven of the dead!

"I was informed that Mr. Joseph May, an old man who retired several years ago in the village of Cyntra, where he spent the last years of his life in cultivating the rarest flowers, wanted to see my assortment. I sent it to him; and in order to become better acquainted with the interior of this land so new to me, I set out on foot to see him. Nothing is more arid than the sections of Portugal which do not have water: such are the environs of Lisbon beyond Maffra, where I stopped to rest. It is an immense convent, situated in the middle of a desert, but the enjoyments of the monks are no less delightful. All that zeal and art could summon for the ease and convenience of these recluses has been carried out there. It is a royal foundation and the fruit of a dream of John V. Never was monarchal idleness more superbly housed. The service of the church was performed there with theatrical pomp. Yet, this cult, so extravagant, belongs to a country which does not produce half the bread needed by the inhabitants. Toward evening, I arrived at Cyntra.

"A long time before the reign of the Moorish kings, this place was known and remarkable for the coolness and the healthfulness of its air. From the Ocean, it was defended by the bases of two natural pyramids, well known by navigators as the rock of Lisbon. The elevation of one is estimated at 2,000 feet above sea level; and that of the other, 1,800 feet. From the middle part of the higher of these promontories, runs a great stream whose waters irrigate the land they enter. The close, the orchards, and the garden of this village are surrounded by myrtle and aloe; on all sides the curiosities of the soil, the variety of groves, the elegant simplicity of the houses, present the most picturesque vistas to the eyes, and to the imagination, the finest and most delightful paintings. It is the sojourn of health, of Flore, and of Pomone; the fruits there are delicious, the vine shoots of an exquisite size and taste, and the flowers, enriched by all the perfumes, decorated with all the gloss that the sun's rays can produce on them. Such are the advantages of the warm countries where one often finds fertility, beauty, and abundance beside uncultivated deserts, savage and repulsive.

"Cyntra therefore owes everything it has to these two promontories:

shelter from the winds of the sea, cool shade, and inexhaustible springs. Without these advantages, everything there would be dry as at Maffra, and the richness and pleasure of foreign traders would never have built these homes, nor planted these groves that one sees there today. The proximity to the capital, the excellence and the abundance of fish, the almost steady evenness of the seasons, the charm of a climate that knows neither the extremities of the north wind blasts nor frosts; the healthfulness of the balmy air one breathes there; such are the features which have attracted so many old people to it, for a long time, and now attract convalescents.

"After acquiring a considerable fortune, and after reaching the age of 60, Mr. Joseph May, member of an English company, captivated by the beauties of this place, left his business to his children, and came to settle here for the rest of his days. This old patriarch saw the fifth generation; his faculties were scarcely a bit enfeebled. Like the Venetian Cornaro, he knew how to prolong his span until the 103rd year, by the regularity of his life, the excellence of the fruits he ate, the moderate exercise that he prescribed for himself, and the reading with which he fortified his mind. What a fine and rare spectacle—that of a man still active and over a hundred years old! How worthy of respect and admiration he seems to me! His sight, somewhat feeble, was still sufficient to permit him to enjoy the beauties of nature; and more than once we were together on a high place admiring the glory of the sunrise and sunset at the time when the rays cross the floating masses of condensed vapors or the transparent clouds. His memory was like an immense ledger whose writing had faded somewhat but on which there was still no trace of illegibility nor of anything defaced. Most of the flowers that he had cultivated himself had come from far-off countries; for almost all the navigators had taken a great deal of pleasure in bringing him the rarest flowers China and the Indies produced. His garden was a terrestrial paradise, where in the shadow of the most beautiful trees and surrounded by the most wonderful waters, one breathed happiness.

"Does happiness then exist on earth?" I asked him. "You appear to me like a privileged being on whom nature, who is so miserly with her happiness, seems to have poured it with full hands.

" 'Yes, I agree,' he answered, 'I have always been happy enough; and although beyond the ordinary limits of life, I feel that I am still happy. Nevertheless, when I think of it, I am ashamed to have lived so long; not that I am tired of seeing the light, but because each must appear in his turn on this great theatre. And what would the spectators say, if the Chinese shades, instead of amusing them by their rapid and varied passage, were suddenly to remain motionless? Would they not have reason to complain? Is the passing of human generations something more important?

" 'But how different is the happiness of old people from that of the young! For almost forty years in the bosom of retreat, I have felt how much my opinions, my enjoyments, and my tastes have changed; and yet I am still the same individual. It is through peace of mind, regularity of life, and mild diversion, that I have prolonged my life; and that is why I avoid with the greatest care everything that could interrupt it and fill me with sad and gloomy thoughts. When I receive newspapers, I always take care to let my secretary read them, so that he can tell me only what will be agreeable to me, for I no longer have the strength to hear with cold-bloodedness, the recital of wars, crimes, and disasters, of which our unhappy race is ceaselessly the victim. On the other hand, in the fear that laziness and inactivity might hasten languor and death, I decided, once upon a time, on a little system of conduct which I have religiously followed since. I threw myself wholeheartedly into the arms of nature; but in entering her sanctuary, I found it so vast, that I devoted myself exclusively to the study of vegetation: I performed a great number of interesting experiments, the results of which I sent to Mr. Collisson, then secretary of our Royal Society. Presumptuous as I was! I sought to discover the mechanism of this powerful and invisible secret, which, by means of the sap pumped by roots, revives the plants and the trees, produces the dazzling enamel of the flowers, the flavor and taste of fruits and the perfumes of the spices; and yet! oh incomprehensible mystery! this sap is only an odorless liquid, swift to evaporate. These studies arouse and absorb admiration and respect. Yes, I feel it, I will live as long as my heart is active enough and has enough warmth to encourage these feelings, as well as by the affection for my dear ones and gratitude to the Supreme Being. I work with my hands as much as strength permits; I take care of and watch over a great number of birds, whose plumage is so soft and whose customs so interesting; they know me and see me always with the same pleasure; it is quite reciprocal, and at my age, one must not neglect the sources of that pleasure, however small they be. By these means, I know very little of the boredom that attaches itself to old age, like rust on iron and moss on old buildings. Every evening I go to bed almost as I have awakened, sometimes even richer in ideas, and in pleasant feelings; especially when letters from my friends or the newspapers have apprised me of some happy news. Another source of my happiness is my numerous progeny, who, out of pity or respect for my age, hide from me their losses or worries. For more than twenty years my heart has felt no violent commotions; the storms of summer, whose noise is repeated by the powerful echoes from the promontories, used to be my only cause for fears and anxieties; but since a celebrated Philadelphian has taught us the art of preserving our homes from lightning, I can admire with perfect calm these majestic and sublime noises, these rumblings so deep and so sonorous. Like the waves of the sea chased by the winds to the most remote shores, they are swift to lose themselves in the far-awayness of the atmosphere. And then! without thunder, I would tell myself, whence would come these refreshing rains, this prime cause of the fertility of our gardens and the healthfulness of the air? Without these atmospheric disturbances which condense and bring us vapors from the Ocean, the rivers of the promontory would dry up and this beautiful greenness by which I am surrounded would fade forever. What more can I tell you about this? The soft and bracing exhalations of the bushes and flowers give the air I breathe a reviving quality whose precious advantage I feel daily. I still have the presumptuousness to hope that my eyes will close 'mid the laughing scenes of the springtime; full of gratitude for the past, little disturbed by the future, I await fearlessly the end of a life that has been long enough. Who would have told me in my youth that already old at sixty, I would still have 43 more years in which to see the sun begin and complete its annual revolution?

" 'The lower of these two lofty headlands, crowned by an old château built by Moorish kings, having become inaccessible through the disintegration of the walks and steps that had been dug in the rock, is today the haunt of vultures. On the crest of the other promontory, the religion of the country in the thirteenth century raised a small monastery, a church, and a hospice. Considering the expenditures that these buildings demanded, the fearlessness of the workers who dared put the bells on the very banks of this frightful precipice, one tries to guess the motive. Was there not room enough on earth without having to scale this great promontory? Yes, to be sure; but the bizarre notions of the times attached to this great elevation something of the mystic. As if, in removing themselves from the ordinary abode of man, these monks had brought themselves nearer what they called heaven.

" 'If these eminences are interesting to see, especially in cloudy weather, how much more so they are after several days of great heat! Then light vapors, like hot breaths from the prairies, rise from their midst; and as if they possessed magnetic attraction, those that float invisible in the atmosphere gradually lift, cling together, and soon become black, thick clouds which bring on the gloom of the night. What a variety in forms, folds, contours, and appearance, occasioned by the violence of winds, which nevertheless cannot detach them from the pyramids around which one sees them circulate! Although streaks of darkest crimson outline and illuminate them, one scarcely hears the thunder; the imposing silence of this scene, sometimes interrupted by the roaring from the ocean, continues to the moment when, finally giving in to the redoubled impetuosity of the tempest, these floating masses disappear from the promontories dividing them in their passage; then streaks of the most vivid light penetrate the deepest black; then these subdivisions, electrified in different ways, receive and discharge, with terrible bursts, the fire contained in them; often even the sun's rays penetrating the densest parts decorate them with all the shades of the iris, with reflections, with jets of light that are extremely striking; and, as if these clouds had become heavier by their division, all of a sudden, they lower and seem ready to burst forth on the village; but attracted invincibly by these heights, they retrogress toward their bases, which they surround again and inundate with their torrents. It is then that one discovers the convent and the Moorish château, like two quiet islands in the midst of waves of the sea in anger. I had seen many storms on land and at sea, but never before did I happen to catch one and follow as distinctly its origin, progress, and end.'

"One day when it was very warm, I was busy breaking off a vine branch whose weight I wanted to know, when Mr. May seeing a little gold locket on my chest, asked me in a serious tone who had given it to me, since when I had worn it and what it contained.

"I do not know who gave it to me," I told him. "I have worn it since my earliest childhood, and never having been able to open it, I cannot tell you what is in it.

" 'Are you a Hollander?'

"I think so, yet without being sure of it, for I remember having spoken English when I was very young.

" 'In what town were you raised?'

"Leyden.

" 'In whose home?'

"In the Brinker home.

" 'Then is your name Brinker?'

"No, my name is Jean de Bragansa and I am known by that.

" 'Whom do you believe yourself to be?'

"I do not know, for, as I told you yesterday, I never had the happiness of knowing either a mother or a father.

" 'Would you entrust this locket to me until tomorrow evening?'

"Gladly; but dare I ask what can be the motive of your curiosity?

" 'Young man, at my age, it is rare that one is curious without cause; but before going into the finer details, I demand that you swear before God to be prudent and discreet; you should know in what land and under what Government we live here.'

"I swear it by His holy name, your hand in mine, esteemed old man.

" 'Not far from here,' he told me, 'lives a man whom I have loved and revered for a number of years; for a long time he has interested himself in the lot of a child who, like you, was raised in Leyden. He has not heard from him in 7 years. Although I am not sure you are the person whose loss he regrets, I think it would be a good idea to tell him that you are here; he alone can unravel this mystery. He himself has experienced a destiny that is quite cruel and quite curious; after receiving an English education and after serving in the Royal Navy of Great Britain, the most extraordinary circumstances forced him to become a monk. What is the religious or philosophical system that can give us the resignation and courage necessary to bear up under such a reversal of life? He owes his life only to his taste for astronomy and to the permission to choose the place of his retreat, and there is none in Europe more favorable for the study of this science than the place in which he now lives. We used to see a great deal of each other at one time. But since he has become ill, and I, more than old, we write each other once a week. Young man, I repeat, be as quiet as a tomb; thank God for having steered your uncertain steps toward this land. To-morrow, accompanied by my son, you will climb the mountain. Unless my eyes have deceived me, my guesses will have a foundation, and you, by your conduct, will merit the happiness that awaits you! This is one of the great moments in your life!'

"In the evening when I was alone, my imagination indulged in a thousand guesses, sometimes they seemed uncertain to me, but more often they flattered my ardent desires, and seemed sure to me. I thought I saw hope in the bearded face that was summoning me from the peak of the promontory; and yet I could not conceive what connection there could be between a Portuguese monk, who believed himself born a Hollander, and me. Very early the next day we left. My guide, who was well acquainted with the entire region, led the way in a manner that permitted me to see these magnificent springs which for centuries furnished water to neighboring regions; the springs spouted in great spurts from the base of a perpendicular rock 30 feet high and forty feet wide and which he told me was higher than 900 feet above sea level. Arriving at what they call the esplanade, we rested in the shade of a myrtle bush, whence we could see at a single glance the Ocean, the town, the Tage, a boundless horizon. From one side, it seemed to me I could distinguish the Azores; from the other, the snow-capped mountains of Galicia. Finally after three and a half hours walk, we reached the gate of this lofty convent, and soon after we saw coming toward us with heavy and measured steps a man of great height who, clad in the garb of a monk, aroused respect. His bald head might have served as a model for a painter; his eyes were blue, his face still young; his appearance and demeanor had something striking about them, quite superior to the typical Portuguese monks; his white hands, especially, betrayed a foreign origin.

" 'Here is a young man whom I present to you on behalf of my father,' Mr. May said to him; 'he has known misfortune.'

" 'Come in,' he said. 'The unfortunate are my brothers even more than other men; here you will find hospitality, friendship, sympathy.'

"But what was my astonishment to see an apartment well furnished and neatly arranged, whence, like an observatory, one saw simultaneously the earth, the sea, and the skies! Several instruments hung on the walls revealing the man's taste for astronomy. In a few moments, we were served coffee.

" 'Here,' he told us, 'is the only luxury I permit myself; the older I get, the more necessary it becomes to me. This drink raises my spirits and sometimes dispels the sadness which overcomes me and which is quite natural in a man so mistreated by fate. But, let us go into another room so that God alone will hear what we are going to say. They told me that you have come from Holland with an assortment of flowers and that you were recommended by the House of Guilde Meister. Is that true?'

"Yes.

" 'That you were raised in the Brinker family in Leyden?'

"Yes, there is a copy of the accounts which they made me sign every year and that of the receipt for the 100 guineas which the Orde House of London gave them every year.

" 'Did you ever know who sent this money?'

"No.

" 'How many years ago did you leave this family?'

"Seven years ago.

" 'What have you been doing during this long interval?'

"Alas! Deprived of paternal counsel, I wandered in the paths of laxity, blinded by the passions of youth, I was led astray, deceived. These wanderings cost me a pretty penny; I ran the whole gamut of misfortune; I came to know all the variations of misery. I have served under the Prussian king; I have sailed beyond Spitzberg in pursuit of whales and the sea was no more favorable to me than the land; I was shipwrecked. Back once more in Rotterdam, I had the good fortune to work for a florist. It is to his advice that I owe the original notion of coming here; it is to his generosity, the fine assortment of bulbs, as well as the honorable recommendation that he procured for me.

" 'Why did you cease corresponding with the Brinkers? And why have you plunged into the cruelest anxiety those who are interested in your lot?'

"Convinced that my misconduct had merited the indifference and oblivion of this family, I ceased imposing on them and I did not think that I was fortunate enough to be worthy of anyone else's interest in my destiny.

" 'How old are you?'

"I learned from the Brinker family that I was born April 27, 1740.

" 'Do you recognize this locket?'

"Why yes! I recognize it! I have been wearing it since the time when I can first remember anything.

" 'Where did you get it?'

"I do not know.

" 'Have you ever tried to open it?'

"Several times, but, unable to succeed, I kept it intact, out of respect for the unknown person who gave it to me.

" 'The time for doubt and cruel perplexity is passed. Yes,' he told me, in a voice stirred with emotion, eyes wet with tears, and holding in his hand a little piece of parchment that he had just taken from the locket whose soldering he had filed, 'yes, you were born in London, April 27, 1740, of Ulrica Stamford and Juan de Bragansa and you were baptized under the name of John in the church of Saint Clement, the 29th of the same month. Read this and let us bless together the chance, or rather the mysterious Providence that brought you to Lisbon, to Cyntra, and finally to this promontory where you now find again a father who intends, by showering you with benefits, to make you forget your misfortunes and begs you to pardon him your birth. Although disguised in this garb, he is none the less a man of honor, virtue, and knowledge, quite superior to the state in which you see him. The degradation to which he has been obliged to submit himself is merely exterior; when you know the man better, when you know better the heart that has palpitated with affection and tenderness for you, you will not blush at avowing and considering him as the author of your days and your best friend. You will learn afterward what his birth and education were. I have 4,700 pounds sterling in English money left me by the tenderest and best of mothers and 7,000 crusados that my esteemed nurse, Dona Theresa H . . . left me on her death.

The pension of 500 crusados that King Joseph gives me annually is more than sufficient to provide for my needs, so I give you the first-mentioned sums, which Doppendal and May, in whose names they were deposited, will turn over to you; but I ask that you join their house, that you write to the good florist in Rotterdam to whom you will pay not only what you owe, but make a present of these 200 crusados. In righting my wrongs toward you, I ask you also to repair your wrongs, and, enriched by an experience that has cost you so dear, to become cautious, wise, active, and hardworking in this new career. At dinner we will talk of astronomy, geography, etc. . . . in order that the lay brother who serves me and my servant will take you to be a pupil whom I am instructing, and thus your visit will arouse no suspicion. The slightest indiscretion would ruin me and you, too; my tomb would be one of the lower depths of the Inquisition. Drop the name of Braganse during the time you are in this country and assume that of Brinker; some day you will know how baleful that name has been to me. It will be very pleasant for me to see you as often as your new occupations permit.'

''My father lived five years longer and was preceded to the grave by only 18 months by his esteemed friend, Joseph May, who nearly reached his 107th year. The death of the latter occasioned such considerable changes in the House of Coppendal and May that I thought it a good plan to leave the country, to go settle in Brazil, where I arrived furnished with fine recommendations.

''What a superb and magnificent land! What richness of soil! What a variety of products! In no other part has nature been as lavish with her gifts, nor has she made greater advances for the happiness of men. Proximity to Africa furnishes them abundantly with slaves which they need; the annual revenue from this slave trade is estimated at 40,000 pounds. But on the other hand, superstition, mother of ignorance covering with its veils these fertile countries, retards the progress of culture and improvements. One can see growing there wheat, sugar, indigo, rice, and every tropical product. I am not referring to the gold or diamond mines; if they have enriched the Mother Country, they have corrupted the customs and deteriorated the industry of part of the colonists.

''In no other country do the clergymen and the lawyers enjoy so much consideration nor exercise a greater influence; they divide among themselves the exclusive monopoly of everything that has any bearing on the interests of this world and the other, and never has a monopoly been more productive.

''If I had by chance been born king of Portugal, I would very quickly have abandoned sterile Lusitania and its wavering throne to establish in Brazil one that is more solid, more respectable, and more brilliant. Instead of sending their merchandise to Lisbon, the European nations would send it to the ports of this new kingdom, which by wise laws one could make in ten years one of the most flourishing countries in the world. What caution and politics have not yet inspired in the House of Braganza, necessity will perhaps force it to think about some day.

"In the office of the captain of the Rio Grande I bought a plantation whose location was charming; two beautiful streams crossed it, and by means of some accidents in the land, I could irrigate a great part: which I did with great success. I was more than a little astonished in seeing how much these innovations, as well as the farming implements, models of which I had brought along with me, displeased my neighbors. I had maps, two globes, a telescope; they asked me a hundred questions about these strange objects; and despite my desire to conform to the ways of the land, my indifference manifested itself; they suspected the purity of my beliefs; some of the most ignorant even called me heretic. At this cry, hate, scorn, and calumny sharpened their barbs; those of my neighbors whom I had most constantly obliged stopped seeing me and became my enemies. Who would believe it? They attributed the success of my harvests to the co-operation of the evil spirit. Alas! it would have been easy for them to see that this success emanated only from my care and my skill in the art of irrigation. I was denounced at the ruthless tribunal, which does not have the power to burn, it is true, but certainly can incarcerate and ruin. I came to San Salvador, to seek the protection of the viceroy. He made me feel with great politeness that it would be wiser to abandon a country with whose customs and religion I could not conform. Finally, after disposing of my property, I embarked on a coastwise vessel, bound for Nicaragua.

"There I found the same religious influence among the people, the same intolerance among the clergy, yet, more refined customs. I was impressed by the extent, the beauty of Nicaragua Lake, which on one side for several miles touches the Caribbean Sea to the south; on the other empties into the ocean through the Saint Joan River. Although deprived of my instruments, for they had not permitted me to take them beyond the Rio Grande, I busied myself studying the relative levels of these two seas and in making a map of the neighboring countries, with the idea of plotting a possible link. This, it seemed to me, would be so useful some day to trade and cost very little. Thinking my enterprise a worthwhile one, I showed my work to some learned people in the town; but soon afterward they invented stories, they attributed motives that I had never entertained; my name of Brinker aroused suspicions; these suspicions were carried to the government of the province, which without even listening to me, condemned me to forfeit all my papers and leave the country within 48 hours. I left for the Bay of Hondouras where I arrived under my real name. The inhabitants of this English colony, quite different from those whom I had left, were concerned only with the exploitation of timber, inlaid work, and dyeing. At the time of the floods to which this vast country is periodically subjected, they go by boat through the forests, often at considerable distances from the sea, to meet and form caravans with the trees which they have felled during the dry season, bringing them to port, where they are exchanged for merchandise and provisions, for these inhabitants cultivate nothing.

"A month later I embarked on a vessel laden with mahogany bound for Alexandria, where after two weeks crossing, I arrived without mishap. This town, formerly known as Belhaven, is situated on the northern bank of the Potawmack, at a little distance from its falls, 136 miles from the mouth of the Chesapeak Bay and 426 miles from the sea. It is the last navigable lap of this beautiful river.

"The streets of this town are symmetrical, the docks well constructed and convenient; already there are 490 houses, and nearly 3,000 inhabitants. Its prosperity is rapidly expanding, above all since the completion of the canals and the locks built to avoid the falls of the river. However, the town has two rivals on the opposite bank: George Town and the new town of Washington.*

"Finally I could breathe freely after becoming a citizen of a country whose Government, protecting all forms of worship, recognizes no church as dominant; where industry is progressive; where each individual, from the very day of his arrival, can exercise his talents; where the writs of naturalization are easily obtained; where the farmer's status is one of the most respectable; a place finally, whose laws are based on the eternal principles of reason, justice, and liberty. How great was my regret at not coming sooner! Guided by the advice of some friends, I crossed the mountains to explore the province of Indiana, a dependency of Virginia. The great number of streams, the proximity of the Ohio, the fertility of the soil, that brotherly and human spirit, which one finds more commonly in nascent societies, where men need one another; all these motives prompted me to buy the ninth part of a district, equivalent to 2,600 acres, located on the Junius River (a branch of the Little Kanhawa). I had the good fortune to find in one of my swamps the remains of a colony of beavers, to

* The federal town.

which I promised the most inviolable hospitality. These families are still there, and without scaring them, I often have the pleasure of seeing them work. As long as I live, the dam on which they have built their dwellings will be respected, and this swamp will never be dried up.

"In exploring the countryside, I was quite astonished to see that nearly all the heights in the neighborhood were covered with entrenchments and fortifications of earth, of a form that was very different from those one knows in Europe. To judge from the diameter of the trees that grow in the area outside, they must date from very early times. I have heard that the same type exists in some of the provinces beyond the mountains of Pennsylvania, as well as Tennessee and Kentucky, on the banks of the Shawanese and the Tiogo, and that the town of Marietta, on the Muskinghum, was built on the site of a vast, entrenched camp. The Sergeant-Major had made a relief map of it to be given the President of the United States.

"Indiana is bound on one side by the Ohio, on another by the Little Kanhawa, the chain of the Laurier, the Monongahela and Pennsylvania, and is 70 leagues from Pittsburgh and 150 leagues from Philadelphia. This little virgin province was ceded in 1768 by the Shawanese and the Mohawk confederation, to a company of businessmen in reparation for the loss of 214,791 piastros in merchandise that had been pillaged by some of their warriors. It contains three and one-half million acres of land, crossed by a great number of streams and little rivers: the soil is good and the trees of the forest are of the greatest beauty. The winters there are less rugged than those of Pennsylvania. One could make a very interesting collection of the flowers that grow wild there. As much of a farmer as I am, I am at work on a *Flora Indianica* that you will probably hear about some day.

"After sharing with my new compatriots the dangers of the revolution which emancipated this great country, I enjoyed the interesting spectacle presented by the prodigious growth of its population and that of the countries beyond the mountains. The principal regions beyond these mountains, the states of Kentucky and Tennessee, have entered the confederation. I am Justice of the Peace in my canton, or rather I am the arbiter and the peace-maker, the mainstay of this fine institution. As often as I can, I help the young colonists of my neighborhood, because I know how difficult and expensive the early years of settlement are. I encourage the establishment of schools. There are no districts in the whole United States where one finds a greater number of schools per capita, taught by the best teachers. The education of youth is the first basis of peace and of public prosperity, as well as the happiness of the families; already we have two academies, to which the Government has granted charters of corporation. The good that I can do is, for me, a field that I love to plant, whose flowers and fruits I love to watch grow. Ingratitude that I have occasionally experienced might keep me from enjoying all this, but, provided I have the pleasure of sowing it, I am satisfied: moreover, having neither wife nor child, I can be generous without doing wrong to anyone. There were only 317 families when I settled in this little province in 1773; today there are more than 5,000 inscribed on the rolls of the Colonels of the militia. On the other hand, one must agree that local circumstances, government, laws, the administration, have been no more favorable to the increase of population than to the industry of men. Instead of going to Philadelphia, our commodities come down the Ohio, and go to Limestone, Kentucky, Colombia, and sometimes even to New Orleans, although it is 691 leagues away. Nothing is more favorable to this fine, long navigation than the two annual swellings of this river: the first arrives at the time of the melting of the ice, the second during the rains which start in the autumn. Then a frigate of 36 cannon, drawing 18 feet of water, could easily go down to the Gulf of Mexico; it would be 8 or 9 days in its passage from Pittsburgh to Louisville, at the rate of 80 miles every 24 hours; between 18 and 20 from this last town to New Orleans. Nowhere on the globe, if one excepts the Amazon, can one see as considerable inland navigation without encountering obstacles. The width of the Ohio is in general from 500 to 650 feet, its depth during the swellings, from 24 to 28 feet.

"Gentlemen, this is the brief outline that you asked me for. But in order to satisfy a little of the interest that it must have aroused, I am going to read to you the story of my father's misfortunes, which I found among his papers, and which he wrote for his esteemed friend M. J. May. Then you will see that, although the colonist of Indiana belongs to the House of Bragance, nevertheless he improves his fields with care and industry; for if necessity made kings, nature has created man and in order to obey his commands, I work." *

* See Chapter I of Volume III for Story of Jean de Bragansa.

CHAPTER XVI

Here I am in New Haven, whence, in accordance with my promise, I send you the details of this little sea voyage, as well as those of my visit in this town: As you know, my education was only that of a man destined for business, so you may expect only a simple account. I know of no sea journey on this continent more pleasant than that of the Sound, especially between New York and New Haven. The shores of this beautiful bay, nearer together in the part I have just crossed than further east, are lined with dwellings, barns, orchards, and well-fenced fields, as well as the remains of primeval forests. To the traveler, they present a series of scenes that are at once varied, picturesque, and interesting. From New York as far as Hellgate, one could chat with the colonists of both shores; but the things that impressed me most before arriving at this famous strait is the contrast of these two shores. On the left, the island of New York is merely a chain of rocks, bare, sharp, wild, and almost all perpendicular, at the foot of which vessels often drop anchor when the wind and the tide are against them; in contrast, Long Island, on the right, boasts a pleasant mixture of cultivated fields and wooded lands with fences and orchards. At one hundred steps from the place where the colonist cut his last shock of wheat or heaped his last stack of hay, he can catch fish; for the waters of this arm of the sea are as fertile as the land on the banks. The houses one sees on the left were built by people of luxury and wealth; those on the right, on the contrary, were built by the industry of colonists, whose barns, sheds, and farmyards attest to their prosperity and comfort. Among these ostentatious avenues of plane trees, sycamores, and tulip trees, one sees only solitary acacias, under whose shade the traveler hitches his horse—or perhaps some old and weather-beaten oak trees, the remainder of primitive forests, with which the river banks were once covered.

How much money had to be spent in leveling off the rocks on the left to make it easy to land, to build spacious, elegant, and comfortable homes; and the extraordinary thing, one of the passengers told me, is that they found springs, from whose waters, along with the rubbish from the town, the owners have been able to make little fields and fertilize these hills. What labors they had to put forth to moderate the slope and fill in part of the valleys! How much had to be cut and filled in order to connect with the main route, fence in the land, build up the slopes, make barriers, and make possible the passing of wagons which 50 years ago could not get through there! The beauty, the vigor of the plane trees and the cedars in front of or around these houses attest to the care and to the perseverance which these projects have exacted. The old and respectable Dutch family of Beekman used to own the three largest houses as well as considerable land on these heights.

This chain of rocks is sometimes interrupted by coves or little bays which serve as shelters to the dugouts belonging to the landowners, as well as favorable sites for fishing; but some miles before Hellgate, suddenly the line of rocks becomes lower, or rather turns inland. Although the outlines of these same river banks are less sharp, they continue to be just as picturesque and delightful, on places where elegant homes have been built, almost all painted white and adorned with porches, surrounded by young trees or old Dutch orchards. The house nearest the strait, whose waters bathe the lowest terrace of the garden, is one of the largest. It has long belonged to a wealthy family, originally from Rotterdam; from the drawing room of this house, one's eyes immediately seek the lovely dwellings on the banks of Long Island, on the Goulet (narrows) the large peninsula, the rocks on both sides of Hellgate, as well as the most dangerous part of this passage. I have heard that it is not rare to see 40 or 50 sailboats crossing, during the last hour of the incoming tide and the first outgoing of the flow.

But the tide being scarcely high enough, we dropped anchor in Long Island Bay, known as Hallet's Cove where there is a fine collection of houses and a good ferry. Hoping to see in a more leisurely fashion this celebrated Gate of Hell (for Hellgate means just that), I disembarked and with the aid of an inhabitant of the neighborhood, a former navigator, I explored the southern shore to the first bend.

Like almost all narrows, this one appears to have been the work of the waters; if one believes the tradition of the Indians from the beginning of the 17th century, it does not date from early antiquity, since they claim that they can recall the earliest Dutch settlers, having heard from their fathers, that their great-grandfathers with dry feet crossed from one island to the other, and that in the high seas of the equinoxial storms, one could see there only a swollen stream. Indeed, the river banks of these two islands, separated from the town of New York twelve miles away, by an arm of the sea 300 or 400 feet wide, gradually come together and form what is called the Goulet, which is no more than 70 feet wide. The long peninsula ½ mile beyond was unable to resist the erosion of waters that carved the passage on the right to the place that I call the elbow. Here once again, thrown back from these granite banks, these waters flow to the left. From there follow the windings, the cross currents and the dangers of this passage, so justly named Hell Gate. If from the moment of their first entrance vessels get caught in an eddy, they swirl about like bits of cork and are soon swallowed up. The speed of the waters in these narrows is much more considerable when one goes from New York to New Haven than in returning from the East, because the tides that come in from the ocean by way of Sandy-Hook have only 18 leagues to run, before they are felt at Hellgate, and those coming from the eastern point of Long Island have more than 40. As to the strength of this multitude of eddies, the direction of the principal currents, the foamings, the swellings of the waters, these phenomena stem from the struggle of the two tides, following their different schedules, as well as from the infractions, the form, and the beds of undersea rocks which occupy the depth of this passageway, some parts of which one can see when the waters are low. Along the banks one sees several leveled-off rocks in whose crevices grow cedars and which at high tide become islands onto which this impetuous torrent suddenly throws the ships it has engulfed.

As to its depth, it must be considerable, for the English vessel, "The Experiment"* of 40 cannon, crossed it several times during the Revolutionary War. One had to be very bold to dare cross these narrows in a ship that drew 18 feet of water, for the high waves, the twists, and the ear-splitting noise arouse involuntary terror. I saw on these rocks two sloops of 70 ton, keel overturned; they had perished, my guide told me, for having had the imprudence to drag some masts behind. Just as I told you, the entrance of the Goulet is no more than 70 feet; and the length of the space at the greatest danger is estimated at 1,000 to 2,000 feet. The rocks are of the hardest quality and like those that one sees today in the great battery of New York, they appear to have been in the process of fusion.

The colonists on this part of Long Island are descendants of the first Walloon and Dutch families who founded the town of New York in 1614. All of them live in fine stone houses surrounded by cedars, and most of them enjoy great ease, a state they owe not only to the profits of their culture, and to their extreme economy, but also to the lobster fishing, so abundant on these tumultuous waters. This fishing is even more lucrative since Hellgate is the most southerly region where these fish live; for they are not found from there to Georgia. The noise of the cannon which the British and Americans emplaced on these two banks during the Revolution had chased them from these narrows. It is only in very recent years that they have returned.

But the tide being high enough, we raised anchor as soon as I was on board; and soon after, still keeping to the middle of the channel, we

* It was commanded by Captain Walace.

entered the Goulet with great speed. The sight of the surrounding objects, which we scarcely had time to consider, the noise of the waters rushing past us, the deep silence that reigned on board, the expressions on the passengers' faces, all that formed a very imposing spectacle for a novice like me. Nevertheless I was not frightened, so great was my confidence in the experience of the captain who had crossed these narrows more than a hundred times.

It does not matter from what direction the wind comes, there must be enough to fill the sails, make the vessel steady and more sensitive to its rudder. Although the speed at which we were sailing permitted me to see only imperfectly the surroundings yet. I still recall distinctly the wide and turbulent current that we kept at some distance on the right as well as a vast space on the left, whose waters appeared to be in a state of the highest seething; we were sailing 'mid a mass of water which some powerful unknown cause raised in great breakers whose long and noisome waves raced afar with a sharp, tearing sound. In less time than I took to write these last ten lines, we arrived at the first bend; that is to say, we made five or six hundred feet in 5 or 6 minutes. From this elbow to the exit of the strait, although the waters are still angry and agitated, they offer no danger, when one takes care to keep midway in the channel. I have heard that inhabitants of the region often cross it in their dugouts, at the precise moment of the ebb tide; the long battle waged between those of the east and the west no longer existing, the currents and eddies are less violent, and there is almost no more danger, especially for the dugouts that draw so little water.

Hardly had we left Hellgate, when the Sound became wider; on the left, one could see several cultivated islands, the mouth of the Harlem River, the houses of Morrissiana, and that long series of fine farms known as West Farms. On the right, we steered our course a little distance from the banks of Long Island, partly wooded, partly under cultivation: they were cut into by wide, deep bays, covered with salt meadows and crossed by rivers that lead to Spring Hill, Flushing, Newtown, etc., whose tide waters, held in by gates, furnish the power for several fine wheat mills.

We were tacking as we rounded the Whitestone promontory on whose height I observed a very beautiful house, when we passed a ship laden with porpoise, destined for New York. Surprised to see so great a number of these fish, that one eats only in small quantities and that only with great difficulty, I expressed my astonishment to the captain. Here is what he answered me:

"Indeed it is only in recent years that several inhabitants of the coastal provinces of Connecticut have devised the means of catching them by the hundreds. It represents what might be called a conquest, or rather a new branch of industry which they are perfecting every year. This fishing is done only in the springtime and part of the summer when the ale-wife * come from the sea and, followed by the porpoises, enter the bays in this part of the continent. They succeed in stopping them on their return with vast nets made of thongs of crude leather, suspended by ropes of considerable size; but as soon as these monsters see this obstacle, they retreat, uniting in tight squadrons and throw themselves with incredible speed on it in order to break the meshes or try to break through the net. The wisdom and daring they use in this moment of danger is an interesting sight to see. You may judge how many boats and men it takes to hold back over a space of 600 to 700 feet the united and redoubled efforts of such agile fish, albeit weighing from 300 to 400 pounds.

"The expeditions which these operations necessitate have given birth to several associations which, having become rich, today possess drawnets and buildings, and venture forth to ply their trade in the southern States as well as wherever they can find convenient bays and sufficient porpoises. The number they have caught in the last 7 or 8 years is considerable. Until now they were believed unattackable, but today, like other fish, they have succeeded in shutting them up in leather pens, which they allow to remain suspended over the side of the boat until the tide is low, and then, by means of hooks and harpoons, one can easily unload them."

"What is the purpose of this fishing, so costly and so difficult?" I asked him.

"To obtain the oil that these fish have in such abundance, as well as their skins. Finer and more water-proof leather can be made from it, than from the hides of a cow or horse. I have seen some whose leather they have succeeded in tanning for fine gloves and short jackets. Each porpoise of ordinary size is estimated to be worth between 4 and 5 piastres. This method of fishing has been perfected by some inhabitants of Nantucket, who find it much more convenient to get oil so near the land, than to put out to sea whale hunting. Moreover, so many have been caught in the last twenty years that their number has diminished considerably; the part of the ocean occupied by the current from the Gulf [1] used to be filled with them; today there are none left; those that survived this terrible disaster took flight into the northern seas, in the midst of ice, which serve them as boulevards. The fishermen of

---

* This fish, whose scientific name I do not know, comes in the spring, in countless schools on the northern coasts, from the Bay of Fundy in Nova Scotia to the waters of the Sound; it weighs from 15 to 20 pounds. One salts it as one does cod. New Hampshire sends much of it to the Antilles.

Nantucket today pursue this enormous fish to the Malouines Islands (St. Mal), in the South Sea, off the coasts of Guinea, and even beyond the Cape of Good Hope.''

We were steering our course with the aid of the tide, for the wind was against us, when, on approaching the long peninsula of West-Chester, known as Frog's Point, the captain shortened sail and prepared to take aboard a passenger whom he said was a Virginian who would wait at New Haven for the Boston stage. Our company was composed of two businessmen from New York who were going to attend a session of the annual literary meeting of the college at New Haven, where their children were; a minister from Stockbridge in the state of Connecticut; a young man who was a member of the legislature of New York State; and some other people. No sooner was dinner over than we went up on deck in order to enjoy the serenity of the day as well as the pleasure of seeing the coast of Connecticut and of Long Island, and of sailing gently over a surface which the wind scarcely stirred. The newcomer told us his political opinions, without even beginning with any of those formalities which are inspired by caution and discretion, in a land where difference of opinions often divides men. He told us of the treaty with England, which had been reverberating throughout the continent for some time and which he inveighed against heavily; of the sovereignty of the people whose deputies to Congress were merely servants; of the great Convention at Philadelphia which, overstepping its powers, had formed a constitution, the aristocratic part absorbing the influence of this same people; and finally, of all those false and superficial ideas, a thousand times reiterated in the gazettes, and a thousand times refuted by experience. He pushed indiscretion to the point of indicting the members of the Government and the senators, whose patriotism and services dated from the beginning of the Revolution: the leading magistrate of the Union was not spared. The general silence which should have indicated to him the disapproval of the company, appearing to stir him up, he continued his diatribe, blaming the administration of finances, too devoted to the whims of the Executive power, the excessive expenditures of the Government; the law about the distilleries; the one which makes the acts of naturalization more difficult to obtain; he ended his long harangue by predicting the ruin of the United States and the necessity of calling a new Convention charged with cutting out of the Constitution of 1787 everything that was too hostile to the interests of the sovereign people.*

* Can one ever forget the conduct of Virginia at this memorable time! Her legislature sent a circular to the legislatures of the other states, as well as to the former Congress, urging them to meet together at a convocation of a general Convention which would be responsible for making a new constitution, more favorable to the rights of the people than the one which had

"A difference in opinions," replied the deputy from New York, "is as natural to man as that of tastes; it is from this difference, in free countries, that enlightenment and new ideas are born; it is the nourishment of real liberty and public spirit; but when these discussions are inspired by rancor and bitterness, and pushed to the extreme where we see them today, then they tend to shackle the progress of Government, to discourage those who administer and to vex that great number of hardworking men who ask only for peace and tranquility. The administrators of whom you speak with so much malice: who were they before they occupied these posts? Were they destined to administer government because of their birth? No, they were summoned there by public vote, or by the Executive Power. Almost all of them clinging to their party by bonds of fortune, are they any more attached to its good fortune, its prosperity, than most eternal critics, cold cosmopolites who have only their venomous pens? Yes, we would have for administrators incarnate angels, whose conduct unable to please all would be heaped with outrages and insults.

"If this freedom to express opinions has sometimes been able to repress, to prevent the malpractice of government, to spread enlightenment, it has also offered disturbed and wicked minds a shadowy asylum, an assured retreat, whence they can spread lies, scandal, and denunciation with impunity. Each day they can sacrifice to their hate, to their passions, to the fury of parties, reward, talents, service, youth, beauty; yes, everyone from the first magistrate to the lowliest clerk— nothing is protected from their invective and their shafts. If the Chinese or the Persians could read our papers, they would presume, from their reading, that we are poorly governed, without protective laws, and that in a word, disorder is at its peak; and if anyone were to tell them that for ten years the Government had imposed no land tax, that we are as free and happy as most human beings; that never before has the progress of population, navigation, and trade been so rapid; then, seized with profound astonishment, they would consider us as bewildered men, or guilty of the greatest ingratitude.

"This unbridled freedom of the press," he continued, "pushed to the excesses one sees it today, is incompatible with the principles of a well-organized society whose laws should assure peace and quiet for everyone; since, on the one hand, these laws permit an unknown person to insult me, to cover me with ridicule, to attack my reputation, which is as dear to me as life, and, on the other, forbid my wreaking

just been ratified. This circular is dated November 20, 1788. History has guarded the memory of the other efforts which this state made to stifle, from its birth, this Government to which the United States owes the peace and prosperity that it has enjoyed since that time. No doubt history will reveal also the motives of these attacks, inspired by the jealousy and ambition of certain families.

a just vengeance; for, under pretext of an imagined advantage, they tolerate a serious violation and refuse to permit its punishment. By the favor of this liberty, the anonymous one reenters a state of nature, which authorizes him to do whatever seems good to him; and I, outraged, grievously wounded, my morale at a low ebb, I can neither complain nor avenge myself; justice, the courts, everything is deaf. This limitless liberty can, then, become a source of disorder, kindle revengeful thoughts, disturb the peace and quiet which are the first prizes for the sacrifices we make in entering the social state.

"Retaliate by writing, they say. And supposing I am not a writer? Must I champ at the bit that restrains me? Must I stifle the desire in order that I lose the hope of a fair retaliation? This right of retaliation, is it not, after all, the very foundation of justice? Considering how difficult it is to restrain men united in great numbers, and to forestall crime, considering also how easy it is to abuse benefits, no matter how much I admire the invaluable privilege of spouting these ideas and opinions, I can consider it only as a beautiful ideal, extremely flattering to our vanity, tempting in theory, but, as is true of so many principles, dangerous in practice.

"How, indeed, are you going to govern men when morning, noon, and night—every hour one can pervert and poison their minds and their hearts by the reading of newspapers and pamphlets, filled with sophisms, lies against individuals, and satires against the head of the Union, his ministers and administrators! What will this Government do? Will it, in the long run, be obliged to justify itself? Then you have a battle which must necessarily impede its progress, diminish its respect, that confidence which is so necessary to it, especially where the executive power is so weak. After all, can one demand that an administration will be as simple as the resolution of a problem in geometry, especially in times as stormy as these? The abuse we make of this liberty is so criminal and so outrageous that it must necessarily lead us to a new order. Yes, I say it while trembling, sooner or later it will lead to tyranny or anarchy, disorganization, or intrusion of violence; and this very feeble system of liberty, and those beautiful hopes for peace, quiet, and prosperity, will pass like a dream, this great and memorable example of reason that we gave to Europe, at the time of the adoption of the new Constitution in 1789, like lightning, will have flashed only for a moment: it will be clearly demonstrated that, in the new as well as the old world, man is not made to taste for long the benefits of liberty; a regime which indeed demands virtues and sacrifices incompatible with the passions and imperfections of human nature.

"If the desire to make a fortune, the greed with which each of us follows the means to obtain favors; if good sense and the national apathy did not reassure me a little, in truth I do not know what I would think of this insanity, this fury that resembles a state of war; as if man were condemned never to know happiness and peace; and to be the craftsman of his own misfortunes, even under the mildest and most moderate of governments.

"How much this boundless freedom of the press stifles among so many people the desire to fill the posts of the administration? For who is the man generous enough or unselfish enough to sacrifice his own peace to the desire to be useful, to that of serving his country when he sees in his imagination this bitch hounded by aggressors and hidden enemies, ready to attack and harass her? How many deputies have not been condemned to silence, betrayed their duty and sacrificed their opinions for fear of being misquoted in newspapers! The number is greater than one thinks.

"On the other hand, how many of your party chiefs do not blush at seeing themselves praised, raised on a pinnacle of fickle popularity? For who can flatter himself long that he is an idol, when one has seen the breath of calumny blast the esteemed name of Washington, considered notwithstanding the founder of this new empire, the father of his country, the man among men, and certainly the one to whose wisdom, to whose moderation we owe so much, but who, like so many other great men, will be appreciated only by our great-grandsons.

"You complain of the Government," continued this young man, "let us speak of the state of things before the time of its birth, but let us see what it has done since. It has brought measure and light into the gloomy chaos of our finances; it has laid the foundations for the public debt, merited confidence by virtue of its punctuality in fulfilling its obligations; it has also fulfilled those of the old Congress, in giving promised military land grants; it has extended and protected the colonies beyond the mountains, terminated the war with the Indians, built forts, fixed the limits of their frontiers, passed laws to prevent the invasion of their hunting grounds. It has concluded treaties with the Barbary powers, brought back the prisoners who were languishing so long in Algiers; it has protected trade, which has stretched as far as the Indies, obtained the free navigation of the Mississippi, as well as the port of the Natchez. In the midst of storms, it has succeeded in maintaining neutrality, starting a navy, building an arsenal, as well as fortifications of ports and harbors; it has built light-houses, obtained the surrender of the forts at Niagara, Oswego, Détroit, and Michillimakinack. Under the influence of this government, towns have increased and become beautified; new ones have been founded; business, coastal trade, fishing industry, farming, inland colonies, population, everything has expanded with incredible speed. Our progress astonishes even Europe. The tonnage of our vessels, which in 1790,* the time of the birth of this Government, was only 500,000 tons, is today estimated at more than 900,000; yet such has been the progress of affairs under the administration of Presidents Washington and Adams. Yet you malign them; and you complain!

"You complain also of the land tax which the Government has just imposed for the first time: and why? Do you wish that our shores be defended, our vessels convoyed, our frontiers protected, without paying for all this? Would you have us enjoy all these benefits without any sacrifice on our part? Be quite certain that we enjoy the advantages of peace, of those of good administration, and the dispensation of impartial and just laws at less expense than any other nation. The excessive weight of taxes burdens and paralyzes industry, I agree; but you will agree that since man is industrious only to the extent that necessity goads him, this tax, far from being detrimental, will be very beneficent; yes, it will be, if it contributes toward diminishing that propensity for dissipation and luxury, that passion for European merchandise that one observes in various States; it will be, if it contributes toward smothering in your state (Virginia) that love of gambling, intemperance, and horse racing, as well as cock-fighting, an infantile and barbaric pastime so unworthy of rational men.

"You regret that the Convention of 1787 has formed a Constitution in which there are principles that are too aristocratic! Would you have wanted instead, then, that the scourges of that war whence we have emerged be followed by the tempest of anarchy which was already beginning to devour us? Have we not, on the contrary, the greatest need for peace and quiet? This peace, this quiet would be even more assured and more lasting, if at this time minds might have been less swept toward extreme democracy. After seven years of dangers and fighting to procure liberty, for lack of knowing all the risks and the real state of things, people feared they did not have enough democracy. A nation that enjoys 500 leagues of coastal land, filled with rivers, harbors, wide bays; whose vessels ply all the seas in pursuit of wealth; a nation which, with the stroke of a pen, can obtain from the Indians entire provinces of new lands; a nation that dreams and concerns itself only with maritime enterprises, speculations, and business, this nation, I say—is it made to live under an Athenian Constitution?

---

* The tonnage of England in 1660 was only 96,000; in 1774, 800,000. That of the colonies, today the United States, was in 1770 already 309,534. People complained then as they complain today; it is an incurable malady.

"Alas! I fear that sooner or later we will pay dearly for the paradox that exists between our customs and the spirit of our Government, a paradox that augments with the increase of our riches and our success. Look at the evil which this delirium of democracy caused in a few years in Georgia, Rhode Island, and even in Pennsylvania. If one already begins to see that these elections, although few in number, bring upheavals, what will it be like in thirty years? These upheavals become more violent; they will produce agitations and convulsions that are extremely dangerous.

"We are certainly no better than those nations who also wanted to adopt constitutions based on too lofty ideas of wisdom, human reason; well! those colossuses, fragile as glass, disappeared before the impetuous breath of passions, and their debris covered the earth with ruin and tragedy. And we would not neglect to profit by these memorable lessons and those, even more instructive, which they give today. Well! if the Government which the Convention in Philadelphia formed in 1787, as imperfect, as feeble as it is, had not been adopted, I ask you, what would have been the consequence of this refusal? After several years, what am I saying, after several months perhaps, of discord, anarchy, and war whose sword was already sharpened in more than one state, either we would have been obliged to take refuge in the arms of our old Mother Country (they expected it in England), or these states would have formed two, or possibly three federations. One or the other of these events would certainly have taken place, if at that time there had not lived a man who succeeded in calming passions by the confidence that he possessed to inspire moderation and by his ability to conciliate, to unite the voters and give some stability to this new Government during the four years of his administration. And you were maligning him! And you would forget the services that he performed for us for twenty-three years of his life! What is one to think of men when one sees them today insult the one whom they overwhelmed with eulogies and blessings only a few years ago?

"Spoiled children of fortune and chance from our very birth, let us tremble in considering the effects which sooner or later will result in the weakness of a Government which people do not hesitate to attack! What a tragedy that the construction of this ship (of state) had not been planned more effectively to resist the inevitable storms of our ripe age, when it sails on a sea even more stormy! What a tragedy that the Athenians of 1787 could bind the hands of those persons who, at the time, saw in the near future the storms, the reefs, and the dangers and wanted to give it a longer keel, greater width, and stability! But these are the same Athenians whose virtues and patriotism are celebrated today! From what source would they have drawn their praise, if these same persons had not succeeded in preventing the union of these states?"

"Not wishing to reply at this moment," retorted the Virginian, "to anything but what you mentioned about freedom of the press, I ask you, what we are to do, when the Government permits arbitrary acts, if you deny a whole nation the right to raise its voice against oppression and abuse? What restraint will you impose then on the ambition of the leader and the malpractices of his ministers? Will you not agree that the strength of this public opinion is the last rampart left to a nation in defending its liberty and its rights?

"If this opinion were really the expression of all the people; if, when there exists a real cause of complaint or censure, man or the group toward which the wrong has been committed appeared with the proof in hand; if personal interest were never to replace public interest; if humiliated vanity, hate, blind revenge would not borrow the language of justice; then you would have reason to inveigh against freedom of the press, the most boundless freedom, and I would join my objections to yours. But the cries of a crowd of malcontents, sedition-mongers, who like kingfish, live only amid tempests; the lying or sophistic declamations of anonymous writers whose poisonous pens stab men of property both by their accusations and eulogies; can all that be considered the voice of the American people? Do you not know as well as I, that nearly three-quarters of these people have no part in these works of injustice, ingratitude, and scandal? Do you not know that what really makes a nation, landowners, farmers, craftsmen, sailors, manufacturers, all those who live by dint of constant and regular work, need only good civil laws, well-organized courts, with a protective police, and that they ask only security, peace, and confidence?"

"You boast of the advantages of unlimited freedom of the press, and I complain of its excesses: this freedom, far from being a benefit for the state, is a craze, which in the long run, creates discontent, insubordination, upheavals and death; it is a lever whose strength it is impossible for a Government such as ours to long resist; it provides the opposition with all the energy and the fanaticism of a new sect, which does not long delay in upsetting the old altar of our country for one of its own. The same is true of freedom that is true of health and strength: to guard them for a long time, one must enjoy them with wisdom, use them with economy; for the abuse of this freedom soon becomes license, the most deadly of all poisons. When one has read history, how happy one has found the nation which is passably governed, above all when it leaves behind the torments of a revolution as long as ours! Especially fortunate is the one over whose destinies caution with all its solicitudes has presided and this you know as well as I—glory with all its dignity. May misfortune beset those whom so fortunate a position leaves without enthusiasm and without gratitude!

"Of all manias, the most dangerous is that of perfection in Governments; and this mania will characterize particularly the end of the century. How many tears, how much blood it has cost humanity! Thank God, the universe is beginning to tire of it. Can there be anything perfect on earth? Was perfection ever given to the weakness, to the misery, to the fearful passions of man? Believe me, leave these cold cosmopolites to die in oblivion, with their futile systems, with their absurd theorizings, escaping from Pandora's box; and we who have the good fortune to claim as our native land a country that we have cleared; we, for whom remoteness from Europe, the form of our Government, and our youth have already procured so many good things, and promise an even greater prosperity, let us fear giving ourselves over to excesses that we would have to pay for dearly! Rather let us bless the circumstances in which the genius of a man placed us, snatching us from the womb of anarchy, from the tragedy of seeing dissolve the union of these states, and civil war break out, and European powers mingle in our affairs. Let us bless the Government which assures us peace, guarantees us the enjoyment of our fortunes and our rights, dispenses justice with impartiality, directs a severe eye to the finances which, in the end, year by year justifies our confidence and earns our gratitude. Let us respect this salutary regime, so recently established, in whose shelter flourish our farming and trade, our colonies inland. Let us not discourage by foolish intrigues, by invective, those who have repaired the losses that we have sustained at the time of our long revolution, those who while we sleep, watch over us and work to heal our wounds and lead us to glory and good fortune."

"But since you blame and fear such unlimited freedom of the press, tell me then, I beg of you, what one must do to hold it within bounds which would stop the delirium and the danger, without muting the echo of that trumpet of public opinion which is so often necessary?"

"It is a great problem which has not yet been solved, and which must occupy our statesmen's mighty minds. My feeble knowledge does not permit me to try it. One can feel the evil, know the cause, and be ignorant of the remedy."

CHAPTER XVII

This interesting conversation, whose ending only did I have time to tell you yesterday evening, lasted until we entered the bay of New Haven, where soon afterwards, our boat was tied to the mooring [1] about two miles from the town where a pier has just been finished, leading to the town wharf. For lack of a favorable wind, we were 10 hours making the trip. The next day I was at the home of Mr. Chittenden, busy examining his carding machine which I was to buy and send to my father, when I noticed a fire engine which they told me was for the town.

"Those fine tubes (nozzles) of copper," I asked of the person who was carding, for Mr. Chittenden was absent, "came no doubt from New York or Boston?"

"No," the worker answered me, "I smelted and turned them; after many attempts, I have succeeded in making quite a few things of copper."

I was congratulating him on his talents when he said:

"Ah, if I were sure of getting my food and clothing for only a year, I could make even more interesting things."

"What, for example?"

"Telescopes and microscopes."

"And where did you learn about these instruments? Certainly it was not when you were serving in the Continental army?"

"The president of our college had the kindness to permit me to see and even to borrow some from the physics laboratory; I have succeeded in making a telescope with which one can discern the satellites of Jupiter, and a microscope in which one can see vinegar eels."

Astonished that fortune had given to this man so little means, and nature so much intelligence, I resolved to take him from this shop, and asked him his name.

"Felton," he replied.

That very evening he brought me his two instruments, with which indeed I could see the satellites of Jupiter and a great many tiny objects. All this amused my fellow passengers enormously.

Instead of returning to my inn by following the street that had been shown me, I took another route, planted with weeping willows of great height. I had gone but a hundred steps, when I saw a potter's shop which I entered to get out of the sun; after speaking to the owner about his art, the clay that he used, and the price of his vases, I was complaining of the heat when he said to me:

"My thermometer reads only 70°." *

Surprised to see in a mere potter's shop such a fine instrument whose scale was of mercury and mounted on mahogany, I asked how much it had cost him.

"I made it myself," he replied.

Imagine my astonishment!

"Where did you learn to blow glass?"

"During my leisure time I busy myself in various undertakings; I have been luckier in glass-blowing than in any other."

"What is your name?"

"Felton."

"Are you by chance the brother of the fellow in Mr. Chittenden's shop?"

"Yes."

I spent some time chatting with this artist, who seemed to me to be as poor as his brother, the pump-maker. He showed me a gun of his making, whose barrel was six feet, and some glass items made from sand that had been recently discovered on the eastern shore of the bay. I bought some items from the former and the thermometer of the latter.

But just as though the number of amazing events had not reached its peak, in following this same street, I saw the frame of a carriage that was being painted: astonished for the third time, I asked for whom this carriage was being made.

"To be sent to Havana," the painter replied; "for what use can one make of it in a town such as this, where there are only 600 houses?"

On entering his shop, I noticed an engraving machine as well as some lapidary's wheels.

"What do you do with these machines?" I asked.

"Because the profession of painting carriages does not keep me busy all year," he told me, "I have become an engraver and a lapidary, every time the occasion arises. I engraved the map of the state of Vermont planned by Major Blodget. I succeeded in cutting the garnets discovered in a mine in the neighborhood of Norwich; they sell very well in Europe. Necessity is a severe mistress, especially when one has a wife and children. By preference, I would rather be working as an engraver; but since I cannot pamper myself, I am obliged to vary my industry. Our country is still so young that it is necessary to know how to do several different things. It will not be the same with our children. Today they receive a much finer education and perform a better ap-

* 16⅔ degrees Reaumur.

prenticeship than did we, raised in the midst of dangers and upheavals of the revolution. The population is increasing; this country is becoming richer; soon craftsmen busying themselves with only a single profession will become more skillful than are we.''

Returning from this little excursion, I presented my letters of recommendation to Mr. H. H., a well-known lawyer, a member of Congress, and surprisingly enough, an enthusiastic amateur farmer. After dinner, he led me to his little farm whose soil, as well as that of all the town environs, is a very productive loam. His fields seemed to me to be well cultivated; he enriched them not only with fertilizer, but with seaweed found in great abundance in a swamp located east of the town, on the shores of the Sound. I also saw several clumps of mulberry bushes and acacia trees, of extraordinary vigor. With much interest, I heard this legislator speak of fuller's earth, improvements, agriculture, alfalfa, and sainfoin, with as much accuracy as though he might have been summing up a complicated case before a jury. He showed me the carriage wheels he had used for 12 years; they were made of knotty oak, found in the swamps; it is the most durable and hardest of the woods of the continent.

Observing wherever we went a great number of mulberry trees that appeared to have been planted with care, I asked him to what use they could be put. He replied:

''For a long time they have been cultivating silkworms in this state. Perhaps you will not believe it, yet we have a small silk factory at Mansfield with which we are quite delighted. It is to one of our most esteemed citizens, Mr. Aspinwall, whom we owe the knowledge of everything concerning the raising of these worms, as well as to the cultivation of the mulberry bushes; it is to him, also, that we owe the first nursery that has ever been in existence in this state. Fortunate is the country where these rare men are born whose passion is to do good. It will take several generations to pay our debt of gratitude. Not content to preach only here this new knowledge, he went to spread it in Jersey and Pennsylvania where he founded several nurseries. That is how he undertook at the same time to spread a great number of mulberry seeds through all the districts of the state and to confide their early beginnings to all the parishes and all the congregations whose number was then 317. He spoke to the President of our college, Doctor Styles, who, praising his zeal, had 317 letters of instruction printed, in which he enclosed 600 of these seeds which he immediately sent to his colleagues; in less than three weeks, 190,200 were planted. That was the origin of the mulberry trees of Connecticut. Many of them have since been planted. This industry in Mansfield has already become so interesting, that, with the idea of preserving its reputation, the legislative body in 1787 granted a corporation charter to the owners of the mulberry trees, authorizing them to elect inspectors among their group and to make any regulations necessary to the perfection of this small business. To be a member of this association, it is necessary to own a certain number of the trees; twelve, if I am not mistaken, in order to have a voice in the council.''

Thoroughly instructed in the history of his country, Mr. H. H. talked to me about its early colonization by three sects of puritans. It appears that these sects were as wise as they were pious; foreseeing that the divisions which began to arise among them would expose them to the vengeance of the Indians, they had the good sense to unite, to obtain from Charles II a charter which today serves as basis for their old constitution; he talked to me about the laws, the customs, the education. In no other part is it so widespread; for according to what he told me, there are not three square leagues in the whole state without one or more schools whose teachers and clergy are paid by the Government.

The inhabitants of this state * are like one big family, wisely and well governed, among whose members one finds the same attitudes and the same inclinations. It is one of the most thriving beehives on the continent: from it five or six thousand young people go forth into other states every year to make new settlements, where land is less dear; perhaps 150 schoolmasters, not to mention men who are destined for the great fisheries, coastal trade, or long sea voyages. Almost all the inhabitants of this state are descended from the first families who came here from England in 1630. Mr. H. H. also told me about the manufacture of cloth at New Haven, where the annual export for Georgia alone was mounting to more than 400,000 els. He concluded by telling us of the manufacture of paper for envelopes, made with what falls from the flax and the hemp when it is cleaned and cut.

The next day being the day for the meeting of the college, Mr. H. H., the two businessmen from New York, and I went to church early; here the ceremony was to take place. Work in the town had ceased; each citizen, dressed in his best, prepared to receive his friends, for the inns were not adequate to take care of all the outsiders who came.

"Today," Mr. H. H. told me, "is one of the days of the year when, like the wife of the good vicar of Wakefield, each housewife puts her-

---

* This state, one of the smallest in the Union, has only 4,674 square miles, divided into 8 counties and 100 districts; and yet, according to an estimate that was made at the time of peace by a committee of the legislative body, it appears that during the war it lost nearly 20,000 men and that the losses occasioned by the ravages of the English amounted to 1,037,450 piastres (8,637,697 pounds). To compensate for so many victims, the Government has given Connecticut the entire reserve of 500,000 acres which it possessed west of Pennsylvania.

self out to make the best pies, the smoothest and richest puddings and tarts, and the most delicious sauces."

But soon the procession arrived; it was composed of the Governor of the state, the lieutenant-Governor, members of the cabinet, as well as the president, the officers of the University, and 136 scholars. After the examinations in English, Latin, and Greek were over, and degrees had been conferred on those who had earned them, the President mounted the rostrum and delivered a speech from which I send you the parts that impressed me; I took them from the original itself, which Mr. H. H. borrowed the very next day.

The exordium was very moving. Imagine a father giving his last advice and paternal benediction to those of his children who, having reached their majority, are about to embark on a tempest-tossed sea; a teacher outlining for his dear pupils from whom he is to be separated lessons which the pupils are soon going to be called on to fulfill. After a brief historical resumé of the transition from colonial state to independence, of the establishment of the new Government, of the effects which these great events had on customs, industry, and society; finally, after paying just tribute of praise and gratitude to the illustrious founders of this new Empire, he said:

"Scarcely ten years have elapsed since those memorable times and already what happy changes we see in the organization of all the parts which compose this great gathering of sixteen states! What a magnificent conception, that of civilization: laws, order, and system to which man owes the distinguished position he holds in this land; security, property, the sciences, the arts, the refinements—in short, the enjoyments of life.

"How much more propitious is this day when you are leaving us to go forth into the world, than the one when we entered this very college! What improvement and progress since that time! No, you will not be considered as citizens of a little neighborhood, of a town, or of an isolated colony, unknown, but as Americans, that is to say, members of the great association of the United States, that new country whose cherished hope you are; to whose glory and happiness the talents you have received from nature and which we have developed, must henceforth be devoted.

"Are you destined to own lands, to cultivate them? Remember: that it is to farming which man owes the early developments of his civilization; these states, their birth and the vigor of their adolescence; that farming is the ancient friend, the companion of customs and religion, a constant source of prosperity, grandeur, and strength; that, more than any other profession, farming is ennobled by the benefits it spreads, for, after all, manufactures are only its daughters. You will draw from the example and experience of the Europeans everything that can enrich and improve our culture, still so imperfect, and which must necessarily be that way until we have become more populous; until the products of the land are sufficient to pay for the expenses of these improvements.

"To repair the lack of foresight of our ancestors, you will have nurseries, and surround your fields with useful, fine trees, those beautiful ornaments of the countryside whose shade and greenness is so beneficial. It is a duty which I hope the legislature will not delay in imposing on us, as well as that of fencing in our fields with hedges; everywhere we see the beginnings of it, for everywhere nature sows, white and black thorns grow.

"You will contribute to the happiness of those who depend on you; and give them the example of industry and order. You will respect old age, whose experience you will often consult; you will spare the indigent the shame of soliciting help. Every time a friend confides a secret in you, you will seal it in your heart with as much care as you would flee the approach of a snake or the knife of an assassin. Likewise, you will push from your mind that frightful and desolating skepticism which attacks the soul, as the ices of the spring smite down the buds in our orchards, imbuing us with an unsociable dried-up egoism, converting our imagination into a barren and arid desert. For what worth is man, surrounded by reefs, dangers, and hardships of life when he does not know, or when he has lost the strength, the resignation, and the courage which inspire the sublime consolations of another life? Like the wretch whose torch has gone out while exploring the catacomb, or the traveler who loses his guide in the midst of endless plains, not seeing on the horizon or rather in the future that shining point that marked his route, and showed him port, he wanders at the will of chance. Does he meet misfortune on his way, then nothing can mitigate this misfortune, nothing can console him since he has lost hope, that precious companion which alone can diminish, and calm the difficulties, pains, and fatigues of the voyage of life.

"As fathers, remember that education is one of the greatest benefits you can leave to your children; it is a sacred duty that God and the laws have confided in you. Remember that the advantages of a good education are the finest fruits of civilization, a power that raises us above the blind and fierce Indian; a light that generates the seed of virtues and talents. The education of this country, which for more than a century had been the object of paternal solicitude of our colonial administration, will receive from time every degree of perfection to which it is susceptible. And look at us now! We, who in 1789, did not even have a national Government!

"Are you destined to fulfill the functions of the ministers of the gospel? Inculcate by your example, your precept, your sincere instruction, the morality of our divine mediator, the most consoling, the one most worthy of respect and veneration of rational beings, that has ever been announced to mankind. Inexhaustible source of peace, charity, and beneficence, the basis of governments, the bond of societies, protector, reformer of customs, alone able to warn of so many crimes and hidden misdemeanors, it supports laws, which, deprived of its help, would necessarily be more numerous and more severe.

"Are you destined to study medicine? Carry into this practice of science, so replete with doubt and uncertainty, all the timidity of caution, which your experience as well as that of others has taught you. Never consider yourselves anything but the humble auxiliaries to nature; let your heart not be hardened at the daily sight of the evils and misery of humanity; apply yourself to the study of botany, that rich treasure so little known, to which, some day, we will owe more than we do to chemistry; repeat a hundred times to your friends, to your acquaintances, publish in all your writings, that after the practice of virtue, hygiene is the holiest and the most useful among men.

"Are you destined to become magistrates, lawyers? Take timid innocence by the hand, unmask imposture, make fraud blush, punish crime. Ah! would to God that lying were among the number of crimes struck at by the severity of laws! Contribute toward stretching the domain of impartial justice, protective aegis of societies, that majestic tree, to use an Indian metaphor, in the shadow of which men enjoy peace, confidence, the fruits of their labors and their industry. Disdain to use those means which slow down the wheels of justice and cause so many costly and futile delays; accomplish in such a way that instead of being a burden to progress, your career in law may become a real benefit. If ever circumstances permit, lend your ear to the general cry, which for a long time has asked for reform of these abuses; see what has already been done in Pennsylvania to destroy those of the ancient penal code.

"If you owe to your country the use of your talents, you owe her also devotion and the courage that you have received from nature; for it is unfortunately that among men. To obtain a greater good, how many sacrifices one must make! Always be ready to carry out your oath, to obey your chief; everytime he calls on you to defend the frontiers, repress abuse of liberty or assure the execution of laws.

"If ever the esteem and confidence of your compatriots send you to Congress, how many talents, how much enlightenment this career will exact! Knowledge of history, of law making, of trade, of manufacture, of the right of nations! What courage, what firmness will you need then to obey the inspiration of your conscience and resist the pressure of political parties, this scourge of countries where freedom reigns; as you will come to know some day, their abuse has caused so much evil among men! Three things must principally occupy your thoughts and become the object of your most ardent desires: to consolidate, to bind firmly the ties of Union; for, like a bundle of sticks, these states will never become strong until they are united; encourage the perfection of agriculture, arts, and education; protect national manufactures and trade, and patronize learning.

"It is from Europe, our old and respectable grande-dame that our ancestors have brought the sacred trust which has kept us from that long and delayed infancy of so many other nations: this trust will also light the way to our maturity. Cultivate this trust, honor it then, as it merits being honored, so that our posterity can shine in all its glory. Born in the Orient, it finds among us on this western continent their last asylum which ends the great circle which our ancestors have run in the space of six thousand years. It is they who taught men, after leaving their primitive period in the forests, to forge iron, to beautify and make fertile the land, to resist the elements, to raise their minds aloft to the author, the conservator of the universe, to know the progress, the distances, the relative positions of the globes of which our planetary system is composed. It is the sciences and arts which have fortified our weakness, with all the resources of mechanics which the sanctuary of chemistry has offered us, and which, finally, have made us savage and ferocious beings come to know the advantages of culture and civilization. With a Congress, a body of magistrates, farmers and soldiers, such as I have just indicated, the peace and good fortune of this new empire will be long and lasting.

"Whatever lies ahead for you, conserve faithfully the piety whose advantage and duty we have instilled in you during your stay of four years in this university. May this daughter of heaven always be your consolation and companion! Meditate often on life whose misfortunes and hardships are so frequent and whose pleasures so fleeting. Raise your thoughts to this future to which you are called and of which this short and tiring pilgrimage is only an introduction, etc."

I was telling Mr. H. H. of the great applause that followed, of the pleasure it had given me and of the Governor's request for a copy, when he said:

"That is about the attitude expressed in the speeches made by most of the college presidents annually in our northern states. There exists among them an extremely edifying emulation. I should be very angry if anything ever caused this tradition to disappear. For it is not to the young people only that these speeches are addressed, but to the entire audience, as well as to the chiefs of state, who like protectors born * of these literary institutions, never fail to be present at these annual ceremonies. Among the thirty-two young people who have left this college, two were from the Bermuda Islands,[2] one from the Bahama Islands,[3] two from Canada, ten from the two Carolinas, and 17 from Connecticut."

After leaving the church, Mr. H. H. and I got into our carriage, to go seven miles away for dinner with one of his friends, a great farmer, and learned man who had traveled widely in his youth; he owned a farm beautifully situated on the southern slope of a hill, bounded by beautiful grasslands. This colonist showed us three mills under the same roof, which he had had built some years before: one was for wheat, the other for oil, and one a fuller's mill. I observed in his pastures several beef estimated to weigh 1,325 pounds by mark weight and some others weighing between 1,000 and 1,200 pounds. Indeed, it is in this state as well as that of Rhode Island, that one sees the finest cattle on the continent, as well as in the western regions of Massachusetts. Thus, one can say nothing more complimentary to the great landowners of these states than to ask to see their herds; quite different are they from those landowners of Virginia, who talk of nothing but horses, races, and cock-fighting.

I was congratulating this colonist on the good fortune of owning fertile fields, of having such vast orchards, of living under a Government so moderate and so thrifty, sheltered from the worries of trade and the torments of politics, when he said:

"Since there is so much evil on earth, how is it that the farmers do not have their share of it? Nothing, indeed, is more tempting than the pastoral life, when one does not know its daily cares, the labor it requires, when one sees it from afar, or in the works of poets: but if these literary men were weighed down by their plows for several days, exposed to the rain and the wind; if they had reaped and tossed the hay of their fields, under the heat of a burning sun, devoured by mosquitoes, tormented by flies; if they had cut their harvests, back exposed to the sun's rays, face earthward, swimming in sweat as we do, they would realize that if sometimes we gather roses, it is only 'mid

* According to the wise dispositions of the last charter of corporation, the governor of the state, the lieutenant-governor and the six oldest counselors are by definition administrators of this college, jointly with the president and the other deans and regents.

thorns and that this father of nature, this star, whose glory and splendor they sing, is sometimes a tyrant of it all.

"And these sudden spring frosts which in a single night destroy our hopes for fruits, apples, and cider; and these electric storms, which in the midst of the burning heat of August, swoop down upon us, and leave us scarcely the straw of our harvests; and this great number of birds that live at our expense! Such are some of the inconveniences rarely mentioned by these learned persons, because they have not experienced them: they are not the only ones; these multitudes of insects, so varied, so voracious, and so destructive, whose generations succeed one another with such rapidity, who are born only to multiply their number, to harm, and then to die! During the warm and wet years, their fertility seems inconceivable and their number incalculable. The instinct of some leads them to gnaw at the roots of the trees, others the leaves, still others the buds; we can neither plant nor sow anything whatever without these insects becoming their enemy; and so that nothing may be spared their ravages, the autumn insects come to devour the fruits whose buds had escaped the voracity of their predecessors.

"And these worms born in the very bosom of the corn stalks and these Hessian flies that lay their eggs under the first stalks of wheat, in order to stop the sap, and these inundations of caterpillars who, like a destructive fire, spoil our orchards and our forests and, in the middle of the summer spread mourning, and in the winter sadness! How can we resist so many enemies, so formidable in number, although so negligible because of their weakness?

"Something even more extraordinary! Their germs and their microscopic eggs survive the rigor of these spring frosts which, in a single night, cause our rivers to stop and freeze over. Yet, if each year had its spring regularly, as well as its summer and its autumn, we would have less reason to complain; but when to the ravages of so many insects, are joined the irregularity and inclemency of seasons, then one must expect considerable losses and bear up under them with courage.

"As for me, if I were a poet, I would entertain myself singing of the peace we enjoy when these numerous enemies are entombed under the winter snows; of the tranquility and leisures of this season, when, like us, the hardworking ox rests in his warm stall, from his long and patient fatigues. I would sing of the impetuosity of the somber northeaster that brings us whirlwinds, these heavy and beneficent snows, a shelter so useful for grains, of prairies, as well as of communications and journeys; season of gaiety, hospitality, and pleasure. I would sing also of the northwest wind, no less redoubtable, roaring down from the polar regions, bringing us hoar-frost, ice, and rime, with which this tyrant of our winters throws solid and durable bridges over our rivers, our lakes, and the arms of our sea, and gives to the snow a dazzling splendor. I should not forget (in my songs) the pipe, now lulling, now meditative, ever calming, nor the joy of cider and ginger,* nor the warmth of a good fire, around which one sees his wife, his children, and often his neighbors. I should mingle in my humble songs the stories of a sailor who tells us of the water spout, of the noise of the cannon, of the enormous column of water pumped by the sun, and suspended in the clouds, or of the whales he has pursued and harpooned from a frail skiff. I would recall also those of the warrior, who, 'mid the piercing cries of the warwhoop, has fought the ferocious Indian on the banks of the Ohio, and has seen his companion scalped. I would speak of the indefinable but real enjoyment that I feel, at the approaches of a cold and gloomy night in December. Everything is closed and tightly shut in when the first squalls of the storm, heralded by the flapping wings of the impetuous north wind, suddenly, redoubling in fury, come like a deluge, thundering over the roof to flash, while scolding over our dripstones, to touch lightly, with different intonations. In their rapid passage, they shake the doors and windows of the house, to thunder down our chimney, whistle through the bare branches of the neighboring trees, and reverberate even longer in our far away forests.

"I would paint the impression of fear and terror which this noise, this sudden turmoil in the atmosphere leaves on the minds of our children; the questions they ask us regarding the unknown causes of violence of these unleashed storms which are nothing more than a violent current of the same air we breathe. I would try to recapture on canvas the impression created by this rain, spring zephyr, or rather divine breath, which lavishes its richness over the earth, in the air, and under water, calling from a void and bringing forth the seeds and sprouts of life and vegetation. Although indescribable, I would try to paint the charms of this season of love and voluptuousness, of flowers and hope; a season which, old as I am, still fills my veins and my heart with happiness and gratitude. I would also try to describe my solitary walks in the forests, in the fields, in the shelter of my orchards, on the banks of the rivers, where I go to enjoy this annual miracle; the swelling, the rapid development of the buds and leaves; I would share, with the birds, so volatile, so gay, and so happy, the pleasure with which they seem to be animated and the vivifying air which they

* Nothing is more restoring than warm cider in which one has mixed a teaspoonful of ginger; especially when it is extremely cold outside and one has just been exposed to this cold.

breathe. I would listen, thoughtfully, to this mysterious voice that seems to address youth at this time and recalls old men to life.

"Such are some of the objects that I would amuse myself in singing about or describing, if my family did not require the sweat of my brow and the work of my hands. If these feeble sketches did not resemble poets' descriptions, enriched by all the colors and all the charms of their brilliant imaginations, at least they would have the merit of being drawn from the great originals of nature, for, despite all the evil nature brings forth on us, the examination of her works excites and arouses admiration and respect. Who would not see in the form, in the organization, and in the instinct of a fly, an insect, a bird, a plant, or moss, an imprint of bursting perfection! Manifest proofs of planned design, such a great profusion of beauty, order, wisdom and foresight, that each object, however small, appears to the thoughtful person like a marvel or rather an immediate emanation of the creative power, the effect of a cause ceaselessly agitating, spread throughout matter, which it is impossible not to recognize and not to admire in silence and contemplation!

"But how many years will have to elapse before we have among us laboratories and lovers of natural history? Today the only thing we can occupy ourselves with is work and industry. Do you see the children around me? Well, all of them must have primary school education, knowledge of a trade or a profession and of the earth, if they prefer farming. The same is true in every family. Ah, how different is our plight from that of the inhabitants of Europe! There, the houses and barns are built, the roads and bridges are made, the mills built, the swamps drained since long centuries into green lands and pastures where orchards are planted; the Europeans have only to entertain, work, and enjoy themselves. Here, on the contrary, there being something to do all the time, we are obliged to be both farmers and creators. The first generation clears the land, the second improves it, and the labors of the third are not sufficient to perfect it. Estimate the expenditures that all these creations exact in a country where it is so easy to become a landowner, and where, consequently, day laborers are bound to be very scarce and very expensive!"

On returning to New Haven from the home of this interesting colonist, I spent the remainder of the day writing; I was busy in my room finishing some letters in the evening, when one of the passengers from the stage coach from New York whom I had observed leaning against one of the drawing room windows, alone and thoughtful, came up to bed (for, as you know, the rooms of taverns always contain several beds). No sooner had he entered the room, when he dropped on his knees at the foot of his bed. I was astonished at the length of his prayers, when I noticed that in getting up, he keeled and was about to fall over; I just had time to hurry to his side and put him in an arm chair where he lost consciousness. The shadows of death, as well as cold sweat soon covered his brow. I summoned help and we put him on his bed. After a half hour of unconsciousness, I heard deep sighs, repeated and labored at various intervals; he opened his eyes again, but his look was still so spiritless and so feeble that he scarcely saw me.

"Oh, My Heavenly Father!" he said in very low voice, "I had reached the doors of Your sanctuary and I am still alive! I had ceased to be and now I must die a second time!"

"What is the matter with you?" I asked. "Where are you suffering? Take some drops of this Hoffman brandy; it will revive you."

"Are you a doctor?" he asked me.

"No, I am only a friend who seeks to console you, since you are far away from your kin."

"A friend! ah, no! You have the pity of an angel!"

I was busying myself wiping the two streams of tears that ran down his face, when he said:

"Let them fall; they relieve the oppression that overwhelms me; they are, I think, the last ones that I will shed here on earth."

I respected his advanced age too much to dare ask him what was the cause of his misery. A long silence followed these last words; the successive heavings of his chest announced a paroxysm, to whose violence I thought he would succumb; a second dose of these drops brought back a calm and then unconsciousness again. He remained in this lethargic state until midnight, when he opened his eyes again, and I had him take a good hot consommé which revived him.

"These attacks," I said to him, "this long crisis which you have just experienced, does it not come from the fatigues of the journey?"

"Oh, no!" he replied, "it is from the misfortunes of life." And the abundant tears began to fall. "Yes" he replied, shaking my hand feebly, "the losses I suffered are irreparable. I was husband and father; these ties and bonds are broken: my heart is filled only with tenderness and affection; these wonderful feelings were the food, the sustenance, and consolation of my old age. This heart is empty; how can I say it? It is filled only with bitterness, regrets, and sobs which will end by breaking it in making their escape."

He stopped speaking; his eyes closed; I thought he was going to lapse again into a second attack, when his hand relaxed, seemed to seek mine, and he said very softly:

"Ah! If the Supreme Being deigns to give ear to my supplications, tonight or tomorrow this broken, worn-out heart, these organs, this body will return to nature to be used better by her, and my soul will go rejoin that of my wife and son. I have no other desires."

I listened to his difficulties; I shared his sadness; again I dried his tears as he said to me:

"Are you married?"

"No," I replied.

"Ah, how fortunate you are! Whatever tragedy befalls you, you will never know the one I am experiencing. What is more worthy of envy, than the lot of a man, wedded to the woman he loves and is loved by! What enjoyment that of having children who bind the knots; that of watching them grow, and guiding their early steps, developing their reason!

"This time of life," he continued, "resembles the spring of nature; it is the season of pleasure and hope. This spring, as you know very well, is followed by the heat, the drought, and sometimes the storms of summer; then the mild autumn whose fruits are exposed to so many accidents and enemies; finally come the ice and the snows of a long and bleak winter; that is where I am now. I lost what I had loved so tenderly; the woman who had been my companion for forty-eight years and the son in whom were concentrated my last hopes, my only future. How can I resist such assaults? How can I bear the poignant sufferings of such a great sacrifice? and yet death and despair in the heart and religion forbid us to leave life! What shall I do on this earth which is today merely a desert, since my friends are no longer here. Alone, as I am, in whose bosom can I pour forth my tears and with whom can I share my woes and moans? Although my eyes witnessed it, I cannot believe that everything I loved is dead; I am more certain that they are only temporarily away, than I am that they have ceased to exist. I can conceive of the idea of absence, oblivion, remoteness; but not that of an eternal abyss, of irrevocable destruction. Ah, since it is so disastrous, so frightful to have loved, why have we been given this wonderful, irresistible disposition, which leads to the unhappiness that I experience.

"I have no desire other than that of falling asleep in the peace and quiet of a tomb; mysterious sleep, during which we pass from death to life, from the shadows to the light; last haven where from every point the debris of humanity come and give themselves up. And why would one fear this haven so much, since in entering it, one puts behind him the sadness, the anguish, and the difficulties of life? Ah! may the Supreme Being transform the drowsiness of this night to eternal sleep! For, death being a benefit to a man who has attained his seventieth year, a quick death, that delivers us from agonies, is even greater still.''

Never will the memory of this long spectacle of tragedy be erased from my mind; nor will its beneficial effect. Ah! May Heaven grant that I never be destined to experience the same misfortune some day! This respectable and unfortunate old man, feeling better after two days' rest, took a more comfortable vehicle than the diligence, and returned home.

I, too, left for Hartford * where I knew that your esteemed friend, Colonel Wadsworth, had just arrived. You had good reason to tell me that he was one of the most interesting men to know on the whole continent. No one is better instructed in anything pertaining to the civil and political economy of his country. I knew all the services that he rendered in the shadow of mystery, at the critical period which preceded the acceptance of the new constitution. His family is the mirror of happiness and union. They had just learned unfortunately that Harriet, his oldest daughter, whose friends had long ago given her the name of Angel, had just died in the Bermuda Islands, whose eternal spring, so favorable to consumptives, had not been able to prolong her days.

Nobody, most certainly, merits better than Mr. Wadsworth the great fortune that he acquired, for there are few manufactures or useful enterprises in this state whose origin he has not patronized. Because his age and health no longer permit him to go to Congress of which he has been a member since the beginning of the new government, he has just resigned his position as representative. I learned in his home that my unfortunate old gentlemen friend of the inn had died two days after his return to Pittsfield in Massachusetts and that, in accordance with his last wishes, his remains had been placed in the vault with his family between his wife and his son.[4]

* Capital of Connecticut. It is located on the west branch of the river of the same name, 50 miles from the sea. It is composed of 500 houses, aligned on a street which is a mile long and 300 feet wide, planted with high trees. This town is divided by a small river, whose banks are extremely picturesque and on which there is a beautiful bridge, from which one can see falls worthy of the brush of a painter.

NOTES TO VOLUME TWO

CHAPTER I

1 LAND OF CHERRYHUM. Either Europe, or the eastern part of America, which is indeed in the setting sun of the land inhabited by the mighty Chérokée nation, formerly composed of many tribes who were almost all equally numerous. The mightiest, who lived south of the mountains, occupied the valleys of the rivers Catahoochée, Tugéloo, Isumdigaw, Salwégée, Oconée, etc. Another tribe, known under the English name of Over-Hills, had spread into the beautiful and fertile valleys of the Ténézée, Kéowée, Highwasée, Chota, etc. This is the one on the continent with whom friendship was possible only by exercising the greatest care and skill; thus the Governors of Carolina were ceaselessly occupied with maintaining the fine harmony which has long existed between the two peoples. This power has disappeared. Almost two centuries ago their ancestors came from a land located west of the Mississippi and seized what is today known as Georgia and Carolina, whose inhabitants they expelled. It was terror over their weapons which made the Séminolle tribes forget their dissension, and to unite in order to block their invasions. Such was the origin of the Muscogulgés confederation, the only one on the continent still in existence; each day it is becoming more respectable.

This state of continual warfare, as well as smallpox and brandy, had already diminished considerably the number of Chérokée warriors when the revolution began; united with the English, at King's Mountain and elsewhere, they suffered substantial losses, from which they did not recover. Weakened, discouraged, those who remain occupy some of their former towns, having sold to the white men seven and one-half million acres of land. Although still masters of a vast amount of land, they are rapidly heading toward extinction; for how can they resist the influence of men who carry the germs of a malady as contagious as smallpox, and the art of making brandy from peaches or from barley? For them the plow, industry, and laws have become redoubtable enemies; and, as an old Missisagé chief said: "The race of sowers of little seeds will, in the long run, expel that of hunters." Sated with this fatal glory which had cost them so much blood, if they had established a government similar to their rivals', the Muscogulgés of Florida, like them, they would have multiplied their number, they would have become respectable, and would still possess their mountains, as well as the beautiful and delightful valleys which they enclose, and the new state of Ténézée, this sixteenth link in the American confederation, would not have been founded.

2 TRANS–ALLEGHENIAN BUFFALOES. Before the settling of the white men west of the mountains, the plains of the Kentuckey region, of the Scioto, Wabash, Illinois, Ténézée rivers were covered with buffalo, only a small number of which were destroyed by the Indians; but since the time when the colonists settled in these regions, there are almost none

left. Buffalo meat is sold at Lexington and Louisville, like beef. Some of the buffalo have gone to join those animals roaming the vast prairies located west of the Mississippi; I have seen some weighing 1,500 pounds. This is the bison mentioned by Buffon.

3 REEDS OF THE PRAIRIES. These canes, or reeds (arundo), are from four to sixteen feet high, and vary in diameter from the thickness of a feather to two inches in diameter; they seek only cool, low terrain; for in crossing these vast plains one notices that wherever there is less coolness and lowness, they cease growing, giving way to red, white, and yellow clover, rye-grass, and buffalo-grass. Seen from afar, these glades look like prairies which industry might have made in the very midst of young forests. These three kinds of clover are similar to those in Europe, although lushness and vegetation make their stalks and their leaves much larger. The reeds reach their optimal growth as early as the first year, but do not bear leaves until the second. They make fine fodder for the horses and cattle. For a long time it has been noticed that the butter and cheese made from the milk of the cows grazing in these savannahs had a quality superior to those products coming from cows grazing on the prairies. These plains were once the general haunt of the buffalo, the stag, and the deer; but hunters have destroyed such a great number of them, that rarely does one find any of them today. It is on the vast plains situated west of the Mississippi where they enjoy abundance and happiness.

4 MAMMOTH. Animal, which according to the Indians, was carnivorous and still exists in the region beyond the great lakes to the north pole. "The great Spirit," they say, "having noticed one day the ravage wrought by these animals among the buffalo, stags, and deer who had come to lick the ground of the great salt swamp (Big bones lick), near the Ohio river, destroyed a great number of them with claps of his thunder, and banished the remainder of them to remote countries."

5 BONES OF THE MAMMOTH. Almost the entire area of this little swamp is covered with the debris of these enormous skeletons. Some have also been found in a salt marsh at the confluence of one of the branches of the Holston and the Ténézée, and in various other places in the north. These remains bear witness to the fact that this animal must have been superior to the elephant, and reasonably the largest animal to have existed on the earth. His head appears to have been three feet long, his ribs seven, and the bones of his thigh five. In Philadelphia I have seen one of these thigh bones weighing seventy-eight pounds. The tusks were one foot long; the molars five inches wide and eight inches long.

What can have been the cause of the destruction of these animals, a destruction which seems to have been very sudden? And why did they perish in the same places, that is to say, always near a salt marsh? One cannot guess anything about this ancient event, since these bones, scattered over the surface of the soil, are not even deteriorated. Whatever the cause of their destruction, it has certainly been favorable to the

happiness of the Indians. Ceaselessly exposed to the fury of this terrestrial tyrant, to how many alarms were they not prey! Indeed, what
resistance could they offer with their bows and arrows to the attacks of
animals five or six times stronger than the elephant? A single mammoth
in one brief moment could knock down and trample over the mightiest
of their villages. One cannot even conceive that the human race could
have survived the effects of its destructive power. At the time, strangers
to dissension and internal wars which have since been so frequent, they
had to unite their efforts against this redoubtable enemy until they succeeded in destroying him. It is probably to the success of this general
confederation that we owe the extinction of a species; this appeared to
form the first link in the chain of co-operation of human beings.

6 MISSISSIPPI. This river is considered the main artery of North
America since it receives the waters of many rivers, which, in their long
course, cross areas perhaps equal to seven-tenths of the width of this
continent; such are the Red, the Black, the Arkama, the Missouri, the
Wadappa-Ménésoter, etc., on the west side; and on the east, the Yasoux,
the Ohio and its branches, the Illinois, the Ouisconsing, etc. Like the
Nile, this river has periodic floods, beginning in March and ending in
July. From the sea-mark at its mouth, in the twenty-ninth parallel, one
encounters no obstacle as far as Saint-Antoine, in the forty-fifth parallel,
566 measured leagues from the sea and 750 leagues by following its
prodigious windings; this gives its extent a coverage of sixteen degrees
of latitude. I am not referring to the area, still little known, which it
penetrates beyond the falls of Saint Anthony, believed to extend to the
fiftieth degree of latitude: the Indians call this part Wadappa-Tongo, the
great Wadappa.

When the water level of the Mississippi is low, its current is only two
or three miles an hour; during the flood it rises to five or six miles an hour.
There is no river known whose bed is filled with as great a number of
islands, whose waters are more healthful, although glutted with mud, and
bogging down a great number of trees, leaves, reeds, and debris, from
which, very likely, its immense Delta is formed.

This river crosses what is perhaps the flattest land on this continent;
from Manchac or Iberville to the region around the Ohio in an area 230
leagues, one does not notice the slightest elevation on the entire west
bank; the same is true from Iberville to the sea; in an area of 68 leagues,
the two banks of the river offer only a vast plain covered with grass or
reeds (except in the cultivated spots), which appear to have been the
work of the waters. This river is destined to become some day the
thoroughfare for the most thriving trade that has perhaps ever existed.

7 VAST FIRES. Most of the savannahs one sees on the banks of the Ohio,
the Scioto, in the northern states, as well as in the two Floridas, are burned
almost every year: the Indians set fire to them in order to secure themselves from the surprises of their enemies; the colonists burn them in
order to assure their cattle blooming and abundant pasture land; for fire,

which destroys only the dried-up cane, speeds up their growth and makes them more tender and delicate.

I know of no spectacle more frightening than these vast fires which, in a short span of time, spread twenty to thirty miles around the plains and devour the thick forests of reeds with which they are covered. These conflagrations represent the most rapid destruction imaginable: a sound, now silent, now piercing, of black fireworks which rise and coil, thick columns of fire rolling over each other, just as the storm precedes and accompanies them. There is no man who, seeing for the first time this unchained element, is not seized with terror and fright; no sooner do these fires die out than one sees a multitude of birds of prey, eagles, vultures, falcons, hawks swoop down to feast on the snakes, frogs, and turtles which the fire has roasted; for nothing is lost, nothing is futile in nature's scheme.

8 SARIGUE. An animal known to the Indians under the name of opossum. The female, a little larger than the cat, has received from nature a double belly, or rather a membrane which she can extend or compress at will. I do not know whether the little ones are born in this kind of pocketbook, I know only that there they are found after their birth, and that from this curious asylum, they suckle their mother, grow to maturity always under her vigilance until they are able to walk, and then, at the first signal of danger, they take flight there and are carried off.

9 SINNICA ON THE KÉOWÉE RIVER. A good-sized town of Chérokées, 16 miles from Fort Prince-George-of-Keowee, 100 from Augusta, and twenty from Washington, in South Carolina. The houses are built on the two banks of the Kéowée river, between that river and a chain of beautiful mountains which rise magnificently and seem to bow down in order to cover the prairies and jut out into the waters. These houses dominate all the settlements placed on the fertile plains bordering the river, as much upstream as downstream, and enjoy the varied view of the opposite heights. There are 500 inhabitants, among whom, one hundred warriors.

CHAPTER II

1 ULTRAMONTANE PROVINCES. The trans-Alleghanian part of Pensylvanie is bounded on the north by New York, on the east by Delaware, on the west by the Connecticut reserve, on the south by the chain of the Laurier. The earliest settlements date from 1763, shortly after the famous treaty of peace which General Bouquet made with the nations of the Ohio and the great lakes, at the forks of the Muskinghum. This territory is divided into four counties: Washington, Westmoreland, la Fayette, and Alléghény. The city of Pittsbourg, founded in 1765, is located at the confluence of the two rivers, Monongahéla and Allégheny: it is here where the junction of their waters forms what is called the Ohio or Beautiful River, which empties into the Mississippi 396 leagues from there. This little town contains 290 houses, the majority of which are brick, and

1,100 inhabitants. It is 107 leagues from Philadelphia, 97 from Baltimore, and 73 from the federal city. Its streets are paved, like those of Philadelphia; it has a printery and some factories.

It is the thoroughfare for all the colonists coming from the north to settle in newly founded colonies on the banks or in the neighborhood of this beautiful river. The fertile plain on which this town was built is surrounded by hills filled with coal, used for a long time by the inhabitants. Quite different from other mines into which one must dig at great depths, in these the chunks of coal are only a few feet beneath the surface. The producing "headquarters" of these remote regions are the same as those of the southern part of Pensylvanie. In bygone times, the inhabitants were obliged to take from the interior all the iron they needed; but for a number of years they have established huge foundries on one of the branches of the Yoyoghémy. The trees of the forests are different kinds of oak, hickory, aquatic ash, chestnut, acacia, platan, and maple sugar. The population of this territory two years ago was 82,568.

2 CYLINDERS. I do not know whether this invention came from Europe or whether it originated in this country. It was in Boston in 1783 that I saw its use applied for the first time to a mill, as well as to the capstan and pulleys of the mast of a ship of 300 ton; sixteen sailors easily hoisted it, whereas formerly this operation required twenty-eight. That is what contributed toward diminishing the number of crews, and consequently the cost of navigation. It is especially in the pulleys of the rudder that this lessening of friction is of great use, when the vessel sails close to the wind, or struggles against the storm. The effect which these cylinders produce is no less remarkable in the frame of sawmills which are far less subject to overheat, and function with greater facility. They are applicable to all perpendicular and horizontal movements.

3 HOSPITAL. This useful establishment, result of public spirit, was founded in 1754 by the citizens of Philadelphia who pledged the sum of 40,000 pounds and to whom the Government granted a charter of incorporation and an equal sum of money: the first building was finished in 1756. According to the privileges of this charter, this hospital is administered by twelve directors, annually chosen from among the subscribers or their representatives and visited by a committee of the legislative body, charged with examining the accounts, as well as the details of administration.

The shape of the building when it is entirely finished will be like an H. The sick and the infirm are cared for there with the greatest attention, and nowhere can one see a greater degree of cleanliness. In building it, care was taken to provide every means to keep fresh air circulating. The building has two stories; the first contains mad people and lunatics; the second, the sick and infirm. No people with epidemic diseases are admitted there; but they are cared for in their own homes by the doctors of the hospital, and furnished with drugs from its apothecary shop. The Government has just accorded to its administrators the sum of 157,000 pounds to be used for the completion of a new building, designed to receive women in childbirth and children. Besides its revenue, this hospital receives annually considerable gifts from public charity. It is located outside the city, surrounded by a high fence inside which there is a walk and a vegetable garden.

4 BETTERING HOUSE. (House destined to make folks better.) This house of correction is also the work of public spirit. A subscription proposed in 1764 by the society of Quakers was soon filled. This building is of bricks and a good size; like the hospital, it is outside of town. Here are gathered the poor, the unemployed, not only of Philadelphia, but from the surrounding area, to be employed in various ways: they are well lodged and substantially nourished. It often happens during the rigors of winter that indigent families leave their homes and take refuge in this asylum where they work until spring. In accordance with its charter of incorporation, this useful establishment is administered by twelve directors, elected every year from among the citizens of Philadelphia; it is maintained by a tax on houses.

5 MARINE SOCIETY. These societies, the majority of which date from colonial times, have been established with the plan of providing for the support of the wives and children of sailors who perish at sea. Into a fund they deposit annually a certain part of their wages, or whatever sum they judge convenient and from which, after six years, they receive considerable interest. Almost all the well-off inhabitants, as well as foreigners, have lost no time in becoming members of these fine and useful institutions; sailors whose industry has been crowned with success leave communally to the society sums which they had put in its fund; this makes it possible for the administrators to give much larger allotments to the widows and orphans. The privileges enjoyed by these societies and the method of administration and election are prescribed and founded on charters of incorporation, some of which are more than 40 years old.

6 TENCHE-COXE. Chief of the office in which is collected all the information concerning manufactures, fishing, construction, progress of settlements, industry, population, in a word, everything pertaining to new discoveries, as well as to imports and exports.

7 WOLVES' HEADS. It is easy to imagine how numerous these animals must be in a land so vast, covered with thick forests, and still so sparsely settled. Their destruction would have been much slower had the Government not offered considerable rewards, to which the districts often add a second. I have known some cantons where each wolf head and ocelot fetched 70 pounds. Despite these wise encouragements, many more years will elapse before we can cease fearing these ancient forest dwellers.

8 EDWARD DRINKER. Born of Swedish parents, December 24, 1688, in the neighborhood of the site on which the town of Philadelphia was built; died November 17, 1782. He often showed me in walking with me through the streets the places where he gathered wild fruit and shot rabbits in his youth. He remembered the appearance and characteristics of William

Penn and the place where the cabin was built in which this famous founder lived for a long time. The very swampy and wooded land which this man had seen in his early years he has seen, in the course of his long life, covered with houses and becoming the leading town in this hemisphere. He has seen churches built on places where frogs croaked and snakes crawled; wharves built and also houses on the same beach where the Indians dried their fish; vessels coming from different parts of the world navigate now on the Delaware which, when he was young, was crossed only by a few birchbark canoes. He has seen a great number of crowned heads come and go; he has seen Penn's company uproot the first tree, clear, and plant the first field in Pensylvania, and eighty-eight years later, this same Pensylvania, as well as other colonies, the majority of which he had seen founded, became independent States.

With the advantages and resources enjoyed by these new States today, who can foresee what will be the rapidity and extent of their progress during the same time spanned by Edward Drinker's number of years.

9 STOCKPORT. Town recently founded on one of the elbows of the Delaware, and only 19 miles from the waters of the Susquehannah, on whose banks Harmony was also founded, a little distance south of the line of demarcation dividing the states of New-York and Pensylvanie. Two years ago Stockport had but seventeen houses; Harmony twenty-one. Although the portage is longer than the one from Cook-House, the region is much more united; this fact made the Government decide to open a road there; and this road brought to birth those two market places, because the commodities dispatched on the Delaware during high tide arrive in Philadelphia in three days; whereas by the Susquéhannah, presuming that the canals of Swatara and Schuyllkill were finished, this shipping mission would take at least ten days.

10 TYOGO. Peninsula formed by the junction of this river with the Susquehannah, five miles south of the great line of demarcation, eleven from the Wappasuning, and twenty from New-town. It is in the region around this peninsula that traces of former entrenched camps have been found, similar to those of the Huron River. Settlements made there are still so modern that they excite no interest.

11 SWATARA. River emptying into the Susquehannah, twelve miles beyond Harrisburg, toward whose sources work is in progress to dig a canal designed to unite its waters with those of Tulpèhoken, branches of the Schuyllkill.

12 CONEWAGO. Another pretty river which empties into the Susquéhannah, five or six miles beyond the Swatara. It is in the neighborhood of the Conéwago that they have just completed a very important canal which will avoid the dangerous rapids with which the bed of this great river is filled.

13 From the mouth of Middletown-Creek to that of the Juniata, the Susquehannah is so covered with rocks and reefs that it is not navigable. The Government is busy removing these obstacles, an extremely difficult

enterprise, for it offers 800,000 piastres (4,200,000 pounds) to the company who would undertake it.

14 The surveyors have no other way of indicating the trails they wish to blaze in the woods than to remove five or six square inches of bark from the trees; this produces a white spot easy to distinguish.

CHAPTER III

1 BEE TREE. The desire to find trees in whose hollows bees have settled has long been the object of an amusing and very simple hunt: it takes place in the autumn and requires only three or four days.

Besides the necessary provisions, one needs a tinder-box, a compass and a watch, and a small quantity of red paint and honey. After finding places covered with high trees, one lights a fire on a flat stone on which drops of honey have been poured, surrounded by red paint. If there are any bees in this neighborhood, the odor of the burned beeswax will attract them quickly; but, because they are unable to approach this honey without particles of red paint sticking to the down with which their bodies are covered, it is easy to recognize them on their return; then one adjusts his compass to determine the direction of their flight, and observes the time they have taken in their flight: with the aid of this information, nothing is easier than to discover the trees whose crests they occupy, and to seize their treasure.

2 SHOES. Of all our clothing, shoes retain the body's odor longest and they are used at night to keep off the wolves and ocelots, especially when the rain prevents lighting a fire. Placed at some distance away on stakes, they make a kind of rampart in whose shelter the traveler sleeps peacefully at the foot of a tree: as soon as these animals have caught their scent, announcing proximity of a man, they shriek with terror and flee.

3 OWLS. The ones living in the forests are the largest, having a five-to-six feet wingspread. Their noisy chatter, especially at night, seems now like the babble of drunken men, now like violent outbursts of laughter. It is difficult for newcomers from Europe not to be deceived by it. The Indians often entertain themselves by attracting them to the tops of the trees near their fires, imitating their loquacious warblings. They eat rats and mice, of which there is a prodigious number.

4 WILD TURKEYS. *MELEAGRIS AMERICANUS*. The plumage of these gorgeous birds is dark brown with no mixture of black; from a distance, their feathers seem to change, and have great gaudiness. Their wisdom, their rapid and light flight make a striking contrast to the stupidity and clumsiness of the turkeys of European stock, which domestication has entirely degraded and stupefied. As soon as the sun sets, one sees them perch for the night on the highest tree, whence the next day they greet the return and rise of the sun with very melodious song, re-echoed throughout the woods. Their ordinary food is the acorn which they seek with great earnestness among the leaves. They usually weigh between twenty and twenty-five pounds. A new species has been bred by

having their eggs hatched by European geese. This half-breed species has become very common among the frontier colonists, but their meat is quite inferior to the meat of those turkeys killed in the woods.

5 FRENZIES OF HUNGER. Not only excessive need, but even the hunger we experience daily produces almost always a very perceptible change in the character and moral disposition of man: there are few who are able to resist long abstinence from food without betraying some evidence of impatience or moodiness. One is more inclined toward mildness, humanitarianism before, than after a long awaited repast: the most severe man is thus inclined much less when well fed than when he was fasting.

I have been acquainted with a magistrate, enjoying public esteem who was unbearable, even with his family, before dinner; scarcely had his appetite been satisfied when, like the sun after the storm, he seemed to resume his serenity. Who would believe it? The Indians always prepare for war by rigorous abstinence in order to be crueler and more inexorable toward their enemies, they claim!

6 GROUNDNUTS. It is the edible ground fungus growth of America, but much smaller and its stem much feebler than the European variety; this makes it difficult to find. Perhaps, by transplanting, one could succeed in increasing its size. The pigs of this land, like those of Europe, are very partial to it.

7 A LIGHT IN THE CLEARING. For lack of another word, the translator has been obliged to use this one to indicate a clearing or rather a spot penetrated and lighted by the sun in the midst of the woods. It is difficult, the author continues, to describe the effect which this comforting sight produces on the minds of those who have lived long in the forests, and even more difficult to describe its effect on the minds of travelers who have had the misfortune to get lost, and to whom this light announces both proximity of a dwelling and the help they need. It is like an unexpected port which the sailor has the good fortune to enter in the midst of the tempest.

8 ALLAGRICHEES. Of all the preparations from corn, the one known as allagrichee is the most nourishing and the most useful to travelers. As soon as they are soaked in milk, the Indians dry them, washing them lightly to remove their skins; after separating the kernels, they pulverize them in a mortar, and add an equal quantity of maple sugar. Such is the panacea which they use, when they find nothing in the woods. Cooked in broth, nothing is more agreeable to the taste, nothing more restoring. Easily crushed, these kernels resemble rice. It was under this name that Penn's first companion sent them to England.

9 BEDFORD. This fort, formerly constructed to protect the mountain passages in the beautiful valley which crosses the main branch of the Juniata, has become the county seat of Bedford County since the time when the ultramontane population pushed the Indians beyond the Ohio. The population of this little town and county is estimated at 18,500.

10 FRANKLIN COLLEGE. See Note A, Chapter II, Volume One.

CHAPTER IV

1 OSWEGO OR ONONDAGA RIVER. This river conducts the waters of the pretty lakes Onéida, Cayuga, Senecca, Otsiko, Oxaruatétés, Owasko, Cross, Crooked, Long, Canandargué, Honéyou, Hemlock, Cornésus, and Little-Senecca into the bay of Oswego in Lake Ontario. With the exception of a portage of 880 toises, fifteen miles from this harbor, it is navigable during the spring and autumn, from Lake Ontario to Oneida. When one considers the number of these little lakes whose waters the Onondaga or Oswego river leads to Ontario, one is astonished that it boasts so little water during the summer.

The same company which has just finished the canal at Stanwick, uniting the waters of the Mohawk with those of Wood-Creek, as well as those of Little Falls, will soon be busy building locks at the falls of the Mohawk River. The falls are only twelve feet high; but this country, five years ago scarcely known and subdivided, still has few inhabitants: we await the time when the west bank, included in the great military land grant, and the east bank, which is the boundary of the new county of Onondaga, is cultivated; at such a time there will be ample reserve.

Considered in all respects, this river, which is the outlet of the Jénézée country, and the only communication between the Mohawk and the Ontario, is of such great importance, that the Government of New-York will make every effort possible to remove the obstacles which disturb navigation from June to October.

2 LAKE ONTARIO. The most easterly of the Great Lakes across which passes the line dividing the territory of the United States from that of Canada. Its length from east to west is seventy-four leagues, its width thirty-five, and its area 2,390,000 acres. The distance from Katarakouy to Niagara is fifty leagues. Although its depth is great, it is less subject to storms than the other Great Lakes. It has been observed that its waters rise slowly over a period of seven years and fall in the same interval of time. It abounds in fish, several kinds of which are not to be found elsewhere: every spring salmon and sturgeon come there from the sea, by way of the Saint Lawrence, whose source this lake is. Fish of extraordinary size have been found there; could they be cetaceous? On the lake shores, as well as the ocean shores, schools of gulls flock to feed from the debris which the storms cast up.

3 PORTAGE FROM ONONDAGA. This is caused by a falls ten to twelve feet high and one hundred twelve feet wide, fifteen miles from Oswégo in ascending the Onondaga River. On this same river there is also a good-sized rapids known as Three Rivers, some miles further. It is on its west bank that the canal planned is soon to be dug.

4 CANAL OF SCHENECTADY. For a long time there has been talk of opening a canal which would start at Albany, a town situated on the Hudson River, and would terminate at this little town of Skénectady, built on the banks of the Mohawk, at the point where the river becomes

navigable, blocked at its confluence in the Hudson, four miles beyond: but the distance, which is four leagues, would call for more funds than a land whose population is still so feeble could afford; on the other hand, the importance and advantage of this enterprise increase in proportion to the settling of the western counties of this State and the rich country of the Jénézées. It is probable that its Government, the richest in the Union, and whose fine spirit is well known, will make every effort to complete this great and useful project.

5 ASSÉDORUS. Name of the two harbors on the southern shore of Lake Ontario, generally called great and little Sodus. The former is a deep bay, which will some day become a very useful port; it is included in the concession of Captain Williamson. The latter has only very little water.

6 BRANCHES OF THE OHIO. Thus does one call the rivers emptying into this beautiful body of water, from Pittsburg to its confluence with the Mississippi: there are more than twenty tributaries, the main ones of which are: the Muskinghum, the Scioto, the two Myamis, the Wabash, the great Kanhawa, the little Kentukey, the Cumberland, the Ténézée, etc. According to Mr. Jefferson, the Ohio and its branches occupy one quarter of the area of the United States.

7 CAPE OF THE MISSISAGÉS. This is the name of the beautiful peninsula which forms the west shore of the harbor at Niagara, formerly ceded by a good-sized tribe of the Niagara nation, from whom the French obtained permission to construct the fort at Niagara. It is on this peninsula that the English today are building the new town of New-Ark which has become the seat of the Government of Upper Canada.

8 COLUMN OF VAPORS. The noise of Niagara Falls, as well as its height, and the distance from which one can see this column of vapors, depends largely on the state of the atmosphere and the force of the wind. I have heard the captain of the royal sloop, "The Erie," say that he had seen it from thirty-four miles distance; it appeared like a white and immobile cloud.

9 OLD ERIE. A stockaded stronghold which the French built a long time ago at the extremity of the portage on the east shore of Rapid Lake in order to store safe from Indian raids merchandise from Europe, and the furs which came from the north country through the lakes. Since that time it has been known, I know not why, under the name of Slausser.

10 LADDERS. These are trees in which notches have been cut to enable descent. The ones known under the name of Indian and Simcoes-Ladders, located on the west bank of the Niagara River, are forty feet high.

CHAPTER V

1 SCARAT. This is the Chippawais and Mohawk name for brandy.

2 ONONTHIO. This word meant "father" in the Indian languages of Canada. From the habit of using it in addressing the French governors has come the custom of knowing them and speaking of them only under this name: from this comes also the custom of designating the Canadians and

Canada as the people or the country of Ononthio; just as one says the people and the country of Onas, in referring to Pensylvania.

3   BUSHY-RUN. Name of a very narrow pass in the Alléghény mountains, where General Bouquet in 1764 defeated a great mass of Indians which enabled him to reach Fort Pitt, at that time tightly blocked by another mass of Indians no less numerous.

4   SAGANASH (red man). This is the name given by the Indians of the Great Lakes to the English, because of the uniform of their soldiers.

5   FIREFLIES. They bear a striking resemblance to bees by their color and size; like beetles, they have two pairs of wings, the upper pair of which appears to be merely a sheath to shelter the lower pair from the rain: when they fly, they produce a third pair which makes the light flash; these flashes give the lower and posterior parts of their bodies the appearance of lighted coal. When they are relaxed, only the lower part is illuminated. This light is not always constant, and seems to depend on their whim. It is only in the months of June, July, and August that one sees thousands of them in the swamps and damp areas, just as soon as the sun has set: they are flying flames that light nearby and even dispel somewhat the gloom of night. Especially when there is thunder and lightning do they appear in all their splendor; it is then when they radiate all the light of which they are capable. They are harmless and never fly over four or six feet from the ground; one can seize them lightly and use them to read by.

6   ODZIZIA. In the Mohawk language this word means "wine."

7   GRASSY PLAINS. Nothing is more impressive on leaving the dense, bleak forests than the sight of these savannahs; it is like a new world. Their growth begins under 38 degrees latitude and increases in extent proportionately as one goes north. Especially in the two Floridas one finds vast areas of them in the midst of which perspective is lost in a limitless horizon; some are fifteen miles wide, covering fifty miles. Their surface is covered only with reeds, clover, buffalo-grass, and often sweet-smelling flowers, whose identity so far is unknown. Some are filled with clear little lakes toward which streams meander. Others have wooded islands which rise no more than a few feet above the plains, pleasantly breaking the monotony. The highlands surrounding these savannahs are covered with the most beautiful forests. These vast natural prairies are infinitely useful to the colonists of Georgia, Kentukey, the valleys of the Scioto, the Wabash, and the Illinois; they furnish these colonists all year long with abundant pasture lands for their horses and cattle. What a magnificent gift nature has made to the inhabitants of this southern part of the United States!

8   FOXES OF THE DAWN-LAND. So often have the Indians been the dupes and victims of the promises and insidious politicking of the white men, that, in order to express the opinion they have of them, the Indians always designate them as foxes.

9   WOLVES OF THIS GREAT ISLAND. Believing themselves very su-

perior to the Europeans, it is under the symbol of wolves that the Indians designate themselves, this animal being for them hunter and warrior. Great Island signifies the continent.

10 CAYAHOGA. This river empties into Lake Erie, 150 miles from Niagara. Its mouth forms a very convenient but rather shallow harbor; it is located in the confines of the land today known as the Connecticut Reserve.

CHAPTER VI

1 RECIPE FOR SMOKED SHAD AND EELS. After opening them and allowing twenty-four hours for the salt added to settle, they are smoked; one week suffices for this process; hung in a storehouse that is dry and ventilated, they can be preserved for a long time. They make very toothsome delicacies, eaten with morning tea or after-dinner tea.

2 SIX TIMES WINE. This expression, synonymous with brandy (scarat), refers to that item.

3 FRESH WATER STURGEON. This fish is smaller than the sea sturgeon, but much oilier; one sees it in all the Great Lakes, and people are beginning to extract sturgeon oil.

CHAPTER VII

1 TONNAWANDA. A pretty river whose very winding course extends nearly thirty miles. It crosses a blooming and fertile land and is accompanied by alluvial lands, known as Bottom Lands, which will some day be converted into magnificent meadows. One of its branches empties into Rapid Lake, and the other, known as Beaver-Creek, not far from the falls. The Indians of the Senecca tribe have a village near its springs which are not far from Buffalo Creek, another river whose waters empty into the Erie, opposite the new English fort of the same name.

2 BEGINNING OF THE PORTAGE. Although the length of this portage is considered as being six leagues, it is really only four; the vessels coming from Lake Ontario ascend the Niagara River as far as Queen'stown, which is only four leagues from the Chippeway fort, whence the merchandise is loaded into bateaux which are transported by pole power as far as the anchorage at Erie.

3 ROADSTEAD. This is located opposite the most easterly cape of Lake Erie, 100 toises from the new fort which the English built there after the surrender of Oswégo, Niagara, etc. This roadstead has no shelter, but the bottom, being excellent, does not bog down the vessels; nevertheless, when the winds are violent, the ships seek refuge in Cape Abineau, ten miles farther west. This peninsula is merely a big sand dune.

4 LAKE RAPID. This lake, which precedes the falls, is estimated to be three miles wide, five miles long, and ten feet deep. Let one try to imagine to himself such a mass of water, flowing at a velocity of two hundred seventeen toises per minute, across countless obstacles, before breaking over the crest of the cataract, and one will have but a very feeble impression compared with beholding actual sight of this vast tor-

rent of foaming waters, which one cannot watch many moments without experiencing a kind of dizziness.

CHAPTER VIII

1 PROMONTORY OF ALASKA. A large peninsula of the continent of America jutting toward Asia: the celebrated Cook determined its longitudes and latitudes.

2 POOTOOTAMIS. A nation once powerful and numerous whose remains occupy the south shores of Lake Michigan and the banks of the Saint Joseph and Theakiky rivers. The French Government had founded on the Saint Joseph River a mission which has long been famous: it has ceased to exist since the conquest of Canada.

3 WINEBAGOS. An old nation whose headquarters are on an island located at the northern tip of Winébago Lake which empties into Green Bay of Lake Michigan, under latitude of 44 degrees. After crossing this lake, one follows the beautiful Outagami river upstream for sixty leagues, at which point a portage of one and three-quarters miles leads to the Ouisconsing, a river which empties into the Mississippi, five hundred measured leagues from the sea. This narrow passage was used very much by the Canadians who traded with the Indians of Upper Louisiana before the conquest of their land.

4 LAKE WINIPEG. This large lake, located under 55 degrees latitude, northwest of Lake Superior, was formerly the last outpost for fur trade. It empties into Hudson Bay. At the head of this lake the English have a trading depot known as Cumberland-House, estimated at 200 leagues from the great portage; but since the discoveries of Makensie, they have established some depots much farther inland; one can have no idea of them nor appreciate their remoteness without the aid of Aaron Smith's maps which Citizen Pierre Tardieu is at work engraving.

5 ARABOSCA. Or, as the Indians pronounce it, Aratapeskow. This lake, which has been known only for a few years, is under the 60th degree of latitude; it is the last height of the lands of this part of the continent, since it empties into a river recently discovered, which in turn empties into a sea which the ices have prevented the English from exploring.

6 LONG PORTAGE. This is the one which the traveler is obliged to make in order to avoid the cataracts that are nine miles long, from a river whose mouth is in Lake Superior and which one ascends for fifty leagues, across four small lakes, in order to reach the highest point in this land; from there a shorter portage across fourteen other small lakes leads to the portage of the Rains, known by the Indians as Tekamionen, or the portage at Lake of the Woods, the furthest boundary of the United States. It is only after surmounting all these obstacles that European merchandise can be exchanged for the fur which is obtained from the Indians who inhabit these cold, inhospitable, little-known regions.

7 MAPLE SUGAR. The forest of the lands bordering lakes Michigan, Huron, Erie, and Sainte-Claire, as well as those of the great peninsula of

Michillimakinack, are so filled with maple sugar trees that a great quantity of it is made every year. This is the work of Indian women, from whom the first Canadian families learned this art, when in 1710 they came to lower Canada to found the town of Détroit. If the population of this town were greater, the quantity of maple sugar exported would be greater; already it is considerable. I have heard many inhabitants of this town say that in a normal year, they sent between six and seven thousand pounds. In former times the nuns of Montreal purified it and made little cakes of it which were sent to Europe. I have seen some made from the sap of the great black birch which connoisseurs could not distinguish from maple sugar: it becomes even more wonderful after being refined.

8 FOUNDING OF A NEW TOWN. During his administration of Upper Canada, Colonel Simcoe had planned to found a town on the Franche River which empties into the Sainte-Claire: this impracticable plan faded out as soon as this Governor was recalled. Only extremely favorable circumstances, and not military projects, can cause colonists to decide to venture so far from their hearths, as happens in the United States; especially is this true in a country like Canada, whose Government, for some unknown reason, grants titles of possession only under duress. Of 100 families, there are perhaps only ten who hold title to their lands.

9 JENEZEES COUNTRY. This is the name designated on maps to the western part of the state of New-York; it is crossed by the Jénézée river. This land, located 250 miles from the Mohawk River, is famous for its soil fertility and the richness of its meadows. Despite its unhealthfulness, colonists come there to settle from all sections: in 1797 there were nearly 10,000. Once populated, rendered healthful and cultivated, it will become one of the most productive regions of this State. Commodities come down the Senecca by boat into the Onondaga (or Oswego), at which point they are taken up Lake Oneida, Wood-Creek, and enter the Mohawk via the Stanwich Canal which has just been finished. This land acquired from the Indians in 1789 contains 2,184,000 acres.

CHAPTER X

1 WHITE CEDAR SWAMP. This tree, remarkable for its durability and lightness of wood, is the species known in the southern States as *Cupressus disticha*. It is found only in special and humid terrain. The coastal sections of Jersey and Pensylvania are covered with it; its vegetative force is so great that its roots need only a little space: that is why the forests of the white cedar are so thick, and why this tree has such a thick trunk. These forests last forever when they are cultivated with care; for as soon as the sun has shone on the sites whose trees have been cut, one sees them spring up by the thousands and grow with the rapidity of the acacia. Its wood is so useful that it is hoped that the day is not far off when the cedar will cover the swampy and coastal terrains of Europe.

2   NEW NAMES. With the exception of names of towns and counties, the Government has submitted to no formality the names given to the burgs, villages, and rivers; it is to chance or to the colonists' caprice that most of the names on the map are due. Each owner of a fair-sized concession names it as he pleases and has the name registered. In general, it is to the surveyors that is due the preservation of those names by which the Indians designated the lakes, rivers, and mountains; except in the States whose early inhabitants lived long in peaceful understanding with them, as in Pensylvania, Jersey, Virginia, and some sections of Massachussetts, where the habit of hearing these names frequently pronounced was instrumental in preserving them. It is to be hoped that it would be thus throughout the continent: however, nothing is more natural than to identify oneself with the land one has just taken possession of, by adopting these ancient and respectable names, the only evidence in centuries to come that will attest to the existence of these nations. This forgetfulness has been even more general in the Spanish colonies.

CHAPTER XI

1   OUTAWA RIVER. Of all the rivers that water Canada, this is the one whose navigation is most difficult; it has thirty-two portages, not to mention its numerous rapids. Despite all these obstacles, it is very useful to people who trade with the Indians of the North. It is formed by two branches which empty into the Lake of the Two Mountains, thirty miles from Montreal. The first of these rivers coming from the heights around Hudson Bay cuts its course into Lake Témiskaming. The second rises several miles from the Neppissing, another lake which communicates with the Huron. From Montreal, it takes twenty days to ascend the Outawa River, and reach the Témiskaming, and almost three months to follow along its riverbanks, to cross the channel of Sainte Marie, to skirt along the northern shore of Lake Superior and finally reach the long portage. The difficulties of this long and painful voyage of 380 miles are very real, according to the seasons and the height of the waters.

It is the Canadians whom the English employ for these inland water expeditions: to courage and perseverance, these men unite patience, industry, and the skill necessary to surmount so many obstacles, to foresee and repair the numerous accidents to which they are exposed. Their constant gaiety in the midst of these somber forests of the north, along these rugged riverbanks, is no less admirable. Encouraged by good results, stimulated by the pipe and some songs, they would go as far as the polar circle. Five years ago it was the Canadians who accompanied Mr. Makensie on the two journeys he undertook to reach the sea through the continent; they traveled over an area of eight hundred leagues. It is to their tireless work that he owed the good fortune of discovering the river, or rather the gulf of Cook, and of reaching its mouth; and finally of returning safe and sound to Montreal.

2   FALLS OF THE PASSAICK. After a quiet, gentle course, this river

suddenly precipitates from the height of a 72-foot high rock, whose width is 130 feet, and which appears to have been broken in the middle by some great shock. It is in the neighborhood of this beautiful falls that the new town of Patterson was founded; here, with the aid of its waters, they were going to set up spinning mills and various other machines; but the upsets in Europe have caused so many changes in trade that this settlement has not prospered. The favorable time for these manufactures will arrive only when the population of these states has become greater than it is today, and when the lands of the interior are covered with settlers.

3 FALLS OF THE JENEZEE. The three falls on this river in an area of 250 toises are much less interesting for the size and bizarreness of their accessories, than for the uniformity and beauty of their sheets of water. As soon as they have precipitated, these waters resume a quiet and gentle course. The first falls has a perpendicular height of seventeen toises, the second five, and the third twelve. The size of these three falls is estimated at 42 toises. This sudden incline of 200 feet in such a short interval is caused by a hill which crosses this region, joining the mountains whence flow the springs of the Jénézée, forming the height of the lands, the water of which on one side empties into the Susquéhannah, and on the other, into Lake Ontario.

4 COHOS OF THE MOHAWK. This cataract of the Mohawk is ten miles from Albany, and three from its confluency with the Hudson. It is 950 feet wide and 50 feet high. During the floods, it is an extraordinary sheet of water which nothing interrupts or divides; when the waters are low, they precipitate with extreme violence across a great number of rocks, whose black hue contrasts with the whiteness of the foamy waves. The sight of this cataract, however, is not as striking as it could be, being considerably weakened by the height of the banks between which it falls. Not far from this falls, a village named Mohawk has been built: a mile beyond is the bridge that an incorporated association constructed a few years ago.

5 MONTMORENCY AND CHAUDIERE. The first of these falls is on the bank of the St. Lawrence, seven miles below Quebec. Its width is 50 feet and its height 240. From a distance one thinks he sees an avalanche of snow, so white is the water. After swishing about in a huge basin surrounded by inaccessible rocks, the water flows quietly into the river. To enjoy more conveniently the beauties of this cataract, General Haldiman, when he was governor of Canada, ordered built on the banks of the east escarpment a pavilion supported by a frame construction more than 200 feet high, leaning against the rocks.

Although the Chaudière Falls are not so high as the Montmorency Falls, their width, which is considerable, the groups of trees, the form of the rocks, the different accessories, all very picturesque, make them more interesting than the Montmorency Falls.

6 PASSAGE OF THE TENEZEE. This passage through the chain of mountains known as the Cumberland is much more interesting, they say,

than the passage of the Potawmack through the Blue Ridge mountains. After bathing these impregnable, mountain bases for more than 100 miles, the river broke through them at the weakest and narrowest point. Its width, before arriving at this point was 460 toises, is suddenly reduced to 50; but at the time it enters the mountain, the sudden spurt from an enormous rock whose resistance it could not overcome gives to its impetuous current an almost circular direction, extremely dangerous for boats, which this rapid whirling absorbs and sinks. It is what geographers call the Whirl or Suck. As soon as the river has issued forth from this mountain, which is only a mile high, it resumes its original width and ordinary tranquility. This place is 510 miles from its mouth in the Ohio, and six miles below the Chérokée villages, situated on the Chikamaga.

Of all the points on a level with the cataract, this is the one most easily reached; it is on the same bank and some feet above the west branch, from which one sees on the right this vast torrent, which after crossing Rapid Lake with an incredible noise and impetuosity, precipitates 'neath the feet of the spectator into a vast abyss, whose angry waves are in continual agitation. Although magnificent and astonishing beyond all conception, the spectacle offered by this falls, seen from below, is infinitely more sublime and more varied, because then one can watch the entire sheet of water, as well as the middle island and some parts of the banks and the east branch.

7 PASSAGE OF THE DELAWARE. This monument to the power of waters must be modern since there still exists proof that this river crossed this same chain 15 miles toward the southeast, at the bottom of a gorge known as Wind-Gap: it still preserves everything that can convince one that it was long the bed of a river; the bottom is nothing but a gravel pit; the rocks with which it is scattered are bare and appear to have been washed; it is still so rugged that people have been obliged to use the route on the old southern bank whose escarpment and sharp juttings attest to the ravages of the waters.

8 STRAIT OF SAINTE-MARIE. This strait, which serves as a drainage canal for the waters of Lake Superior, is estimated to have a length of 40 miles. The canoes coming from the Huron can ascend it as far as three-quarters of a mile from Lake Superior; but from that point, they are obliged to make a portage. The amount of water which this strait empties into the Huron is not as considerable as one would believe, considering the immensity of this interior sea and the great number of rivers which feed it. This strait serves as a haven during the wintertime for an innumerable quantity of fish.

9 NATURAL BRIDGE. The details relating to this singular phenomenon, which the author had inserted in his notes, having appeared very inferior to those of Chastellux, the translator thought he should replace them by those of Chastellux. SEE Volume II page 305.

"Natural Bridge forms an arch fifteen feet long, of the kind known as bulls horns. The span of this arch is seventeen toises above bridge and nine below. The right arch is such a flat ellipse that the small arch is not even one-twelfth the size of the larger. The solid mass of rock and stone in this arch is 49 feet on the keystone of the curve and 37 on the smallest stone; and since one finds nearly the same difference in the leveling off of the hill, one can believe that the arch is on a level with the length of the keystone. It is not futile to make the observation that this mighty rock continues over the entire thickness of the arch, and that on the other side, it is only 25 feet at this point of greatest width and begins to narrow down.

"The entire arch seems to make one single stone, for the kinds of joints one sees above bridge are indeed the effect of a thunderstorm which struck this region in 1779. The other side does not have the slightest seam and the intrados is so united that the martinets flying around there in great number cannot cling to it. The abutments have a very slight declivity, are extensive without being flat, and they all have the polish that a current of water would give to a rough stone at the end of a certain time. The four rocks adjacent to the abutments appear to be in the most perfect homogeneity, with a small declivity: those on the right bank of the stream are 200 feet above the water level, the intrados of the arch 150 feet, and the two rocks on the left bank 180 feet. These rocks are of calcareous matter. This bridge is 10 miles from Fluvana."

10   AREA OF THE LAKES ABOVE THE FALLS. Here is an estimate of their areas; I obtain this information from a member of Congress who is very well informed on the geography of the interior of the continent.

	SQUARE LEAGUES
LAKE ERIE	3,000
LAKE SAINTE-CLAIRE	380
LAKE HURON	7,420
LAKE MICHIGAN	4,780
LAKE OF GREEN BAY	475
LAKE SUPERIOR	12,756
THE FOUR LAKES OF THE LONG PORTAGE	1,740
THE 14 LAKES LEADING TO THE LAKE OF THE RAINS	2,240
LAKE OF THE RAINS	2,175
RED LAKE	2,000
LAKE OF THE WOODS	1,900
TOTAL	38,866

11   CHIPPEWAY RIVER AND FORT. It is at the mouth of this river which empties into the west arm of Rapid Lake, 3 miles from the falls, that the English have just constructed a small fort and storehouse; it is

at the end of the portage. Twenty miles west of Cape Abineau, another river by the same name empties into Lake Erie.

12 QUEEN'STOWN. Pompous name which the English have given to a very small village located on the Niagara River, 3 leagues from Lake Ontario, last navigable point of this lake, where they have built a wharf and storehouse. At this place the portage begins.

13 NEW-ARK. Town recently founded by the English on Missisagès Cape, opposite Fort Niagara. Despite the founders' pride, the public has come to know it only under this name.

14 KÉWASSA. Indian name of an insect known as the Woodtick. This insect in its sleeping state resembles a lentil seed in color and size. Quite different from the others, the female cannot give life to her little ones without losing her own, for this purpose she lights on the end of a branch nearest the paths and roads, and from there she darts forth on everything that passes by her: but so violent is this move, that she breaks open while approaching the object, and in this way scatters her numerous progeny on the man or animal she had seen. These particles immediately imbed themselves in the pores of the skin, where they very soon cause inflammations, which can be made to disappear only by the application of tobacco leaves.

15 DAY (Lake) FLIES. "As soon as these mosquitoes have left the bosom of the waters, some fly toward the land; the others, feebler, light on the grass until they have acquired the strength to follow their comrades. This resurrection from the depths begins early in the morning and ceases as soon as the sun has risen. At the approach of twilight, one sees them flutter about in great swarms, like clouds hovering above, as they gradually approach the river, little by little, they come down toward the surface of the water, deposit their eggs there and end their lives. Those feeble flies immersed in a viscous liquid, float on the surface for a while and then sink to the bottom. The baby fly, as soon as he is hatched, sinks into the mud where he grows and lives until spring: stimulated by the warmth of the season, he then changes into a nymph (pupa) and makes his entry into the world. What a singular destiny! One year is the term of his existence, and of this number of days he spends 360 in a hideous form, groveling in the mud, scarcely able to move in this prison; for each larva is endowed only with a narrow cell which he never leaves, and in which he can make only a perpendicular movement toward the water surface to feed on various particles, to seek a little air and to see the light of day; again on this short voyage he must carefully watch out in order to avoid the tooth of the enemies by which he is ceaselessly surrounded.

"Summoned suddenly from this dark and miserable existence, to a more brilliant life, these insects are endowed with the happiest faculties, bedecked in nature's most beautiful colors, delicate shapes, free, light as the pure air they cross: they flutter about in the midst of flowers at the setting of the sun; then they go forth to die. But during this short interval, they have known the pleasures of love, they have lived a year and have had but one happy day."

(EXTRACT FROM THE FINE TRANSLATION BY CITI-
ZEN BENOIT OF THE VOYAGES OF JOHN BARTRAM
INTO THE TWO FLORIDAS; Volume I, page 55) Translator's
note

CHAPTER XII

1 MARIETTA. Town founded in 1787 at the confluence of the Muskinghum
with the Ohio, 58 leagues from Pittsburg, and 160 from Philadelphia,
by a colony of soldiers from Massachussetts, under the command of generals Parsons, Putnam, and Varnom. It is the first settlement made by
the United States on the northwest bank of the river. These officers,
having been associated with several other people, under the name of the
Ohio Company, bought from the Government a great quantity of lands
bordering on the ones they had received as reward for their services.
In accordance with this ancient custom, these million acres have been
divided into districts of six square miles and these districts into thirty-
six lots of a mile, each containing 650 acres. Two of these lots have been
reserved for future schools and two others for religious purposes. Never
was a colony founded on wiser principles, nor under more favorable
auspices. The lands had been legally acquired from the Indians; among
the hardworking colonists there is not one man with bad habits. I venture
these details with so much confidence, for I was closely associated with
the founders: they took with them a minister and a schoolmaster. Thus,
despite the Indians' war, the colony soon prospered. Today there are
nearly twelve thousand inhabitants on the banks of the Muskinghum.*
They have even built factories for the necessities which remoteness from
the coastal towns promptly made flourish. This town, which already boasts
118 houses and nearly 500 inhabitants, was built on the site of an old retrenched camp, worthy of arousing curiosity because of its size and high
antiquity. Fortunately the founders, very learned men and soldiers for a
long time, have carefully preserved the most remarkable parts.

2 STATE OF WASHINGTON. Although this name was not legally given
to that beautiful ultramontane part of the United States, I am conform-
ing with the intentions of the founders from whom I have several letters
dated from Marietta, State of Washington, on the Ohio. Today this name
applies to all the region acquired from the Indians; including the area
stretching from the Wabash to the Illinois rivers. In order to be able to
establish a provisory government, as well as the administration of justice,
Congress divided it into four counties: Washington, Sainte-Claire, Hamilton, and Knox, which are large enough to form individual states. This
ruling dates from the 13th of July, 1787. A Governor, three Judges, and
a recording Secretary were sent there; they were authorized to introduce
such laws of the old States as they thought necessary to maintain peace.
These laws, these provisory rulings will continue to be observed until the
first legislative Assembly of this new country has adopted them, or has
promulgated new ones; at the rate of 500 voters per representative,

* In 1798 there were nearly 20,000 souls.

when this assembly has 25, it will be able to send a delegate to Congress; and when the population is 60,000, this new State will be taken into the Union, and will enjoy all the privileges of the other members of the Union. As soon as population permits, the provisory Government will be composed of a Governor, without whose consent there will be no law, a legislative body composed of five members, and an assembly of deputies. The laws, like those of the old States, will be based on civil and religious liberty. There will be no slavery, the lands will be free and clear. Such is the faint outline of the wise ruling which accompanied the settling of the first American colony on the northwest bank of the Ohio River in 1787.

3 LAKE ERIE. The distance from Fort Erie to the mouth of the Miami, thirty miles wide, is estimated at 100 leagues and only 25 fathoms deep. That is why its crystal-clear waters lose their transparence as soon as the wind stirs their surface. On the north shore shelter can be found only at Cape Abineau and on the long peninsula; yet they cannot always be depended on in certain seasons of the year. The south shore is a vast sandy beach on which one finds Presqu'ile, the mouth of the Cayahoga and Sandusky; but these harbors have only ten feet of water. Just as the shores of the ocean, the lake shores are covered with gulls and other water birds. The sand dunes, which the winds and the waves have piled up on Cape Abineau, resemble from their cliffs the great waves of the ocean. The islands occupying the western part of this lake are remarkable for the enormous thickness of the trees with which they are covered; nowhere does one see red cedars of such a great diameter; but it is dangerous to disembark there because of the prodigious quantity of snakes and reptiles which seem to have become masters of these somber and thick forests. This lake is filled with excellent fish, and especially sturgeons, from which they are beginning to make oil.

4 DANCES. The Indians know only the ones relating to war; these are pantomimes which, when well done, depict it admirably; one is not confused by them: typical are the ones of discovery, combat, victory, and retreat.

5 CASTORS. Since the greed of the Indians has been excited by the greed for gain, they respect no more, as they used to, these animals, some of which they always permitted to escape; they destroy every one they meet: that is so true that in Quebec in 1797 at the time of the arrival of the furs, there was a decrease of 15,000 skins.

6 THE MONTHS. The Indians divide the year into twelve moons, to which they have given the following names.

Months	Moons
January	Cold
February	Snow
March	Poetry
April	Plants
May	Flowers
June	Warmth

July	Roe
August	Sturgeons
September	Corn
October	Journeys
November	Beaver
December	The Hunt

7   WARWHOOPS. After piercing the flesh of their victims with a great number of little pieces of resineous wood, which they light, they watch, as they utter great bursts of laughter, the indescribable torments of these wretched creatures.

8   SONG OF DEATH. In general, they contain only the account of their prowess, or their ancestors' in war and at the hunt; but when they go to the fatal kettle, these songs are abuses and insults addressed to their tormentors. Here is one of the songs, translated from the Shawanese:

"I am about to die. I see the cowards, as well as the fire and the boiling water which is going to snatch life from me. When they speak of me in the village of ———, the warriors will say: 'N——— died like a brave, scorning the fury of his enemies; let us sharpen our tomahawks, to cover his body with scalps; if they have drunk the soup of his flesh, we will drink the soup of their flesh, and we will give their bones to our dogs.' Tie me up tight, do you understand? Torment me as I would have tormented you; you will see whether I am a woman ... No, N——— fears neither suffering nor death. My brave ancestors await me in the land of the West; I am going to join them. But who will replace me in the village?"

9   In the former wars of Canada, an Onondaga chief, having been taken by the allies of the French, was put in the Kettle, according to custom; he insulted the spectators so severely by singing his song of death, that a young Huron, transported by rage, plunged his knife into his belly several times.

"You are a big fool," the captive told him quietly, "for you are unable to moderate your fury; do you not realize that in shortening my life, you shorten your time for vengeance, while giving me the time to show you how an Onondaga chieftain bears up under the sufferings of death?"

10   PETER OTSEQUE. Six weeks after this young Mohawk had returned from Paris, where he had spent three years with Monsieur de la Fayette, and had received all the education he was interested in, he cast aside his European garments, quickly clad himself in the garb of his compatriots and wished to keep only the high collar he had received from his benefactor. Shortly after this metamorphosis, he married, and resumed so completely his Indian way of life, it was as though he had never left his forests, nor lived in the chief city of Europe.

11   SONGS. Just like the dances, the songs of these nations relate only to war. Although they have not had, like the Ancient Celts, Scandinavians, and Germans, any poets to compose their chants of victory and combat, they have been able to express all the ferocity of their feelings in the songs of cannibals. Their antiquity proves that in all times, to devour the vanquished, to drink the soup of their flesh, has been considered one of

the rewards of victory. If this barbarous custom has ceased, it is not because they feel its horror, but because the trading of furs, and the rapid diminishing of their numbers have dried up the source of their dissensions and their wars. I confess, it is not without difficulty and disgust that I recount here those frightful impressions, those yowlings of cannibals, to which they give the name of songs. The first was translated from the Mohawk; the second from the Arcansa; * this proves that the Indians of Louisiana, although living under such a beautiful sun and on such a fertile soil, were also acquainted with anthropophagy, that shameful smear, that original sin of the human race.

MOHAWK WAR CHANT

Let's raise our tomahawks
Hang our kettles;
Grease our hair
Paint our faces
Let's sing the song of blood
That soup of warriors
Let us find amusement by killing
Let us cover our dead braves—to conceal them
And call lustily
To tell them they will be avenged.

Refrain
Let us drink the blood
And eat the flesh of our enemies.

ARKANSA WAR CHANT

I go forth to war to avenge the death of our braves,
Like the ravenous wolf, I shall be inexorable;
I shall exterminate our enemies, and devour them;
I shall tan the hide of their bloody skulls
Like the hail, I shall crush their women and children
And like lightning, I shall consume their villages.

Refrain
I go forth to war, to avenge the death of our braves;
Like the ravenous wolf, I shall be inexorable.

CHAPTER XIII

1 The first European child to see the light of day on the territory today owned by the United States was born in Roanoke, in lower North Carolina, of Ananias Dave, August 18, 1587, 189 years before the Declaration of Independence: this child was a girl who was named Virginia, from the name which Sir Walter Raleigh had suggested giving to this part of the Continent in honor of Queen Elisabeth; several companies had come here and been massacred by the Indians. The last company was obliged to embark again and go down the Chesapeake Bay under the leadership of Lord Delaware.

* A nation once numerous and powerful, and one of the mightiest in Louisiana, next to the Natchez. It owned all the country which crosses the great and beautiful river to which it has left its name, and which empties into the Mississippi, 223 leagues from the sea. The extent of the vast grassy plains that it waters has not yet been determined by astronomy calculation: it is believed that they extend as far as the waters of the Rio del Norte.

2   Owner of considerable property, Mr. Bull did not believe, after the capture of Charlestown, that he should expose his riches to the rapacity of the English; he left, at the head of 200 Negroes, and followed by a great number of wagons which carried his property and provisions for his little army; thus he crossed the two Carolinas and a part of Virginia, pitching camp every night in the most suitable spot. Thus he arrived in Tukahoe, on the James River, in the home of Mr. Randolph, rich inhabitant of Virginia, and his former friend. This man gave him some property near his home, on which he soon had a house built by his Negroes; and he lived there quietly amid his slaves and his flocks. Does one not see these old patriarchs emigrate with their families, sure of finding everywhere a land which will receive them and feed them? (Chastellux, Volume II, page 115) Translator's note.

2A   SAVANNAHS. One sees all sizes of them: the ones that cross the Mississippi are of such a vast extent that, up to the present time, their limits are still not known. Their soil is uniform, level, covered with grass or reeds; one sees trees and bushes only on several islands. The savannahs are moist in the spring. They are the constant haunt of buffalo, deer, bear, numerous flocks of turkey and a great many snakes.

3   THE AUDACIOUS KING-BIRD. *Lannius tirannus.* Of all the birds of this land, he is one of those who possess the art of flight in the highest degree of perfection. Impatient, jealous, arrogant, above all when he has little ones, he lives in a state of perpetual war, not only with the birds of his neighborhood but with those that chance brings into his neighborhood; he fears neither falcons nor hawks, which he knows always to attack in the windward. Nothing is more interesting to watch, especially when the wind blows with violence, than his long and bloody combats with the crows, which he obliges to take to the woods. Happy is the colonist who has some as guardians of his corn fields. He can be assured that their extreme vigilance, their indefatigable perseverance, and their audacity will put his domain in the shelter from all kinds of depredation; but on the other hand, he destroys the bees and chases away the birds whose plumage is so interesting, especially in Virginia, where his lovely melody is more common than elsewhere. The climate not being as warm as in the two Carolinas, nor as cold as in the northern States, it is scarcely astonishing that these delightful musicians have chosen it as their favorite land.

4   THRUSHES. "At sunset I stopped one time to watch two red thrushes that appeared to be challenged at the song, like the shepherds of Theocritus. This bird seems to be considered the nightingale of America. He resembles the European thrush only in shape, color, and habits; but he is twice as large. Although his song is similar to the latter, it is so varied and so perfect, that if one excepts the smooth, plaintive notes of the nightingale, one could take one for the other." (*Journey of Chastellux* Volume II, page 79) Note of the Translator.

5   MOCKINGBIRD. "I had gotten up before sunrise, and while they were preparing breakfast, I walked around the house; the birds were singing; but my attention was caught soon by a very fine song which appeared to

come from a neighboring tree; it was the mockingbird who was greeting the rising sun. At first I feared I would frighten him; but quite to the contrary, my appearance seemed to please him; he sang better than ever, fluttering from branch to branch. This curious bird, as remarkable for his agility as for his plumage, raises and lowers himself continually. One can never reproach him for tiring his listener; for nothing is more varied than his song. Has *he* just heard the lark or the thrush? It is the lark or the thrush that *you* hear. Does he hear someone singing? He will sing like him. If they are Scotsmen, he will repeat the air of a soft and plaintive romance; if they are Germans, one will recognize the gaiety of a Souabe or of an Alsatian. Sometimes he cries like a child or giggles like a girl. As he had reason to be happy with me, he hid from me none of his talents; one might have said that after giving me a delightful concert, he still wanted to present a comedy for me; indeed, he began to copy different birds; this he did in the most recognizable manner. When I returned home, he followed me from tree to tree, still continuing his song, now his own, now the songs he had learned in his flights." (*Journey of Chastellux,* Volume II, page 7) Translator's note.

6   CRANES. "This interesting bird is nearly six feet long, and from the toenails to his beak, he measures five feet; his wings have a span of eight to 9 feet; his tail is very short, but the feathers that hang from his two sides are long, pointed, of a delicate texture and soft as silk. The under part of his head is decorated with a sturdy, black skin. The legs and thighs, which are very long, have no skin as far as well above the knees. The plumage of this bird is in general ashy grey, shaded with light brown and sky blue. It is the brown color that dominates on the back and shoulders. The stems of the top feathers of the wings are wide and long, and when one snatches them, a big hole is left where they had been imbedded. All the bones of this bird are small and contain a great medular receptacle. When flying, he moves his wings slowly and in cadence. It is an interesting spectacle to observe that order and intelligence which reign in their numerous and peaceful societies and nothing is sweeter to the ear than their harmonious songs, when they are raised to the heights of the atmosphere." (*Journey of John Bartram,* Volume I, page 378) Translator's note.

7   WACHOVIA. Beautiful Moravian settlement, located between the Dan and Yadkin rivers, in North Carolina. It contains 100,000 acres which the Moravian Society bought in 1751 from Lord Grenville, and divided into six districts: Béthabara, Béthany, Hope, Salem, Fried-Land, and Fribourg. This colony is very flourishing; remoteness from the seaports having given a great degree of prosperity to the numerous manufactures which were established there.

CHAPTER XIV

1   CROCODILES. "This beautiful spring has other peculiarities which have not the slightest interest: its basin is filled with countless schools of fish, some of which have beautiful colors. There one sees the voracious croco-

dile, watching the spectator with an audacious and disturbing greed; the gar-fish, the trout, the bream, the fearless sting-ray, the bass, the skate, and a school of other kinds, all in separate groups, all moving fearlessly among each other. Among them one sees no sign of enmity, no attempt to destroy or to attack one another. Each group keeps apart from the other, to give the others the space necessary.

"This sojourn of peace and delight seems to be to the fish what terrestrial paradise was to men on earth, not that they change nature, but because the environment in which the fish move is so transparent, that it puts them all on the same level with respect to the need of protection against attack. Indeed, one knows that all fish in fresh water seize their prey by trickery; all of them ambush in some corner, to await the opportunity for surprising their victim; but this fountain, having neither shade nor shelter, the trout passes freely within reach of the crocodile; likewise the bream." (Bartram, volume 1, page 289) Translator's note.

2   SALT SPRINGS. The discovery of these springs on the banks of the Ohio, in Kentukey, Ténézée, etc., has contributed greatly toward increasing the number of inhabitants, and toward accelerating the farming of these beautiful lands. In Kentukey, there are already five springs from which salt is extracted.

3   DOGS. "Do they not often approach by their devotion, their fidelity, the strength of their attachment, and their patience, to what human nature considers as being most praiseworthy? Of what astonishing degree of intelligence are they not capable? In my youth, I had made a pact with mine; when I journeyed into the woods, he kept watch while I slept, on condition that as soon as I awakened, I would give up my place on the bearskin; never did this faithful friend fail me." (This note was found in *Memoirs of a Carolinian*.)

4   MOUNTAIN PASTURE LANDS. The custom of burning leaves every spring is known in many States; regularly it is done in the mountains which divided Upper Jersey from the State of New-York, and they furnish during the summer abundant food for the cattle sent there. The same situation exists on the salt meadows. Those one finds, when crossing between Bergen and New-Ark, are like that too; it has been observed how much this combustion speeded up the growth of the hay and improved its quality.

5   WEEPING WILLOWS. I have seen this kind of willow only in the town and environs of New-Haven; like the other willows known under this name, the branches of their tops bend and make a vast cradle. The leaf of this tree is a trifle larger than the leaf of the ordinary willow.

6   WATER ASH. This species is extremely precious; it makes excellent fireplace wood. After felling the trunk, they remove the thin, light branches from which durable baskets are made. It is from this wood that the springs used in wagons and several other kinds of carriages are made. This wood is excellent for carriage building and wheelwright work. From its roots, very sought-after, vases are made.

7   VEINED MAPLE. The sap of this third species gives scarcely any sugar;

it is remarkable only for its wood, which is extraordinarily hard, and so veined when it is polished, that despite the evidence of touching, the eyes are sometimes deceived by it : it takes as fine a polish as mahogany. It is common only in the neighborhood of Lake Champlain, where I have seen some maples two feet in diameter.

8 KNOTTY OAK. This species flourishes only in the most humid swamps and in some that are covered with water. Its leaves are small, its branches brown, and its appearance extremely lugubrious. It is bristling with black thorns, whose scratch is very dangerous : it is the ebony of this land, the hardest wood known here. So much is it sought after to make wheels, that it is becoming rare.

9 MOSS. The seed of this peculiar species of moss clings, like the mistletoe, to the bark of branches, taking root there, and in a short span of time, produces long garlands, that rock to and fro at the will of the wind, giving the trees an appearance of old age and decrepitude. But soon these parasites bog the branches down with their weight, and crush them. In the winter time the deer and cattle eat the branches which storms have detached. Moss is also used to fill mattresses and seats. The slightest particle put on the branch of a tree grows there with rapidity.

CHAPTER XVI

1 CURRENT OF THE GULF OF MEXICO. The important discovery of this great current is due to the whalers of Nantucket; the knowledge of its swiftness under different latitudes and its different widths is due to the extensive research and perseverance of Captain Folger, one of the principal privateers of Nantucket. After several years of observations and experience, he drew a map which he presented to Doctor Franklin, then agent of the colonies of Pensylvanie and Massachussetts for the British Government. This was in 1772, I believe.

I have often heard this learned person say that the Gulf current was caused by the trade winds which, blowing between the tropics almost constantly from the northeast, accumulate waters of the sea, along the shores of South America, causing them to flow back again into the Gulf of Mexico, from which point they return to the northern Ocean by way of the strait of Bahama. Although the waters of this current are between eight and ten degrees warmer than those of the sea, one does not see them sparkle during the night, as sometimes happens elsewhere. As for the heat, it is not astonishing that a mass of water as deep, and several leagues wide, coming from the tropics, can retain it for twenty or thirty days, that is to say, until it has reached beyond the banks of Newfoundland. This mass is too great to be suddenly cooled while passing through a less warm atmosphere. As a result of this difference in temperature, the air surrounding becomes lighter, rises, and is replaced by heavier air which comes in from all sides to replace this void; from there we get whirlpools that are sometimes violent, and those waterspouts so common in these parts of this current.

Just as vapors which rise from a pot of boiling water, scarcely distinguishable in warm living quarters, become visible as soon as the door is opened, the vapors of this current, imperceptible in warm latitudes, suddenly condensed by the cold of 45 degrees, produce those fogs which almost continually fill the banks of Newfoundland.

It is to this current that we owe the height of our tides, when the wind blows, for a few days in the northeast sector, which is opposite to its direction. This current passes by only 70 miles from the coasts of our northern States; but the further North it goes, the further from our shores it flows. Its swiftness is estimated at four miles an hour, from the strait of the Bahamas, to Cape Hatéras;* it is no swifter than two and a half miles an hour across Cape Cod.** Toward this latter latitude, it heads for the Azores, which it crosses, and from there to the coasts of Africa, where it fills the void produced there ceaselessly by these same trade winds. Such is the circle which the waters of this current describe. One can easily distinguish it on the open sea, by the quantity of sea plants known as racemes, by which it is covered; these plants have been detached by the violence of the current as it passed over the rocks, the keys, and the lowlands of the Bahama archipelago. Its width, only 40 or 50 miles on the maps of Georgia, increases as one heads north; it has also been observed that the northeast wind limits and then increases the swiftness of the current, but the northwest wind has just the opposite effect.

If ever a passageway is opened between the Ocean and the South Sea, by way of Lake Nicaragua, an undertaking that would not cost 300,000 guineas, and which would avoid circumnavigation of Cape Horn by 3,000 leagues, then the waters of the Atlantic, constantly held higher, because of the trade winds, than those of the Pacific Ocean, would escape through this new canal; they would then cease accumulating in the Gulf of Mexico, and would come out of it through the strait of Bahama.

It is to the knowledge of this current and its eddies that the navigators of Nantuket owe the promptness of their return from Europe; it is not rare to see them return from London to Boston in twenty or 30 days; this is the ordinary time of a voyage from the second to the first of these cities.

CHAPTER XVII

1 GREAT BLOCK. The shallowness of the waters of the Bay of New-Haven prohibiting vessels' approach to that town, a few years ago a block or cone was built two miles and several hundred feet from the shores, where the vessels load and unload their cargo. It is from this cone that they have just built a breakwater to the town; it facilitates the transportation of commodities and merchandise of the land, as well as the disembarkment of passengers. It is wide enough for vehicles to come and go conveniently.

* Cape Hatéras, located under 35°, is formed by the elbow or salient angle of a very long cliff of sand (sand dune) which protects Pamlico Sound from the furies of the Ocean.
** Cape Cod is the extremity of a peninsula 300 miles long forming the western entrance of the great bay of Massachussets, known by the inhabitants as Race-Point, off which is a depth of thirty fathoms.

2 BERMUDA ISLANDS. This little archipelago, which is merely a dot in the midst of an immensity, is located under the 32nd degree of latitude, a thousand miles from Madère, and three hundred miles from the continent. It is composed of several fertile islands, and a great number of reefs and barren rocks. The largest, known as Saint-George, is only sixteen miles long, and two or three miles wide. It is toward the middle of the salient angle of this island that they have built the capital, whose population—black and white—together with that of the other islands is mounting to 20,000 souls.

All the houses are of stone, extremely soft when they leave the quarry, but soon hardened by the sun. Like the former English colonies of the Continent, this island is ruled by a Governor, a Council, and a Chamber of Representatives. The greatest number of inhabitants, sailors from their very birth, are engaged in making voyages to our chief towns or to the Antilles, whence they return at the time of the hurricanes. No vessel more durable, nor sloop more excellent is known than the schooners and sloops which they build with the cedars of their island; nor are there better navigators than the Bermudans.

The formidable reefs surrounding this archipelago are impregnable ramparts which put the inhabitants in the shelter from invasions from their enemies, and protect them against the furies and ravages of the Ocean; located between zones crossed by the trade winds and changing winds, they often experience frightful storms, which may some day destroy this little archipelago. I confess, in my lifetime I have never experienced as deep a feeling of terror as in 1767, when, in the shelter of a rock located on the crest of a height some miles from town, I watched the struggles between the atmosphere and the Ocean. More than once I thought I felt the earth shake 'neath my feet when the enormous weight of those waves rolled forth to break on the banks of that island, which they threatened to swallow up. The violence of that hurricane would long be remembered by the inhabitants. At every moment or so, from the bosom of those purple-tinged clouds issued, not claps of thunder, but torrents of fire, accompanied by terrible explosions. The air I breathed was like electrified fluid above me, as the unchained elements made implacable war, by the flash of lightning, I saw in the valley nature reclad in her most brilliant colors; on one side, I watched the horrors of what I thought was to be my last night in the world; on the other side, by the light of these same lightning flashes, I saw the magnificent verdure of the forests surrounding me.

The climate of the Bermudas is one of the most pleasant and healthful known; the sun, whose heat day and night is tempered by the refreshing breezes of the sea, produces the most astonishing effect on the human constitution and on vegetation. This mild warmth seems to be like a life-giving and creative power which ceaselessly strains to bring to birth, to develop, to embellish everything it produces; also, the women there are extremely fertile and Bermuda blood is as fine as the blood of Massachussetts.

Located 300 miles from the rigors and torpor of winter, the gardens are always filled with vegetables, and the trees covered with flowers or fruits: the art of gardening is unnecessary here. Forever animated by this mild temperature, birds make their songs heard from the beginning to the end of the year. What a pity the nightingale has not been introduced there! Under the influence of this smiling climate, its egg-laying and melodious songs would have succeeded one another, like the flowers and fruits of the trees in which they would have made their nests; this lover of spring, never feeling the necessity to emigrate elsewhere, would have remained forever on these islands.

I am not the least bit astonished that the bishop of Cloyne (Barclay *) has chosen this haven to woo his muse. He had planned to found a university where the young people of the continental colonies would have been educated.

At the time of the visit he made there (1754), the customs of the inhabitants were as pure as the air they breathed. It was really the Golden Age; but unfortunately these islands, becoming during the revolutionary war the rendez-vous of various frigates and English corsairs, the sailors introduced there the taste for gambling, dissipation, and everything that is called pleasures in the coastal cities. Since that time, hospitality, industry, innocence, and moderation of desires have disappeared from these beautiful islands like a dream. Of everything that used to be admired there, only the mildness and charms of the climate remain. This saintly bishop would no longer recognize the customs of the inhabitants which had impressed him so deeply.

3 BAHAMA. The islands known by this name (there are 500 of them) form an archipelago much larger than the Bermuda archipelago: it occupies almost the entire area included between the eastern coast of Florida and the island of Cuba. Among the great number of islands and keys, there are only sixteen that are fertile and of considerable area. The most remarkable are Aethèra, Bahama, Lucaye, Saint-André, and Providence. The latter is the most highly cultivated, and also the seat of the English Government which seized it in 1667, after chasing out the pirates and the buccaneers, for whom the islands had served as asylum for nearly a half-century. The favorite occupation of the inhabitants of Providence, in wartime, just like their predecessors, is to equip the corsairs and scour the coasts; they are the most eager and pitiless of all men, these men who engage in this activity. No doubt they owe this taste to their location, 'mid this vast labyrinth of islands and reefs surrounding them. Sure of collecting booty from the debris of shipwrecks, very frequent in this

---

* The Reverend James Barclay, Bishop of Cloyne in Ireland, not content with the good accomplished in his diocese, wanted to extend its sphere; for this purpose, he embarked, planning to explore the colonies of this continent. He visited the colleges and academies, revived those that were languishing, aided those that were just starting, enriched many libraries with considerable gifts. Since the beginnings of the colonies, it was the first time a prelate had been known to leave his see, to cross the ocean and spread the seeds of good. Having heard in New York about the Bermuda Islands, he embarked to visit this little archipelago, then ignored, and virtually unknown. Impressed with the beauty of the climate, as well as the customs of the inhabitants, he resolved to found there a college, whose President and instructors he was to import from England. I do not know what prevented the execution of this plan. This same prelate discovered and taught us the use of tar-water.

dangerous archipelago, one can see them rejoicing after a storm, like the farmer at the approach of the harvests. The Government is like the one of the Bermudas. These islands are also the native land of the tortoises, and their favorite haunt; from here they are taken to all the chief towns of the continent. I have seen some that weighed from 50 to 260 pounds.

4   VAULTS. The ancestors of most of the prosperous families of the northern States, as well as New-York and New-Jersey, have built vaults in the town cemeteries, or in the vicinity of their country homes. These vaults are distinguished by the number of flat stones which cover the steps. The bodies enclosed in two coffins of oak and mahogany, on which have been engraved in copper or silver the name and age of the deceased, are near each other. It is the custom that every time a member of a family dies, the survivors go down into the vault, to contemplate for a few minutes amid the remains of their ancestors: I have often watched this gloomy and soul-stirring ceremony.

It is also the custom in the Southern states to have in reserve a certain number of large planks of cedar from which the coffins are made; each member of the family puts in a special place the ones which are destined to bury him some day.

END OF VOLUME TWO

VOLUME THREE

CHAPTER SUMMARIES

VOLUME THREE

CHAPTER IV   461

Several days later, Mr. Hazen sends the two travelers the following details:
    Coalition of the nations of the Ohio and Great Lakes against the English,
after the conquest of Canada.—General Bouqet is named commander of the
army destined to raise the siege of Fort Pitt.—Devastation of the frontiers.
—Deplorable state of the interior of Pensylvania.—The General arrives at
Carlisle.—Fright of the inhabitants.—The general reaches the pass at Bushy-
Run in the Alleghény mountains.—Bloody battle against a group of Indians.
—He defeats them after a seven-hour battle and arrives at Fort Pitt.—Crosses
the Ohio.—Penetrates into the forest as far as Tuskaraway.—Peace proposals.
—The General is dissatisfied with the first speeches of the chiefs.—He arrives
at the forks of the Muskinghum.—Treaty.—Speeches of some chiefs.—Arrival of several hundred prisoners.—Touching scenes.—Reluctance of some of
the prisoners to return.—What one of the chiefs says to the general in giving
up some children.—Great ecstasy of the mothers over finding again some of
the children whom they believed lost.—Irresistible effects of sympathy.—A
soldier from Maryland recognizes his wife.—Effect of his first exclamation.
—Anxieties over the fate of a child of three.—A new convoy of prisoners
arrives.—Distraction of the woman mentioned: on seeing her other child, she
drops the child she has at breast.—Powerful effect of tears to calm great
shocks to the soul.—Affection of the Indians for their prisoners.—Devotion
of a young Mingo warrior.—Antipathy of some of the children for their
parents.—Many prisoners escape to rejoin the Indians.—Speech of one
of the women to the general.—Return to Fort Pitt.—Reflections on the
Indians.

CHAPTER V   474

Astonishment of a young Shawanese warrior on seeing transcribed onto birchbark what he had dictated.—Interesting thoughts on the art of making men
speak when they are not present, or after their death.—Reply of General
Butler.—He fears that the following item does not merit being sent.—Warriors are more common among these nations than prose writers.—Regrets
that such a fine nation refuses everything that has been done to civilize it.—
Duty to conserve Indian names, more sonorous than most of those given by
the Europeans.—Difficulties of translating their harangues.—Necessity of
introducing new words.—Indians less susceptible to friendship than the
white men.—Reasons.—Reflections on their way of life.—Observations of
various chiefs on the foresight and anxieties of the future.—Their astonishment at seeing the white men work day and night.—Lament of Panima, seated
at the foot of a great birch in the moonlight, addressed to Ganondawé, his
friend, who had gone to Pensylvania.—The lament is in 8 parts.

CHAPTER VI   483

Visit with Chancellor Livingston.—Departure from Clermont for Albany and
Skénectady.—The travelers go up the Mohawk as far as the mouth of the
Oriskany.—Reflections on the great changes which have taken place since

1789.—They take four Indians to serve them as guides and purveyors.—They arrive at Lisandre, one of the districts in the great military concession.—Meeting with a family recently arrived on its lands.—Favors done for them.—They leave for New Geneva.—Arrive at the farm of a colonist from New-Jersey.—Worries of his wife over the sight of four hunters.—She summons her husband by a piercing blast of a conch-shell horn.—Her husband arrives.—He points out the surveyor-general's camp.—Departure.

CHAPTER VII   494

They cross through regions covered with pines and hemlocks.—Newness of the clearings.—Sterility of the soil.—Encounter with some Cayuga chiefs.—They arrive on the shores of Sénecca.—Thoughts aroused by the glimpse of the small marketplace of Geneva.—They cross the lake.—They find abundance and cleanliness at the inn.—Conversation with one of the founders of this new settlement.—Reasons that made them decide to leave their native land.—Praises of Colonel Williamson, from whom they bought their land.—The travelers embark on the first sloop ever constructed in Geneva.—Departure.—They cross the districts of Ovid, Lake Cayuga, and arrive at the surveyor-general's camp.—Details on apprenticeship, the subdivision of lands, Roman names given to the districts of this military concession.—Chart of canals finished, begun, or planned in the United States.—Chart of population of these States at different times.—Chart of the annual progress of this population.—Error of those who believe that this population increase springs from European emigrations.—Progress of clearings in the north and northwest parts of the State of New-York in the last eighteen years.—Thoughts of Mr. Herman.—Return to Skénectady.

CHAPTER VIII   508

Ancient pyramids, circuses, and causeways in Georgia and the two Floridas.—Thoughts of Mr. B., member of the United States Senate about the obvious traces of an ancient population, as well as the entrenched camps and tombs located west of the Alléghénies: the ancient Floridans must have enjoyed peace for a long time; the ancient Trans-Alléghénians, on the contrary, must have existed in a continual state of warfare.—Traditions of the Cherokees. These works were in the same state of preservation two centuries ago.—Enormous layers of oyster shells.—Oyster fossils in the land of the Chicassaws.

CHAPTER IX   523

Details on the acts of incorporation.—On the public spirit which they arouse.—It is to this spirit that is owed everything useful in the United States.—Churches, hospitals, colleges, academies, literary societies, bridges, canals, etc.—Inviolability of these charters: as respected as property.—Subject to forfeiture.—Details of things founded in New-York and in the interior of the State by incorporated societies.—At Philadelphia, in Connecticut and Massachussetts.—Origin of the great hospital of New-York and of the marine society.

CHAPTER I

STORY OF JEAN DE BRAGANSA

"You ask me to retrace the chief events of my life from the pleasant twilight of youth to the somber mood of this evening. What a sad and painful task your friendship imposes on me! How can I recall the memory of so many injustices and outrages without once again accusing blind destiny which subjected me to them? It is true, some ideas remain, just as one finds sparks in the midst of a pile of cinders, but the organ of speech, or rather the mold is worn out. Do you not realize that style, which is merely the physiognomy of the mind, either warms and stimulates one or grows cold and lifeless, according to the feelings of the soul or the different periods of life? Is it at my age when the ices of winter have paralyzed the imagination, frozen the memory, extinguishing this early and sacred fire which rouses our intelligence, that one can turn to writing? No, like these flowers whose glory cold has dispelled, whom the weight of storms bends toward the earth, I have arrived at that age where life is nothing more than the remains of vegetation. But your friendship exacts it and I impose no other conditions to my acquiescence than that of secrecy, for you do not know what the consequences would be of the slightest indiscretion.

"After being nourished and tenderly cared for until the age of three, by Dona Theresa H . . . , sister of Bishop . . . , my mother, who was in England, summoned me and some time later sent me to the country, where I remained until grown up, when I entered Eton. Whatever might have been the talents I received from nature, or whatever special care they might have taken with my education, I was not long in making rapid progress, and earned the esteem of my superiors. One day when the chancellor according to his custom arrived to make his annual visit to the college, to my great astonishment I was presented to him as one of the scholars who was deserving of the king's protection (George I then reigned). This flattering and unexpected circumstance delighted my mother so much that she decided to have me enlist in the Royal Navy, and in the following year I was admitted to the school at Greenwich. After three successful years of study I was honored by His Majesty with a commission on board the 'Alfred,' commanded by Captain Walton, brother of my mother; on his books I was inscribed as John Braganza, a fatal name to which, as you will see, I owed in consequence all the misfortunes that befell me.

When one thinks how imperceptible are the early causes, the early events that influence our lot, and the pivot on which turn the destinies of men, it seems evident that we on earth are the toys of what some call chance, others fate. Alas, how frightened we would be if, setting forth on the obscure paths of life, we could anticipate the influence of our early steps and figure out the links of this indestructible chain of all human events!

"Shortly after my arrival on board the 'Alfred,' that ship was assigned to the Mediterranean, where it remained for three years. We put in at seaports of this terrain once so celebrated: Smyrna, Alexandria, the islands of Cyprus and Candie, the ports of Africa and the Moree; we even went as far as the Dardanelles which we left by ship's cutter several times to get to Constantinople. I still re-read with pleasure the details of these excursions and the observations which the sight of so many objects inspired in me; for despite the dissipations of youth, I did not neglect to record them every evening, and later to copy them. Full of health, hope, and strength, joy and pleasure raced in my veins and shone in my eyes: I was happy with the joy of living.

"My greedy eyes sought out everything that was great and beautiful; my imagination became inflamed: that astonishing column at Alexandria, the Athenian buildings, the old ruins which one meets on the two banks of the Hellespont, whose origin is lost in the darkness of time. My admiration extended to ecstasy reflecting on the taste, the boldness, the patriotic spirit, the richness of these ancient peoples, who, better than the moderns, knew how to infuse in their buildings the spirit of immortality. But it was especially among the Greeks that I recalled what history has transmitted to us of this celebrated people whose aquiline noses, outstanding type of beauty, mouths with crimson lips and teeth of enamel, sparkling eyes a thousand times more expressive than words. I seemed to recognize these figures which the genius of Praxiteles and Phidias committed to marble 3,000 years ago; some of them have been preserved until now.

"At the prescribed time, we received orders to return to England, stopping on the way at Gibraltar and at Lisbon. The day after our arrival in the latter city (in 1736), there was at the Court a gala party to which, according to custom, the ship's officers were invited. Scarcely had we entered the reception room of the palace, when one of the major-domos came to greet us and in a very polite tone said:

" 'Gentlemen, protocol demanding that I present your names to the Secretary of State, I beg of you to tell them to me.'

"Instead of writing mine down, as he had done the others, he stared at me closely and disappeared. The crowd was so large that I followed my comrades without paying much attention to it. I had been a half hour in the great drawing room when I was arrested and taken before one of the secretaries of the palace. There I was submitted to a long interrogation relative to the name I bore, my mother, what I had done since the age of reason, etc. In vain did I refer them to my captain and to Lord Kinnoul, then ambassador from England: where they took me I cannot recall, but there I stayed nearly seven months until one day a man appeared in my room and said:

" 'Are you not a little bored here?'

"How can one ask such a question of one who repines so long in a captivity whose causes he knows nothing of? Who are you? Who sends you here?'

" 'Those who are interested in your lot, your superiors and mine.'

" 'I know of no superiors other than his Britannic Majesty and the captain of his ship, the "Alfred." '

" 'Until now you have been right; but things have changed for you. Understand that you owe allegiance to the British nation only through your mother and that your father is a Portuguese lord. He reclaims you and adopts you as his son, but on condition that you will serve in this country's navy: a commission of lieutenant awaits you on board a frigate ready to leave for Goa; are you willing to accept it?'

" 'If actually this lord reclaims me as his son,' I said to him, 'why has he kept me so long in these four walls? What reproach can he be making me? Why does he not permit me to see him, to deserve his kindnesses? By what right has he deprived me of my freedom? All of that is an enigma which I cannot comprehend.'

" 'I am not permitted to tell you more,' he replied, 'but if I may hazard some advice, it would be for you to accept these propositions. After all, would it not be better to be a lieutenant on active duty than to languish here as a victim of circumstances that will be unknown to you for a long time?'

"He left me, telling me that he would return the next day to learn what would be the result of my decision.

"I spent the night in an agitation that bordered on delirium, busy recalling what this stranger had told me, wondering who this person could be who claimed me again as his son, and by what chance my father was a Portuguese lord; I, whose mother, a lady of quality, was English. Left to myself, impatience and boredom made me decide to follow the advice of this messenger. Arriving at Lisbon, I soon found out that I was being closely watched, although treated more politely. Moreover, they permitted me to write to my mother, as well as to my friends in London, but no sooner had I sent my letters than I was taken on board the frigate and presented to the captain who was awaiting me on the deck. I was busy exploring my new surroundings and going over the papers I had left on board the 'Alfred,' when I saw a letter from Captain Walton, written three days after my arrest, in which he expressed his regrets, told me the futile efforts he had made in my behalf, and promised to apprise the admiralty of what had happened to me. As soon as I had donned the Portuguese uniform, my commission was read to the crew; but what was my astonishment to learn that instead of my name, they gave me that of Jeronimo de Sousa.

" 'Why this change of name?' I asked the captain.

" 'I cannot answer that question here,' he replied. 'I am obeying instructions.'

"After exhausting all resources of conjecture, and engaging the captain in long conversations, I made my decision and left this mystery to time for revelation. I associated with my colleagues and busied myself seriously with my duties. Nevertheless, I missed my friendships with those with whom I had served on the Mediterranean, whose language, customs, and nautical knowledge were so different from those of my new companions.

"Our frigate, careening at full speed, was shipping so much water that the captain was obliged to put in at Mozambique, whose governor was a Negro. Finally, after 102 days crossing, we arrived at Goa, in the island of Salsette. Tired from such a long passage, I was preparing to make a tour of the town, when the captain said to me:

" 'I have received definite orders to hold you on board; but in order that you will not be chagrined by that, I shall frequently have company, and we will go fishing any time you like. I advise you to accept this slight annoyance with patience and courage.'

" 'In the name of heaven,' I told him, 'who can have given you such inconceivable orders? Am I not lieutenant of this frigate? As such,— aye as a man—have I not the right and privilege to do as I like after fulfilling my duties? Is this an example of the interest that he who calls himself my father takes in me, seeming to be my father for the sole purpose of chaining me and holding me in bondage? Are these the marks of his affection? Why did he not leave me on board the "Alfred"? There, at least, I was free and happy. No, this man is not a Portuguese; but an Arab, a Moor.'

" 'You are more fortunate than you think, imprudent young man,' he replied. 'For, if what you have just said were known by someone other than I, you would be lost: be more discreet or you will force me to be more severe, do you understand? Despair is the lot of old age, but at your age!!!'

"Among the people whom the captain often invited on board, were two Indians, serious persons, venerable by virtue of their age as well as the unchanging gentleness of their expressions.

" 'Are you fathers?' I asked them one day when they were alone with me on the deck.

" 'Yes, we are,' they replied, 'for a long time.'

" 'How old are your first born?'

" 'More than 30 years.'

" 'Why do you not bring them here some time? I would be delighted to know sons of such worthy fathers.'

" 'The youngest are in Benares; the others in Persia. Could you have something on your mind that you would rather tell them than us? If it is thus, and the difference in our ages inspires neither timidity nor distrust, our hearts are as open to you as our hands; relieve your soul. Through your heart's outpourings, lift the weight and bitterness of your worries, if you have any.'

"Influenced by such a moving overture, I told them the story of my life, up to my arrival in Goa.

" 'Worthy and interesting young man,' they said to me, 'born of an unknown Portuguese who, according to your belief, enjoys great consideration, and of a mother belonging to one of the highest strata of English society, neither justice of Heaven, nor that of men, nor your conscience, has the slightest reproach to make you, and yet you are unhappy. In Europe as here, destiny seems to summon men onto this great stage only to make them toys of its whims. What to do? Leave life, or learn to bear up under its disgusts and bitternesses. We know the captain of a ship bound for Lisbon; the day of his departure we will procure for you the means of leaving this frigate, your name will be Gasparo Vitello, which you will keep until your arrival in England. Concern yourself with the means of getting there as soon as you reach Portugal; otherwise misfortune awaits you every place.'

"The very day I disembarked at Lisbon, I saw the man who had come to speak to me in my prison at Evora. Thunder falling at my feet could not have caused me greater fright. All my precautions to avoid him were in vain. The following day I was arrested on the wharf where I was to embark and led to the common prison. Irritated by this new arrest, considering this land as none but a land of slavery and injustice, I allied myself with an Irishman, accused of some irreverence before a madonna of a village. Three days later, with the aid of a rope made from remnants of our sheets, we reached the foot of the wall located on the bank of the river, which we swam until we reached the English ship. Fortunately, the captain who was on board, received us and treated us with fine feeling.

"What a day, what a moment, the one, when finally free, I disembarked at Falmouth! How sweet and fresh the green of this beautiful country seemed to me! The dotted fields, these orchards of Pomona, the appearance of the inhabitants, what inexpressible joy the sight of all these objects excited in my heart! But I craved only to see London, where, a few days later I found myself clasped in the arms and wet from the tears of the tenderest of mothers. Leaning against her knees, my hands in hers, I was consoled by the prospect of a far happier future. Indeed, the very next day, she presented me to Queen Caroline, who, two months later, named me one of the undersecretaries of Lord Stairs, ambassador to Paris.

"As soon as I was in that capital, I started to study astronomy, whose elements I had learned at Malta, during the various trips the 'Alfred' had made there. But thunder was rumbling over my head and was to burst forth in my mind. After spending eighteen months in Paris, I was informed that my mother was breathing her last. Torn by frightful presentiments, I returned to London, where I arrived—alas —only to close her eyelids. And I have been able to survive this cruel loss! And the anguish of despair did not even break my heart! O tender and beloved mother! Sweet and revered soul! I can still see the features of your face, object of beauty that death has not been able to destroy! I can still hear the sound of your voice, organ of that unalterable softness which, with kindness, formed the basis of your character. I still recall your first lessons, those outpourings so sweet of maternal affection. Will our spirits one day meet again? Some day will your unhappy son be able to share your happiness, that of the just? But could I admit this cruel doubt? No, it would crush my heart as well as my fondest hopes; it would destroy the courage and resignation with which I bear up under the harshness of fate and the sufferings of life. Ah, if I could believe that bold, profitable crime, protracted suffering, and virtue were merely names, that remorse had its course only in education; that everything must equivocally disappear in the shadows of death, then I would say:

" 'Of all creatures who breathe, man is the most wretched, since he can hope for no compensation for the innumerable sacrifices that his stay on earth exacts. The God of nature, this father of sensitive beings, whom we invoke daily, does not exist, or is merely the passive organizer of matter.'

"Two days after this fatal event, the executors of the last wishes of Lady Anne Fitz...sent me an authentic copy of her will and a letter written entirely in her handwriting informing me that King John V of Portugal was my father. This secret, like a ray of light, clarified for me the reasons and motives for the severity with which I had been treated. But, instead of flattering my vanity, the revelation of this mystery made me tremble, for kings often have opinions and prejudices peculiar to their position. In her will my mother left me her house and the income from her estate, which, while these were not considerable, were none the less precious, since they represented the last testimonial of her tenderness. She departed from this life at a time when my life was to be overflowing with new bitternesses.

"King Joseph I, annoyed by my escape, as well as by the protection I had obtained from the English government, instructed his English ambassador to inform him of all the observations he could obtain regarding my employ under Lord Stairs, as well as to the time of my return. This ambassador was so well acquainted with all these details, that he scarcely allowed me time to dry my first tears. He suggested to the Secretary of State, that, out of respect to the memory of King John, who had just died, his successor wished to attend to the fortune and progress of the son whom his father had had by Lady Anne Fitz... ; that, despite the renewed efforts and offers of kindness, this young man had constantly refused them, without anyone's guessing the reason; that, in the case where his disdainful refusals might come from affection for his mother, one excused him; that, out of respect for her, the king had closed his eyes to this stubborn resistance, but, this lady being no longer alive, he, the king, wanted the intentions of the young man's father carried out. In consequence, he charged the ambassador with returning him to his real country, where he would be advanced in the service and honorably treated. Lord..., then Secretary of State, deceived by these fine promises, was duped, and I was the pitiful victim, for no sooner had I disembarked at Lisbon, than they took me to prison, as guilty of having resisted the wishes of the king. And if this king had been the Dey of Algiers or emperor of Morocco, what would he have done with me?

"I spent hardly a week in this prison when the jailer entered my room and said to me with a mysterious air:

" 'I know that I am risking my life in bringing you this letter, but I could not resist the solicitations of a holy bishop who charged me with giving you this: if you are discreet, it will not be the last.'

"The letter was from Dona Theresa Hen....

" 'I am the woman who twenty-six years ago nursed you with the milk from her breast, and although I have never seen you since, heaven is witness that I have not ceased a single day to interest myself in your fate. As happy as it was, I contented myself in rejoicing in secret, but now, that you have incurred the anger of the King and lost your mother, I want to take her place: count on my earnestness. They have made this feeble person, imperiously governed by his confessor and his minister, believe that it was wicked that a man in whose veins flows the blood of his father, dared live anywhere but here, and dared carry his name to England. Rest assured: someone will send you 400 crusados and some pounds. Rely on the tender interest of your good nurse and friend, Dona Theresa Hen. . . .'

"The traveler, overcome by fatigue and almost dying of thirst in the midst of deserts, experiences no keener joy when he comes on a well and some trees in whose shade he can rest, than that which the reading of this letter filled my heart and mind. Everything around me shone and my prison was no longer so dreary, nor the passage of time so slow and painful. Hope sprang forth to dampen my burning eyelids. Every week I received most consoling letters from this worthy woman. Finally, I learned that her brother, the Bishop of B. . . . had found the means to awaken the conscience of the king, representing to him the injustice of my detention, the necessity of treating with less severity a young man whom no one could reproach. He even dared to advise him to send me to the abbey of M. . . . , where I would enjoy greater ease, telling him that there people would concern themselves with my safety and give any instructions needed for a man who had spent so many years among the heretics. I was transferred there.

"Thus, blind destiny, chance, or I know not what unknown cause, plays with the happiness, with the lives of small or great men, poor or rich, wicked or virtuous. From one of the most cultivated lands in Europe, bosom of a nation renowned for its riches, its industry, its trade, and its power, I found myself transported and almost enchained in one of the most arid, most uncultivated places, among the most ignorant people—in a word, a Portuguese convent. In reflecting over the death of my mother, and of all that had happened since, I recalled the fable which I had heard repeated by the good Indians of Goa.

"Long before time began, Vishnu existed in thought and this thought stretched over space. To fill it up, he divided it into fifty layers. As soon as he had reached the earth's layer, he called forth his two winged dragons: one was red and the other white. 'Create for me,' he said, 'a solid and firm soil which can hold trees and harvests, on which you will put two-footed men, four-footed animals, birds, insects and snakes.' And to the second, he said: 'Create for me a sea which can be deep enough to hold the waters, and let these waters be of salt. You shall fill it with great and little fish, some with shells, some without. May all have eyes to see with, ears to hear with, and enough intelligence to make their way.' But as he spoke, there appeared the

Irrevocable (eternal necessity) ; she presented to each of these dragons a chest filled with leaves from the tree of good and evil.

" 'Why mix one with the other?' Vishnu asked her.

" 'Because they are inseparable.'

"Satisfied with this reply, they went off toward one of the highest spheres to order the creation of another world, but no sooner had they arrived when a frightful storm devastated the greatest part of the continent which the red dragon had just formed. This threw him into such a terrible anger that he sought out Vishnu.

" 'The first leaf that has left the chest of the white dragon,' he said, 'being the one from evil, leaves only one half of my work.'

" 'You will be satisfied,' replied Vishnu, and at that moment he appeared on the upset earth. He whistled and the winds ceased, he whistled again and the submerged continent reappeared. From there he took a flight toward the moon where Necessity had already arrived. There they resolved that the day when the red dragon dropped a leaf of good from its element, the white dragon would do as much for him and even for the leaves of evil. No sooner had they emptied half their chests, when there was a terrible explosion, the debris of which filled these boxes. Then chance, which had hidden itself, arranged things so effectively that the greatest number of first leaves were lost in the vagueness of space and the second leaves, windborne, spread themselves out over land and sea. That is why, from ancient times, there is more good than evil in the land and why sometimes both happen in equal parts.

"It was at the abbey of M.... where for six long years a man was to exist without dying from the experience; a man who, by birth, education, and talents, had believed himself destined one day to enter the English navy. This abbey enjoyed an income of 60,000 crusados. There was a library there, curiously enough. It contained decretals, legends, stories of miracles performed on the coasts of Africa by missionaries, and various editions of the lives of saints, somewhat different from those of the worthy Plutarch. What an expense to lodge, feed, and support 42 persons in laziness! Like a bottomless pit, this house absorbed the greater part of the nutritious juice of the neighboring regions, and that in a country where half the land is being cleared and the other half cultivated by the most unskilled hands. When the rains did not fall, the hope of the inhabitants was lost, and they had no resource other than the gates of the abbey, where bread and garlic were given them.

"At this time, each community, like every church, had its favorite saint, its religious fancies, its formulae and its miracles. The house where I lived was famous for its stigmata: all the monks had received these nocturnal favors, and those whose wounds were deepest, passed to be favored by heaven. Everything appeared quite extraordinary and quite new to me; but in reflecting on the nature of man, for whom, in this valley of tears and misery, one needs consolation and hope, whose eyes can watch neither the sun nor the truth, except through clouds and illusions, I became accustomed to this form of worship with much less repugnance. Of all these monks, I saw only the prior and the master of novices. The former always had his eyes toward heaven or fixed on the earth, an emblem, I was told, of seraphic ecstasy. The marks of respect consecrated by custom approached adoration. This devout creature had six names, which added the same number of holidays to the calendar of the abbey; on these days, they threw flowers at his feet, then genuflected before him after paying homage to him.

"The master of novices, a hypocrite, a knave when he thought it necessary to be, governed the house, the prior, and the novices. Although from his fertile brain spurted mystic ideas about the virgin, and although some were extremely mild and bore the quality of love, he himself was hard, irascible, and pitiless, a misfortune to whoever displeased him, especially to those in whom he believed he saw doubts or incredulity: they were sure to expiate their sins in the most obscure hideout. The other monks, unclean by habit, ignorant through education, and according to their temperament, fanatical or superstitious, lived together not only in the most perfect indifference, but often amid quarrels, hatred, and jealousy. One might just as well have introduced the sap of vegetation in the dried up trunk of a tree as to introduce any feelings of friendship or of affection in the hearts of these monks. The majority were prone to the most brutal passions, which in this hot climate, are no less active for being cloistered. Such were the men with whom I lived six years, losing neither reason nor life; moreover, by virtue of instruction, I became enlightened, even learned.

"But in the midst of these catechisms, they noticed that I had some English and French books, as well as some land maps and star charts. This discovery occasioned a general fomentation in everybody's mind for never, since the founding of the convent, had such a situation existed. I was accused of studying the occult sciences prohibited by canon law, of being an atheist, unbeliever, and impious, and the very next day, all these details were sent to the tribunal of the holy office, and until judgment was passed, I was shut up in a dungeon. After I had spent twelve days in the shadows of despair, they read the following pronouncement to me before the assembled community:

" 'It is forbidden to Jeronimo de Sousa, to apply himself to the study of geography and astronomy, under punishment prescribed by the holy office; this knowledge pertaining only to the Holy See which alone can know the different parts of the world whose visible head it is. As to the study of astronomy, he is guilty of believing the earth turns around the sun; that is the system of the heretics, whom God condemns forever. He is forbidden to predict eclipses; it behooves only an atheist to seek to know what is not yet known. As to the study of the stars, it is pure sorcery, one reads in the heavens only to deprave his soul. It is ordered that his books and his maps be consumed by fire and he be condemned to six months solitary confinement. May the sentence of this tribunal of mercy and justice be read to the assembled community, so that each may profit by it.'

"The king, to whom they reported these miseries, was so angered, that he said:

" 'This Jeronimo de Sousa, is nothing but a refractory creature, a heretic; were he my son, I would not pardon him. Have them take him to Angola.'

"This cruel sentence would have been executed, had it not been for the intercession of the patriarch and of Bishop B....

" 'Well, then,' said the king, 'see that he enters the monastic order; I shall see that he gets an income of one thousand crusados; I want to hear nothing more of the matter.'

"Words that anger provokes in kings strike down and destroy like thunder. When I learned of this fatal resolution, everything, all my courage and strength abandoned me. Alas, tired of life, why do people not know enough to leave it, as one leaves a house, ready to fall, as one leaves a vessel ready to hit bottom? Finally, I gave in. Unable to die, I professed ignorance and superstition for the rest of my days. What a fate for the natural son of King John and Lady Anne Fitz.... !

"After tasting the joys of liberty for several days, I hastened to see Dona Theresa, from whom I had often received letters during my stay in the Abbey at M.... In embracing her for the first time in my life, I wet her old cheeks with the most enthusiastic gratitude; she deigned to wet mine with the same feelings of sensitivity. My dried up heart, crushed by the adversity and pitiless hardness of mankind, had not experienced in a long time such sweet feelings.

" 'Do you remember Lady Anne Fitz.... ?' I asked her.

" 'I do indeed! She was the most beautiful woman I ever knew.'

" 'And I, her wretched son, will never forget that she was the best. These sad and bitter memories are all that remain to me of those happy days when in the shelter of her wing, I explored gaily the early paths of life. What a difference, dear Dona Theresa, between the lot that was mine then and what I am experiencing today.'

" 'Forget what you might have become in order that you may bear up with more resignation under what has been done to you. Call to your aid courage and steadfastness; they will come to help you, to steady your steps, until the sponge of time and the balm of habit have softened the bitterness of these early moments.'

" 'Reason, dear Dona Theresa, is dumb; courage deaf to my voice under this vilifying livery; but since my fate is not yet irrevocable, why should I submit to it? I need only one remedy; I know where to find it.'

" 'This livery that you scorn so much,' she said to me, 'is nevertheless the one in this country which leads to power, riches, and consideration. What does it matter to you the bases on which all that is founded. Think of the vows you have just uttered, and fear perjury, at least.'

" 'When the heart, the spirit, and the mind contradict simultaneously what the passive mouth has been forced to utter, can one fear perjury? Can an absurd vow be obligatory? Heaven and my conscience have absolved me.'

" 'Fear, at least, the anger of the king, the myrmidon of the Holy See, and the vengeance of the patriarch who saved you from the prisons of Angola.'

"In Bengal or Philadelphia I will brave their hatred, as well as their threats and soon they will forget me.

" 'But, my dear Don Juan, how do you expect to leave this country? Are you ignorant of the fact that leaving this country without permission is forbidden and that these orders are executed with the greatest severity?'

" 'Yes, I know that Portuguese nobles crushed under the yoke of one of the most shameful servitudes, are masters neither of their will nor of their actions. They are the descendants of the ancient conquerors of India whom they have succeeded in enclosing in a park like a lowly herd. With money and wisdom I shall be able to scale the wall.'

" 'But if luck does not favor you, do you know what the consequence will be?'

" 'Fate, dear Dona Theresa, is tired of following me since it has caused me to become a monk.'

" 'But are you not of the class of those from whom one chooses the chiefs of the abbeys, the prelates, and the bishops?'

" 'If the riches attached to the crosier and the mitre could tempt me, then I would be perjured.'

" 'You would be no more guilty than my brother and so many others.'

" 'Your brother, as well as your other bishops, received an education that is quite different from mine; we did not breathe the same air.'

" 'Since destiny, which controls everything on earth, wills it thus, submit to its sway; it is irresistible; profit by the circumstances which call you to riches and sacerdotal dignities. But, old as I am, what can I say that will console you and persuade you? Fifteen years ago I could have opened the gates of this land to you and pardoned you for having taken your father's name to England. Nevertheless, I still have enough influence to obtain the choice of the convent in which you may wish to live, some enjoyments and privileges analogous to your tastes. I have a considerable sum of money in Saint Anthony's church; we will share its income and on my death, I shall leave it all to you. In the name of that great saint, do not expose yourself to new dangers. Remember that at the slightest suspicion, the dungeons of Angola await you. Rest assured that from here on for the remainder of your years, your moves will be strictly watched, for this is the land of spies: the Government, the patriarchate, the ministry, the Holy See each has its spies, and there are no hirelings better paid.'

"Won over, without being swayed by what this fine woman had just told me, weakened, worn out by the decline of my health which alone might have sustained my strength and courage, I resigned myself to the orders of dictatorial necessity. Ah! how many times since have I not regretted the patience with which I gave in! I should have perished or broken my irons.

"In accordance with the advice of Dona Theresa, I went to see the patriarch, who granted me permission to choose the convent, or rather the prison in which I was to spend the rest of my days. I still reproach myself for the adulations, the lies, the shameful subterfuges to which I was obliged to resort: it was the first time in my life I had degraded myself in my own eyes. I came to see this celebrated old rock, its location, high and imposing, the small number of monks who occupied this house, the feebleness or rather ineptitude of the ones who governed it, and the proximity to the sea, and the capital, where through strangers, I could procure from London and Paris books and instruments I needed; finally, the hope of keeping in touch with the world through the tales of travelers, and by a few moments spent in the company of enlightened men; such were the motives that made me decide to establish my residence here. Finally, abandoning hope and almost desire to see England again, I invested what my mother had left me in public property of this kingdom, and Don Juan de Bragansa, resigning himself to the providence which had treated him so rigorously, shut himself up for the rest of his days in this little monastery. My income, what my mother and my worthy nurse had left me, even put me in the way of helping our monks; I mitigated their harshness by acquainting them with pleasures to which they had not become accustomed. In order to obtain some consideration for this, I neglected no means for becoming useful to them. On the one hand, convinced that in avoiding shocking them, I would improve my lot and assure its tranquility, I made every effort, despite my repugnance, to fulfill the duties of the state I had been forced to embrace. But when the trumpet of departure sounds, of what importance is it that I was a monk or pontiff, slave or emperor, whether I lived in a palace or on the summit of this rock?

"At the time when the shaking hand of your old friend was busy writing these lines, the last to leave his dried-up pen, I was completing my seventy-third year, and the forty-sixth year of my captivity. I am reaching the time when langours, infirmities of the body, and the dulling of faculties all make us wish for eternal repose, as the woodcutter, exhausted from fatigue, sighs after the balsamic sleep of the night. Quite different from you, my worthy friend, whom nature by an extremely rare miracle has exempted from this sad tribute, and for whom she still makes gladden some flowers 'mid the wintry ices.

"The relaxation of reading, the care of my garden, filled with the rarest and most exotic growth, the conversation of travelers and learned men, as well as the study of the movement of the stars during our beautiful Chaldean nights, have all contributed substantially toward filling the emptiness of my monastic existence, in shortening and softening the passing of time. Indeed! What an inexhaustible source of ideas, thoughts, conjectures in raising us above the ordinary sphere of our desires, our chagrins and our miseries!

"What a field for meditation, what an expanse for the flight of thought—the solar system offers us, when, with the aid of a good telescope, we cast our bold glances toward those far-off regions and cross the spaces wherein whirl the planets of which it is composed. Tired of these latter limits, we throw ourselves into the depths of the universe and admire its order and movements.

"How many times have I not been elated in thinking about the nature of the human spirit, which, with the aid of marvelous power of calculation, can seize, follow the rapid progress, announce appearances, know distances, determine the velocity of spheres so remote, and even predict the return of some comets whose elliptical and mysterious paths, so different from other celestial bodies, appear to be placed far beyond our intellect.

"Would a knowledge, which from the obscure and foggy regions of the earth, can reach great heights and is susceptible to just as great conceptions, be perishable as matter which serves as an envelope for it? Does not the genius of a Newton announce that this knowledge is an emanation of that spirit, of that divine fire which animates the universe, since it has succeeded in raising itself towards its author and discovering some of the laws according to which He governs it?

"Can it be that this universe is an entity existing by itself, and not the result of a cause, the work of creative and conserving power? The immutable order of this marvelous ensemble does it not, on the contrary, indicate the design and vivifying presence of a God whose hand serves its equilibrium and duration and maintains its propelling power? Without the ever-agitating power of this prime principle of things, would not the irregularity of some of the movements necessarily have resulted in general disorder and plunged nature once again into the darkness of chaos?

"In observing that just as on earth, the planets have a dual movement: that of a diurnal rotation around themselves and that of a periodic revolution around the sun, and that, as on our planet, they have inclined poles; that several are accompanied by satellites; that, consequently they must have a succession of days and nights, seasons and years, whose length is proportionate to the size of the orbits they travel, one is forced to believe that there exists some affinity, some rapport between their inhabitants and us. For analogy of cause must produce effects. In that case, we were not the only ones who were moving across the plains of space. Like the vessels that ply the seas, each planet of which our system is composed, carries its own cargo of sensitive and thinking creatures, animals, birds, vegetables, whose forms and organization are adapted to their distance from the sun and to the density of their lands, and like our globe no doubt is submitted to the chances of destiny and vicissitudes of life. Thus, do I instruct myself and associate in my imagination with these unknown companions of existence.

"Often, carrying afar the meanderings of my dreams, I wonder:

"Did the combustion of the sun precede the formation of the planets? Is it contemporaneous to it or posterior? Will they become extinct some day? If ever that happens, what will become of these planets? Dragged down by the enormous weight of their mass, will they arrive from the ends of the universe to precipitate themselves into this common center of their gravitation, and rekindle their fires? They say that the same cause which separated them from it thousands of years ago, will still detach them to resume their former stations, travel their former orbits, and become again, as today, the abode of existence and life! Has this catastrophe not already happened in some of the solar systems by which we are surrounded? Is it among the probable or possible things?

"Penetrated by the keenest admiration, dazzled by the sight of so much magnificence, so many marvels and wonders with which the unlimited plains of space are filled, I adore its unknown cause, which I dare to call the father of nature, and I raise myself tremblingly to the foot of His throne. Has He deigned to concern Himself with the lot of His children? Has He prescribed duties for them? Did He promise rewards for those who would accomplish them? Have I had the good luck to know them and acquit myself of them? Conserver of this universe, would He not also be the protector of oppressed innocence? Could it be that life then, is but a fortuitous accident? Is it not, on the contrary, a link in a long chain of lives to which we are called?

"These are some of the objects of my frequent meditation and flights of my feeble intelligence. Convinced that the one thought which stirs me will survive the destruction of bodies, I forget the hardships of my destiny, the injustice of men, and prepare myself to appear before the Great Judge, who, as fair as He is powerful, will reward virtue and punish crime."

CHAPTER II

During our stay in Wilmington,[1] we had the pleasure of meeting Mr. Wyning, one of the most eloquent speakers in Congress; only recently, at the time of the origin of the new Government, named United States senator. To this happy coincidence we owed the good fortune of learning everything relating to the culture and industry of this little state, Delaware, as well as the technique of building a levee which would hold in the waters of the Delaware that used to flood the vast low lands. He also told us of the advantages which result when landowners form a corporation for the speedy repair of damage caused by muskrats [2] or by the rising of the waters.

"The same situation exists," he told us, "at Salem, at Sweedsbourg, at Goshem, etc. in Glocester and May counties, located on the southern bank of the Delaware. Before anyone thought to petition the Government for charters that unite the interests of the landowners, damage and considerable loss were suffered. It is to the Quakers in Salem, owners of vast tracts of this property submerged at one time, that we owe this useful example. The peninsula formed by the confluence of the Skuylkill and the Delaware, a vast swamp forty years ago, has become in the last few years solid ground covered with cattle and bringing great income. This was accomplished by means of levees built and maintained by communal funds. How true it is that from union comes strength."

He showed us the windmills of Brandywine whose construction and operation surpass in perfection anything we had seen until then and in which more than 300,000 bushels of wheat (180,000 quintals) are annually ground into flour.

"We are the feeblest state in the Union," he told us; "but as members of this great and fine association, we have the same representation in the United States senate and we enjoy the same rights, the same privileges as those states which are more populous. Our location on the Delaware, the proximity to Philadelphia, the superior quality of our flour, the richness of our pasture lands,[3] compensate for our political weakness. As for me, I do not regret it; I like mediocrity; in it one finds virtue and repose.

"Tomorrow I shall introduce to you the most interesting man in this region; a skillful farmer who served as aide-de-camp to General Fouquet in the war with Canada. Deeply affected by domestic losses suffered in Europe, to which he had returned at the peace of 1763, he came back to this continent sometime later in order to forget so many bitter memories. Chance having led him into this part of the state,[4] he was so impressed by the exemplary industry, the temperance, and the wisdom of the colonists, that he bought a well-built and fairly well-cultivated plantation.

"For I know too well," he told me, "the fatigues and disgusts of a new settlement to dare expose myself to one at my age; those back-breaking clearings are neither the Elysian fields nor the groves of Thessalie, as they are sometimes pictured by the imagination of a newly arrived European, who judges according to what he has seen and what he knows.

"His example and his lessons have been extremely useful to us. To wise practice, he joins much theory from which he makes innumerable experiments performed in his leisure time. During his trips his brother, possessed of European mentality, replaces him. Like the Chinese, both of them excel in the art of irrigation. To this industrious colonist, we owe almost all the planting of the mulberry trees, the acacia, the plane-trees and the hickory [5] which shade our roads and are beginning to fill waste lands. For, accustomed to consider trees only as injurious and harmful things, the inhabitants of these states until now have neglected to repair the inattention of their ancestors. Public esteem would have sent Mr. Wyning to Congress a long time ago, if he had consented. He has just returned from a long trip whose interesting journal he has presented to the President of the United States. Although overwhelmed with the thorny problems of the supreme magistracy, General Washington is vitally interested in the progress of the settlements in the interior, especially those of agriculture. Right now, he has two persons in Europe, charged with transmitting to him the fruit of their observations on everything that has any bearing on this foremost among the arts, which he considers, very justifiably, as the purest, the most abundant, and most inexhaustible source of happiness, wealth, and splendor of a state.

"Tomorrow we shall see an old soldier; hark! *see* him did I say? We shall spend several days there, for he does not like short visits. If we can succeed in dissipating the clouds of melancholy that often envelope his spirit, you will see with what elegance he tells what he has seen and to what extent honest and sensible souls find themselves delighted to chat with him. For him our President has a special esteem, evidence of which he gives him every time he visits him either in Philadelphia or Mt. Vernon, where one can say, as far as agriculture and other things relating to it go, this great man preaches by his example."

The next day after journeying for fifteen miles through one of the most cultivated fields Mr. Herman and I had ever seen, decorated with elegant and well-painted houses, fine orchards and pastures filled with animals, we arrived at Mr. Hazen's home.[6]

"I bring you two travelers," Mr. Wyning told him. "Although they have experienced and observed a great deal in all the places they have explored, there are still many more things for them to know; I hope you will permit them to draw from your interesting stories, the knowledge they need."

"I often travel in order to divert myself and ease a weight which grows in solitude and idleness. I am never so little ill at ease as when I am busy; work and activity, you see, are the consoling factors in the hardships of my life. But, I know nothing more pleasant than the exchange of ideas. I shall gladly share mine, such as they are, with those of these gentlemen."

And after several reciprocal questions, he continued: "As soon as the Peace of 1763 was concluded, I felt the need to see my native land again; the one of all the countries whose government, laws, customs were most agreeable to me, the one where I had the greatest number of friends; I was afire with the desire to see again this beloved country whose very name had swelled my heart with the tenderest affections; to wander once again over those mountains where our industry has carried culture as high as possible; to cross these valleys beautified and made fertile by the rays of the sun; these glaciers at the foot of which the plow often traces its furrow .... and where one sees the cattle grazing. How shall I explain to you? I saw once again the canton of Glaris with inexpressible pleasure, and from the moment of my arrival, I decided to drag the tottering steps of my old age there and to die on the very hill where I was born and where I had spent my early years. It was there that happiness awaited me, without my suspecting it. I married one who was to help me experience all the joys of life; I became father of three children. But can one analyze, define these enjoyments so exquisite, so unutterable, which spring from marriage and accompany fatherhood? Everything smiled on me, in my home as well as in my fields, everything around me became beautiful: for I had become a farmer. The change of seasons, the storms, the snowfalls had no element of the disastrous for me, as before, because the good fortune I enjoyed compensated for all these inconveniences. The companionship of a beloved woman who had chosen me above all other men, to make her happy; the presence of our children, the pleasure of seeing their talents and the germ of their reason grow was for me a series of joys which abundance could not destroy. Alas! this period, these years have fled away on the wings of the sparrow.

"Blind as we are! we walk confidently to the edge of a precipice, without seeing it. I was ignorant of the fact that the happier one is, the more he should tremble; that the happiness of a father and of a husband above all, founded on a great number of understandings, is extremely fragile. I was praising heaven when a catarrh epidemic occurred, annihilating these high hopes and these exquisite enjoyments! My three children succumbed; and, as if my losses had not been great enough, nor the wounds of my heart deep enough, pitiless destiny also struck their mother. And to think that one survives such a wrench! And after losing four-fifths of his happiness and his life, one can still breathe the air and see the light of day! Our frail constitution, which a slight accident, a cold even, destroys in a short span of time, resists the torments of despair, the bitterness of regrets so poignant and so long! Life then is merely a stormy sea, whose very ports even are not sheltered from storms! Or rather, it is merely a distressing dream, a series of chimeras, a fortuitous combination of illusory benefits and real evils. One must admit: it is not a light task, that of appearing in the theatre of the world, and living there to a very advanced age, above all in these times when men, through their senseless wars and their discords, still add more to the inevitable calamities of nature. Who, then, has summoned the human race to this globe to be the victim of so many scourges and tragedies?

"Wretched enough not to give nature back the miserable breath she had lent me, I abandoned the places where everything reminded me of things so dear and memories so sad. I returned to this continent, long a haven for unfortunate people whom Europe casts up as the sea casts on its shores the debris of shipwrecked people. I wandered for a long time without knowing where I would settle; I even dreaded the notion of making a settlement. Yet, when I came upon the cultivated fields which formerly I had seen covered with thick forests, when I chatted with men whose work some years previous brought them scarcely bread enough for the day and cost them sweat and infinite pains, and when I saw them as immigrants suddenly becoming good and useful colonists, I confess my heart opened to softer sensations: by sharing their happiness, I became less wretched. For can one help smiling upon the early light of hopes founded on the protection of laws, on the possession of lands, the business of farming? What spectacle can rouse more effectively one's sensibilities? The association with educated people, the sight of so many interesting things, the change of air, all those causes which no doubt had a great influence on my health, also recalled my courage and dissipated somewhat the somber shades of melancholy that I had brought with me.

"I was exploring that section of the state when a rather serious fall

obliged me to spend several weeks in the household in the neighborhood. The fine and saintly hospitality with which I was received and
treated there, the assiduous care they took of me, the extreme cleanliness, serenity, the mild gaiety, the ease, the comfort that reigned there
impressed me and pleased me highly; yes, everything, even to the
language, for the 'thee' and 'thou' used there seemed so friendly, and
possessed of something so fine. The relationship between servants and
masters was that of deference, rather than subordination. I soon
learned that this respectable family was a member of the religious
society of Quakers or Friends, just as was the great number of those
who lived in this region. Curious to probe the fundamentals of a sect
that admits, they tell me, of a single mystery of the incarnation of the
Christ, and which does not exact, like so many others, a blind, limitless
faith, here is what I learned from informed people:

"Founded in the very bosom of liberty, it knows nothing of the
hierarchy of powers, nor consequently the spiritual thunders and
pains of excommunication. The elders of each church content themselves, after several admonitions, to erase from the board the names
of the members of the church whose conduct is immoral or who desire
to leave the fold. The only exterior rite they practice is to assemble
every Sunday in a building of the simplest architecture, where nothing
impresses one, save the whiteness of the walls and the cleanliness of
the seats. There they often spend whole hours in prayer and meditation,
until one of them, man or woman, rises to expound on some pages of
the Scripture or on some religious subject. Admitting no sacrament,
what use could they make of dogma? The practice of good deeds, the
constant exercise of justice, charity, and friendliness are the only deeds
they believe to be acceptable to the Supreme Being. A cult as reasonable and as simple has no need of leaning on grounds of theology or
of controversy: it is a duty that is inspired rather than written. That
is why they do not know anything of bitter and burning fanaticism,
a source of so many wars, discords, and hates. They consider and treat
all men like brothers; hence this use of 'thee' and 'thou' and the general appellation of 'Friend' which they use in their conversation;
hence their aversion to lawsuits, dissensions, quarrels, and war; hence,
too, their love of peace which they consider as the foremost blessing.[7]
The inhabitants of this region are well-to-do craftsmen or good farmers. Content with their lot, they do not know, like so many others, that
fever of anxiety, that eternal desire to be better, which so often prevents one's ever considering himself good. Each one follows his profession or cultivates his land, with order, intelligence, and industry.
Does some cause for dispute arise? The old people of the church, born

arbiters, end them without delay or cost. They have no ambition other than to live in ease, to raise their children properly, to leave them a sufficient heritage, either in the share of their farms, or in the purchase of wooded lands or in the knowledge of a livelihood which they begin to learn at the age of fourteen.

"Each church or congregation possesses a sum called a treasury for the needy formed by the tenth part of each of the members' annual income given voluntarily. It is designed to prevent or alleviate tragedies or to help the weak. Supposing a young man leaves his apprenticeship without capital enough to make the investments necessary to start his business? This treasury supplies his needs for a stipulated time without interest. Supposing a colonist has lost some cattle; or perhaps his barn or home has burned. Maybe he has just suffered a costly sickness; or maybe he has become an invalid. He finds in the treasury of his church ready relief. There is not one among them who has a more sacred debt. But if it happens that the same person experiences new misfortunes, the debt is cancelled; it is no longer a loan, but a gift. That is why one never sees among them indigent persons, nor men reduced to servile labors. Like summer rains after a long drought, like spring freshets after the rigors of the winter, this admirable and fertile institution sows and fosters good deeds.

"What a great deal of individual happiness and general prosperity has it not produced among the branches of this society throughout these states? It is incalculable. I know some entire regions whose terrains, still wooded, were bought from the funds of this little treasury and given to the young people of the congregation who went there to found new settlements. How many misfortunes and devastations committed by the English during the Revolution have been repaired by these funds from an inexhaustible generosity. One must have observed it nearby as I did, to be able to appreciate it.

"Another trait characteristic of this society is the religious care they take of the education of their children, of the establishment of schools provided with the best teachers in the country as well as in the cities. When you return to Philadelphia, go see the building where those of the wealthy, and the less fortunate, girls as well as the boys, are educated. They consider the upkeep of these schools an indispensable and sacred duty, not to fulfill this duty would make them feel guilty of negligence. That is why one sees some of them always busy visiting the most remote regions, to carry help to the colonists who are not yet in a position to maintain themselves as they should. For a long time Warner Mifflin and his wife devoted their time and their fortune to this: angels of goodness, one sees them now in the south, now in the north of the Union, inspiring by their advice and money, all the places where members of their society have settled.

"No doubt you know that the Friends are the first to preach and recommend liberty for the Negroes; they do even more for these Africans; they make them worthy of this benefit, raising their children on the principles of morals and religion and teaching at a certain age a profession or trade. Perhaps you have heard about Antoine Bénézet? Not content to give a part of his fortune for the establishment of these schools, he died, the director of the one which he founded at Philadelphia.

"Another trait no less striking, of the sect, is the order, the regularity, the perseverance which they put into their administration, as well as their domestic affairs and their agricultural labors. This subject reminds me of an event which took place when the English were in Philadelphia. An officer was charged to go as head of a party to burn down the house of Charles Thompson, member of that sect. Thompson, who was the first director of the great Quaker school of that city, had been called to be secretary of Congress. The officer having arrived at this farm, not far away, found the house, the arrangement of the hedges, the fences, the enclosures, the fields and orchards—everything so different from what he had seen prior to that, that he did not wish to carry out his orders: perhaps he was too generous by nature to become an arsonist. To a precision, a special restraint in their ideas as in their action, they unite a simplicity just as respectable as it is touching. Their customary dispositions are both mild and serious, human and sensitive. They love work and industry. Neither their mind nor their capital is ever lazy, especially in the towns where they develop in their youth the habit of business. It is rare that one does not see the names of some members of this group on the lists of the numerous subscriptions by means of which so many useful projects in this land are carried out. They are no less distinguished in their charitable dispositions and there is no more tolerant sect.

"'Why do you subscribe with so much haste to the construction of this church, which does not belong to your faith?' I asked one day of a member of this society.

"'Since one must adore the creator of all things,' he replied, 'of what consequence to me is the name that they give to it and the cult that one must observe in it?'

"They have a great respect for laws. The Government has no citizens more devoted to it, none who fear innovations more than they do. How shall I express it? They worship with sincerity a God who, in his goodness and justice will reward virtue and punish crime. That is why

449

they keep from public employ those who see no reward at the end of a life, however good or bad.

" 'It is possible that they are good farmers, peaceful citizens, fine family men; but a morality that is not based on that salutary belief, offers no guarantee.'

"Well, so frugal and so simple a cult, devoid of ostentation and ceremony, admitting no altars, no pontiff; knowing neither sacraments nor expiations, neither dogma nor mystery, recommending only good works; this cult united with careful education, fortified by the example of parents, has nevertheless the happiest influence on conduct and customs."

"It is the masterpiece of the human mind," Mr. Herman said enthusiastically. "If I were to decide to stay on this continent, tomorrow, I would become a member of this worthy society. According to what I observed in Philadelphia in their haven for the penniless and the old, it would seem to me impossible to push Christian charity and humanitarianism further; they enjoy concurrently ease and good lodgings kept with the most meticulous care. It is to the indefatigable zeal of some members of this society that we owe the origin and beauty of several useful settlements, as well as the exploitation of ways of extracting sugar from the maple, the reform of the penal code, the new system for the prisons, solitary confinement, etc.

"Such were the details," continued Mr. Hazen, "that made me decide to take up my abode in this happy neighborhood of peace and industry, where through kindnesses of some friends, I had the good fortune to buy a plantation. The house, being commodious enough, and the fields in good condition, my brother and I had only to follow the order of harvests established by my predecessor; but knowing from experience how useful irrigation is, humidity and warmth being the prime agents of vegetation, I had a great well dug near the summit of the hill which you see; in it I put three pumps: a machine as simple as it was inexpensive, run by wind power [8] turning forty barrels a day. This water in my reservoir is easily piped to my kitchen garden, to the foot of my trees, into my pasture lands and wherever else it is useful. I enrich it as much as I can with the tanner's bark thrown into the ditches, and with salt, of which we have an abundance hereabouts, and with limestone; in a word, anything that can saturate it with elements which will enrich vegetation.

"Wood being rare in this region, I planted a considerable nursery the second year of my settling here: it was the first one they had ever seen hereabouts. Such was the effect of the irrigation on the roots, that instead of nine years, it was ready for cutting the sixth year. My example and my successes opened the eyes of my neighbors and my nursery furnished the means of surrounding their fields, as I had, with trees that were useful as well as pretty. Up until that time they had known only the necessity of felling trees: they were ignorant of the pleasures of planting them and seeing them grow. Already, as you have been able to observe, the mulberry tree, the plane-tree, the acacia, the hickory have raised their tops along the way and begun to bend their refreshing shadows toward tired travelers. I taught them the use of mud plaster for the improvement of their pasture lands, the growth of wheat, and the cultivation of corn. What a pity that they have not discovered it in this state! Before I came, they had never heard of using tar-pitch and charcoal for protection against wormholes in the wood which they use in the construction of vessels, mills, factories, and levees. What a fortuitous discovery for the coastal states! Furthermore, this tar-pitch prevents rust. So, for several years, they have been using it in the timber yards of Boston, New York, and Philadelphia.

"I confess, for me it is a source of great satisfaction to think that I have been able to be of some use to these peaceful and industrious settlers whose minds, not yet subjected to the tyranny of old habits and routine, easily open to truth. Among them there is a fairly large number who are well informed; several even, have traveled. I know nothing more respectable than a prosperous farmer who knows how to mitigate hard work through study and who, when he is tired of guiding his plow and sowing his wheat, relaxes over reading the history of the revolution to which he owes the liberty and independence of his country, the Congressional gazettes to which he is indebted for the laws that maintain peace and order, and encourage agriculture, fishing, manufacture, and commerce, and the newspapers of Europe which he cannot browse through without congratulating himself on being twelve hundred leagues from there."

Since it was late, Mr. Hazen waited until the next day to relate what follows.

CHAPTER III

"Almost all my summers are devoted to journeys and the winters to domestic duties: it is then when the days are too short for the active man and then when he takes care to shorten the nights. I have come from Philadelphia, where I presented to the President of the United States, the journal of the trip I have just made through lower and upper Virginia, Tennessee, Georgia, the land of the Muscogulges, Chectaws, and Chikasaws,[1] as far as the land of the Natchees [2] on the banks of the Mississippi. It is a token of my respect and veneration for the one among all the men whom I know to be worthy of it. With what admirable talent he knows how to divide his time between the duties of the supreme magistracy, the care which the large-scale farming of Mount Vernon (which he directs, although the seat of Government is 100 miles from there), and the reading of everything people send him relative to the progress of the inland colonies, to the perfection of skills, industries, and learning. Although cold and reserved, his conversation is no less interesting, for without being eloquent, he has a power of depth and clearness which rings true and carries conviction. The other day in speaking of political objectives to some strangers who had been presented to him, he said:

" 'Virtue and justice are to a good Government what the sun is for living Nature. There exists in the order which nature has established, an indissoluble union between these two factors and happiness, between duty and real interest, between the pure maxims of an honest and generous people and the solid rewards of prosperity and public welfare. Heaven never permits a favorable glance on a nation which tramples under foot laws of order and justice which it has established.' "

"What motive can have made you decide to undertake such a long journey?" asked Mr. Wyning of Mr. Hazen. "I think there are at least 1300 miles between here and the land of the Natchees."

"For a long time," he replied, "I have had the greatest desire to see Tenessee [3] that country which is so modern, whose population, in the span of a few years, has risen to nearly 40,000 despite the storms and obstacles that accompanied its infancy, occasioned by the repeated attacks of the Cherokees and the discords which arose among the early settlers. I wanted to explore that mountainous region which resembles Switzerland somewhat, crossed by that beautiful river whose name it borrowed and which is navigable for nine hundred miles, with the exception of the Mussle-shoals and the Whirl: [4] moreover, I knew that a road had been opened from Richmond in Virginia to Knoxville on the Holston,[5] and beyond even as far as Nashville [6] on the Shawanese or Cumberland, over a space of 640 miles. What was my surprise, after following this road, to find along the first of these rivers a furnace and three great smithies in use. Without the discovery of this mine, the progress of that beautiful colony would have been much slower, for what is man on earth, when he does not know iron, nor how to procure it? The salt springs have already furnished a great supply of salt; the people still need coal, and some has just been discovered on the banks of the Clink.

"I have often stayed in the Cherokees' villages, where live the remainder of that nation, long so formidable; like others, they soon will be extinct. The chiefs today realize how wrong they were to have become involved in the white man's quarrels, to have neglected farming, toward which, nevertheless, everything was in their favor: richness of soil, navigable rivers, fine location, and the example of their neighbors.

" 'Situated as we were, in the middle of the continent,' Oweecome-wee, one of the Sagamores of the great village of Cussatee told me, 'masters of this vast chain of mountains, we would have been able to shut off its barriers, if we had wanted to cultivate its valleys; and if the wave of the white man had not engulfed us. We walked, we slept on iron, and yet we have not learned how to arm ourselves with its power, as they have. How many times have I not said to our warriors:

" 'Let us bury the bones of our dead ones so far down that the thirst for blood and the desire for vengeance can no longer grow in our hearts: we have feasted enough on the flesh and the stew of our enemies; let us plant the tree of peace; carry this spirit to everything surrounding us; may the high top of this tree shelter the wigwams of our villages, from Keowee to Nagutchee. Then our young people will fish and hunt, and our old men will smoke under its thick foliage. May each one at work and play, take care lest he wound the bark, for, like the bite of a snake, which, at first appears to be nothing at all, though in reality is fatal, the slightest wound becomes deep and soon reaches the heart. If the tree falls, you will see how the fury of war, devours; just as in the past. What have we gained by wiping out the people of Ouasioto,[7] by treating like women the hunters of the Ohio, by chasing the whites out of Kentucky, by making the two Carolinas tremble? The blood of our warriors has become the food for flies, their bodies, food for our enemies and for wolves. After having had the strength of the oak, we are no longer anything but dried up reeds, which the first spark can consume. What became of the memory of our victories and triumphs? It has passed, like the wind that blows, like the voice of the echo which dies away in the mountains; but what will never pass is the regret of having been for so long a time, blind and senseless, and of being no longer what we have been: the leader among nations.

" 'That is what I told them. Their ears were open; but their hearts and their minds were shut. You see what remains in our villages. Well, in a few more moons, there will be no more old men and women—in a few years more, nothing, no one. The plow of the white men will break the ground over which my fire burns today, where my bearskin is stretched; the brilliant sun of the Cherokees is in its decline and soon will set forever.'

"The soil of Tenessee is so richly varied; the lowlands so rich, that some day its inhabitants will cultivate simultaneously wheat, cotton, mulberry bushes, the olive tree and the wild grape. They will have cattle in abundance. I love mountainous countries, not only because they resemble Switzerland but because men are made of finer fiber there than on the plains. Prouder, more indomitable, they are worthier of liberty. History has not strutted in its pageantry what these brave mountain people did at the time of the invasion of a formidable band of Cherokees and royal troops at King's Mountain, as well as at Guilford in North Carolina. This fine colony, which is about to join the union as the 16th state, owes its very survival, no doubt, to these mountain people. If these mighty enemies had triumphed, everything would have been over for the colony of Tenessee; they would have burned all its farms and massacred all its inhabitants. I observed with pleasure that the founders had expressed their gratitude to the generals and chiefs of the revolution by giving their names to the towns and subdivisions of this great land. I have recorded in my diary everything that has any connection with its extent, the height of its mountains, distance of its mountain chains, temperature, minerals, farming, etc.

"After penetrating as far as the settlements permitted, we decided to go over the mountains to Keowee, in order to reach Georgia. I arrived in Augusta, the capital, some time after the Government had ceded to several companies the immense territory which it claims from the Creek frontiers as far as the Mississippi. One can imagine only with difficulty how it happened that concessions could become the property of private owners, for according to the Constitution, the Federal Government should have possessed them; since the constitution had charged the Union with assuming the debts, contracted by this State during the War.[8] Whatever the case, the Seminoles vigorously opposed the invasion of their territory and more than once Georgia had cause to deplore the misfortunes of their cruel depredations. This immense region stretching from Savannah to the Mississippi, and embracing at least nine degrees of longitude, will some day grow almost all the products of the tropics. The beauty of the climate, the depth of the soil, the natural meadows, so much like those of Eastern Florida, the great number of gentle and navigable rivers, some of which empty into the Ocean, others into the Gulf of Mexico, the streams which one meets, especially in the land of the Creeks, such are the conditions which promise a great prosperity to this vast region.

"Accompanied by several travelers who were going to Uchee, capital of the tribe of that name,[9] we crossed the Ockonee and the Ockmulgee, upper branches of the Alatamaha [10] and some time afterward, the Apalachicola,[11] the Flint, the Chatta-Uche, the Talapoosa, the Alibama, and the Tombechee, branches of the Mobile, on whose banks we stopped off to spend several days with a Frenchman, grandson of one of the early colonists. He told us about the connecting link that would be made some day with the states in the interior, between the sources of the Tombechee and those of the Occochappo which empties into the Tenessee; this would lessen the distances considerably. He showed us the map of the intervening country. According to the map, a distance of only thirty miles appeared to separate the navigable waters of these two rivers.

"Supplied with the information we needed for lodging (for the path was well beaten), we crossed through part of the land of the Chika-saws, a delightful, cool region, irrigated by a great number of streams, as far as the River of the Pearls,[12] where we rested for twenty-four hours, to avoid one of the most frightful storms I had ever seen. From there, we arrived without mishap among the Natchez eighty miles away, after covering 586 miles in thirty-seven days from Augusta. We found much to praise in the hospitality of the natives and the whites, with whom we found refreshment for ourselves and our horses, and a most brotherly reception—just as they had predicted in Augusta.

"Of all the aborigines on the continent, the Creeks and Chectaws are the most civilized; they cultivate corn, breed cattle as well as horses, in their great savannahs, and live abundantly. They have chiefs, equal justice, some laws though not written, at least well-known. Their land, fairly well cultivated and beautified by lovely hills, meadows, lakes, fertile valleys through which run numerous rivers will some day be-come the Arcadia of this continent. Their great chief Macgillivry [13] had gone to St. Augustine; [14] so we did not see him.

"After resting in the home of Mr. B. Lintot, one of the first settlers in the Natchees country, I explored at my leisure all parts of this beautiful and fertile colony which, although situated way beyond the limits of Western Florida [15] is occupied by a Spanish garrison, from

New Orleans. Its elevation above the Mississippi, estimated to be 200 feet, the fertility of the soil, the richness of its products, the ease of communication with the capital, located only eight miles from this place—everything has resulted, since the annihilation of the Natchee nation in 1737, in attracting French, English, German, and American colonists. The Georgians claim it as being within their boundary; the Spanish own it.

"From one of the lookouts of Fort Rosslie, built on a very high parapet 116 leagues from the sea and 486 miles from St. Anthony's cataract, I saw the Mississippi, its deep, still waters rolling majestically throughout the plains that knew no boundaries, dotted with islands that were broken occasionally by river banks; I admired these banks covered with sycamores, cypress, magnolias, tulip-trees of the greatest height and diameter, the like of which I had never seen. In reflecting on the length of its course (for its headwaters are perhaps a thousand miles from where I was), on the great number of rivers which bring their waters to it, on the prodigious stretch of this inland navigation, on the trade whose center this river will be some day, on the richness of this beautiful part of the globe, my imagination projected into the future to meditate over everything that industry, population, educated minds, and freedom will bring about some day. Already it seemed to me I could see this immense surface divided as in ancient Egypt, into nomarchies linked by causeways, surrounded by canals, and planted with trees whose shade and coolness will be so healthful. More fortunate than the Egyptians, the settlers of Louisiana will not have their lands inundated by the waters of the river; for so great is the depth and the fertility of the soil, that their harvests will not need to depend on the river's overflowings. These settlers will be born at the time when men will have attained the highest degree of civilization, when the arts, the sciences, mechanization will direct and accelerate their labors. Thus I wandered through the vastness and variety of a prospect which will perhaps be a reality before two centuries. Tell me, is it not better to occupy one's thinking with bright futures and new speculations—so interesting to humanity—than to wander through the uncertain and questionable paths of antiquity, only to contemplate tottering ruins, demolished buildings, or the effects of devastating revolutions?

"The sight of these plains, grassy or covered with reeds, was even more interesting to a man like me, born in the midst of the mountains and glaciers of Switzerland and coming from northern climes, where the rigors and the freezing spells arrest any progress and vegetation for four months of the year. In Louisiana the soil, refreshed almost all year by summer breezes, warmed by the fertile power of the sun and the rains, scarcely permits an interval when nature ceases to produce; her bosom, like her bounty is tireless. In Switzerland as in the northern states, the wooded regions have a wild and savage appearance which is displeasing and repugnant. Here, on the contrary, these green plains, these islands, and these beautiful river banks covered with magnificent timber, give a more inviting impression attracting and compelling men to make settlements and improve the land. What riches will result when this region, today mere waves like the sea, is peopled with settlements, shaded by the sycamore and the cypress of the Mississippi,[16] their enormous size attesting to the fertility of the soil! Then Louisiana will become the rival of ancient Egypt, so renowned for the wisdom of its laws and for its progress in the sciences. What an understatement I am making! It will surpass Egypt in extent, number of inhabitants, as well as in navigation and commerce, whose very center it will be. What a difference, indeed, between the narrow limits of Egypt, bound by the Theban rocks and the burning sands of Nubie, and the vast and fertile region through which the Mississippi turns and twists. In width, it stretches from the River of the Pearls on the east bank to the North River in the heart of the Gulf of Mexico, over an area of more than 120 leagues; and in length, from the sea-mark at the end of the first outlet, 566 leagues away beyond the St. Anthony River. They say that five-ninths of this immense region consists of high, wooded lands; the rest, estimated at 218,400,000 acres of fertile plains or natural prairies, of which scarcely one half is exposed to the floods.[17] That is the brief summary of a vast land open to the efforts of posterity.

"Egypt is irrigated only by the Nile; everything these waters do not reach is arid and uncultivated; in contrast, the Mississippi has innumerable tributaries emptying into this great river only after they have fertilized vast regions. On the east, these include the little Yasoo, rising in the land of the Chectaws; the great Yasoo, in that of the Chikasaws; the Ohio and its branches, which include more than 400 leagues; the Illinois, the Ouisconsing, the Chippaway, etc. On the west, the Black and the Red rivers, the Arcansa, the Missouri, which rises in New Mexico, the Nadooasses, from the Wadappa-Menesoter, etc. What a great quantity of commodities, of timber, minerals, produce of all kinds, this network of waterways will transport to the sea some day when these vast regions are inhabited! This area, shaped like a parallelogram whose cultivable surface is at least 67,920 square leagues, is located in one of the most favorable latitudes, from the 29th to the 45th degree.

"I know of no subject of contemplation more interesting, nor more worthy of occupying the minds of men, who, like us, find themselves in the cradle of nations whose posterity will some day cover this part of the northern hemisphere. Whatever its population and power, I hope that on the soil of Louisiana haughty pyramids of superstition and slavery will never be raised for they are witnesses of so many revolutions that have survived history and even tradition. Like those of the Nile, the delta of the Mississippi makes entry difficult, everchanging and sometimes even dangerous. From the sea-mark to New Orleans, vessels must drop anchor near the bank, for fear of being battered by the trees floating in this river.

"But the Manchac or Iberville [18] River (which is a drainage of the waters from the Mississippi near Lakes Pontchartrain and Maurepas during the time of floods that often rise 90 feet), offers to the ingenuity of future generations an alluvium that is much more certain: it will be like the canal that connects Alexandria with Cairo. Then the capital will necessarily be moved to this area which is higher and more healthful than the present site of New Orleans, which is too low and too damp. At this junction of the two rivers the English built fine shops and some very attractive homes during their sojourn in this area. Like the great river of Egypt, the Mississippi has a tremendous delta [19] which widens every year with the accumulation of trees, reeds, and leaves, as well as with the great quantity of mud which the river washes along.

"One day as I was going up the Arcansa River [20] in a boat, we were at Lanca, off the west shore, when I saw some smoke which seemed to rise from the middle of a vast plain.

" 'It is coming from the dwellings of many Arcadian families,' [21] one of the French passengers told me. 'These Arcadians were driven from their country, a flat, picturesque island. They are nomads, for with the exception of corn and cotton which they cultivate only in small quantity, their riches consist only in the number of their cattle. Instead of raising them laboriously, as is done in northern regions in the fenced-in area of a township, they turn them out to pasture, to rove the plains. Everything around them is big and free. The boundaries of their homes are those of the horizon, or some of the natural canals, which in flood times serve as drainage for the waters of the river. Their cattle lack only shade, which they frequently seek on the wooded island of their master, or under the sycamore trees which these colonists sometimes take the trouble to plant. Here as with you, they govern and restrain these animals by their need and appetite for salt. Ah, if it were possible for men to be happy anywhere, they could be happy here—so little do they need for their well-being. They are nourished on milk and cheese as well as on the flesh of their animals and often from the product of their hunting and fishing. The different preparations for rice take the place of bread. The women spin the cotton and weave the clothing which their families need. They live without worries, without anxieties, without being exposed to those fatigues, without shedding that sweat which is the price one pays for ease and independence. But on the other hand, having no obstacles to overcome, nor difficulties to vanquish, these men often become unwary and lazy. When they complain (for that is man's lot), I say to them:

" 'You are guilty and ungracious; you do not deserve the happiness you enjoy; learn to know it and to feel it; that is all you need.

" 'We have a colony of peaceful Acadians who settled several years ago on the summit overlooking our river. Several of their families, having become wealthy and discontent with the soil of their islands, have surrounded by ditches some parts of the neighboring plains where they cultivate corn, sainfoin from Malta, etc. Nowhere can one see such luxuriant vegetation; but something even more striking: there are two rows of cypress and poplar trees from the Mississippi which they have planted on the other side of the ditches. On a warm day the eye and the imagination relax with an inexpressible pleasure in the shade of these fine trees to which the fertility of the soil gives a vigor of growth that can be seen only in Louisiana. It is shade like this which the interior of the continent lacks.

" 'All my life I was employed in trade,' continued the French passenger, after telling me at great length of his journey into Upper Louisiana. 'But since the war—what am I talking about! Since the general convulsion on the continent of Europe, destroyed it, I live on the banks of the Arcansa in happy retreat from men and affairs. My books, neglected so long, have become my friends. From time to time I receive newspapers from the United States: for in New Orleans, printing them is prohibited. With how many doubts and reflections my mind is filled at the sight of these unexpected events which suddenly change the destiny of empires and nations! In vain one seeks to probe the cause; only the effects appear. Who can keep from weeping tears at the sight of the miseries with which these revolutions inundate the earth? How can we conceive that they are at one with the scheme of the Great Director. And if he is too powerful, too haughty to interest himself in our lot, what other power presides then?'

"That, gentlemen, is all my memory recalls of that moment; the special details, the geographical sketches that Don Pedro De Casanorte, surveyor-general of Louisiana, wanted to give me, information from the most informed sources, observations that I made daily are in my diary; for however miserably I was lodged, ordinarily I wrote in my diary every evening, lest time erase my fresh impressions. Often had I experienced that one gets a true picture only of the object at hand the very day and that those of the day before are forgotten. My journey lasted eight months and during this interval I was not sick once, although nearly all the settlers on the banks of the Mobile [22] had been attacked by fever when I passed through there. I owed a great deal to the hospitality of the colonists with whom I lived as well as to that of the Muskogulges, Seminoles, Chectaws, and Chikasaws by whom I was received and treated as a brother and friend. They were astonished to learn that curiosity was the sole motive of my journey.

" 'What is curiosity?' many among them asked me.

"Indeed it is a feeling of which they have no idea."

"Ah," said Mr. Herman, "if I had had the good fortune to have known you then, I would most certainly have accompanied you. What enjoyment to record in peace and calm the myriad of observations which the sight of so many objects inspired; to describe such extents of solitude, forests so beautiful, these rivers, those soils so varied, the climates so mild, destined some day to be the arena of industry, of movement and activity, the sojourn of opulence and good fortune. Moreover, men compressed in spaces that are too small, injure one another, become bored and suffocate; here they will multiply, stretch out for centuries. Some time ago, in going through a collection of old papers, I came upon some details relative to the celebrated campaign of General Bouquet whose aide, Mr. Wyning told me, you were. May I ask you whether you recall some details of the scenes that took place at the time of the arrival of the prisoners at Muskingum? Doctor Smith, then president of the University of Philadelphia, published several articles which I have been unable to find among the Libraries."

"Although the impression of these scenes can never be erased from my memory," replied Mr. Hazen, "today I could tell you only part of it. Because I should have to recall not so much the things I saw, as a mass of sensations which I experienced and which it would be impossible for me to recapture. I made a brief outline of it for the General, immediately after the interpreters had given me the translation of the wild harangues from which he made notes at the scene of the conference. The report merited the General's approbation as well as that of my friends among the officers of the army. But, such is the disorder of my papers, that I would lose considerable time in finding it. If you wanted to see it, it would give me great pleasure to make a copy of it and send it to you in a few days."

He kept his promise and a short time after our return to Philadelphia, we received the following details.

CHAPTER IV

"The conquest of Canada produced in the minds of the great nations of the Ohio and the Great Lakes country an extraordinary revolution which was to leave in its wake the most tragic consequences for Pennsylvania, Maryland, and Virginia. As though a ray of light had suddenly made them see that until now, they had been the dupes or victims of the whites, their chiefs resolved to unite forces and throw off this yoke. To this end they formed the great plan of seizing all the forts in the interior, formerly constructed in their land to command the portages, straits, as well as the principal haunts of hunters, and they carried the plan out with a promptness, co-operation, and a courage of which no one had believed them capable. Unanimity, constancy of their efforts, as well as the inconceivable fury of attack demonstrated plainly that if thirty years sooner they had known that from union comes strength, these colonies would not have penetrated beyond the mountains until a much later time. The union of these nations, then numerous, and led by daring and skillful chiefs (they had some of extraordinary calibre), might have founded a federated republic similar to that of the Seminoles. Perhaps by experience they would even have succeeded in directing a part of their nations' industry toward agriculture and soon they would have had workers and warriors. All that might have changed the state of affairs on this continent. The progress of these colonies might have been extremely retarded; they would have lost for a long time navigation on the Great Lakes, as well as the possession of beautiful lands beyond the Alleghanies.

"Some attributed this formidable eruption to the withholding of ordinary wants; others to the usurpation of great portions of lands which had not been bought previously. The fear of being slaves of a power which, since the conquest of Canada appeared to them to have become tyrannical and oppressive, was the real cause, and above all the realization that British garrisons of these little French forts would soon become the germs of so many colonies,[1] for the Indians fear our plow even more than our arms. Indeed game disappears as soon as a canton begins to be cleared.

"The nations of Sandusky, Munsy, Cagnawaga, Outawa, Wyandot, Winebago, with those of the Ohio country, played the principal role in this war, whose first idea, they say, was conceived by Pondiack, Outawa chief, long celebrated for his wisdom and eloquence in council as well as for his fearlessness and courage in war. To starve out more effectively the forts and posts and cut them off from all communication with the cultivated provinces, these nations resolved that a part of their strength would be deployed in subduing them; while the other, at harvest time, would produce a general uprising on the frontiers of Pennsylvania, Maryland, and Virginia whose inhabitants they would massacre, whose cattle they would kill, and whose barns they would burn.

"In accordance with this bold and bloody plan, they seized all the merchants who were in their villages; a great number of whom perished for daring to resist. At the same time the frontiers were invaded by parties of Indians, armed with torch and tomahawk, destroying everything in their path. I explored districts where not a single inhabitant remained, nor a single home. These tigers transformed into deserts a region that was beginning to be well cultivated. My pen refuses to write and my memory refuses to recall such horrors.

"Almost at the same time they seized the forts at Le Boeuf, Venango, and Presqu'île on Lake Erie; La Baie on Lake Michigan; Pheakiky on the river of the same name; Myamy on the Miamy; Ouytanon on the Wabash; Sandusky on Lake Junondat, and finally Michillimakinac.

"Relying on the general peace which had just been negotiated, far from help, separated from cultivated provinces by great distances, these feeble garrisons succumbed to their fate and their plight offers history bloody pages and terrible recitals. This depressing news as well as the unheard-of ravages committed along this long line of frontier, spread consternation in every heart. Those of the colonists who could escape the devouring flames and murderous tomahawk, abandoned their homes and took refuge in the interior: all these districts, abode of peace and of happy industry, soon presented only the image of desolation, misery, and ruin. Never, from the founding of these colonies, had they sustained tragedy as great, as unexpected, and as deplorable—never before had the implacable hostility, the cruel hatred, and the ferocious vengeance of the Indians, shown itself in such true character.

"Detroit and Fort Pitt were the only places able to resist; the strength of their garrisons was much greater and they knew better how to defend themselves; moreover, they knew only too well the lot which awaited them: to surrender or perish. They owed their safety to the intelligence of their commandants, as well as to the patience and courage with which they bore all possible kinds of distress and misery before anyone could send them help. Niagara, defended by formidable artillery, was not even attacked.

"The conduct of the little army destined to raise the siege of Fort Pitt was entrusted to General Bouquet, whose aide I was.

" 'As soon as you are in Carlisle,' they told him before his departure, 'you will be furnished with provisions and horses enough to continue your way.'

"But what was his astonishment on arriving in that part of Pennsylvania, to find the inhabitants plunged in the greatest consternation and ready to abandon their homes. All work had ceased; fear had frozen minds and paralyzed arms; everywhere harvests awaited the sickle and there were no harvesters.

"The roads were covered with weeping families who had not even the barest necessities. Instead of receiving help which the General expected and which, at a less disastrous time would have been furnished with great haste, the voice, or rather the cry of humanity, obliged him to give what aid he could to these unfortunate ones.

"Nevertheless there was not a single day to lose, for Fort Pitt was so besieged that the garrison could neither receive nor send any word. It was in the midst of such crushing circumstances that he undertook to reach the forts at Bedfort and Ligonier [2] before these important posts fell into the hands of the savage Indians. Arriving at the latter, situated on the Loyalhanning (branch of the Keskiminetas) he resolved to leave there his convoy of wagons and take only his pack horses. Before him were the dangerous passes of Turtle Creek commanded by precipices; but no sooner had he arrived at Bushyrun, several miles beyond, when the savages, uttering bloodcurdling cries, attacked him on all sides. This stubborn and bloody battle lasted from one o'clock in the afternoon until nightfall. It took the bravery and coldbloodedness of the troops and the skill of the General to deceive indefatigable vigilance and to elude the traps of enemies and to resist the astonishing impetuosity with which they repeatedly swooped down on us. Never before had they been as daring nor as formidable. After this signal victory concluded in May 5, 1763, to which Pennsylvania owes its safety, the army, although considerably diminished, joyfully arrived in the environs of Fort Pitt; there the savages took flight at our approach.

"Wishing to profit by the terror which this memorable defeat occasioned among them, the General resolved to cross the beautiful River (Ohio) and penetrate to the forks of the Muskingum,[3] whence he could attack the villages of the Mingos, Wyandots, Delawares, and even those of the Shawanese along the Scioto, although situated 80 miles further on. After packing several portable forges, provisions, and necessary tools, he left, commanding 1,500 infantrymen and a corps of cavalry.

It was the first time since the founding of the colonies that so great a number of trained troops had dared plunge into the depths of the forest so great a distance from cultivated provinces. At the end of sixteen days march, during which time we were obliged to blaze trails, build bridges, and fill in ravines, we reached Tuskaraway without interruption from our enemies.

"Very much astonished at seeing themselves attacked in their homes which, until that day, they had believed inaccessible to the European troops, these proud children of nature finally decided to ask for a Council meeting; the General consented. With the intention of making this ceremony more impressive, he had built in the middle of the camp a large cabin covered with bark and open on all sides. Here, in great military pomp, he appeared surrounded by most of his officers.

"The Senneccas sent Kiashuta, accompanied by fifteen warriors; the Delawares, Custaloga and the Great Castor, with twenty warriors; the Shawanees, Keyssinocta, one of their leading sachems, with thirty warriors; the Piancachas, chief of the Mingos, with thirty warriors. The Tuscaroras and the Wyandots did not arrive until several days later. At the very first meeting, the Mingos freed eleven prisoners and gave the General eighty-three pieces of wood indicating the number they still promised. But the speech of Keyssinocta, delivered in cool anger and humiliated pride, as well as those of the other chiefs, seemed to the General merely means of stalling in order to starve the army and attack us on our return. He decided to penetrate even further into the wilderness; eight days later we finally reached the forks of the Muskingum, located seventy miles from the mouth of that river in Ohio and one hundred miles from Fort Pitt, a much more convenient and central site, since some of the principal villages are only seven or eight miles away. This bold penetration contributed not a little toward making these tribes listen more favorably to the reasonable terms the General had offered them at the camp in Tuskaraway.

"He had four great strongholds built; the space between was scrupulously cleared; they also built a storehouse for the provisions and several houses and barracks to lodge the officers and the prisoners who were to arrive; and soon this little camp became like a town, in which the finest order, cleanliness, and law reigned.

"For almost two weeks that this Council lasted, the General often met with the chiefs, heard their speeches, received and sent messages in the neighboring villages relative to the progress of the treaty and especially of the exact liberation of the prisoners, the principal object of his solicitudes: 83 finally arrived from the Mingos; 206 from the Cagnawagas; 104 from the Shawanees and 87 from the Delawares. To give you an idea of the style as well as the sentiments expressed in the speeches which the chiefs made in delivering these prisoners to the Congress, I will repeat what Kiashuta, great chief of the Senneccas said:

" 'Father of the white warriors, in accordance with our promises, we give you back your flesh and blood. Some of these persons have been united by bonds of adoption for a long time; although we give them back to you, these bonds are not broken; we shall always consider them as relatives and friends. We have taken the same care of them, shown them the same affection as though they had been our flesh and blood. There they are; ask them if they have not found warmth by our fires; if they have not eaten from our kettles; if they have not slept on our bearskins. Let them answer! Do you hear what they are saying to you? Show indulgence for them now, for they have forgotten your customs and your practices, and some even your language; they are going to return to their land, where perhaps they have no more friends and they are abandoning our land where friends are not lacking. What will they do then? They will regret the day when you came so far to force us to give them back to you. Treat them with goodness we exhort you; perhaps that will persuade them to stay among you. Here—here is a branch of blue and white wampum so that my words will be ever present in your mind and so that you may not forget to convey them to their relatives and friends if they still have any in their old country.'

"All the prisoners being finally delivered and the conditions of the treaty accepted and ratified according to their customs, the General decided to extinguish the Council fire. For this occasion, accompanied by his officers and military music, he entered the conference cabin located in the heart of the camp, and for the fourth time took the chiefs by the hand and smoked with them the great pipe of peace. However, extremely discontent over the conduct of Nettohatway, chief of the tribe of the Tortue in the Wyandot nation, who, until that day had not wanted to appear, he forced that tribe to elect another sachem. It was the last act of authority he exercised among them.

"Don't smile at this, for although this expedition was not accompanied by circumstances as spectacular as those of a Nabob, it proves to what degree of humiliation these proud warriors were reduced, and what were the talents, the poise, and courage of the General who knew how to penetrate so far into the depths of these solitary forests, abode of the chieftains' power, and to impose on these indomitable men to the point of making one of their foremost sachems fall from power.

"The most distinguished orator was Red Hawk, chief of the Delawares. His speech offered such a striking mixture of pride and submission that I cannot deny myself the pleasure of reciting for you some of the characteristic passages.

" 'Father of the bearded warriors, chief of long and short-knived men [4]—listen; my voice speeds to your ears. Will you hear us, we who are your younger brothers? Seeing in your eyes sign of discontent, we wipe them with this belt of blue and white wampum in order that you may see more clearly what we have been and what we are. People have told you many lies about us; with this second belt we clean your ears so that they may hear better what is true and throw far away what is not. We purify your heart with the smoke of this pipe, so that it can resemble that of Ona (William Penn) whom evil never approached. You have come here because your tomahawk was longer and stronger than ours; however, we have spared neither our lives nor our blood—you recall that. But perhaps your victory emanates from the will of the Great Spirit which has long favored the white man. We, your young brothers, are warriors as mighty and brave as your own. Although unhappy, we snatch this tomahawk from your hands to throw it upward to the one who lives way beyond the clouds, so that he may dispose of it as he wishes; perhaps he will bury it fast under earth; perhaps he will let it fall into a bottomless lake; then, Father of the warriors from the land of Onas, we say to you:

" 'Take one end of this branch of peace and friendship and let the other be held by representatives of the tribe present now. You, chief of the warriors in the bearded tribes, would you want to burn the wigwams, destroy the provisions of our wives, of our children, of our old men who have never done you any harm? Well, they are speaking to you through me. As for our warriors, they can do without your pity since they know how to live from hunting. But old age, feebleness, and infancy!—here as among your people, they need rest and fear famine. Therefore take pity on them, since you have succeeded in coming so near our villages; may the war cease and may peace begin with this very moment.'

"But what language shall I use or rather on what palette shall I find the colors and the hues appropriate to paint the most touching sight I have ever witnessed? I refer to the time when the colonists who had obtained permission from the General to accompany the army after the Battle of Bushyrun,* recognized among the prisoners whom

---

* After the victory of Bushy Run, a great number of colonists who had escaped the fury of the savages, obtained from General Bouquet permission to accompany the army, hoping that in the treaty of peace which would necessarily follow, all the prisoners would be returned. Several women who had taken refuge in Fort Pitt, accompanied him as far as Tuskaraway.

the Indians freed, some their wives or their children, others, brothers, sisters, or friends. How to transmit to your heart the deep impression made on mine by the manifestation and the first utterings of a happiness both great and unhoped for? Sublime impetus of nature, expressions of the finest sentiments that ever ornamented the heart of man! Here one could see among them those hesitating steps and wandering eyes betokening extreme inquietude, meeting in the midst of the crowd wives, whom they had believed massacred, throw themselves into their arms and virtually inundate them with tears; yonder, brothers or friends escaped from the fire of their dwellings and the tomahawk of fury, recognizing one another after a few moments of doubt, calling each other again by name, expressing with a thousand different indescribable nuances, the happiness of having escaped so many dangers, and that of finding themselves in the midst of these somber forests; farther on, mothers, who in the intoxication of their emotions, had just snatched their children from the arms of their adoptive parents, succumbing under the excesses of maternal tenderness while pressing these cherished beings against their heaving bosoms.

"Ah! in the contemplation of this solemn spectacle, how much the painter, the poet, the philosopher would have found these objects worthy of their artistic touch or their deep thought! How beautiful and sublime human nature seemed to me then! No, I do not think there is a person on earth whose heart and soul would not be moved by it!

"Among the prisoners who were hastening to pay their gratitude to the General, some were so stirred they could scarcely articulate a few words to the General; others, more eloquent, poured forth only silent tears; here one could see groups of persons, eyes raised, thanking aloud the Supreme Being for the good fortune of having found their loved ones or friends; there, other groups who, to avoid importunate questions, fled into the woods. But I was so moved by it, that it is not astonishing that a myriad of recollections has escaped me! And how could I have painted them! Like a powerful lover, sympathy exerted itself on the souls of spectators with an irresistible force.

"Those of the children who had partially forgotten their maternal tongue appeared almost insensible to the happiness of seeing again their parents and of being caressed. Those who had lost them altogether, refused to leave their adoptive friends, or submitted to this separation only after repeated pleas. Often it happened that this repugnance aroused in them the most crushing doubts whose relief the unhappy parents could effect only after discovering some of those marks which colonists on the frontiers make on their newly born at birth. No sooner had they seen them, when exclamations of happiness burst forth, but when the instinct of nature was deaf or when they discovered nothing that confirmed their early suspicions, then the air was rife with groans of grief. On the other hand, it was a triumph for the Indians to whom the white man had promised to abandon those who were neither claimed nor recognized.

"But if on the one hand, shades of the loveliest hues embellished these happy meetings, on the other, shadows of the cruelest disturbances appeared on the faces of those who did not find their wives or children. One could see them at the arrival of each new convoy of prisoners running hither and yon, to find out the lot of their loved ones, even though they trembled to learn it. Those persons whose doubtful hopes were dissipated, struck dumb with grief, leaning their heads against a tree, would burst forth into sobs. This variety of circumstances, this mixture of good fortune, uncertainty, hopes, and regrets, excited in our hearts so much emotion and anxiety that we were overcome by it. Officers, soldiers, pioneers—everyone appeared deeply moved by this crushing spectacle, which I find impossible to describe. Some, unable to stand it, had to withdraw; others put a handkerchief to their eyes. General Bouquet himself, who from the long and bloody battle at Bushy Run, never lost his poise—whose face during the seven hours of this conflict that hung long in the balance, had not manifested the slightest change—like so many others, was very much moved, and could not stifle the tears that overcame him and which he did not blush at shedding abundantly. Never before had I realized how much power tears have for assuaging great shocks to the soul. An old soldier near me told me he had not cried since infancy; like me, he experienced tremendous emotion at the sight of all this.

"The savages themselves, those children of such untamed nature, forgetting their opinions and their customary ferocity, contributed much toward making this spectacle even more touching. Who would have believed that hearts as hardened by example and rearing, could give way to such touching and generous emotions? They gave their adopted ones up only with the greatest regret, and in shedding profuse tears; it was a sublime struggle of tenderness between them and the parents of these children.

" 'Rest assured,' one of the Shawanese chiefs said, looking proudly at the General, 'rest assured that it would have taken more than your victory at Bushy Run to force me into making the sacrifice I've made today.'

"With what zeal they recommended the adopted ones to his protection! Their attention to them did not stop there; it lingered as long as they were in the encampment. Each day they came to visit them, to bring them corn, skins, furs, in a word, everything they had given them during their sojourn with them, at the same time lavishing on them tokens of the tenderest affection. Some even sought and obtained freedom to accompany them as far as Fort Pitt and to give them the daily product of their hunting and fishing.

"One young Mingo pushed his attachment even further and gave the army proof of tenderness and devotion rare in any land, especially in the heart of the woods. Among the prisoners returned to camp, was a young girl from Virginia, from the Fairfax country. He fell madly in love with her. He called her his wife; despite everything people told him at the fort regarding the danger of approaching frontiers, he resolved to follow her, to serve her, at the risk of being killed by the survivors of those who had been massacred, or whom the last devastations had ruined.

"In the number of prisoners, there was one woman from the region around Potawmack in Maryland; she had a child at breast. No sooner was she brought into the conference room than a soldier from that very province on guard, recognizing her, cried out:

" 'God of mercy! God of pity! She is my wife!'

"With as much speed as that discharged by electricity, this exclamation reverberated in everyone's heart, exciting their most vociferous shouts, and producing among the bystanders although under arms, the murmur of applause and the smile of pleasure. After congratulating the husband and wife, the General permitted the soldier to take his wife to his tent, where she changed her savage attire for the clothes of a European.

"But no sooner did they begin enjoying the first effusions of happiness at having found one another again, when a dark cloud suddenly obscured this beautiful sun: it was the distress over the fate of another child, aged three, taken with the mother, and separated from her in the division of prisoners. Forgetting in a single moment all that Providence had done for them, they were consoling each other 'mid sobs when someone came to tell them of the arrival of a new convoy of prisoners under the leadership of the Wyandot chiefs. At the sight of this, the couple, their eyes wild and searching, were presented with a child about that age. The mother, pale and frightened, anxiety and fear virtually painted on her face, having caressed this one and futilely called him by name, was seizing another child, when, turning about, and staring again at the first, she felt the cry of motherly instinct; in her frantic state, she forgets the child at her breast, to seize the one whom she has found again, takes him in her arms, shedding a torrent of tears. Sublime distraction of maternal tenderness! triumph of instinct, that first gift of nature, over the cold precaution of reason!

"Like her, the husband, drunk with joy, accompanied her to his tent, incapable, either of them, of acknowledging the congratulations heaped on them by the officers and soldiers surrounding them. She owed the good fortune of not losing her second child while finding the first, to the promptness of Captain Perceval who was near her and prevented the child's falling.

" 'May heaven bless you a thousand and a thousand more times!' she told him. 'In the state I am in, how can I know what I am doing?'

"On our return I was often witness to the dismay and desolation of parents whose children watched for the moment when they could run away, or would approach their parents only with disgust. These children were far from sharing the happiness of their parents and spent the first few days sobbing, often refusing food offered them. If, by chance, they saw the Indians, to whom permission had been given to hunt in order to bring food to their friends, one could scarcely restrain them.

"What a situation for these wretched colonists, who at the risk of their lives, had come to fetch them back, to buy them back, had that been necessary, and bring them home; above all for those tender mothers whose caresses they disdained or repulsed. It is not the first time I have observed the almost invincible remoteness and aversion to civilized life which the young whites who have spent part of their infancy among the Indians always preserve: that abode, that second habit superimposed itself on the former trait, leaving with them a new one which becomes indelible; they are lost to society as well as to their parents whom they abandon as soon as they find the opportunity. How many similar examples the history of the colonies offers! And even among the older prisoners whom we repatriate, a great number of them regret very openly the Indians from whose society they had been snatched, and whom they call their best friends. You would be astonished if I were to repeat here everything I have heard them say about the happiness they enjoyed among them; one of the Shawanese chiefs swore to the General that he had been obliged to tie the hands and feet of some of them before leaving in order to return them to their friends. In spite of the vigilance of the officers and soldiers, forty-seven of these men, for whom we thought we were performing the greatest service, rejoined their new compatriots; and what will seem even more astonishing to you: the women deplored their miserable lot to us, just as did the men because it removed them from the Indians' villages.

"What a vast subject of thought for those who have entertained such frightful and extraordinary notions about the customs and the way of life of these children of nature! This incredible tendency which one can observe for more than a century in the South as well as the North, would it not seem to indicate that the forests were the early cradle of human nature, that this innate taste, stifled by social education awaits only favorable circumstances for its manifestation? Among the women who were brought to camp was one who, more courageous than the others, dared address the following words to the General. She was born in Ireland and had been seized on the banks of Toby's Creek, in the province of Indiana.

" 'You have won, General, not because you are braver than our warriors, but because your weapons were better than theirs and because you commanded men who carried long knives. Our people have devastated the frontiers because these lands belonged to them; they have seized some of your forts because you wished to gain control of their trade. If you say that they are wrong, I shall reply that their ancestors walked over this soil, hunted over it, owned it long before the arrival of your ancestors. Your farmers need peace and quiet to repair their losses! Well, now! you will have both if you do not demand anything of our people that will humiliate them. You know them; one of the conditions of the treaty of Tuskaraway is that they will return their prisoners: do you not know that they do not have any—and that the whites who live among them are their relatives or their friends? Eleven years ago I was captured; since then I have been happy; I am a mother. If you force me to follow, I shall return as soon as I find the opportunity, for once in my own province, I shall be as free as you. Those are my intentions; they are the same as those of a great number of persons whom you forced our chiefs to deliver to you. To the glory which you have just acquired by your weapons, it is well to add the one of humanity; but since it destroys our happiness, be generous enough to permit us to return to our friends.'

"Astonished, amazed by the boldness of this woman and by what she had just said, he consulted us: almost all the officers were of the opinion that every one was master of his own destiny and should seek happiness wherever he believed he could find it, the General permitted her to go back.

"Now then! these inhabitants of the forests whom we call children, the younger brothers and sisters of nature, because they do not wish to leave their primitive state of hunting, have they not, 'mid their ignorance and their barbarism, some qualities which merit esteem and respect? Yes, indeed. What a volume one could fill of their fine deeds! Do you recall what happened to Colonel Bird in 1774? During the time of his ambassadorship to the Cherokees beyond the mountains, some Virginians, having killed two warriors of that tribe, the young people demanded of the chiefs execution of the law of retaliation; it was accorded them. Shiloue, one of the first sachems, was opposed to it.

"He told them, 'Before killing this white man who has smoked my peace pipe, slept on my bearskin and whom you have recognized as chief sent by Virginia, you will kill me.'

"Indeed, he protected him by standing in front of him and the young people respected him. This fury which stimulates them in war, these blood-thirsty and ferocious dispositions which make tigers of them, are to be attributed to the ill effects of their education which infuses in them such false notions of courage and heroism. Consider the invariable gentleness of character, of which in the villages they are the most perfect model, their inviolable hospitality, their fidelity in promises, their friendship, their unselfishness, examples of which we are well acquainted with. Consider their virtues (for they have them), and we will know very well that nature has made them, too, susceptible to culture and to what we call civilization, and that they would be worthy of becoming our brothers, our neighbors and our friends.

"Let us not forget those feelings so worthy of praise: their respect for old age, as well as for the memory and ashes of their ancestors. Here is what Tongastoutack, chief of a tribe of Anier Indians said in 1696 to the Marquis of Vaudreuil, then governor of Canada:

" 'Ononthyo, you have said to the Aniers, "Sell to the white men the lands which border the Misiskouy River,[5] from the waters of the lake to the great falls." Here is what they answer you through me: These lands are the site of our villages, in which were born the fathers of our ancestors, and our ancestors, too. Here still live some of their sons, whose children we are; can we say to each of these old men:

" 'Roll up your bearskin, extinguish your fire, embark in your canoe and come with us to raise your wigwam far from here!

" 'Can we say to those venerable bones which repose in the shade of the neighboring trees: "Rise, leave your tombs, and follow us into a strange land!" '

"It is true, they are cruel and terrible to their enemies, by habit and example; nevertheless, every time they listen, excited by various motives, to the inspirations of compassion and of humanity, whose germ nature has put in the hearts of all men, in giving them life, they never fail to accompany this present with everything that can render it fine.

" 'Take courage,' says the warrior to one whose life he has saved; 'from the prisoner you were, I have unbound you; do not be evil-hearted; soon you will console yourself for having lost your dear ones and for being so far from your own land. From this day on, consider my fire as yours, and my kettle too.'

"On returning from their expeditions, when some of their prisoners are adopted, a frequent occurrence, they say to the adopting one:

" 'Here, here is something to compensate for your loss; whether you wish to drink the soup of this living flesh, or permit the victim to share your bearskin, you can dispose of this captive whenever you wish, and as you see fit.'

"If they spare the life of a woman, it is only for reasons of generosity, since we have no incident where they have violated her honor. As for the children, they love them, they treat them and raise them as their own. The idea of perpetual slavery, that of making them serve as prisoners, never entered the heads of these northern tribes. The one whom their affection, their caprice, a dream or any other motive decides to spare, immediately becomes a member of the family of the captor, as well as the tribe of which he is part; he lives with the family and as they do. I have seen them severely reprimand the children guilty of insulting words or scornful deeds toward these newly adopted ones. Among them so great is the power of adoption, that often this bond has seemed to me more difficult to break than that of marriage.[6]

"This expedition of General Bouquet, to whose success Pennsylvania owed her safety, led with as much courage as wisdom, closed the temple of Janus in this hemisphere. The devastations of the frontiers were soon repaired. For a long time now, the population has crossed the Alleghanies and has penetrated beyond Ohio country. Today the plow traces the furrows, harvest is gathered on the very site of our two camps at Tuskaraway and the forks of the Muskingum.[7] All that has been the work of thirty-two years, during seven of which this country has had to live through the war which separated it from Great Britain."[*]

Christiana-Hundred

Frederic Hazen

[*] The travels of Henry Timberlake among the Cherokees and those of the trader John Long among various tribes of Indians in North America, include a great many details positively confirmed by those given here by Mr. Frederic Hazen. See the translations of others published in the Year II and in the Year V, by Citizen Billecocq (Note of the Editor).

CHAPTER V

In accordance with your wishes and my promise, I am sending you, in care of Mr. Jay, minister of foreign affairs, the little article I mentioned to you last year in Philadelphia. It is the fruit of a vine, crude, wild stock which, aided by grafting, might perhaps have bred a better product. If its novelty does not give it merit, may it at least have that accorded to rare things imported from afar; for you may recall that among these nations there are more hunters and warriors than writers or poets, and that this village is at least 300 leagues from New-York. I wrote it, as dictated by the author, if I may use the expression; he was a young Shawanese warrior, from the village of Waccakala, settled in the village of Chillichate. If he appeared astonished when I asked him to recall this plaintive ballad, he was more astonished when I read him what he had just dictated to me.

"What!" he said to me proudly, "with a quill from a goose, held by only three fingers, you can say to my words, 'stay on this piece of birch bark!'—and they stop.[1] Anytime it strikes your fancy, you can say, 'repeat these thoughts to me,' and they will be repeated to you! Why—with our ten fingers, are we not able to do the same? How can these lines, lifeless as the ones our children trace on the sand of the river bank, repeat the living words of an absent man or one who has departed this earth for the West? It is making him speak without his mouth opening, and even after his eyes have ceased seeing the sun of life. What is the meaning of these little black tracings which you are making so rapidly? Could they see something there while mine, which are as good as yours, see nothing at all? How is it that they can transmit a sound, or an idea? Is it possible that they have a soul—or a voice? Or do you infuse your own? Perhaps they are speaking into your ears! Let's listen ... I do not hear them! Do you hear them?"

"No."

"Well, then, if they are as mute to you as they are to me, what did you do in order to repeat what I have told you? Is it because your memory is keener than mine and has suggested all this to you? ... No, you say? Well, I don't understand it. Perhaps like the spring dew, after the long winter freezes, like the fruits, after the warmth of summer, like the sunlight after a storm, this comes from the Great Spirit who taught this art to the white man? If this is true, why did it not do the same for the Nishy-norbay?"

"Take a goose quill, write the thoughts of your mind on a piece of birchbark; this bark will repeat them to posterity, and it will become learned:

"Like the Nishynorbays," I replied, "the first men from the Dawn-land * were born in the forests and were hunters of long standing. Exploring the earth, chance led them to iron, and necessity taught them to forge it. Such was the first source of knowledge they acquired, and the origin of their military strength. Without this metal, like your people, they would still sail in canoes, still be hunting in the forests, and would never have crossed the great salt lake, nor discovered your land. Instructed by our example, why did they not arm themselves with its power, without which man is nothing, in the plains as well as the forests?"

"Perhaps," he replied, "the Great Spirit, lives in the plains of the eastern sun, as being the source of light, and prefers the men nearest him. Perhaps those of the setting sun are not his children, since he refused them knowledge of this metal, whence, you say, springs strength and knowledge; or perhaps above the clouds there are Oke-maws, one as big as a mountain, powerful as the northwest wind of the winter,[2] whose dwelling would be on the east shore of this lake; the other smaller and more feeble, which would occupy the western shore. All that is a black night, through whose thick shadows the eyes of my mind cannot distinguish anything.

"Before my departure for Chillichate," he continued, "I should like to have you give me a copy of what you have written on this birch bark. Perhaps some day it will speak to me, as it speaks to you today. Perhaps when I am old, it will remind me of the thoughts which came to mind at the foot of the great Nemenshehelas (black birch) just as you, Pématuning sent by the great chief of the land of Onas (Pensyl-vanie) who gave me a rifle and a red coat."

That is the conversation which the transcription of this plaintive ballad aroused between this young warrior and me. Various other in-habitants of the village participated, attracted to me by the stir of curiosity and novelty. How bizarre the thousand and one reflections with which they assailed me, would appear to you! I did not wish to bore you with them.

Despite all my research, this feeble essay is the only one which has come to my attention since I have been residing here as agent of the Government, except the one which Cosmogonie ** collected almost a century ago from Kèlappama, ancient Schawnese chief, whom Wil-liam Penn summoned to his side. The Pemb family must have given

* Europe, which, relative to America, is East.
** This chapter, whose preface only was found, is probably among the great number of those which were lost, through negligence of the pilots of Hellégaland (Translator's note).

you a copy. In reading it, you will perhaps find, that it did not merit being translated. I have long wondered about it, I confess, but considering that you wanted some information, I decided to send you this for lack of anything better.

What a shame that that nation, one of the most numerous on the continent, among whom one sees a great number of men of very great stature, and whose language is harmonious and pleasant, has constantly opposed itself to all the efforts made to inspire in it the taste for a sedentary and farming life. Like so many others, it will disappear and leave for the rivers and mountains of this beautiful nation, only names which our geographers have carefully conserved.

It is a task which I have frequently recommended to the founders of the new Trans-Allegheny colonies of Indiana, Washington, the great Ménéamy, Kentucky, Wabash, Tenezee, etc. This respect for these names would have been prescribed by law; for after all, since destiny has decided that the European nations have been civilized for centuries, that our plows have replaced the bow and arrow of the Indians, that we have converted these regions, until now uncultivated and covered by forests, into prairies and fertile fields, we give to posterity their primitive names; then we shall prevent remembrance of these tribes, from being lost to the darkness of time, and we shall immortalize the only witness of the gratitude we can give and very certainly one we owe to the ancient owners of this continent whom we have tricked and deceived. Besides, these names—already consecrated by the passage and imprint of many centuries—are they not more appropriate in all respects and infinitely more sonorous than those of our common nomenclature? What a difference among these: river Margo to the Moelle, Franche, Trippe (in Canada), Liking, Sandy, Muddy, Turkey (in Kentuckey), and those of Pottwamack, Ténezee, Monongahéla, Alleghany, Keskéminétas Cahyahoga, Junondat, etc., rivers of Virginia and Pennsylvania.

Despite all my efforts to translate this little passage as literally as I was able, I confess that I have been obliged to use some words which were not in their language, such as, for example, that of soul, which they replace by life, animation; shadow, by black figures; absence, by distance; it is because of the lack of aptitude in conceiving metaphysical notions of some of our words, that they have never been able to understand some of the truths and historical points of religion.

"We are not children—we are warriors," they answer with their characteristic pride.

And they have more pride than you would suspect. That is why our missionaries have been able to convert only a small number of them. Their taste for the nomadic life is another obstacle no less insurmountable. What can they remember of their instruction, these men, who spend six months of the year hunting castors, bear, and wolves? And besides, what confidence can we flatter ourselves in inspiring in those who distrust everything we tell them, and who have for us as much scorn as hatred?

You will recognize in the expressions of Panima, those of Nature such as one observes in the forest; a mixture of bushes and some high, upright trees; of some odoriferous flowers, and of a great number of things barren and lacking in odor. You must often have noticed in their public speeches a kind of eloquence, which sometimes sparkles and rises with the aid of metaphors borrowed from everything that strikes their imagination. I know some who in their expression of sentiment, even approach the sublime; the harangue of Mingo Logan, in the peace of 1773, the reply of Tongaskootack to the governor of Canada in 1696, and seven others which fortunately have been collected.

"Although their way of life and the customs resulting from it, keep friendship among them from being a sentiment as keen and as cultivated as among us, I have seen touching examples of it, notes of which I shall show you some day at the first opportunity. It is impossible to imagine, without having lived among them for a long time, to what extent their civilization contributes in retracing the circle of their affections and their morale. They scarcely know the pleasures of love which they consider, on the contrary, unworthy to the ways of a hunter and warrior.

"He who would strike his enemy long and hard," they say, "must have long since scorned the bearskin of a woman."

Inertia, the inactivity of this first impetus of our existence, makes their imagination cold, sterile, and stupid; nothing means anything to them; nothing ever stimulates them; although, often lazy, they never feel that excess zest for life which among us sometimes produces boredom, the origin of so many useful enterprises and worthwhile discoveries. That is why people have found among them neither stories, fables nor apologues. They have only songs destined to celebrate their victories and the sating of their implacable vengeance; they are utterances of ferocity, as well as of their barbarous pride, rather than of happiness and pleasure.

Indeed, what understanding can attach a man of this kind to his fellow man? Sufficient unto himself by his adroitness in hunting as well as fishing, occupied solely in filling his kettle, he means nothing to his neighbor, and his neighbor means nothing to him; it is as though they lived on two islands separated by a branch of the river. The only joy of which they have an idea and of which they love to speak is rest, or rather the most complete inactivity; for you must know that their wives have the exclusive responsibility of the household chores.

"Ah, my brother" said Nangooarcala, Nimwha, Maratenza, and some other chiefs who were dining with me, "you will never know as we do the happiness of thinking of nothing and of doing nothing; next to sleep, there is nothing more delightful. That is the state in which we, before being born, had the misfortune to be; that is how we shall be after death. Who," he continued, "put into our heads, this perpetual desire to be better fed, better clad, and to leave so much land and money to our children? Do they fear that the sun and the moon will never rise for them? That the dew from the clouds will never fall for them? That the rivers will dry up, that they will leave for the West? Like the fountain which spurts from the rock, like the waters of our rapids and our falls, they never sleep; as soon as a field is harvested, immediately they harvest another, after felling and burning one tree, they proceed to fell and burn another and as though the sun's day were not long enough, I have seen some who have worked by the light of the moon. What then is their life compared with ours, since the present means nothing to them? It arrives; blind as they are, they let it pass. On the other hand, we live only for that rest after coming back from our wars and our hunts. Like the smoke which the wind dissipates and the air absorbs, the past is nothing, we tell ourselves; as to the future, where is it? Since it has not yet arrived, perhaps we shall never see it, therefore, let us enjoy today for what it is; tomorrow it will be far away.

"You talk to us afterwards of foresight, that torment of life: do you not know that it is the evil jinn who gave it to the whites in order to punish them for being wiser? Relentlessly it wounds and needles them without ever being able to cure them, since it can never prevent the arrival of evil, which attaches itself to children of the earth, as thorns do to the legs of the traveler."

Thus do the inhabitants of the forests reason or rather feel, and in their crazy pride, they believe themselves wiser and happier than we. I have known some who would push their scorn to pity, which proves that happiness can take all forms, live in any climate, and find pleasure under birch bark as under magnificent marble. How can we convince such minds of the necessity and the advantages which result from agriculture and industry? As to the studies of this language, which you have asked me about, they are in the hands of Mr. Maddisson, member of Congress for Virginia. He promised to give them to you for me.

In the village of Kispoko, July 4, 1786

Richard Buttler

Panima, seated at the foot of the mighty Nemenshehelas (birch tree), the moon being full and resplendent, addresses Ganondawé, his friend:

"The threshold of your wigwam has been seized, the ashes of your fireplace been dispersed, and your fire extinguished, brave Ganondawé! You have abandoned your wigwam and the village to go to the land of Onas, from which the whites have removed the shade and coolness. Why they do not even know, as we do, how to live from the hunt, to sleep on a bearskin and to drink from the water of a stream. They would not be thirsty for our lands, and we would be neighbors and friends.

"Beware of their fine talk. Like the ice of our rivers at the return of spring, he who puts any faith in their talk is lost; like the treacherous eddies of the Alleguipy, the unwise traveler who approaches them is swallowed by them. Never do they say what they think, and never do they think what they say. Do you know why? Because trickery and lies drool from their lips like the putrid sap of a tree whose heart is hollow and rotten.

"But to whom do I speak, since you are no longer here to hear my words? Could my voice reach yours and yours—like that of an echo, could it reach mine? I am listening . . . it is only the rustle of the wind which passes, or the pounding of the falls which dies away in the depths of the forests nearby. It says nothing in the ear of my attentive soul. I listen again . . . it is only the woodpecker against the dried up trunk of a tree or the pheasant summoning his mate as he flaps his wings. Yet I would like to speak with the you who lives in my thoughts, whose image the eyes of my mind see.

"Ganondawé, where are you? Could you not hear the voice of Panima, your friend?

"I shall imagine I am speaking to you since your absence, like the thickness of a mountain, hides you from my eyes; and since like the winter ice, it has closed my mouth. When I think of you, my arm stretches out, my hand opens to meet and shake yours. During the light of day, I seek you and find you no more; even your shadow has left me. During the silence of nights, my thoughts turn to you, and like the surface of the waters, they reflect your presence. Unhappy and saddened as I am, my arrows no longer pierce game; fish pass on and no longer see Panima's hook. I put the peace pipe to my mouth, but, like the waters of the stream, stopped by the dam of the beaver, these thoughts of mine which your absence retains in my head, are no longer happy and gay; they are becoming sad and gloomy.

"Ganondawé, where are you? Could you not hear the voice of Panima, your friend?

"Since you are no longer here, how long it seems from morning until night (how long the days seem)! And without the oblivion induced by sleep and the distraction of dreams, how much longer, even the time separating night from morning seems! When will you return, bring the gaiety which followed you, the skill and the patience which I need in order to live? When will you return to remove the leaves from my path and to chase the breath of misfortune which I encounter everywhere? If I run through the forests, I get lost; if I venture on the water, I cannot steer my canoe, if I light a fire on my hearth, it gives more smoke than warmth; if I leave my wigwam, the snakes of the earth and the birds of the night seize it; if I practice hurling my tomahawk, it falls before reaching the bark of the tree.

"Ganondawé, when will you return? Can you not hear the voice of Panima, your friend?

" 'When you speak,' our old men say, 'the ears of your audience listen attentively.

" 'Yes,' they say, 'his voice is sonorous like the echo of the forests, like the voice of the crane amid the clouds, or that of the curlew in the midst of the savannahs. Like drops from a fall, each of his words has weight; he has the heart of Poohagen, his ancestor, and the language of Sagagoetchè, his father; never has a black lie left his red lips. He is wise and quiet like the swamp beaver, cunning as the foxhound, brave and bold as the starved panther, as fleet of foot as the pursued stag; his eye is as keen as the bald eagle's; and his hearing equal to that of the elk with the forked antlers. Like his rifle, his judgment never misses aim. May the leaves of his tree of life shelter for a long time the wigwams of the village and those of our tribes!'

"That is how the people who knew you spoke of you, from the forks of the quiet Scioto to the waters of the great Ohio and beyond.

"Ganondawé, where are you? Could you not hear the voice of Panima, your friend?

"Do you remember that from our earliest youth, we have always paddled the same canoe, pursued the same game, and shared the same dangers? When one said yes, the other said it, too. That when we lighted a fire on your hearth or mine, friendship was always there to blow on it? Do you remember that I had given you my confidence just as the sick man gives his to his healer, as the traveler gives his to the faithful and steady current which guides his canoe? Do you recall that when they came to hear you, silence closed the door, and that the strictest attention lurked in our ears? Do you remember that in the fear of interrupting you, they even neglected to replenish the fire with wood? Do you recall how our words were like those of one person, united like the smoke of our peace pipes? Do you recall that everyone acclaimed you, saying:

" 'Let us follow him wherever land and waters carry him. He knows how to speak, think, and lead in the light of day as well as in the shadows of the night.'

"Ganondawé, where are you? Could you hear the voice of Panima, your friend?

"I am brave and fearless; you are, too. I fear neither death nor suffering; neither do you. I am a patient hunter, skillful and indefatigable; so are you. I am a man; as such I fear neither the tomahawk nor the kettle of the enemy; the same is true of you. When I stumble over stones in the path, I lean on your shoulder; you do the same. When my courage wavers you look at me; my strength doubles. When I intone my war chant, I sing it with more energy when I think of you. How strong two men are when they make only one! It is like the wings which support the bird, like the canoe paddled by two braves in the midst of a rapid; if it is directed only by one, soon fatigue and worry pursue and overtake him; he loses the course of the current, capsizes and for lack of a friend, becomes the unfortunate one, a piscatorial picnic ground.

"Ganondawé, where are you? Couldn't you hear the voice of Panima, your friend?

"I should like to know whether, when the sun rises in the land of Onas, its first rays make you rejoice, just as when you left your wigwam to greet it; I should like to know whether the shadows of the night cover the earth with dew and your eyes with sleep. I should like to know what you think of these bearded men who kill themselves with work and are never happy; to whom so much is necessary for happiness, and who do not live any longer than do we, who have only our rifles. What do you think of their God, to whom they speak so often, and who does not forbid them to work our lands and chase game from them? He is an evil God since he permits them to invade our villages, to expose the bones of our ancestors to the wind and the rain, to give us waters of fire and fury to consume, and fine crafty words to deceive us.

"These sad thoughts, like a day in winter, bring to birth even sadder ones. If Panima goes to war, who will drag him from the tooth of his enemy? If his canoe capsizes, who will help him chase away their memory? If the spirit from on high smites him with his arrow, who will cover his body with earth? Whatever I do to chase these ideas from my head, the melancholy which hid behind the mountain, when you were here arrives, bringing me even sadder and gloomier thoughts. Since your departure, my face is as somber as the water which runs 'neath our black pines; my mind is lost in the midst of shadows, like the hunter in the midst of forests; silence closes my mouth, my ears no longer hear the warbling of the muskawiss [3] and my eyes look without seeing.

"Ganondawé, where are you, could you not hear the voice of Panima your friend?

"I speak to you and you do not hear me! I look and see only myself at the foot of the Nemenshehelas! Who, then, will serve as witness to the utterance of my living words? The moon, that modest maiden, daughter of the radiant sun, to her I confide them. But who will bring you the voice of my lament and the substance of my memories? Will the wind, breath of the great Manitou, a messenger, often inconstant and fickle, carry them to you faithfully? I pledge it.

"Hasten to return in order to hear these laments from the mouth of your friend, and tell us how these men of Cherry-hum-Sagat received and fed you, how they took you ten times by the hand, or smoked with you, to deceive you ten times better in your exchanges, as often happened to me. Hasten to return to your wife, to your children, to Panima who awaits you seated on your father's threshold.

"Come back to your threshold, light your fire again and hang your kettle. May my ears hear you hail and may my eyes see your canoe rounding the cape of Kittagamick, long before the corn is ripe!

"Ganondawé, where are you? Couldn't you hear the voice of Panima, your friend?

"These are my words, which I confirm by three cuts on the bark of Nemenhéhélas, in the village of Chillichaté the fourth day of the moon of the squirrels.

Panima"

CHAPTER VI

Mr. Herman and I stayed for a time at Clermont with Mr. Livingston, chancellor of New York State, enjoying the interesting conversation of this honored man, one of the founders of the independence and liberty of his country. From the porch of his fine house on the east bank of the Hudson, we watched the many vessels continually ascending or descending the beautiful river, adapting their courses to the tides or the prevailing winds. We reflected on the already immense production of agriculture and industry in a country inhabited but a few years before only by hunters and Indians. Our visit was brought to a close by a letter to my companion. A company in which his family had holdings wished to acquire one of the districts in the military land grant, the said district to be located as advantageously as possible in relation to the waterway of Lake Ontario, or to inland roads.

We needed a guide; fortunately, Mr. Livingston, who had taken a strong fancy to Mr. Herman and was anxious to see him settle in the neighborhood, provided us with a young man who had accompanied the surveyor general when the boundaries of the great tract were established and who was well acquainted with all its subdivisions. In a few days we left for Albany, from which town, after a twenty-four-hour halt, we easily made our way to Schenectady. There we bought a large boat, which in seven days carried us up the Mohawk to its junction with the Oriskany. Since we hoped to travel rapidly through the forests, we hired four Indians, who would at the same time serve us as guides and provide us with game, thus constituting, as Mr. Herman remarked with a smile, a sort of ambulating inn.

What changes had taken place since our expedition to Onondaga in 1789! The Little Falls Canal, then not even thought of, was almost finished. Already, a short distance from the falls, a pretty town had been laid out on the outskirts of which we observed several elegant houses, a fine flour mill had just been built, and the new Stanwich Canal was already being dug. I counted thirty-two houses in the little town of Whitestown (White's town), the point at which the Mohawk becomes no longer navigable. The Oneidas had sold their land, with the exception of 100,000 acres. The Onondagas had kept back only 65,000; and the Cayugas, about the same amount, toward the upper end of the lake which bears their name.

"Thus are accomplished," I said to Mr. Herman, "the predictions of old Keskétomah, and those even older sayings of Menesage-Korey-hoosta; thus have disappeared the hopes of the Oneida chieftains; thus, by treaty and purchase, and without even resorting to force, the whites will always be able to extend their territory as their population, or rather their cupidity, increases. To this military concession of a million and a half acres, and the acquisition of Colonel Williamson, which is said to be almost as large, and the holdings of Dutch and Flemish companies—you have, all told, a country as big as Silesia, purchased for less than 20,000 pounds. The famous Mohawk league is destroyed! And, almost inconceivable! of all its members, not one has become a landowner and farmer; not one said to himself, ''I shall keep back for myself 1200 acres on the banks of such and such a stream, I shall sell half of it for 2000 piastres, with which I shall build a house and buy horses and tools. Like the whites, I shall sow and reap, like them I shall raise my children in the habits of labor and industry; like them I shall leave to my descendants my orchards, my fields, and my name; and like them, my seed shall multiply upon the earth!—who can help seeing in this blind obstinacy, the will, the hand of destiny?''

Equipped with an excellent map of this portion of the state, just published by Mr. De Witt, and preceded by our guides, we made our way to the district of Camillus, at the northern end of pretty little lake Oxaruatates (Skaneateles), not without suffering both the hardships which arise from sleeping in the forests, and, in spite of the skill and zeal of our hunters, the inconvenience of having either more food than we could eat or not enough.

Just as we had been told, we found, on the banks of the little stream which connects the waters of this lake with those of Lake Cross, a family of recent settlers. They had flour, pork and peas, two cows, two yoke of oxen, and a few chickens—which the foxes feasted on occasionally; but they were still without a house. Since we planned to make this spot our headquarters, we resolved to come to their assistance, for there were seven of us; and within four days they had a shelter 14 feet wide by 25 feet long. It is true, this building was crude, constructed as it was of logs; but it was snug enough, with a good roof of oak bark which our hunters pitched on the rafters with great dexterity and willingness, for the Indians are the most obliging and serviceable men on earth, if only one has the knack of stimulating and directing them; then they will do for their friends what they would not do for themselves, since in those circumstances they do not consider such labor dishonorable.

After having passed ten days in carefully examining the nature of the soil, the quality of the trees, the streams and falls, the marshes and low lands of the adjacent districts, Mr. Herman, on the advice of the young surveyor whom the chancellor had hired for him, fixed his choice on the district of Lysander, bounded on the south by the Seneca River, on the north by the district of Hannibal, on the west by that of Cato, and on the east by the Oswego or Onondaga River, which empties into Lake Ontario, and by which, in spring and fall, it is possible to reach Lake Oneida and the Mohawk. After we had made this decision and obtained all the necessary information, as well as a topographical map of the district, we were on the point of returning to Oriskany, following the trail which our guides had prudently blazed, when the desire to add to our knowledge of this new and interesting part of the state made us decide to go on to New Geneva, a town thirty-five miles from Lysander, at the head of Lake Seneca or Canoderago. From there, it would be easy, taking the government road, to return to Schuyler or to Palatine on the Mohawk. In this way, we would go through the districts of Brutus, Cato and Aurelius, the Cayuga Reserve, and the districts of Romulus, bathed by the waters of Lake Seneca.

During the first days of our journey, still accompanied by our Oriskany men, we struggled against the multitude of obstacles which characterize country wooded with hemlock and pine; for the enormous height which these trees attain does not always indicate a fertile soil. The paths were obstructed by trees which high winds had felled; the marshes were difficult to cross; at night we were tormented by microscopic insects called gnats; the settlers whom we met, all newcomers, could offer us only corn cake.

As we traveled, we reflected on the cause of the astonishing variation in soil, not only in the same district, but in the same field; on the use that some day would be made of the many waterfalls along our way and on the nature of the rocks over which they precipitated themselves; on the eventual drying up of so much marsh land and the large extent of pasturage which would eventually recompense the settlers for the present worthlessness of their woods; until we entered the district of Brutus, covered with chestnuts, elms, oaks, hickories, and sugar-maples—indications of a much more fertile soil: and indeed, the district was more settled than that through which we had passed. As we approached the junction of the little Owasco with the Seneca, we spied a dwelling, a crude one, to tell the truth, a mere shelter, but with a shingled roof.

The mistress of the house, respectably dressed, her head ornamented by a Bermudan straw hat, surprised at our arrival, and especially at our four native hunters, answered our questions and invited us, with much timidity and embarrassment, to dismount. Nonetheless, she was polite enough to lead our horses in under what she called a shed. This was a roof of bark, mounted on four poles and weighed down with stones to prevent the wind from carrying it away.

"Not exactly luxury," my two companions said, "but at this time of year, one does not need much to be fairly comfortable, and this comfort is offered us so politely that we ought to be satisfied and grateful."

As we talked with this young and pretty American, who was making tea for us (for one finds tea everywhere), her husband, summoned by the piercing blast of a conch-shell horn, arrived, covered with sweat and black as coal.

"What on earth have you been doing?" Mr. Herman asked.

"Burning out a great mass of roots, bushes, and weeds, with which nature has covered this soil. How powerful nature is, to bring forth from nothing so many useless products. If the land were encumbered merely with trees, our task would be a good deal less unpleasant and less difficult: by ringing the bark we cut off the sap, and the giants die as they stand, offering no resistance. But this incredible mass of bushes, trailing vines, briars, and creepers, whose shoots spread with amazing vigor for two or three years—that is what retards our progress, and often makes us lose heart. It's a real labor of Penelope, destroying those hardy plants! Our successors will be fortunate! They will pay a bit more for the land, it is true, but the enormous and difficult work of stripping, grubbing, and burning will be done with: the land will be cleared; it will be their task only to perfect our rough beginnings, to enclose the fields, to work them, and to enjoy their fruits. I assure you that a colonist needs more than courage to leave his native place, to renounce forever the example and the help of his neighbors and friends. If only he were sure of succeeding! But quite the contrary: here more than anywhere else, we are exposed to the risk of accidents and of bad luck, whose evil influence accompanies man everywhere. Yet, nonetheless, blinded by the illusions of hope, forgetting the misfortunes of those who have failed, we dare to found new homes and to struggle against a multitude of obstacles."

"If it is not courage, just what is it that inspires and sustains you?" M. Herman asked.

"A sentiment, or rather an impulse, which, fortunately, is not premeditated, but instinctive. The love of our wives and children—which is synonymous with the love of ourselves; the desire to lead a comfortable and independent life—that is the source of my industry and perseverence. Perhaps I need such an impulse more than most men, having spent my early years with a book in my hand rather than an axe. At the time when I was to enter the ministry, I was unhappy enough to lose a beloved father. That event so affected my heart and mind, that I left the paternal roof and became a whaler. For five years, I pursued and harpooned that enormous fish; I would be pursuing it yet, had not this sweet and pretty housewife one day forbidden me to. Perhaps she was right: she thought only of the mutual happiness which we have found in our marriage. I admit, however, that without her and the children whom she has given me, I would not be as industrious as I am. But when my heart fails me, I wake to a new effort, to prove to her that I am worthy of being her husband. And, though she has never spoken of it, I know that she does the same; yet she (no more than I), was not reared to lead such a rugged existence.

"Alas," he continued, "what would become of a settler in these mournful wastes, if he were not accompanied by a dear companion to lighten and alleviate his hardships, to excite and sustain his emulation, to prepare his food? How would he resist the boredom, the disgust that these remote and deserted places inspire, especially during the early years when the sight of a human being is a novelty, and only a long journey will bring a man to a neighbor? The emptiness he feels in his house—even more, the emptiness he feels in his heart—leads him inevitably to seek some object which can fill that void. What reason has he for industry, if he works only for himself? However insensitive he may be, he would be ashamed to enjoy a comfort and happiness which he could not share with someone. Yes, if I had neither wife nor children (and I thank Providence for such a worthy mate), instead of farming, I would become a savage—an easier and more material step than people think—and like the natives, I would live happily and carelessly by hunting and fishing, untouched by the continued worries, the anxieties about the future, which spring from property and are inseparable from the duties and responsibilities of organized society. I would do coldbloodedly and reflectively what these children of nature do instinctively. At the present time, when the reasons for their former wars and relentless feuds have passed away, if fire-water, the only source of their present dissensions and bloody quarrels, could be banished from their villages, peace and happiness would descend from heaven and take refuge among them.

"To acquire, through the ownership of a certain amount of land, the rights of a citizen: to elect and be elected, to participate in the making of laws, to fill the various municipal offices; to obtain, through farming, comfort, independence, and respect; to become a husband and a father—those are the dreams which, every year, lead so many young couples to leave the family firesides to create new homes far away, and which give them at the same time the fortitude to endure such struggles and hardships."

"However painful your work may be," said Mr. Herman, "you are nevertheless on the path to happiness—if there be any upon this earth. Surely none shall find it more easily or in more durable and less precarious form than the man who tills his own fields. A few more years of courage and perseverance and it will be yours; a few more years and your barns will be full, your pastures covered with herds, your orchards heavy with fruit. Here you cultivate fresh, free land, you work only for yourself, you pay neither rent nor taxes. You have only the roses of liberty; the wise government which protects you has removed all the thorns.

"Sometimes your troubles are great, I admit, but they are only those of the body. Once the day's task is done, the night's repose, that restoring balm, comes to seal your eyelids, to restore your strength, to give you new energy to sustain the tasks of the morrow. If sometimes hope lags behind you, often she precedes you, summons you, takes you by the hand, and says with a smile:

" 'Each night, after having lifted the eyes of your intelligence to the sovereign master of the universe, giver of fruitful dews and rains, father of farmers, picture to yourself the fair banks of the Owasco covered with hemp and corn; imagine half of the forests which surround you changed to fertile well-fenced fields; imagine the young trees of your orchards bent under the weight of their fruit. Your humble shelter has become a spacious and commodious house; your little shed, a fine large barn. You shall be loved and cherished by those children whom you have carefully reared in the love and salutary fear of a rewarding and revenging God, in whom you have planted the respect and thankfulness which you owe to the Government which protects your life and property and which encourages your industry without demanding a single ear of your harvest or a single apple from your orchard, and to fill with overflowing the greatest happiness that man can enjoy upon earth, you and your wife shall see arrive very gradually, the last of your days, as you bless the moment when you met her, and she exults in never for an instant having repented that she chose you as a husband. Indeed, I promise you, this consoling vision will come to pass, and at no distant day. Only continue as you are, hard working, God-fearing, and grateful.'

"You are certainly right," Mr. Herman continued, "if ever bravery and industry deserved a reward, first settlers deserved it for they, like the advance guard of an army, cut the first paths, build the first bridges, clear the fields, raise the first crops, and open the way for the mass of society which will soon follow in their footsteps. But why have you settled on land so difficult to clear?"

"Because a large part of this concession consists of alluvial land, which, in a few years, will have increased in value tenfold. Twenty acres are enough to make a family rich. This gift of nature seems to have been formed during the course of centuries as the waters receded, leaving a deposit behind them. I have dug trenches to various depths, and in the space of nine feet I have counted up to twenty-eight layers. They alternate: marl, black sand, clay, and vegetable debris of various colors. The mixture is inexhaustibly fertile; the land will yield corn ten feet high, hemp, flax, oats, peas, and hay in the greatest abundance."

"What is your native state?"

"New Jersey."

"Why did you leave it?"

"Because my father, who had nine children, left me only 72 acres of land. What young man would vegetate on such a modest holding when by emigration he could secure a much larger tract? Here with my axe and the help of Heaven, I have enough for a little fortune—that is, to live comfortably and to leave to each of my children either a hundred well-cultivated acres or the knowledge of a trade."

"Is there no affection for the family homestead here, no attachment to the native land?"

"Much less than in Europe, and naturally so. To begin with, the family homestead is always reserved for the youngest son, who supports the parents in their old age. Furthermore, are we not all members of one great family—the United States? Is not a citizen of one state a citizen of them all? Do we not speak the same language, have the same weights and measures, obey the same laws? Do we not have the same customs, and almost the same religion, from Maine to Tennessee, from the shores of the Atlantic to the plains of Scioto? What does it matter whether a man lives in Virginia, Pennsylvania, or Maryland? I would go to Kentucky, to Illinois, or to the banks of the Wabash with no hesitation, provided I were happy there in the possession of a few hundred acres of fertile land."

"Why do you need so much land to be content?"

"Because labor is so dear that we are forced to compensate the crudeness of our cultivation by the magnitude of our fields—that is to say, to make up by extent what we lose by method. And then too, a man with children thinks about setting them up for life. If I have four more years of health, the future will not worry me."

"Was the price of the 72 acres which your father left you enough to pay for the 320 you own here?"

"Oh, I did not sell them. This fine piece here comes from the government, as payment for having carried the chain for the surveyor-general during the great project that he and the surveyor general of Pennsylvania have just finished: establishing the boundary between the two states. That official was too generous not to reward us with the best land.''

''Are the laws good, and are they enforced?''

''They say that there are magistrates, judges of the lower court, and a sheriff in the district; I myself know no more than that. Peace reigns among us; our neighbors are our friends—though unfortunately there are not many of them. Everyone is busy clearing his land, getting it in good shape, and planting it. Like everyone else, our judges have their work to do and are busier about their farms than in hearing cases. Fifty years from now, things will have changed. There will be more people here, living closer together, and the salutary reign of law will be more necessary. All we really need now are good roads or canals. The government is taking care of that, and we are grateful that it is doing so without demanding any tax.''

''How, then, does it get the money to make the necessary expenditures?''

''From the interest on the large sums it has deposited in the Bank of the Union. Here we pay the state only a very moderate amount to serve as bounty for the destruction of wolves and panthers—a tax which we suggested ourselves. But how unfortunate, gentlemen, that you did not arrive a day earlier. You would have found here the surveyor general, Mr. Andrew De Witt, who would have explained such matters much better than I can.''

''Does he live in this district?'' I asked.

''His office is at Albany, but just now he is only thirty miles away, in the district of Tully, on one of the branches of the Owego River. He is finishing the subdivision of this great military concession, destined for the contingent of the Continental Army which this state furnished during the War of Independence.''

Delighted by the chance of meeting a man as praiseworthy for his virtues as for his talents, I secured my companion's consent to make this little detour, after a rest in New Geneva. As we crossed the Cayuga Reserve, we met several aged chiefs of that nation who gave us some of the fish they caught in the lake. On the second day, we entered the district of Romulus. Since an epidemic of fever was in progress among the settlers, we hastened on to gain the east shore of Canoderago or Seneca, from which point we could make out the town—or rather the humble hamlet—of Geneva.

''If it were proper to compare the small with the great,'' said Mr.

Herman, "I should say that this sight calls up thoughts of the new Salente, founded, like this town, in the middle of a forest, by men, who, like these natives of Geneva, were forced to flee from their fatherland. How powerful the reasons must be that led these families to cross the ocean and settle among a people whose very language was unknown to them! What sacrifices they must have made to give up their old customs and occupations to become hard-working settlers! What privations they will still have to suffer before they live in comfort!"

"It is thus," I said to him, "that the poverty, dissension, and frequent wars of the old world help to settle this one. In how many ways America has been useful to Europe! Parts of this continent have served as penal colonies where the criminals have reformed. Here the unfortunate have found asylum and rest; the persecuted, toleration; the unemployed, a new field of industry; all, liberty and the protection of law. The many obstacles which the new arrivals meet during their first years serve only to provoke their courage and skill. Those who do not succeed as farmers lose none of their utility in becoming artisans or workmen, whose labor commands a high wage."

When we reached the town, its one inn, which also served as a store, was pointed out to us. We found it clean and well-stocked. "You have come a few years too soon," the host said in French. "As you see, we are still in the midst of the inconveniencies and hardships of a new settlement. We have been here less than four years; you can still see the tree stumps. We are undergoing the fate of all new settlements, but with the help of Heaven, we, like so many others, will some day enjoy the fruits of our labor, and our children after us. Indeed, it requires more perseverance than one thinks in Europe to get decent houses built, fields, yards and gardens cleared, and the grain, vegetables and fruit harvested. Except for those settlers who reach a great age, it is only the second generation that is able to enjoy cultivated land, good orchards, and fine roads."

"What led you to settle so far from the sea?"

"The facility of communications, the fertility of the soil, and, I must say, the reputation of Colonel Williamson. He is the owner of an immense grant which extends to Lake Ontario, covering a vast territory. Besides the virtues of the man, he possesses all the talents, all the energy, generosity, and honesty as well as the qualities necessary to the founder of so large a colony. We acquired the township from him. He threw into the bargain two hundred acres of land, one hundred for the church which we are going to establish, and one hundred for the school, which is already built. He thinks of everything and foresees everything, down to such details as improving the breed of our horses and cattle. The settler who does business with him is fortunate. We respect him like a father; he loves us as his children. Consequently, the price of his land goes up every day. We know that he has asked the legislature for a charter of incorporation of our growing town, and he ought to get it at the next session. It will contribute a good deal to our prosperity.''

''Of what advantage is a charter?'' asked Mr. Herman.

''It will assure the regularity of our labors, prevent a diversity of interests, unite our efforts, support the police force and civil order, secure for the town the ownership of the lake shore out to a certain depth, as well as the piers which we have already built. And, to tell the truth, it will flatter our pride by identifying us in a special fashion with this town which we have founded, this soil which we have purchased, this country which has become our new native land.''

''Why did you leave the shores of Lake Leman to settle on those of Canoderago?''

''We feared that the eruptions which in 1790 shook all of France would throw their fearful lava on our city, which as you know is but a dot in the immensity of Western Europe. Subsequent events have only too obviously justified our foresight and prudence. When flames devour your neighbor's house, is it not wise to leave your own, carrying to safety your most precious possessions? We depended completely upon commerce and industry; it soon ceased as the relations of our city with the rest of Europe were completely destroyed.

''Besides, we were tired of a democratic regime whose turmoil gave us no more than ten or twelve consecutive years of peace and quiet. We sought, for a long time, a country where there was room to expand, a country whose government and laws were stable and protective, where every man could make a living without being exposed to arbitrary taxation, where, finally, we could escape forever the furies of demagogues, the conflagration of war, the terrors which are so common in the old world. We flatter ourselves that we have found these advantages here. They certainly have cost us dear; but desperate situations call for desperate measures; and a man must have the fortitude to bear them or perish. Of what is he not capable when he has a wife and children who depend on him for protection, safety, livelihood? If there is any irresistible motive for action in a man's life, it is that one. And so far, thank God, we have suffered only hardships and have had no losses.

''This new Geneva,'' he continued, ''like the old, is situated on a lake, as long as Lake Leman, but not so wide; and since it is not surrounded by mountains, storms are rarer here. Already the shores are fairly well cultivated. There are even a few orchards producing excellent cider. That which you are drinking comes from Ovid where last year they built a fine schooner of 70 tons to carry their produce to our warehouse, from which it is shipped on the Seneca. That river, as you know, flows into the Oswego or Onondage; from it the boats go up Lake Oneida and enter the Mohawk River through the new Stanwick Canal, 270 miles away.

"Its location should in time make this young town a depot for all the products of the surrounding country, and they will increase as the population grows. A very short canal, joining the little Seneca River, which flows into the southern part of this lake, to the Tiogo River, will link us to the interior of Pennsylvania. Colonel Williamson has had the land surveyed and estimates that the canal can be built for 20,000 pounds.

"Return in ten years and you will not recognize this district which today you probably find wild and savage. Our humble log houses will be replaced by fine dwellings. Our fields will be fenced in, and the stumps will have disappeared.

"From this vantage point, as from a quiet harbor, we look out, not without fright, at the storms which have laid waste the land we have left forever. May the victims of so many innovations and revolutions, like those former victims of the long and bloody wars of religion which once devastated Europe, seek the shores of this hospitable country and, like us, find peace and land."

He went on to tell us about the new town of Canondaga, capital of Ontario County, twenty-five miles west of Geneva, at the head of the fine lake of the same name; about the hamlets of Bath, Canonwaga, Ontario, etc. lately founded near the Genesee River; about the numerous settlements made in that district during the last few years; about the fertility of the plains along that river; about a colony which Colonel Williamson had just set up at Sodus, a large harbor on the southern shore of Lake Ontario, thirty miles from Oswego and ninety from Niagara; about the bilious fevers to which the colonists were more exposed than in other parts of the state and his conjectures as to the causes of the disease as well as his hopes that draining the marshes and clearing the woodland would make the region more healthful. We also discussed the former owners of this land and the brutishness and degradation into which the abuse of spirituous liquor has plunged them—an abuse which is rapidly leading them to extinction.

The remarks of this settler were so accurate and sensible and his speech was so correct that we soon realized that he had not been born to keep an inn. But to what extremes does not imperious necessity drive brave and energetic men, especially in this age of tempestuous passions which overthrow empires and light the flames of civil war!

CHAPTER VII

After we had rested three days in this budding town (Geneva), some of the founders there suggested that in order to shorten our route, we continue by water as far as the district of Ovid, twenty miles away. This proved to be a charming excursion, made on the only schooner of the lake, whose name it bore. Having crossed this region in which we met several families who had settled there two years ago, we reached Cayuga, which is only two miles wide, located five leagues east of Canoderago or Seneca. Still accompanied by our hunters, we explored the districts of Milton, Locke, and Sempronius until we arrived finally at Tully, where the surveyor-general was camping.

It was indeed quite a camp; four tents raised in the shade of the tall oaks, formed a kind of enclosure some distance from the banks of the little Oswego, whose waters empty into Lake Oxaruatetes (Skaneateles). In one of these tents, we saw several persons busy tracing subdivisions on the large map of this great military concession.

"Are all the lands surveyed in this manner?" asked Mr. Herman.

"This particular method," replied Mr. Duwitt, "was introduced only since the independence of this country; as soon as the boundaries of these patents are determined and fixed by some lasting mark, they are divided into districts of six square miles, known as townships, each having 23,400 acres. Each of these townships is then subdivided into 36 lots, each one mile square and containing 650 acres. This wise method, which puts great order into property, came to us from the surveyors of Connecticut and Massachusetts, and was unknown in colonial times. At that time nothing was more irregular, nor more arbitrary than the form and division of lands and a great number of lawsuits were the consequence. Since the time of independence, the divisions into squares or parallelograms was adopted. What a contrast with the present time, when everything is free and clear, to the time when the British crown exacted annually a tax of seven denier for each acre! The purchasers of new lands paid the Government neither rights nor rents beyond the initial purchase price; they are subject only to land tax and up until now, this State, which enjoys considerable revenue from funds which it put in the Bank of the Union, has not even exacted any land tax.

"Everything which belongs under the military concession," continued Mr. Duwitt, "known under the name of military bounty, is likewise given without restrictions or rents or claims, with the exception, however, of three lots in each district, 650 acres apiece, for the purpose of encouraging schools and religious establishments; but all over the reserves are the same: the buyer, or the one to whom this donation is made, knows very well that instead of 23,400 acres for each district, he can buy or receive only 21,450. I am engaged now in dividing this concession into twenty-five cantons or townships of ten square miles, containing consequently 65,000 acres apiece. The land which it includes is located between 42 degrees 25 minutes and 43 degrees 30 minutes latitude. All the waters from the lakes and rivers included in this area, empty into the Ontario through the Onondaga River, which empties into the Bay of Oswego. It is the highest region in the state and the one with the most productive and most vegetative soil. With the aid of canals, some day people will be able to reach Pennsylvania through the Susquehannah, and to go to New York by way of the Mohawk and the Hudson rivers. From looking at this map, judge whether or not this land is not well irrigated; here are fifteen lakes varying in size from ten to forty miles in length, and in width from two to five miles. One of these little lakes, whose waters are salty, is already furnishing a great abundance of salt.''

''Why does this military concession exist?'' asked Mr. Herman.

''Congress,'' replied Mr. Duwitt, ''having promised the officers and soldiers of the continental army a certain amount of land, which when peace was signed, was to be given them as reward for their services, the other states in whose territory Congress found unoccupied land, shortly afterward did the same for the troops which they had sent to the army. Since that time, various other parcels of land have been put up for sale, known as donation lands, in order to liquidate three kinds of military certificates whose value, before the ratification of the new constitution was null. But these details accompanying the chaos in our finances before this memorable epoch, would be too long and too dull: it is to the great and rare talents of Colonel Alexander Hamilton that we owe this escape from the abyss into which the feebleness of our first confederation had plunged us; it is to the wisdom of General Washington that the nomination of this young and adroit financier is due. What makes Mr. Hamilton a truly extraordinary man is that he is considered one of our foremost orators and one of the most learned legal counsels on the continent. Leaving this ministry as poor as he was on entering, he resumed his profession of lawyer.

''The object of this military concession which I am engaged in subdividing is to fulfill the obligations of that state toward its contingent of the continental army. If the services of these brave soldiers have been long and painful, on the other hand, never before had they received rewards so full and so honorable: it is both the acquittal of a public debt and evidence of public recognition.''

"Why did they give Greek and Latin names to these subdivisions?" asked Mr. Herman.

"The Government, in order to facilitate the administration of justice and the establishment of municipal laws, wanted the entire State to be divided into townships of six square miles or two square leagues. It left to the owners, to the surveyors and often to chance, even, the business of naming them. Our soldiers, having a great veneration for the ancient heroes and the other great personages of Greece and Rome, sent me this list. In a few years, a traveler will be able to breakfast in Hannibal, dine with Lisandre, and sleep in the home of someone in Camillus; the next day he will be able to do the same at Fabius, Homer, and Virgil. Assuredly it would be difficult to find better company on the way.

"I confess," he continued, "this notion has pleased me in a very odd way; it recalls a myriad of memories of olden times, whose story made the delight of my youth: I am flattered at the happy coincidence which permits me to replace them in the memory and in the mouths of men, and to consecrate anew such revered names, in attaching them to the portions of a continent of which the Greek and Roman philosophers had not the slightest inkling.

"I see by the gazettes, that they built in the new state of Tenezee, a town destined to be the capital of another military concession, given by South Carolina to its contingent of the Continental army; they are going to name it Cincinnati. We shall soon learn the famous names of antiquity given to the subdivisions of this great concession.''

"But how does it happen," queried my companion, "that South Carolina can concede lands to Tenesee, a sovereign independent state which has just been recognized as the sixteenth link in the confederation of the United States.''

"Because in its act of cession, North Carolina has reserved the right to confirm all the locations of lands, as well as the promises it had made before freeing this part of the land lying beyond the mountains. The same was true of Kentucky (a division of Virginia) as well as in the cession which many of the states in the Union, of all federal lands, situated on the two banks of the Ohio and elsewhere.

"If I could transform my wish into law," continued Mr. Duwitt, "it would be from ancient history, according to the appearance of the place, according to Indian lore and legend or perhaps from some local circumstance that the settlements would take their names; our language furnishes an inexhaustible variety. This would perhaps wound the pride of our little founders of towns and districts, who never miss joining to their own names some hideous sounding suffix such as that of bourg or town or ville, such as Cooper'stown, White'stown, Harrisbourg, Nashville, etc. or those who have recourse to even more trivial sounding names such as Newbourg, Newlondon, New York, etc. What will posterity think when it is obliged to add the adjective new to the name of a capital or a land which will be five hundred years old? It was convenient to borrow some names from our old country when we were mere colonies, but today! it is time that we have a national nomenclature, just as we have laws and a Government that are strictly ours. I have heard the same observation made by various ones of our representatives to the legislative body. One must hope that some day it will concern itself with these matters."

"Are the costs of surveying very heavy?" asked Mr. Herman.

"Much more than they would be in a land already explored. The difficulty of tracing lines through thick forests or impenetrable swamps, through all sorts and kinds of obstacles, and the innumerable inconveniencies of which only those who have surveyed a long time have any idea, the lawsuits, the observations on the quality of the soil, the kind of trees, the streams, the falls, the maps demanded by the co-owners of a land grant; these are the factors that make surveying here more costly than in Europe. One must be young and vigorous to resist the fatigues of a long expedition. You would be astonished if I showed you the long series of observations and the detail of the operation which had to be made to determine the outlying boundaries, as well as the subdivisions of this great concession; they constitute a volume in folio."

Mr. Duwitt showed us a hydrographical map of the lake, rivers, and creeks in the state. This map had been ordered by the Government to make available knowledge of the utility and the possibility of canals whose construction it is planning. He told us of the difficulties he had met in completing the surveying of this state whose area is estimated at 35,474,000 acres (from the point where the 45th degree of latitude cuts across the St. Lawrence River).

He showed us also the great line of demarcation which divides the states of New York and Pennsylvania; it was traced on a roll of paper 50 feet long by eighteen inches wide. On it one could see the milestones, the peaks and the valleys, the creeks, the streams and the rivers, ten toise either side of this line. The beauty of the sketch, the exactness of the astronomical observations blended with the novelty of the idea. This line of demarcation is almost 260 miles long (86 leagues).

"Although this State whose capital was in the hands of the English for seven years, may have suffered more than the others," observed

Mr. Duwitt, "it is nevertheless the one which repaired its losses most promptly; no doubt this is due to the immensity of its territory, to the navigation of the beautiful Hudson River, as well as to the excellent attitude of our legislature, quite different from what it was during colonial times. The emulation inspired by the advancement of learning, by public spirit and the astonishing progress of Pennsylvania have contributed substantially to it also. That is why our Government lavishes so much aid and encourages companies which undertake the building of bridges, the opening of roads and canals. Of all those of the Union, this state is the first to copy the fine example of Pennsylvania in the reform of the penal code and the administration of prisons. The prison it has just finished building is most assuredly the most beautiful one in this hemisphere: its site occupies 640 square rods and cost 950,000 piastre (4,987,500 francs). Just as in Philadelphia, the inspectors are members of the Society of Friends. This prison is intended to receive criminals from the different sections of the state. Our legislature has also just granted 1,600 acres of very choice lands to the new college which is to be built at Schenectady [1] as well as a charter of corporation to the subscribers for 42,000 piastre destined for the construction of this building. You probably know what the State did at the time of the ratification of the new constitution in 1789, toward the beautifying of the State house of our capital to make it worthier of housing the new Congress; to be sure, it was quite inferior to the state capital at Philadelphia, known as State-House.[2] They have just established a dispensary [3] to the subscribers of which a charter of corporation was given. This establishment is founded on the same bases as the one which has existed in Philadelphia for a long time, and which every year renders such great service to suffering humanity.

"Who would have believed it," he continued, "the industry, activity, the successes of the founders of the city of Hudson,[4] the wise measures which have just been adopted by the founders of Esperance [5] have finally opened the eyes of the inhabitants of Albany [6] and made them emerge from their long lethargy. Extreme prudence, or rather timidity, that disposition for rigid economy, which their ancestors had brought from Holland, was extremely necessary in a country where nothing being plentiful, the slightest imprudence could have tragic consequences; but over here, where there are so many spaces to fill, where everything grows and flourishes with astonishing rapidity, one must permit oneself more than audacity, activity, and energy in speculations. In order that agriculture flourish, it is necessary that the intelligence and the enterprises of the businessmen continue to contribute labor-saving devices; that is what has started to take place.

They are at work clearing out the mud at Over-Slaugh [7] and soon there will be seen in Europe, in Jamaica, at Saint-Domingue, vessels built and loaded at Albany. The presence of the legislative body in that town has contributed measurably to the happy changes which have been evident. To what degree of prosperity is it not summoned when the bridges, canals, and roads already begun are finished and when the population of this part of the state will be increased tenfold, in the not too distant future, considering the great number of foreigners and colonists who arrive there every year!

"The same progress manifests itself also in many other States of the Union, especially those to the north. The Government of Massachusetts is constantly concerning itself with any project which can contribute to interior improvements and useful settlements. Where in these States can one see bridges as fine as those at Charlestown, Cambridge, Winesimet, Salem, Piskataqua, etc. The latter is 2,290 feet long, 50 feet wide, 52 feet above the river level, and the middle arch is 245 feet span. The arch of the bridge at Merrymack near Newburyport, measures 130 feet. These fine works were engineered by a man (John Coxe) who had no training whatsoever, but owes all his knowledge to an instinct for building.

"Last year, Mr. Osgood, director-general of the post, told me the revenue which in 1790, the time of the birth of the new Government, was only 4,000 piastres, had increased to 73,000 in 1796; and this, despite the considerable expenditures made by order of the president of the United States, to establish branches of the post office in regions still only sparsely settled. He also told me that the number of gazettes printed each week in this same state, was mounting to 67,000 without including those of Pitts'bourg on the Ohio, Lexington in Kentucky, and Knoxville in Tennessee. In a few more years," he continued, showing me a record of canals begun, finished and planned,[8] "most of the states will enjoy inland navigation from the Sounds at Albermarle, Pamlico, Currituck, as far north as the Bay of Massachusetts,[9] and from the Ocean as far as Lakes Erie and Ontario."

The next day Mr. Duwitt suggested an excursion on little Oxaruatetes Lake, only four miles from his camp, by way of the Owege River. We left, accompanied by companions from Oriskanny, whom he had often employed as hunters during his early expeditions. This pretty lake is only from 1,000 to 1,200 toise wide, and empties into Crooked River, an extension of the Senecca River; with the exception of several high points of land, its shores are uniform and composed principally of what are called Bottom-Lands. But what was our surprise, when instead of a canoe, we found ourselves starting forth on a raft with an improvised shelter attached, supplied with a bed of leaves to shade us from the hot rays of the sun; there was also a small improvised fireplace over which we were to cook the fish!

"Who designed and constructed this charming little raft?" asked Mr. Herman.

"One of my apprentices," replied Mr. Duwitt, "a young man who combines with his mathematical knowledge, skill and very special good will. This raft, made from various slabs of white cedar, was the work of only one day: I confess, however, that if I had been forced to linger longer in this region, I should have had a canoe built, with one of the beautiful pines which grow on the banks of this river; it would have taken from eight to ten days. But this ingenious substitute is adequate for my purposes."

"Did you say one of your apprentices?" queried Mr. Herman.

"Yes, why does that surprise you? Among the young men whom you saw in my camp, some are my assistant surveyors, others apprentices, to whom, by legal agreement, I am obliged to teach the little I know and who, by this same agreement, are obliged to survey, to sketch, and to record for me, for a certain number of years."

"Don't you find all this troublesome?"

"No, during the winter they learn trigonometry, design, the use of instruments, a little astronomy; and during the summer they put into practice what they have learned. I have only excellent pupils whose education has been very carefully looked after; moreover, if there are inconveniencies, they are compensated for by the tuition of one hundred guinea which they pay me. The same situation exists with apprentices to doctors and lawyers. As for the craftsmen, they are bound by contract to clothe their apprentices until the expiration of their services, and sometimes even to give them a rather considerable sum of money, according to the stipulations which have been negotiated by the parents of the apprentices, their tutors, their friends, or by the charitable societies which have put them in apprenticeship."

"Then this is the customary procedure throughout this country?"

"Yes, especially in our northern states. They consider teaching their young people a trade or profession, an indispensable and sacred duty which gives them knowledge frequently more useful than a mere inheritance. What would become of the young people in a land like this, where the great number of children and the smallness of fortunes necessarily require the acquisition of some ability which can lead them, if not to riches, at least to an honest subsistence? Besides, during the formative period of their lives, is it not necessary that they be guided? That is often the only fortune which the father of a large family can leave to his children; this is so true that the knowledge of a trade is always considered in their will as equal to one hundred acres of land. It is a resource against the reverses of fortune. On the other hand, if fortune smiles on them, they quit the trade they have learned. I know a man, famous during the revolution, who, since that time, has made a large fortune in business; his name is found everywhere among the associations whose aim is public welfare. Well! far from blushing over what he once was, he tells everyone who speaks to him of his successes, that he served his time (apprenticeship) in a marshal's establishment. I repeat his very words.

"If, by some extraordinary revolution, it happened that this custom were interrupted suddenly, the present state of our whole social structure would be completely upset; we would cease to be what we are, a hard-working nation, active and enterprising; we would fall into a state of paralysis, and our progress toward a more respectable order of things would be delayed. Moreover, one can see children who from their infancy have been accustomed to using their time gainfully, becoming almost invariably useful citizens—good family men. Apprenticeship is the great seed plot whence sprout every year our lawyers, our doctors, our businessmen, as well as our manufacturers, sailors, pilots, and craftsmen."

"What is the method for assigning young folk to apprenticeship?" my companion asked.

"For this purpose, we have a special legislation, over which the mayor of the town or some chief judge presides. It is in their presence that these arrangements known as "indentures" are made. Before these same judges the litigation rising between masters and apprentices is conducted. Everything is reviewed and regulated by their decision: the instruction, the feeding, the number of years, the vacation, the pay and the clothing which the masters are obliged to give to the apprentices at the expiration of the apprenticeship; as well as the hours assigned to them to attend schools during the autumn and winter months in order to learn to read, write, and count. Have you not observed in the towns, signs placed over certain doors, with these words, 'Evening Schools?' Well, those are schools designed for apprentices who belong to the lower classes. What good fortune, for example, for the son of a poor immigrant who in his old country led a useless unemployed life, to be learning a trade, with which, if he is wise, he will be certain some day to make his fortune, especially in a country like this, where workers are so rare and so dear, because of its rapid growth?"

"Since you mentioned growth," said Mr. Herman, "may I inquire what has been the increase in your population? So far I have been able to obtain only vague and uncertain information.''

"Surely," replied Mr. Duwitt. "The part of this hemisphere occupied by the United States, bounded on the north by the Sainte Croix, which divides it from the former French Acadia * and on the south by the St. Mary River, which separates it from eastern Florida ** and which at the beginning of the century, had only several thousand inhabitants, today has more than five million. The widely circulated opinion that we owe this increase to immigrations from Europe, is without foundation, as you will soon see. 14/15ths come from our own stock. But, you ask, what can be the cause of this progress? These: our customs, our habits which are those of a new and agricultural nation from the very beginning; the ease of acquiring land and of becoming a landowner; the absence of feudal and sacerdotal hierarchies; the numerous branches of industry, which on all sides offer ways of getting started, settling and raising a family; the lightness of the taxes; the flourishing state of our trade and our agriculture; added to all that, the form of our Government, so adapted to encourage, stimulate and develop all the germs of prosperity and growth.

"The greatest number of Europeans coming over in a single year has not exceeded 10,000; this was in 1792, two years after the new constitution; the growth of our population, that same year was about 149,971. In examining carefully this chart, result of long research, documented from the most informed sources, you will discover that our increase depends on no foreign cause; that the increases were different at different times—more rapid in some states, less in others. For example, the very sudden settling in the western counties of Virginia, whose population in 1780 was only 45,760 persons, and which grew in only ten years to 151,235, sprang from a great number of German families who left Pennsylvania. The same was true in Kentucky, which drew its population principally from Virginia, its mother state, and from the two Carolinas; although Kentucky also receives a great many colonists from Europe, as well as other sections of the Union. The first tree in Kentucky was not uprooted until 1775 and today this state contains 167,425 inhabitants.

"In examining this chart with attention, you will see that at certain times and in certain cantons, the population doubled in the span of 16 to 18 years; moreover, during a span of 20—22—24 years, that it shrank considerably during the war, especially in the states of New York, Connecticut, Massachusetts, and Rhode Island, which had fur-

* Today, New Scotland (Nova Scotia).
** Owned by the Spanish.

nished two-thirds of the Continental army. You will notice that the same cause has produced the same effects in the general population, from 1774 to 1782; you will notice also that the number of inhabitants of Rhode Island, has increased to only 8,000 in the course of nine years, that is, from 1774 to 1783; this is due not only to the great losses it suffered during the war, but also to the exaggerated form of its democracy in Government which disgusted perhaps 10,000 families who are now spread throughout the states.

"I am sorry that I was unable to procure more precise information to complete this chart; it would make it more interesting, but I wanted to compose it only from authentic facts on which you could rely. That is why I did not include, for example, the total population in New Jersey, except for the year 1785, having access only to certain details of the population of subsequent years.

"It is as the result of these examinations that I arrived at the average term of 20 years for calculating the annual progress of our increase in population just as the businessmen do, who add annual interest to capital, the rate of $3\frac{1}{2}$ per cent thereby doubling the capital in a 20-year period. According to certain evidence, this seems to me to be the nearest approximation, especially since the establishment of the Federal Government. This is the one, I have been told, which General Washington has adopted in the great work which he has just completed on this important subject: I am extremely flattered to find myself in agreement with him on my calculations and conjectures.

"This chart, based in part on the census of 1790 and in part on the result of the latest information submitted to the President of the Congress, seems indeed to give the rate of $3\frac{1}{2}$ per cent. Some times even, this rate has been higher in certain states: for example, the population of Pennsylvania, which in 1760 was 159,545, increased in 1780 to 329,045, which makes a difference of 9,165; furthermore, in 1790, it was 29,891 less; this was caused by the flood of emigration into Northern Virginia, Kentucky, and the Muskinghum River Valley. I am awaiting further details to know whether it will be more or less than this rate. If my calculations are right, the population in Pennsylvania must be, at the end of this year (1798) around 566,455. I know that at the end of last year the militia strength was 122,000 men. This number is further confirmed by the progress of the population of this state (New York), despite the war lasting seven years, the seizure of its capital by the British, and the devastations which they committed in several of its richest counties.

"The amount of cleared land in the United States is estimated at 31,602,000 acres: these are the bases on which are founded the survey of the progress of these annual yearly conquests. Let us take for example the growth of the general population from 1796 to 1797; this was 172,088; I have deducted from it half for the women, that leaves 86,044 for the male population; from this number I take one-third for those men who become craftsmen or sailors; that leaves 57,363, half of whom, I estimate settled on new lands; and half of the other go to work in new establishments, where the wages are very high. For a number of years, it is noticeable that as soon as there are 20 persons per square mile, or 32 acres per capita, or from 150 to 200 acres for each family, the surplus population migrates: I am supposing that each individual clears only six acres (the ordinary estimate) the first year of his settling; then the number of acres well or poorly planted, or covered with grain, will be 171,786. In supposing further that only half of these 57,363 emigrants in a position to buy these new lands are married (and it is rare that they venture forth to found a new settlement before marrying), then there will be in this year 28,631 thatched houses or logg houses, built in the entire span of the United States, and a comparable number of young households started.

"Such is, if I am not mistaken, the rough estimate of our yearly progress with respect to the population and new clearings based on contributions long pondered by our finest minds, and which I myself have followed with all the attention of which I was capable. Therefore, you have in the span of ten years, nearly two million more acres plied by plow and scythe and 286,310 more households, not to mention the marriages performed during the same interval in the other states.

"It is not astonishing, then, that the price of new lands is rising, if not in the same proportion as the number of small colonists, at least substantially. Lands worth 2 dollars an acre four years ago, today sell for from 3 to 3½ and even 4 to 5, according to the fertility of the soil, and the proximity of the rivers and roads. In general those lands having 20 persons per square mile, are considered valued at 14 dollars or 3 guineas an acre. On the other hand, the increase of the value of actual money and the revolutions in Europe have also contributed to its increase.

"431,662,336 acres is the estimate for the amount of land which is neither occupied nor sold, more than half of which is located beyond the Ohio, giving 100,000 acres per 1,139 persons. According to the annual increase in population by 3½ per cent, the chart below indicates the probable date at which these vacant lands will be inhabited at the rate of 20 persons per square mile or around 32 acres per capita; of course, after these have been acquired from the Indians.[10]

"I admit these results neither are, nor can be mathematically cor-

Pennsylvania contained in

Year	Number	
1750	89,945	
1760	159,945	
1780	329,045	} Settlers
1790	434,773	
1798	566,455	

The four northern States, conjointly with State of New York, contained in

Year	Number	
1750	444,000	} Settlers
1790	1,348,000	

The Western Counties of Virginia contained in

Year	Number	
1780	45,760	} Settlers
1790	151,235	

Massachusetts contained per square mile in

Year	Number	
1750	32	} Settlers
1790	60	

Connecticut contained per square mile in

Year	Number	
1750	20	} Settlers
1790	50	

Rhode Island contained per square mile in

Year	Number	
1750	23	} Settlers
1790	52	

In 1750, Number of Settlers

Massachusetts	197,685
Connecticut	104,000
Rhode Island	29,500
New Hampshire ...	34,000
New York	78,782
New Jersey	66,000
Pennsylvania	89,945
Delaware	12,224
Maryland	102,545
Virginia	254,545
North Carolina ...	82,300
South Carolina ...	110,400
Georgia	10,500
Total	1,171,426

In the Following Years the Thirteen States Contained:

Year	Number
1750	1,168,235
1774	2,141,307
1782	2,389,300
1790	4,000,000
1798	5,267,001

Taxable in Pennsylvania the Following Years:

Year	Number
1760	31,667
1770	39,765
1779	54,683
1786	66,925

Population of New York the following Years:

Year	Number
1756	96,775
1771	152,420
1773	168,007
1776	178,840
1784	212,468
1786	238,897
1790	354,120
1798	502,638

Number of Inhabitants in City of New York in

Year	Number
1697	4,302
1756	10,881
1771	21,863
1786	23,614
1790	33,131
1798	37,420

Population of Connecticut the Following Years

Year	Number
1756	129,994
1774	197,856
1776	204,935
1782	208,870
1785	217,524
1790	231,400
1795	249,140
1798	272,241

Population of New Jersey

Year	Number
1738	47,369
1745	61,403
1784	140,435
1790	184,139
1798	237,290

Number of Free-Holders in Massachusetts in

Year	Number
1772	71,779
1777	82,962
1783	90,575
1787	101,220

Population of Rhode Island

Year	Number
1774	51,897
1783	59,678
1790	52,543
1798	64,400

Population of Massachusetts

Year	Number
1763	241,024
1776	349,094
1784	357,510
1790	440,561
1798	560,790

rect; but they are probable—and sufficient, I hope, to show you the point whence we have come, where we are, and the one toward which we are rapidly going. It is reasonable to assume that toward the middle of the next century, our population will be between 28 and 30 million. Long before this time, labor having become scarce and more costly, people will be engaged in manufactures, for which we have in abundance raw materials such as iron, copper, lead, vitrifiable sand, wax, cotton, silk, vineyards, etc...... Then agriculture will be more scientific than it is today, considering the dearth of labor; for man does not become truly industrious until need pursues him and needles him.''

Then Mr. Duwitt showed us some of the reports he had made to the Government, and from which it appears that for 18 years, more than 22,000 families had settled in the north and west of this State. 173,000 acres of land had been cleared, 2 great forges built, 65 wheat mills, 102 sawmills, 47 fulling mills, and 11 oil refineries, not to mention the numerous factories for potassium and maple sugar. Bridges had been built, public roads opened in a land which in 1780, with the exception of a few scattered regions, was occupied only by wolves and bears.

''How much more interesting are these details of conquests made under the auspices of such a paternal Government, and those details on the savage and wild nature of marshy thickly forested lands than the details of the life of men who have laid waste the land, steeped it in ruin, crimes and misery, and who, instead of using their power to imitate nature by planting, fertilizing, and making things grow, used it only to destroy and ravage! One shudders, one's heart breaks, in exploring the bloody pages of history; it quivers and becomes faint at the sight of so many new creations and rapid developments of this young nation, scarcely 30 years old. Its period of transition from colonial state to independence has become an epoch doubly memorable, both because of the independence and the influence which this independence will already have had on the destinies of the world some day. How true it is that everything is linked, everything is involved in the life of individuals and in that of nations! Who would have been able to predict in 1766 that the discontent of the colonies, then strongly attached to their mother country, and so proud to belong to her, a discontent occasioned by the sending of a few rolls of stamped paper, and by some cases of tea, would have detached them from her forever? Who would have been able to predict that a cause so feeble might produce everything we see today? What will it be like within a span of time equal to that which has elapsed from the day when these first sparks were ignited, sparks which Great Britain might so easily have extinguished in putting a little more justice and a little less pride in her conduct?

"As for me," concluded Mr. Duwitt, "who was an eyewitness to the birth and development of these seeds, I can give you no more information on the subject. It is probable that if we do not experience too many great reverses, that if we have the good fortune to see our wise Government, obtain gradually the conservation of time and the dominance of habit; that if the dangerous mania of ideal perfection disappears, a mania founded on the alleged dignity of human nature; that if, in a word, the tutelary genius of some great man can some day cause calm and peace to follow the agitations rampant, or to put it better, the tempests which are upsetting Europe; it is probable, I say, that we will fulfill our destiny, which summons us to populate, to clear, to beautify this continent to its last cultivatable limits."

CHAPTER VIII

I have the following details, relative to the pyramids, the artificial mountains, and the arena one sees in Georgia, and the two Floridas, from Mr. B. . . . elected member of Congress since the birth of the new Government and in the last four years, United States Senator. At the risk of repeating some of the observations which have appeared already in the course of this work, I shall change nothing in the account of this worthy person. His observations are all the more valuable because he has lived in Georgia for thirty years and has himself seen some of its old monuments.

I shall close these details by copying faithfully what other persons have told me or what has already been published regarding the fortifications, the entrenched camps, and the tombs recently discovered on the banks of the Ohio, as well as in the neighborhood of Lake Erie. The reader will then have before his eyes the account of everything I have learned on a subject so new and so interesting.

"In examining these pyramids, these causeways, these amphitheatres dug in the ground, and these artificial mountains and the cantons in which they are situated, the first observation they present is that the creations are all at a considerable distance from the sea, located on sites that are remarkable for their fertility, and which appear to have been the centers of population, and finally that these are not military fortifications at all.

"What was the object of them? Were these monuments of religious significance or purely attractions? Were they observatories, altars, or tombs? As to the causeways, it is obvious that they were built to hold back the river waters or to make little lakes. The second reflection is that the forms of these works, being the same from the mountains of Tenesee to western Florida, it is beyond the realm of doubt that this part of the continent was inhabited by a nation, or by the union of several great tribes who spoke the same language and who had the same customs and the same religious beliefs; that these tribes must have enjoyed the advantages of peace for several centuries, since, although they knew how to build such remarkable pyramids, they left behind them no traces of their military labors and finally that they must have been quite numerous, civilized, and subservient to a powerful Government which could form and execute such vast projects and unite and feed so great a number of workers.

"But on the other hand, our colonists, in destroying some of these works, having found neither instruments of iron nor cut stones, nor brick fragments, how can we suggest that without the aid of fire, these pyramids could have been built to such a height, to form and consolidate these causeways? Did these ancient nations know what degree of civilization they had reached? Quite probably, but this is impossible to decide, located as we are, at so great a distance from them.

"We know from the tradition among the Cherokees, that at the time of their ancestors' arrival from the mountains of Mexico, these great works existed almost as one sees them today, and that the most ancient among the vanquished Savannucas,* did not know when and by whom they had been raised. This invasion took place toward the end of the fifteenth century. If one supposes that among the nations of hunters, 300 years suffice to erase the very last traces of tradition, then the existence of these monuments dates back to the twelfth century. How regrettable that its feeblest lights were extinguished! Did they emanate from the high antiquity of these works or from the stupid ignorance of our Indians?

"Was this nation aboriginal? How many centuries must it have existed as a nation before being able to raise these pyramids and dig these arenas? For what purpose were they destined? What is the degree of civilization to which man can aspire without the knowledge and use of iron? What were the religious opinions for which these pyramids were designed? What was the plight of these nations? Could they have been destroyed by some great catastrophes of nature? That is not reasonable since their works entirely built on earth still exist. Could they have been exterminated by the barbarous newcomers from the interior of the continent? If that is true, how can we conceive that a numerous people, capable of raising such imposing and massive monuments, can have been completely annihilated and that the knowledge and enlightenment they acquired may have perished with them without being carried elsewhere by those who escaped—or at least the conquerors keeping alive some of its sparks?

"Does its existence predate or postdate the existence of that ancient people on the banks of the Ohio who built there and elsewhere entrenched camps which have been discovered in recent years? According to the careful examination made of these, and likewise of the earth around them, in the first, as well as those on the Ohio, there is no evidence of iron nor of cut stones; therefore, one could believe them to be contemporaneous. If one can conceive that a peace-loving people such as the one which inhabited this state and the two Floridas, can have been destroyed by barbarous nations, to what cause can one attribute the entire disappearance of the warring nations of the Ohio country,

---

* This was the name of the ancient Indians of Georgia and the mountains of Tenessee.

who were able to erect such formidable boulevards and choose such strategic war sites? If these works date from the same epoch, which would seem to me quite reasonable, the same unknown cause must then have destroyed both the warring and the peace-loving tribes, although separated by a distance of more than 200 leagues.

"Like the pyramids of Egypt, these traces of the existence, the industry, the civilization of the ancient peoples are merely useless and silent witnesses, whose connections with the ancient state of this part of the world are enveloped, lost in the vague shadow of the past. However, although these entrenched camps, these works are merely imperceptible points, little hillocks, compared with the grandeur of those rivals built on the banks of the Nile, the observer beholds what North America reveals of the most ancient, the most extraordinary, and the most worthy of being closely examined.

"I consider these worthy ruins as the background of a great tableau, through whose light and vaporous shadings one can distinguish objects and whose foreground represents the recent arrival of the Europeans in this land, as well as everything they have done here in the last century. But, unfortunately, like the horizon at sea on which one can see neither rocks nor breakers, nor any objects by whose aid one can appreciate distances, the span separating these two great epochs, deprived of intermediary points, is merely a vast desert with neither trees nor bushes on which the observers' eyes can rest. One seems to have been the end, and the other the renewal of things.

"I would be quite curious to know the opinion of the learned minds of Europe whose enlightenment, works, and thought often reach me across the Ocean to enlighten and instruct me; whether, like me, they considered attentively these ancient works on the same land where a great population swarmed and cultivated in unknown bygone times; whether like me, they observed, admired these oaks of enormous height growing today on a soil which once upon a time was covered with harvests.

"But since after all we can form no more reasonable conjectures, one must believe that these industrious and peaceful nations must have been exterminated by barbarous hordes from the interior of the continent, which in the course of centuries, were destroyed by other tribes no less ferocious; the latter chased by the Cherokees from the mountains of Mexico; and these in turn by men coming from Europe. Such has been the fate of almost all nations; all have suffered nearly the same vicissitudes; all have had to struggle or have been the pawn and the victim of the caprices of that fearful and unknown, which we call destiny, fatality, or chance.

"Twenty-five miles west of Wrights' not far from the banks of the Little River, one can see in the middle of a fertile plain several artificial mountains, whose bases are from 700 to 800 feet in circumference, and from 30 to 40 feet in height; a pyramid whose dimensions are much more considerable; 4 terraces in the shape of a square, 10 or 12 feet high; and finally a sunken arena surrounded by four tiers of benches which, as far as one can surmise, must have contained 3,000 spectators; and even further on, the obvious marks of benches and ancient plowed ground on which have grown enormous oaks; I have measured some which had diameters of 4 feet 7 inches. The pyramid alone, whose height is about 55 feet must have taken the work of several thousand men: thanks to its shape, to the thick bushes as well as to the roots of trees which cover it, it still exists almost intact.

"Further on, toward the west, on the banks of a great natural prairie, one sees works identical with these I mentioned, but whose dimensions are smaller, or which have been more affected by weathering.

"At some distance from the banks of the Oakmulgue, whose meeting with the Oconee forms the Alatamaha, one sees also the obvious traces of the habitation and the long and persevering industry of an ancient people, such as remains of terraces, arenas, hillocks, and pyramidical elevations, near which have been found fragments of pottery of a far more perfect kind than those used by our Indians.

"The most amazing works and the ones worthiest of exciting curiosity, are found in the neighborhood of Fort Dartmouth on the banks of the Keowee (east branch of the Savannah River), 100 miles beyond the town of Augusta.* The first object the traveler beholds is a circular pyramid whose base is almost 1,000 feet in circumference, whose height is seventy feet, as far as I am able to judge—without the aid of instruments—and whose summit is crowned with cedars. One climbs up there by a spiral-shaped path on which at the different heights and at the four cardinal points, one finds four niches. From the height of this pyramid, one can see several minor ones. Some are square, others form parallelograms; some are 200 feet long, and from five to twelve feet high. But what seems more astonishing, is a causeway more than three miles long, which the river waters never submerge, although they bathe the base of the pyramid with frequent inundations. How did this ancient nation defend itself against these floods which took place three or four times a year before raising this causeway above their level? What reason did they have for building this pyramid? If it was to

---

* Capital of Georgia, built on a beautiful plain at the extremity of the sea-going boats of the Savannah River, 100 miles from the sea; on the route which leads to the Creek nations and to the Mississippi.

shelter themselves from the waters, why the necessity of giving it such great height? These vast terraces and causeways—were they not sufficient, and besides, why did these people choose such a low place?

"Six miles further, one enters another valley known as the Cullsate —just as beautiful and just as blooming—in the midst of which one sees great and long terraces and two pyramids 30 to 35 feet high. This valley is not exposed to the inundations from the Keowee.

"Further on in the mountains not far from the site of the old town of Sticoe one sees another pyramid whose circumference is 800 feet and whose height 48, with a very considerable embankment. The same objects exist at Cowee, principal town of one of the most fertile valleys in the Tennessee (as well as various cone-shaped tombs). An old Cherokee chief told me that at the time of the invasion by his ancestors, these tombs and artificial hillocks existed in almost the same state.

"Several miles from Fort Prince George at Keowée one sees also several cone-shaped elevations which are believed to be tombs, and four artificial mountains covered with trees and bushes. At Watoga, a Cherokee town of considerable size, there is a pyramid, whose height the inhabitants have reduced to twenty feet, on which they have raised their rotunda, or council place. Old Oweekamwée repeated what I had heard at Cowee about the tradition of the ancient Savannuccas.

"Not far from the town of Keowée, they have recently discovered some other ancient works, the only ones to bear the imprint of the hammer: they are composed of four stones six feet long and three feet wide; two of these stones are placed edgewise and in a parallel direction, a third covers them and the fourth strengthens one of the ends.

"A long time ago in the two Floridas, monuments similar to the ones mentioned were discovered, as well as causeways which appear to have been raised to form ponds, and roads aligned on the same level leading to the neighboring savannahs; also some fragments of elegant pottery and urns. The most considerable of these works are located not far from Lake George on the St. Joan River, as well as at Taenza, on the Mobile River; at Otassée, at Ufalée, Talasée Muclassée on the Talapoosa or Oakfuska, at Kiolége on the Coosa at Uche on the Apalachucla, etc. Is it not surprising that the Indians considered with the greatest indifference, these ancient and respectable witnesses of the long habitation and the industry of the nations which preceded them and who in bygone days lived and farmed this beautiful part of the country? The same is true of the whites who carry on trade or live among them. One young man, a good surveyor and passable draughtsman, had undertaken to make the plans of these works and to sketch views of them; but unfortunately several Seminolle hunters found him and took him to be someone who had come to survey their land stealthily (something which to them is an unpardonable crime); they were on the point of killing him when he had the presence of mind to show them his pictures. They took him to the Myco of their village who released him; but out of deference to these hunters, they threw into the fire his drawings and his plans and he was forbidden to return among them with any instrument."

Details concerning the ancient fortifications located on the Huron or Bald-Eagle River which empties into the southern part of Lake Erie. Sent to General Washington June 29, 1789, by A. Steiner.

"The foremost of these fortifications, number 1, is located 220 toise * from the east bank of this river, 8 miles above the mouth of this lake. It is a plateau of 300 feet diameter and medium height surrounded by a circular platform 3 and one-half feet high, and 7 to 8 feet thick. Twenty-four feet beyond this first rampart one sees another like it, part B, having the same height and the same thickness, but this is nothing more than a semicircle. Just like the first, it is surrounded by a ditch 4 to 6 feet wide, still filled with water. On this esplanade there are no stones or any vestiges of ancient buildings. The entrance C is not defended by any protective breastwork. Toward the northeast, one sees 34 tombs at D, 60 to 70 feet in circumference and 3 to 4 feet high, whose shapes are partly circular, partly elliptical. The first ones are only 5 feet from the ditch; there are four others at D toward the northwest, whose dimensions are the same.

"Two miles below on the banks of the escarpment E of the little stream which empties into the Huron, one sees a hillock, number 2, surrounded by a double platform and ditches beginning and ending on the banks of this same escarpment; the only difference is that instead of the one entrance, this little entrenched camp has three at G. Toward the south there is another platform at H, also with a ditch, but whose shape is not a perfect circle, and which does not appear to have been erected for any purpose other than to cover the two principal entrances. Not far from the most southerly entrance are two elevations on land K and I which converge at the wall or platform. The first, which is circular, is 50 feet in diameter and only $2\frac{1}{2}$ feet in height; the second is a square of the same height and 70 feet on the sides. There are few tombs in the neighborhood of the entrenched camp; one sees a few more scattered further away and in the same direction.

"These ancient fortifications are covered with bushes and with trees

* toise—6.39459 feet.

whose trunks are 18 to 26 inches in diameter. On the crest of the tombs, I saw a dead oak 30 inches in circumference. The soil in this region is clay on which there is a very feeble vegetative growth. The forests consist of white and red oak, beechnut, and linden trees. The Indians, a mixture of Chippaways, Delawares, and Wyandots, told me that according to tradition, these military works had been raised by men who were much taller and stronger than they are; that at the time all the tribes were in a continual state of warfare, that their hunters had discovered various other fortifications: some similar to these, others more extensive; and that these ancient Indians used the shoulder plate from the stag and the elk [1] as we use iron shovels.''

Report of J. Hart, captain in the First Regiment, concerning the ancient fortifications discovered on the banks of the Muskingum at a half mile from the confluence of that river with the Ohio.

''For the sake of greater clarity, I shall call the town number one, the fortifications number 2, and the pyramid number 3. The town is a square of 220 toises surrounded by platforms which are 6 to 10 feet high, and 20 to 40 feet wide. Three openings divide these platforms into four almost equal parts. Those facing the river seemed to me to be a little larger. Nothing covers the four corners of this town; one of the openings of the west side serves as an exit to road M, 120 feet wide, leading to the lower parts of the river by a gentle slope of 60 toises: this route is closed in on two sides by a platform which begins 60 feet from the platform at the town, and rises as the passage to the rivers lowers, in such a way as to keep constant the river level. The bed of this road appears to have been made by shelvings on both sides, and is accompanied by two ditches which perhaps served as the drain of the waters from the town.

''Toward the northwest corner of this same town one sees an elevation B, in an oblong shape 37 toises long, 22 wide and 6 feet high; the surface of it is perfectly uniform. Four ramps or inclined floors, I, converging toward the center, I, from four sides, lead to it; they appear to correspond identically with the openings of the platforms or walls of the town.

''Not far from this wall toward the southwest one sees another elevation G, 25 by 20 toises; but instead of 4 ramps, it has only 3 :I, I, I. The site of the fourth R, appears to have been dug. A little further to the northeast is a circular-shaped elevation surrounded by four little excavations, K, placed at equal intervals. Toward the southeast one sees another, H, whose form is a parallelogram 9 toises wide and 18 long; it is much more deteriorated than the others. The most southerly corner of the town is covered by a work of a very special type: it is a fairly high hillock N accompanied by two semi-circular parapets X. It is probable that the three other corners of this town were defended by works similar to this and destroyed by time.

"The fortifications, number 2, form an almost squared grouping which, like the town, is surrounded by platforms whose entrances are defended by the hillocks S. Those of the openings TT are double. Between the fortifications and the town one sees excavations, some circular heights Z, and tombs W, number 3. The pyramid B is almost circular; it is 50 feet high and 390 in circumference; it is surrounded by a ditch five feet deep and 15 wide as well as by an exterior parapet, A, which is 759 in circumstance. This rampart has only one opening, R, and is preceded in the direction of the Ohio by some breast-works, C and D.

"Several other hillocks have been discovered, excavations and platforms covered with bushes and trees whose ensemble is not visible in its entirety; that is what made me decide not to include them on the drawing of the map.

"The trees covering these ancient works are oaks 2 to 4 feet in diameter, hickory, maple sugar trees, ash, sycamores, acacias, planes, pines, etc. The vegetative soil on which they grow seems to be as fertile as the one nearby. The tombs, 11, are little elevations in which human bones have been found. It appears that the bodies had been inhumed with much care and placed in the direction of east and west. On the chests of some of the bodies chalk has been found. The bones of others have been calcified or dried in order to preserve them. Here have been discovered also stones which bear the imprint of fire, as well as carbon, arrows, and fragments of pottery.

"Elsewhere, scarcely no iron was found, nor anything else which can lead one to guess that this ancient people knew this metal. The uniformity, the regularity of these boulevards, their advantageous location, the height, the width of these platforms, all attest to the fact that they were built by a numerous, powerful nation, considerably advanced in civilization. Doctor Cuttler, famous botanist, who has carefully examined the oak trees which have fallen from decay, as well as those which are still in full vigor, believes that the latter belong to a second generation; this would date the time of the building of these fortifications to perhaps one thousand years ago.

"Imagine my surprise, when in setting forth for the first time in the midst of these ancient and venerable forests, the sight of these tremendous works told me that at a very remote time in the past, these places, today solitary, had been alive with the presence and activity of a very numerous, industrious, and warring nation. The regularity of these fortifications, the enormous quantity of earth with which these ramparts and this pyramid have been formed, all these objects, although certainly very striking, astonished me, however, much less than the total disappearance of this ancient people and the passing of their tradition.

"It is probable that this part of the continent was heavily populated, for if the extent of these entrenchments was proportionate to the number of people whom it defended, it was also to that of the attackers. If ever they were attacked, I do not believe that the number of besieged ones and the besiegers can ever have been less than 10,000; and if one out of ten was a soldier, the surrounding countryside then must have contained 100,000 inhabitants. The same reasoning being applicable to the other entrenched camps discovered in Kentucky, on the two Miami river branches, and elsewhere, it is obvious that the land watered by the Ohio and its branches contained a great number of people. What has become of all those people? How did it happen that the newcomers, who at the time were merely barbarians, preserved none of the arts nor the knowledge which the conquered must have acquired? How can we conceive that so vast and fertile a region is today inhabited only by a few hordes of hunters scattered at great distances from one another with whom one sees no traces of culture nor industry, except some fields of corn planted by the women? I leave these vague conjectures to the research and meditation of the savants of Europe and of our capital cities, who have a thousand times more knowledge and leisure time than I."

Cross-Creek on the Ohio, May 4, 1789 *

"It will probably seem astonishing to you, sir, to learn that a country which until now we have never believed to have been occupied by any people other than our Indians and their ancestors, offers clear and indisputable proof of the long habitation of ancient nations, old tribes, which must have been numerous and far more civilized than the ones of today.

"On the southwest branch of the Ohio, almost opposite this little colony, fortifications of earth have been discovered whose shapes are very regular, although quite different from those in Europe; I saw them during the autumn of the year 1787; but the trees, the bushes,

---

* This letter, written to Doctor Wetherspoon, president of the college at Princeton, by one of the inhabitants of the little colony of Croosic Creek on the Ohio, is a new proof that this continent must have been formerly inhabited by populous tribes. I have transcribed it with so much fidelity that I have not even wished to cut out certain other observations, although they have nothing to do with the discovery of the ancient fortifications.

and the herbs, by which they were covered, prevented me from examining the entirety with as much success as I would have wished. Thus, I have decided to see them once again in the spring before the budding of the leaves in order to send you more precise details about them.

"Not far from the mouth of Grave Creek one sees two tombs or conical shaped elevations, in which human bones have been found. Mr. Worth, a well-educated man, who has explored these regions, told me that he had discovered in this very neighborhood, the ruins of a town as well as those of walls or platforms of earth by which the town was surrounded; since these two cone-shaped elevations were only a short distance from the town as were some other entrenchments, he believes that they were designed as lookout places for marksmen who could effectively disturb the inhabitants of this town.

"On one of the branches of the little Kanhawa, they have found two grindstones from a mill, remains of a dam, and traces of a little canal which brought water to the place. Mr. Worth also told me that he had seen on one of the branches of the Monongahela, a rock whose surfaces seem to have been polished with such care, and which bore, engraved in six columns, faces of men, birds, and fish. On it one could see several lines written in characters which were unknown to him as well as to those people who have seen them since. In several other regions they have discovered tombs containing human bodies enclosed in coffins of baked and glazed earth. The bodies' arms and legs were likewise in a kind of cylinder of the same earth, soldered at their furthest extremity to the body in the coffin. The sheaths for these legs were 18 inches long.

"In digging in a salt pit on the banks of the Yoyogheny, they discovered six feet underground, a collection of china and a funnel of wood as well as several fragments of pottery and bowls. It appears in certain regions that the ground must have been cleared. All the trees covering it are young and in full growth; one sees none, as elsewhere, which are declining, withered, or fallen into decay. What, then, was that nation, today extinct, which inhabited this region for several centuries? According to the Shawanese traditions, it was a Mexican colony. But on the other hand, it is obvious that there was at one time another nation, perhaps aboriginal, perhaps coming from some other part of South America, and whom the state of continual warfare in which they lived for a long time, obliged to keep arms constantly at hand; for, without mentioning these entrenched camps, nor these regular fortifications which have been discovered in several places, one meets on almost all the heights neighboring these waters, traces of redoubts—lines of defense of a considerable extent.

"All that we know is that the Indians who occupied this land 200 years ago, did not know by whom these entrenchments had been raised and who had inhabited them at the time of their arrival. Whence came these hordes? It is a question to which their descendants cannot reply. One becomes lost in conjectures stimulated by inspection of these venerable witnesses, as well as the contemplation of this ancient state of things.

"Here we have nothing which merits the attention of travelers, except fountains and our trees. Among the former, there are some whose waters are extremely salutary: but who among us is qualified to analyze them? The height and the thickness of the trees of our forests are truly extraordinary; one sees none like them in our northern country. The principal species are the white oak, the red oak, the black oak, the white birch, the walnut tree, the black and the white ash, the yellow and white hickory, the two types of beech tree, the elm, linden, sugar maple, sassafras, poplar, wild mulberry, the sycamore, etc. Almost all the plants and flowers they cultivate in your country with so much care, grow wild here; wild allspice, ginseng, sasparilla, snakeroot, ginganvre (ginger), several kinds of mint balsam, mint, sage, etc.

"One notices on the banks of the little Kanhawa, a very peculiar gaseous spring; it gives forth fumes which attach themselves to surrounding objects and seem to breathe a sulphurous substance. But in the third year of the founding of these colonies beyond the mountains, you must not expect these interesting details on everything novel and curious which this climate and beautiful nature offer the eyes of the botanist and the naturalist. One must first, as you know, clear, sow, harvest, build dwellings, plant orchards, dig wells, before concerning himself with scientific objects. We are only at the first period of our existence, that of work and industry. How many years will elapse before we have among us men whose leisure time will permit them to acquire knowledge and who will be in a position to answer all your questions in a satisfactory manner!"

For fear of being accused of whimsical judgment, I thought before submitting the account of Captain Isaac Stuart to the reader's eyes, that I should inform him of the following details. According to an ancient tradition in Wales, it appears that at an unknown time some chiefs of that nation led a number of their compatriots across the Ocean and disembarked in the land known today as Louisiana. For several years, many travelers are sure they have discovered the posterity of these Welsh people; I do not know how it happened, but their stories have been forgotten. However, since the evidence of the existence of this ancient colony may have some connection, or may cast some light on the time when the ancient monuments which I just mentioned to you were built, I believed I should transcribe in its entirety, the account of Captain Stuart, after previously informing the reader of the varying degrees of authenticity which accompanied its publication.

Mr. Stuart, officer in the colonial cavalry of South Carolina, having embraced the royalist party from the very first moment of the revolution, embarked on board the English war vessel, the "Peacock." On the recommendation of Lt. Colonel Cruger, he obtained the command of a detachment of sailors of this vessel. The details he supplied to the captain of his former journeys into the interior of the continent, relative to the discovery of the nation of Indians who spoke Welsh, seemed so interesting to this officer that on returning to Charles-Town, he had them published in the gazettes of that town. This account excited public curiosity, and the following certificate was inserted in the newspaper of New York, then occupied by the British troops.

"I, the undersigned, certify that the account published by Captain J. C. Ecuyer * commandant of His Majesty's Ship, the 'Peacock,' in the gazettes of Carolina March 1782 conforms to the details with which I supplied him, and is in reality the true story.
Signed in New York, June 2, 1783, Signed, Isaac Stuart

Another certificate from the captain of this same vessel, dated from Sainte Marie in eastern Florida, October 17, 1784, adds even more weight to the authenticity of this discovery.

Although since that time, I have heard nothing pertinent to it, I thought I would not neglect making a faithful copy of this very exact account concerning the fertility, the richness, and the magnificence of the plains, through which run all the rivers emptying into the western branch of the Mississippi.

No doubt one will be astonished to learn that neither the Government of the United States, nor the literary societies have conceived the notion of dissipating these doubts, if they are not founded, or of verifying such an interesting discovery. Perhaps the expenses of a journey to the sources of the Red and the Arcansa rivers which are only 700 or 800 leagues from Philadelphia, would not have amounted to more than 400 to 500 guineas. With what enthusiasm the savants of Europe would have sent learned men to see if indeed this Welsh nation existed, and to bring them back details concerning the extent, the fertility of these lush plains, details about the plants of a soil located in the most favorable latitudes, on the nature of the trees in the forests by which

* Thus did the commandant of the vessel, the "Peacock" designate himself in the gazettes.

that part of America is shaded—treasures unknown to the Spaniards, masters of so many regions which will be long useless to them. One must agree, the region stretching from the Mississippi to the mountains of New Mexico, from Santa Fe, from California, is almost as little known as the interior of Africa, although crossed by many great and magnificent rivers.

One will be even less astonished at this oblivion, or rather this indifference, in recalling that the political existence of these states dates back scarcely twenty-two years; that the existence of the Federal Government, true epoch of their union and their prosperity, did not begin until 1790; that this age is one of youth, of activity, of enterprise; that nobody here is lazy; that everyone is busy with his own affairs, his own speculations, trade, means of increasing his fortunes and never before, has such a vast field of industry and activity offered itself to men; that the spirit of the Government is rather one of protection than of action; and finally that literary societies are composed only of individuals who, like others, are busy with their own affairs, and scarcely have time to attend their meetings. Things will not be this way in another half-century.

Narration of Mr. Isaac Stuart, published in the gazette at Charles-Town, in March 1782, by the commandant of the British war vessel the "Peacock."

"I was taken prisoner by the Indians about 18 years ago, being 50 miles west of Fort Pitt. With several other whites I was led to one of their villages, located on the Wabash. A few days later, my unfortunate companions were massacred with the most horrible barbarism. My good fortune directed me to inspire some interest in one of the women of this village, who adopted me and gave a horse as ransom for me. After a stay of two years, a Spaniard arrived, claiming to have come from New Mexico, and to be traveling in order to make discoveries. Having need of two rowers, he obtained permission from the chief to take me into his service, along with a certain John Davey, a Welshman by birth. Soon afterward, we embarked and went down the Ohio and the Mississippi as far as the mouth of the Red River. After resting several days there, we went upstream for about 700 miles (233 leagues) and entered one of the Red River branches (Post River) where, to our great astonishment, we found ourselves in the midst of a nation whose people were white skinned and had red hair.

"The very next day after our arrival, John Davey sought me out to tell me that these Indians spoke the language of his country very well and he had decided to stay among them. Extremely astonished at what he had just told me, I went to the wigwam of one of the chiefs whose language indeed seemed quite different from the language of the nations with whom I had lived. They told me, through John Davey, that their ancestors had come to settle on the banks of this river some time after the conquest of Mexico by the Spanish, and the invasion of western Florida, where they were then settled; and in order to convince me of this story, they showed me several rolls of parchment enclosed in a beaverskin, on which were a great many characters written in blue ink; but since I knew no Welsh, and my comrade was unable to read, I didn't know what they contained, nor could I verify what the chiefs had told me.

"This nation is divided into two classes: warriors and farmers. The former are brave and fearless and their women more beautiful than those of other nations. After spending some time among these Welsh, the Spaniard and I embarked once more and continued up the Red River as far as the village of another nation, the Wyandottes, who claimed they had never seen white men nor firearms. While exploring a little stream which, after crossing a great plain, plunges into the cavern of a mountain, we discovered the skeleton of an animal which must have been of an enormous size, if one can judge it by the length and width of its ribs, its vertebrae and the weight of its molars. The Wyandot nation lives in the neighborhood of the Red River, not far from its source. It was there that the Spaniard discovered gold dust, which surprised me very much, not having ever seen any before: he was busy picking it up when someone told him that further west lived a nation among whom this metal was so common that the warriors decorated their arrowheads with it. Before arriving there, we covered 500 miles: we had to cross a chain of mountains whose streams ran in a westerly direction. Happy and content, my Spanish companion resolved to travel no further but to settle in this land; as for me, I had a wife and children. I left him and in the company of another white from Louisiana, we crossed several immense plains which led us to one of the branches of the Missouri, from which, by going down the river we reached the Mississippi. After resting at Pancore, I reached the land of the Chikasawa on the banks of the great Yazou, from there to the Chectaw country and finally among the Cherokees, whence I returned to Fort 96, in South Carolina.

"I do not know how to describe the lands I explored west of the Mississippi; one would have to be astronomer and geographer to be able to determine the extent of them. What idea can I give of these plains, so fresh and so fertile? Some are covered with reeds across which a horseman can wander or often lose himself: others by some gramineous plant whose name I do not know, and especially with yellow and red clover three feet high. The trees in the forest announce by their very height, the fertility of the soil on which they grow. It is the haven of a great number of deer, roe, bear, and buffalo which come to spend the night there, after exploring during the daytime these endless savannahs. I have sometimes come upon vines attached to these prune, apple, and wild orange trees whose fruit at so great a distance from cultivated lands seems delicious to me. I do not believe that there is in the land soil more productive for the raising of corn, tobacco, indigo, and rice. One settlement, located near the sources of the Red and Arcansa rivers could easily furnish enough for all of Europe. Compared with the soil of our colonies, the latter is like the Garden of Eden. As to the transportation of these commodities, nothing could be easier; they would build, with the fine wood of the neighborhood, great bateaux which would carry the commodities down the river to the Mississippi and even to New Orleans. I noticed in some places rocks in whose formation there is much salt, which all the animals of the land come to lick during the heat of the summer. The shapes of the hollowings which they have made with their tongues in the long course of centuries, are so bizarre that at a certain distance they resemble bas-reliefs and offer the imagination, the likeness of men, animals, trees, landscapes, and often even fantastic objects.''

Although the following details have no connection with what I have just said, persuaded that they have bearing on the condition of the continent in bygone times, and besides, having seen in the office of Mr. Edwards of Stockbridge, the object about which I am going to speak, I thought I would insert the details here.

''They have recovered from the bottom of the Chemung River or Tiogo (branch of the eastern Susquehanna) ten miles above its confluence, the bone or the horn of an unknown animal. It is 6 feet nine inches long, 21 inches around at one end, and only 15 inches at the other. One can see at the larger end a hollow which is 6 inches deep and 2½ inches in diameter, similar to a bull's horn which has been removed; the rest is all solid. The exterior is uniform and white as ivory, a little bronzed at one place only. The color of the interior resembles calcified limestone, burned, but not yet dissolved. The form of it is round without any mark which would indicate that there was a joint of any sort. According to the broken appearance of the two extremities, it appears that the total length of this horn must have been considerable. Its curvature is that of a large circle. When it is rubbed, it gives off an odor which resembles that of the horn or of a burned bone.''

CHAPTER IX

Incorporation is a bill or an act of the legislature under an appropriate name, which unites in a corporate body a certain number of persons and grants the permission which they have requested for the execution of a given project. This bill is contained in an official charter with the great seal of the state; its preamble always announces the object or aim of this bill in the most precise manner.

There are several kinds of bills. Charters destined to incorporate young colonies, towns, villages, and counties are quite different from those which sanction business associations whose aim is the propagation of knowledge or public welfare, such as colleges of medicine and literary, religious or philosophical societies; the founding of churches, hospitals, libraries, chambers of commerce, marine or charitable societies, large schools, savings banks etc.; or those institutions in short whose sole aim is special interests, such as insurance houses, banks, construction companies for the building of bridges, canals, highways, etc.

They give to the subscribers or members of the associations the authority to assemble, to deliberate, to register their decisions, to elect a president, a treasurer, or several secretaries, to make all the rules (known as bylaws) necessary for the administration and execution of the project. They fix the value of personal and public property owned by these groups and give them a seal with which their acts must be stamped; and finally, according to circumstances, they invest the societies with the right of renewal, as well as the right to transmit and regulate, and bequeath their vested interests.

When it is a question of public works, these charters prescribe the conditions for them, or the rents or the tolls of the usufruct—either for a limited time or forever—according to the nature of the enterprise or the will of the legislator. But the reasons for which one seeks and obtains these charters are so varied that it would be difficult to define all types. As soon as the signers or subscribers have become a corporate body, they form in the eyes of the law one single body or individual, which through its president or committees can attack or defend, can be prosecuted in courts, invest funds, float bonds, recover debts, buy or sell as an individual would. Each member is responsible only for the amount of his own investment.

The use of these charters is very ancient, as one sees in the history of England. They have served as bases for the establishment of most of the colonies, as the foundation of the towns and counties. Even today the constitution of Connecticut, for example, has undergone no changes, although like the others, this state has become independent and sovereign. Thus, one can say that it is still based on the same rights and contained in the same charter, accorded in 1662 to its founders, by Charles I.[1]

Nothing is more inviolable nor more sacred than these charters. They are concessions, solemn and irrevocable pacts between the governments and the citizens, which neither laws nor courts can annul, except in the case of forfeiture. Among the great number of wrongs which Congress alleged as motives for the famous Declaration of Independence,* one of the most substantial was the violation of these charters, on the faith of which the earliest colonists had left England.

As to those charters intended to incorporate cities, they are concerned with the manner of electing municipal officers, naming justices of the peace, magistrates, the police and prison officials, with the collection of municipal taxes, with the granting of different privileges, such as those of sending to the legislative body a certain number of representatives. They deal with the ownership and the improvement of navigation rights on the rivers and waters, the possession of inundated lands and public property; the power of establishing ownership of this public property is considered mortmain. The municipal property in the city of Albany is 12,500 acres, and that of New York, likewise very large. In general, the incorporation of the large towns ** whence emanate their prosperity, and the rights of citizens, are acts of the greatest importance. The charter of Philadelphia is a model, a masterpiece of wisdom, enlightenment, and expediency, perfectly adapted to the spirit of the new Government, of which it is a miniature, so to speak; it would serve to administer a good-sized region.

Public prosperity, being nothing more than the total of family and individual prosperity, these charters which unite and concentrate the efforts, the means, and the interests of a great number of persons, and direct them toward a common end, which sanction pious and praiseworthy views, or useful projects of these associations, these charters, I say, have contributed substantially in this young land to the development, progress, and perfection; and to cap the good fortune, the spirit of the Government, even in colonial times, has always been more kindly disposed toward protecting than governing.

Next to the laws of safety and justice, there are none which are more useful. How many churches, religious institutions, charitable societies; how many savings banks for the use of widows and orphans,

---

* July 4, 1776.
** Before being incorporated, they are known as towns; and after the incorporation, they are known as cities.

asylums for the indigent, literary societies, schools known as academies, how many have been supported by these? How many bridges, canals, and other worthy projects have been made possible by the ease of obtaining these charters, and the confidence which they inspire, especially since the independence and adoption of the Federal Government?

One can say that the greatest share of religious, civil, business, literary, and charitable institutions in the United States owe their origins to these private associations, sanctioned by law and consecrated by charters of incorporation: churches, hospitals, factories, canals, dispensaries, colleges, etc.

The colonial Government, as well as the one which succeeded it, having never exacted any but the most indispensable taxes for the expenses of administration, has laid the foundation of these useful establishments, these beautiful institutions to public spirit. These charters are one of its principles; for they are, as well as being the property, also holy arches, placed by opinion and law above the reach of the Government as long as the associations conform to the text of these charters, which otherwise, can be annulled.

Without this fortunate expedient, what would this country be, whose several states have not more than thirty years of political existence to their credit, whose regions, longest inhabited scarcely more than a century, and nine-tenths of which are still covered with forests? Most assuredly, affairs would not be so far along, although they are still inferior to what they will be some day. Too young to bear up under the weight of taxes, what would the Government have done to construct these buildings, found these societies, build these bridges, dig these canals? Public spirit, that curious mixture of love and good weal, personal interest, and vanity have filled this need.

And what does it matter whence it comes, this weal, so rare on earth and so difficult to obtain? If the waters of my stream are good and clear, if they are abundant enough to irrigate my trees and my pastures during the hot month of August, it interests me very little to know that the stream source runs down the side of a mountain or comes from the depths of a swamp.

And even if these governments had been able to raise the necessary sums, what difference is there between giving voluntarily or being forced to pay? One offers with pleasure what might have been demanded of him. What a difference, above all, between the most total civil nullity and the noble pride of contributing to the various establishments of one's country, of participating in the advantages which come from it, or in the welfare which then bring it to fruition?

It is then that one is doubly a citizen, for one clings to his country, to his region, to his native town, by a great number of bonds.

One must have lived in the countries where man is nothing and the government is everything, in order to appreciate the happy influence which these associations have sanctioned by law. What good will they not accomplish some day when the progress of population, culture, and industry will bring forth a greater number of new creations, and when riches, enlightenment, sciences, and arts will have multiplied the resources and means of perfection?

A brief survey of the institutions, fruits of the piety, charity, or of the public spirit, in the city and the state of New York, authorized by these charters, will contribute perhaps toward making what I have just told you more intelligible.

Almost everything good and useful that one sees there is the work of chartered associations, except for the three Anglican churches, founded and endowed by Queen Anne. The others (there are sixteen of them) were built by societies to which these charters gave perpetual ownership, as well as self-administration; that is to say, one of benefits which have been given or which could be bequeathed immediately by these churches. Such are the magnificent hospitals founded during colonial times by a subscription, considerably increased by new gifts and by the Government, which assures its existence, and according to the advice of the society of doctors has prescribed for it the wise administration which one sees today.[2]

The marine society, whose aim is to give pensions to widows, and to raise the children of those who perish at sea on an annuity proportionate to the amounts that have been put in the chest. Most of the foreigners assume it a duty to become honorary members, averaging an annual subscription of 42 francs; and the sailors whom fortune favors, leave their savings to augment the funds of the society and to enable the administrators to put them where they will do the most good.[3]

The society of pilots contribute some of their earnings in order to insure, like the others, by the annual sacrifice of a moderate sum, subsistence for their wives and children. The Port-Warden, chosen among the most respectable sailors, is automatically president of it. This institution is put under the special inspection of the Government, from which emanate commissions known as branches, sealed with the official seal of the state. Without these and without an apprenticeship of seven years and several qualifying examinations, no sailor is permitted to present himself as pilot on board the vessels.

Nothing is more wisely organized than this association. The pilots are divided into a certain number of classes, each possessing a schooner of 60-foot keel and 60-foot mast whose construction and rigging are the fruit of long experience. No one knows any vessel which sails better nor closer to the wind; they draw 8 feet of water stern and 4 at the bow, they are sturdy craft and cost between 16,000 and 17,000 francs. Each of these schooners gives its name to the class to which it belongs; it is under this name that the accounts are kept and reviewed every month by the Port-Warden. At first they estimate what the graving and the upkeep have been; finally the total which, according to the rules of the associations, each pilot owes to the chest: the rest is divided among them.

The religious societies known as congregations (there are ten sects). Besides the temporal administration of these churches, accorded by their charters of incorporation, each one of them directs a school, in which the principles of religion, reading, writing, and arithmetic are taught to the children. The richest of these societies dress those of the poor and often assume the responsibility for putting them into apprenticeship.

An Irish society, called St. Patrick, has been established to help the immigrants from that country, who arrive in a destitute state or who need advice.

The Scotch society whose object is the same for people coming from Scotland is called St. Andrew; the English society is called St. George.

The society of Craftsmen is charged with administering its treasury in which the members of this association are obligated to put a certain sum every month and from which they can draw assistance in their illnesses.

A society to encourage the freeing of slaves, and to protect those who have become free. It has founded a school where they teach the children the principles of religion, reading, writing, and counting. The present governor of the State is its president.

A society to assist the prisoners, and to pay the debts of those who have been arrested only for negligible amounts.

A society for the library, destroyed during the war and rebuilt since. It was formed anew in 1786 by a great number of subscribers to whom the Government granted, a short time afterward, a charter of incorporation, and the municipality gave beautiful rooms in the city hall (formerly Federal Hall).

Columbia College founded in 1754 by the most respectable persons in this colony, aided by the current legislative body of the time, and by the city church. The Government has since richly endowed it, given it a new charter, making it a university of which the several academies, founded by public spirit in the various counties of the state, are constituent members. These academies are:

Flatbush, founded in 1786 by the inhabitants of that fine district of Long Island; it is known and has been incorporated under the name of Erasmus.

The Academy at East Hampton, founded in 1787 by the colonists of the county of Southampton, at the eastern extremity of the same island, known and incorporated under the respectable name of Clinton, who was then governor of this State.

The Academy at Goshem, founded in 1787, by the inhabitants of Orange County, known and incorporated under the same name.

Eight others founded in various parts of the State, which like the ones mentioned above, are under the surveillance of a permanent committee, chosen every four years by the majority of the subscribers.

Literary Society, established in 1788; as yet it has not published anything.

Society of Medicine, one of the most useful and best organized on the continent.

Society of agriculture, whose representatives to the legislature are automatically members.

Society for the encouragement of manufactures.

Society of the Dispensary; this is the headquarters for apothecaries who furnish drugs, medicines, and cordials to those who bring a certificate from one of the subscribers. This society pays an apothecary and a doctor whose responsibility it is to give consultations and to visit the sick. The number of those whom it helped from the very first year of its founding was 972. The small subscription is for 5 piastres (26 francs); the large for 50 piastres (262 francs). It was incorporated shortly after its birth.

The Government chartered in 1792 an association which had formed the project of opening a communication by water with Albany, to Lake Ontario (it is partially carried out), and the same year another company which was to unite the waters of Lake Champlain with those of the Hudson and to perfect the navigation of this upper part of the river.

A charter has just been granted to a third association which from the district of Cortland, is to bring to the town a part of the waters from the Brunks (Bronx) a good-sized stream, located 25 miles away, and which by means of an aqueduct will cross the river at Harlem, whose width is 170 toises.

All the churches of the little towns in the interior, as well as those of the counties, are the fruit of the piety and zeal of the associations which have been incorporated. Many of these churches have been endowed by the Government or by private donors; that is to say, they possess the rectory and the fairly extensive land for the use of their pastors. In 1773 one could count in this colony 192 incorporated churches.

There are several other little associations, charitable and literary, which I do not mention, since they are not incorporated.

These establishments are much more numerous at Philadelphia[4] and at Boston.[5] One is astonished, however, not to see yet any dispensary in the latter town; it is probable that the good done by the ones at Philadelphia and New York will make the inhabitants of all the towns in the Union imitate such a fine example.

Since, after all, it is only in associating with one's fellowmen that man can find strength for his weakness and help in adversity, is it not astonishing that these institutions are so rare—the desire to forge a protection to safeguard from attacks of tragedy as well as tap balsamic springs where the sick can benefit by salutary waters—and is it not also extraordinary that these common funds are not more widespread among the different classes of society, especially in the capitals of Europe?

There, nothing is more common than to see workers in these capitals, like the Indians here, spend in wild orgies the fruits of their industry. The latter, in order to relax, they claim, from their long and arduous winter hunts plunge themselves into a delirium of drunkenness and even boast of so doing; the Europeans under pretexts equally frivolous, often consume in one day the savings of the future and the subsistence of their families. Although raised in the midst of civilized societies, surrounded since childhood by religious precepts and salutary counsel, they are just as careless, just as heedless as the children of nature placed by her in the bosom of the forest. This disposition, then, is in nature itself, since it resists the influence of education and the precept of example.

Yet nothing seems to me easier to create than these institutions, which sooner or later, will become in all civilized lands, the support of the weak, the consolation of the wretched, and the resource of impecunious persons. Suppose 500 workers deposit in a chest two cents a day (and there are none, especially in the capitals who cannot afford this little sacrifice); there, from the very first year is a saving of 36 francs per capita and consequently a capital of 18,000 francs which can be advantageously allocated to public funds; and if in this city there were a dispensary to which that particular town subscribed 500 francs, for example, that is to say 20 sous for each society, it is obvious that being able to obtain from this apothecary's shop, the consultations and all the medicine necessary, a great number of sick persons would be relieved or cured at very little expense and for them that is a very appreciable advantage. The same reflections can be applied to all other establishments, whether charitable or financial, which in uniting a great number of small savings would form an inexhaustible treasury of aid to help the needy and ease the weight of the miseries of life. The idea alone of being cared for in the bosom of one's family and not at the hospital, would it not bring to birth in all hearts the desire to see these beneficent societies becoming general?

How many other advantages would result from the creation of common funds? Activity, industry, sobriety, emulation, purer customs. Like a faithful monitor, the desire to increase the financial total of each month, would of necessity lead to disintegration and dissipation; these associates would become better fathers, better husbands, and consequently more respectable and more useful citizens.

Could I terminate this little sketch without mention of the promulgation of the new penal code and of the new prison regime of Pennsylvania in 1793? No. The following details, I hope, will give some idea of it.

The prison built several years ago in Philadelphia is a good-sized building. One of the wings contains the cells built according to the plan suggested to the legislature by various members of the Society of Friends. Spacious courtyards, filled with workshops, occupy the interior of the yard.

In accordance with the new penal code, the pain of death is inflicted only in the case of premeditated murder; other crimes, even that of high treason, are punished by solitary confinement whose duration is proportionate to the enormity of the crime. This punishment, it has been observed after a successful experiment lasting several years, has much more effect and inspires a greater degree of terror than death.

Indeed, the criminal, alone in an abode of shadows, silence, and solitude, prey to inactivity and boredom, is not long in feeling the prick of remorse and bitterness of repentance. Thus, the wisdom of the legislature has achieved the aim it set for itself: of reforming rather than punishing the guilty. This is a sublime notion which no legislator had ever conceived, and which no criminal code had ever put into practice!

As soon as a prisoner has entered, they shave his head, wash him, give him new clothes. Then he is shut up in the kind of cell prescribed by the court which condemned him. Is his crime among those which used to prescribe the death sentence? That cell is very dark; he can neither hear nor see anything; it is the void of a tomb. Every morning, the jailor to whom he is strictly forbidden to speak, brings him his pittance of bread and water. There he expiates, during the prescribed time, 'mid the cruelest reflections, the crime he has committed, or the wrongs he has committed toward society.

Such is the most extreme degree of severity which the new laws of Pennsylvania permit to operate for all crimes which do not include premeditated murder. The second degree is a cell: just as solitary, but lighted. The third degree a larger cell in which the prisoner is permitted to read and busy himself. The fourth degree permits the prisoner to work with others.

With the exception of the part occupied by the cell blocks, all the rest of this prison resembles a great factory in which no one is idle; here one sees tailors, shoemakers, weavers, gunsmiths, locksmiths, and nailmakers. They are paid wages comparable to those in town. These wages provide for their daily needs. Whatever is left, they may keep. Some have been known to come out far richer than they had ever been in their lives. Everywhere silence and decency reign; they are not permitted to laugh, to sing, nor even to speak, unless it be for something indispensable. The terror inspired by solitary confinement as well as the diet to which the prisoners are exposed, softens the most hardened characters and maintains everything in the most perfect order.

This prison is governed, or rather administered, by directors chosen annually from among the citizens of the town; and it is always on the most respectable that the choice falls. Three of these directors constitute a committee of inspection making bi-weekly and sometimes daily visits to the prison. The new criminal law stated that the Governor of the State, the Mayor of the town, and the Judges of the Supreme Court will automatically be the inspectors. On the basis of the report which the committee makes to the general assembly of directors, when it is supported by the judges, the fate of each prisoner is decided; these reports—more or less favorable—are based on the conduct and on the progress of his penitence; for mild hope has not been banished from this institution, which has become more a place of retreat than one of punishment. What happy results emanate daily from this effective discipline?

Twice a week the prisoners change their linen and are shaved; twice monthly they are taken to the baths. Their daily diet consists of soup and pudding from corn meal; only Thursdays and Sundays are they permitted meat, and under whatever the pretext might be, they have only water to drink: an admirable regime which keeps the mind and the body in a state of quiet and calm that is very efficacious to the progress of their regeneration! An idea worthy of Pythagoras!

The women prisoners, numbering only a few, separated from the men, devote themselves to occupations suitable to their sex. Every Sunday, the prisoners not in solitary confinement go to Church services, which, according to custom, always include a sermon. The ministers do not limit themselves to this duty: they mingle with the prisoners, conversing with them, consoling them, encouraging them, and instructing them. It is difficult to get an idea, without having been witness to it, of the good performed by the penetrating and inspiring influence of these contacts. It is the dew from the heaven which revives these plants, long withered; it is a healing balm of Gilead applied to chronic ulcers.

And these altruistic inspectors, whose zeal and boundless charity I have often admired! How much they contribute, by the potent force of hope, whose sole dispensers they are, as well as by the veneration which their virtues inspire, toward directing gently these lost men to a feeling of penitence, and God-fearing, and to making them worthy of resuming their places as useful members of society! For, when the conduct of a prisoner has long merited their approbation, not only do they consider it a duty to recommend him and to place him advantageously as soon as the period of his expiation is over, but sometimes they are instrumental in shortening his sentence!

No one can enter this prison without express permission, signed by one of the inspectors; this is difficult to obtain. There is a large and beautiful infirmary where the sick are well cared for; but sick people are rare here. The diet of work, cleanliness, and sobriety to which they are subjected, has become an admirable preservative of their health.

I should consider myself guilty, if I were to end this feeble narrative without mentioning the person to whom United America, and some day Europe, I hope, will owe the reform of the penal code and that of the prisons whose customs and regime thus far have been so barbarous. Could I name Caleb Lowndes, that virtuous man, that respected member of the Society of Friends, whose piety, founded on the most sublime principles, as well as love of fellow men, has inspired the zeal, the constancy, the perseverance necessary to effect such a great change? For good is accomplished only with difficulty in all times and in all places. And how many obstacles he has had to surmount! With what gentle patience has he not borne denials, ridicule, and contradictions!

Finally, having had the good fortune to communicate to one of his friends,* the sincere belief that absorbed him, and to kindle in his heart the desire to perform great good, these two persons whose names will never be forgotten, succeeded in persuading the judges and in enlightening the legislative body which lost no time in passing the law unanimously for this dual reform, one of the most important and most memorable of this century.

May it be permitted to a foreigner, long a witness of their courage and their efforts, long an admirer of their generous devotion, to extol them as the shining example of their country and worthy of men's gratitude.

Will I ever see some of these germs transplanted to my country? Its soil, which for so many centuries has nourished so many wild and exotic plants, would certainly be as favorable to their growth as is this one. If the sea and winds are favorable, I will see it again, my native land, before a year. There I received my education, there I lived; in her bosom are the remains of my ancestors, near whom my remains will be buried.

Like a little bee which, fleeing its hive at dawn, returns only toward dusk, bringing the most precious findings, on my return after an absence of so many years I shall dare speak of what I have seen, of what I have observed in my long travels, unknown though I am. My too feeble voice will not be heard, I fear; but what does that matter! I shall have fulfilled a sacred duty, acquitted myself of a compulsory obligation. Other travelers, more distinguished than I, by virtue of their talents, but not by their zeal, will write and will be favorably heard; I do not despair, therefore, of seeing the Pennsylvania criminal code adopted, as well as the new regime of its prisons, the sailors' societies, the repositories of benevolent funds, the dispensaries, etc., in a country where one has only to express a desire to see miracles accomplished.

Moreover, are we not nearing the end of the 18th century? Does not everything announce that the next century will bring in its wake one of the most memorable and one of the greatest epochs, designed to bring to birth ideas and inventions until now unknown, unforeseen, as well as everything which is good and useful that human ingenuity and industry can produce?

* Mr. Bradford, attorney general of Pennsylvania.

CHAPTER X

For some time I had been visiting Mr. G., head of one of the first families of New York, and my old friend, whose farm is located on the fertile banks of the Passaic[1] in the State of New Jersey. Mr. Herman, whom I then believed to be in Nantucket, where he was to visit for several weeks, sought me out and invited me to share the pleasant hospitality and the instructive conversations which I enjoyed in the home of this worthy colonist. Although he was trained to enter business and had spent part of his life at Ste.-Croix,[2] Mr. G., wiser than so many other businessmen whom greed and habit hold to their counters until old age, had set himself a limit to the fortune he would make. As soon as he reached this limit, he left his business and came to this charming retreat to enjoy its riches and attractive leisures; if one can call leisurely one who busies himself with the chores of farming or irrigation devices, nurseries, inspection of a large garden, and finally the reading of good books, that delightful nourishment for the soul.

Mr. Herman entertained us with the numerous observations he had made during his sojourn in Nantucket, a sandy isle, enriched by industry and the maritime enterprises of the fishermen who live there. It is indeed remarkable to have been able to increase, in the span of seventy years, possession of a few whaleboats,[3] with which their fathers went eight or ten miles along the coast to harpoon whales, to a fleet of fifty sailing vessels which venture forth in all latitudes to pursue and harpoon this enormous fish.

Although my companion was well acquainted with everything concerning the Society of Quakers, he was nevertheless very impressed with what he saw among the inhabitants of this island of 25,000 acres. The first two days he talked of nothing but their intelligence, the daring of their enterprises and of their successes. This journey had enriched his diary so considerably that Mr. G. could not imagine how this little plot of land could have given birth to so many pages of ideas.

This did not astonish me in the slightest, when I recalled the effect which the contemplation of these same objects had produced on my mind more than twenty years ago. Mr. Herman told us that the families from Sherburn who had settled at Dunkerque in 1785 had just arrived from there, the reason for their stay at Dunkerque having been destroyed by the war, and that on the return of peace they planned to return there. He was telling us about the boats which come and go along this island to the continent, the commodities, the property, about the person who had brought him to New-York, when Mr. G. communicated to us the following observations.

"One must agree, the number of these ships has increased considerably since the consolidation of the new Government; that is truly astonishing. It is only at this time that a liaison was established—a close bond among these states, on land and at sea. In every direction, especially in the center and the North, new roads are being opened, present roads are being improved, bridges are being built; one sees diligences and coaches making their way. In all the ports they have started maritime lines whose ships are busy transporting from their region to the capitals people as well as commodities. These vessels constitute a fleet which extends from one end of the United States to the other, that is to say, from the bay of Passamoquid * to the north as far south as the Altamaha and Ste Marie rivers. The number and tonnage of these vessels are greater than one thinks.

"In 1785, 1,068 ships put in at Philadelphia, of which 567 were coasters coming from different states. In 1788 there were 857; 410 which were coasters.

"We have three wharves on this river, which is scarcely navigable for fifteen miles, and each one of them has at least two ships employed all year long in transporting to New-York the products of industry and farming. The same is true on all the creeks which empty into the Great Bay or flow into the Ocean. Thus, one sees hundreds of them arriving at and departing from New-York at each tide. Some come from Connecticut, from Massachusetts, Rhode Island, Long Island, etc., others from more southern points such as Nantucket, Philadelphia, and Albany, as well as the different landing stages on the Hudson River which furnish more than 300 vessels.

"But to give you a more precise idea of the importance of this coastal traffic and of the codfishing off the Grand Banks, I want to show you the chart on the details of our economy which I made with the aid of a very well-informed man. Consult the chart immediately following; you will see, not without some astonishment, that the tonnage of the fishing schooners and coastwise vessels constitutes nearly one-third of our navigation. These two branches of industry form a nursery or rather school whence leave every year a great number of excellent sailors.

"I am sorry I was unable to obtain authentic information in order to distinguish among the vessels dispatched to our ports those destined

---

* According to the postal registers 1,710 miles (510 leagues) are figured from the Bay of Passamoquidy below which falls the Ste Croix River which separates the United States from New Scotland (Nova Scotia) as far as the Ste Marie River which separates Georgia from eastern Florida.

Chart showing sea-going and coastal vessels and fishing schooners
of the United States, from 1790 to 1798.

	SEA-GOING			COASTAL		
Year	*Vessels*	*Crew*	*Tonnage*	*Vessels*	*Crew*	*Tonnage*
1790	1,814	19,047	362,823	1,415	8,490	113,181
1791	1,819	19,099	363,854	1,331	7,986	106,494
1792	2,073	21,766	414,629	1,513	9,078	120,997
1793	2,194	23,037	438,864	1,771	10,626	141,639
1794	2,635	27,667	527,194	2,049	12,294	192,686
1795	2,901	31,460	580,277	2,149	12,894	171,918
1796	3,375	35,437	675,046	2,505	15,030	200,372
1797	3,457	36,298	691,447	2,600	15,600	208,058
1798	3,601	36,910	720,247	2,694	16,164	215,520

FISHING SCHOONERS OFF THE GRAND BANKS

Year	*Schooners of 70 Tons*	*Schooners of 40 Tons*	*Total Schooners*	*Number of Fishermen*	*Tonnage of Schooners*
1790	300	138	438	3,228	26,622
1791	402	110	512	3,876	32,542
1792	396	109	405	3,832	32,062
1793	450	167	617	4,602	38,177
1794	337	92	429	3,248	27,260
1795	422	114	536	4,060	34,102
1796	480	118	593	4,548	38,320
1797	480	120	600	4,628	38,400
1798	476	129	605	4,582	38,480

	TOTAL SAILORS AND TONNAGE		FOREIGN TONNAGE	GENERAL TONNAGE
Year	*Number of Sailors*	*Tonnage at Departure of Vessels*	*Taken at Arrival of Vessels*	*Foreign & American Tonnage*
1790	30,765	502,520	464,563	767,089
1791	30,961	502,890	238,466	741,356
1792	34,676	567,688	244,278	811,966
1793	37,168	618,680	163,226	781,906
1794	43,209	747,140	82,974	830,114
1795	47,314	786,297	63,200	849,497
1796	55,015	913,338	47,846	964,184
1797	56,626	937,905	57,490	995,395
1798	57,656	974,247	not yet known	

for the Antilles[4]: the quantity and variety of commodities which we supply to these islands, are prodigious for it is to this continent particularly that they owe their prosperity based on the ease of feeding their Negro population.

"In 1788 the city of Philadelphia alone sent to the British Antilles 58,287 barrels of flour, and the entire exportation from Pennsylvania that same year was only 220,605; imagine what the islands belonging to the French, Danish, Spanish, etc. must have received from the other states. These annual supplies are put at six or seven hundred thousand pounds sterling.

"Here is another summary of the interior and exterior navigation of the port of New-York for that very same year 1788 two years before the establishment of the new Government, a time when I was retiring from business; you will see attached here another chart of the boat-building industry from 1784 to the end of that same year, 1788. I know how much better qualified you would be to judge our progress, if I had the same detailed information for that year! I was unable to get it because I have been busy with the cultivation of my fields and my acacias. Thus, you will judge from the point where we were ten years ago and the one where we were four years before that. This point of departure was zero; for the British, in sacking our city, November 25, 1783, left us not a single vessel, not a single schooner, not a single sloop.

"Supposing that most of these things were tripled, others doubled, then you will have a fair idea of our trade, our shipping as well as our agriculture and population.[5]

"I am convinced that the tonnage of the vessels belonging to the city of New-York has reached 220,000 tons today. The navigation on the Hudson alone uses more than 300 sloops of from 40 to 70 tons. This town, moreover, is famous for the thoroughness and promptness with which it makes repairs and improvements. That is why every year so great a number of European vessels put in there."

"In reflecting on the dearth of labor," said Mr. Herman, "one has difficulty in realizing how that has happened; I should think, on the contrary, that the ships could be repaired cheaper in European ports."

"Yet there is quite a difference," replied Mr. G., "because of the price of the masts, tar, and wood, items which this continent furnishes much cheaper than does France or England. Pennsylvania, Virginia, Maryland, and Massachusetts enjoy the same advantages, but New-York, being located in the center of the continent, has only eleven leagues of coastline; it is much easier to arrive there. Moreover, we enjoy the inestimable advantage of a ready and much needed supply

CONSTRUCTION

VESSELS

Name	Size	Wood	Price **		
Clinton	300 ton^n·	Live-oak *	9^l·		
Ann & Susanna	350 "	oak	7		
Betsey	300 "	Live-oak	10		
Favorite	275 "	"	7	12^s·	
New York	235 "	oak	6	5	
America	700 "	Live-oak	7	2	6^d
Betsey	275 "	"	8		
Mohawk	300 "	"	8		
Olive Branch	220 "	oak	6		
P. B. Espagnol	255 "	Live-oak	8	2	
Total—3,210 "					

CONSTRUCTED AT HUDSON

Vessels	Tonnage			L	S
2 Vessels	200	400	oak	5	5
6 Brigantines	150–180	990	"	4	18
6 Sloops	—65—70	402	"	3	18
Total Tonnage—1,792					

AT HUNTINGTON, LONG ISLAND

4 Brigantines	150–180	650	oak	4	5

AT COW BAY, LONG ISLAND

2 Brigantines	120–170	290	oak	4	18

IN OTHER PORTS OF LONG ISLAND

71 Sloops	45–70	4,047	oak	3	10

* LIVE-OAK, evergreen-oak; OAK, ordinary oak. The former comes from Georgia and North Carolina. The latter is found in great abundance in the inland states.

** The price of the construction of a vessel is always determined by the weight in tonnage of the vessel; this price includes the masts, the topmasts, the sailing yards, the rudder, the capstan, the

C H A R T

Showing shipbuilding and ship repairs made in New-York City and
elsewhere in the State of New York, from the first of
January 1784 to the end of December 1788.

C O N S T R U C T I O N

BRIGANTINES

Name	Size	Wood	Price
Mercury	150 ton^n	Live-oak	7^l
Young	90 "	"	6 10^s
Silva	70 "	"	7 1
Betsey	70 "	oak	5 10
Eole	80 "	"	5 10
Total—460			
Schooner, 1	60	oak	6
Sloop, 1	70	"	4 18

PILOT BOATS

Name	Keel (ft.)	Wood	Price
Fortune	49	Live-oak	775^l
Trimmer	50	"	810
Greyhound	49½	"	820
Le York	50	"	850
Total—160			

CONSTRUCTED IN NEW ROCHELLE

The Morris	320	Com. oak	6^l 12^s

CONSTRUCTED AT KAAT'S KILL

The Sally	320	Com. oak	6^l 4^s

S U M M A R Y
TOTAL CONSTRUCTION SINCE PEACE WAS DECLARED

In New York	Tonnage
10 Vessels .... estimated ...	3,210
5 Brigantines	460
1 Schooner	60
1 Sloop	70
4 Pilot Boats	160

At Eusopus

1 Brigantine	120

At Hudson

2 Vessels, 6 Brigantines, and 6 Sloops	1,792

At Kaat's-Kill

1 Vessel	320

At New Rochelle	Tonnage
1 vessel .... estimated...	320

On Long Island

6 Brigantines, 71 Sloops	4,997

On the North River

135 Sloops	6,075

On Staten Island

25 Sloops	1,300

bowsprit, as well as the quantity of iron used in the construction of the vessel.
 The pound in New-York was composed of 20 schellings, the schelling was an eighth of a piastre and this piastre was worth five pounds, six sous tournois; therefore, the pound in New-York is equal to thirteen pounds, 6 sous tournois. By means of this calculation one can see that the price of construction was from 33 to 135 pounds at this time. As for the so-called pilot boats, those fine schooners were designed to unite speed with sturdiness of construction, and are built with extreme care.

C H A R T (Continued)

R E P A I R S

TWO-MASTED BRIGS		ENLARGING A BRIDGE	PLANKING & TOPSIDE	ORDINARY REPAIRS
1st Ton$^{n.}$	2nd Ton$^{n.}$	Repair #1	#2	#3
1	95	150	120 vessels of	61 vessels	350 vessels of
2	90	150	100–150 Ton$^{n.}$	cf 100–300	varying sizes
3	120	160		Ton$^{n.}$	
4	90	125			
5	95	150			
6	70	130			
7	80	145	work has begun on the repair of a		
8	90	140	vessel of 250 ton$^{n.}$		
9	75	120			
10	90	140			
	895	1,410			

RESULTS OF TONNAGE

14 vessels	4,250
18 brigantines	2,520
238 sloops	11,894
4 pilot boats	160
1 schooner	60

Total Tonnage—18,884

Increase in Tonnage in ten 2-masted brigantines   515

19,399

REPAIRS

No. 1 Vessels of 100–150 tonn.	120
No. 2 " of 100–300 "	61
No. 3 " of all sizes	350

Total Vessels Repaired 531

from Georgia, cedar and mulberry from Virginia; this is a great boon
for a sea-going nation. The vessel in the construction of which one
uses these items is more costly, it is true, as you can see in the attached
chart, and it must be thus in view of the strength and long duration
of these woods. A vessel whose topsides are of cedar, resinous pine, or
mulberry, almost invariably sails better because these woods are very
light, although as sturdy as though ordinary oak had been used in their
making.''

After exploring Mr. G.'s fields, covered with wheat, corn, and clover
and returning along the bank of the Passaic up which a full-rigged
sloop was sailing, we spoke of the pleasure, of the advantage of living
near this pretty river, and of being only a short distance from New-
York. Mr. Herman said to him:

''How much you can congratulate yourself on having learned so
early in life to prefer the tranquility, the sweet independence of life
in the country to the chaos and worries of business and trade. That
is true philosophy: to make one's fortune when one is young and to
enjoy it in the decline of one's life. I know on the banks of the Hudson,
Mohawk, and Connecticut, more impressive locations than this, but I
have never seen any so pleasant. Each tide brings you the fish you
need by means of the ingenious nets placed at the extremity of this
wire fence. There is nothing happening in Europe which you cannot
hear about in the span of a few hours: everything you send to the
market leaves your wharf with great ease; you enjoy without any
inconvenience all the advantages offered by proximity to a large
town.''

''I agree,'' replied Mr. G. ''the contours, the gentle slopes of this
river, the fertility, the improved condition of the land through which
it winds, from its cataract, to its mouth—all that resembles, somewhat, places I have seen in Europe. You are not the first foreigners
who have appeared astonished to see such prosperous dwellings, fields,
and orchards so well tended. Do you know that with the exception
of some settlements on the banks of the Cohansey at Tenecum, Christiana, Wicococ * founded at the beginning of the 16th century by the
Swedes and some Finnish families, the clearing of this region is one
of the earliest in this part of the United States? Almost 168 years ago
the first tree was felled. The richness of the soil, the proximity to New
York, easily reached in three hours, since the bridges and embankments have been completed, the proximity to New-Ark,[6] the most
beautiful village on the continent, where workers and craftsmen are

---

* This is the name given by the ancient Lenopys to the peninsula on the part of which
Philadelphia was built; this site was occupied at the time of the arrival of William Penn, by
several Swedish, Dutch, and Indian families.

541

easily found; such are the causes which have contributed toward making this part of New-Jersey very habitable and much more carefully cultivated in the interior.

"This land is filled with red and white cedars with whose wood a very popular coopery is made; the mud of the river, the earth taken from the ditches of these vast meadows of New-Ark, as well as the seaweed which they produce, have long been an inexhaustible source of fertilizer with which we cover our land during the winter snows. Besides our vegetable soil which is deep, on a layer of clay everywhere, one finds streams used a great deal by industry; that is why the trees of the open forest and the orchards here grow with such rapidity and are so productive. You must have heard people praise the cider of this region, whence annually a considerable quantity is sent to the southern states. I have drunk some of it in Georgia, and it seemed even better than the cider here. Two months ago I had the pleasure of offering some to General Washington when he came to New-Ark. The orchards of this region were then in bloom; he found it almost as delicate as the cider made in Virginia from wild apples, and which is known as Crabb-Apple-Cyder."

"What!" exclaimed Mr. Herman, "you had the good fortune to receive this worthy man under your roof and chat with him! The keen interest, the respect which his name and his virtues inspire, have made me seek since I have been on this continent, every means of being presented to him; my efforts have been futile; I was able to see him only at church. More fortunate than I, a young businessman from St. Malo, whose voyage across the Ocean had no other aim, having been charged with an interesting mission on behalf of an agricultural society, had the good fortune to be presented to him and even to be invited to dine with him. His mission took him ten or twelve days, at the end of which he embarked to return to his country. A painter whom he had brought with him, stationing himself in the church opposite the general, succeeded in catching a very striking resemblance of him in the portrait he painted. If you know any details of his personal life, you would oblige me very much by telling them to me. How interesting must be anything concerning the private life of a man so famous—his habits and his way of living. As to his public life, I have read with the greatest attention, what History has already written in its records of his great deeds."

"Here is what I have heard about him," replied Mr. G., "and what I myself know of him. No one has ever known better the value of time and the art of using it, than General Washington,[7] he is very hard working, yet without being a slave to his work.

" 'It is not in doing too much all at once, but in doing regularly what each day demands, that one succeeds in accomplishing a great deal,' he says.

"All year long, he rises at five in the morning; as soon as he is up, he dresses, says his prayers with great meditation. Some time later he goes out to see his horses, looks them over carefully, often exercises them, and gives orders to the stable boys. After the visit to his stables he retires to his study where he works until breakfast, which consists almost always of tea and corn cake which he himself butters. He is not the only Virginian whom I have seen prefer the use of corn to that of wheat. From breakfast he returns to his study, summons his secretaries, and goes over their work carefully.

"As to his proclamations, his speeches to both houses of Congress, his replies to the numerous addresses which are made in his honor, and the letters he receives, he writes them himself, something of which it is easy to convince oneself when one knows his style, which has rhythm and a very special phrasing. His first speech as President of the United States is a model not only of declamation and eloquence but also of wisdom, depth, and lofty thoughts.

"Almost every day, he invites for dinner delegates to Congress, senators, public officers, as well as the foreigners who have been presented to him. Everything that leaves his tables destined for the use of prisoners is immediately taken to the jail; this rule has been constantly observed during the time when he lived in New-York as President of the United States, for it was during his stay in that town that I had frequent opportunities to see him and to know his family intimately. He never had any children, those one sees in his home are the grandchildren of his wife, who was a widow when he married her. In my day, he never went to the theatre without them. I have seen them on his knees.

"Almost always grave and serious, it is only after drinking two or three glasses of wine, and after being stimulated by conversation, that he becomes gay and his face brightens. They say that during the war, no one ever saw him laugh and that even by himself he rarely smiles. His great height * and the reserve, or rather the dignity of his bearing, give him a very imposing appearance during Congressional sessions. He seems much less serious at the teas of Mrs. Washington; then, mingling with the crowd, he chats more freely with the people he knows—and sometimes with the ladies. I have often seen him on fine summer days leave town, accompanied by some friends, to go walking in the country.

* He is five feet nine and one-half inches, English measure.

"He always wears homespun clothing and at his table uses only American-made linen, plates, and utensils. And these owners lose no time in giving him their first products. Sundays, he never misses going to church service, accompanied by his family. His mind, being more solid than brilliant, he seems to conduct himself according to the inspirations of a sense of right and natural wisdom rather than from knowledge acquired by reading. It is at the school of experience and meditation where he equipped himself for administration and affairs. The revolution having given him the opportunity to meet or talk with a great many people, and to appreciate their talents, his choices have all been fortunate.

"However, out of respect for those who recommended friends to him, he made a note of it on a special memorandum. This is something I have seen him do many times.

"Brave without ostentation, human without weakness, generous without recklessness, how many times in the course of the revolution, did he not come to the rescue of the unfortunate and how many times did he reward courage and good deeds? How many tears did he not drop in the silence and obscurity of the mysterious, a mystery which was revealed only by the voice of gratitude! He unites the qualities and virtues which honor man, citizen, and great magistrate: wisdom and moderation, enlightenment, humanity, modesty; virtues which have earned him the esteem and veneration of his compatriots and assure him that of his contemporaries as well as of posterity.

"Such was he as Commander in Chief from 1775 to 1783, as a private citizen from 1783 to 1789—finally as President of the United States from the last epoch until his retirement from the Presidency in 1796.

"From the time of his appointment as Commander of the Continental Army, he had the good fortune to silence slander, to mollify exhibitions of jealousy, to unite the opinions of his fellow countrymen; and through the confidence he inspired in them, he knew how to direct their efforts toward a single, united aim in freeing his country.[8] This singular good fortune was even more remarkable when the new constitution was ratified. Well! Who can say today what would have happened if by a marvel of unanimity he had not been elected to the presidency; and especially if during the early infancy of this constitution, the supreme magistrate, had not, like a great lover, attracted so many people, concentrated so many scattered wishes, and gradually enfeebled the influence of those who feared the union of great interests of this land under an effective government?

"What would England not have done—or even Spain? What would

not have been done by so many other persons whose customs and principles, ease and fortune had been destroyed by the war—the number of them was considerable. How many I have seen calculate with greed all the probabilities of the nonacceptance of this new form of government?

"Never do I think of this memorable time, of this unexpected event which finally invested this continent with legislative power, without blessing a thousand and a thousand times this marvelous chain of circumstances and happenstances which I have long observed with all the interest and the attentive calm of a good citizen. It is probable that, after being able to resist the dangers of novelty, as well as the crises which have assailed it since, this Government, which has repaired so many tragedies, so many hopes, opened so many sources of industry, enterprises and prosperity, will consolidate itself and will finally merit the respect and gratitude of the inhabitants; unless, blinded by passions, by the craze and fury of political parties, at the risk of burying itself in its own ruin, they destroy their own work: then one would have to despair of human nature, and like so many others, believe that it is not worthy of enjoying the benefits of liberty, and believe that finally a popular and wise government is a chimera."

The next day in going down the river to fish for salmon towards the bay in New-Ark, the pretty craft of Mr. G. struck a reef which the pilot had not noticed. The tide was going out rapidly so we needed great time and effort before being able to put ourselves afloat.

"It is my fault," said Mr. G., "that this accident happened to us, for I have known this reef for twenty-two years; in vain have I hoped that the violence and ices of winter would rid us of it. It is not a rock, but the stern-post of one of the vessels which were sunk here sometime before the British army landed on Long Island in 1776. Among the privateers of New York, some sent their ships up the Hudson; others, more fortunate, led them to this river, where after unstepping the masts, they sank the ships in twenty-seven feet of water, on a muddy bottom. In 1784 they were raised, drained, and brought to New-York where they were soon repaired."

"Never having heard of these operations," said Mr. Herman, "I would take great pleasure in learning by what means all this was accomplished; would you be kind enough to instruct me. These operations would seem to me to be difficult and dangerous."

"Nothing is simpler to effect than these," replied Mr. G.; "by means of holes drilled in the bottom of the hold, these vessels were sunk in two hours; of course, after they had been completely unrigged and the masts unstepped. As to the operations of raising them, you may well imagine that it must be more difficult. The owners, accompanied by their friends, arrived here, supplied with tenders, cables, and pumps which they had borrowed from the town; divers attached one end of the cables to the hooks with which these ships were equipped, the other was attached to the hand winch; after much effort, and aided by the tide, they were raised to water level with the exception of the one which we struck. With the aid of pumps, the deck was soon dried so that one could walk on it. This operation took much time and trouble, because the slightest movement of the vessel caused it to ship water. As soon as this drying operation was finished the pipes of these same pumps were placed in the hatch of the large hold, the hull was emptied in the space of a day and the holes were immediately plugged. On the tide of the third day, they were taken to New York, where they were put in drydock until the sun had dried them. You may judge what an enormous quantity of mud must have covered and filled them. The effect of this immersion was to harden the beams to such a degree that they are still in use.

"As to the hull already used in this early time, it was replaced, as well as some parts of the topsides; but what will perhaps seem astonishing to you, is that the gunwales made of acacia had not even been damaged. Indeed, this wood is everlasting, particularly under water. That is why such an extensive use is made of it; that is why every year so many of these trees are planted; their yield at the end of a few years is considerable. In walking over my land, you must have noticed how careful I have been to cover every bit of land with them which the plow cannot work. I know a doctor who in his youth had the presence of mind to plant a field of sixty acres *; today his income from it is a thousand to twelve hundred piastres yearly; with no expense other than the maintenance of fences. It is on Long Island and in the state of Rhode Island that one sees forests planted by man's hand.[9]

"After these submerged vessels have been repaired anew, remasted, and painted, one would never believe that they had spent eight years in the bottom of the Passaick. Two of these brigantines which were sawed in two and lengthened twelve feet, are still boats used in the commerce with South Carolina."

"What—sawed in two!" said Mr. Herman. "What could be the reason for an operation which certainly must have weakened them and also have been very costly?"

"It was done in order to give them a larger hold, and often even to increase their speed."

* At Hyde Park on the Hudson.

"That would seem to me to have been very dangerous; for in acquiring a great length of keel, and in conserving the same width of bow, it would seem to me they could no longer be rigged with the same sized sails they had formerly used."

"In this country such an operation is performed only on those which were too wide in proportion to their keel. You will notice on the chart that in the span of four years, ten brigantines were sawed and lengthened, and that their capacity which was only 895 tons, increased to 1,410 as a result of this operation. What would you think of a merchant in New-York whose vessels are renowned for their speed (I do not refer to those of medium size), who submits them to this operation when they return from their first voyages. The prosperity of his business depends on this speed, and he spares neither expense nor trouble to have the best vessels possible. He is the man who furnishes the inhabitants of Havana, Jamaica, as well as those of several others of the Antilles apples from Newtown—pippins [10]—whose odor and taste are so delicious, especially in the torrid zone. I do not believe that the gardens of the Hesperides have ever produced any as good. When they arrive, fresh and well preserved, each in its own paper covering, they often sell for six to eight piastres a dozen. The same is true of the sirloins and other parts of choice beef which they pack in this country in little oak containers, hermetically sealed and filled with a special brine by means of which they are conserved until their arrival on these islands; you see how important it is to have fine vessels.

"This continent," continued Mr. G., "is the foster father of this great archipelago. Not only does it furnish the inhabitants with edibles, material necessary in the construction of their homes and mills, kettles, and cylinders for their sugaries, but also horses and carriages, such as phaetons, cabriolets, etc. The last time I was in Cartagena and Havana, I observed with pleasure that in those towns there was not a single carriage which had not come from Boston, New-York, or Philadelphia."

Gradually carried by the tide, we soon discovered a bridge which had been built over that river by the same incorporated company, whose works one also finds at Hackensack, as well as the 4-mile dam which extends from Bergen to New-Ark.

"The soil on which these two bridges were built," said Mr. G., "is so soft and unsubstantial, that the foundation bridge was very costly. Who would believe that this coastal terrain, completely submerged at all high tides, is twenty feet deep? Yet it is quite true; it rests on a foundation of white sand, whose waving surface attests to the activity of the waters which inundated it once upon a time. Seven feet below this bed of sand, one finds a clay terrain whose odor is extremely fetid, filled with the debris of various fossils, quite different from the form and size of those we see today on the shore of the sea. The governor of this state keeps in his office the shell of an oyster which contains a little less than a pint of water; larger ones were discovered when they dug a ditch in Monmouth county, fifty feet down. The astonishing thing is that the terrain on which the oysters were found, appears to have been an old swamp. What changes in the surface, as well as in the level of the seas these continents must have undergone at some unknown time!

"This new road whose right of way was conceded to posterity by the Government, is the only one leading from New-York to Philadelphia; thus it is heavily traveled and it is said that this undertaking cost 300,000 piastres and that the subscribers realized considerable interest returned on their investment. Never was a road tax paid with greater pleasure; prior to its building, it was no easy task to cross these wide meadows and get over the Hakinsack and Passaick rivers. This new route has become very useful to the village of New-Ark, the starting and ending place for southbound diligences. It is a continual stream of traffic; baggage and mail are also served by it. That is why one sees such a great number of inns there.

"After enjoying abundant fishing, we were going back up the river at eventide, when such a violent storm came up that we were obliged to disembark very hurriedly at the dock of Mr. Schuyler, the owner of a copper mine operating over a century; here we were urged to spend the night. This dock is located opposite the village of Acquakanunck, on the east bank of the Passaic."

"This mine," one of Mr. Schuyler's sons told us, "was discovered five years after the arrival of the first Dutch in New-York, that is to say about 1624. Some sailors who had disembarked at Sandy Hook [11] were taken by the Indians, and led to this same village of Acquakanunck, and according to custom, put in the pot to be boiled, with the exception of one of them, who had the good fortune to be adopted by one of the women of the village. Some time later, this Indian woman noticed the buckles which were attached to the shoes of her new husband, and she told him that on the other side of the river she knew a place which was filled with this same metal. The very next day, unknown to the village, she took him there.

"This man, ignorant as he was, soon figured out that this green earth was indeed concealing a rich mine in its bowels. Returning home, he made friends and promised to bring back clothing like his, brandy, and guns, if they would permit him to go along with his fellow countrymen to New Amsterdam.* The chiefs consented. This smart sailor kept his promise with so much zeal and good faith that they gave him a second and third permission. Profiting by his ascendancy over the minds of his new friends he had the good fortune to make peace between the two nations and to obtain from the sachem at Acquakanunck, concession of the peninsula on which this mine was located, and which today, as you have been able to see, is covered with magnificent farms and beautiful orchards. But instead of cultivating the land which they had just given him and introducing the new seeds from Europe, he worked to exploit this mine, summoned workers from Holland and, ere long, experienced considerable losses. Forced by circumstances, he sold it to one of my ancestors, returned to his village, where he had a house built on the site of the wigwam in which he had been adopted in 1618; it is still owned, as well as the lands surrounding it, by the descendants of this sailor, whose great grandson served with great distinction during the Revolutionary War, and is today an excellent farmer and magistrate of this canton.

"If the English company of Liverpool had not, according to what my father told me, burned our pump, this mine would still be in use, but the devastations of war until now have prevented us from resuming these worthwhile works. We are going to build a blast furnace for the purpose of melting a great quantity of mineral which has remained scattered for a great number of years, in the neighborhood of this mine; already they are beginning to plate the copper at the great refinery of Charlotte'sbourg."

The next day instead of following the ordinary road, which the storm had rendered impassable, we crossed the great swamp of white cedars. These trees belonged to this same family and netted them a tidy income. I noticed that part of the swamp, burned four or five years previously, had already been covered with a considerable number of cedars, growing wild, four feet high; I noticed also that the soil on which they grew was black, swampy, a little odoriferous and almost like the soil of the coastal meadows nearby, although somewhat dryer.

With what ease then will one grow cedars near the sea and in certain boggy regions inland, on which I have seen them grow as well as here. The two kinds of cedars, the acacia, the mulberry, not to mention the oak, are trees valuable in the construction of vessels; the Government of this country will some day encourage their cultivation. And why would they not cultivate these three species in the coastal and sandy regions of Europe? Twenty years would suffice for the growth of these trees, which bear seed as quickly as the onion.[12]

* Today New-York.

What vegetative strength would not the white cedar have, for the closer together they are planted, the more rapid is their growth. Generally, two or three thousand per acre are planted; several uses in ship-building are made of them; ladders, gutters, shingles, planks, fences, etc. Their wood is important also in this country in the manufacture of barrels, of which a great quantity is exported to the East Indies.

On returning to Mr. G.'s plantation, he told us of the coming in 1614 of the first Dutch colonists, among whom were two of his ancestors. He told us that, originally French, they had been driven from their country for having addressed their prayers to God in their mother tongue, and not in the language of an ancient nation which had not existed for centuries; that one of them, a learned man, had been the first recorder of the town of New-York, and had been kept in this position after the conquest of that colony by the English in 1663.

"In reading the gazettes," he added, "how different things are today; the Government no longer busies itself with the beliefs of men; the influence of laws extends no further than the business of this world; each man can adore God in his own fashion—provided that he worship—that is all that is asked of him. Who could have predicted such a sudden and unexpected change? Is it the fruit of wise politics or philosophy? How different would the state of affairs be today if such had been the reigning notions for 200 years! What a difference, in Europe, as in this country if at the time of the wars of religion, Calvinism had obtained superiority? Royal power which reigned in France would have been restrained in more narrow limits, and the form of Government would have changed considerably. Then with what rapidity would the same France have not become sea-minded and industrially minded! It would have surpassed England by more than one century, since it was the French, driven from their country, who first introduced the art of making hats, paper, tin plate, silk stuff, and—the Huguenots—that of making cloth.

"On what did all this depend? On a few musket shots, better aimed, or rather on the conquest of Mexico, whose gold was procured for the Nero of the South, that burner of men through so many means of bribing and corrupting. On what did the conquest of such a powerful empire depend? On the experiences and discoveries of an obscure German monk. Such are the imperceptible sources of human destiny. And one can foresee, one can organize the events of the future, as though they had not been necessarily foreordained, engendered by the past. Nevertheless, all these events must have taken place in order that my ancestors be obliged to flee their country like criminals; in order that I have the pleasure of receiving you beneath my roof, and that I might hear the interesting stories of your journeys into the interior of the continent, which is as unknown to me as though I had been born in Europe.''

Informed of the arrival of a schooner at the port of embarkation, Mr. G. left until the morrow his instructive conversation and hastened to receive the company which he expected from New-York; this was Sunday.

CHAPTER XI

"When I recall all I have heard you say about the interior of the continent, our great lakes and the colonies of the Ohio," said Mr. G., as soon as the numerous and brilliant company which had come to dine with him had left, "I confess I feel a little mortified. But the time for curiosity which presupposes leisure, ease and some instruction, has not yet arrived; we are and for a long time will continue to be in a state of agitation and excitement, which permits us to think only of means of repairing our losses and of acquiring a fortune; that is the universal desire. From there springs so much activity, so many enterprises, projects, and speculations; from it also springs that spirit of cupidity of which a great number of strangers accuse us. Do they not know that the same is true of the existence of nations as that of men; that each period of this existence has its tastes, its passions, and its errors? Do they not realize the critical situation in which these colonies found themselves in 1783 after their independence? Do they not appreciate the struggle fraught with so many sacrifices made in order to be rid of the common enemy? Are they not aware of the thousand of unforeseen germs of rivalry, jealousies, discord, and ever internal warfare which were manifest? The war and the paper money issue had destroyed all fortunes; eleven of our cities, destroyed by the enemy, were still smoking; our finances were merely chaos; the ties, which during the moment of crisis, had united these thirteen states, were but a thread, ready to break; the weight of these old debts contracted in Europe overwhelmed the business houses which sought to establish themselves; no longer was there any credit, public or private; Congress was merely a shadow, ready to fade away; our flag was defiled, and our customs became deteriorated by the scourge of paper money, as well as by the habit of war. Such were some of the principal circumstances which made this long interregnum so alarming that a great number of people considering as illusory the brilliant hopes which they had founded on the independence of the continent, languished in the bitterness of their hearts, and regretted that so many sacrifices had been made, and that so much blood had been spilled futilely.

"How did it happen that their fears were not justified? One must have known, as I did, the designs, the plans formed to overthrow the new form of Government which the convention of Deputies assembled in Philadelphia proposed at the end of 1787; one must have seen, as I did, the devices and the tricks trumped up to deceive the inhabitants of the countryside, especially in the States which regretted seeing the substantial revenues from their customs * almost disappear from their continental treasury, in order to be able to appreciate the chances and risks which these states ran of not being united, and perhaps of falling again under the yoke of their mother country. And despite the force of the most urgent circumstances, despite the energy and unanimity of the good citizens, their hope would have been dashed, anarchy would have triumphed, without that last article of the constitution which declares that as soon as nine states adopted it, it would be put into effect and have authority for these states. Without this clause, New-York whose deputies to the Convention at Philadelphia had retired early ** and whose own Convention purposely assembled later, would have rejected it, in accordance with the plan of the majority, a plan well known long before the opening of the debates.

"The numerous malcontents of Massachusetts and Pennsylvania and probably also those of Rhode Island and North Carolina whose legislators had not wished to send delegates to Philadelphia, and among whom the opposition had agents, would soon have taken up arms again to uphold its plans. On the other hand, the old soldiers of the continental army, the inhabitants of the coastal towns, a great number among the people of the country, would have united to oppose those who wanted to prevent the union of the States; then this new civil war would have destroyed everything the revolution had not upset. What might have been the consequences of this new conflict? A paragraph of three lines upset all these historical combinations. New Hampshire, the ninth state, accepted the new Constitution during the sessions of the convention and New-York found itself forced, although regretfully, to ratify it also.*** On such do human events depend.

"From this long state of crisis, confusion, and turmoil resulted the one in which you see us today, just as the waves of the sea roll a long time after the tempest has ceased; add to all that the obstacles and the difficulties which normally accompany the newness and youth of a popular Government, the birth and the bewilderment of the

---

* The duty at New-York in 1788, amounted to 72,000 pounds, equal to 180,000 piastres (954,000 francs).

** Of all the deputies of this state, there remained only Colonel Hamilton; no sooner had they returned, than the first ones justified their conduct in a long letter which they addressed to the Legislature and to the Governor, in which they disapproved of the new form and the principles of the proposed Government. Most of the delegates having been re-elected members of the Convention of the State of New-York, which was to decide on the ratification or refusal, it is obvious that from the origin, they had decided to reject it.

*** It was of such great importance that they were informed at Poughkeepsie (one seat of the sessions of the Conventions of the State of New York) about the ratification of New Hampshire, whose deputies were assembled, before the majority of those of New-York, certain of victory, pressed the closing of their sessions, which a great number of young men, in the states of New York, Connecticut, Massachusetts and New Hampshire, mounted on horseback, placed themselves on the highway ten miles apart, by means of which the news of the ratification was transmitted in four hours. The distance was 124 leagues.

parties, the shock which it has experienced from the dogmas which almost upset the Old World, the bonds of an almost exclusive trade which we were obliged to make with our former mother country since the war has destroyed almost all manufactures and closed to us almost all the ports of Europe, the irritation caused by the seizure of a great number of vessels, the arrival among us of a crowd of foreigners of all castes and kinds, the creation of public funds, these are some of the causes to which we can attribute, on the one hand, this delirium of speculations, this thirst for riches, this spirit of speculation in which, however, greed has no part; on the other hand, this lukewarm attitude and this indifference to science and the arts are fully apparent.

"Just like the Europeans, we will sigh for peace, and like them, we will feel more and more its need; it alone can replace the commerce of the universe on its former basis, restrain our maritime speculations within their just limits, calm the bitterness of political parties, and gradually consolidate our Government, our fine institutions, and our national character. Then we shall have among us savants, literary men, geologists, amateur botanists, naturalists. Then we shall know everything of novelty and interest to us the forests and the bowels of this continent conceal; it is the work of a few years of peace. To the indecision, to the storms of youth, will succeed the consistency and the logic of mature age.

"If my long sojourn in the West Indies, if the circumstances incidental to my return have not permitted me to explore the interior of our coastal states nor the region beyond the Alleghanies, if I have not yet seen the Great Lakes, Niagara Falls, Natural Bridge, the same will not be true for my son. He is coming from Tenesee [1] where he had gone to see the military grant of three million acres, which Carolina gave a few years ago to its contingent of the Continental Army, as well as to obtain the title of the part of that concession which belongs to him, having married the only daughter of a colonel of that same state, who died three years ago.

"He was so delighted with the mildness, and the evenness of the climate of this new land, that he decided to settle there. Surprised at such an extraordinary plan, I tried to show him the inconveniences of founding a settlement in a region so far from the sea, where everything coming from Europe and the coastal states must necessarily be very high-priced, and where labor will be dear for a number of years yet, since everyone works for himself; and finally, where men cling for a long time to the provincialism which their fathers adopted in their labors and the solitude of their isolated settlements. I have calmed this first outburst, so natural to youth, whose eyes, for lack of experience, see only the attractive side of things.

"These remote colonies," I said to him, "are suited only to men who know a trade and who are accustomed to work; they are happy and content, wherever they can procure land cheap; but as for you, to whom I have given the very finest education one can receive in this land, you who are destined to enjoy an honest fortune, it would be the greatest imprudence to expose yourself to such serious risks. Tell me, do you think nothing of the distance you would be from me, whose consolation you are? Keep your military lands, valuable witness of public gratitude toward your father-in-law; but stay here, where you will have only trees to plant, well-fenced fields with high hedges to cultivate, and orchards in full bloom to look after. Settled three leagues from New-York, you will enjoy the delights of life, you will participate in the progress of human thinking and you will study the sciences; for I hope you will be too wise ever to expose a well assured fortune to the risks of trade.

"His tender affection for me as well as my own judgment, had all the effects I had hoped for; he will close my eyelids for I shall not die far from the person dearest to me, who unfortunately lost his mother some time ago; for you know one does not advance in life; each year one sees a relative or friend disappear from life; and if one does reach an advanced age, one finds himself isolated, like the old oaks which have survived all the trees of their neighborhood.

"I have sent my daughter's son, whose tutor I am, to the college at Dartmouth [2] in the western part of New Hampshire. The distance from towns, the healthfulness of the climate, the enthusiasm of his instructors, who appear to be grateful when one sends them students from so far away—such are the reasons which made me decide to separate myself from this child. Judge of their force, since I am only thirty miles from the college at Princetown, and even nearer the college at New-York.

"How regrettable that the latter was placed in a coastal town where business, dissipations, and the activity of trade are very annoying distractions for the muses, to those who like solitude, the silence of the countries, the sight of falls and cascades, the shade of trees, at the foot of which one invariably finds composure, father of meditation! At the time of the founding of this college, this town, to be sure, was only a large marketplace; yet it was easy to foresee that, located in the center of the continent, at the mouth of a river in which the tide extends as far as fifty miles, it would grow with rapidity; that is what happened in the lifetime of some of the generous founders. They made the same mistake in Philadelphia. I never go to New York without the sight of this fine institution renewing my regrets and my desire to see it transported to Eusopus, in the neighborhood of the Blue Mountains, or at Hampton at the eastern end of Long Island, in full view of the ocean.''

''Since your ancestors were among the first to come from Holland,'' asked Mr. Herman, ''could you tell me the name which the Indians gave to the Hudson River? I have sought it in vain in your public archives.''

''I think it is lost,'' replied Mr. G., ''the same has happened to various other rivers and mountains of this state. Most of the men sent here by the Dutch East India Company, to whom this land had been given, were not Dutchmen at all, but Walloons, men from Liège and from all the little provinces bordering the United Provinces. Some of their leaders were learned men, I agree, but thwarted by a Government in which they had no part, each one busied himself with his own interests and means for bettering his plight; that is why one finds in our archives only acts of land cessions, establishment of churches, wars with the Indians, and nothing concerned with the geography and the natural history of the land and nothing worthy of the annals of history.

''The first governor was a Courlandais officer to whom this wretched job was given for the loss of a leg in the siege of the town of Dordrecht. Without the ceremony of baptism, most of the early colonists would not even have had a name. Their descendants are not known in some cantons by anything other than nicknames, and what will seem even more extraordinary to you is that each individual has three: the first, by which he is known in the fields, the second at church, the third when he receives neighbors in his home.

''About forty years ago, an adventurer arrived from Holland who had brought a long list of names. He decided to put them up for auction. Those preceded by the *van* were worth two dollars, the others only one. From this curious speculation a mass of lawsuits resulted about the identity of individuals. These lawsuits cost far more than the names, and it is possible that even the present generation will not see an end to them. What useful observations can one hope for from men whose descendants were still so ignorant forty years ago?

''Nevertheless, how instructive were the details relating to the arrival of the first colonists, of what preceded and followed their disembarkment! With what interest would one not read today those of the first interviews with the Indians, those in a word, of the means which they adopted to house themselves and live on the sterile point of the Isle of Manhattan? For, just as intervening space surrounds with illusions far off objects, time adds much to the importance of events, excites curiosity, and even meditation, when one considers the influence which they had on the infancy of this colony. It is only since the time when this colony received in 1683 the civil laws of England and a legislative body * that its history becomes interesting.

"The close alliance which Great Britain contracted at the time with the Six Confederated Nations, an alliance which has persisted in the beginning of the Revolution, permitted the inhabitants to extend their clearings, build towns in the interior and multiply their number. It experienced in the course of all this a great expansion by the successive arrival of Germans, Irish, Flemish, Palatins, and French driven from their country by the revocation of the Edict of Nantes, that shameful blot on the reign of Louis XIV.

"What a difference between these early colonists of whom I have just spoken and those who founded New Plymouth in the Bay of Massachusetts in 1620, origin of the peoples of the four northern states, which today are estimated to comprise one-fifth of the population of the United States! Instructed by the revolutions which they left, enlightened by the theological discussions then so common, having been persecutors and persecuted, these men were quite superior to those whom Holland sent here also, they very carefully kept track of their progress, the form of Government which they agreed on among themselves before embarking, the solemn pledge which they made to keep the laws which they promulgated, their meetings, their discussions, and their wars with the Indians; for, except in Pensylvanie and Maryland, the early fields of all the colonies have been steeped in human blood.

"The variety of religious sects, which were not long in rising among them, was the source of so many little settlements that soon they became flourishing towns, such as Boston, long known under the Indian name of Shawmut; Salem, as Naumkeag; Charlestown, as Agawan, and finally Ipswich, names which they did not lose until the time of their incorporation. Time has not erased any of these traits, characteristic of religious opinions of that time. Their fanaticism was so extreme that the chief motive of a great number of those distinguished by their birth and their enlightenment was less to form settlements and to acquire lands than to enjoy in the bosom of these bleak forests all the liberty of their cult. This religion was the object of their daily conversations, the soul of their existence; but often, also, the cause of disagreements and separations. History never speaks of the founding of new settle-

---

* Twenty years after the conquest of it made by the English in 1663, in the name of the Duke of York to whom this land had been conceded.

ments without indicating the name of the minister which led this new flock into the desert, to found there a new church. Thus were colonized the coastal part of Massachusetts, all of Rhode Island and Connecticut, not to mention New Hampshire.

"Today when the spirit of the century is so different, the descendants of these old Puritans can scarcely form an idea of the importance which their forefathers attached to the interpretations of certain texts of the holy scripture, as well as to the rigid forms of a religion which had such a great influence on their conduct and their actions. One could not be elected to any civil function, nor even be elected member of their societies, without also being a member of their congregations. From all that sprang a spirit of intolerance and hypocrisy for which they have been blamed long and unjustly. What a difference today! The Mohammedans could build a mosque among the great-grandsons of those who, a century ago, had several Quakers executed for refusing to renounce their religious views. What will it be like in another century?

"However, in the midst of these ardors, the outbursts of this burning fanaticism, one can see eminent virtues and great qualities shine, not only among the chiefs of these illustrious ones but even among themselves; never was a colony founded by less ignorant men. A very few years after arriving in the Bay of Massachusetts, they devoted their desire to further advancement and knowledge to the founding of the University of Cambridge,* that alma mater for whom their descendants keep the greatest respect and tenderest affection, as well as by the founding of schools in the country as well as in towns,** a great and memorable example which William Penn himself did not follow until his arrival in Pennsylvania sixty-two years after the first colonization of Massachusetts.

"I confess, never in history, do I meet without some feeling of admiration the names of these illustrious founders who crossed the ocean to lead their companions to this continent, at that time covered with dense, wild, and savage forests, filled with ferocious animals and cultivated by men equally fierce.[3] To how many dangers, fatigues, and inconveniences of all kinds the first generation was exposed, when houses were merely cabins, with almost no furnishings; and when there were

---

* The University of Cambridge or rather Harvard, the name of its chief benefactor, was founded in 1638, eighteen years after the arrival of the first colonists, and received a charter of incorporation in 1650. It is favorably situated three miles from Boston; its buildings are vast and beautiful. It is the oldest, the most richly endowed, and in every respect, the outstanding one on the continent.

** The law obliges inhabitants of districts where there are fifty families, to have a school where they teach the children reading, writing, spelling, arithmetic, and the English language. In those districts where there are over 2000 inhabitants, there is another school in which one teaches Greek, Latin, as well as English grammar. The tuition is from 30 to 100 piastres (150–530 francs).

no roads, no bridges, and no communications.[4] Who would recognize today the former condition in traveling through this country, so well cultivated and generally so picturesque? If courage is needed to go and live on the Ohio River at one hundred leagues from kith and kin, how much one needed this same courage to abandon one's country, one's friends whom the colonists were never to see again and from whom they were separated by a vast Ocean. With what energy must religious opinions have endowed them at that time? Most of them were wealthy and belonged to distinguished families; it is perhaps to this that their posterity owes the energy which still distinguished them from their compatriots and manifests itself in such tireless activity, industry, and boldness of their enterprises and speculations on land and sea.

"Five years elapsed before the arrival of the first cow; it was a day of great festivity throughout the colony. Without including the other cattle, today in the State of Massachusetts alone there are 391,-254.[5]

"I confess, I recall, the names of Cabot, Raleigh, Argal, Popham, Damer, Hudson, and so many other famous navigators with more veneration than those of men to whom history had given the title of hero. What a difference between the memories which the names of Delaware, Fairfax, Baltimore,* Penn, Carver, Indicot, Vane, Vinthrop, etc., and those which awaken the names of Paul Emile, Marius, Sylla, Tamerlan, Attila and so many other conquerors. The first of these have opened a haven where the wretched and oppressed have found a refuge; the others have used their glory only to destroy or ravage. The former have cast the foundations of this vast temple of civil and religious liberty and to do it, so to speak, have summoned men from a void; the others have conquered only to subject nations to the yoke of iron. The first have promulgated laws of justice and peace, founded villages and towns, established maritime trade, cleared the fields of this hemisphere where science and the arts, those fine fruits of civilization, begin to be cultivated and encouraged; the talents and the genius of the other have served them only to upset, subjugate, and enslave.

"Pardon me, gentlemen, for the length and the triviality of the details which I permitted myself to drag in only in order to answer your many questions; details which you owe to the special study I made of the origin of almost all our colonies. If I were a literary man, I would be worthy of writing of their origins; I have made a collection of every-

---

* When Lord Baltimore (Cecilius Calvert) was secretary of State in 1622, he obtained from James the First a very sizeable concession on the island of Newfoundland, to which he gave the name Avalon, after the one of the manor he had in Somerset. He went there twice, built a great house, and cleared a large piece of land, and spent 25,000 guineas; but the French having devastated his domain, he abandoned it and obtained in 1632 from Charles the First, the grant of Maryland, estimated to contain 9,170,000 acres.

thing that has been published in Europe and over here relative to the discovery of the continent, as well as the histories of almost all the colonies. What an interesting account a skillful writer could make of the great series of events, efforts, and adventures more or less fortunate or unfortunate; from the first colonists whom Sir Walter Raleigh led to Roanoke in 1577 and of whom no one has ever heard since, to the colonizing of Georgia by General Oglethorpe [6] in 1737, and the founding of the inland colonies of Vermont, Kentuckey, and Tenezee. I know scarcely any subject more worthy of the brush of a great painter; and if to the details of these long and painful beginnings he were to add those of the progress of these colonies until 1775, those of their emancipation, confirmed in 1783, those, finally, of the posterity of these states since 1790, I believe there are scarcely any readers in whom this work would not inspire a great interest. It would be the history of the most interesting event in modern times, the discovery and the population of this hemisphere, whose new destinies must necessarily influence those of the old world.

"No map of the country has been published in Europe which I do not own; I even have a copy of the one of Sir Martin Béhem,[7] made for King John II of Portugal more than 300 years ago, as well as that of Purchas, published in 1625, on which were traced the first discoveries of the Cabots, from the Gulf of St. Lawrence to the capes of Delaware.

"Next to Mr. Hazard, to whom we owe the conservation of our maps * that of the acts of Parliament, the decrees of the Council, the decisions of the ministers relative to the colonies; the treaties with the Indians, in a word, what are called State papers, I am perhaps one of the persons on this continent who has most carefully concerned himself with everything relative to our beginnings; thus, I have become a member of the Society of Antiquaries, founded at Boston in 1782. I have done even more: at great expense I have procured plans of our capitals, such as they were at various stages of developments. For that I have been obliged to rely on the memories of their oldest inhabitants. It is truly a very interesting thing to see today what Charlestown, Philadelphia, Boston, New-York, etc., were like 30, 40, 50 years after their founding. I have had drawn on separate sheets of paper pasted on one large sheet, a plan of New-York [8] at the time of its conquest by the English, almost as it was in 1663, in 1683 when the government of this colony became royal, in 1710, in 1764, in 1776 when it was taken

---

* It is to the knowledge, the zeal, and the indefatigable perseverance of this worthy person that the United States owes the fine collection in-folio of the charts and acts of government, from the origin of the colonies to the revolution. This valuable collection will not be presented to the public until toward the end of the century.

by Lord Cornwallis and partly burned, and finally as it is today.[9] What tremendous growth! I could scarcely believe my eyes! It no longer resembles what it was in my youth. The Bayard and Delancey farms, formerly covered with harvests, cattle, and pasture lands, are today covered with elegant homes, streets, sidewalks, and pumps. The great prison which the Government has just built occupies four acres of the former Delancey grant; this section is one of the most beautiful in the city.

"What a desolate and bleak appearance this western end of Manhattan Island must have had where our ancestors disembarked! The ridge (today Broadway) was only 400 toises wide from the waters of the Hudson to those of the Sound; the rest, toward the South, was merely a muddy area on which reeds and seaweeds grew. Broad Street was a natural but inaccessible canal in which the tide rose almost to the city hall. Most of the terrain on which the city was built offered only lagoons covered with waters from the sea.

"As to the beautiful street of Greenwich, which is sixty feet wide and two miles long, only eleven years ago the Hudson River waters covered a portion of the site which it now occupies; it was the anchorage of all the oyster vessels of the town; the houses extended four hundred feet further along this river. Considering this town only as it was in 1784, I think one can be assured that a quarter of the terrain on which it was built was man-made.[10] That is why the well water is not good; that is why, rather than setting up another fire pump, the first of which the English destroyed during the war, people thought it would be preferable to bring a great stream from twenty-five miles distance; that is the plan of a company which has just been given a charter of incorporation by the Government, which gives everlasting rights of usufruct to this enterprise. I am curious to see how they will build this aqueduct which is to conduct the waters of this stream across the Haarlem River, and especially how they guarantee the piers from the violence of ice. This enterprise will be costly and is worthy of the ingenuity of the people whom the subscribers have chosen from among them to be its directors, among whom one finds Colonel Burr, famous lawyer, long United States senator, who, during the war, was one of our bravest officers. His father died, president of the college at Princetown."

"How can one become master over these inundated lands with so much ease?" asked Mr. Herman. "By what means does one make a watery soil solid enough to permit the building of houses? Must one transport rocks, whole mountains, even? It seems to me that it must be as costly as it is difficult to execute."

"These operations are much less costly than you imagine," replied Mr. G., "because we have a great abundance of wood and stone, and because everything is transported by water. The necessity which faced the first colonists in building their shops and homes as near as possible to the navigable waters forced them to resort to these embankments, whose notion, it is reasonable to assume, they brought from Holland. From there came the skill which they acquired in this kind of industry; today it is so perfect that I have seen them drop foundations forty feet below water level with as much ease as at ten.

"For this operation, trunks of appropriately squared fir trees or hemlocks are used; with these frameworks, built according to the dimensions of the watery lands conceded by the corporation of the town to which they belong, they let them down gradually and perpendicularly until they touch bottom; then they heap on stones brought on specially constructed barges; this operation requires great speed. As they are filled they have to shore up the sides with reinforcements, placed diagonally and secured by large iron pins, especially on the parts which are most frequently exposed to the force of the ice. As soon as they have been heaped to a point about the level of the sea, they cover them with gravel and earth. In my youth I recall having seen at Greenwich a pier thirty feet long, which, being useless, was planted with lucern grass and this alfalfa lasted a great number of years.

"As soon as these artificial lands are consolidated, wooden frame shops and, a few years later, brick houses are built there. Such was the beginning of nearly all the southern section of New-York. The site on which they built the great restaurant, which today serves as the Stock Exchange, and where the bonding houses are, in 1763, was the anchorage of average-sized ships. This fine building is now five hundred feet from the ocean. Two rows of houses on two streets have been built along there.* This invasion of the waters was so considerable that today vessels pass between Governor's Island and Nassau,** a span of land which I have frequently crossed during my youth, without getting my feet wet. Twenty feet of water cover this place, where formerly one could scarcely see a stream.

"The same situation existed in almost all the coastal cities of the continent. To obtain a greater depth of water, at the other end of their jetties, the inhabitants made substantial frameworks. At Newport in Rhode Island, one sees tremendous works of this nature, as well as at Boston. The main jetty of the latter city, famous as Longwharf, is fifteen hundred feet long and eighty feet wide; on the left of it, a long

* Water and Front streets.
** This island constitutes the eastern harbor.

series of magnificent shops have been built, opposite which ships are loaded and unloaded: it is there where one sees in all their bustle, this sea-faring people. This jetty was built forty years ago by an incorporated company to whose agents one pays the rights of wharfage prescribed by law.

"What a pity, you will say, that these works were not made of stone! Such a sight would be more pleasing to the eye, and you would think actually more durable; but remember that these foundations were not built by kings, who, like the Czar of Muscovy, would have sacrificed tons of gold and thousands of men, but by private individuals, or by associations who could employ only ordinary methods. Moreover, I am convinced that the ice would have taken a greater toll on the corners and surfaces of stone-built foundations than do they on these wooden piles which are repaired so easily, without the entire structure suffering the slightest upset.

"It is probable that in a century or so, people will concern themselves with adding a little style to the construction of these works; manpower will be more numerous than in Europe; our posterity will enjoy greater resources than our feebleness permits us to tap today. Until now we have sought only means of being able to load and unload vessels with promptness and ease. You will agree that these jetties to which these vessels are moored are a considerable item; why, the carriages approach the very gangway of the ships!

"And what business do we have busying ourselves with these embellishments, we, whose real emancipation dates only from 1790; we whose name, whose very existence as a nation with a Government have not yet felt the impact of a great number of years? What were we before this time? A nation covered with the rust of prejudice contracted in its infancy, although suddenly arriving at its majority by the most extraordinary of events; a nation which but recently, knowing no affection or interest other than those of the colony which gave birth to it, has not yet had time to raise, through education, the opinion and feeling to the great character which is to distinguish the members of the new family of the United States. What were we forty years ago, when in the interior one could see only isolated dwellings, separated from each other by thick forests, or by vast swamps or bridgeless rivers? What were our towns like? Small market towns inhabited by men, happy in the truth (for the infancy of these colonies was their golden age), but only slightly educated; men whose speculations and trade, dictated by the mother country, did not extend beyond a narrow circle. Therefore, one should not find it exceptional, as do the majority of travelers, that what they observe among us is inferior—is so inferior to what they have seen in their own countries. Can one hope that a tree will bear fruit before acquiring the necessary growth? Thirty more years of peace with the universe and tranquility among us, then they will see how much more perfect all this will be."

"Since the long visit which I made two years ago with Chancellor Livingston," said Mr. Herman, "I have never heard so interesting a conversation. What good fortune for a foreigner like me, to have been introduced to so many people in whose homes I have enjoyed both the charms of hospitality and the pleasure of hearing details as new as they are instructive! After six months of study, I could scarcely learn what I have just absorbed in a few hours. It is to this worthy traveling companion," he continued, "that I owe the wonderful opportunity of having the esteem and friendship of so many educated persons. Just as you, Sir, he has known this land in its colonial state; just as you, he has seen these events breed and spread, luck and fortune have brought this interesting section of America to emancipation. If he is sad at growing old, he is somewhat compensated for it by the rapid passing of life when one has the good fortune to appear on the scene of the world at as extraordinary an epoch. What a change in the opinions of mankind since 1774! This short period of twenty-four years has been the most fertile in great events, and above all in the causes of events still more important, than many other previous centuries. The beginning of this will be considered in the course of time as a new era. Tell me, I beg of you, how long you have owned this beautiful and fertile farm, so delightfully, so pleasantly situated on the banks of this river."

"It has been in our family," replied Mr. G., "since 1690, the time when my great-grandfather purchased it from the last Indians of the village of Aquankanunck. The ownership is quite legitimate, as you see. Obliged to become a farmer, after the disappearance of game, one of the chiefs of the tribe, Wepeeton, sold for the allowance of fifty piastres, the section of land due him at the time of the division with the other inhabitants of the village, of whom only sixty-seven remained. My grandfather, a fair-minded man, had a fine little cabin built for him with a good-sized garden in which the women planted their corn. With these resources and that of fishing, this family lived in ease until the death of Skeesakon, the last descendant, who died in 1730.

"I am attached to this paternal soil," continued Mr. G., "and I would be extremely pained if I ever thought that my son were to get rid of it. With the idea of making it more valuable, I imported from Europe a great number of fruit trees of the very finest and rarest species in that land, where the taste for gardening is still in its infancy.

Like you, I have an excellent Dutch gardener, to whom I refused nothing he needed for the improvement of the soil and guarantee of my trees against the rigors of winter; I even have several twines of vine which are already beginning to bear berries. Would you believe it? This man is a practical philosopher in everything concerning the vegetation and conduct of his garden: his enlightenment, his experience, and his conversation have taught me a great deal; for, when I was working at my desk in Santa Cruz, I never would give a thought to the movement of the saps of trees, nor to the influence of the sun and the seasons.

"At my age, this man acquainted me with a new kind of happiness of which I had not the slightest notion and one goes to seek this happiness under the frosts of the north, and under the extreme heat of the torrid zone while at our very doorstep, neath our very windows, in our very gardens, there it is! In placing a pruning knife in my hand, my gardener taught me to feel interest in and even affection for my trees. He gave me some lessons in botany. Could I ever tell you about the astonishment, the respect, and the admiration that these wonders of nature filled me with! 'Wretch that you are,' I would tell myself, 'you have lived as long as fifty years, and you do not know this sanctuary under whose veil nature hides the mysteries of the propagation and reproduction of plants.' Nowadays I rarely go to New-York; I have less need of frothy society, luxurious food; I prefer dining with my friends whose tastes are analogous to the tastes this honest Dutchman has inspired in me. I spend with him a part of the time which I devote neither to reading nor to the cares of farming. As much as possible, I have my son accompany me; I try to inspire in him the same tastes. This fine gardener has taught him to grow and graft plants.

" 'These wild vines,' I say to my son sometimes, 'which owe you their cultivation, will someday be more valuable to you than the other plants of this garden; some day their fruit will seem better to you, and you will experience renewed pleasure, I am sure, when, in presenting to your friends a beautiful peach or a succulent pear, you will be able to say to them, "I grew these." ' "

"Several years ago some distance from my house, I had a small sepulchral vault built which I surrounded with red cedars and acacia trees in which the remains of my ancestors were brought from the old Dutch church of New-York, and I have left instructions in my will that mine be placed there some day. Having inspired early in this young man a religious respect for the consecrated places for the repose of the dead, I flatter myself that all these reasons will contribute toward ridding his mind and his heart of the idea of selling this land and will cause him to consider such an action as shameful and sacrilegious. This respect with which all forthright souls are involuntarily filled is more the effect of instinct than of thought, since one observes it in Indians, in whose memories the places where the ancestors' or friends' bones have been buried, have become geographical markings in the minds like torrents, falls, and mountains. Besides, how many useful reflections do not owe their birth in the mind of a son to the sight of the trees which his father has planted, of the fields which he has cleared, or the streams whose waters he had conducted to irrigate his pasture lands and his orchards!''

"I think your son is too fortunate in his inheritance," I said to Mr. G., "not to heed your last wishes and the considerable bonds which attach him to this holding whose fifth owner he will be, from father to son. Little doubt that one would meet in this state a dozen families who can boast such long ownership."

"It is rare indeed," he said, "especially in a nascent society established so recently on such a vast continent; besides, the inclination of my compatriots for emigration, an inclination determined by the natural desire of becoming landowners, since the families are quite large, the children, on the death of the fathers are often obliged to sell their paternal possessions in order to divide the inheritance.

"How much these things influence the perfection of agriculture! Indeed, what man would carefully raise and plant his trees, improve his fields, fence them with high hedges, if he could foresee that at the end of a few years they might pass into other hands? Such is the inevitable consequence of youth in our societies, and not of ignorance, as so many travelers have alleged. In other countries people often complain of the surplus of population per square mile; here, on the contrary, farming, manufacturing, the completion of roads and canals—everything languishes, everything is retarded for lack of manpower; it will not be thus in a few years.

"Blind as we are, we sigh, we complain about the imperfection of our learning, the slowness of our progress! How much happier is our lot than will be that of our great-grandsons when this country is as heavily populated as Europe! They complained in this fashion in colonial times; for that is the lot of mankind; that epoch, however, was the real golden age of this new part of the world. Everywhere there reigned abundance, peace, moderation in wants; everywhere one could see the real seeds of happiness spreading; the benefits of liberty had not yet been soiled by deliriums or tempests: everywhere one could see paternal administration, laws founded on justice and salutary customs. If the eyes had not been dazzled by this spectacle of great fortunes, hearts would never have been crushed by that of misery and poverty.

The failure of a merchant was something unknown. Nothing was rarer than executions; in the span of twenty-seven years only one man was put on the rack in the state of Massachusetts and this man was a sailor from Genoa.

"Such were, with a few exceptions, the happy circumstances which accompanied the infancy of these states; such were the causes to which we must attribute the rapid progress made in the course of a century by these colonies whose origin is due to intolerance, to long and bloody wars of religion which desolated England and a great part of Europe in the seventeenth century. It is probable that if the new doctrines of Luther and Calvin had not appeared, the basis on which these colonies were founded would have been less favorable to liberty and would not have had such a rapid growth. On what did the silencing of these doctrines hinge for so long a time? On the fact that Pope Leo X had not planned to glorify his reign by building the basilica of St. Peter, as well as the various degrees of wisdom and moderation in the mind of that pontiff and in the minds of his council."

"Was it you who planted these fine cedars on the slope whose waters bathe the escarpment?" asked Mr. Herman.

"No," replied Mr. G., "they are the children of nature; that is why you see them so high and their heads so pyramidical. According to tradition, it seems that they were in the same state of grandeur 178 years ago at the time of the arrival of our ancestors. That fact proves the astonishing longevity of these trees which, like oaks, enjoy even longer centuries of existence after reaching their greatest growth; I did not want to permit the felling of a single one after the death of my father, who, like me, admired them and respected them and had tulip trees planted near them.

"It is under their pleasant shade that I sometimes go to dream, to meditate on our destiny, on life, that eternal circle of vicissitudes; now of order, now of peace and good fortune, now of wars, misfortunes, disorders of all kinds; on that swift circle from birth till death, annihilation, and reproduction. What was the past like, I have often asked myself, in the shadowy wave of which events, generations, centuries plunged themselves? Like the waters of rivers in the depths of the Ocean? And this future which is nothing before arriving, and which leaves us the very moment it arrives; toward which, however, our imagination transports us at every moment that we may pin on it our tiniest hopes? And the present—fleeting, like the wind that blows, and which we scarcely enjoy, before it is gone? Placed between these different points which surround and escape him relentlessly, what is man?

"But, tired, even frightened by these presumptuous flights of my intellect whose feebleness will never be able to break its bonds, I stop and come down to earth, so to speak. I admire the elegance, the beautiful colors of the butterfly, that child of the sun that comes to light on me in the shade of these cedars. With the aid of a magnifying glass I examine the riot of emeralds which ornament these deadly and ferocious mosquitoes, which after spending the winter buried in the midst of our meadows, come forth to frighten, to desolate, to pursue our beasts during the heat of August. And that variety of insects whose forms and abilities are so various and so marvelous! And those microscopic atoms which appear to enjoy all the boons of existence! Animated, stimulated by the heat of the sun, their generations succeed one another with extreme rapidity, until, warned by the approach of autumn, they seek the most convenient places to bury themselves in the form of chrysalids or to die after laying their eggs. And this periodic movement of the waters, to which we owe navigation on so many rivers; which each day quietly conducts to New-York and brings back from there our dugouts and our sloops! This ebb and flow, is it due to the activity of the moon or to the melting of the polar ices? And that fine vegetation by which I am surrounded; and the development of so many seeds! What an inexhaustible source of astonishment and admiration!

"When during the summer, the storms of my mind are relaxed, and my soul has become susceptible, I know not why, to the slightest impressions, it seems to hear under these refreshing shades an ethereal concert whose sounds appear to be near or distant, to be born, to grow, or to die, according to the strength of the sea breeze which passes with some force through the leaves of these trees. Now it is the sonorous echo of many harps; now it is the seductive sound of the flute, or the mere buzzing of a bassoon. I find nothing so enticing as this blending of sounds, sometimes vague, uncertain, and almost always harmonious; nor anything more conducive, gently, softly to this delightful oblivion of oneself, which is nothing but thoughtful sleep.

"Moreover, these cedars bear witness to the prosperity of the Indians who inhabited this region once upon a time, as well as to the arrival of the Europeans; witness also to the incredible decadence of the Indians and of the growth, no less equally incredible, of the Europeans; they must seem very impressive to the travelers and certainly worthy of being preserved. These are our meditations and although they are not covered with the rust of centuries, like those one sees in museums in Europe, they are covered by bark and moss."

The time we spent under Mr. G's. roof, divided between the pleasures of fishing, walking, and conversation, elapsed like enchanted days, that is to say, with the speed of lightning. Besides the special esteem which our host had conceived for my young friends, the facility with which the latter spoke Dutch, had produced such an understanding between them that our sojourn at Acquakanunck found itself prolonged well beyond the limits which we had set ourselves. When finally he had to leave, Mr. G., as a last token of the affection he bore my companion, had placed in his garden a stone of New-Ark, engraved with the following verses which my companion had written on one of the window panes:

Enchanted places, sojourn of peace and happiness
O Passaick, lovely and delightful river!
It is here on these banks that a true sage
Enlightened my mind, inspired my heart.
Haven of virtues home of hospitality
Orchards where nature unfolds her bounty
Majestic trees, rich river.
Host even more dear, adieu for ever!
I shall never see you again but my saddened heart
Swears sacred friendship, eternal memory.
Adieu! How many times, from the bosom of my country
My thoughts will blend with yours.

Mr. Herman had wished for a long time to see the carding machine which Mr. Chittenden built for him, so we separated at New-Ark, he to spend a few days at New-Haven, where this engineer lived, and I to return among my friends at Shippenbourg.

"Sir, I have received a letter from my father informing me that his health no longer permits him to stand the burden of business. He needs me and urges me to leave this continent without delay. Although I cannot hesitate for a moment between filial devotion and friendship I announce this news to you only with the feelings of deep regret. If the approach of the equinox were not so imminent and above all the distance separating us were not so great, I would not embark before shaking hands with you and expressing to you personally all the gratitude I owe you for the innumerable favors and services you have done me and the countless proofs of friendship you have showered on me.

"Never shall I forget that I am indebted to you and to your friends for having seen a great part of the interesting things this continent offers; these young farming societies, scattered in almost every direction, the general activity from the banks of the Ohio to the sea, those majestic rivers, those magnificent cataracts, those mediterranean seas, the numerous Transalleghaney settlements, those canals and the rapids being opened in every direction, that long series of states both coastal and agricultural, whose capitals already resemble some of the ones in Europe. This vast ensemble is like an everchanging picture to which new lines and new colors are added every year. Without mentioning the other states, what changes have taken place in New-York since our journey to Onondaga in 1789! Scarcely was the country of the Tenezee then known, even less those of the new Catarakouy, Castorland,[11] Oswegatchie, Rieland, etc., the towns of Little Falls, Whiteston, Barne-welt, Roterdam, Rome, Leyden, Castorville, etc., were not even founded then, nor were the canals of Wood-Creek and Stanwich dug. Not a single dwelling was built on the banks of the great bay at Niahoure.[12] The same was true in Pennsylvania and in the states of the north; everywhere one observes movement and industry, activity and specu-lations. This progress is so rapid that the things one hoped for yester-day, are today almost always realized, and tomorrow will bring again what one hopes for today: symbol of youth, which each day, sees in-crease what it already possesses.

"If the too democratic form of the Government, if the reaction of the new principles which have just missed upsetting Europe have given birth to parties, those fermentations which one sees especially in the towns have no influence on the progress of the clearings of the inland colonies or on those of trade. These discussions, these differences of opinion, hinder neither the departure of vessels nor the activity of plows, nor, in a word, the emmigrations which every year, leave the northern stocks to form settlements in the west and the south of the Union. They are even more prone to solicit the favors of fortune than to pay attention to what is said and done in Congress.

"Never shall I forget that it is you who took me through the great forests of the continent and into the humble cabins of the early settlers; that is you who had me cross their fields, rid of stumps, to observe the work and the progress of their first clearings, to know the munici-pal laws of these nascent societies and finally their first magistrates.

"Never shall I forget that, under your auspices, I lived for two weeks and chatted with the Indians of Onondaga, those children of nature on whose minds the great spectacle of agricultural industry and civilization has made no impression for more than a century. Never shall I forget these men who to cannibalism, and to ferocity unite in their domestic societies generosity, tranquility, and the refinement of civilized men. Just as though they returned from the war to their villages and immediately changed their natures!

"Never shall I forget the happiness I have known in the great num-ber of families with whom I shared with you all that hospitality and the most flattering esteem and confidence offered; to whose conversations I owe so many interesting tales of the wars with the Indians, the successive pushing back of the frontiers, the birth, the progress of these colonies, as well as of everything relative to England's attitude toward them and to reasons for the war which separated them from her.

"How happy I should be on the shores of the Baltic, if I could be useful to these worthy personages and prove to them that the distance which will soon separate us from them, will chill neither my gratitude nor my friendship!

"As for you, my guide and my friend, who have instructed me, enriched my youth, who have taught me to appreciate life and things, as well as to know men, you who have rendered me worthy of the esteem of so many eminent people: my heart wells, tears dim my eyes. Could it be that we are destined never to see one another again? I neither can nor will admit this crushing possibility. If war, if the misfortunes which one of the most beautiful parts of Europe has undergone have saddened you so, realize that these tempests have just followed calm and peace; that moderation, steadfastness, justice, clemency, and enlightenment, today replace ferocity, crime, blindness, and barbarism.

"Until the time when the one to whose ingenuity, to whose happiness, these early miracles are due may have had time to accomplish even more, come share the house of a friend, in town and country, in the bosom of security, peace and abundance. Together we shall observe the striking contrast which the customs, laws, the Government of my old country present with that which this young family of republics and states directs. I shall renew this invitation which my heart addresses to you, before embarking, and I shall renew the tenderest farewells from your companion and young friend,

Gustave Herman"

NOTES TO VOLUME THREE

CHAPTER II

1 WILMINGTON. Good-sized town in the State of Delaware, pleasantly situated on a gentle slope a mile and a half from the Delaware River, twenty-eight miles from Philadelphia, and a short distance from the Christiana or Christine River. It has 400 houses and more than 3,000 inhabitants. In Wilmington I saw many colonists from St. Domingo, obliged, by the fire and havoc wrought by the Revolution, to abandon their native land. Vast was their praise of the inhabitants' hospitality, as well as the abundance of provisions and provender. The less affluent found refuge and assistance with Christian houses of charity. An academy was founded there, chartered since, and attended last year by fifty-four scholars. The Government plans to set it up as a college. This town is only a short distance from the mouth of the Brandy-wine on the Christiana along which there are four flour mills whose ingenious mechanism, perfected by Oliver Evans of Philadelphia, was very much admired by connoisseurs. The first of these mills was built nearly seventy years ago. It is a pleasure while strolling on the bridge, to see this group of twelve to fifteen factories, with the whimsicalness of the wind from which they get their power, the charming little straggling town of Brandy-wine, the vessels laden with flour, wheat etc.—all this makes for a lively, interesting, and very picturesque sight. The proprietor of the largest mill near the bridge—it has twelve millstones—told me that in 1795 he had milled 600,000 bushels * of wheat, which had produced 114,000 barrels of superfine flour,** 12,000 of second quality, 18,000 of third, 6,000 of fourth, and 180,000 bushels of bran, weighing 34 to 36 pounds.

2 MUSKRATS. So-called because of the odor which they leave wherever they have tarried. Although much livelier and more humble than the beaver, they have the same industrious nature, the same talents, and appear to be miniatures of them. But not being strong enough to fell trees and build dams, they content themselves with building their dwellings with the wood and earth which they bring up from the shallow lakes, a short distance from the shores. The damage which they cause in the making of the dikes is often considerable and requires prompt repair. Their underfur, like the beaver's, is used in the manufacture of hats.

3 PASTURES. The lowlands, such as the islands that abound in the Delaware River from Philadelphia to Chester, the peninsula of Moyomensing, several coastal swamps in Sussex county and in Jersey, which a long time ago were drained and protected from the waters of the Delaware by means of dikes, have become of great profit. People think their fertility comes

---

* The bushel used in the United States is the Winchester bushel: it contains 60 pounds of wheat.

** According to the measurements of barrels prescribed by law, each of these barrels weighs a quintal and three quarters.

not only from the silt from which they have been formed in the long course of centuries, but also from the saltiness of the water. Most of these pastures produce today a gramineous element (known popularly as black grass), whose origin is unknown, and which grows nowhere else. It yields from three and one half to four and one half tons of hay per acre (7,700 to 9,900 pounds). Without the aid of any industry, it has replaced the milkwort (*glayeuls*), aquatic weeds, and the rush, all very common in all coastal regions of the middle states. These gramineous plants are so healthful that often horses from inland are sent to regain their health by grazing on these drained lands. These feeble conquests are nothing yet compared with the vast stretch of lands, either marshy or inundated, that one sees along the banks of the Delaware and large rivers, from one extremity of the United States to another. We must wait until the progress of population multiplies available manpower. The little state of Delaware will then be able to enrich itself by extremely fertile land, whose extent is reckoned at 6 or 7 thousand acres.

4   This little neighborhood is located five miles from the Christiana or Christine, seven miles from the town and in the Hundred of the same name.

5   HICKORY. Nut of which 4 kinds are known: the shellbark, the pignut, the keskétomah, and the wild hickory. It thrives in moist lands; then it grows like the oak. It is the finest burning firewood known. But although weighing as much as the former, it is apt to be riddled with hollow spots. Its nut, whose taste is delicious, has a very hard shell which requires a hammer to break. The Indians of the South make from it a milk with which they season many dishes. This tree can be found from Connecticut to western Florida. Some day it will be carefully cultivated, just as the sugar maple is.

6   QUAKER FARMERS. For a long time it has been observed that the colonists who live in the neighborhood of large Quaker and Moravian colonies are much more industrious and more serene, have moderate customs, and a more careful education than people of almost any other place. Such is the happy effect of a good example, which, if it were better known, would serve to convince those who, in their crazy pride, have believed that the teaching of religious precepts was useless; how much, on the contrary, these very precepts serve to make men more industrious, happier, more submissive to laws and better citizens.

I knew Mr. Johnson, a member of the Colonial Council of New-York, founder of one of the districts of Duchess County * in the State of New-York. Well-informed of the salutary effects of a religious education, this gentleman took with him only colonists of Quaker faith. How many times have I not shared his happiness in seeing the prosperity of this beautiful and fertile region swell rapidly, and these hardworking, modest, intelligent men become well-to-do and even opulent landowners?

7   QUAKERS IN THE TOWNS. Having little ambition to obtain employ-

* District of Nine-Partners.

ment, fill public offices that require oath, they devote themselves almost exclusively to business and manufacturing. In some respects, therefore they are apt to be, indeed they are, quite different from the Quakers who cultivate the land.

8   HYDRAULIC MACHINE. Its mechanism is so inexpensive and so simple that it is astonishing not to see it more frequently used in the great gardens of Europe. It consists of 2 platforms, 5 or 6 feet in diameter, mounted on 4 vertical standards to which the lower one must be solidly attached. The platform above is held and revolves over the first by means of 3 blades leading into a circular groove 2 inches deep. This platform is supposed to receive a small iron axle 5 or 6 feet in diameter, having in its middle a crank whose height must be ½ the play of the motion, that is to say, 4 inches; at one extremity blades are attached; under the other is a piece of wood inclined. This serves both as counterweight, and also to turn the mill. To this is attached the upper part of the spear of the pump, furnished with a handle, like a carbine-swivel. It is easy to imagine without going into elaborate detail that the wings of this axle, once they are put into motion by the wind, must necessarily make the pump go (or— must create torque). The length of these wings is proportionate to the resistance, which is not very great, unless one wishes to multiply the number of pumps, which, if the well has a copious yield, can be increased to 4.

CHAPTER III

1   CHECTAWS AND CHIKASSAWS. The Chectaws are formidable and numerous: they inhabit the beautiful land watered by the branches of the Tombéchée, the Alibama, and the Passagoola, whose waters empty into the Gulf of Mexico. Of all the Indians of this hemisphere, the Chectaws are the most advanced in civilization and in farming. Located on a fertile soil, surrounded by majestic forests, filled with fragrant bushes, and plains filled with game, they lead a quiet, peaceful life. Their houses are well-built and quite comfortable; the majority are surrounded by orange, cherry, and plum trees. A great number of Europeans have settled among them. The Chectaws came, as did the Seminoles, from the lands located west of the Mississippi. Some say that the hate, or rather antipathy, that exists among these nations dates from remote times. Some of these tribes occupy coastal regions watered by these beautiful rivers. Like their neighbors, they are fond of the dance; one might even say they have perfected it, and, surprisingly enough, one finds among them poets who produce poems for the great feast of the new fire. They have a religion and many tribal ceremonies. Their number is estimated at more than 20,000. Some of their wives are truly comely and quaint, even by European standards; they have sparkling eyes, aquiline noses, and a complexion that is not so dark as the northern Indians' color. It was among the Chectaws that the Natchez took refuge, when in 1730, they had the good fortune to escape the vengeance of the French.

The Chikassaws, coming from the same western lands, occupy the river-heads of the same rivers mentioned above, as well as the banks of the Yazoo, which empties into the Mississippi River, 163 leagues from the beacon. They are even more numerous than their neighbors and less civilized. For a long period of time these two nations harassed the French colony along the Mississippi and intercepted numerous convoys that plied up and downstream between New Orleans and the land of the Illinois. Their land, located under 34° and 35° latitude, watered by innumerable streams forming the Alibama, the Tombeéchée and the Passagoola, is one of the most healthful and fertile one can find. I owe all these details to Mr. Bernard Romans, Swiss officer whom Great Britain sent as geographer to this area a few years before the Revolution.

2 NATCHEES. A nation once famous and prolific. Not only was it the most civilized, but also one of the most advanced in skills of prime necessity. Its religion had a certain resemblance to that of the Peruvians. Headquarters of this nation was a big and beautiful plain known since as the Natchées' Plain, on the east bank of the Mississippi, 124 measured miles from the beacon, and 80 miles from New Orleans, under latitude of 31° 40'.

With warm hospitality the Natchées received the French colonists who came to settle among them and lived for a long time on good terms; but certain causes of dissension having arisen between these two peoples, the natives massacred a large number of their new neighbors, against whom they alleged they had much cause for grievance. A short time after this event, a detachment of troops from New Orleans destroyed or dispersed the entire nation. Since that time, 1730, this beautiful region has become very flourishing and is one of the best cultivated in Louisiana. The settlers are a mixture of French, English, Germans, and Americans. The healthfulness of this plain is due to its great elevation, estimated to be 200 feet above the level of the waters of this great river. It is along the bank of this ECORE, where Fort Rosalie was built. From there one's gaze embraces a vast horizon of grassy plains covered with sweet rush, the majestic Mississippi, a great distance off to the right and left, and islands covered with trees, which occupy some of its bed.

3 THE TENEZEE. This river, almost 300 leagues long, is formed by the joining of various branches, the Clinck, the Holston, the Nolachuky, the French-Broad, the Highwassée, etc.; on its banks the first settlements were made; to them the Ténézée gave its name. On one side these river branches flow from the chain of the Alléghénies, known under the name of the Great-Iron-Hills (Great Mountains of Iron); on the other side from the Chérokées or Cumberland, separated by a distance of twenty to thirty leagues. This river crosses the Alléghénies at a place known to geographers under the name of Suck or Whirl. In general, these waters are rapid as far as this crossing; but from that point through land scarcely mountainous at all, they are navigable as far as the Ohio. Near the sources of the Ténézée, one can still see ruins of former villages of

Chérokée, Tellico, Chatoga, Chata, Chillhowee, Talazée, Cowée, former headquarters in the beautiful valley of the same name; and near the sources of the Highwassée, one can see ruins of the ancient villages of the Chéwassée, New-Tellico, Nowée, Quanussée, etc. It is impossible to imagine locations that are cooler, more fertile, more delightful; richness of soil, healthful air, mild temperature—these are some of the advantages.

4 MUSSLE-SHOALS. Under this name an extension of the Ténézée is known. It is covered with islands and bottomlands which make crossing difficult for boats in certain seasons of the year. This little lake is near the center of the great elbow which this river forms—better known as Great-Bend.

5 HOLSTON. Main branch of the Ténézée that waters an extremely fertile area, and on the banks of which several towns have been established: Hawkins, Greenville, Jones'borough,* etc. In Holston one can also see several great forges, some salt mines which furnish the colonists with all the salt they need and a great number of mills. This is the part of this new state that was the first to be farmed.

6 NASHVILLE.** Town founded in 1783 on the south bank of the Chérokee or Cumberland; chief town of the district of Méro,*** one of those making up the State of Ténézée. There one can see an academy, named for its founder, Davidson, almost 300 houses and 1,400 inhabitants: in the surrounding area the finest cotton known in the States is cultivated. Nashville is located 375 leagues from Philadelphia, 231 leagues from Richmond in Virginia, 61 leagues from Knoxville, capital of this new state, 64 from Lexington in Kentukey, 14 from Clark'sville,**** built further down and forty leagues from the mouth of the Chérokée River on the Ohio. Discovered some distance from this town was a salt-works with remains of furnaces, whose design, shape, and full details were sent to the Duc de Rochefaucauld in 1787.

7 OUASIOTO. Great chain of mountains estimated to stretch twenty leagues and separated from the Alléghény chain by a great valley. For a long time the mountains have served as a haven for the remnants of the small nations whom the Chérokées have destroyed and of whom there remain only a few bandits, without village and without permanent homes. Driven out on all sides, they took to brigandage and thieving, and for a long time have been scourges to the emigrants who left Virginia for the new states of Kentukey and Ténézée. Inasmuch as people have stopped talking about them for quite some time now, it is quite probable that the frontier settlers whose scourge they had become, have destroyed them.

8 LANDS OF GEORGIA. In 1795 The Legislature of Georgia, composed of the most unscrupulous men in that State, whose constitution was then completely democratic, took it upon themselves to put up for sale the lands between their frontiers and the Mississippi. This, they said,

---

* Names of generals who distinguished themselves during the War of the Revolution.
** So-called after General Nash, killed in the Battle of Germantown.
*** So-called after the Spanish Governor of New-Orléans.
**** From the name of General Clark.

amounted to some forty or fifty million acres, without reckoning that two-thirds of these lands belong to the bellicose nations of the Creeks, Séminoles, Chectaws, and Chikassaws and that according to the federal constitution, they must return to the general Government of the Union, as soon as the Indians have sold them. Such a thing will probably not take place for many years. The first act of the Legislature that replaced the first, was to nullify this shameful transaction. We must hope that the new form of Government which has just been adopted, very similar to that of Pensylvania will re-establish order, decency, and respect for laws without which absolutely no kind of prosperity can exist in a civilized nation. It would be better to adopt a savage way of life than to be a member of a society so disorganized and to obey a Government without restraint and balance. These flaws, this instability will disappear with time.

9 UCHEE. Big and beautiful town Muscogulge (or Creek), with 1,500 inhabitants; is located on the banks of the Chattachée River, a branch of the Apalachicola, some distance from the juncture of the Pinchlucco. It is the headquarters of a great tribe of the same name, belonging to the Creek federation. Constantly one sees evidence of farming, as well as animals and horses that graze in the nearby grassy areas; thus they live in great abundance. Although very devoted to the cultivation of their fields, they do not neglect hunting, which seems to be their favorite occupation, and they are as skillfull in this pursuit as the Indians of the North. Their houses are good, solid frame dwellings inside as well as outside. Nowhere in the world will you see more gaiety and happiness.

10 ALATAMAHA. Great and magnificent river of Georgia which, after a course of one hundred fifty leagues, empties into the ocean at three outlets: opposite the islands of St. Simon, Jékill, and Sapello, thirty-four leagues south of Savanna. This river, navigable for nearly sixty-four leagues, is formed by the union of more than twenty branches which come down from the great chain of the Alléghénis, known in this State as the Apalachés. It is on their bases, low and fertile, that many of the Muscogulgé confederation live, under the name of Creek, because of innumerable streams which water this beautiful region giving it a freshness and beauty surpassed only by the voluptuous valleys of the Ténézée.

11 APALACHICOLA. Another big and beautiful river which empties into the Gulf of Mexico beyond the bay of the Apalaches. Like the Alahatama, it is formed by the union of various good-sized branches, the chief ones of which are the Flint, the Chata-Hoopsa, the Uchée, the Chata-Uchée, the Pinch-Lucco, etc. The mountains from which they flow being about one hundred fifty leagues from the sea, and the land only slightly mountainous, nearly all of them are navigable to their very sources to small boats and dugout canoes. At the juncture of some of these branches one sees many villages of the Muscogulge confederation; at that point they have easy access to the Gulf of Mexico, even going to Havana, where they take their deerskins, their honey, and other products of their land.

The Apalachicola divides the two Floridas. Fifty leagues from the sea several Seminole tribes have settled; they are known as inferior Creeks.

12 PEARL-RIVER. This river, navigable for seventy-five leagues, empties into Lakes Pont-Chartrain and Borgnes, located on the west branch of the Gulf of Mexico. Once upon a time the ancient nation of Yazoos lived near its source. Today they are extinct and only their name remains, given to a good-sized river which empties into the Mississippi, one hundred sixty-five measured leagues from the marker.

13 MACGILLVRY. His father, an Irishman by birth, had married a Seminole woman and lived in Georgia a long time before the Revolution. This young man, having been obliged to abandon his country at the beginning of the war, because of his devotion to the cause of the King, withdrew among the Creeks, his maternal kinsmen. Irritated by this, when peace came, the authorities, instead of recalling him, which was the custom in other States, outlawed him and deprived him of his patrimony. He became a Creek and shortly afterward, was raised by his new compatriots to the rank of Myco, king or chief of the Muscogulge confederation. Since that time he has fullfilled his duties with much energy and dignity.

In 1791, invited by the President of the United States to send deputies to Philadelphia in order to end the differences that had existed for a long time between the Muscogulgé nation and Georgia, he was represented by twelve warriors who embarked at Savannah and arrived without incident at the seat of Government. The shortest of these ambassadors stood five feet six inches. Their costume, strength, and the athletic vigor of their bodies, in addition to their noble bearing, were all greatly admired. I had the pleasure several times of dining at the home of General Washington, where, save for a few minor blunders, these Indians conducted themselves with great decorum. Quite different from the Indians of the North, they scarcely blushed at showing some degree of astonishment on beholding those churches, that market—one of the cleanest and most beautiful in this hemisphere—the streets, the sidewalks, the pumps, and especially the great number of vessels which abound on the Delaware. Their eyes sparkled on the day when the General, whom they called King or Chief of the United States, received them in a public hearing, with a happy combination of dignity, ceremony, and simplicity.

14 ST. AUGUSTINE. Chief town of eastern Florida, built at the foot of a bay of that name, protected from the Ocean by the Island of Matansa. The houses in the region are all built of stones taken from Saint-Anastase. The harbor, like all those in the south, is sometimes exposed to half-submerged rocks and has a bar which vessels cannot clear without the assistance of pilots.

15 WESTERN FLORIDA. This Spanish province is bounded on the south by the Gulf of Mexico, on the north by a line which begins at thirty-one degrees latitude on the Mississippi and runs parallel a distance of one hundred fifty leagues as far as the Apachicola, which separates it on the east from eastern Florida, and on the west by the Mississippi. With the

exception of a few coastal settlements, it is entirely in the possession of different tribes of the Seminole nation.

16 TREES OF THE MISSISSIPPI. Only in Georgia and certain regions of Florida does one see trees as high as those that shade the banks of this great river and the islands with which it is filled. The majority are magnolia, ash, holm oak, sycamore and cypress. I have journeyed in a dugout canoe made from the trunk of this latter type. The craft was sixty-one feet long, four feet nine inches wide, and carried forty men. It is difficult for travelers from the north to imagine the growth of these trees, their height, the extent of their branches, the picturesque beauty of their tops, as well as the vegetative strength of such a rich soil under a very warm sun. In general, the sycamores are taller than the cypress, but since their wood is light and much less durable, it is rarely used.

17 FORMER HEIGHT OF MISSOURI FLOODS. How were these vast grassy plains, these savannas formed? Some might have been lakes, similar to those in eastern Florida, whose waters in the spring drain into subterranean canals. But the growth on most of them is higher than that on the wooded lands which surround them. A Mr. Willing, major in a detachment of Continental troops that captured some Illinois during the War of Independence, told me that at some distance from the mouth of the Missouri in the Mississippi one can see on the banks, rocks whose tops, seventy feet above the level of that river, bear horizontal marks showing the former height of the waters. Similar marks can be seen on rocks not far from French-Broad, on which one hundred feet above their base, travelers believed they could distinguish the faces of animals and birds. Going back up the Tombéchée and the Alibama rivers, more than three hundred miles from the sea, and in many inland sections of Georgia, men have discovered enormous banks of oyster shells. From these the Chikassaws make lime and pottery works. Still further, in the direction of the mountains, fossils are visible. All this points to the fact that the surface of this continent has undergone great changes, since a time not too remote, for these oyster shells still exist, and also, the water level is considerably lower in the interior; all this was caused by the breaking away of the mountains in the interior, as well as the receding of those on the Ocean.

18 MANCHACK. On going back up the Mississippi from New Orléans one meets on the east bank of this river, thirty-seven leagues from that capital of Louisiana, a great opening whose bottom is elevated during dry spells to the extent of fifty feet above the level of that river. This is Manchack during its swellings, which elevate it to more than ninety feet; its waters flow through a canal into the bay of Perles, across Lakes Maurepas and Pont-Chartrain. The distance of this river to the navigable waters of the Yberville and the Amit being only three leagues, one could, by digging out this canal, which is dry six months of the year, open communication with the Mississippi; this would eliminate the dangers to vessels of the muck near the sea-mark and the difficulties encountered in going upstream for a distance of forty leagues.

Manchack is not the only canal through which the mighty waters of the Mississippi flow during floods. There are a great number, especially on the west bank, in going upstream as far as New-Madrid, a town, recently built opposite the mouth of the Ohio, three hundred leagues from Manchack. Immediately the river swells, these openings become like rivers overflowing their banks, leading these vast swellings into the San-Bernardo, whose mouth is in the Gulf of Mexico. It was at this very mouth, which they took to be the mouth of the Mississippi, that LaSalle and most of his companions perished.

19 DELTA OF THE MISSISSIPPI. If one can judge it by its soil, this Delta stretches nearly twenty leagues toward the East and just as far to the West and from the shores of the sea as far as Manchack. In this entire stretch one can find the kind of mud and the same debris on a deep bottom of white sand, which had been stirred up by the waters of the gulf. The progress of this Delta toward the mouths of the river is estimated at a league each century, or twenty-five fathoms a year; this conjecture is based on the distance to the marker which the French established at the time of their first colonization, and which is more than 2,000 fathoms from the spot where the Spanish fixed their marker. This swelling will cause no astonishment if one stops to think of the immense number of trees, reeds, canes, leaves, and mud which this river continually brings down. Once on the lowlands, these trees stop and become obstacles in the midst of which the waters deposit their endless débris. Soon raised to water level, these quicksandy areas produce watery plants that perish every year and contribute toward the raising or consolidating of this new soil.

20 ARCANSAS. A big and beautiful river on the west bank of the Mississippi, two hundred twenty-three leagues from the marker. Its sources, like those of the Missouri, which are still relatively unknown, are in the neighborhood of the mountains of Santa-Fé. During its long course, the Arcansas receives a great number of secondary rivers; the plains these rivers cross are inhabited by many nations that hunt on horse and come to exchange their game and pelts for the merchandise from Europe with the Spanish who have a fort near the mouth of the Arcansas River. These plains are filled with buffalo. The river has been explored upstream as far as two hundred leagues in the region of the Panissas, headquarters of a nation known by that very name, at 95° longitude and 36½° latitude.

21 ACADIANS. About the year 1745 Great Britain, to whom France had just ceded Acadia (today New Scotland—Nova Scotia), instead of keeping it for its former inhabitants, in accordance with the capitulation, snatched from its native land, under some frivolous religious pretext and without compunction at the sight of such a great crime, this gentle and hardworking people, men, women, children, old people, and sent some to Canada, others to New-York, to Maryland, and elsewhere. Some of the most well-to-do families chartered a vessel and came to settle in Louisiana, then a French colony, where they introduced the pastoral customs and

habits in which they had been raised. Poor, but honest and industrious, they settled near the grassy plains—most of them possessing but a single cow, whence have descended the great herds which they possess today and which have become the principal source of their wealth. These animals live all year on these fertile savannas; they are lost to sight, forgotten, their masters certain they will return to seek salt when this desire makes itself felt. The sky line is their parish.

Only a very small number of these inhabitants raised themselves above this primitive state to the point where they prefer the cultivation of rice, indigo, and tobacco. They retain the simplicity of customs and hospitable virtues of their ancestors. Satisfied and content with bare necessities, they know scarcely anything of the fever of desires that leads sometimes to prosperity through a thousand hazards and dangers, and more often to reverses and repentance. I have known some who, under this beautiful sky of Louisiana, on its fertile soil, still missed their cold, damp, and foggy land (an indestructible feeling, especially among upright and virtuous folk), and something even more astonishing, the French Government at that time did nothing for these subjects who were so deserving and so devoted.

22 THE FRENCH COLONY OF MOBILE. At the time when the French settlers began to farm along the banks of the Mississippi, a number of families of that nation established a good-sized settlement on the southern extremity of the island formed by the Tombéchée and Alibama rivers, and in the course of time they cleared several districts along these fertile river banks. One hundred leagues from this town at the junction of the Coosa, you can still see parts of cannon and evidence of houses. The descendants of some of these families who went from French to English to Spanish domination still retain their language and their former customs.

There is no land in the country more fertile than the land drained by the Alibama and its numerous branches; nature is as productive as in the torrid zone. There one can see everything from an apple tree to a pistachio tree. Today the region is inhabited by Creek tribes by whom travelers are always sure of being well received.

CHAPTER IV

1 CANADIANS. These people scarcely farm at all. The young Canadians, almost constantly busy paddling their canoes, laden with merchandise for the north country whence they return with furs, know very little of farming details and in this respect have much less experience than do the American colonists. Almost all those who spend their lives making these long journeys speak the language of the natives very well and have been accustomed to their ways. That is why in these respects as well as several others, of all the whites whom the Indians know, they like and admire most the Canadians. To be born in Canada is a reason for preference and protection; hence, the English employ no other agents in their trade. On

the contrary, wherever English troops are garrisoned, soldiers busy themselves with small-scale farming. The officers, to keep from becoming bored, build little rural retreats, which, in the eyes of the Indians, was "taking over" (something not rightfully theirs) and moreover, contributed toward frightening away game.

2 BEDFORD AND LIGONIER. The first of these forts was formerly constructed to protect the mountain pass; the second to protect the approach to Loyal-Hanning, on the road leading from Philadelphia to Pitt'sbourg. By slow degrees the region around these forts was farmed by the various garrisons; settlers came; municipal laws followed and these military sites have become true centers of the region.

3 FORKS OF THE MUSKINGHUM. This is the designation on maps by geographers of the point where this pretty river empties into the Muskinghum; it is about thirty miles from the forks, according to the route taken by the army commanded by General Bouquet.

4 LONG AND SHORT KNIVES. This expression means the bayonet of the infantry and the saber of the cavalry. It was with the aid of the latter army that the mountain-dwelling colonists of the Ténézée repulsed on several occasions the vigorous attacks of the Chérokées during the War of the Revolution, and forced them to make peace. The greatest difficulty these cavalrymen had to overcome was that of feeding their horses in the woods for nearly a month.

5 MISISKUOY. A big bay on the east shore of Lake Champlain, today included in the territory of the State of Vermont. The boundaries of Canada, fixed at 45° latitude, are only a short distance. From the time of the French settlers, more than half of this state was part of Canada. This bay is navigable way up the shore and well inland and very abundant in fish, especially in salmon, which come down the St. Lawrence, the Richelieu River, and Chambly Rapids to enter this lake every year.

6 BONDS OF ADOPTION. Several years ago in a birchbark canoe, guided by two Abénakis from lower Canada, I had the misfortune to be shipwrecked at the headwaters of the St. Lawrence, whose falls, six leagues long, we had just cleared. The first snows had just fallen. Without axe and without any means of lighting a fire, reduced to eating raw the few fish we had the good fortune to catch, we resolved to walk south, and, in order not to get lost in the woods, to keep the river in sight on our left. Dying of cold, spent, and exhausted, we had reached the third day of this arduous journey and had just eaten the last morsels of our last fish, when to our great joy we thought we saw in the distance evidence of smoke. It was coming from a big village of Christianized Mohawks near the mouth of the Osswégatché River, widely known then by the same name and today included in the territory of the United States. As soon as we had arrived within call, my companions crouched and let out howls several times. At these cries of pain some Indians from the village came to see who we were and soon, touched by our misery, they took us to their village without a word and placed us in three different families. Chance placed

me, a white man, in the wigwam of the one who was both chief and sachem of this village and who, consequently, united the pre-eminence of age with the authority of a chief. After taking my hand and offering me the great tribal peace pipe, this old man said to me:

"Welcome, no matter whence you have come. Rest your bones on this bearskin, warm yourself and eat."

He spoke a little English and French: his family consisted of four women and three men. The next day, after I had informed him from whence I came and whither I was bound, he said to me:

"Winter approaches, as you see; already the great river sweeps along broken ice; ice has formed solid on our river; it is impossible to go to Montreal ere spring. Put aside the little bit of clothing that you still have and dress as we do; our people will like you better thus."

Scarcely had I consented by shaking his hand, when the women approached with eagerness, and laughing the while, cut my hair, painted my face, brought me clothes I would need. They did not even forget to give me a name. After a few days getting used to things, I realized I was as well-housed and clad as though I had been among friends in Montreal; one adjusts so easily to everything when one is young. Like the others, I went fishing morning and night, sometimes through the ice, sometimes with a net, according to the temperature or amount of snowfall, and I was proud indeed to be able to help fill the pot. In addition, we had corn aplenty and potatoes, for since the time when this tribe became Christianized, they have cultivated the soil with greater care and foresight. With the inner bark of the birch tree I made myself a huge book in which I carefully wrote all the words of their language whose meanings I could fathom. This seemed to bring them as much pleasure as though I had rendered them an important service.

Time passed without tedium in the midst of all these pursuits; toward the end of January a young man arrived, laden with furs and frozen meat. It was one of the sons-in-law of old Minickwac and the husband of the woman who had been most eager to cut my hair and paint, and even tattoo me. Already I understood enough words of their language to be aware that the newcomer spoke Mohawk almost as badly as I. Surprised at this, I asked the reason of old Minickwac; here is what he told me:

"This man, Kittagawmick, of the ancient tribe of Ouasioto, was taken prisoner several years ago by some of our warriors. Having arrived in this village, he was adopted by one of my daughters, whose husband had been drowned coming down the long falls of the great river. He is one of our most skillful hunters, as you can see from the quantity of beaverskins he has brought. After a few years' stay here, his first wife arrived in the land of the Mohawks to reclaim him—something even the most ancient had not seen happen: a message was sent here which surprised us a great deal; a return message was sent from here; the winter passed. For my part, I did not know what to think and Kittagawmick knew nothing. Missionaries became involved in matters. Some of our people wanted to send this woman back to her country; others, on the contrary, wanted her to take back Kittigawmick, her first husband. Finally, in order to do only what was fair, Henrique Nissooassoo, great chief of the Mohawk tribe, lighted the council fire at Oriskany, where he invited the sachems, the old men and the thinkers: I, too, was there. In spite of what the priests and the white men said, here is what was decided after several peace pipes had been slowly smoked.

"The day when Kittigawmick was taken prisoner, he could have been killed or put in the pot, and, according to custom, his marriage with Cattaw-Wassy would have been dissolved; but having been taken to the village of Osswégatchée and adopted by Kippokitta, and enjoying a new life, which he owed to his second wife by adoption, the first no longer meant anything to him.

"This is what I learned in 1765. After grieving over this decision for a long time, Cattaw-Wassy consoled herself by marrying one of the Indians from Oriskany with whom she lived for a long time. Sir William Johnson, as well as many other whites, who admired the courage she had shown in coming alone from her country a distance of more than two hundred leagues, showered many presents on her. She was the first woman of this large village who had a cow, a horse, and a house, where one could find milk, butter, meat, and two beds. What even slightly informed man in colonial times has not heard the name of Cattaw-Wassy? With further education, she would have become a distinguished woman."

I could cite several other examples of the respect which the natives have for adoption, if that were necessary—especially the most ancient nations, such as the Outawas, the Shawanèses, the Chérokées, etc.

7 The military concession given by the former Congress to officers and soldiers of the Massachussetts league, as well as the acquisitions they have made from the Government since that time, including almost all the land watered by the Muskinghum and its branches, and those two ancient military sites of the army of General Bouquet, are inhabited and farmed today: for, in spite of the war with the Indians that lasted three years, this colony of former soldiers has increased considerably; it is one of the most flourishing of all those one can see today along the banks of the Ohio, except for Kentukey, founded in 1772.

CHAPTER V

1 BARK OF THE BIRCH. This is one of the most beautiful and most majestic trees that one meets in the forests; the further north one ventures, the greater their height and girth. It is not rare to find them in Canada and in the province of Maine, from three to three and one half feet in diameter. It is with its bark that the Indians cover their wigwams and sheathe their canoes. They have a knack of removing only the first layer, without wounding the tree, which after a few years replaces this layer. I have seen some birch layers four feet wide and six feet long.

2 NORTHWEST WIND DURING WINTER. The impetuosity, cold, and continuance of this wind, which in a single night can freeze over the sur-

face of the rivers, is a truly extraordinary phenomenon. I have heard tell of several ships captains who, after trimming their sails at Sandy-Hook, had been chased by this wind as far as Europe, and with phenomenal violence. One day when I asked Dr. Franklin what could be the cause of such a powerful effect, he told me this:

"I believe that these are the winds from the south, which after having stirred up and agitated the waters of the Gulf of Mexico with so much violence, rampaged over the plains of Louisiana as far as the sources of the Mississippi; perhaps they even got as far as Lakes Bourbons and Assiniboels; there they meet the wind from the north, no less impetuous: from the balance, or rather the conflict of their strengths, results a diagonal direction, which is, of course, northwest."

"But," I said to him, "why is this wind less violent in the lands beyond the mountains than it is here? It seems to me that it would be even more."

"It is," Dr. Franklin replied, "because it takes on added strength and impetuosity in breaking loose over the Alléghény mountains from the top of which it swoops down over our north Atlantic States."

3 MUSCAWISS. This strange bird, big as a male falcon, has brown feathers with spots of dazzling white. It appears only one or two hours before sunset; then from all directions one can hear the noise of its capers, its darting about, its sudden and rapid falls which give rise to the notion of cunning and madness. Its strange flight resembles none other that I have ever seen; one can conceive of nothing lighter, but scarcely do the shadows of night begin to cover the land, when these birds descend from on high, perch on the lower branches of the trees, on the fences, often even swooping down in the middle of fields, where they pass away the hours of the night repeating their monotonous and gloomy tones, which the Indians represent as *muscawiss* and the colonists as whip-poor-will. It is also known by muskito-hawk. No one knows on what it lives, where it lays its eggs, or what becomes of it in winter time. Nothing is more amazing than the extreme agitation of its movements, the nimbleness, the speed of its flight and its constant immobility, as well as the sadness of its tones all through the night; these tones seem to be those of pain or of deep anxiety.

CHAPTER VII

1 SKÉNECTADY. This town is located 14 miles from Albany, on the Mohawk, where the lower section of this river begins to be navigable as far as its junction with the Hudson River, being obstructed by the Falls at Cohos, as well as by a long series of rocks. The town was built about a century ago in this fertile region, by a mixture of Dutch and Flemish families. In Skénectady merchandise to go up the river is loaded, and also, products from the whole northwestern part of the state are unloaded at this town, to be taken overland as far as Albany. In order to facilitate this hitch in the water transportation, the people of this region are talking of opening a canal that would unite the waters of the Mohawk and the

Hudson rivers. Since the legislature of this State has established itself in Albany, it is hoped that the Government will encourage the completion of this great and useful undertaking.

2   STATE HOUSE. House of the State. It was built in 1746, 64 years after the founding of Philadelphia. The columns and the posts of the doors and casement windows, which are of marble, were sent by the Society of Friends of Philadelphia: but what makes this building much more interesting in the eyes of the observer, other than its clumsy style of architecture, is that 94 years after the arrival of William Penn, the independence of the colonies was proclaimed, and under the venerable roof of this State House, 11 years later (in 1787) the Federal Convention assembled. To the deliberations of this body the United States owes the wise Government that directs its affairs.

3   DISPENSARY. Apothecary's shop founded and maintained by contributions; from it, medicines and restoratives are distributed free to the sick on presentation of a certificate from one of the subscribers. This association, which has just been incorporated, also pays an apothecary and a doctor whose duty it is to hold consultations, and even to visit the sick, when necessary. There are two kinds of annual subscriptions. The first is only 5 piastres, the second 50. The greater the amount subscribed, the greater the number that can be treated. The following chart will give an idea of the good that can be accomplished by these admirable institutions; the chart represents the number of sick persons who have been received at the Dispensary in Philadelphia during the first 44 months of its establishment, that is to say, from April 12, 1786, the time of its birth, to December 12, 1789. What relief it has lavished since!

April 12, 1786–December 12, 1786

NUMBER OF SICK PERSONS INSCRIBED
ON THE REGISTER, 719

Idem. Cured	562
Idem. Dead	32
Idem. Relieved	33
Idem. Dismissed for bad conduct	7
Idem. Hospitalized	2
Idem. Incurable	1
Idem. Not yet cured	82
Total	719

December 12, 1786–December 12, 1787

NUMBER OF SICK PERSONS INSCRIBED
ON THE REGISTER, 1,653

Idem. Cured	1,297
Idem. Dead	69

Idem. Relieved	137
Idem. Dismissed for bad conduct	24
Idem. Hospitalized	6
Idem. Incurable	4
Idem. Not yet cured	116
	Total 1,653

December 12, 1787–December 12, 1788

NUMBER OF SICK PERSONS INSCRIBED
ON THE REGISTER, 1,596

Idem. Cured	1,294
Idem. Dead	81
Idem. Relieved	84
Idem. Dismissed for bad conduct	27
Idem. Hospitalized	13
Idem. Incurable	0
Idem. Not yet cured	97
	Total 1,596

December 12, 1788–December 12, 1789

NUMBER OF SICK PERSONS INSCRIBED
ON THE REGISTER, 1,863

Idem. Cured	1,561
Idem. Dead	85
Idem. Relieved	88
Idem. Dismissed for bad conduct	19
Idem. Hospitalized	12
Idem. Incurable	2
Idem. Not yet cured	96
	Total 1,863

Thus, in a period of 44 months, 5,831 persons received aid from this Dispensary and were cared for in their homes.

4 HUDSON. This town was founded in 1784 by Seth and Thomas Jinkins, Quakers from Rhode Island, on the east bank of the river whose name it borrowed, eighteen leagues from Albany and forty-eight leagues from New-York. Never has speculation been more skillfully combined to realize the hopes of the founders, and extraordinarily enough, they received from the Government a charter to incorporate, and were named chiefs of this new municipal body, even before the first house of this town was built, so great was the esteem that the integrity and talents of these strangers had inspired! * The location of this town, whose streets are wide and

* I was present when Governor Clinton promised it to them.

lined up, is about a thousand square (toises), divided into thirty shares. Each of these subdivisions contains two rows of thirty parcels; each parcel is fifty feet wide and one hundred twenty feet deep. The first task with which these skillful people busied themselves, was to lead a brook here from a distance of three miles, by means of an aqueduct, not elaborate, it is true, but good and solid. There are eighteen feet of water at the town wharves; already the town boasts seven hundred fifty houses and from four to five thousand inhabitants; several distilleries, some whale oil manufacturing works and a sailcloth company, etc. Herring fishing, which they know how to smoke in the Dutch style, is very abundant hereabouts. Last year there were fourteen vessels used in foreign trade, four whalers, and six sloops, busy in transporting to New-York the products of a fertile land that stretches to the western part of Massachussetts.

5 SPERANZA. Town newly founded on the west bank of the Hudson, 49 leagues from New-York, and 17 from Albany, in the district of Lunnenbourg, inhabited by descendants of Palatine families, whom Queen Anne sent after the destruction of the Palatinate. Already there are 27 houses, several log houses, and 2 sloops to transport the products of the land to New-York. The prosperity of this young town depends on the progress of the clearings inland, still not far along, but the long and beautiful road which the Government is opening as far as the land of the Jénézées, branches of which the town founders have undertaken and already begun, will not be long in attracting colonists who will spread and give fresh life to its trade. The depth of the waters at the wharves of the town is from 16 to 18 feet. This town has just been incorporated; the municipality is already organized, as though the population were considerable—and there are scarcely 300 souls.

6 ALBANY. A big and beautiful town, second in the State of New-York, located at the end of the maritime navigation on the Hudson River, 66 leagues from that capital and 78 from the sea. In the beginning it was only a small fort, long known under the name of Fort Orange, intended to protect the fur trade of the early Dutch settlers, who, in 1623, founded the colony known as New-York. It was incorporated in 1686. There are 1,300 or 1,400 houses and 9,000 inhabitants. Albany's location at the head of such a beautiful river, in the midst of a vast region whose clearing, farming, and improvements are increasing every day, all promise great prosperity to this second capital of the State. Additional favorable factors: the navigation of the Mohawk River extended as far as Lake Ontario and the land of the Jénézées by the opening of the canals at Little-Falls and Stanwick; the roads being opened by the Government, the bridges built in recent years, the arrival of a great number of colonists from the northern States and from Europe, the competition which arouses and spurs on the persevering work of the inhabitants of Troye, Lansingbourg, and Hudson, towns founded since peace; lastly, the residence of

the Government. Less than twenty years ago only Dutch was spoken there; everything was dead or inanimate; the young people were inclined neither toward business ventures nor knowledge. Nothing was narrower than the sphere of their activity and projects. Timid carefulness made them prefer an idle and monotonous life to the risks of even the most feeble speculations, a state of mind remote indeed from the spirit that motivates the inhabitants of a land where everything is growing and progressing with astonishing rapidity. The surveyor-general, Mr. Du-Witt, had established a reading-room; no one used it. What a difference today! The language, the customs, the very shape of the houses—everything has improved there. One single obstacle interfered with navigation on the river (the Over-Slaugh); they are working to raise the water level with machines such as those that were used several years ago on the Connecticut River.

A bank was established in Albany; it has been incorporated. The fertile lands bordering the river yield abundantly, but the winters are long and severe. The outskirts of the town are filled with mills and manufactures, powered by water.

7 OVER-SLAUGH. This is a good-sized sand bar located 6 or 7 miles from town and caused by the great stretch of water as well as by some low and sparsely wooded islands. Public spirit, which is beginning to awaken among the inhabitants of Albany, especially since the residence of Government and the arrival of a great number of foreigners, has shown itself through a large subscription, the income from which is being spent on work to narrow the bed of the river and remove the sand bar.

8 CANALS. See the following table.

9 INLAND NAVIGATION. With the aid of a map of the coastal parts of the United States, it is easy to see that as soon as the Norfolk canal is completed (it probably is now) from the mouth of all of the rivers that empty into any of the sounds of North Carolina, one could easily reach the strait of Currituck and from there, by means of this canal, the Delaware Bay. From the waters of this gulf, one could enter the waters of the Delaware River, proceed upstream and cross the Choptang, which leads to the Bohemia River; from the mouth of this, it will be easy to make one's way upstream on the Delaware to the Assompink, from whose headwaters the planned canal will conduct boats to the Rariton River, whose waters mingle with those of the Great Bay of New-York. From this point an arm of the sea, sheltered from the ocean by the island of Nassau (actually Long Island's first and official name) and several others, leads to the very heart of Buzzard's Bay, located west of the peninsula formed by Cape Cod. Proceeding up Herring River, one would enter Barnstable Bay, which is part of Massachussetts, by the Bowdouin canal whose pitch on one side is only 34 feet and whose cost has been estimated, according to data I saw in the hands of Governor Bowdouin, at only 107,163 piastres (562,606 francs). Such is the brief picture of this navigation of nearly 400 leagues, which in war time, will be of the greatest

use, since it could compensate for coastal trade then. Besides the advantage of bridging considerably the distance by crossing Bowdouin canal, one would avoid circumnavigation of the entire peninsula of Cape Cod, which is more than 100 leagues long and very dangerous.

10 It is estimated that the land owned and acquired from the Indians by the Government up to the beginning of the war, in 1791 amounted to 35 million acres, in which we must include the military concession of the Muskinghum, of 1,500,000 acres, purchase of which the same soldiers made from the Government, to the extent of 4,901,480 acres; the three districts of Salem, Gnadden-Hutten and Schoenburn, granted to the Moravian brothers for use by their native converts, and located on the Muskinghum and Némenshéhélas rivers, of 22,000 acres; the 3,000,000 acres sold to the colony of Colombia, located on the Ohio between the two Miami rivers, established in 1784 by Colonel Symmes; as well as other military and private concessions.

I do not know what amount the Government obtained by fixing certain boundaries agreed on between the United States and the Shawanèse, Mingo, and Wyandot nations on the occasion of their peace negotiations in 1794. Judging them from the location of Forts Defiance, Recovery, Waynes, Lawrence, etc., built to determine and assure these boundaries, this amount is to be quite a bit greater than what the Government owned before this war, in which these nations were unfortunately involved through English politics.

CHAPTER VIII

1 ELAN. The elk. This animal has the height and hair of the horse; his tail is very short; his horns are of prodigious size and are not branching like those of the buck; rather, they are flat and 8 or 10 inches wide. He is remarkable for his speed. One sees him only in the forests of the Northern States and in Canada.

CHAPTER IX

1 ACADEMIES OR BIG SCHOOLS IN CONNECTICUT. Those of Greenfield, Plainfield, Norwich, Windham, Pomfret, etc. are all heavily endowed and famous for their instruction. Two grammar schools founded in 1657 by Governor Hopkins, one at Hartford and the other at Newhaven; their purpose, according to the dedication:

"... in order that the young people of this colony, who constitute its fine nursery, which is the hope and heritage of the colony, can be properly instructed."

Besides these academies, in all the districts there are schools financed by the Government. These institutions are so respected, that the annual amounts allotted to them are always included in what is called the civil list.

Here is the summary of the charter of incorporation granted to the college of Newhaven. The Government of the State, the Lieutenant-

State of New-York

Finished	Little Falls	to avoid a rapid over the Mohawk
Finished	Stanwick	To unite the waters of the Mohawk, with Wood-Creek and the Oneida
Planned	Onondaga	To avoid the falls of the Onondaga
Planned	Three Rivers ...	To avoid a rapid
Planned	Schenectady	To unite the waters of the Hudson and Mohawk
Planned	South-Bay	To unite the waters of Lake Champlain and the Hudson

Pennsylvania

Finished	Conewago	To avoid a rapid in the Susquehannah
Half-finished ..	Swatara	To unite the waters of the Swatara with the Tulpéhoken, branch of the Schuylkill
Begun	Schuylkill	To unite the waters of the Schuylkill with the Delaware, in the vicinity of Philadelphia
Planned	Juniata	To avoid obstacles in the Susquehannah at its junction with the Swatara
Planned	Presqu'Ile	To unite the waters of the Erie with those of the Allegheny, through the Vénango
Sketched	Bohemia	To unite the waters of the Chesapeake with those of the Delaware.

Maryland

Begun	Maryland	To unite the waters of the Susquéhannah, with those of the Chesapeake, eight miles above Havre de Grace; government enterprise.

Virginia

Finished	Washington	To avoid the first falls of the Potawmack
Finished	Potawmack	To avoid the second falls of the Potawmack
Finished	Richmond	To avoid the long rapids of the James River
¾ finished	Norfolk	To unite the waters of the Chesapeake, with those of Albémarle Sound, in North Carolina

North Carolina

Finished	Skupernong	To unite the waters of the Skupernong with those of Dismal Swamp, in the county of Currituck

South Carolina

Finished	Charlestown	To unite the waters of the Santee River with those of the Cooper
Planned	Peedee	To unite the Peedee with the Santee
Planned	Wateree	To unite the Wateree with the Santee

New-Hampshire

Finished	Hampton	To channel the waters of the Merrimack

Connecticut

Finished	Hadley	To avoid a rapid on the Connecticut River

Vermont

Finished	Bellows	To avoid a 30-foot rapid on the Connecticut River

Massachussets

Planned	Bowdouin	To unite the waters of Buzzard's Bay with Herring River, which empties into Massachussets Bay; this will avoid a circumnavigation of more than 100 leagues around Cape-Cod.
Planned	Massachussets ..	To unite the waters of the Connecticut River with those of the Charles River

New-Jersey

Planned	Assompink	To unite the waters of the Delaware with those of the Raritan; this would complete an inland navigation of more than 350 leagues, from Edenton, in North Carolina, as far as Boston

Governor and six of the first members of the council of State, in conjunction with eleven ministers of the Bible, form the deliberating body of it; it can own property in free hold land; it can perpetuate itself through vote; it can draft all regulations necessary to matters temporal of this college, as well as make academic laws which will contribute toward perfecting the teaching of sciences. The executive power, entrusted to the president and a fixed number of professors, can confer all the degrees of a university.

2   ORIGIN OF THE BIG HOSPITAL OF THE TOWN OF NEW-YORK. On May 22, 1769, in accordance with custom, the anniversary of this hospital was celebrated in the college of this town. Among the speeches made was that by Samuel Bard, a young Doctor who had come from Edinbourg, where his parents had sent him to complete his studies. The speech attracted attention and deserved the applause of the audience, as he gave clear indication of the necessity of establishing a hospital on a high, spacious, and convenient spot, which he designated. The usefulness of this project, together with the animated style of the speaker, made such a strong impression on the group, that the Governor (Sir Henry Moore at the time) immediately opened subscription by contributing 100 guineas and promising a charter of incorporation in the name of the King. His proposals were accepted and his example followed with eagerness.

A short time afterward the Legislative assembly of this colony, in sanctioning this fine foundation, gave the subscribers a considerable sum and the very next year the building was begun, located one mile from the town and a short distance from the Hudson.

3   ORIGIN OF THE MARINE SOCIETY OF NEW-YORK. Another establishment no less useful has rendered this year remarkable in the annals of this city. Several days after a violent storm had thrown a number of ships on the nearby coast, the widows of the sailors who had perished appeared with their children at the chamber of commerce, to beg for aid, which they needed. Deeply moved by this saddening sight, the members clubbed together to raise money and gave them pensions.

On thinking over the dangers to which sea-faring men are exposed, the members of the chamber of commerce conceived the idea of establishing a permanent fund from subscription by citizens who might encourage this institution, as well as a portion of the wages and allowances of sailors desiring to assure their families a decent living after their death. A committee was named. After drafting a programme, it called a meeting of all the townspeople, by means of the newspapers. A great number of persons were eager to subscribe and the sailors made arrangements assigning a portion of their wages for the cause. Two months later the Government granted the organization a corporate charter. Such was the origin of the Marine Society of this town; its capital has become considerable. The excellent administration by its leaders is above my feeble praises. Although I am not a sailor, I am honored to be a member of this worthy association.

4 LITERARY SOCIETIES; CHARITABLE INSTITUTIONS OF PHILADELPHIA. I think one can regard Philadelphia as the town on this continent where there are the most useful institutions and associations, proportionate to population and wealth. The following summary will prove this.

Founded 40 years ago by Dr. Franklin with various other persons, the university, whose first subscriptions have been augmented substantially by the Government, which has granted it a charter of corporation, is one of the most respected bodies in the land.

Philosophical Society, founded in 1769 by Dr. Franklin and others; incorporated in 1780. Its charter permits it to enjoy a net income of 10,000 piastres (52,000 pounds). The spirit expressed in the preamble of its charter is so splendid, that I believe I should quote an extract for the reader (see Note 4A following).

Dickenson College founded at Carlisle in 1783 by the Government at the request and during the administration of the worthy Dickenson, then governor of Pensylvanie. In 1797 there were 142 scholars.

College of Franklin for German young people, founded in 1787 by the Government at Lancaster, in accordance with the suggestion and during the administration of Dr. Franklin, then Governor of that State.

York Academy, founded in 1783 by the inhabitants of this town, incorporated by the legislative body. In 1797 there were 92 scholars.

Academy of Germantown, founded before the Revolution.

Academy of Pitt'sbourg on the Ohio, founded and incorporated in 1787. It is the furthest inland academy in the state.*

There are others, which, like this one, have been established and endowed by public spirit. The legislative body has just given 60,000 acres of land for schools, and 60,000 additional acres for literary institutions.

Society founded in 1787 for the purpose of research and study of politics.

COLLEGE FOR DOCTORS, founded in 1787, incorporated in 1789.

PENSYLVANIA HOSPITAL, founded by contributions in 1750; enlarged in 1751 and 1756.

THE DISPENSARY, founded in 1786 to furnish free medicine to all those appearing with a certificate from one of the subscribers. A committee, composed of several members, and some doctors are in attendance there every day. More than 2,000 persons were treated there last year. From this one can see, not without astonishment, the miracles that the accumulation of small funds can make possible, for the subscription is only 1 guinea and there are between 600 and 700 subscribers.

SOCIETY OF PENSYLVANIA for the abolition of slavery and for the protection of Negroes unjustly held in bonds of servitude, founded in 1774 and incorporated in 1787.

MORAVIAN SOCIETY, whose aim is to spread knowledge of the Gospel and of civilization among the Indians. It is impossible to possess more zeal, courage, and perseverance than do these pious missionaries.

* The town of Pitt's bourg, on the Ohio, is 140 leagues from the Delaware capes.

SOCIETY TO ENCOURAGE USEFUL ARTS AND MANUFAC-TURES. It is supported by the generous contributions of men, zealous for the prosperity of their country. It is a precious seed which has already borne fine fruits and which will bear many more, as soon as population has increased. The object of this splendid and useful group is to encourage the manufacture of silk, cotton, linen, wool, iron, leather, lead, pottery, furs, etc. It is presided over by a president, 4 vice-presidents, 12 administrators, 2 secretaries and a treasurer, elected annually.

In 1787 it gave 15 prizes, 3 of 50 piastres, 2 of 30, and 10 of 20: total 410 piastres (2,152 pounds).

In 1789 it awarded 17, to wit: 15 gold medals, each weighing 5 guineas, as first prizes; 15 silver as second prizes of 200 piastres (1,050 pounds) and one for 100.

In 1790 the Society offered 2 prizes, each medal of gold weighing the equivalent of ten guineas to the persons of any nation who wrote the finest report on the following subjects:

What is the best system of taxation for a growing country whose prosperity is founded on the progress of agriculture, commerce, and manufacture?

To what extent should the Government make regulations for this branch of administration?

This society was followed by another, established in colonial times; its object was the cultivation of silk and in the society's registry, one can see the following details for the year 1771:

SILK

RECEIVED FROM JUNE 25 TO JULY 3	817 pounds	15 ounces
From the 4th to the 10th	580	7
From the 11th to the 18th	92	10
From the 19th to the 24th	174	10
From the 25th to the 1st	47	2
From the 8th to the 15th	41	8

SOCIETY FOR SHIP INSURANCE.
ANOTHER SOCIETY for the insurance of houses. The usefulness of this society is felt even in the inland towns.

SOCIETY FOR IMPROVING THE LOT OF PRISONERS. Since the introduction of solitary confinement and the change in the penal laws of the State, this Society has become less useful.

SO-CALLED SOCIETY OF HUMANITY. To revive persons who have been shipwrecked; founded in 1770.

SOCIETY OF ST. PATRICK, ST. ANDREW AND ST. GEORGE. To help assist the emigrants of Ireland, Scotland, and England.

SOCIETY OF AGRICULTURE. This association is the fruit of the most active zeal and of many contributions. The rewards that it offered in 1789 were a plaque of gold, weighing 56 guineas bearing an inscription; 13 gold medals, each weighing 5 guineas and 13 silver medals. Its location is impressive and was given to the association by the Government.

SOCIETY FOUNDED FOR THE BENEFIT OF GERMAN EMIGRANTS.

MARINE SOCIETY, SIMILAR TO THE ONE IN NEW-YORK.

SOCIETY FOUNDED FOR THE BENEFIT OF WIVES AND CHILDREN OF PRESBYTERIAN MINISTERS.

THE SOCIETY OF QUAKERS' CHARITY. Never has an institution fulfilled more effectively the aim of its founders. Nothing has been forgotten that could mitigate the harshness of misfortune and poverty or console old age. The interior of this establishment is one of the most interesting things one can see in Philadelphia.

DR. KEARSLEY'S ENDOWMENT FUND. For the purpose of feeding, clothing, and housing 12 widows of the Episcopal clergy.

Just as in New-York, each religious group has its charitable institutions, for the benefit of widows and orphans of its clergy and for those who have made contributions.

ASSOCIATION OF CAPTAINS AND OFFICERS OF MERCHANT SHIPS. To assure, in case of misfortune, a decent living and haven for their old age.

SOCIETY OF PILOTS. Similar to the one in New-York.

ACADEMY to instruct young ladies in the humanities. Those whose parents are not in a position to pay, are admitted free. The annual meeting of this splendid institution attracts all of the most respectable persons in the town. The closing address is always made by a prominent person whose oratorical talents are well known.

SCHOOL FOR YOUNG NEGROES, where they are taught the elements of religion, reading, writing, and arithmetic; the young Negresses are taught to sew, knit, etc. It was founded in 1780 by Antoine Bénézet of reverent memory (see Note 4B following), who bequeathed the society 50,000 francs. Since then, this institution has received various gifts from different parts of the continent, and even from London. That worthy citizen, Bénézet was its first teacher.

SUNDAY SCHOOLS. To forewarn of the abuse made by the young people of the liberty they enjoy on that day.

PUBLIC LIBRARY, founded 40 years ago by Dr. Franklin and a great number of associates; its subscriptions go toward maintaining and expanding it. The setting for this library is very beautiful.

SOCIETY OF CARPENTERS, JOINERS, ROPE-MAKERS, TAILORS, CLOCKMAKERS, WIGMAKERS, etc., whose aim is the establishment of postal savings banks intended to aid the members of these associations during their illnesses. In 1787 the legislative body of Pensylvania passed 15 laws for incorporation of churches, schools, and other establishments.

"Some time after arriving in Philadelphia," Mr. Herman told me, "after seeing a man whom I did not know enter my home, I asked him what he wanted of me."

"To dress your hair," he replied.

"Why didn't N. come today?"

"He had the misfortune to fall on the deck of a vessel. I was sent to replace him until he is feeling well enough to walk."

"Who sends you?"

"The committee from our society."

"What society are you talking about?"

"Society of hairdressers. In order to remedy the double misfortune of losing both health and business, they formed an association in whose treasury each member deposits the fruit of his savings which, however, cannot be less than 2 shillings per week (1 pound sixpence): these amounts are invested in government stocks, where we already have almost 500 piastres (2,600) pounds. When one of the members becomes sick, he is cared for at the society's expense; care is taken immediately to replace the amount used. Rarely does one meet persons who refuse this little obligation."

"Dress my hair well," I told him, "and do not fail to come back tomorrow. I would have a poor opinion of anyone who would not admire these fraternal associations, unfailing sources of consolation and goodness; and who would not bless, as I do, the person who first conceived the idea, or brought the idea from whatever country he came."

4A "Whereas, in all ages and in all civilized lands, the study of useful knowledge has contributed greatly toward perfecting industry, agriculture, and commerce, improving society, increasing happiness, and providing a more bountiful life.

"Whereas, the immense sweep, the variety of soils and climates, the internal treasures of the land, until now unknown, as well as the great number of lakes and rivers scattered over the surface of this continent, which divine Providence has bequeathed to us, promising to the United States one of the vastest expanses for farming and improvements that has ever been offered human industry.

"Whereas, societies composed of scholars meeting without regard to nation, creed, or cause contribute toward the dissemination of knowledge and enlightenment, toward the propagation of *l'esprit philosophique et humain,* in arousing young people to persevere in the quest for wisdom and truth.

"Whereas, many citizens of Pensylvania and of other States of the Union, aroused by public spirit and true patriotism, have voluntarily met, for a great number of years, under the name of members of the AMERICAN PHILOSOPHICAL SOCIETY, and through their projects and research have extended the reputation of their country to the most enlightened nations of Europe, where many learned men have expressed the desire to become associated with their projects.

"Whereas, finally, that the meeting of this society, interrupted so long by the calamities of war, is the expressed wish of public opinion; moved by all these reasons to encourage them, to arouse them to pursue, as before, the study of knowledge which will one day contribute to the glory, to the prosperity of our land, as well as to the honor of humanity, in accordance with their request of this day, we, the Representatives of the good people of Pensylvania, do forever incorporate the aforementioned persons into a body politic under the name of AMERICAN PHILOSOPHICAL SOCIETY, and do accord to them all the privileges and immunities necessary to fulfill its aims, etc., etc."

4B   EXTRACT FROM THE FUNERAL ORATION DELIVERED BY DR. RUSH, THE DAY OF THE BURIAL OF ANTOINE BENEZET.

This State will long lament the loss of a man in whom reason and sensitivity had combined to produce a degree of moral excellence rarely found in mortals. This estimable person, regarding men as children of the same father, whether they be white, black, or bronze, whether they speak his language or a strange dialect, finally, whether their religion accept or reject ritual—I repeat, this estimable person regarded them all as his brothers and object of his benevolence. If ever the United States promulgates laws to banish slavery entirely from this country, if ever the Kings of the world publish edicts abolishing the blasphemous slave trade, if ever schools are built in Africa; if ever seeds of civilization are planted in these unfortunate lands, future generations will remember that this happy revolution will be due to the publications and perseverance of Antoine Bénézet. His entire life is vivid proof of the good that one individual in society can do, and how much in the short span of their own lifetime good and virtuous men can accomplish that is great and useful.

5   LITERARY AND CHARITABLE INSTITUTIONS IN THE TOWN OF BOSTON AND THE STATE OF MASSACHUSSETTS. The University of Cambridge, was founded in 1638, 18 years after the arrival of the first colonists. It is the oldest, most respected, and most highly endowed institution on the continent. In all its legislation, the Government refers to it only as Alma Mater.

ACADEMY OF SCIENCES AND ARTS, founded in 1780, it has already published several volumes of its Transactions.

DUMMER ACADEMY, founded in 1756, incorporated in 1782, it is the result of bequests from a former governor of the same name.

PHILIPES ACADEMY, founded in 1778 by a citizen of that name, incorporated in 1780. The building is huge and well laid out.

LEICESTER ACADEMY, founded by contribution in 1780, incorporated in 1784.

THE ACADEMIES OF WILLIAMSTON, TANTON, DERBY, etc., founded in various counties of the State by private contributions and incorporated by the Government.

SOCIETY OF MEDICINE, incorporated in 1781, the aim of which

is to extend the knowledge of medicine and surgery, and to correspond with the most celebrated doctors on the continent and in Europe.

HUMANE SOCIETY, founded and incorporated in 1785 to revive shipwrecked persons. On the islands and rocks of Massachusetts Bay nearest points of shipwrecks, the society built 8 or 10 little houses in which were placed clothing, food, wood, straw, and fuel for fire. All these items were put there under safekeeping of the general public, by announcements published in the gazettes.

SOCIETY FOR THE SPREADING OF THE GOSPEL AMONG INDIAN NATIONS, founded in 1787.

SOCIETY OF AGRICULTURE, incorporated in 1792. It has considerable financial backing and has already accomplished a great deal of good.

HISTORICAL SOCIETY, whose aim is to gather together all data that can serve the State of Massachussetts since its founding, which dates from November 11, 1620. Its findings are also to extend to anything pertaining to the Indian nations.

BOTANICAL AND NATURAL HISTORY SOCIETY. This is composed of a great number of members, most of whom live in various counties of the State. What I have seen of these works at the home of the learned Doctor Cuttler, seemed very interesting to me. The first notion of this useful institution is due to the enthusiasm of the late Mr. Bowdouin, former governor of the State, who died in 1789.

SEVEN LARGE FREE SCHOOLS established in Boston during the last century are under the immediate inspection of a committee of the town and are maintained by a tax on houses. Greek, Latin, English, Elements of Geography and Navigation, Accounting, and Penmanship are taught in them. The students in these schools are examined 4 times a year by the same town committee and hold a meeting attended by the Governor, the Magistrates, the Judges, and outstanding citizens. Nowhere does one find schools that are more useful or better organized. In 1797 they had 502 young ladies and 846 young gentlemen.

CHARITABLE SOCIETY founded in 1724, incorporated in 1784, for the benefit of Episcopal clergy, or such other unfortunate persons, no matter what religion, who are recommended by the majority of members.

CHARITABLE SOCIETY OF MASSACHUSETTS, founded in 1779. This is a large fund maintained by annual subscription, as well as by collections made in the churches and destined for the relief of Indians. This worthy association has recently established a school for the instruction of their children, especially the girls.

SOCIETY OF ARTISANS, similar to the one in New-York—"One of our greatest enjoyments," some members of the association told me one day, "is to deposit in this fund a month's savings; the larger the amount, the happier are we, because the hope that after we are gone, our wives and children will have a more assured living, renders the prospect of death less bitter."

CHAPTER X

1 PASSAICK. This pretty river flows from a swamp located in Morris County; its winding course waters a fertile land, crossing beautiful meadows before reaching its cataract of the same name. This falls is 20 miles from its mouth in the great bay of New-Ark, whose tide rises for 12 to 15 miles. In this state there is no more delightful or better culti-vated region than the one stretching from this lovely village, and even from Elizabethtown to this falls. In all directions one sees well-made houses, barns well cared for, orchards, and fertile fields. I have heard many travelers say that the region resembled certain parts of Europe. A great many of the landowners are well-to-do persons who have been busy beautifying their homes, and whose farming is carried on in-telligently.

This cataract, which is 72 feet high and 350 feet wide, is the first thing that stirs the curiosity of almost all foreigners; it is only 18 miles from New York. The mixture of orchards, cultivated areas, and things still in a natural state makes the surroundings interesting and pictur-esque. The inn of this region is one of the best in the land. It is at the foot of this falls where factories and mills were established in 1790, but the high price of labor and the upsets in Europe have kept it from becom-ing successful. The location is so favorable that some day this useful project will be completed.

Although this state is not large, since its estimated size is only 5,500,000 acres, although the part of its territory bordering the sea is very sandy and covered with cedars, the industry of the inhabitants located between the two large towns of Philadelphia and New-York makes it annually more productive. There are 1,200 factories, one half of which are devoted to converting grain into flour, the other to platinizing and forging iron, extracting oil from linseed, fulling cloth, sawing wood, turning the ham-mers of forges and the blowers of many furnaces. There are also many good-sized tanneries; those of Elizabethtown and New-Ark are well known. This State also has some copper mines. Despite the devastations of war and the emigration of 8,000 families, who settled along the Ohio, Ménamy, Muskinghum, and Kentukey rivers, it has 237,290 inhabitants.

2 ST⁰. CROIX. This island, one of the Antilles, belongs to Denmark, yet one notices only a small number of individual natives from that kingdom. Most of the colonists have come from the continent and especially from the town of New-York, with which this island has always had the closest bonds. English is spoken there more commonly than Danish.

3 WHALE-BOAT. A kind of sailboat of a very special construction whose design and lightness are well suited for speed while sailing on the water, especially since they are specifically for whale-catching. Its keel is only 18 feet, its shell light, with ribs of holm-oak and sheathing of cedar plank made fast with screws. Although two men can easily carry it, its crew consists of 4 rowers, a harpooner, and the skipper. The bow and stern

being exactly alike, it matters not from which end the whale boat is steered.

After the great birchbark canoes * used by the Indians none is known that travels so fast on the water. It is on such fragile and light craft, of which each vessel carries two, that fishermen often go great distances in pursuit of this enormous fish which, at the slightest shock could overturn them. As soon as they see whales, they put these boats in the water, so that in case of misfortune, witnesses of the struggles can go to the aid of their comrades. Of all undertakings, that of approaching 12 or 15 feet and harpooning this Leviathan, is one of the most rugged; one slight disobedience of the harpooner's signals, one single false pull on the oars, or the slightest error in the manipulation of the harpoon not only can defeat the mission, but also bring these whaleboats to inevitable destruction. To appreciate the daring and skill of these rugged navigators, one must have watched them struggling against the violence of the winds, maneuvering their boats over the crest of the waves that buffet them about. I have watched races on the Sound (Long Island) some miles from New-York; it is then that one can judge the speed of which they are capable.

4 SUGAR ISLANDS. I thought I should insert in this little note the following details to prove to what extent the provisions and other articles of trade produced by this continent have contributed to the prosperity of the Antilles. It is estimated that the United States furnishes them annually 120,000 barrels of flour, 12,000 barrels of biscuit, 30,000 of rice, 18,000 of bacon and salted beef, 400,000 bushels of corn, not to mention beans, peas, and oats, 150,000 quintals of dry fish, 30,000 barrels of salt fish. Besides these essentials and indispensable provisions, this continent also furnishes them wood, such as beams, joists, squared timber, planks, tenters (for looms), all valued at nearly 5 pounds sterling the thousand foot. In an ordinary year 2,150,000 feet of such assorted wood are sent, 20 to 25 million feet of cedar clapboard to cover the houses, 16 million feet of caskwood of different sizes worth 8£ sterling the thousand; from 14,000 to 16,000 packages of finished staves, sperm oil candles, iron tar, fish oil, sheep, poultry, beef, pack mules, horses, etc.** Without the increase of farming and population of the continent, what would these islands have been! On the other hand, without the islands, the inhabitants of the United States would not have found elsewhere as advantageous a channel of trade for a host of items which have become useful to them.

5 PROGRESS OF POPULATION AND FARMING. Since this time (1784), such has been the number of emigrants coming from the northern States of Europe, that the Government has been obliged to create 6 new counties: Herkimer, Otségo, Tyogo, Bath, Ontario, Onondaga—which, with the other 14, form the 20 large divisions of this State, subdivided into

---

* The largest birchbark canoe I have seen among the Indians was 23 feet long, 4 feet wide, 26 inches deep and carried 1,200 pounds of goods. Two Indians could easily carry it on their shoulders.

** From 1786 to 1787 New London exported to the Antilles 6,671 beef and horses; from 1787 to 1788 6,919. The town of Middletown exported 2,177 horses, beef, and cows.

19 townships or districts so that distributive justice can be more generally and more promptly exercised toward the inhabitants. The population, which at the same time was only 212,468 souls * according to the last census, increased to 502,638.

6 NEW-ARK. This large village, located not far from the banks of the Passaick and in the neighborhood of the vast meadows separating the Bergen peninsula from the rest of the State of Jersey, has long been considered one of the most beautiful villages in the State. It consists of a well-planted street, 7 to 800 feet wide, and almost 2 miles long, a veritable green carpet, with a church at either end; the one on the south, built of stone, is one of the finest in the State. Almost all the houses are separated from each other by gardens and orchards whose cider is well known, as well as everything else made in this State. Around the houses, this village, which has become the county seat, boasts fences, gentle hillsides covered with apple trees, and pasture lands. In the spring New-Ark is a delightful place to stay; a veritable Flore and Pomone. A great number of houses are built of brick or stone, of which one finds inexhaustible quarries in the hills of the vicinity. The quantity of these stones, sent to New-York and elsewhere, is considerable and fills many sloops. This stone, of a rust color, takes quite a fine polish. It is used to make corners of houses, bricks for plinths of columns, side posts for doors and windows, flights of steps, and sidewalks, as well as for tombstone inscriptions.

The inhabitants of New-Ark have long been known for their activity and industry. The tannery of this village furnishes leather for the manufacture of shoes; annually 90 to 100,000 pairs are exported. Another has just been established which is no less interesting—a factory for carding wool and cotton, a branch of industry considerably increased since the invention of Chittenden's machine the teeth of which cut and card thousands of yards daily.**

At some distance from New-Ark, the ground rises in fertile hills and from a gentle slope watered by several brooks, many mills are operated from this source of waterpower. It is in this cool, healthful region that one sees elegant homes, delightfully located, commanding far-off views of the bay, harbor, and town of New-York, as well as several large islands and lands extending as far as Sandy-Hook. The inhabitants of New-Ark, like those of Elizabethtown, have a community herd, which, under the care of one shepherd, wanders way off to graze. This village is the arrival and departure point for all baggage and stages for Philadelphia, which accounts for the great number of inns one sees in Passaick.

* The war of the Revolution, which had just terminated, had occasioned this great diminution in the population.
**This machine, whose mechanism is very ingenious, was invented in 1782 by Mr. Chittenden of the town of New-Haven; it costs 25 guineas. It is to this machine that the inhabitants of this land owe the ability to card at the rate of 50 (à 50 pour 0/0) more cheaply than is possible in Europe. There are machines of varying degrees of fineness, from number 1 to number 12: the quantity of them that people exported last year from Boston and surrounding towns, amounted to 71,000 *paires*. These factories employ 800 women and children and have implemented the existence of many others for brass (binding?) wire.

7 WASHINGTON. As though the United States were not worthy of having given birth to him, the English Gazettes in New-York announced during the war, that having been born in Great Britain, George Washington was doubly rebellious. Nothing is less true than this assertion, for his ancestors came over to settle in Virginia about the year 1657 and he is thus, third generation English; he was born the 11th of February, 1737, in the parish of Washington, one of the districts of the County of Westmoreland. His father's family was very large. He was the oldest of a second marriage bed, but having lost his own father at the age of 10, he was raised by his older brother of the first marriage and by his mother, who did not die until 1789. This brother, colonel in the provincial regiment, sent to the siege of Carthagène in 1745, conducted himself in a manner that was so distinguished, that he earned public praise from Admiral Vernon, whose name he gave to the splendid estate of 16,000 acres he owned on the banks of the Potowmack. Upon the death of his brother, which occurred shortly after his return from that siege, George Washington inherited the property. He was then only 20 years of age. We know how he conducted himself as major from Virginia, under the command of General Braddock in 1755, and with what presence of mind he saved the rear guard of the English army defeated on the banks of the Monongahéla, by the French and their allies.

After being cured of pneumonia, believed a long time to be fatal, he married Mrs. Custis, a wealthy widow, born the same day he was, and by whom he had no children. Since that time, he has been continually deputy to the legislative body of this district, magistrate of his district, and judge of the lower court, until the time when his compatriots deputized him to the first Congress of 1774, as well as to the one that assembled the following year in Philadelphia, by which he was named Commander in Chief of the Continental army. We are acquainted with the speech he delivered on this occasion and the reluctance with which he accepted this important commission.

After the misfortunes he experienced toward the end of 1776, the Congress raised a cabal against him which did not lessen public confidence in him a whit. The Trentown affair during the great winter of this same year stifled the murmurs of his enemies. Finally, came the surrender of Burgoyne, which decided the alliance with France, an alliance that contributed so powerfully to the surrender of Yorktown and to peace. One would have to have known some of the persons who lived close to him in order to know with what joy he learned that his labors were over; that the liberty and freedom of his country were assured; with what recognition he received from his neighbors and his friends so many evidences of their friendship and interest. We know that he constantly refused the many gifts which the States of Pensylvania and Virginia wanted to offer him; although they were offered in the most delicate manner, he did not even wish to accept the 50 shares in the incorporated company formed to perfect navigation of the Potowmack, offered to him by the State of Virginia.

The great role he had just filled on the world scene; the uniform stead-fastness he had shown in the midst of dangers, and especially in the most calamitous situations; the courage with which he had overcome them; the happiness of having been able to reach the day of triumph and peace; his moderation during the time when he was charged with the burden of war; the eagerness with which he left public life—such were the memories that accompanied him in his honorable career at the end of 1783.

The desire people had at that time in Europe, as well as America, for letters from him was so keen, that people wrote him from everywhere and often under the most frivolous pretexts; each author, before publish-ing his work, hastened to pay him homage; on the continent nothing new was invented before the inventors solicited his approval or sent him plans of their inventions. The same situation existed in Europe, from which a great number of rare items were sent to him.

Among the extraordinary things accomplished by him, we must not forget the tireless patience with which he answered all the letters he received. Had he not known how to economize his time with so much method, he would never have been able to fulfill such tiresome tasks, receive his friends and see to the cares of his great plantation.

Until the time when he was called to the supreme magistracy of the Union, nary a foreigner of any calling or qualification who has not been to see this modern Cincinnatus and spent some time under his roof. Not a member of Congress has not been in Virginia without an eagerness to go to him to express his deep devotion. He was as great, as respected in his retirement, as at the head of his armies.

If, in the final years of his presidency, so many foreign circumstances made difficult and stormy the impure breath of calumny and lies, if violence of partisanship, if mercenary pens, paid, we know by whom, to fill this hateful task, have attempted to defame his reputation, recall to yourself the plight of Aristides, of Phocion, and that of so many other illustrious personalities. In a few years his enemies, his calumniators will be forgotten, will return to the dust of nothingness, and the palms which this great man has so justly acquired will flourish over his grave, will carry to the most remote posterity his name, with its fine example and virtues.

8 PROOF OF CONFIDENCE. Among a great number of proofs of this boundless confidence which General Washington inspired for Govern-ments, as well as for individuals, I shall cite only the following incident which I witnessed. When the Continental army was virtually on the eve of no rations, instead of appealing to Congress, which would have taken too much time, General Washington contented himself with writing to the Governor of Connecticut (J. Trumbull). Here are the last paragraphs of this letter, dated from camp at Morris-town, August 4, 1777.

"In consideration of the extremely imperious circumstances which I have just discussed with you, I beg you to send me 800 beef in as many shipments as you deem necessary. Knowing as I do, the confidence which the Legislative body of your State has in its worthy chief, I imagine that this cargo will arrive promptly; for, after all, my dear Governor, before all else, we must concern ourselves with the subsistence of those who are concerned with defending our country." The 800 beef arrived.

9   USE FOR ACACIA. It is on Long Island, in Rhode Island and in Providence that one sees good-sized plantings of acacia, for there are no trees among these species, more sought after by animals. Those whose stems and branches are winding, are more expensive than the others; various means have been devised of trying to make them take the proper angle; those whose height and diameter permit the making of (étambot), are also very expensive. I have seen one for which 45 piastres (338 Fr.) were paid. Use is also made of the hoops; there are none more tenacious, nor more durable. As to the use of this wood for pegs for sheathing, it has already long been in use. The earliest ones planted on Long Island came from Rhode Island, whose primitive forests were full. Before the war, all the roads of Rhode Island were lined with them; nothing was more beautiful, or fresher: the English did not leave one of them there. In Hamstead, I know some gates, whose posts were planted with acacia in 1683, and they are still healthy. The rapidity with which these trees grow in a light or sandy terrain, is unbelievable; I know some whose roots had grown young shoots 60 feet away. Animals always prefer the grass that grows under their shade, to that of the neighboring trees. I have not mentioned the excellent syrup made from their flower; next to oak, it is the most useful tree one can cultivate in a coastal country.

10   APPLES FROM SPITZENBERG AND PIPPINS FROM NEW-TOWN. These 2 kinds of apples, like so many other things, are the products of chance. Some Walloons and some people from Liège, having grafted onto the wild vine the sprouts they had brought, discovered in the forests of their concessions, that from this alliance 2 kinds of apples resulted. These have been known here for more than 80 years under the names of Spitzenberg and New-Town pippins; from the region of Long Island, where the finest orchards are located. They are remarkable, especially the latter, for the fineness of their skin; the delicacy of their pulp and an extremely sweet odor, reminiscent of pineapple. I have seen some that were 14 inches in circumference. Usually they are about 9 to 11 inches. The desire to eat these fine fruits having become common among the inhabitants of the very warm areas, people have already spread their cultivation considerably in the central part of the States; where they grow as well as on Nassau (Long Island), their native habitat. It is not rare to see them on the tables of New-York as late as the month of May. These apple trees are remarkable for the uniformity of their branches, their rotundity, and the evenness of their bark. By enclosing pigs in these precious orchards, one sustains or renews their vigor. These apples are always picked by hand and separately wrapped in gray paper when they are shipped on vessels. I have sent more than 3,000 grafted shoots to

Europe, ¾ of which have arrived as sweet-smelling as those of this country.

11 SANDY HOOK. A great sand peninsula covered with red cedar which, as one moves in a westerly direction, forms with the dunes in the East, the entrance to the port of New York City. It is on the tongue of this peninsula that the Government has erected a lighthouse 100 feet high, although this part of the land belongs to New Jersey, which did not give authorization. It is facing this lighthouse that the first bar is located, which is only 21 feet of water in ordinary tides; after crossing it, one enters what is called the horseshoe, which is only 11 leagues from the town. It is along a wharf constructed on the lee side of this peninsula where the pilots' schooners are kept; of these there must always be a certain number.

In the middle of this sandy area, covered with high cedars, one sees a gravestone raised to the memory of the Gardes-Marines of English war vessels. "L'Assistance," having strayed in pursuit of deserters on the night of December 31, 1783, the crew perished, overcome, buried under the weight of one of the most memorable snowfalls anyone has seen in 40 years. One cannot read without sadness the expressions of tenderness and regret, engraved on this marble block sent from such a great distance by their parents. The heir to the ancient Scotch family of Mortons, a young man of 20 years was among the victims.

12 THE GROWING OF 2 KINDS OF CEDARS AND ACACIA. In the hope that the following details, relative to the planting and growing of these 3 species of trees will be useful, I am going to transcribe them in the light of my own experience, because instead of sending the seeds to Europe, I have raised some in big tubs until they were three years old, and then sent them to their destinations. Nothing is easier to raise than the seeds of the 2 kinds of cedar, as well as the acacia. The red cedar, which requires a rich, damp earth, does not appear until the end of 2 years; this length of time is compensated for by the wonderful results, however. Because its growth is so bushy, it is necessary to prune some of its lower branches every year, taking care not to cut them beyond 1 or 2 inches from the trunk. Few trees have a greater number of roots and root hairs. That is why they revive so quickly when they are transplanted; they cannot stand the sun and must be carefully kept from it for the first two years. Although this tree is found in rocky, damp, or sandy earth, as well as in crevices of very high rocks, a slope whose soil is rich is better suited to it; what men plant requires much more care than what has been planted by nature.

All the white cedar needs is choice of soil, for it thrives on black, foul-smelling earth, somewhat marshy and yet compact. The lands that seem to have been formed by ancient deposits of sea water, as well as by the destruction of coastal plants, are better suited to it, although I have seen forests of them in the interior of the continent growing on the banks of great natural prairies. It thrives in the shade, especially during its early stages of growth and if one wishes to see it sprout early, after seeding, one must keep it from the summer sun from the hours of ten to four. Its transplanting requires more care than that of the red cedar; it must be done at night, and then you must take the greatest care with its tap-root, on which depends the great elevation which it is supposed to attain. But, quite different from the first, which loves isolation and solitude, the latter thrives surrounded by other growth.

As to the acacia, if one wishes to see it growing from 16″ height from the very first year on, one must give it a light, oozy warm soil, exposed to frequent irrigation and much shade in the middle of the day. One can put it in a nursery from its third year on. I have seen some raised on layers of leaves, instead of manure; they reach 2 feet in height from the first year on.

CHAPTER XI

1   TENEZEE. This new State's line begins on the summit of one of the mountains of iron and the intersection of the boundaries of North Carolina and Virginia. From this point to Clearfolk in the Cumberland, the distance is 112 miles; from there to the first ford near the mouth of the Obey, 105; from this mouth to the second ford of that very river, 130 miles; from there to the Ténézée 9 $\frac{1}{4}$; from there finally to the Mississippi, 60. Its width, being a degree and $\frac{1}{2}$ of latitude, or 104 miles, the surface of this State contains 24,570,240 acres. Before it was freed, its mother state, North Carolina, gave to its first colonists 4,464,195 acres; to its contingent of the continental army, 3,000,000 acres; to several others 500,000 acres. Now there remain 16,606,446 acres, still in the hands of the Cherokees, from which one may deduct 5,000 as being noncultivatable. The new State will concede 11,606,046 after acquiring them from the Cherokees. Discouraged, humiliated, since the Cherokees are no longer a warring nation, and surrounded by whites from whom the Indians obtain, with fatal facility, intoxicating liquor, the Cherokees will disappear as the others have; in 20 years, and perhaps less time; one will see them no more. Such will be the swan song of a nation long powerful and famous, and one of the most numerous of all those that came from Mexico. The population of this sixteenth State, newly entered in the confederation whose origin is so modern and whose childhood has been so stormy, mounted one year to 63,800 persons.

2   DARTMOUTH. This college, founded and incorporated in 1769, is located on the frontier of New-York under latitude of 43 degrees 30 seconds, 80 miles from the Canadian border, in the midst of a fertile plain and at a little distance from the banks of the Connecticut river. What a long recital of efforts of perseverance and of courage its tardy childhood extracted from Dr. Wheelock, its founder! He had at first planned to raise and civilize the young Indian youths, several tribes of which were living at the time in those remote regions, but all the efforts of this missionary zeal having failed, and its attempts fruitless, he dedicated

the college to the education of white people. That is why he located it, at the beginning, so far from European settlements, which had grown much closer since peace time. Last year it had 207 scholars.

This college is composed of 2 groups of buildings located on a promontory from which one can see, off at a great distance, the turnings of the river, as well as the Green Mountains that cross the entire State of Vermont. In front of these buildings is an expansive lawn on both sides of which many pretty farms have been built. The second of the buildings, built in 1786, is 150 feet long, 60 feet wide, and 3 stories high. The library of this college contains at the present time only 3,000 volumes. It has some globes and a few other objects of relatively little importance. The physics laboratory does not yet amount to much. The countryside is very healthful and the winters there are very rigorous. Travelers are not a little astonished to come so far from the sea upon a region so recently settled, with such a substantial literary Mecca.

"This temple, dedicated to the Arts and Sciences," one of my friends told me, on his return from that remote area of the United States, "seemed to me a beautiful rose tree in the midst of a desert and in 10 years this desert will be converted to pasture lands under cultivation and covered with rich harvests."

One very remarkable item is that Dr. Wheelock had the good fortune to live long enough to enjoy the realization of his hopes and to obtain the reward of so many cares and concerns. In a journey which he made to England to seek aid, what he received from Lord Dartmouth, then Secretary of State, was so substantial, that, with the idea of showing gratitude, he gave his name to this college, or rather to this university, since its charter of incorporation accorded to him all rights, privileges, and immunities.

3   FEROCIOUS INDIANS. A few chiefs must be excepted; gratitude has preserved their names in history; among others, Massasoit, sachem of Pakonet * Maskonome, sachem of Numkèag,** who welcomed the first colonists with great kindness, and were a great help to them. But however pious and respectable these first families, we know too well the arrogance, so indigenous, of the Europeans, to believe that this harmony can last long. The more land and woods they gave the white men, the more they demanded.

The new colonists, pressed by need, demanded the same privileges relative to hunting. In the wake of injustices, some acts of violence were committed; an attempt was made to rectify them; this proved fruitless. The Indians complained anew; imperceptibly they became irritated; vengeance was ignited; then the whites, authorized by the law of retaliation, sacrificed some of these very men who had received them so

---

* Today known as Salem, this pretty town, boasting 12,000 inhabitants has considerable trade and navigation.
** Today New-Plymouth. This is the place where the first English disembarked and where they built their first houses. It is the largest town in the district of that name.

cordially. To the scourge of war was added smallpox, and soon a good part of these Ichthyophagic tribes disappeared.

However, despite the superiority which skill with firearms gave them, with men who knew only the bow and arrow, it is probable that the whites would not have settled in these regions with so much ease, if the number of Indians had not been considerably diminished by the smallpox which had wiped out ⅔ of their population 15 or 16 years before the arrival of the Europeans. This terrible calamity extended its ravages from the Baie des Chaleurs in the Gulf of St. Lawrence to the Poohatans of Virginia.

It must be told: immediately a government was formed, forceful enough to unite and restrain these scattered groups, the object of the laws that it passed, was to remove from individuals the means of buying lands belonging to the Indians and the attention of covering part of those lands which the colony owned by acts, bearing the signature of the principal sachems. Some of these can still be seen in the archives of that State. Missionaries united in various districts the remainder of these tribes, from whom this same Government hastened to wrest the inalienable lands. They translated into the Nattick language, not only the catechism and book of prayers, but also the entire book of prayers. I saw a copy of it at the University of Harvard (Cambridge) printed in 1633. The missionaries taught them some principles of farming, as well as morality, something of the Gospel, few examples of which were observable in their way of life.

"Since we are brothers, you say, and since the God of the Sun is the father of all men who inhabit the 2 extremities of the great salt lake," the old Siccacius said one day to Dr. Eliot, "why did you come from so far away to invade our lands and our rivers, kill our game and our fish? Why do you poison us with your sicknesses and kill us with your firearms every time we follow our inclinations, as do your people; it is to this same free will that you owe the first pieces of wood with which you warmed yourself, the first fish on which you feasted. Why do you act toward us in a manner that is so different from the one you use with your companions. Explain that to me."

When one thinks about the effects produced by so many circumstances of violence and invasion, one realizes how impossible it was not to expect that injustices, dissensions, and wars would exist. If, as in Pensylvania and Maryland, these various associations had been led by a chief who, alone, would have acquired some lands and negotiated treaties, then, few violences would have been committed. The settling of this colony, founded on equality and justice, would have been more legal and more in conformance with the inspirations of humanity. Well! Despite the fine leadership of William Penn with the Indians of Pensylvania, one can still see a far greater number of them settled permanently in Massachusetts than in Pensylvania. I do not know the reason for it.

4 BRIDGES AND COMMUNICATIONS. The 4 northern colonies and Maryland and Pensylvania grew through their own strength—governed themselves according to the privileges accorded the first founders without

the mother country mixing in their affairs; and that is why their progress has been so rapid. Everything was the work of the Governments which they gave themselves: establishment of colleges, schools, literary societies; foundations of towns, small scattered villages, police protection of frontiers, bridges, canals—everything emanated from the wisdom of these Governments and from the public spirit they had aroused and carefully cultivated.

The independence enjoyed by these colonies (except their trade, directed by the mother country) founded on the charter which they obtained from King James I, Charles I, and Charles II was more remarkable, even in Connecticut. According to that, what must one have thought of the conduct of George III, when in 1774 he wished to treat with harshness the colonies to whom his predecessors had granted similar equal immunities a century and a half before.

Although the dénouement of the great scene that opened in Philadelphia on July 4, 1776, might be impossible to foresee, it was nevertheless natural to think that the colonies, whose Governments were what people then called charter Governments, would offer great resistance to the encroachment of their rights; indeed, the colony of Massachusetts was the first to take up arms. It was a few miles from Boston where the first English and American blood mingled. It was with 10,000 or 12,000 men that Great Britain wished to bring into subjection the descendants of those former Puritans who had overthrown the throne of Charles I. These descendants lost no time in proving that they had not degenerated and that it would not be so easy as the Parliament had been assured, to cross the continent with a body of 7,000 to 8,000 men. In order to declare themselves independent, these colonies had but a single bond to burst: the one that enchained and directed their commerce.

5 ITEMS TAXABLE IN THE STATE OF MASSACHUSETTS AC-
CORDING TO A VERY LOW ESTIMATE FOR THE YEAR 1798.

Number of inhabitants	560,794
Houses of substantial value	72,164
Barns and other buildings	48,485
Log houses & houses of 5£ evaluation	13,440
Distilleries and refineries	51
Roperies	75
Potash works	168
Shops	941
Mills of all types	2,391
Large forge	79
Shallow walls of wharves, jetties and other lands built over water	498,783 feet
Land under cultivation	389,870 acres
Meadows	366,149 idem.
Pasturelands	270,905 idem.

Coastal meadows	62,549 idem.
Pastures	840,047 idem.
Lands in wooded areas	766,344 idem.
Lands not yet cleared	4,850,760
Lands not liable to be cleared	692,390
Barrels of cider	218,870
Tonnage of vessels, including cod fishermen's,	
buildings used in offshore & inshore coastal traffic	289,500
Horses	64,254
Beef and other cattle of various ages	334,708
Cows	391,254
Sheep & goats	548,614
Pigs	357,013

Taxes being levied in this State on all manner of property, real and personal, resulted in a more specialized knowledge of these items than existed in other States, where different methods of levying were adopted. Sometimes it happens that these results are published by order of the Government; it is from this source that the above table of taxables was drawn. These taxable items are evaluated at a fair rate and it is on the sum of these evaluations that so much per 100 is deducted for each individual; this constitutes his tax.

6 FOUNDING OF GEORGIA. With the plan of protecting the frontiers of South Carolina from the frequent invasions of the Creek and Seminole nations, the people resolved to secure from these Indians part of the territory which today comprises this thirteenth coastal State and to establish there a Government whose inhabitants would be both soldiers and farmers. Under orders of General Oglethorpe, a great number of Germans and Swiss, as well as some English families, to whom lands were given, a military régime was set up; but this form of government, it was soon realized, would not suit a land that had to be cleared and peopled; this growing colony needed peace, liberty, and above all, good civil laws. From these false principles stemmed the discouragement, discontent, and dissensions that they could not extinguish, after the experience of several years, except by the establishment of a royal Government like the one in South Carolina, and in some colonies that had not been founded on charter, composed of a legislative Council and a Governor.

It is only since that time, that Georgia (named for George II, who was reigning then) increased its clearings and its population and that it finally began to prosper. Its immense territory is one of the most fertile in the continent. Some day it will yield wine, oil, cotton, silk, tobacco, indigo, and perhaps even sugar. Without the serious and too democratic inconveniences of the constitution, which the colonists adopted on the occasion of their first effervescence, the Declaration of Independence, this country would be further along than it is today. But, profiting by a long series of disorders and disasters, it has just adopted a much wiser constitution which, in the long run, will repair all these misfortunes and will erase the shameful errors of General Oglethorpe's demagoguery.

Almost the same situation existed in Pensylvania, where Dr. Franklin was the lawmaker.* His work, like that of the famous Locke (although established on bases and principles that were quite different) produced only tempests, at the time when anarchy, was raging worse than ever; enlightened men of the legislative body called a convention composed of deputies sent by the various counties of the State; this convention adopted the principles on which the General Government of the Union was founded, to wit, 2 houses, executive power without council, and judges appointed for life so long as their conduct is irreproachable; this proves how different things are in theory from what they appear to be in practice.

Led on no doubt, as were so many others at this memorable time, by the idea people had of the excellence and dignity of human nature, Franklin, although 80 years old, was convinced that men meeting in little clubs could sacrifice their interests to public welfare and exercise moderation. Its single house, whose laws were to be published and discussed for one year before being passed; its council of censors, which could suspend the court of justice, could summon the legislative body to its chambers, reform the constitution, etc.; its executive power, composed of 17 persons, its frequent elections, all that proves quite obviously the high opinion he had of men and particularly of his compatriots.

Something even more extraordinary: it is only after having seen and felt the dangers and inconveniences of this form of Government during the 3 years that he was president of Pensylvania, he carried these same opinions to the Federal Convention, to which he was elected a delegate. This seemed astonishing to those who knew the depth and wisdom of his genius. It was only in his last speech, less famous for eloquence than for the wisdom of its ideas, that he helped to reform the present form of the general government by sacrificing private opinions.

7 MARTIN BEHEM, native of Nuremberg, from which, after studying geography for a long time, he went to Portugal during the reign of John II. He discovered the island of Fayal, got concession of it, and lived there several years. From this island he reached the Kingdom of the Congo, and in 1484, he discovered the coasts of Brazil, as well as the strait of Magellan. His letters dating from 1486, in the archives of his native city, speak of his discoveries and voyages undertaken six years before Christopher Columbus', who did not set sail from Palos until August 3, 1492. It was Martin Béhem who gave that famous navigator the first idea of a continent to the west.

As for Magellan, he did not decide to cross this strait until after he had seen in the hands of King John a map of this part of America which Béhem had drawn and given to that very king. Jérôme Benson speaks of this map in the history of America which he published in 1550. After being knighted in 1485, Béhem returned to Nuremberg in 1492 and had a

---

* A short time after his return from France in 1786, Franklin was elected President of the executive Council of Pensylvania: the word *governor* at this time was as proscribed among the hot-headed patriots as was the word *basiléos* among the ancient Greeks.

globe made on which he traced the discoveries that he had made and to which he gave the name of "Western Lands." This globe was finished the very year that Christopher Columbus left on his first voyage. For the second time the chevalier Béhem, left his native city and returned to Lisbonne, where he died in 1506.

8 MAP OF NEW-YORK. The map of this town, as well as those of several others which were in the same packet, has become so damaged by sea water, that all the lines of it were obliterated, and the colors so confused that the result no longer represented anything. The same fate would have befallen the other drawings in this work, if the author had not put them in several protective covers.

9 NUMBER OF HOUSES. Today there are 4,700, and 37,420 inhabitants in this town where, in 1763, there were only 1,769 houses and 14,154 souls. It must not be forgotten that in 1776 New-York was half burned, the same day the British seized it, and that they occupied it until November 25, 1783, without repairing a single house.

10 LANDS BUILT ON WATER. Frequently I have heard several members of the corporation of this town say that according to the surveys they had made of lands granted since its earliest beginnings, but particularly since its incorporation in 1683, it appeared that the surface of these lands that were made by the hand of man, on which wharves, houses, and streets had been constructed, was 432,000 square feet. If one multiplies this surface by 8 or 10 feet depth, one will have some idea of the work required for enlargement of the site on which the town of New-York was built.

To what point will the Hudson river extend yet? Perhaps to 2 or 3,000 feet beyond its present course; for I do not know what water limit was granted this town by its charter of incorporation, and beyond that limit, its Magistrates can grant nothing without exposing themselves to maladministration, a danger which they will avoid risking; the more irrevocable are the immunities, the privileges, and lands originally granted by these charts, the more dangerous it is to exceed these boundaries; excess would lead to legal proceedings, fines, or to cancellation.

NOTES ON THE LETTER FROM MR. HERMAN *

11 CASTORLAND. This northern part of the State (New-York), whose 3 big districts are known under the names of Richland, Katarakouy, and Castorland, is bounded on the east by Washington and Clinton counties and Lake Champlain, in the middle by the new districts of Oswégo, Onondaga, and Herkemer; almost the entire length of this northern part is crossed by the Black River which is navigable for 40 to 50 miles to its falls, located a short distance from its mouth in Niahouré Bay, on Lake

---

* The Editor, having learned that one of his friends had just received a letter from the agent charged with the establishing of large grants of lands which he owns in this part of the State of New-York, thought that it would not be disagreeable to the translator of this Work, absent for quite some time, nor to the public, to see inserted here some of the interesting details contained in this letter, dated September 4th last.

Ontario: in its course this river receives several brooks and good-sized creeks, filled with fine sites for setting up factories.

With respect to outlets, this region is very favorably situated. On one side, it communicates with Canada by the St. Lawrence, with English settlements on the right bank of the river, as well as those of Kingston in Katarakouy Bay; on the other with the Ontario through the bays of Niahouré and Cat-Fish, and finally with the land of the Mohawks by a road which has just been opened, passing through Richland, Rome, and Castorville: another has just been blazed from this chief town to the first navigable waters of the Osswègatchée, at whose junction with the St. Lawrence, Major Ford has founded a substantial colony. Long Lake, whose waters flow almost parallel to the great river, offers another outlet for those who might want to go to Ford'sbourg and lower Canada.

With the exception of the mountains, the soil is deep and fertile, as best one can judge it from the elevation and variety of the trees in the forests. The lands bordering the river from our Katarakouy to the line which separates us from Canada (the 45th parallel) abounds in oaks, a tree that is all the more precious since it is very rare in Montreal and in Quebec. In the other districts, one sees a mixture of elm, sycamore, maple, butter-nut, hickory, beech, ash, and linden trees. There too, one finds the hemlock, white pine, the different types of spruce, wild cherry, red, and white cedar. From the branches of the spruce, that beer, so praised by Captain Cook, is made; it is known to be one of the best treatments for scurvy.* As for the sugar maple, it is very common in several districts where it constitutes one-third of the trees. Not only can we extract all the sugar we need from it, but also vinegar of an excellent quality.**

Just as in almost all the northern countries, this area is filled with wooded swamps and natural prairies: which afford us pasture land in the summer and provender for the winter. In many places one finds limestone, clay, and an iron ore that is extremely malleable. We are still too young to think of constructing furnaces and great forges. It will not be thus in a matter of 10 years; it is probable that at that time we will be in a position to furnish these needs to the inhabitants of northern Canada who, having no contracts whatsoever to assure them landownership, cannot dream of such enterprises.

Already we are beginning to cultivate corn, wheat, flax, and even hemp since the time when people observed the height to which the lands reached,

* After boiling for 2 hours 12 or 15 pounds of spruce leaves, one pours the extract into a large barrel to which one adds 2 pots of syrup and as much water as is necessary to fill the barrel. Put in bottles after having fermented, this infusion acquires, if not strength, at least the sparkle of brewers' beer. I have known some persons who, in order to make it more whole-some, filled the wide-mouthed, short-necked bottle of one of those ingenious machines used in London to fill a certain amount of spirits in a certain quantity of water. If I were a doctor, I should speak of the admirable results (marvelous curative powers) of these spirits taken internally, as well as the great number of wounds that I have seen healed with the sole aid of these same spirits.

** Toward the end of the month of April, when one observes the sap lessening, then, instead of making sugar from it, after half boiling it, fill a barrel with it, placing the barrel in the sun or under the roof of the house: this liqueur soon sours and becomes vinegar of the highest quality.

once inundated by beaver dams; but not yet in our fourth year, the details of our progress cannot be very interesting.

An event as unfortunate as it was unexpected, has retarded considerably the prosperity of this colony. The death occurred of a young man, full of talents, whom the Castorland company had sent from Paris to make a country wild, and until then unknown, suitable for a newborn settlement, divide the lands, open communications, begin plowings, build bridges and mills, devise machines in that area where manpower is scarce. Victim of his zeal to complete the leveling of the river, he perished while trying to cross it above its great falls. His comrades, grief-stricken enough at not being able to rescue him, composed a memorial describing this disastrous event; I could not read it without a feeling of deep emotion, and so I send you a copy.

Our rivers abound in fish and our streams in trouts. I saw two men catch 72 in one day. Of all the beaver colonies that occupy this land and have built dams, only a few scattered families remain, for we have destroyed this little society, image of happiness, in whose bosom reigned the most perfect order, peace, prudence, precaution, and industry. The wiliest wolves, more warlike than the beavers, live at our expense and until now have avoided our deadly lead.

The same is true of the orignal. No longer are any of them to be seen in this part of the State and soon our hunters will have caused all of them to disappear, for, as you know, wherever man moves in, this tyrant wishes to reign supreme. Among the birds, we have the pheasant, the gélinote,* the ring-dove, the different species of ducks, the geese, the wild turkey, etc. Our chief town, built on the banks of the pretty Castor River, and because of that, so justly named Castorville, is beginning to grow. As you have good reason to believe, it is nothing but a collection of primitive houses; but finally some families of artisans arrived, of whom the new colonists have so frequent a need. Several shops located in favorable spots are beginning to be popular. Canadians from the right bank of the river come to Castorville to buy the things they need, as well as sugar and rum, whose duty is lower in our ports than in Quebec. The region near these French settlements is infinitely useful in several respects. Cattle are less expensive than in our own land, as well as manpower. Such are the bonds that exist between the inhabitants of the two banks of the St. Lawrence, a rapport which the English Government cannot possibly prevent.

Our colonists here, as well as everywhere else, are a mixture of various nations; we have some Scotch and Irish families from the northern States; these as you know, are the *officina humani generis* of this continent. Many of these colonists have already made considerable clearings. One of these families coming from Philadelphia, besides fencing 100 acres, has built potash works, where the cinders of the region are washed; another from the Quaker sect has settled on the route from Katarakouy, where already it has built a sawmill and a substantial maple sugar estab-

* Drumming partridge.

lishment; last year it turned out nearly 16 quintals. The head of this family is a model of intelligence and industry; the merchandise he brought with him has procured for him the means to employ many hands profitably. He pays 12 piastres per acre for clearing his land and ½ the ashes;* besides that, to the potash workers, he furnishes the huge iron cauldrons, plus the labor, and takes in return ½ the salt, whose value, with that of the first wheat harvest, pays more than enough for the expenses of clearing, fencing, and harvesting. The average yield of an acre being 24 to 28 bushels, and the price of wheat from 6 to 8 shillings, it is easy to see that he still has a margin to provide for accidents; the second harvest is entirely profit.

Among these families, we have some who, chased from their land by fear and tyranny, came to this country to seek in this asylum of peace and liberty, if not riches, at least calm and security and gentle ease. One of them, settled on the banks of Rose-Creek, had come from San-Domingo, where the family owned a good-sized plantation; he shows courage and a degree of perseverance worthy of admiration. One of the landowners has a daughter who, as interesting by her face as by her industry, adds simultaneously economy of housekeeping to the pleasures, or rather happiness, of life. Still another landowner is an officer gifted with a quick and original mind. Born in the burning climate of India, here his health has become more robust. He directs the clearing of 1,200 acres of land which his two sisters, French ladies, have entrusted to him and to which he has given the name, Sisters' Grove. Already he has had cleared more than 100 acres, built a substantial house, and fenced a garden in which he works with exemplary perseverance. He has 2 Canadians, whose ancestors were natives of the same province as he. Far from his native land, the slightest circumstances sometimes become reason for recrimination and regret; those who have never experienced these emotions cannot possibly have any notion of them.

As for the cattle, the young ones that are sold for only 9 piastres a team at the end of one year are worth 70 piastres when they have reached their 4th year. Fat beef, ordinarily weighing 7 to 900 pounds, sell on an average of 5 piastres per 100 pounds. Pigs living almost continually in the woods, a colonist can own as many as it is possible to fatten in the fall. He must not neglect to give them an ear of corn from time to time in order to attract them to the farm and to prevent them from becoming wild; for then one cannot tame them; they get bored, regret their roving life, and do not fatten, no matter what one feeds them. Butter is as costly in our region as in the regions earliest farmed: it sells for 1 shilling per pound.**

Contrary to most people's thinking, we have nothing to fear from the nearby Canadian settlements attracting our colonists. The lands of Canada all belong to the Government or to individual lords: both give them freely, I agree; but they give no title; as a result, numerous dif-

---

* One acre yields normally 200 bushels of ashes, which would be worth 8 sols per bushel.
** 13 sous 6 deniers.

ficulties arise when one wishes to sell, or give away the lands. Moreover, they are encumbered with quite a considerable number of conveyance duties, redemption rights for lack of heirs, taxes, or reserved for religious reasons, lumber or mining monopolies, restrictions unknown in the United States, where all lands are free and clear. Therefore, it is probable that sensible colonists will always prefer, to precarious ownership, sure ownership which can be given with neither rights nor formalities.

This land, bounded by the St. Lawrence and the Ontario, will see population increase more rapidly where men can spread out over vast territory, as in certain districts of Pensylvania, along the Ohyo, the Wabash, etc. What people here call Katarakouy, or the numbers 1, 2, 3, and 4 of the great Macomber concession, will always be the outermost boundary, the ultima Thule of this part of the State of New York, and our land will be the next to the last stage; that is why the lands which, in 1796 were worth from 2 to 3 piastres per acre, have increased in value from 3 to 4.

The banks of our great river are not the only ones to which people flock. Already those of Swan's-Creek are beginning to fill. Had it not been for the death of M. P., we should have been further ahead in our colonization, for we had to wait until another engineer arrived to finish the major land-surveying and the subdivisions. Our winters are cold, less cold, however, than those of New Hampshire; but the beneficent snows of this climate prevent the ice from ruining our grass lands and our rich rolling land. It is truly an admirable sight to behold the promptness with which vegetation develops, a few days after the snows melt.

I have located your dwelling not far from the great falls, well protected from the fracas the falls make falling from 3 different heights. The picturesque sight of the chain of rocks across which these waters fall, their tumultuous movement, the natural meadows in the region, the great forests which surround the settlements on the opposite bank, the traffic of travelers, arriving at the trail-bridge I rigged—these things lend interest to the location. This interest will heighten when farming, industry, and time have had a chance to beautify the wild, rustic region still so remote from resembling the sylvan serenity of Thessalia. The house is solid and comfortable; the gardens and yards well fenced.

I have put a French family in charge of the shop and I am very pleased with the way things are going, However, I think the family will return to France, whose new Government finally banished injustice, terror, and crime, replacing them with a reign of reason, clemency, and laws.

Fishing on the great lake (Ontario), which interests me keenly, furnishes me with plenty more than I need of shad, salmon, and herring. We have ample manpower. You who live in a land where there are so many lazy people, or people whose labors are so fruitless—would that you could send us hundreds of these men! The void they would leave would be imperceptible; over here they would fill the spaces that need to be animated, livened by their presence. What conquests they would make in 10 years and what a difference in their plight! Soon they would become freeholders, heads of respectable families.

The other day a young Frenchmen, my neighbor, 7 miles away, settled for several years on the banks of the river, said to me:

"If it is good fortune for one to enjoy rest, the fruit of one's labors, ease, after escaping the risks of revolution, how much more fortunate it is for one to *share* these enjoyments! I am waiting for a friend, rather a brother; this is one of the boons nature alone bestows. What pleasure shall I not enjoy in showing him the evidence of my first tilling; in watching him count the successive cycles of its growth and the progress of my prosperity!—but especially in proving to him that I have never forgotten him. The things around me, I shall say to him, attest to this truth; this hillside on the right, covered with somber pines is indicated on my map under the name of Hyppolite's-absence: the brook crossing my meadow is known as Brother's-Creek; the old oak which I couldn't bring myself to fell at the fork of the 2 paths, one of which leads to my house, the other to the river, is known as Union Creek, the site of my house on Blooming-Slope; soon he will arrive from San Domingue where Toussaint-Loverture has permitted him to recoup some of his fortune."

12 BAY OF NIAHOURE. Big and beautiful bay located on the east shore of Lake Ontario, 30 miles from where that lake narrows, forming the beginning of the St. Lawrence; it boasts a width of 8 miles and a depth of 12 to 15. At the bottom of this gulf, the Black River falls, forming a harbor in the shelter from the winds and sheets of water of the lake, which, during time of the southwest winds, roll like the ocean waves. The right, or south shore of the bay is extremely fertile; it is one of the coolest wooded areas one can see. The north shore is barren and rocky. This roughness continues to the mouth of the Catfish, a good-sized river that empties into the lake and forms the deepest, finest harbor on this shore. From there to the angle of repose, where the St. Lawrence begins, is a long series of dunes, resembling those between Dunkerque and Ostend. These dunes are topped off by rocks of red granite that seem to stretch to Katarakouy, and form what are called the thousand islands. It is there that wealth will some day come to remove blocks of stone to make from them busts and monuments. In the harbors and bays every spring, fish such as herring, shad, and salmon arrive from the sea, although it is nearly 300 leagues from the gulf of St. Lawrence. As to the *maskinonge* (muskellunge—or pike) that one finds only in the Ontario, the colonists catch some of these almost year-round. Those who settled in the Bay of Niahouré already have some boats and good dug-outs, by which they go to Oswégo and to Kingston. This part of the Katarakouy and Castorland districts may properly be considered coastal lands.

DATE DUE

DATE DUE			
0816 '67			
GAYLORD			PRINTED IN U.S.A.